Transferring Wealth and Power from the Old to the New World

This book contains a collection of essays comparing the evolution of the fiscal and monetary regimes of the Old World colonial powers – England, France, Spain, Portugal, and the Netherlands – from the seventeenth through the nineteenth centuries with the experiences of several of their former colonies in the New World of the Americas: the United States, Canada, Mexico, Colombia, Brazil, and Argentina. The objective is to see how such fiscal and monetary institutions were modified or replaced by new ones. The case studies in the collection consider the experiences of the colonies after they became independent countries. The case studies also examine the factors that allowed efficient fiscal institutions to develop in some countries, while in others such development turned out to be unsuccessful. They consider the reasons some governments were able to live within their means and provide public goods, while for others expenditures frequently exceeded revenue, often leading to fiscal crises. On monetary issues, the collection considers the evolution of institutions designed to save on transaction costs, the extent and the manner in which sovereigns would resort to seigniorage, and the effects of this instrument on economic stability and development.

Michael D. Bordo is Professor of Economics and Director of the Center for Monetary and Financial History at Rutgers University, New Jersey. He held previous academic positions at the University of South Carolina and Carleton University in Ottawa, Canada, and has been a visiting Professor at the University of California in Los Angeles, Carnegie Mellon University, and Princeton University and a Visiting Scholar at the International Monetary Fund and the Federal Reserve Banks of St. Louis and Richmond. Professor Bordo is also a Research Associate of the National Bureau of Economic Research in Cambridge, Massachusetts. He has published many articles in leading journals and ten books on monetary economics and monetary history, including *A Retrospective on the Classical Gold Standard 1821–1931* (with Anna J. Schwartz, 1984); *The Long-Run Behavior of the Velocity of Circulation: The International Evidence* (with Lars Jonung, Cambridge University Press, 1987); *A Retrospective on the Bretton Woods International Monetary System* (with Barry Eichengreen, 1993); *The Defining Moment: The Great Depression and the American Economy in the Twentieth Century* (with Claudia Goldin and Eugene White, 1998); and *Essays on the Gold Standard and Related Regimes* (Cambridge University Press, 1999).

Roberto Cortés-Conde is a professor at the Universidad de San Andrés, Argentina. He formerly served as a professor and director at the Instituto Torcuato di Tella in Buenos Aires and has held visiting positions at the Universities of Cambridge, Oxford, Wisconsin, and Texas. The recipient of Argentina's National Prize in History and a Guggenheim Fellowship, Professor Cortés-Conde is a member of the Royal Academy of History of Spain and the author or coeditor of several books, including *The Latin American Economies: Growth and Export Sector, 1880–1930* (with Shane Hunt, 1985) and *Dinero, deuda, y crisis: evolución monetaria y financiera en Argentina* (1989).

Studies in Macroeconomic History

SERIES EDITOR: Michael D. Bordo, *Rutgers University*

EDITORS: Forrest Capie, *City University Business School*, U.K.
Barry Eichengreen, *University of California, Berkeley*
Nick Crafts, *London School of Economics*
Angela Redish, *University of British Columbia*

The titles in this series investigate themes of interest to economists and economic historians in the rapidly developing field of macroeconomic history. The four areas covered include the application of monetary and finance theory, international economics, and quantitative methods to historical problems; the historical application of growth and development theory and theories of business fluctuations; the history of domestic and international monetary, financial, and other macroeconomic institutions; and the history of international monetary and financial systems. The series amalgamates the former Cambridge University Press series *Studies in Monetary and Financial History* and *Studies in Quantitative Economic History.*

Other books in the series:

Norio Tamaki
Japanese Banking
0-521-49676-4

Competition and Monopoly in the Federal Reserve System, 1914–1951
Mark Toma
0-521-56258-9

The Strategy and Consistency of Federal Reserve Monetary Policy, 1924–1933
David C. Wheelock
0-521-39155-5

Banking Panics of the Great Depression
Elmus Wicker
0-521-66346-6

Monetary Regimes in Transition
Michael D. Bordo and Forrest Capie, editors
0-521-41906-9

Canada and the Gold Standard
Trevor J. O. Dick and John E. Floyd
0-521-40408-8

Elusive Stability
Barry Eichengreen
0-521-44847-6

Europe's Postwar Recovery
Barry Eichengreen, editor
0-521-48279-8

continued after last page of index

Transferring Wealth and Power from the Old to the New World

Monetary and Fiscal Institutions in the 17th through the 19th Centuries

Edited by

MICHAEL D. BORDO

Rutgers University

ROBERTO CORTÉS-CONDE

University of San Andrés, Argentina

CAMBRIDGE
UNIVERSITY PRESS

PUBLISHED BY THE PRESS SYNDICATE OF THE UNIVERSITY OF CAMBRIDGE
The Pitt Building, Trumpington Street, Cambridge, United Kingdom

CAMBRIDGE UNIVERSITY PRESS
The Edinburgh Building, Cambridge CB2 2RU, UK
40 West 20th Street, New York, NY 10011-4211, USA
10 Stamford Road, Oakleigh, VIC 3166, Australia
Ruiz de Alarcón 13, 28014 Madrid, Spain
Dock House, The Waterfront, Cape Town 8001, South Africa

http://www.cambridge.org

First published 2001

Printed in the United States of America

Typeface Times New Roman 10/12 pt.   *System* QuarkXPress [BTS]

A catalog record for this book is available from the British Library.

Library of Congress Cataloging in Publication Data

Transferring wealth and power from the old to the new world: monetary and fiscal institutions in the 17th through the 19th centuries / edited by Michael D. Bordo, Roberto Cortés-Conde.
p. cm. – (Studies in macroeconomic history)
Includes bibliographical references and index.
ISBN 0-521-77305-9
1. Economic history. 2. Europe – Economic conditions. 3. Fiscal policy – Europe – History. 4. Monetary policy – Europe – History. 5. International economic relations – History. I. Bordo, Michael D. II. Cortés-Conde, Roberto. III. Series.
HC51.T678 2001
330.9 – dc21   00-046756

ISBN 0 521 77305 9 hardback

Contents

Contributors

Marcelo de Paiva Abreu
Pontificia University
Rio de Janeiro, Brazil

Michael D. Bordo
Rutgers University
New Brunswick, New Jersey, USA

Forrest Capie
City University Business School
London, England

Marcello Carmagnani
University of Torino
Torino, Italy

Francisco Comín
Fundación Empresa Pública
Madrid, Spain

Roberto Cortés-Conde
University of San Andrés
Buenos Aires, Argentina

Albert Fishlow
Council for Foreign Relations
New York, New York, USA

Herschel I. Grossman
Brown University
Providence, Rhode Island, USA

Jaime U. Jaramillo
Banco de la República
Bogotá, Colombia

Luis A. Corrêa do Lago
Pontificia University
Rio de Janeiro, Brazil

Jorge Braga de Macedo
Nova University
Lisbon, Portugal

Adolfo R. Maisel
Banco de la República
Bogotá, Colombia

Carlos Marichal
The College of Mexico A.C.
Mexico, DF

George T. McCandless
University of San Andrés
Buenos Aires, Argentina

Angela Redish
University of British Columbia
Vancouver, British Columbia, Canada

Álvaro Ferreira da Silva
Nova University
Lisbon, Portugal

Rita Martins de Sousa
Institute of Economics and Management
Technical University of Lisbon
Lisbon, Portugal

Richard Sylla
Leonard N. Stern School of Business
New York University
New York, New York, USA

Gabriel Tortella
University of Acala de Henares
Antiguo College of Minimos
Madrid, Spain

Miguel M. Urrutia
Banco de la República
Bogotá, Colombia

Jan de Vries
University of California
Berkeley, California, USA

Eugene N. White
Rutgers University
New Brunswick, New Jersey, USA

1

Introduction

Michael D. Bordo and Roberto Cortés-Conde

The chapters in this collection examine the factors that allowed efficient fiscal and monetary institutions to develop in some countries at certain moments in time, while in others such development turned out to be unsuccessful. They also deal with the reasons why some governments were able to live within their means and provide public goods, while for others expenditure often exceeded revenue, financial difficulties were the norm, and, in the face of extraordinary shocks, fiscal crises arose.

On monetary issues, the collection considers the evolution of institutions designed to save on transaction costs, the extent and the manner in which sovereigns resorted to money finance (seigniorage), and the effects of this instrument on economic stability and development.

The collection compares the evolution of the fiscal and monetary regimes of the Old World countries from the seventeenth to the nineteenth centuries with the experiences of countries in the New World. The objective is to see how such fiscal and monetary institutions were transferred from the Old World to the New during the colonial era and how old institutions were modified or replaced by new ones. In addition, the chapters in this collection consider the experience of the colonies after they became independent countries.

The creation of efficient fiscal institutions involved the transition from regimes where sovereigns financed themselves with resources derived from their own lands (the demesne) or from their feudal rights (the patrimonial state) to a new regime where the rising expenditures of the new national states required resources to be exacted from their subjects (the tax state).

At the beginning of this transition, in the face of extraordinary circumstances such as wars, duties consisting of aid and requisitions were imposed. Later on they were demanded on a more regular basis, finally evolving into taxes. While the sovereign could dispose of his own property at will, this was not the case when the decision involved his subjects' property.

It should be remembered that in the feudal world, the sovereign's relations with his subjects, like those of the lords with their vassals, involved (mainly) an exchange of services. These obligations arose from the customs of the manor. It then became necessary to define a new set of property rights by which the sovereign could bind his subjects. Although property rights had been gradually defined over time, there was still an ambiguous area where the sovereign and his subjects continued to struggle for their respective rights. The sovereign claimed his right to receive aid in the case of needs of state (e.g., wars), while his subjects demanded the right to be consulted concerning the actual existence of such needs and the implementation of taxes.

This struggle gave rise to a process that led to a new set of property rights and to the creation of a competitive political environment where those affected were entitled to take part in the decision making that generated the expenditures and the distribution of the burden. This process, in turn, involved the creation of institutions of political representation that were quite rudimentary in some cases and more advanced in others (e.g., "no taxation without representation").

The degree of participation in decision making over taxation varied considerably across countries. In some cases, taxpayers' representation was wider, as in the Low Countries (de Vries, this volume) or the British Parliament after 1688 (Capie, this volume); in others, it was more nominal than effective, as in the Spanish courts (Tortella and Comín, this volume); and in still others (paradoxically), nontaxpayers were represented, as in the French parliaments of the eighteenth century (White, this volume).

However, it is evident that, regardless of the identity of those legally empowered to create taxes, the revenue collected was higher and the costs were lower if there existed consensus on the part of the taxpayers. Lack of consent resulted in tax evasion and the fiscal uprisings that were common in Europe.

The legitimacy of decisions had a bearing on their effectiveness. The negotiations between sovereign and subjects and the agreements reached on taxes depended on a series of circumstances. In the first place, they depended on the traditions of the country, the degree of evolution of its institutions and its economy. In the cities of northwestern Europe, where commercial activities had been widely established by the Late Middle Ages, the need to establish a set of property rights arose earlier than in predominantly agrarian societies, and in the urban environment the citizens' obligation to support their governments was already widely established.

At the same time, commercial activities yielded a surplus that permitted the creation of capital markets. The early formation of debt markets for urban governments was a consequence not only of the existence of commercial surpluses but also of the fact that their citizens, among them rich financiers and merchants, unlike the sovereign, could be prosecuted for their debts (Ehrenberg, 1973).

The experience of the cities was the basis for the tradition continued by the seven provinces of the Low Countries in granting taxes and creating a debt market (de Vries, this volume). In England, the tradition of "dialogue" between ruler and subjects that led to parliamentary democracy can be traced back to the Magna Carta of 1215 (Capie, this volume), and it extends to the long conflict between the king and Parliament, with the latter's success in the Glorious Revolution of 1688.

A second circumstance involved geography and related economic characteristics (Landes, 1998). England's geography gave it the peculiar feature of a tightly interwoven territory that facilitated the early formation of homogeneous markets. Its insular nature facilitated the development of a variety of ports through which a more controlled trade took place. France, by contrast, was a continental country with a wide territory divided into several regions that were not always connected. This gave rise to segmented markets, quite autonomous regions, and lower trade flows. The Netherlands benefited from its small scale, from its location as entrepôt of the trade between the North Sea and the Baltic, and from its subsequent expansion overseas. It was the need imposed by the peculiar geography of The Netherlands that led to the creation of cooperative associations, such as those for drainage, which in turn established a precedent for collective action (de Vries, this volume).

At the same time, Spain consisted of a set of kingdoms with diverse features. Castile had a powerful central government, with the influence of the Cortes (parliament) continuously diminishing, while Aragon had an autonomous government with greater popular participation (Tortella and Comín, this volume).

The discovery of abundant mining resources in Spanish America, by alleviating the tax burden on the inhabitants of the Spanish metropolis, allowed the king of Spain to avoid entering into the agreements with his subjects necessary to establish sound fiscal institutions. On the one hand, the easy access to American treasure meant significant cost savings; on the other hand, it meant the postponement of fiscal reforms. Further reform finally became unavoidable when mining resources became insufficient. Thus the precious metals represented a source of significant royalties for the king of Castile. This windfall also permitted him to manage his debt quite carelessly.

The fiscal experience of Portugal was determined by its geography and history. Portugal was a small country having, consequently, no significant regional differences, with a large waterfront on the Atlantic Ocean and a preeminence of the urban sector. The need to consolidate the national state in the face of the foreign menace facilitated the acceptance of reform leading to the modernization of the regime (de Macedo et al., this volume). These circumstances, according to the authors, allow a comparison to be made between the Portuguese and British cases.

Excises existed in Portugal from 1387, and the *dezima* applied to all sectors, including the nobility, from 1641. With the Cortes, there was a representation mechanism related to tax decisions. However, Portugal, like Spain, based its revenue on remittances from the colonies (on trade monopolies and the *quinto*), which accounted for 50 percent of the total revenue and helped alleviate pressure on the metropolis. When the court migrated to Rio de Janeiro during the Napoleonic Wars, colonial remittances dropped and expenditures (mainly war expenses) rose, and a fiscal crisis occurred that led to the liberal revolution of 1820. The attempt to finance expenditures through the issue of debt (tax smoothing) failed and the crown took to inflationary finance, which damaged its long-standing monetary stability. Nevertheless, this situation improved by the second half of the nineteenth century thanks to the implementation of the gold convertibility regime.

1.1 THE TAX REGIMES

Although during the seventeenth century a transition from a patrimonial tax regime to one based on the subjects' contributions occurred in most of the European countries surveyed, the path followed displayed idiosyncratic characteristics in each country, with many features of the old regimes often surviving. This transition required the modification of existing fiscal institutions or the creation of new ones. These institutions, in turn, were designed to deal with difficult aspects of the fiscal function: the creation of taxes, the generalization of the tax burden, the centralization or decentralization of taxes, the administration of revenue, and debt management.

1.1.1 Tax Creation

The decision on the taxes to be levied depended on each country's traditions and circumstances. In the cases analyzed in this book, direct taxes on income, production, or wealth and indirect taxes on consumption via both internal and external trade were imposed. In almost all countries both types were applied, although in different proportions, depending on the circumstances that made collection easier. Direct taxes demanded complex assessment mechanisms, while indirect taxes were easier to implement, provided that centralized markets existed. For this reason they became the most substantial source of revenue. Direct taxation was common in Spain (*tercios*), France (*taille*), and Portugal (*dezima*). Taxes on local consumption were levied in Spain (*alcabalas*), Great Britain and Portugal (excise), and France (*gabelle*, *traites*, and *aides*). The amount of the contribution depended on the general economic situation, but also on the simplicity and cost efficiency of the evaluation mechanism, the collection method, the degree of consensus, and generalization, that is, the fact that the tax burden affected all subjects.

To a considerable extent, the geography and the economy of the country conditioned the success of tax collection. In countries with a wide territory such as France, taxes were mostly levied on local production, while the insular nature of Great Britain made it easier to impose taxes on foreign trade. Custom duties and excise taxes constituted the most significant part of British revenue. During the Napoleonic Wars, following a decline in import duties, Great Britain was successful in imposing direct taxes on property and income from a wide sector of the community, including the nobility (Capie, this volume).

Spain based its resources on direct taxes such as the *tercios* and on indirect ones such as the *alcabalas*, but the revenue derived from the mining activities in the colonies (the *quinto* and later on the *decimo*) were of fundamental importance. Spain found a source of income in the colonial mines that were included in the patrimony of the king of Castile. In addition, taxes were imposed on colonial trade, which was also monopolized for the benefit of the Spanish crown (Tortella and Comín, this volume). Portugal was another example of a monarchy that exacted resources from its colonies. The Iberian example is in contrast to that of Great Britain, Holland, and France.

Economic growth in the sixteenth century and the growth of international trade raised the issue of who would levy taxes on the new activity. In the case of taxes on consumption, incidence depended on the elasticity of demand and supply; in the case of taxes on domestic sales, incidence fell on local producers or consumers; in the case of import duties, it was supposed that they were a burden solely on foreigners. For this reason, they were resisted less, and sovereigns understood that as long as they were not imposed on their subjects, there was no need to consult with them.

This was the source of a painstaking debate between the British monarchy and Parliament, in which the latter was successful and rules were set forth requiring consultation with taxpayers via their representatives ("no taxation without representation"). This outcome had favorable consequences, concerning not only revenue but financing as well, since it was then possible to place debt in the capital markets, as it was guaranteed by Parliament (Capie, this volume).

As regards the implementation of a long-term public debt market, the British adopted institutions successfully applied by the Dutch since the seventeenth century (de Vries, this volume). The Dutch monarchy, in placing bonds in the capital markets, in turn, had made use earlier of the experience of medieval cities (de Vries, this volume). When, as in the case of Great Britain, Parliament began to guarantee sovereign debt, the fear that the sovereign would repudiate it decreased (North and Weingast, 1989). Thus, it was possible to lower the sovereign risk. As credit standing rose, the risk premium and interest rates declined.

1.1.2 Generalization of the Tax Burden

One of the characteristics of the modern tax state was the elimination of the numerous tax exemptions that had survived from feudal times. These had a social dimension, since certain estates (the nobility and the clergy) were not bound to pay taxes on their property. Since feudal times, the nobles were bound to arm themselves in defense of the king, which in turn exempted them from the burdens imposed on those not rendering military service. However, by the seventeenth century, the monarchies of the new nation-states found that to be successful in war, both a complex technology and the professionalization of the army were necessary. Thus, as the nobility ceased to render blood services, their traditional exemptions became anachronous. In France the nobility strongly opposed generalization of the tax burden and found support in the parliaments; during the seventeenth century they managed to dismiss any fiscal reform aimed at taxing them. This failure to widen the taxable base brought great financial difficulties to the monarchy during the course of that century (White, this volume).

But generalization of the tax burden was a question related mainly to those regimes mostly dependent on direct taxes. Indirect taxes on consumption, because of their very nature, were paid by all members of the community, as was the case in Great Britain and, to a lesser extent, in Spain (*alcabalas*) and Portugal (excise). Curiously enough, contrary to present practice, indirect taxes were (for this reason) more egalitarian than direct ones. During the Napoleonic Wars, because of the decline in custom revenues, Great Britain depended more on direct taxes and succeeded in making them universal to include the nobility (Capie). According to de Macedo et al. (this volume), Portugal also taxed its nobility.

1.1.3 Centralization or Decentralization of Taxes

Who would be entitled to collect taxes: the central government or the local authorities? In the European monarchies, where the transition to the tax state paralleled the consolidation of the nation-state, the tendency was to empower the monarch, that is, the central government, to collect taxes that in some cases previously had been local. Where there was no nation-state, as in the German principalities, the taxes continued to be local. The Dutch monarchy itself was a federative association of seven provinces empowered by the cities to collect taxes (de Vries, this volume).

Thus, in the Old World, the trend was toward centralization, although local regimes, different from those of Castile, continued in force in Spain in its relations with Aragon, Catalonia, and Valencia. The experience of the New World was different, as in the United States, Canada, Mexico, Brazil, and Argentina. There the newly independent governments tended to establish decentralized systems in which the right to collect taxes sometimes rested with the central government and sometimes with the local authorities. The demarcation between authorities, in turn, was closely linked to the political regimes of these countries.

1.1.4 Tax Administration

Tax collection may be either centralized or decentralized. It may be performed by the administration itself or commissioned to third parties. In general, those systems with weaker collection capacity were more dependent on tax farming. The principle that the state's revenue should equal the future income of the farmer seldom was enacted in reality, although it came closer to it when farming was subject to bidding. In most cases, with scarcely transparent markets, this gave rise to mutual fraud between the sovereign and the farmers, ending in a great burden on the taxpayers and leading, in turn, to frequent tax revolts. Spain applied a farming regime in the seventeeth century (Tortella and Comín, this volume), but the most remarkable case was that of France (White, this volume).

1.1.5 Debt Management

The answer to extraordinary circumstances such as the frequent wars of the period, demanding unusual resources, required complex institutional engineering. In the past, this problem had been solved by resorting to savings generated in earlier periods of peace (the war chest) or else borrowing directly from the suppliers of material or from bankers. Generally, these were short-term debts claimable in full. The idea was that at the end of the war the victorious party would acquire the defeated party's resources. However, it was not always possible to take everything from the loser, and as wars became more drawn out, the problem became how to schedule the debt so as to repay it over longer terms.

The needs of an increasingly complex and bureaucratic military structure increased the states' extraordinary demands and their need to search for new sources and forms of finance. Spain, during the seventeenth and eighteenth centuries, dependent on Genoese and German bankers, bound to repay short-term debts, and with no access to a capital market, went into repeated defaults. Something similar happened in France, with several defaults during the eighteenth century. The Low Countries and Great Britain were far more successful since they managed to place long-term debt in the markets.

De Vries (this volume) points to a special feature of the Low Countries that allowed them to organize a debt market. This occurrence reflected, first, the early rise of financial centers in Antwerp and later in Amsterdam and, second, the fact that the House of Orange took over the authority of the cities, which had earlier pioneered the issue of public debt. As Ehrenberg (1973) has pointed out, the cities had a patrimonial responsibility that made them more trustworthy in the eyes of investors. In England, according to Capie (this volume), the solution, in 1676, to Charles II's default ("stop of the Exchanges") was to create the annuity, a long-term investment instrument.

1.2 THE POLITICAL INSTITUTIONS

In the tax state, the government is sustained by the taxpayers instead of deriving resources from its own property. As tax levies impinge on taxpayers' property rights, the perception of the legitimacy of the tax regime becomes a key factor for the efficiency of the system. This is intimately connected to the political regime, that is, the regime that establishes who decides who must pay, the amounts owed, and the allocation of such funds. All this is essentially a political issue.

In both the Dutch and British experiences, a mechanism was achieved through parliamentary representation that involved taxpayers in the decision making concerning taxes and fiscal control. Such a principle, of decisive importance in the transition in the early modern period from an absolute monarchy to a limited constitutional monarchy, was made sacrosanct in Great Britain.

The importance of this political institutional structure in the development of an efficient tax system and in the formation of capital markets has been well established (North and Weingast, 1989). In this sense, the successful consolidation of a tax state coincided with the political transition from the ancient regime to limited government. Such political transitions, which occurred first in Great Britain and Holland, took longer to achieve in Spain and France. In Spain it took place only in the nineteenth century, thus contributing to a deeper crisis, both in the metropolis and in the former colonies. In France, failure to attain a consensus over tax reform brought about a series of crises during the eighteenth century and led to a summoning of the States-General and the French Revolution in 1789.

1.3 MONETARY INSTITUTIONS

All of the Old World countries under consideration were on a specie standard in the period covered by our study. With the exception of France in the brief John Law affair, none resorted to the issue of inconvertible notes (the inflation tax) as a form of revenue. The Spanish and Portuguese monarchies had, however, on different occasions engaged in debasement of the coinage. Philip III of Spain began the debasement of silver coins (reales de plata). These coins were displaced by an alloy of silver and copper (reales de vellón). Debt instruments such as *juros* and *vales reales* were also used as quasi-monies. Portugal after the restoration also resorted to debasement. Banks, other financial institutions, and financial markets also developed in The Netherlands, Britain, and France but not in the Iberian countries.

1.4 THE COUNTRIES OF THE NEW WORLD

The European colonies in America were recipients of the fiscal and monetary institutions of their respective metropolises. They adapted these institutions to their own resources and circumstances, population, customs, cultures, and distances. Did they modify them or did they create new ones instead? What was their experience as they became independent? Did they reject colonial institutions as an expression of their opposition to the ancient regime and adopt other institutions, which they considered more consistent with the ideology that had inspired those proclaiming their independence from the European monarchies?

In the cases studied, all outcomes prevailed in varying degrees. In the beginning, the colonial powers – it couldn't be otherwise – transmitted their institutions to the New World. These were the institutions familiar to them, but the distances were so large and the differences between the new territories and the metropolis so marked that they had to be adapted to the new circumstances. Later on, the colonial masters adapted to the new situation but also to the fiscal goals of the home country and to the special concerns of their colonies. This was not so much the case in the North American colonies, where little of the wealth discovered in Latin America was found.

1.4.1 The United States

Along with this process of adaptation of institutions and the creation of new ones, perhaps the most remarkable case was that of the English colonies of North America. The representation principle in force in the metropolis after 1688 was upheld within the sphere of the governments of the 13 colonies (later of the states), but a typically American political innovation was added: that of local administration. The difference was relevant because the activity of government in the colonies was rather limited, while the local administration incurred most of the expenses to provide services, such as security and education. The British colonial governments collected taxes on foreign trade as well as some indirect excise taxes, but their expenses were very small. The local administrations instead collected direct taxes on property and wealth. Indeed, the English settlers in America did not directly support the central administration in London. Great Britain subsidized defense expenses because settlers were not represented in Parliament. When the Crown attempted to transfer these expenses to the colonists, the revolts that led to American independence broke out. Thus it was of great importance that the provision of basic public services occur at the local level and that, in their cities, the American settlers take part in making decisions concerning expenditure and taxation.

America not only took up the principle of no taxation without representation within its local governments, but also added to it the participation of taxpayers in local assemblies (Sylla, this volume). A correspondence between expenditure and taxes was established that not only legitimated taxes but also made their collection more effective and easy. These were largely taxes on property, and local officials were the ones who best knew the value of the taxable items and could make an accurate assessment, under the surveillance of the other settlers.

This regime was passed down to the independent Republic with a modification: the emergence of a federal government that undertook defense expenditures (and servicing of the national debt) and that, in turn, was empowered to collect taxes on foreign trade, a faculty formerly vested in the colonial administrations. The latter (the states) continued to collect indirect taxes and some direct taxes, while local governments concentrated mainly on property taxes.

According to Sylla (this volume), local government was perhaps the single most innovative and durable contribution of the North American colonial past.[1] The fact that increases in expenditure were decided upon by those who would benefit from them not only granted legitimacy to the system but ensured tax collection as well. Expenses at the federal level were minimal, since the eighteenth-century vision of the federal government was of a minimal state. It was not responsible for social security and education services, which fell within the sphere of the local governments, and because almost its only burden – defense – was of relatively low cost. National defense was based on state militias, not a standing army, and wars were few and of relatively short duration until the Civil War. Thus the U.S. federal government ran repeated surpluses, and when extraordinary circumstances arose that led to deficits, the latter were easily financed by means of debt issues that were repaid with the surpluses of normal years.

The 13 colonies developed a unique monetary system based on bills of credit and land bank bills to overcome the perennial shortage of specie (since the British Navigation Acts prohibited the colonies from having a mint and from importing British specie). Most bills of credit were issued to finance government expenditures during the frequent wars with the French and the Indians. These bills, issued in convenient denominations, thus served as money and in some colonies the issues were inflationary.

Overissue of bills of credit to finance the Revolutionary War (the continentals) and the use by the states during the confederacy period of competing seigniorage led to a major reform of U.S. monetary and fiscal institutions embedded in the Constitution of 1789. Under the brilliant tutelage of Alexander Hamilton, according to Sylla's account (this volume), the new nation quickly adapted the best fiscal and monetary institutions from Britain, institutions which did not exist when Britain ruled. These included a stable unit of account. The dollar was defined as a fixed weight in both gold and silver. The federal government was given the exclusive power to coin money and regulate its value, as well as the power to levy customs duties and excise taxes.

Hamilton also was instrumental in creating a long-term bond market on Dutch and British lines following successful funding and conversion of outstanding wartime federal and state bonds. Hamilton's final contribution was the creation of a national bank, the First Bank of the United States. It was chartered as a public bank rather than a central

[1] While the federal system consisting of the federal and state governments established by the U.S. Constitution of 1789 was adopted by Mexico and Argentina, the American local government system (the third level) was not.

bank to provide short- and medium-term finance to the government, to promote a uniform national currency, and to finance economic development. The First Bank of the United States and its successor, the Second Bank, each lost its charter in the ongoing struggle between federal and state power.

As the nineteenth century evolved, a clear demarcation developed between federal and state fiscal and monetary institutions. The federal government raised customs and excise taxes and sold land to finance its minimal activities. In wartime it sold bonds and engaged in tax smoothing. During the War of 1812 and the Civil War it also issued paper money. The state and local governments raised revenue primarily from property taxes to finance local public goods. They also chartered commercial banks, which proliferated and were not always sound. Other financial institutions and markets (e.g., commercial paper, stock markets) developed and expanded rapidly in an environment of limited government regulation.

1.4.2 Canada

Canada's legacy of fiscal and monetary institutions came from two colonial powers: France and England (Bordo and Redish, this volume). The fiscal system of New France was part of a French tax farm including the West Indies. The revenue derived from customs and excise taxes and feudal dues was considerably less than government expenditures, largely for military purposes. Continuous transfers in specie from France filled the gap. Like the British colonies to the south, New France had a perennial shortage of specie. Like the British colonies, the problem was solved by financial innovation, the issue of playing card money.

Under the British colonial regime, as under the French regime, expenditures on infrastructure and the military exceeded indirect tax receipts. The balance was made up largely by transfers from Britain, although as the nineteenth century progressed, the Canadian government increasingly issued debt. During the War of 1812 a significant deficit was financed by the issue of army bills. However, unlike the U.S. experience, there was no suspension of convertibility or inflation. At war's end, the bills were redeemed in specie.

The Canadian monetary system in this period was based on multiple currencies which were exchanged at different exchange rates in terms of the British unit of account. In 1853 the Canadian dollar was established as a unit of account at par with the U.S. dollar. After the War of 1812 the Canadian chartered banking system was established. It was modeled on the Scottish system, with note issue, branching, and high capital requirements.

The Dominion of Canada inherited British colonial fiscal and monetary arrangements. The first 50 years were a period of rapid growth and development. Foreign borrowing and a national tariff financed massive expenditures on railroads. The monetary system was based on the gold standard and the chartered banks. There was no central bank.

The Canadian experience was unique among New World colonies in that its monetary and fiscal institutions were always very conservative. There was less monetary experimentation than in the 13 colonies, with the principal exception of playing card money. There was also a chronic dependence on fiscal transfers from Britain, in comparison with the 13 colonies to the south during the eighteenth century. This legacy of dependency extended to the post confederation period, with the government always playing a larger role in the economy than was the case in the United States.

1.4.3 Latin America: Mexico and Argentina

At first, the Spanish Crown established the metropolitan institutions in its colonies. However, the resources as well as the Crown's purposes were different in the colonies than in the home country as a consequence of the discovery of the extremely rich silver mines in New Spain and Alto Peru. In spite of the fact that the complex tax system of Castile was handed down to Latin America, nontax resources prevailed, such as those derived from the monopoly on colonial trade; but it was Crown royalties for the granting of mining rights that constituted the main source of income in America and represented a significant part of overall revenue. The Crown in Castile received remittances from America once the expenses corresponding to the maintenance of colonial administrations had been deducted from them. As time went by and conflicts with other European powers increased, local expenses came to represent a large proportion of the revenue and remittances dropped. Only those from New Spain (Mexico), where precious metal resources were greatest, remained at a high level (Marichal and Carmagnani, this volume).

Other taxes such as *alcabalas* were collected by the local administrations (subordinate treasuries), which also deducted their own expenses before sending the (ever-decreasing) remainder to the capitals of the viceroyalties and from there to Spain. But, unlike the British colonies, the local administrations paid only for the royal bureaucracy, and settlers had no part in making decisions regarding these taxes. These bureaucracies were, in practice, sufficiently autonomous to withhold resources. When the colonies declared their independence, such control allowed them to constitute local autonomous governments (states and provinces) that became the basis of the federal regimes in Mexico and Argentina. In fact, the spatial organization of the Cajas was the antecedent of the federal organization in those territories.

While the colonies had a permanent fiscal surplus with regard to the metropolis, Mexico subsidized the Caribbean (*situados*), and the Alto Peru did the same with the River Plate.

The extra resources derived by the Spanish Crown from the royalties from the mines in the New World saved the Crown from having to reach an agreement with its subjects over taxation. This delayed tax reform and encouraged lax debt management. The same phenomenon occurred in the colonies, since the local bureaucracy was paid out of the mining resources. This, in turn, created a culture that established no link between taxes and expenditures. However, the Spanish colonies were liable to other fiscal burdens such as taxes on foreign trade and trade monopolies, which led to violent protests, as well as taxes on domestic trade, which contributed to the segmentation of the market as a result of the high transportation costs, a situation that continued to affect the new independent nations during most of the nineteenth century (Cortés-Conde and McCandless, this volume).

With the formation of the new independent republics, as silver resources began to decline, the need to negotiate agreements to distribute the burden of supporting the state was added to the double political crisis derived from the need to legitimate the new state and the transition from an absolutist government to a constitutional one. This happened because in the River Plate and in other Latin American countries, the mines remained outside their territories and the subsidy regime from the metropolis (*situados*) ceased after independence. The countries with depleted mineral resources, such as Mexico, also entered into a deep crisis (Marichal and Carmagnani, this volume).

The new countries were unable to create a cohesive polity to negotiate the agreements and create the fiscal institutions that could provide them with the resources needed to make their governments viable. The wars that derived from such conflicts and that, at the same time, made the conflicts last longer were evidence of these deep and repeated crises in Mexico and the River Plate.

1.4.4 Latin America: Brazil and Colombia

Brazil inherited the Portuguese institutions but adapted them to the specific nature of its resources. The monopoly for this exploitation of Brazil wood, the *dezima* on the production of sugar, the *quinto* on gold production in Minas Grerais, and the monopolies of trade were the main sources of revenue. In some cases, taxes were farmed; in others, they were directly collected.

During the empire, the main taxes were those levied on foreign trade, either on exports or imports. In spite of the fact that the Constitution of 1824 did not admit it, the provinces collected export taxes (because of a geography that allowed the existence of multiple ports) (Abreu and do Lago, this volume). When export duties were imposed on coffee because of its dominant role in the world markets, the tax fell on foreign consumers. This made these duties easier to collect locally and granted greater stability to the fiscal system, which until 1890 remained free of inflationary finance (Abreu and do Lago, this volume).

Colombia had the same tax system as the other Spanish colonies, that is, *alcabalas*, *diezmos*, and a head tax imposed on the natives (Jaramillo et al., this volume). However, unlike Mexico and Peru, and later the River Plate, Colombia was a poor colony, with no access to the resources derived from silver mining. The heavy burdens on local trade in the form of *alcabalas* led to the commoners' revolt in 1781, a precedent to independence. Jaramillo et al. claim that this brought about successful modern reforms by replacing *alcabalas* on internal trade with taxes on foreign trade.

1.4.5 Monetary Institutions in Latin America

The Latin American colonies all followed the Spanish and Portuguese bimetallic monetary standards. None engaged in the issue of paper currencies, as was the case in North America. After independence, Argentina and Brazil adopted paper currencies issued by government-chartered banks of issue. Inflationary finance was periodically used to finance continuous civil and external wars. By contrast, Mexico and Colombia used specie convertibility throughout most of the nineteenth century.

In conclusion, the chapters in this collection contain a wealth of information on the fiscal and monetary institutional experiences of both the Old and the New Worlds. They also raise issues that may be the subject of future research.

REFERENCES

Ehrenberg, Richard (1973). *Capital and Finance in the Age of the Renaissance: A Study of the Fuggers and their Connections*. New York, Augustus M. Kelley.

Landes, David S. (1998). *The Wealth and Poverty of Nations: Why Some Are So Rich and Some Are So Poor*. New York, W.W. Norton.

North, Douglas and Barry Weingast (1989). "Constitution and Commitment: Evolution of Institutions Governing Public Choice." *Journal of Economic History*, December, pp. 803–32.

PART I

THE OLD WORLD

2

The Origins and Development of Stable Fiscal and Monetary Institutions in England

Forrest Capie

2.1 INTRODUCTION

There are many explanations for the emergence of the nation-state, and then perhaps many more that try to account for the subsequent material success of these nation-states. Sensibly, since of necessity most of these explanations are complex and roam over the whole range of religious, political, cultural, social, and economic factors. The purpose of this chapter, despite its fairly grand title, is much narrower. It is to investigate one area of explanation that has been offered and to follow a particular aspect of that explanation. The explanation is Douglass North's, on the rise of the West (North, 1981; North and Weingast, 1973). The particular aspect of that explanation is to consider how the core of North's thesis relates to the emergence of stable/successful fiscal and monetary institutions in England. Most of the explanations of the nation-state take some account of the fiscal dimension. Certainly, successful fiscal regimes underpin the role and scope of state activity. And stable monetary arrangements underpin economic growth. They do that by providing financial intermediation, which aids growth, and by contributing more generally to macrostability.

The chapter first sets out (Section 2.2) the essence of the North thesis as it relates to the emergence of institutions in England. This section outlines the role of property rights and transaction costs in the context of the origins of growth in England. Evidence on these aspects is not easy to provide, but the concepts are insightful and suggestive and we try to illustrate how. Section 2.3 provides the fiscal story, beginning with the growing fiscal problems of the state from the fifteenth century on (something that is not contentious) and the resolution of these, in England but

I thank John Hatcher, Steve Jones, and Larry Neal for comments on an earlier version, and I am deeply indebted to Patrick O'Brien for guidance.

not in other major powers, in the seventeenth century. But the story does not end there, for something that needs explaining is the remarkable rise of tax and debt in the eighteenth century – something that is pursued in Section 2.5. Before that, Section 2.4 provides the monetary element, which, of course, is closely connected to the fiscal. We outline the growth of the monetary economy and the beginning and development of the principal institutions. After examining how the monetary and fiscal regimes operated in the course of the two centuries or so after the 1680s (Section 2.6), we show briefly in Section 2.7 how these British institutions found themselves adopted in many other countries.

2.2 A FRAMEWORK

What follows here is a brief summary of the North thesis insofar as it relates to England, and an indication of the implications of this thesis for the emergence of fiscal and monetary institutions. For our purposes here, the North agenda can be abbreviated as follows. The optimizing assumption of the neoclassical model is a powerful one, but it depends upon perfectly operating markets. The key part of it is that it assumes an incentive structure that allows individuals to capture returns, and it is one where private and social costs are equated. For these conditions to obtain, well-specified and enforceable property rights are essential. Security of property rights is important for the rate of saving and for capital formation.

There would seem to be three key elements. The first is property rights and how such rights are defined and enforced. (A frequent example of how such rights stimulate economic growth is patent law.) The second and closely related element is institutions – closely related in that it is a set of institutions that clearly specify property rights, and these, in turn, allow the appearance of institutions that play a part in growth. Efficient institutions (rule structures) are those that provide individuals with strong incentives to work, save, and invest, and are essential for growth (necessary but perhaps not sufficient). Some countries had more efficient institutuions than others. Given a favorable incentive structure, investment and innovation are encouraged, as are a whole series of subsidiary arrangements – such as the joint stock company. The third element is transaction costs. When these fall, for whatever reason, greater possibilities for growth exist. Transaction costs appear with property rights. If the conditions allow transaction costs to fall, then the groundwork is laid for more efficent tax collection; and monetary institutions can emerge that can facilitate financial intermediation and so raise welfare.

North and Weingast's argument for the rise of the West, particularly England, if the following caricature can be allowed, is the following.

Starting from a state of institutional nature and working with the fundamental axiom that running through human society is a preference for more rather than less, we pick up the story in the tenth century. As people sought to improve their lot, protection was needed – to allow production and exchange to take place unhindered or at least with as little hindrance as possible. Implicit contracts were struck with lords who held land in exchange for armed services (from knights) and labor services (from peasants). In the absence of money and of well-functioning markets, it was cheaper to provide labor services. A manorial system that provided law and order in exchange for labor was a cost-effective institutional development. Secondary institutions emerged to support primary institutions. Population growth and economic development followed. Markets and market networks developed apace, and as transaction costs fell, further development continued. Knowledge of market prices meant that money wages could be substituted for labor services. And as with labor services, knight services were commuted for money rents (scutage).

Given the economies of scale in the provision of public goods, the role of provider moved from the manorial lord to the Crown. There were some hitches and reversals in this process (something to make the medieval historian cringe!), but as far as England is concerned, by the sixteenth century all men were free. Much of what was true for England was also true for The Netherlands but not for France or Spain. By the time we get to the seventeenth century, the possibility of greater differences opens up.

There were widespread crises in the seventeenth century across Europe, where wars and falling wages were accompanied by social upheaval and religious strife. The causes of the crises have been argued about, but the key for North is that England escaped crisis because of property rights. Property rights provided the incentives to use factors efficiently, and could be found in England and The Netherlands but were notably absent in France and Spain. It was the rise of Parliament that caused the nature of English property rights to diverge from the continental European pattern. It is difficult to date these things precisely, but the Glorious Revolution is said to have marked an important shift to private property rights secure from government confiscation and so created the preconditions for the Industrial Revolution. The theory is therefore a strong one. That is, relatively little is being asked to account for rather a lot.

Property rights of different kinds have, of course, existed for millennia. The question is, at what point did they become sufficiently well defined, enforceable, and extensive to allow/promote economic growth? Some have argued that by 1300 England had an independent judiciary, and the beginnings of security were laid. For O'Brien (1994), "a viable basis in law and behaviour for a market economy was already in place by the Restoration (1660). By that juncture (indeed long before) private property rights in land, minerals, houses, transport facilities, agricultural, industrial and commercial capital, and in personal skills and labour power had already been established and accepted" (p. 229) (also see Burt, 1995). The framework of laws and codes of behavior may have taken centuries to mature, but such a framework was widely accepted by the second half of the seventeenth century. At the same time, O'Brien (1994) argues, the Hanoverian state (to move into the eighteenth century) "failed to provide proper legal conditions . . . conducive to the operation of efficient markets . . . for raising long-term capital, and for the regulation of credit supplies" (p. 230). O'Brien concludes that Hanoverian governments did not protect persons or property effectively from crime, nor was their control of production and trade properly secured against the resistance of those who opposed free markets. "[T]he acceptance and safety of private enterprise may have depended more upon traditions of behaviour and deference than upon the political and legal system" (1994, p. 241).

In an attempt to give more precision to the timing of the impact of property rights, Clark (1995) tries another approach. He takes as a starting point that the political foundations of modern economic growth lie in the period 1540–1800. He argues that one way of testing the sufficiency of the property rights hypothesis is to examine rates of return. In times of uncertainty, great political turmoil, and otherwise adverse conditions for property rights, rates of return would be high; investors would want a premium for such increased risk. Then, as security of property rights was established, the rates of return should fall. Clark therefore looks at rates of return across a very long period: 1540–1770. He uses "real property (land, houses, and tithes) rent charges, and bonds and mortgages." He finds that there was no fall in the rate of return and concludes that England had well-established property rights long before the beginning of modern economic growth. He concludes that the political changes that came in the late seventeenth century had no impact on the private economy – that rates of return were uninfluenced by the Civil War of 1642–9 or the Glorious Revolution of 1688. Thus, while security of property rights may well be a necessary condition for growth, it is not a sufficient condition.

However, before we accept this conclusion, there are some points to make about rates of return. First, the fragility of the data cannot be overstressed. Second, the nature of the test – a long list of dummy variables to capture war, revolution, the South Sea Bubble, and so on – is less than ideal. Third, there is the fact that a number of different elements determining rates of return could be operating to offset each other. Fourth, it may be that the difference between expected and realized rates is what explains matters. At the same time, we need to leave open the possibility that private property rights in England were quite well defined and enforceable by the sixteenth century. That would leave us looking for what, if anything, there was in the late seventeenth century that made a difference.

The other principal element in the thesis is transaction costs. Transaction costs are made up of search costs involved in finding buyers and sellers; negotiation costs that determine prices and other costs of exchange; and enforcement costs to ensure that deals are kept. In the absence of markets, transaction costs are generally high and trade and activity are lower than they would otherwise be. Trade was therefore restricted in the main to local exchange. Markets were appearing increasingly after the tenth century (Britnell, 1993), and the English economy was to experience relatively rapid growth in the thirteenth and early fourteenth centuries. At that time, the service sector appears to have experienced huge productivity gains. However, diminishing returns set in in agriculture, population fell dramatically, and there was a decline in trade and activity more generally. Since transaction costs are subject to increasing returns to scale, a reduction in scale meant that costs rose in the fifteenth century. But that setback was overcome and the pace of activity again picked up in the sixteenth century.

Still, it is clear that in the sixteenth and seventeenth centuries England was one of the lesser European powers. Something changed, and by the middle of the eighteenth century it was the preeminent naval power, whose dominance continued to grow until it reached its high point toward the end of the nineteenth century. What we do next is set out some of the principal changes that occurred in the seventeenth century and try to suggest where some of the important reasons for these lie, particularly in relation to fiscal and monetary institutions.

2.3 FISCAL INSTITUTIONS

2.3.1 Background

The purpose of this section is say something about the nature of the fiscal problem and the relationship of its resolution to property rights. In brief, the argument is that an efficient tax system depends on well-defined and enforceable property rights. With these in place, tax collection is facilitated.

There is some debate over what comes first, money or taxes. Certainly, without a monetary economy taxation is difficult – very difficult from a public expenditure point of view. Nothing, however, should be read into the fact that we give fiscal matters precedence in this chapter. There was a monetary economy in England for a long time before we get to our period. There is in any case, as is common, a two-way relationship, with money paving the way for taxes and taxes giving birth to new financial instruments.

The setback in the fifteenth century that reduced activity brought a reduction in duties and tolls, to the detriment of the Crown's revenue. The Crown was also suffering from a fall in rents, so fiscal crisis loomed. Part of the solution to this widespread problem lay in territorial expansion, which of necessity involved war-making. Unfortunately, the rising scale and cost of military technology (but see Black, 1982, who argues for changes in organization rather than scale) meant that fiscal requirements expanded; the minimum efficient scale of the state increased, and there followed the emergence of the nation-state. England was unified under Henry VII, but the struggle for command of resources was to occupy the next century and a half.

There is nothing new about taxes, but in seventeenth- and eighteenth-century England there is something new about their scale and means of collection. The Romans taxed on a large scale, and the collectors were a despised and secondary class of citizens; then in the Dark Ages feudalism reached its high point, and central authority was eroded to the point where taxes virtually disappeared. It was in the Middle Ages, with the revival of a monetary economy, that taxes reappeared. But they were viewed as an unaccustomed encroachment on both liberty and property. Thomas Aquinas, in the thirteenth century, in his *Summa Theologica* posed the question of whether it was possible for robbery to take place without its being a sin. He concluded that it could, "whenever a sovereign ruler levies Taxes in accordance with the demands for justice to promote the general welfare" (quoted in Grapperhaus, 1989, p. 67).

A number of steps were taken in the Middle Ages that led to improvements in state finance. For example, the signing of the Magna Carta by King John in 1215 (itself the outcome of a power struggle between the barons and the king), which guaranteed the liberties of English subjects, contained some clauses on taxation that specified that the king could tax only in cases of necessity (Dowell, 1884). The concept developed into *national defense* and *war* and became very elastic (Harris, 1975). Nevertheless, the Magna Carta can be seen as the first step toward a dialogue between ruler and subjects that led toward parliamentary democracy. From that point on, there were various developments that led in the direction of improved state finance. The Hundred Years' War is often cited as a major step. Not only was the importance of customs revenue raised, but parliamentary taxation rose, and it also forced new means of collecting taxes (Neal, 1990). But the real changes had to wait for the seventeenth century.

For the sixteenth century, it is not clear to what extent Parliament had the right to influence the monarch's policies. Under the Tudors the center of power shifted somewhat from the House of Lords to the House of Commons. The Tudors had moderately good relations with Parliament, with the power of the king being limited by magistrates upholding case law and by Parliament; and the Stuarts therefore inherited a strong position. The king controlled the *fisc* – the complex of estates, revenues, and rights. In addition the king got import duties.

Under the Tudors, ordinary – that is, recurring – revenue came from Crown lands and feudal dues (the demesne) and customs. Extraordinary – that is, supplementary – revenue for a particular purpose came from parliamentary agreement. And large amounts of Tudor revenue came from expropriated church property and debasement of the currency. In the first 40 years of the seventeenth century, there was increasingly a blurring of distinction between these forms of revenue as public finance came to be based on tax rather than on demesne revenue. In the second half of the century, England ceased to be a demesne state and became a tax state, with the resolution of the tension between demesne and tax coming in the 1640s (Braddick, 1994). This was, of course, Schumpeter's famous thesis: that the early modern period saw the creation of the tax state on the ruins of the demesne state – effectively, the emergence of the state.

The first half of the seventeenth century is a story of the tension between the king and Parliament over the raising of funds, with Parliament becoming increasingly self-confident. The Crown had growing difficulty in finding ways to raise finance for war. It was in these conditions that a number of new tax ideas were floated – for instance, a proposed excise on beer. The Petition of Right was introduced in 1629 and, next to Magna Carta, was the most important piece of constitutional law. It delineated the king's power with respect to Parliament. No one could be forced to pay anything without consent of Parliament. Much of the country was encouraged by this and refused to pay tonnage (an import duty per ton of wine) and poundage (an import duty per pound of goods). In the late 1630s, John Hampden (a Puritan) refused to pay a fee to the sheriff of Buckinghamshire, and while he lost his case, the public was given more encouragement and refused to pay ship money. At the same time, there was growing discontent over the sale of monopolies.

The key to the possibilities for growth in tax collection can be found in the excise. In 1641 Pym, with the background of civil war and fiscal crises, proposed the excise, and the Long Parliament of the 1640s introduced it. Again there were various antecedents, but in the Civil War and Interregnum it was established as a system. In the 1650s 25 percent of all revenue was excise, though it should be said that it was mostly in London and mostly from beer. This was a period of administrative preparation for the fiscal state (O'Brien, 1988).

Before 1688, Parliament met infrequently and its legislative output was low. After 1688, it met annually and its output was high. It had a new place in economic life, and acts relating to finance were many and particularly successful, with growing transparency and accountability (Hoppitt, 1996a).

2.3.2 Origins and Principles

According to Adam Smith, the four maxims governing taxation should be equality, certainty, convenience, and economy in collection. That was stated in the late eighteenth century, after more than a century of evolution in the development of modern taxation. These principles were certainly not what governed practice at the beginning of our period.[1]

The beginnings of taxation in its modern form can be found in the middle years of the seventeenth century. If precision were demanded for the starting point for modern public finance it would normally be taken to be 1688, at which time parliamentary control of finance was established. In spite of some claims for the 1650s, both monetary and fiscal affairs had been shown to be inadequate in the Dutch wars of the 1660s. When there were no funds to pay sailors and there was no scope for further borrowing, the English navy was defeated in 1667. It was time to reassess government finance. Many English practices were adopted from the Dutch (see de Vries, this volume).

Nevertheless, there are some significant points before 1688 that can be noted. In earlier times, taxation was regarded as a public charge against the benefits derived from protection from the state. In normal times, indirect taxes were used for the ordinary expenses of the state. Apart from customs duties, the first such indirect tax was the excise, which was considered the best tax and the easiest to collect. In emergencies or in wartime, which is what that usually meant, direct taxes tended to be imposed. Prior to 1688, the principal direct taxes were the poll tax, the house taxes (called *hearth money*), and the monthly assessment.

[1] Andrew Hamilton set out some other contemporary views on the subject and on the "best example of the application of statistical reasoning to finance that had then appeared", see McCulloch.

It is worth bearing in mind that even from very early times, some of the practices that might be considered quite modern today were already in force. For example, the practice of exempting specific amounts from persons with the lowest incomes was quite common. The idea that a minimum amount of money was needed to provide the necessities of life goes back a long way – at least to the thirteenth century and probably the eleventh. So too does the principle of graduation, that is, that there should be a rising scale of taxation to parallel rising income.[2] This principle of graduation became firmly established as a central feature of the English tax system. A further feature that has developed more recently is the differentiation between earned and unearned income. All the modern elements are based on notions of equity and welfare.

2.3.3 Revenue and Expenditure

According to O'Brien and Hunt (1996), the Tudors and Stuarts raised and spent something like 6 percent of gross national product (GNP) in wartime and 3–4 percent in peacetime. These figures clearly have to be treated with great caution but they provide some starting point. In the long century that followed the Stuarts, from 1689 to 1815, there were eight wars of varying length. In the first of these, spending ran at around 12 percent and subsequently in the region of 19–20 percent. In this 127-year period, Britain was at war with France for 65 years. Across that period, taxes rose 16-fold and borrowing about 240-fold. Something remarkable happened that allowed the British government to tax and borrow on these unprecedented scales. Tables 2.1, 2.2, and 2.3 and Figures 2.1 to 2.5 provide some orders of magnitude on these variables for this period. These figures provide some indication of the scale of raising and spending (1690 was a war year, while 1730 and 1790 were years of peace and 1815 marked the end of the long Napoleonic Wars).

There had been a relatively long evolutionary process in the specification of tax and its collection to which we have already alluded. What is interesting is that from the seventeenth century to the twentieth century the principal items of government revenue were remarkably stable. The one significant change over the three centuries was the replacement of the land tax (important in the sixteenth, seventeenth, and

[2] In the 10th and 15th centuries goods had quite high and variable exemption limits, which meant that the great majority often paid nothing. The modern justification for graduation comes from Edgeworth, as well as the concept of diminishing marginal utility, the argument being that the utility of successive income increments diminishes at a more rapid rate than that at which increments increase. Therefore, in the interests of equality, higher income groups should be charged at a higher rate.

Table 2.1. Fiscal State, 1580s–1815

	1600	1650	1690		1730		1790		1815	
Nom. GNP (£m)			46		57		130		320	
Natl. debt (£m)			3.1		51.4		244		745	
As % of GNP			6		100		185		220	
(annual borrowing)					1.2m		3m		20m	
Tax rev. (£m)			2.05		6		16		63	
As % of GNP		3.4	7		10.7		12.3		18.2	
Tax def. 1675 = 100			3		6.3		12		28	
Expenditure (£m)			4		5.5		16.8		112.9	
As % of GNP			9		10		13		35	
Tax breakdown										
Excise (£m/%)			.9	30	3	49	7.5	43	23	36
Customs (£m/%)			.7	23	1.6	26	6.3	36	19	30
Dir (with. £m/%)			1.4	47	1.5	25	3.6	21	21	34
Expenditure										
Military (£m/%)				79w		39p		31p		61
Civil (£m/%)				15w		17p		13p		9
Interest (£m/%)			.6	6w	2.3	44p	9.4	56p	30	28

Note: w = war, p = peace.
Source: Mitchell (1988) and O'Brien.

eighteenth centuries) with property and income taxes in the nineteenth and twentieth centuries. At the beginning of the period that concerns us, revenue came from three main sources: customs, excise, and land. In addition, post office and stamp duties always provided significant amounts.

Net income rose from around £5m in 1690 to around £20m in the 1790s (i.e., of the order of 10 percent of national income if we use Colquhoun's figures). Total expenditure, which was of course similar, rose from about £5m at the beginning of our period to about £20m at the end. However, the pattern of the latter is both different and interesting. The striking difference is the peaks that appear with war years. Even before the Napoleonic Wars there are several sharp peaks: 1710, 1749, 1763, and 1784.

The principal items of income were excise, which rose from around 30 percent at the beginning of the period to around 50 percent, where it remained for most of the century. Customs made up about 25 percent but was falling sharply at the end of the period for obvious reasons. Land taxes made up close to 20 percent and stamps and post office duties the balance. The main items of expenditure were debt charges – wildly fluctuating, but about 40 percent. Civil government showed a similar erratic pattern that is more difficult to account for but about 10 percent. The civil list was in decline and below 10 percent. Military expenditure oscillated wildly, and unsurprisingly, and took around 50 percent of all expenditure.

In the nineteenth century, customs and excise duties continued to be important; together they supplied around one-half of total gross income. Land taxes had virtually disappeared, and property and income taxes emerged to make up about 10 percent of the total. In the twentieth century, the main change in the composition of the principal constituents of government revenue was the growth of property and income taxes. Together they made up close to one-half of the total by midcentury. Customs duties still provided around 25 percent as recently as 1965, while excise had fallen to an eighth; profits and death duties together contributed about 5 percent.

2.3.4 Direct and Indirect Taxes

As the state searched for ever more sources of revenue over time, almost every good imaginable was the subject of taxation. The recent poll tax was an obvious repeat of an earlier (and equally unpopular) tax. And the more recent proposal for a tax on houses based on the number of bedrooms has direct parallels in the seventeenth century with the window tax. The latter was originally imposed in 1662 on every house, at 2s for every hearth and stove.

By the middle of the seventeenth century, the need for government revenue for the purposes of defense saw the introduction of *ship money*, initially levied on selected seaports but soon extended to the whole country. And as noted, it was also in the middle of the seventeenth century that the first excise duties were imposed in England by the Long Parliament. Excise duties were simply indirect taxes on goods for domestic consumption at the point of sale. Dr. Samuel Johnson described the excise as a "hateful tax levied upon commodities and adjusted not by the common judges of property but wretches hired by those of whom excise is paid."[3]

Currently, excise duties are associated with wines and spirits, but that practice is comparatively recent. *Excise* simply meant a cut. It is true that the first such duties were levied on beer and cider, but they were very quickly extended to groceries, silks, furs, tobacco, and so on – anything that raised revenue effectively. The argument for excise taxes

[3] Johnson had much more to say on taxation, notably on the colonies, a subject that generated its own literature.

Table 2.2. Principal Constituent Items

	Total Net Income	Customs		Excise		Stamps		Post Office
	1	2	2 as % of 1	3	3 as % of 1	4	4 as % of 1	5
1692–1695	4,008	845	21.02%	983	24.51%	46	1.12%	61
1696–1700	4,441	1,175	26.29%	1,161	26.53%	72	1.62%	70
1701–1705	4,977	1,458	30.06%	1,519	30.23%	91	1.87%	69
1706–1710	5,283	1,299	24.58%	1,646	31.14%	92	1.74%	59
1711–1715	5,523	1,460	26.42%	1,985	35.94%	132	2.37%	86
1716–1720	6,107	1,666	27.27%	2,214	36.32%	145	2.37%	93
1721–1725	5,966	1,576	26.43%	2,663	44.65%	146	2.46%	93
1726–1730	6,184	1,636	26.43%	2,725	44.25%	157	2.54%	96
1731–1735	5,701	1,555	27.31%	2,857	50.25%	142	2.48%	94
1736–1740	5,824	1,490	25.55%	2,911	49.99%	137	2.35%	90
1741–1745	6,451	1,258	19.53%	2,867	44.42%	132	2.05%	87
1746–1750	7,074	1,379	19.38%	3,285	46.47%	133	1.89%	83
1751–1755	7,038	1,672	23.76%	3,561	50.63%	135	1.91%	101
1756–1760	8,057	1,886	23.45%	3,652	45.49%	250	3.09%	82
1761–1765	9,999	2,181	21.81%	4,848	48.58%	300	3.01%	111
1766–1770	10,556	2,589	24.52%	4,849	45.98%	319	3.03%	161
1771–1775	10,846	2,642	24.37%	5,001	46.14%	342	3.16%	162
1776–1780	11,499	2,044	17.96%	5,542	48.23%	456	3.95%	146
1781–1785	13,693	3,286	23.83%	6,058	44.38%	869	6.31%	191
1786–1790	16,432	3,796	23.15%	7,142	43.43%	1,278	7.79%	308
1791–1795	18,606	3,888	20.90%	8,807	47.31%	1,443	7.76%	407
1796–1800	17,965	3,397	20.36%	7,918	41.77%	1,544	8.50%	606

[a] In £ thousand sterling.

rather than some other form of taxation or borrowing was advanced by Charles Davenant at the end of the seventeenth century. It was added to significantly by Horace Walpole in the 1730s, particularly with proposals to convert customs duties to excise duties, though there was no shortage of opposition. Excise duties were placed on all kinds of goods over the years: tobacco and wine were popular for revenue; salt was another widely used item and on occasion was subject to very steep rates of tax; other items ranged as far as whale fins. Such duties meant that the burden was heavily regressive since the great part came from products in wide demand. In modern times, they have been consciously aimed at goods with, in the jargon, low price elasticities of demand and high income elasticities. This raises their effectiveness as a tool of fiscal policy.

Holland was the major economic and financial power of the second half of the seventeenth century; frequently, new practices adopted in England were often simply copied from Holland (see de Vries, this volume). Thus the 1690s were years of great financial

	Land and Assessed Taxes[a]		Total Net Expenditure[a]	Debt Charge				
				Total[a]		Funded[a]		Terminable Annuities[a]
5 as % of 1	6	6 as % of 1	7	8	8 as % of 7	9	9 as % of 7	10
1.53%	1,776	44.35%	5,413	361	6.47%	60	0.97%	151
1.59%	1,614	35.90%	5,586	1,179	25.52%	168	3.79%	330
1.43%	1,739	34.47%	5,033	1,086	22.65%	257	5.21%	340
1.11%	2,042	38.65%	8,423	1,666	19.66%	307	3.68%	733
1.56%	1,717	31.11%	8,357	2,672	37.76%	814	11.90%	1,280
1.53%	1,619	26.45%	6,294	2,956	47.21%	1,306	21.03%	1,316
1.57%	1,345	22.52%	5,895	2,981	50.88%	2,563	43.79%	278
1.55%	1,521	24.41%	5,838	2,470	42.48%	2,161	37.19%	201
1.66%	969	16.90%	5,426	2,141	40.05%	1,870	35.02%	184
1.54%	1,153	19.82%	5,404	2,088	38.95%	1,788	33.36%	182
1.34%	2,078	32.22%	8,644	2,125	24.70%	1,764	20.52%	167
1.16%	2,166	30.69%	10,586	2,815	27.94%	2,345	23.43%	206
1.43%	1,541	21.85%	6,513	2,848	43.95%	2,495	38.50%	212
1.03%	2,036	25.10%	13,476	2,956	22.73%	2,604	20.07%	226
1.10%	2,297	23.05%	16,316	4,522	30.46%	3,874	26.20%	427
1.53%	1,981	18.90%	9,838	4,851	49.47%	4,209	42.93%	485
1.50%	1,869	17.24%	10,148	4,646	45.84%	4,122	40.64%	455
1.28%	2,329	20.22%	17,913	5,197	29.38%	4,332	24.64%	624
1.38%	2,616	19.18%	25,726	8,048	31.55%	6,417	25.16%	1,226
1.87%	2,939	17.89%	16,323	9,395	57.61%	7,909	48.50%	1,225
2.19%	2,973	15.98%	24,455	9,631	42.98%	7,948	35.52%	1,306
2.46%	3,165	17.04%	41,449	—	29.53%	10,248	24.07%	1,353

changes and also of considerable fiscal experimentation often based on Dutch experience. The first stamp duties were implemented in 1694, being duties on official forms and legal transactions, such as deeds of conveyance and settlements. In 1695 there was a proposal for a tax according to rank on marriages, births, burials, and even bachelors; in that same year, there was even a proposal for death duties.

Taxes also fell on newspapers, first in 1712 (and in the process provided a means of censorship). A lot of discussion followed on "taxes on knowledge." Local taxation was another subject that generated discussion throughout the nineteenth century and has seldom been out of the discussion in the twentieth century. At the turn of the twentieth century some of the debate had shifted to the tariff (Ashley, 1903) and remained prominent in the years between the world wars (Beveridge, 1931).

The principal direct taxes were on land in the early years and then increasingly on income. By the 1790s the discussion on taxation was

Table 2.3. Principal Constituent Items

			Civil Government									
	Unfunded		Total		Civil List		Army	Navy	Ordnance	14 + 15 + 16		1–7
10 as % of 7	11	11 as % of 7	12	12 as % of 7	13	13 as % of 7	14	15	16	17	17 as % of 7	18
2.52%	256	4.73%	702	13.13%	691	12.90%	2,231	1,797	323	4,350	80.38%	—
7.01%	674	14.55%	717	14.14%	672	13.37%	1,423	1,534	188	3,145	53.54%	—
6.88%	494	10.63%	645	13.34%	630	13.02%	1,513	1,653	136	3,303	64.02%	–56
8.63%	593	6.99%	840	10.01%	728	8.71%	3,509	2,139	269	5,917	70.33%	—
18.33%	541	7.18%	789	10.90%	749	10.33%	2,153	2,591	152	4,896	51.34%	—
20.91%	320	5.04%	907	14.49%	827	13.20%	1,297	1,012	121	2,430	38.30%	–187
4.79%	125	2.07%	1,069	18.22%	976	16.63%	858	886	102	1,846	30.91%	71
3.46%	103	1.75%	1,012	17.38%	830	14.25%	1,211	1,005	141	2,357	40.14%	346
3.43%	85	1.56%	962	17.90%	885	16.49%	980	1,139	204	2,322	42.04%	275
3.40%	117	2.18%	913	17.06%	841	15.72%	1,070	1,147	185	2,403	43.99%	420
1.96%	168	1.93%	864	10.04%	766	8.91%	2,639	2,669	346	5,655	65.26%	—
2.03%	203	1.98%	1,049	10.21%	855	8.33%	3,051	3,185	486	6,722	61.86%	—
3.28%	136	2.12%	1,057	16.32%	814	12.59%	1,194	1,271	143	2,608	39.72%	526
1.73%	110	0.80%	1,159	9.13%	838	6.54%	4,837	3,942	581	9,360	68.14%	—
2.90%	170	1.10%	1,143	7.47%	895	5.82%	5,541	4,583	526	10,651	62.06%	—
4.95%	144	1.46%	1,170	11.91%	920	9.39%	1,593	1,833	271	3,697	37.47%	717
4.49%	144	1.42%	1,082	10.68%	822	8.11%	1,578	2,076	334	3,988	39.27%	699
3.41%	221	1.24%	1,375	8.00%	1,064	6.11%	5,742	4,288	897	10,927	60.29%	—
4.81%	347	1.36%	1,354	5.30%	1,033	4.05%	5,541	9,138	1,203	15,882	61.42%	—
7.50%	281	1.73%	1,583	9.71%	1,127	6.91%	1,996	2,387	465	4,848	29.64%	109
5.89%	325	1.42%	1,722	7.81%	1,132	5.04%	6,505	4,990	1,105	12,600	46.94%	—
3.70%	438	0.97%	1,887	4.53%	1,008	2.36%	—	—	1,769	26,868	65.10%	—

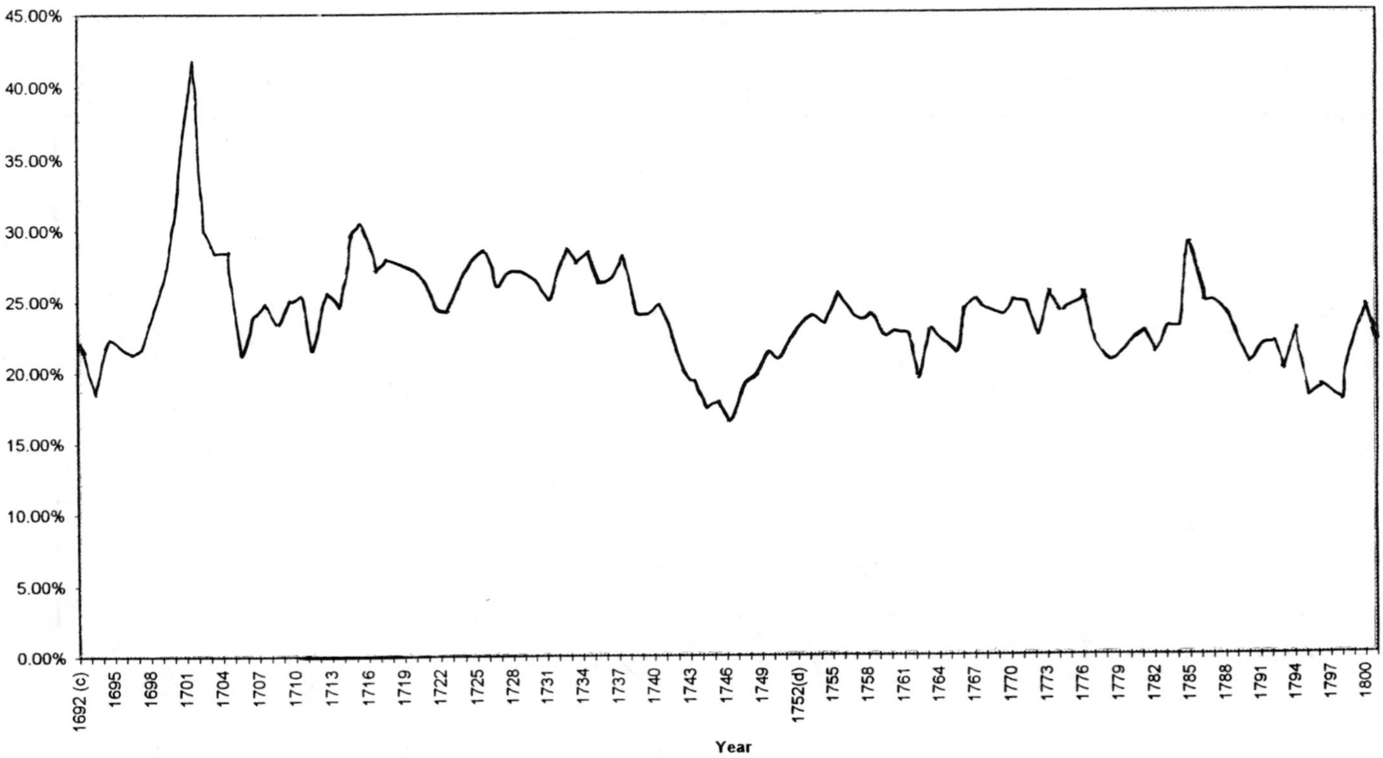

Figure 2.1 Customs as a percentage of total net income, 1692–1801.

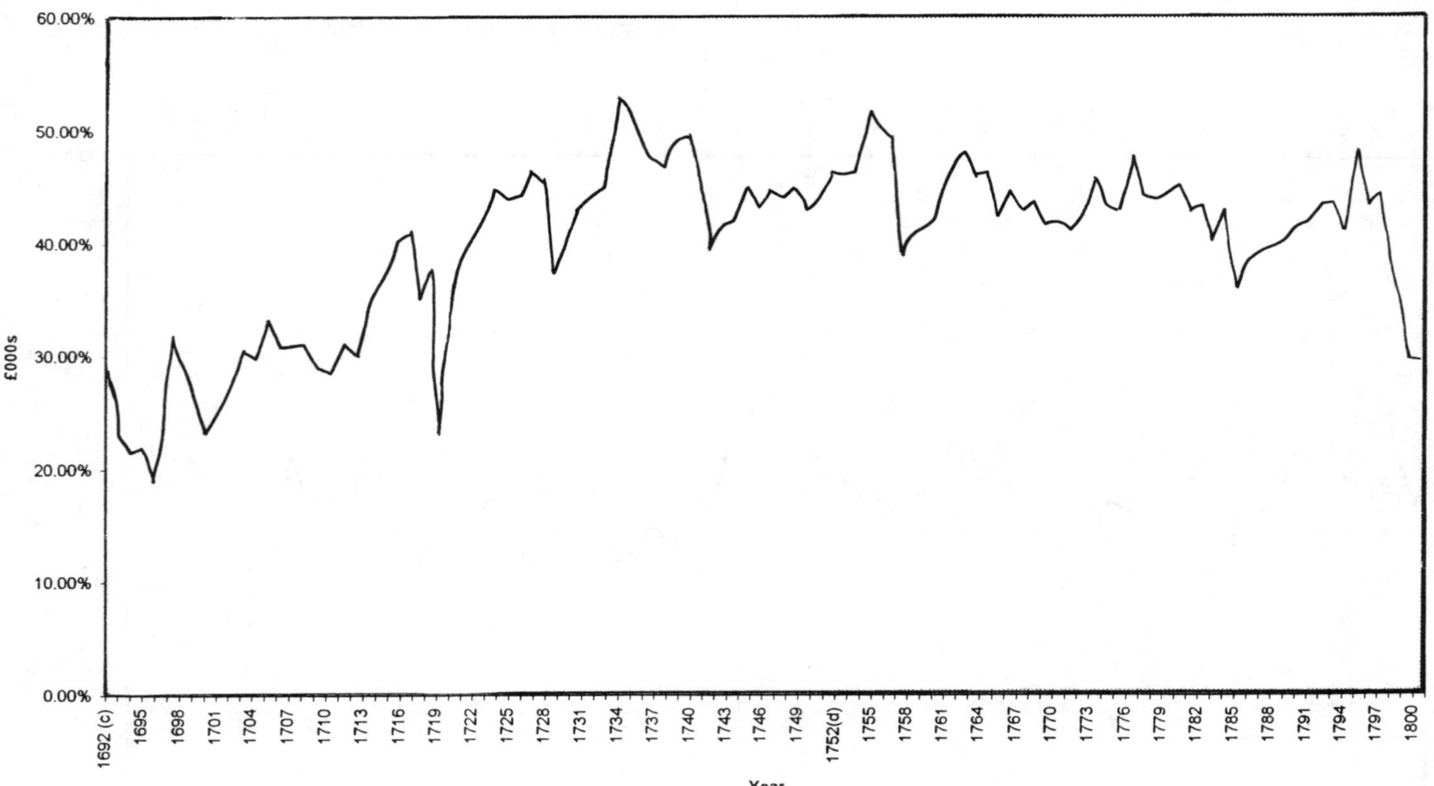

Figure 2.2 Excise as a percentage of total net income, 1692–1801.

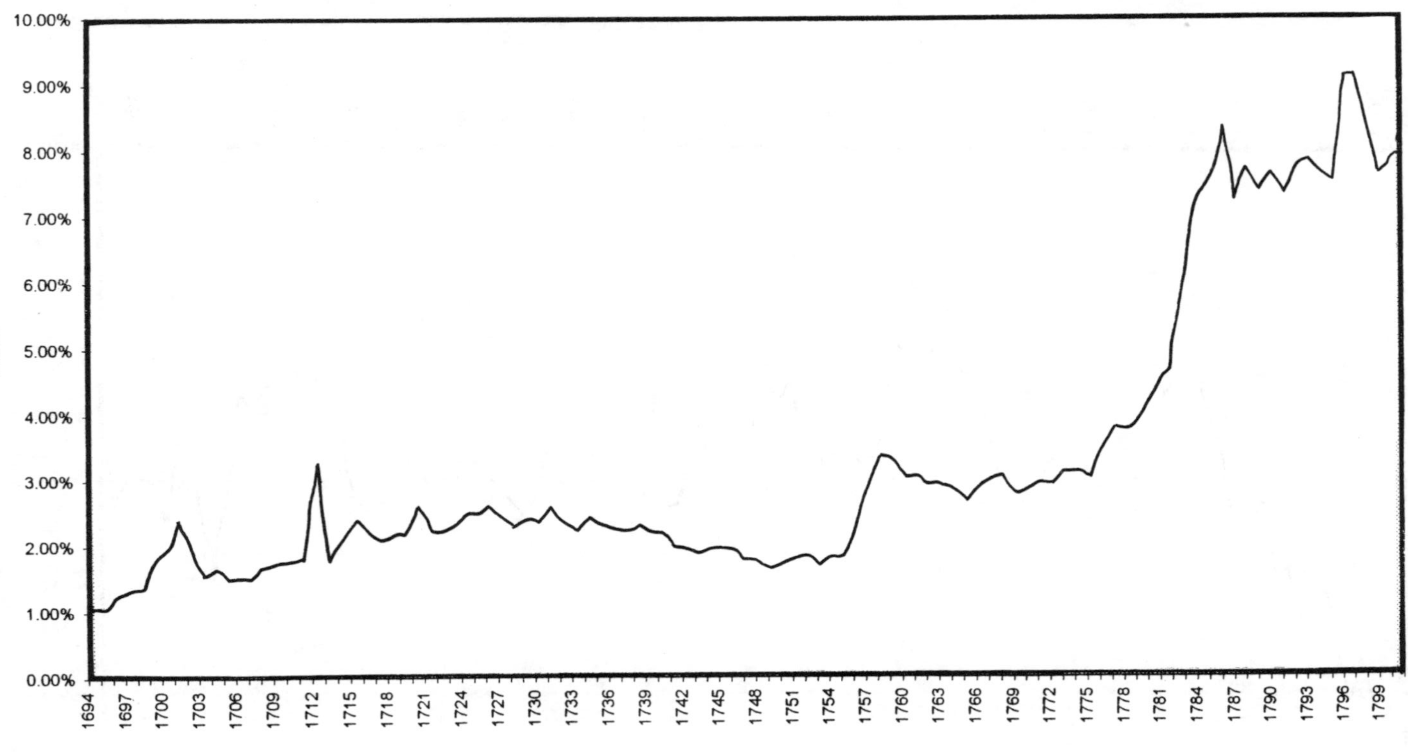

Figure 2.3 Stamps as a percentage of total net income, 1694–1801.

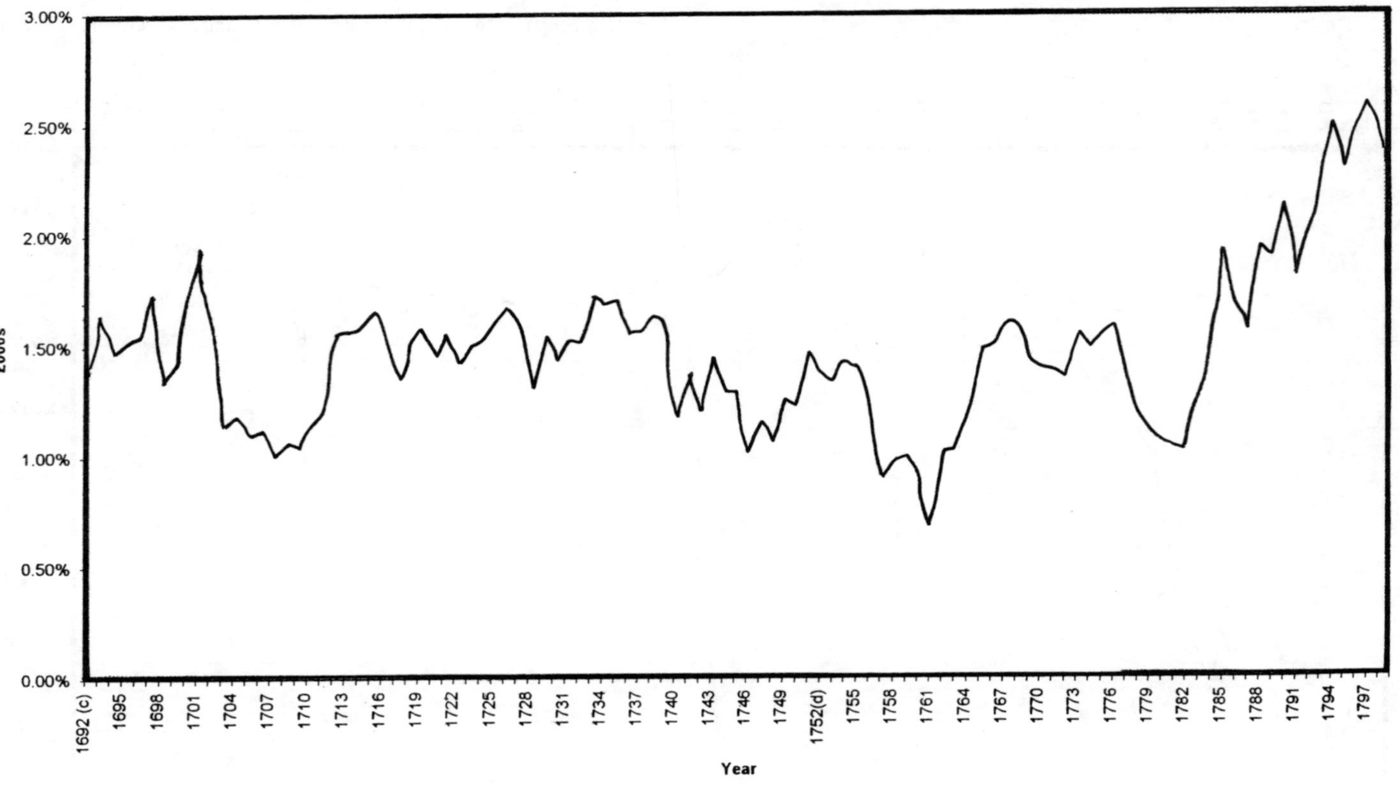

Figure 2.4 Post office as a percentage of total net income, 1692–1799.

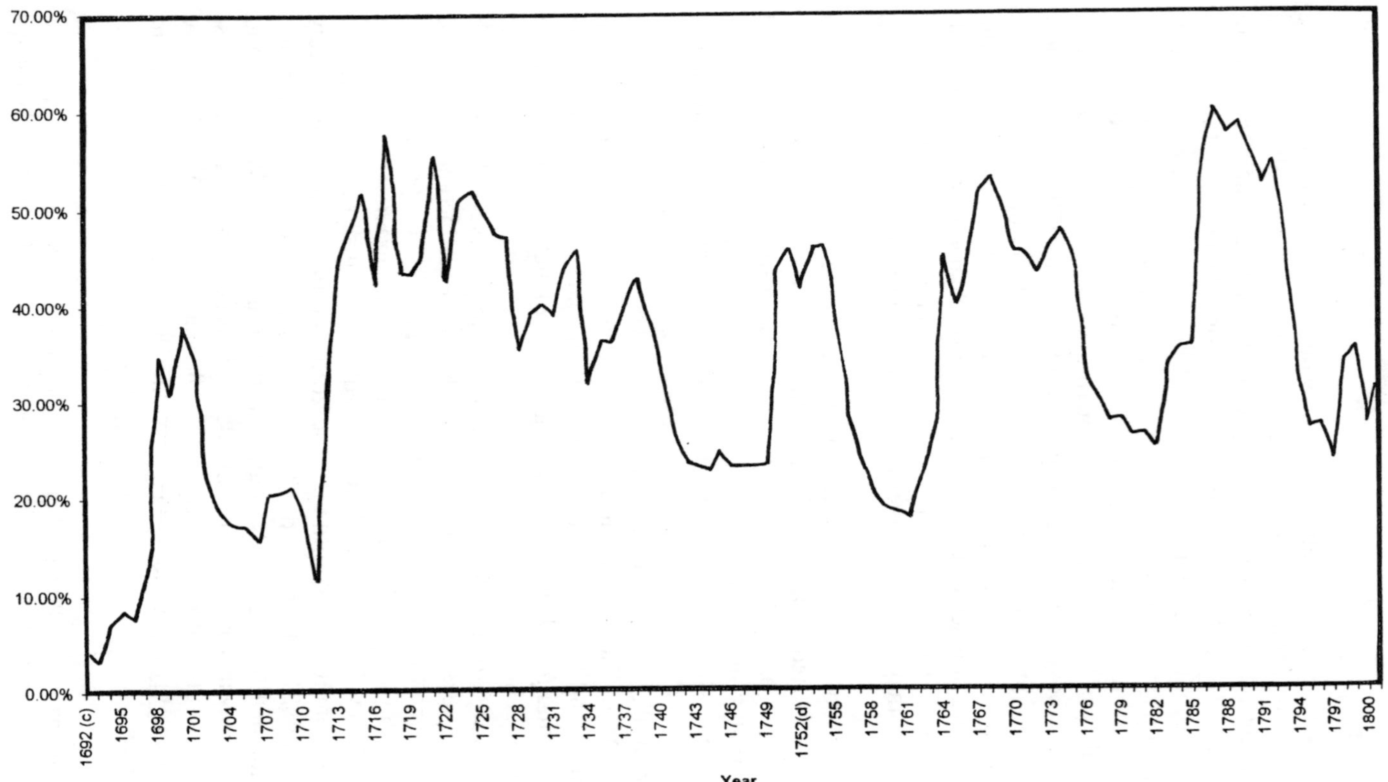

Figure 2.5 Total debt charges as a percentage of total net expenditure, 1692–1801.

largely in terms of income tax, for obvious reasons – the sharp decline in a principal source of revenue, customs duties, in time of war and the comparatively easy avoidance of assessed taxes. Additionally, there were reduced exports to the Continent and a consequent fall in the willingness of continental merchants to accept English bills of exchange. This meant that the market for the government's short-term debt was hurt. Earlier, there had been proposals for a tax of this kind, for example by Fauquier in 1756, suggesting a capitation tax levied on all those with incomes above a prescribed level. But it was in the 1790s that the most urgent proposals were being made. In 1799 William Pitt introduced the first income tax. This did not quite represent a complete break with the theory and practice of the past, but the final changeover from expenditure tax to income tax was certainly prompted by the pressures of wartime; they were both inefficient and easily avoided (see Kennedy, 1913).

The Napoleonic Wars were expensive, and income tax was imposed on a graduated scale from 2d/£ on an income of £60, rising to 2s/£ on an income of £200, with incomes below £60 exempt. The tax proved remarkably successful as a source of revenue. In its first year it raised £6m, and while Pitt's estimate had been £10m, that was a little ambitious. In the years when it was in force during the wars, it raised one-sixth of all revenue required; it was repealed in 1816 at the end of the wars. David Ricardo produced one of the most distinguished works on taxation and greatly favored keeping the income tax (and even levying a once-and-for-all wealth tax) as a means of helping to redeem the national debt.

The needs of government were limited in the course of the nineteenth century. Nevertheless, it had become clear that the income tax was the wave of the future, and it was reintroduced in 1842 (in part in anticipation of the repeal of protectionist duties) and thereafter was renewed annually by Finance Acts. It was raised in the course of the nineteenth century, but it was not until the First World War that it was raised sharply (Stamp, 1921). The numerous tax enactments were consolidated in legislation of 1918.[4] The rates went up again in the Second World War and PAYE (pay as you earn – regular deductions rather than annual assessment) was also introduced. By the middle years of the twentieth century it was the highest-yielding tax, providing 40 percent of all government revenue.

[4] Royal Commission, 1919–20. Stamp was called as one of the first witnesses before the Commission and, following his brilliant reply, was immediately invited to join the Commission.

It was also in the Second World War that income tax began to be regarded as an instrument of fiscal policy in the Keynesian sense that it could be used to help regulate the course of aggregate national income. Increasing the tax served to reduce disposable incomes and so dampen consumption expenditure, and decreasing taxes reversed that pattern. And of course, income tax has also been used increasingly as an instrument of social policy in the redistribution of income.

Let us return to the beginning of our period and pick up on what concerned the state in the late seventeenth century – tax collection. There was wide discussion on tax collection and at an early point a privatized system was opted for, that of tax farming. Discussion followed on how to monitor tax farmers. Between 1658 and 1671 there was a lot of tax farming under rules set by the state. The origins lie in the management of land, and it was a system favored by parliamentarians. The 1660s and 1670s witnessed struggles between the farmers and the king, with Charles II wanting a hike in rent and the tax farmers wanting assurances on foreign policy. The Treasury developed a tight system of control with three-year leases in London, and kept squeezing the farmers. Finally, the last lease for excise was for 1680–3. Tax farming was a necessary part of the process of learning about collection. The excise was to evolve into the most efficient department of state: the basis of the Victorian civil service (see Roseveare, 1991). Customs was different where the opportunities for corruption were extensive.

2.3.5 National Debt

Taxation consistently failed to provide sufficient revenue to cover expenditure, and the great growth of the national debt is testament to that fact. Borrowing has almost always been needed to support government spending.[5]

The origins of the modern British national debt can be found, like much of this story, in the late seventeenth century with the establishment of superiority in the position of Parliament over the Crown. When Parliament had to approve and guarantee all loans to the state, the basis for the modern national debt was laid. The foundation of the Bank of England in 1694 with a specific loan to the state is often taken as the official date of birth.

In the early days of the national debt in the 1690s, the total amounted to less than £10m. This has risen for most of the time since, though there

[5] Currently, lotteries are being used as a further source of revenue. It is of interest to note that they were a popular means of raising revenue in the eighteenth century.

were long periods of comparative stability and even, on occasion, some actual decline.[6] The spectacular growth came in the eighteenth century, with the financial needs of war being responsible for almost all of the major jumps in the debt. In the mid-eighteenth century it stood at £78m, and following the wars of the second half of the century it rose to £240m by 1790. The Napoleonic Wars then drove it up dramatically to £840m by 1820. Not surprisingly, the issue of the debt generated some discussion. Measures for coping with it were proposed frequently, and on occasion suggestions were made for abolishing the debt altogether.

Most of that first decade, the 1690s, was taken up with war and, as is usual, a number of different fiscal measures were employed. But as is also usual, these measures did not cover the costs, and borrowing was resorted to at an early point. Short-term loans were raised but at ever-rising interest rates, and by 1692 the situation was critical. Three new techniques were then employed: lotteries, tontines, and annuities. The latter two were long-term instruments and mark the beginning of deliberate long-term borrowing. But these were all dwarfed by the borrowing organized in the foundation of the Bank of England.

There was considerable debate on the debt in the course of the eighteenth century. The views of the distinguished figure David Hume are well known; he was deeply apprehensive about the viability of the state. Adam Smith too worried about it but, accepting it as a fact of life, he took comfort in the superiority of the British tax system and felt that it ensured Britain's growth in spite of the high debt. "Great Britain seems to support with ease, a burden which, half a century ago nobody believed her capable of supporting" (Smith, 1776).

It may be of interest to note that in the eighteenth century Austria, Bavaria, and Wurtemberg succeeded in preventing their debt from rising. France reduced its debt by 30 percent between 1716 and 1771. Tuscany repaid some of it, as did Venice (Bonney, 1996, p. 532).

The nineteenth century was essentially one of peace and of relatively stable prices throughout, but even so, it is remarkable that in 1850 the total outstanding debt had fallen to £790m, and that by 1900 it had fallen further to £570m. It then rose in nominal terms to £670m in 1910. It rose startlingly in the First World War to £8,000m in 1920, was still £8,000m in 1940, and then, following the Second World War, climbed to £26,000m in 1950. In the inflationary times since then, it continued to grow in nominal terms to £33,000m in 1970 and £95,000m in 1980.

[6] Part of the job description of the governor of the Bank of England was to reduce the national debt.

Of course, what really matters is not the nominal value of the debt but the ability of the state to service it. Therefore it is the percentage of national income that the debt makes up that is a better guide to the problem it presents. For the 1690s, in the absence of national income figures, a reasonable estimate puts the proportion in the region of 15 percent. A century later, following various wars, it was around 100 percent. Following the Napoleonic Wars it had risen to 250 percent. Thereafter, with economic growth and peace, it fell fairly steadily, so that by the beginning of the twentieth century it had come down to a very manageable 35 percent. The First World War pushed it back to around 150 percent and the Second World War took it to around 240 percent. These latter two enormous rises severely constrained government policy (both fiscal and monetary) for long periods in the twentieth century. But the share again fell steadily in the post–World War Two period, so that in 1990 it was down to the level of a century ago – around 40 percent of total income.

For our present purposes, however, what needs to be explained is what it was that allowed such growth in tax and debt. We return to that issue after introducing another essential ingredient in the story – the monetary dimension.

2.4 MONETARY INSTITUTIONS

2.4.1 Some Antecedents

There are always antecedents, and again, some of them can be found in preceding developments in The Netherlands (Feaveryear, 1963, sets out some of these, as does Horsefield, 1960, and de Vries in this volume). Neal has provided a useful catalog of some of the essential ingredients. Something of interest happened in the price revolution in the sixteenth century: prices rose more rapidly than the flow of new specie. Therefore, money must have been been used more efficiently. And in support of that, the nominal interest rate seems to have fallen. With the new discoveries came new profit opportunities, but these could be realized only after periods of waiting, and so new forms of finance were needed.

Charles V's levying of excise and property taxes (1542) gave rise to new financial instruments and to markets for long-term securities. Van der Wee (1993) points to the perfection of the negotiability of the foreign exchange bill in the late sixteenth century in Antwerp, particularly the serial endorsements, as being of key significance. This innovation was transferred to Amsterdam when Portuguese Jews and various Protestants were expelled from Antwerp in 1585. Innovations spread with such migrations – as did the flow of financial capital – and England began to benefit as a recipient. William III gave active encouragement to this process and gave foreigners high status. Wartime needs continued to fuel these developments, as it gave emigré bankers new opportunities for large profits.

According to some, there was by the early 1650s a sophisticated credit mechanism in place, as well as substantial taxation, and these lay at the root of the English naval success in the first Dutch War.

2.4.2 Background

Following the establishment of parliamentary government in England, substantial changes in the financial system occurred, and they continued for much of the next century. They were followed for another century by industrial and economic changes, all of which resulted in Britain's becoming the world's foremost economic power, with a highly developed financial system. Britain was to remain at the heart of the world economy until around the outbreak of the First World War.

The period, in Dennis Robertson's words, is one in which we see in the seventeenth century "the London goldsmiths discovering that they could, in the most literal sense, make money by lending out their own promises to pay, and so filching from the Crown its immemorial right to determine, subject always to the vicissitudes of foreign trade, the volume of the country's money supply." And this period continues until just after the 1844 act, when Robert Peel tried "to recapture the right of the Crown by giving a virtual monopoly of note issue to the Bank of England. . . . But alas, or rather perhaps fortunately, the banks had already invented a dodge even neater than the note, namely the cheque, which enabled them to escape from Peel's net" (quoted in Dennison and Presley, 1992, p. 59).

Discussion has seldom faded on the respective beneficial and adverse effects of money, and hence by implication of banks. The introduction of money to an economy raises welfare by removing the inefficiency of individuals having to search for coincident wants. The use of money and its smooth transmission helps promote efficient production and consumption. That much is positive. On the negative side there can be excess money in relation to output, and the consequent inflation introduces inequities into debtor–creditor relationships. All that has been known for a long time, though some of the niceties of the process continue to be debated.

Heads of state have long used money for their own ends. In England the Tudor inflation was in part attributable to the debasement of the currency – taxation without representation – the practice being to produce coins with a lower metallic content than their face value intimated. Governments everywhere have been unable to resist the temptation to produce too much money and hence subject the population to the inflation tax – a tax that is impossible to avoid and one that even the weakest government can impose. On the other hand, there were several recoinages when attempts were made to restore order.

The late seventeenth century brought quite dramatic changes in the monetary economy. The scale and pace of change in financial innovations were particularly concentrated in the decade of the 1690s. What happened then is said to have constituted what can truly be called a revolution. The word *revolution* has perhaps been overused in economic historical studies, but perhaps this is an occasion when it is appropriate. How far outside that decade the term could be taken to apply is more problematic. Clearly, several essential conditions were laid down in the preceding decades, and the ramifications of the changes of the 1690s carry on through the first few decades of the eighteenth century. When the subject was first set out with such clarity by Dickson (1967), the whole period of financial change carried the dates 1688–1756. In the most recent view (Roseveare, 1991), the dating has been extended somewhat to 1660–1760 and the emphasis placed on breaking the sharper discontinuities that had previously obtained.

The background to the revolution was the change that had taken place in the nature of the state (importantly, Parliament's control of finance). The responses in banking and finance were remarkable. There followed the well-known institutional innovations in the founding of the Bank of England and the origins of the national debt. It was also at this point that the stock market properly emerged, though there had been trade in stock prior to this time.

The military defeat at the hands of the Dutch in the 1660s was not unconnected with the financial inadequacies of the government. And yet, by 1760 Britain was indisputably the leading world power. Its financial power rested on a complex set of factors, many of them intangible, such as the confidence and trust that were the necessary prerequisites for good credit. A host of factors could be arrayed as part of the necessary background to the changes that came in the late seventeenth century, but high on that list, and probably crucial, was the initiative of 1665 to facilitate the government's wartime borrowing. Parliament was obliged to guarantee loans made to the king, and in exchange for loans, lenders were given official receipts that could be traded. This was the beginning of the gilt-edged security, and it also marked the beginning of accountability.

The system was not, of course, reformed at a stroke. Bankers continued to earn huge profits and public opprobrium, and since one ambition of the 1665 initiative had been to allow government to borrow directly from the public, further measures were introduced. Certificates called *Treasury Orders* were created in the years 1667–71, when Sir George Downing was secretary to the Treasury.

When in December 1671 Charles II decided to defer repayment of debts (known as the *Stop of the Exchequer*), the beginning of another financial innovation occurred. The debt that was frozen was owed in the main to the less than popular goldsmith bankers, which undoubtedly mitigated the effects of the action at the time. Nevertheless, the king had irreparably damaged the Crown's credit and at the same time destroyed a generation of bankers. The solution to the problem, which came in 1677, was the creation of annuities. The bankers were reimbursed, but there was an obligation on them to repay their depositors. The origins of the national debt were laid; on the positive side, the annuities became the first long-term investment instruments. An active secondary market in these developed in the 1680s. There were positive and negative elements arising out of the stoppage. Although one group of bankers was destroyed, a new group came to the fore, and they avoided the business of the Crown and gained greater credit from the City for that. Child's and Hoare's and the forerunner of Martin's were all born at this time.

As far as the Crown was concerned, many other sources of funds were still available to it, especially the large joint stock companies such as the East India Company. But the Crown was of diminishing importance, and the point to stress is that the basis of the nation's financial strength lay in the development of the Treasury as a powerful department of state and in the parliamentary control of finance (Bridges, 1964).

The 1690s is when most of the interesting action took place. It was a decade of extraordinary financial innovation. The great achievements of the decade in financial terms were the establishment of long-term borrowing, the founding of the Bank of England, and the recoinage of the metallic currency and the circulation of paper money – based on metal. Progress rested on acceptable government finance; indeed, it was underpinned by such finance. Neal (1990) provides a full account of these developments and what they meant for annuities, and what in turn they meant for the development of financial markets.

It is worth noting here a view on the subject of property rights in relation to credit. Zahedieh (1996) argues in her examination of the availability of credit in the late seventeenth century that in the absence of sufficiently well-defined and enforceable property rights, credit depended on intimate knowledge of the parties and hence on trust.

Groups that developed tight networks of contol to enforce good behavior and provide accurate information secured an advantage. It was for this reason that religious groups did particularly well, especially in the more difficult areas of trade (such as foreign trade), and why Quakers and Jews in particular prospered.

2.4.3 Banks

The precise origins of modern banking are still the subject of debate. A number of possible claimants compete for the source – scriveners, goldsmiths, and the older state financiers – but what is clear is that by the beginning of the period covered here, the practice of deposit banking was established. Private banks prospered, especially in London, while joint stock banks were prohibited by law. Country banks were the product of, and the contributors to, the process of industrialization in the provinces. They developed a close and profitable business with the London private banks (Pressnell, 1956), while joint stock banking had to wait for the change in mood of the nineteenth century and the gradual erosion of the Bank of England's monopoly.

Forms of deposit banking had existed in continental Europe from medieval times, but English deposit banking had its beginnings in the middle of the seventeenth century. Deposit banking was different from what was commonly regarded by contemporaries as banking, for they saw banks as money lenders and brokers rather than the more modern concept of institutions making money by the creation and use of deposits.

The earliest explanation of the origins of deposit banking (and one that went unchallenged for almost two centuries) was that the goldsmiths some time in the seventeenth century began to act as cashiers. When they later began to hold cash (or deposits) they paid interest on it, and a natural next step was that they loaned these reserves out at higher rates of interest than they paid to their depositors. Tawney (1912), for one, disputed the view that the goldsmiths were the source, arguing that the Elizabethan scriveners took deposits from graziers and lent them out at a profit. His view therefore broke the line between private banking and state banking. The real authority on the origins of banking is Richards (1929), who provided a more eclectic view, holding that the state bankers' experience was transmitted to the goldsmith bankers, and that neither should be excluded in a full account.

Scriveners, brokers, and goldsmiths had long performed some of the functions associated with banking and made their profits from the fees they charged for their services. But they had stopped short of the key function of modern banking: the creation of deposits. Evidence is not easy to assemble, but it is clear that the practice, albeit in nascent form, was developing in the course of the seventeenth century. Sir Robert Clayton, whose origins were with the scriveners, was one of the first such bankers, holding deposits of almost £2m in the mid-1660s. At that time, goldsmith bankers were also making loans with their clients' money.

This then is where the origins of the London private banks lie, and a key question is, what was it that prompted them to begin behaving as they did? There were around 30 of them in the early eighteenth century, and most of them were to survive for a long time. In fact their numbers grew modestly in the course of the eighteenth century, there being 50 in 1750 and 70 by 1800, some of which still exist – names such as Hoare's and Child's. These latter were "west end" banks, as opposed to the City banks. The former dealt with wealthy clients, usually in the aristocracy, and specialized in mortgages, while the latter's balance sheets were biased in favor of trade bills and stock exchange securities. The City private banks also played a significant part in channeling the funds of the provincial private banks, into the London money market. Note issue was never of any significance to the London private banks, and by the 1770s what there was had died out altogether.

We return, however, for a moment to the question of origins. From the Restoration of the monarchy with Charles II in 1660 to the year of the establishment of the Bank of England, 1694, is the time when private banking emerged, prospered, and became established. There was the transferability of debt; interbank clearing; institutional arrangements for facilitating the payment of taxes; problems of investing in large-scale debt; and connections with the international bullion market. There are connections between some of these, but no necessary logic taking us from one to the other and linking them all.

The goldsmith-bankers created a web of intermediation that linked the monetary and financial institutions of the time in both the public and private sectors. This produced an integrated system, though of course there were some negative aspects. For example, while interbank clearing of debt helped with a core function of banking such as delegated lending, it created other problems, notably that of asymmetric information and the problem attaching to fractional reserves, the potential for runs (Quinn, 1997).

Christopher Hill (1969) remarked that for finance the Middle Ages ended in 1643. Two new taxes were introduced then (excise and land), and this helped to transfer command over resources from landowners to moneylenders. But he might have dated the transition at 1640. For when Charles I closed the Mint in 1640 and seized the bullion that was there, it was the end of trust in the monarchy and the real beginnings of private holdings – in a way, the true beginning of the active goldsmith-banker. Even though the revenue from new taxes aided Charles II, the Crown's expenditure (largely war finance) ran ahead of income, and borrowing from City institutions became necessary. A combination of the needs of government finance and the distrust of the Crown meant that funds flowed to merchants, who then lent to the Crown and to others.

In the middle of all this lay a desire both to bring down interest rates and to increase purchasing power (often couched in terms of alleviating poverty) – a theme that runs throughout this period and beyond. And there seemed also to be a widespread belief that emulation of Dutch practices would help to bring this about. All the key elements of modern banking therefore emerged in these decades. Bankers did not quite come into favor for what they could do, but they made themselves indispensable without perhaps becoming popular. They were then severely damaged, and some bankrupted, by the Stop of the Exchequer in 1672 (though some staggered on for some time); but then the 1680s was a decade of relative calm before the war needs of William once again resurrected the chronic problems of public finance (Wilson, 1969).

And yet, whatever the antecedents of the financial revolution were, the revolution could not be completed until after 1688. That was because James II's pro-French and pro-Catholic policies frightened what were predominantly Protestant bankers and investors, whose support was needed. As noted, bankers such as Hoares were Protestant and were established at this time (in 1672).

A key element in the evolution of banking was the system of bilateral settlement in interbank debt that evolved, rather than a centralized system; this decentralized system worked effectively to minimize transaction costs and also allowed the monitoring and discipline of members. This picture (from Quinn, 1997) is derived in the main from the records of Backwell, and Barnaby of the most distinguished and successful of these goldsmith-bankers. Changes in Backwell's accounting system are identified as facilitating clearing with other bankers. An examination is made of three bankers' accounts with Backwell for the eight-year period 1665–72. The means of settlement devised by these bankers is said to have expanded the circulation of bank debt (notes and checks).

The emergence of banking in general is usually expressed in terms of the needs of the state and the distrust of the Crown. But something else that might be considered is the following. The period 1510–1660 was a long period of inflation. Several generations had become accustomed to gentle inflation, and that petered out around 1660. The second half of the seventeenth century was one in which there were calls for an increase in purchasing power (as they expressed it) – that is, for an increase in the money supply or in credit. Was the emergence of these bankers and the greater tolerance of bankers in part a response to these calls, and indeed to the complicated effects of the Free Coinage Act of 1666? We do not know with any precision what was happening to the state of economic activity, but it was expanding. The likelihood is that the general level of prices was falling, and the difference between output and prices might explain the pressure for, or the tolerance of, fractional reserve bankers who were creating money.

Something else that can be added to this story is that these bankers were increasingly successful in taking up the task of tax farming – that is, collecting taxes. This was to improve their banking business enormously for a number of reasons. It extended their deposit base and the use of their notes, and in the process generally raised the awareness and acceptability of notes and banking. When banks collected taxes, they increased their knowledge of the local economy – information on local borrowers and depositors – and that increased their efficiency in the banking business. In other words, if a proper taxation system depends on security of property rights and this came decisively with the triumph of Parliament over the Crown, and if a key element in the growth and success of banking was this operation, then secure property rights indirectly promoted private banking. That, in turn, paved the way for improved financial intermediation and hence for growth.

2.5 EIGHTEENTH- AND NINETEENTH-CENTURY DEVELOPMENTS

What was truly remarkable about the eighteenth century was that heavy wartime borrowing was accepted with such little discussion. It would be wrong to suggest that a complete transformation in finance and behavior in markets had been effected by the opening years of the eighteenth century. As is well known, financial markets were still in their infancy and there was still at that point little certainty in transactions. Indeed, bribery and corruption took place on a huge scale and were central issues in the eighteenth century even if the scale was less than that elsewhere. The corruption was in part less because there was a superior means for taxing and borrowing. The ability to tax and borrow on the scale outlined earlier undoubtedly had to do with the honest and efficient tax administration.

Brewer (1989) explains the eighteenth-century developments in the following terms: "The 'new' administration did not replace but was added on to existing institutions. Its rules and practices were not accompanied by wholesale reform of older departments, many of which contained sinecurists, pluralists and officers whose chief source of income took the form of fees. Rather administrative innovation in Britain, as elsewhere in Europe, either worked around existing office-holders and their interests or reached an accommodation with them by combining the old and new to their mutual satisfaction" (p. 69). The new government agencies "rewarded full-time employees with salaries rather than fees and offered a career ladder of graded appointments with progressively higher renumeration which culminated in a government pension. They also expected administrative loyalty and sought to encourage an ethos of public duty and private probity" (p. 69).

Nevertheless, what still needs explaining is what enabled governments to borrow and tax on the scale shown. The principal part of the explanation must rest in the establishment of reliable bond markets backed by the credibility of Parliament. As we have already noted, wars, of which there were many, were financed by the issue of debt – usually unfunded debt. This was made up of various short-term bills – army bills, navy bills, and ordnance bills – and increasingly by Exchequer bills. The funded debt – that is, the long-term securities that were used to retire the short-term obligations – was less expensive, came in stages, and was improved enormously in midcentury by the establishment of the irredeemable 3 percent consols. Funding was carried out during and after wars.

It should also be noted that the availability of liquid assets in the form of government debt in bank portfolios enabled bankers to take on riskier loans in the rest of their portfolio or to roll over short-term loans more readily to the private sector.

A number of experiments were carried out in the early years of the eighteenth century as a search for more acceptable instruments was continuously made. The South Sea promotion was an illustration of this. While the plan eventually produced the South Sea Bubble (in part at least a function of corruption – Clapham, 1994), it did nevertheless convert most of the outstanding irredeemable debt of the time and helped bring about a reduction in interest rates – and hence reduced the burden of debt servicing. While the bubble was something of a setback to the establishment of credibility and hence government finance, it did lead the way to the establishment of consols between 1749 and 1757.

The trend in interest rates in the eighteenth century was down, with little jumps at various points associated with war. But it was the establishment of consols that determined the long-term borrowing rate (Pressnell, 1960). That rate influenced rates across the board as investors switched between gilts, East India stock, bonds, land, and in due course turnpike and canal shares. The successful borrowing that was thus made possible at lower interest rates allowed further borrowing, and as reputation and credibility improved, so did the possibilities of ever-further borrowing. The proportion of war expenditure that was financed by borrowing rose from 51 percent at the end of the seventeenth century to over 80 percent in the American War of Independence (O'Brien, 1988, Table 3).

Nevertheless, the huge rises in debt during the Seven Years' War (1756–63) and the American Revolutionary War (1776–83) did result in fear of financial distress and brought about steep rises in taxation. Further, the Sinking Fund was established in 1786, and over the next few years of peace budget surpluses were used to reduce the debt. This was a way of showing the public that taxation would be brought down, and so it further enhanced the government's future borrowing power. This was just as well because Britain was about to embark on its costliest period of war ever, and over the years of the Napoleonic Wars debt rose staggeringly to £800m – roughly 220 percent of national income.

O'Brien (1994) reports that borrowing during the Napoleonic Wars accounted for 90 percent of war expenditure. The sale of government securities forced interest rates up sharply. Unfunded loans as a share of total loans increased from 19 percent in 1797 to 76 percent in 1808 (Bordo and White, 1994, p. 256). The fact that interest rates rose in wartime should not, of course, cause surprise. As the state bids for scarce resources the price is bound to go up, but additionally a rise in real interest rates should reduce consumption and leisure and promote saving and labor effort.

British war experience in the eighteenth and nineteenth centuries might be seen as an early example of what is now called *tax smoothing*. If future government expenditure were known with certainty, the current tax rate would be set to reflect that expenditure and remain constant over time. In the real world, where future expenditure remains uncertain, taxes will follow a martingale process[7] as the government tries to predict the future course of expenditure and sets taxes that are consistent with such forecasts. Then only unpredictable events will mean changes in the tax rates.

The credibility of eighteenth-century governments grew steadily from faltering beginnings after the Glorious Revolution and the Hanoverian Settlement. Foreign purchases lend some support to this (see Neal, 1990).

By the nineteenth century there was supposedly a tradition of raising taxes rather than loans, and direct taxes rather than indirect ones; this was regarded as proper behavior. It is not clear where the notion arose

[7] That process is analogous to the residuals in a regression, where what remains unexplained should reduce to change variation.

that wars were once paid for as they were fought. Certainly, in the eighteenth century that was not the case. The colossal growth in the national debt as a result of war finance has already been noted. The nineteenth century may have been fortunate in being one of relative peace (for England at least), with the Crimean War being a comparatively small-scale affair. Certainly, as William Gladstone dominated fiscal affairs in the middle of the nineteenth century he became, rightly or wrongly, identified with complete fiscal rectitude; Gladstonian finance was very much of the Mr. Micawber variety. A small budget with a small surplus was regarded as the key to happiness. If ever there was a time when the financial markets operated with more or less complete trust in the state to keep spending low and stable, this must have been it. It was after all the age of laissez-faire and relatively little government activity. The financial system was, apart from some statutory guidelines, left to its own devices, and increasingly it monitored and policed its own activities in what were effectively clubs.

The banking system whose origins we have described was to continue to evolve beyond the essentially unitary structure of the eighteenth century. In London, as noted, the private banks retained their strength, and in the rest of the country banks flourished from the first half of the eighteenth century. Provincial, or country, banks grew up in tandem with the economic changes that took place in the provinces in the course of the century. They were clearly an important part of the industrialization process. Their origins can be found in a number of different kinds of businesses, from manufacturing to retailing and service firms. Thus there were brewers and distillers, drapers, tax collectors, and solicitors all prominent in the nascent banking business, all for slightly different reasons but essentially because they had idle balances that they wished to put to work. There were perhaps 12 of these country banks in 1750, and these had grown to 120 by the 1780s, and even more dramatically to almost 400 by the end of the century and possibly as many as 800 by 1810. Precision is not possible since definition is not straightforward. These banks provided a remittance business in bills on London (dealing with the private London City banks). They created credit and the circulating medium for their local communities by issuing notes, and once they had built up the necessary confidence, they were trusted with deposits and their contribution to deposit banking began. They took up the Scottish innovation of lending on overdraft.

2.6 JOINT STOCK BANKS

A number of factors lie behind the change in legislation that allowed the emergence and great growth of the modern joint stock banks. As noted, there was considerable antipathy to the Bank of England at the beginning of the nineteenth century and public opinion was strongly opposed to the Bank's monopoly position. Further, the collapse of hundreds of banks in the recession that came at the end of the Napoleonic Wars persuaded many that there was a need for institutions with a stronger capital base and that the restrictions on size were in need of revision. Also, the growth of the economy and the increasing size of some enterprises undoubtedly added more weight to this force.

In 1826, following another burst of failures, an act was passed that finally allowed joint stock banking. There was not complete freedom, however. These banks were institutions with unlimited liability but, more important, they could operate only outside a distance of 65 miles from London, and they were thus denied access to some of the most lucrative business in the country. The act of 1825 also encouraged the Bank of England to establish branches in the provinces to export good practice and to provide competition for the anticipated new joint stock banks.

In 1833 a further act was passed allowing joint stock banks to operate in London for all kinds of banking business except the issue of notes, which was to remain the preserve of the Bank of England. In the next few years following that act, some of the great joint stock banks were founded. The 1844 act provided the concluding piece of legislation.

The system then moved fairly steadily to a highly concentrated structure with just a few banks dominating but with thousands of branches (branch banking was another Scottish innovation). This provided a highly stable structure with banks with well-diversified portfolios, across all sections of the economy and across all geographical areas. The stability was pronounced, with no banking panic after 1866 and no financial crisis. By the third quarter of the nineteenth century, to some extent, stability rested on the behavior of the Bank of England.

The Bank of England was established as a joint stock company completely separated from government and without the obligation to meet cash needs on demand. When central banks are discussed, they are usually referred to as being the government's bank, and in addition the banker's bank, and while they do indeed fulfill these functions, their precise nature needs to be carefully specified. None of these issues was being discussed when the Bank was being set up, nor did it crop up as a subject of serious discussion until the nineteenth century. The Bank lent to the government and to a host of private customers and enjoyed a monopoly of joint stock banking until the second quarter of the nineteenth century. The evolutionary path to its modern form took a long time and had to await some developments in monetary theory. The directors of the Bank resisted for a very long time the idea that they could influence the price level.

However, in the course of the nineteenth century, with the Bank acquiring a monopoly of note issue and assuming its principal macro function of stabilizing the exchange rate, its private function as a profit maximizer began to come into conflict. The public responsibility came to dominate, and the Bank's private business declined in importance. It gradually took on the role of lender of last resort to the system.

2.7 EXPORTS

Very briefly, this section indicates how these institutions were transmitted to or adopted in other countries, though it should be said that this is mainly a job for others – those on the receiving end. The adoption of British practices across a range of activities should surely not be surprising. In the middle of the nineteenth century, when it was obvious that Britain was the dominant power, it seemed that there were lessons to be learned from it. Even free trade, notoriously difficult to achieve on any scale for any time, was quite widely adopted for a while, since Britain seemed to have prospered under such a policy. The widespread adoption of the gold standard too is associated with the desire by some to join the prosperous and civilized club led by Britain. It is not surprising therefore that monetary and fiscal institutions similar to Britain's should be imitated, too. Some countries were affected directly as a consequence of the British Empire. British banks, or banks headquartered in London, or banks with very close connections with London were often the principal financial intermediaries in these countries (the white dominions being the most obvious but not the only cases), and so became the transmitters either implicitly or explicitly of British practice.

Further, the growing dominance of the gold standard in the late nineteenth century coupled with the strength of sterling meant that many empire countries worked on what was in effect a sterling standard. Sound finance was in effect exported by these means. In other cases, it was achieved through currency boards. So it was with fiscal institutions, where Britain had pioneered much of the territory.

What is perhaps somewhat surprising (if I have picked up on the correct literature) is that more countries, and perhaps particularly some in Latin America, did not adopt more explicitly British practice. Take an illustration from Argentina. Britain and Argentina had long had close connections, particularly after the Treaty of 1825. But in the 1850s, when Argentina struggled with paper currency stabilization, it seems to have repeated the mistakes made by Britain 50 years before. That experience appears to have had remarkable parallels: war, blockades, excess issues, depreciating currency, and so on. And of course, a great debate erupted and was accompanied by an explosion of literature on the cause of the inflation/depreciation. Yet none of this seems to have been referred to in the discussions in Argentina in the 1850s. My recollection of Brazil in the 1880s suggests something similar. This contrasts with the situations in both the United States and Canada (see Sylla and Bordo and Redish in this volume). In the United States, under the tutelage of Alexander Hamilton, British practices were adopted, including an imitation of the Bank of England in the Bank of the United States. In Canada there were similarities too. Both cases may reflect the fact that in North America property rights were secure, whereas in South America they were much less secure.

However, the main point here is that this is a subject for others. British experience can be said to have derived in good part from the long period of gestation in the development of property rights and in falling transaction costs. However, it has to be remembered that at important points there were other significant ingredients in which the accession of a Protestant monarch in the late seventeenth century must be included. But the range of financial instruments available and the relatively good behavior of a government constrained by a democratic Parliament were paramount. On that basis, reputation and credibility were allowed to develop.

2.8 CONCLUSION

In the Middle Ages the revenue base of European monarchies was neither large enough nor secure enough to allow large, permanent debts to be accumulated. Thus, as Bonney (1996) puts it, "the test of a state's capacity to modernise was not simply its ability to accumulate debt but to restructure it" (p. 15). From 1688 to 1815, as we have noted, Britain was frequently at war and became, like its main rivals, a fiscal-military state. But Britain was better at it than most. And the reason for that, in the argument of this chapter, is that it developed stable fiscal and monetary institutions before the other nations, based on well-established and secure property rights.

Such rights do seem to have been quite well established at an early date, and we may conclude that they were necessary but not sufficient for further development. In the second half of the seventeenth century, significant improvements in the organization and governance of state finances, in tax imposition and collection, and in monetary matters all pushed things along further. Then, in the decade of the 1690s, there were some further dramatic changes. It is difficult to escape the conclusion that 1688 was a date of considerable significance. We have noted the truly startling increase in the number of joint stock companies that followed and the concomitant growth in the number of investors. And, the establishment of a stable, reliable market in long-term securities was important. These developments were supported and facilitated by parallel developments in banking, which in turn were connected to the collection of taxes. The practice of banks holding highly liquid debt grew. This was important in a number of ways, and not least for government debt sales.

What the eighteenth-century experience demonstrates is that the government was able both to tax – essentially by the excise – and to borrow on a huge scale, and to do that both domestically and internationally. Credibility improved, reputation was established, and that allowed increasing taxation. Credibility is a simple concept but one that is difficult to demonstrate empirically. In a modern setting with abundant and robust data, we might measure it in terms of the difference in real bond yields across countries. Such data are relatively scarce for the period that interests us, but it is probably not without significance that English bond rates were falling across the long period when borrowing and debt were rising steeply. The London securities market is said to have contributed to low interest rates and to the stability of the banking system.

The export of these good practices came in the main with the second empire in the nineteenth century when British military policy had, in the words of O'Brien, "moved away from the Hanoverian view that high levels of expenditure on the ground forces of Britain and her allies were essential in favour of 'blue water' policies".

REFERENCES

Ashley, W. (1903). *The Tariff Problem* (P. S. King & London).

Beckett, J. V. (1985). "Land tax or excise: the levying of taxation in eighteenth century England," *Economic History Review*, Vol. C, pp. 205–308.

Beckett, J. and M. Turner (1990). "Taxation in the eighteenth century," *Economic History Review*, Vol. XLIII, pp. 377–403.

Beveridge, W. (1931). *Tariffs: The Case Examined* (Longmans, Green & Co.).

Bisschop, W. R. (1912). *The Rise of the London Money Market 1640–1826* (London: Stevens and Haynes).

Black, Jeremy (ed.). (1982). *The Origins of War in Early* (Edinburgh: John Donal).

Bonney, R. (ed.) (1996). *The Origins of the Modern State in Europe from the Thirteenth to Eighteen Century: Economic Systems and State Finance* (Oxford: Clarendon Press).

Bordo, M. and E. White (1994). "British and French finance during the Napoleonic Wars," in Forrest Capie and Michael Bordo (eds.), *Monetary Regimes in Transaction* (Cambridge: Cambridge University Press).

Braddick, M. (1994). *Parliamentary Taxation in Seventeenth Century England* (Woodbridge, U.K.: For the Royal History Society).

Brewer, J. (1989). *The Sinews of Power: War, Money and the English State 1688–1783* (New York: Alfred A Knopf).

Bridges, Lord (1964). *The Treasury* (London: George Allen and Unwin).

Britnell, Richard (1993). *The Commercialisation of English Society, 1000–1500* (Cambridge, UK: Cambridge University Press).

Burt, Roger (1995). "The transformation of the non-ferrous metal industries in the seventeenth and eighteenth centuries," *Economic History Review*, Vol. XLVIII, pp. 23–45.

Capie, Forrest (ed.). (1993). *A History of Banking* (London: Pickering and Chatto).

Clapham, J. (1944). *The Bank of England* (Cambridge, UK: Cambridge University Press).

Clark, Greg (1995). (American Economic Association Meetings).

Clay, C. G. A. (1984). *Economic Expansion and Social Change: England 1500–1700* (Cambridge, UK: Cambridge University Press).

Dennison, S. R. and John Presley (eds.) (1992). *Robertson on Economic Policy* (Macmillan).

Dickson, P. G. M. (1967). *The Financial Revolution* (London: Macmillan).

Dowell, S. (1884). *A History of Taxation in England from the Earliest Times to the Present Day*, 4 vols. (London: Frank Cass Edition, 1965).

Evans, Eric (1996). *The Forging of the Modern State: Early Industrial Britain 1783–1870* (Longman).

Feaveryear, Sir Albert (1963). *The Pound Sterling* (Oxford: Oxford University Press).

Fenn, Ch. (1837). *Compendium of English and Foreign Funds* (London: Gilbert and Piper).

Grapperhaus, Ferdinand (1989). *Taxes, Liberty and Property* (Amsterdam: Meijburg & Co.).

Harris, G. L. (1975). *King, Parliament and Public Finance to 1369* (Oxford: Oxford University Press).

Hartwell, M. (1981). "Tax in Industrial Revolution," *Cato Journal*, Vol. 1, No. 1.

Hill, C. (1969). *Reformation to Industrial Revolution* (London: Weidenfeld and Nicolson).

Hoffmann, P. T. and K. Norberg (eds.) (1995). *Fiscal Crises, Liberty and Representative Government 1450–1789* (Stanford, CA: Stanford University Press).

Holmes, Geoffrey (1993a). *The Making of a Great Power: Late Stuart and Early Georgian Britain 1660–1722* (London: Longman).

(1993b). *The Age of Oligarchy: Pre-industrial Britain 1722–1783* (London: Longman).

Homer, S. and R. Sylla (1991). *A History of Interest Rates* (New Brunswick), NJ: Rutgers University Press).

Hoon, S. (1968). *The Organisation of the English Customs System 1696–1786* (David and Chales: Newton Abbott).

Hoppitt, Julian (1990). "Attitudes to credit in Britain, 1680–1790," *Historical Journal*, Vol. XXXIII, pp. 305–22.

(1996a). "Parliamentary legislation 1660–1800," *Historical Journal*, Vol. XXXIX, pp. 305–22.

(1996b)."Political arithmetic in eighteenth century England," *Economic History Review*, Vol. XLIV, pp. 516–40.

Horne, T. A. (1990). *Property Rights and Poverty: Political Argument in Britain 1605–1834* (University of North Carolina Press: Chapel Hill).

Horsefield, K. (1960). *English Monetary Experiments* (London: G. Bell & Sons).

Jones, D. W. (1988). *War and Economy in the Age of William III and Marlborough* (Oxford: Oxford University Press).

Kennedy, W. (1913). *English Taxation 1640–1799* (London: reprint 1964).

MacLeod, Christine (1986). "The 1690s patent boom: Invention or stock-jobbing?" *Economic History Review*, Vol. XXXIX, pp. 549–63.

Mann, M. (1988). *State, War and Capitalism* (Oxford: Oxford University Press).

Mathias, P. (1959). *The Brewing Industry in England 1700–1800* (Cambridge: Cambridge University Press).

(1979). "Taxation and industrialisation in Britain 1700–1870," in P. Mathias *The Transformation of England* (London: Methuen).

Mathias, P. and P. K. O'Brien (1996). "Tax in Britain and France 1715–1810," *J.E.E.H.* 601–50.

McCloskey, D. N. (1978). "A mismeasure of the incidence of taxation in England and France, 1715–1810," *Journal of European Economic History*, Vol. 7, pp. 209–11.

Mitchell, Brian (1988). *Abstract of British Historical Statistics* (Cambridge: Cambridge University Press).

Neal, Larry (1990). *The Rise of Financial Capitalism* (Cambridge: Cambridge University Press).

North, Douglass C. (1977). "Markets and other association systems in history: The challenge of Karl Polanyi," *Journal of Economic History*.

(1981). *Structure and Change in Economic History* (N. W. Norton & Co.).

(1994). "The evolution of efficient markets" in J. James and M. Thomas, *Context of Capitalism* (Chicago: University University Press).

North, Douglass C. and Robert Paul Thomas (1973). *The Rise of the Western World: A New Economic History* (Cambridge U.K.: Cambridge University Press).

North, Douglass C. and Barry Weingast (1989). "Constitutions and commitment: The evolution of institutions governing public choice in seventeenth-century England," *Journal of Economic History*, Vol. 4, pp. 803–32.

O'Brien, P. K. (1967). "Government revenue 1783–1815" (D. Phil Oxon), unpublished.

(1988). "The political economy of taxation, 1660–1815," *Economic History Review*, Vol. XLI, pp. 1–32.

(1994). "Central government and the economy, 1688–1819" in Floud and McCloskey (eds.), *The Economic History of Britain since 1700* (Cambridge: Cambridge University Press).

O'Brien, P. K. and P. Hunt (1996). "Excises and the rise of the fiscal state in England 1586–1688," in R. Bonney (ed.), *The Rise of the Fiscal State in Europe* (Oxford: Oxford University Press).

Powell, Ellis (1966). *The Evolution of the London Money Market 1385–1915* (London: Frank Cass).

Pressnell, L. S. (1956). *Country Banking in the Industrial Revolution* (Oxford: Clarendon Press).

(1960)."The interest rate in the eighteenth century," in L. S. Pressnell (ed.), *Studies in the Industrial Revolution* (London: Athlone).

Quinn, S. (1997). "Goldsmith-banking: Mutual acceptance and interbank clearing in restoration London," *Explorations in Economic History*, vol. 34, 411–32.

Richards, R. D. (1929). *The Early History of Banking in England* (London: Staples Press Ltd).

Roseveare, H. (1973). *The Treasury 1660–1870* (London: George Allen and Unwin).

(1991). *The Financial Revolution 1660–1760* (London: Longman).

Sacks, D. H. (1994). "The paradox of taxation," in Hoffman and Norberg (eds.), *Fiscal Crises Liberty and Representative Government, 1450–1789* (Stanford, Calif.: Stanford University Press).

Scott, W. R. (1910). *The Constitution and Finance of English, Scottish and Irish Joint Stock Companies to 1720* (Cambridge: Cambridge University Press).

Sinclair, J. (1785). *A History of the Public Revenue of the British Empire* (London: Single Works).

Stamp, J. (1921). *The Fundamental Principles of Taxation in the Light of Modern Developments* (London: Macmillan and Co.).

Tawney R. H. (1912). *The Agrarian Problem in the Sixteenth Century* (London: Longmans Green).

Tilly, C. (1975). "Reflections on the history of European state making," in C. Tilly *The Formation of National States in Western Europe* (Princeton NJ: Princeton University Press).

Van der Wee, H. (1993). *The Low Countries in the Early Modern World* (Aldershot, U.K.: Ashgate Vasiorum).

de Vries, Jan and Woude, van der (1997). *The First Modern Economy* (Cambridge: Cambridge University Press).

Ward, W. R. (1953). *The English Land Tax in the Eighteenth Century* (Oxford: Oxford University Press).

Wilson, C. (1969). "Taxation and the decline of empires – an unfashionable theme," in *Economic History and the Historian.*

Wright, J. (1997). "The contribution of overseas savings to the funded national debt of Great Britain, 1750–1819," *Economic History Review*, Vol. L, pp. 657–74.

Zahedieh, N. (1996). "Credit, risk and reputation in late 17th century colonial trade".

Zell, Michael (1996). "Credit in the English pre-industrial woollen industry," *Economic History Review*, Vol. XLIX, pp. 667–91.

3

France and the Failure to Modernize Macroeconomic Institutions

Eugene N. White

Like the other great European powers, France laid claim to a colonial empire in the Americas at the beginning of the eighteenth century. Yet, these territories were quickly lost, and there was little transfer of French institutions to the New World. While military failures were centrally important for this loss, France's flawed macroeconomic institutions imposed critical limits on the Crown's finances. This chapter examines the origins and operation of the French *ancien régime*'s fiscal and monetary institutions. The weakness of these institutions contributed not only to France's difficulties in projecting its power overseas but also to the crisis and ultimately the collapse of the monarchy.

3.1 THE THEORY OF OPTIMAL MACROECONOMIC POLICY

The grand ambitions of the French Crown were held in check by its inability to conduct a more efficient macroeconomic policy that would raise the needed revenue while minimizing economic distortions. Theories of optimal macroeconomic policy and sovereign debt offer some insights into the weaknesses of French policy and what reforms were necessary.

In the simplest setting (Barro, 1987, 1989; Mankiw, 1987), optimal monetary and fiscal policy requires that the government satisfy a present value budget constraint where the outstanding current real government debt equals the sum of all present and future real tax revenues less all present and future real government expenditures. This may be restated as follows: the existing debt must be fully funded by cumulative budget surpluses. In the absence of tax collection costs, the government would set a constant tax on output (an income or sales tax) to satisfy this constraint. Substantial increases in spending, such as wartime expenditures, would be financed by debt funded by peacetime surpluses. This *tax smoothing* policy avoids intertemporal distortions and minimizes the intratemporal policy-induced distortions. The presence of collection costs (Bordo and Vègh, 1998) adds a new distortion that makes the use of seigniorage (the tax on real money balances) part of the next best policy. The government now has two policy instruments – the tax rate and the inflation rate – that cause deadweight social losses; and the government must choose the tax rate and the inflation rate to minimize the present value of these social losses subject to the budget constraint. The optimal policy here consists of fixed tax and inflation rates for tax smoothing and inflation smoothing, where the marginal social costs of taxation and seigniorage are equal. The mix of taxation and inflation may change if disruptions, most likely civil or foreign wars, raise the cost of tax collections. Higher collection costs increase the distortionary effects of taxation and induce the government to switch to a higher inflation rate – a more distortionary policy. Similarly, a less desirable policy will be employed if borrowing is costly, where capital markets are not perfect and risk premiums are assessed. A government will respond to this situation by substituting higher taxes and inflation for borrowing.

From the sixteenth to the eighteenth centuries, Western European countries were on a specie standard and were subject to large fiscal shocks in the form of frequent wars. Although the coinage was sometimes debased to generate revenue, seigniorage was usually a modest source of revenue for the French Crown, as suggested by the theory of optimal macroeconomic policy. Adherence to a specie standard may also have been a commitment mechanism that allowed a government to follow a time-consistent policy, where in the absence of inflation debt retained its real value (Bordo and Kydland, 1995). Without such a commitment to price stability, it would be difficult for a government to use debt finance. Ceding control of the inflation rate, the French Crown gained some limited seigniorage and was left with the tax rate as the major policy instrument.

The ability of a government to issue debt is central to tax smoothing. While expenditures and tax revenues might be reasonably predictable during peacetime, the uncertain duration and intensity of wars make wartime expenditures extremely variable. To ensure tax smoothing, the government will incur debt when faced with an unexpectedly large increase in spending and adjust the tax rate to fund the debt over a long period. In the period examined in this chapter, the rising cost of warfare required major fiscal innovations for major powers with colonial ambitions. Examining eighteenth-century Great Britain and France, Barro (1987) and Bordo and White (1991, 1994) found that Britain came closest to following an optimal fiscal policy. Taxes were smoothed, rising not just for the duration of the war but also during and after the war, and wartime budget deficits induced increases in interest rates that brought about needed short-term adjustments in consumption and investment.

The French Crown's policies appear to have been inferior, with greater use of seigniorage and higher borrowing costs, thus constraining its ability to finance war. Special interests obstructed many reforms essential to improving the efficiency of fiscal policy. In spite of attempts to reform the tax structure and produce a unified national system, rates varied considerably by regional and personal legal status, producing large economic distortions. Linked to the tax structure was the tax collection system, which produced lower revenues, reflecting the Crown's difficulty in monitoring tax collectors and its own risk aversion. Central to France's fiscal problems was the absence of national institutions representing taxpayers that could legitimize tax increases and reforms. Instead judicial officials checked the Crown's efforts. In contradiction of the tax smoothing tenets of optimal policy, the officials insisted that there could be no permanent increase in taxes and that taxes could rise only for the duration of any war.

The ability to borrow in peak times of spending was essential to the conduct of an efficient macroeconomic policy. Higher than expected expenditures not matched by tax increases violate the present value constraint. Unable to cut expenditures or raise revenue, a government may default to reduce its servicing of the debt, thereby satisfying the constraint. But, the prospect of default will drive away potential lenders unless there is an enforcement mechanism to induce repayment. The problem for sovereign debt is that there is no internal legal or external enforcement device; only the desire for continued access to loans induces a government to service its debts.[1] To maintain its reputation, the government must service its debts to fulfill the lenders' expectations. However well intentioned, a government may still find it impossible to repay the debt in full if huge wars unexpectedly drive up expenditures and taxes cannot be raised sufficiently. This possibility might deter lenders unless they consider sovereign debt as a contingent claim. This type of financial instrument allows partial shifting of risk to the lender in the case of excusable defaults, that is, defaults where lenders understand that there are potential bad outcomes (Grossman and Van Huyck, 1988). This arrangement gains the government some insurance against disaster, shifting risk in the form of partial defaults and permitting borrowing soon afterward. Unjustifiable debt repudiation, including a complete abandonment of the debt, would not allow a quick return to the

[1] Models where deterrents and external enforcement mechanisms exist (Bulow and Rogoff, 1989a, 1989b) are not appropriate here.

Table 3.1. French and British Income and Taxation

	France	Britain	France	Britain
Year	**1715**	**1715**	**1788**	**1788**
Population	19,250,000	7,129,000	26,596,000	9,369,000
Nominal GNP, livres/pounds millions (millions of pounds sterling)	1,760 (116)	46.2	6,977 (280.8)	134.8
GNP per capita	91.4 (6.0)	6.5	262.3 (10.6)	14.4
Tax revenue, livres/pounds millions (millions of pounds sterling)	166.0 (11.0)	5.8	472.4 (19.0)	16.8
Taxes to GNP percent	9.4	12.5	6.8	12.4
Taxes per capita, livres/pounds (pounds sterling)	8.6 (0.6)	0.8	17.8 (0.7)	1.8

Note: All GNP figures are nominal. The figures for 1788 were obtained from Weir (1989). For 1715, Mathias and O'Brien (1976) provide most statistics. Their figures for commodity output are raised by 20 and 32 percent to account for rest of GNP in the French and British economies (Lévy-Leboyer and Bourguignon, 1985, the Table A-1, and Mathias and O'Brien, 1976, p. 608). Livres tournois are converted into pounds sterling at prevailing exchange rates (Bouchary, 1937; McCusker, 1978).

markets.[2] The French Crown borrowed under these conditions, but its frequent defaults imposed a substantial risk premium that raised the costs of financing deficits.

These many deviations from optimal macroeconomic policy reduced France's revenue, hindering the greatest power on the European continent from acting as a truly great colonial power in the Americas. The magnitude of the revenue problem may be seen in a comparison of France and Britain in the eighteenth century.

3.2 THE FISCAL DEMANDS OF A GREAT POWER

As a great power seeking to project its influence and plant colonies in the New World, France needed to generate revenue. But its fiscal system had a limited capacity to grow. Table 3.1 illustrates France's revenue generation problem vis-à-vis Great Britain, its chief eighteenth-century rival. France was by far the larger power, measured by population and national income at the beginning and end of the eighteenth century. Yet, even considering the fact that its subjects had lower per capita incomes,

[2] Efficient risk shifting may be hindered if the sovereign has a high probability of losing power, a high rate of time preference, or low risk aversion.

what is striking is that the French fisc produced proportionally less central government revenue than that of its smaller rival. And this disparity grew over time. In 1715, France's population was triple Britain's and its national income was less than triple, yet tax revenues were only double. Taxes and taxes per capita were a smaller fraction of gross national product (GNP). By 1788, Britain's population had grown a little faster and its national income was nearly half that of France, widening the gap in per capita incomes. Total British tax revenue now nearly approximated total French tax revenue. France had increased its per capita taxes slightly, while British subjects bore more than double the rate their cross-Channel contemporaries paid. Westminster may have raised taxes but the share of taxes to GNP was unchanged, thus milking the growing economy. Versailles failed to do so and saw taxes to GNP slip from 9.4 to 6.8 percent.

Mathias and O'Brien (1976) looked at this problem in real terms over time and found that the pattern held in spite of economic fluctuations and the demands of war. Table 3.2 shows that over the course of the eighteenth century, the burden of taxation did not increase in real terms in France. Considering either 1715 or 1725 as a base year, tax revenues in current livres more than doubled by 1785. In constant livres, there was a much smaller increase, perhaps 50 percent, once war years are isolated. However, the real per capita level of taxation was nearly constant. It rose in wartime but declined afterward to approximately the same level. A similar result was obtained by Riley (1987) using slightly different data.[3] In contrast, nominal British tax revenues more than doubled but total real revenues almost doubled. There is also a modest rise in the real per capita level of British taxation. For The Netherlands, Fritschy (1990) found that in Holland and in the smaller, poorer province of Overijssel, nominal tax revenues changed little, although price declines propped up their real value in the middle of the century. Contrary to the experience of Britain and France, Dutch per capita tax revenue declined, reflecting low economic growth and efforts, until 1780, to keep out of war.

While acknowledging the fragility of their data and the absence of data on services that bulked larger in the British economy, Mathias and O'Brien also compared taxes as a share of commodity output. They found that French tax revenues as a share of commodity output scarcely changed over the course of the century, as seen in Table 3.3, hovering above 10 percent. In Britain, taxes commanded a higher share of output,

[3] Riley's data are extended to cover 1775–85, using tax revenues from White (1989) and Labrousse's index (1970), Vol. II, p. 387. Hoffman (1986, 1994) shows a similar pattern in real total and per capita taxes measured in grain equivalents.

Table 3.2. The Growth of French, British, and Dutch Tax Revenue

Year	France Tax Revenue (millions of livres)	France Real Tax Revenue (1715 = 100)	France Real Tax Revenue per Capita (1715 = 100)	France Real Tax Revenue per Capita (1730 = 100: Riley)	Britain Tax Revenue (in million pounds)	Britain Real Tax Revenue (1700 = 100)	Britain Real Tax Revenue per Capita (in pounds: (1715 = 100)	Holland Tax Revenue (in million guilders)	Holland (Overijssel) Real Tax Revenue (1750 = 100)	Holland (Overijssel) Real Tax Revenue per Capita (1750 = 100)
1715	166	100	100		5.8	100	100			
1720					6.1	110	110	19.1	81 (89)	74 (115)
1725	198	125	124		5.9	100	101			
1730	186	144	130	100	6.2	113	113	19.5	93 (120)	87 (142)
1735*	236	174	155	120	5.7	108	109			
1740*	201	139	124	113	5.9	98	100		(74)	(80)
1745*	245	160	144	137	6.6	127	124			
1750	207	127	114	106	7.3	127	122	22.0	100 (100)	100 (100)
1755	253	156	134	117	7.2	117	110			
1760*				160	8.7	146	132	22.6	100 (103)	100 (98)
1765	320	173	138	127	10.0	146	128			
1770	318	137	106	109	10.4	149	126		(73)	(67)
1775	362	164	126	101	10.7	143	117			
1780*	419	199	145	124	12.6	170	135		(82)	(76)
1785	424	183	132	113	14.6	190	144			

Notes: The asterisk (*) denotes a war year. The dates stand for the nearest year to the available budget. The real values are calculated using Mathias and O'Brien's (1976) grain index.

Sources: Mathias and O'Brien (1976), Tables 1 and 2; Riley (1987), Tables 3 and 4; White (1989), Tables 1 and 3; Labrousse (1970), Vol. II, p. 387; and Fritschy (1990), Tables 1 and 2.

Table 3.3. French and British Taxes as a Share of Output (Percent)

Year	France: Taxes as a Percentage of Commodity Output	Britain: Taxes as a Percentage of Commodity Output
1715	11	17
1720		17
1725	13	16
1730	15	18
1735*	17	18
1740*	13	16
1745*	15	20
1750	11	18
1755	13	16
1760		20
1765	12	19
1770	9	18
1775	10	18
1780*	12	21
1785	10	22

Notes: The Asterisks (*) denote war years.
Source: Mathias and O'Brien (1976), Tables 3 and 4.

beginning at 16 to 18 percent and rising to 18 to 22 percent. Thus, taxes rose faster than the economy grew in Britain. This comparison adds to the evidence that France was not mobilizing sufficient resources in its political and military struggle in Europe and overseas.

The question arises of why France was unable to generate more revenue and enhance its power in war and overseas. Although it may have been constrained somewhat by its lower income per capita, there is – ignoring for the moment the political economy of taxation – no reason why part of the gap with Britain could not have been closed. In a simple counterfactual, if France had kept its tax share of GNP at 9.4 percent (well below the 1788 British level of 12.4 percent) instead of letting it fall to 6.8, government tax revenue would have been 656 million livres instead of 472 million. Such an increase would have provided ample funding for war and colonial expansion. Even if the Crown revenues had slipped to 8 percent of GNP, taxes would have provided 558 million livres, a figure that would have closed the pre-Revolutionary budget gap of 100 million (White, 1989). Instead of 18 livres, French subjects would have paid 21 livres or 24 livres out of a per capita income of 262 livres. Even at a lower standard of living than the British, this would not seem an intolerable burden. However, French macroeconomic institutions and the political economy of macroeconomic policy had evolved in such a way as to limit even apparently modest changes capable of strengthening the French state.

3.3 THE ORIGINS AND STRUCTURE OF THE FRENCH TAX SYSTEM

The French fisc had multiple problems. Its key features were determined by the evolution of the French state. Territorial expansion from the Middle Ages on absorbed new regions that retained separate fiscal regimes, producing a great diversity of taxes and tax rates. Further complicating matters was the ability of regions, groups, and individuals to obtain tax exemptions. Over time, this patchwork quilt of taxation produced a sense of general inequity in the tax burden and resistance to the imposition of new taxes or reduction in tax privileges. The ability of the Crown to gain new taxation was hindered by the absence of a national representative institution that could grant new taxes legitimacy. Furthermore, the tax collection system was operated by contractors who had considerable autonomy. The Crown was heavily dependent on these tax collectors to provide short-term funding in anticipation of taxes, although it gradually gained access to the market for long-term lending. Because government finance was linked to the system of tax collection, reform became more difficult. Changes that could have improved efficiency and provided increased revenues proved to be extremely difficult given the complex political economy of French finance. Several times an invigorated Crown initiated new reforms to centralize and simplify the tax system, but in the long run the government had limited success in altering the basic tax structure.

The evolution of the French state shaped the character of the fiscal system. Regular, direct taxation first appeared in Western Europe in the late thirteenth century, when the fiscal pressure of wars forced the Crown to seek resources outside the royal domain and commute service obligations into tax payments. In France, the greater wealth of the royal domain and the absence of an effective central representative institution delayed the imposition of direct taxes (Ormrod, 1995).[4] In both England and Castile, there were assemblies – the Parliament and the Cortes – representative of the secular nobility, the Church, and the towns that met with some regularity and judged the king's requests and granted taxes. The assent of representatives of some taxed subjects conferred legitimacy and acceptance of changes in taxation.

[4] Conditioned by their support of the Crown for crusades, the clergy paid regular taxes in England, France, and Spain, negotiated by their representative institutions, judging the king's requests.

France never developed even modest representative institutions. Composed of delegates from the nobility, clergy, and third estate, the Estates General drew up lists of grievances to be presented to the Crown and advised the king on legislation. In the fourteenth century, France had two Estates General, one for the north (Languedoil) and one for the south (Languedoc). By the fifteenth century, there was one body for the whole country, in addition to provincial estates. Although it did not vote on legislation and the monarchy created new taxes without its approval, many French jurists claimed that only the Estates General could vote new taxation (Collins, 1995). Its influence was limited, partly because it met only four times, in 1484, 1560–1, 1588, and 1614–15. The inability of the three Estates General to agree on the reform of the government in 1615 led to its dissolution and abdication of authority to the king (Mousnier, 1980). It vanished from the scene until 1789, and the vacuum was filled by the Parlement de Paris and the regional *parlements*, composed of privileged noble judges who managed the judicial affairs of the Crown (Doyle, 1974). The preeminent Parlement de Paris had authority over central France. By tradition, it legalized all royal acts of taxation or loans by recording them in its registers in formal plenary sessions (Stone, 1981). The ceremony of *enregistrement* was required to legitimize a monarch's edicts, making them enforceable at law throughout the kingdom. Simultaneously, the *enregistrements* confirmed the legality of the Crown. If the *parlement* decided that an edict was illegal or harmful to the kingdom, it read a *remonstrance* to the king and refused to register it, making the edict legally unenforceable. However, a monarch could force registration by calling a special parliamentary session, a *lit de justice*. If the *parlementaires* still proved recalcitrant, the Crown sometimes closed *parlement* or exiled its members. Flexibility in fiscal policy was limited by the theory most *parlementaires* held that no new permanent taxes could be decreed, except by the nation as a whole as represented by the Estates General (Stone, 1981).

When it expanded its authority to new territories, the French Crown often confirmed traditional liberties and granted privileges to new provinces, producing a great variation in taxation, with provincial authorities often retaining power to determine the form of the taxes. The original core of the kingdom, represented by the Estates General of Languedoil, had relatively uniform taxation, but the provinces added later, such as Brittany, Burgundy, Dauphiné, and Provence, and many enclaves retained relatively autonomous systems. Particularism remained a central feature of the tax system and of many other aspects of the French state (Collins, 1988). France stood in strong contrast to England, a smaller realm, one where there was one Parliament that met frequently, taxes were universal, and royal courts handled almost all important cases.

Permanent taxation by the central state began in France only when the state was threatened by capture of the king, John II, in the battle of Poitiers and by the bands of demobilized soldiers after peace with the English in 1360. To raise money, a package of two *aides* – a 5 percent sales tax and a one-thirteenth tax on wholesale wine – and the *gabelle*, a 25 percent salt tax, were instituted. Together with the hearth taxes (*fouages*), which commuted military service for commoners, they formed the core of Crown taxes (Collins, 1988).

Out of the hearth tax, the *taille* was established, which became the principal direct tax levied by the Crown. The *taille* was a geographically apportioned fixed sum tax. It was assessed on landed income and took two forms. In northern France, payment of the *taille personnelle* depended on personal status. Nobles and some bourgeois of privileged towns were exempt from the *taille*.[5] Exemption from the *taille reélle* of southern France depended on whether the status of the land was noble. Originally, the nobles had not been exempt; but Charles VI, a weak king, granted them exemptions from the *taille* and the *aides* for production on their properties in 1388. Gradually tax privileges spread to magistrates, royal officers, and the leading bourgeois, leaving a heavier tax burden on the peasants and artisans (Hoffman, 1986, 1994).

To apportion the tax, the total sum of the *taille* was divided among the regional financial districts or *généralités*, numbering 4 in the fourteenth century and growing by the acquisition of provinces and subdivisions to over 25 by the late seventeenth century. The tax officials or *receveurs-généraux* in each *généralité* divided the tax obligations among the *élections* in the *généralité*, which were supervised by *élus*. Each *élection* divided its portion among the parishes. Within the parish, the parishioners assessed and collected their parish *tailles*. Each unit was collectively responsible for the total contribution. The structure allowed for variations in taxation and incentives to enforce collection and monitor avoidance. Parishioners named four to eight tax collectors, who were paid a commission of 2.5 to 5 percent to assess and collect taxes. They sent the money to the *receveur* of the *élection*, who paid some local expenditures. About 90 percent of the revenue was forwarded to the *receveurs-généraux*, who made payments assigned by the king, passing on a fraction of collections to the central treasury. These tax officials enjoyed the substantial benefit of the use of tax funds until they were obliged to remit them. Thus, they were able to provide short-term credits

[5] If a noble worked his land with servants, he was exempt, but if tenants were sharecroppers, the tenant's share was taxable.

to the king. Overseeing the system in the Estates de Languedoil, the Cour des Aides sat in judgment on tax cases and the Cour de Comptes audited the accounts of tax officials (Collins, 1995).

In the sixteenth century the *taille* was augmented by additional levies – the *crue*, the *grande crue*, and the *taillon* – for the military, postal service, dike and levee repairs, and roads and bridges. These usually took the form of surtaxes. While the *taille* itself was levied only on the Estates de Languedoil that had originally consented to the tax, these later additions, collectively called the *tailles* or the *tailles et crues y joint*, were paid by the whole kingdom. The newer provinces also had their own local direct taxes. To administer these taxes, the newer provinces had their own *receveurs-généraux*, Cour des Aides and Cour de Comptes but no *élus* (Collins, 1988). Regional control of taxation remained strongest in the *pays d'Etats* that had representative Estates, in contrast to the *pays d'élections* of the North and Center.[6] The *tailles* were leading sources of royal income. In the early 1520s, Francis I had a regular income of 8 to 10 million livres, of which approximately 5 million was obtained from these direct taxes.[7]

There were three main forms of indirect taxes in *ancien régime* France: the salt tax or *gabelle*, the sales tax or *aides*, and the transit fees or *traites*. The Estates General voted the salt and sales taxes in the 1360s, and the *traites* evolved from the king's overlordship rights. Except for some salt-producing areas, the sale of salt was monopolized in most of France. In the *pays de grandes gabelles* of the north, the king had salt warehouses and each household had to purchase a minimum quantity of salt. In the south – the *pays de petites gabelles* – taxes were levied on salt upon leaving the region of production and the salt was traded freely upon arrival. The regional variation in taxation induced smuggling. The government responded by forming a large military force to police the *gabelles*. The sales taxes were levied on selected goods, notably wine. There were taxes on imports and exports (*douanes*), but there were also transit fees levied on goods moving from one province or region to another. The numerous taxes on traded goods encouraged considerable smuggling to avoid what often constituted punitive taxes. This system had some economic logic, attempting to keep collection costs low and maximize revenue. For example, Brittany was a major salt producer and paid no salt tax, as monopoly sale would have been very difficult. Wine had

[6] In 1600, the *pays d'Etats* were Brittany, Burgundy, Languedoc, Provence, Dauphiné, and the southwest. By the early seventeenth century Dauphiné and the southwest lost their estates.

[7] The clergy's *décime* yielded 1.1 million livres, the *aides* 825,000 livres, and the *gabelles* 460,000 livres.

to be imported to the province, and Brittany paid high wine taxes. On the other hand, the province of Burgundy, which produced wine but no salt, paid low wine taxes and high salt taxes (Collins, 1988).

While most direct taxes were managed by royal officials, most indirect taxes were collected by tax farmers. The choice of tax collection methods by the Crown reflected its ability to manage the "principal–agent" problem inherent in tax collection (White, 1997). Tax yields varied from year to year with economic fluctuations. Furthermore, revenues might be reduced if tax collectors were not properly motivated. The monarchy had three basic choices of contract, each offering a different incentive: (1) establish a government tax bureaucracy where tax collectors were paid a fixed wage for delivery of all revenue from a tax to the Crown, (2) create a tax farm where the tax collectors paid "rent" of a fixed sum to the government for the right to collect a tax and keep the revenue, or (3) create a revenue-sharing tax farm where the government would lease the right to collect a tax to tax collectors for a share of the revenue. Some of the factors affecting the choice of contractual form would have included the technology of tax collection, the ability of the government to monitor the tax collectors, and the degree of risk aversion exhibited by the government and its tax collectors. If the task of collecting taxes is well known and collection can be costlessly monitored, a fixed wage is an efficient incentive to motivate employees. By absorbing the risk, the government will also maximize the revenue it receives. As most of the process of assessment and collection of direct taxes was assigned to the localities, the Crown assigned fixed wage officials, *régisseurs*, to manage the system, creating a *régie*. However, lacking the techniques and ability to monitor tax collectors and averse to the risk of fluctuating tax revenues from indirect taxes, the Crown most often used either form or a combination of the two types of tax farms to collect indirect taxes, accepting a lower yield to avoid risk and the monitoring problem.

In the beginning, most tax farms were individual farms, limited to small areas whose boundaries rarely coincided with other fiscal divisions. Leases were for one year, and continuity of management was difficult. In the fourteenth and fifteenth centuries, the monarchy used competitive bidding to award leases in the hope of driving up lease prices. The growing need for increased resources in the sixteenth century moved the Crown to seek larger consolidated tax farms, *fermes-générales*, operating on a regional basis. The new *fermes-générales* consolidated each type of tax, but even these mergers did not cover the entire kingdom. The drive to consolidate tax farms was slow and halting, with many retreats in the face of political instability and financial crises.

Venality of office was a distinctive feature of French government that included the tax officials. In the thirteenth century, the Crown found that it could sell the right to handle royal finances, justice, and other aspects of government to officials. Depending on the office, an official benefited from management of royal monies, fees from litigants, an annual payment or *gage*, exemptions from taxes and social distinction. Secure tenure for life in an office was conferred in 1467. Besides loss of office by death, resignation, or forfeiture, the king retained the right to suppress offices (Doyle, 1996). When in 1604 Henry IV established the *paulette*, he made property rights to transfer an office secure by an annual payment of one-sixtieth of the official value of the office.[8] The king also fixed the official value of the offices and salaries or *gages* (Collins, 1995). Growing from 4,000 to 5,000 officers in 1515 to 15,000 a century later, this venal system produced a large vested interest in the preservation of the fiscal system.

At the apex of the tax system was the central treasury, created in 1523 by Francis I. This treasury was created to reduce the dominance of the *receveurs-généraux*, who previously had controlled tax collection. They had collected, borrowed, and disbursed funds with little oversight from the Crown, often at considerable individual profit. With the flow of funds centralized, all receipts had to be delivered to the treasury after payment of the costs of collection and any assigned expenses, which later included debt payments. Disbursement of funds required written orders from the treasury. However, the bureaucracy of the central administration remained modest. The regional fiscal officers continued to enjoy considerable autonomy, even though they were subject to some monitoring. Overseeing the system was a superintendent of finances, a controller general, and several *intendants* of finance.

3.4 ATTEMPTS TO REFORM THE TAX SYSTEM

In the sixteenth, seventeenth, and eighteenth centuries, the tax system created in the Middle Ages came under pressure to deliver more revenue to finance state and empire building. Successive kings attempted to increase revenue by (1) the centralization of tax collections, (2) the reduction of tax avoidance and evasion, and (3) the increase of tax rates. However, these reforms were often partly or wholly thwarted. Tax officials did not willingly concede their profitable operations to kings and ministers seeking to raise revenues. The Crown's dependence on borrowing from these officials further limited its ability to pursue reform

8 Before the *paulette*, if the office holder died within 40 days of transferring his office, it reverted to the king.

projects. Efforts to raise revenue by cutting exemptions and raising assessments were fiercely opposed by elites and regions that benefited. Finally, the absence of representative institutions raised high political barriers to changing the structure of taxation or tax rates. Three rough periods in the evolution of the fiscal structure of the *ancien régime* can be discerned: (1) the mid-sixteenth to mid-seventeenth century, (2) the era of Louis XIV, and (3) the eighteenth century.

3.4.1 Frustrated Reforms of the Sixteenth and Seventeenth Centuries

In the late sixteenth century, Henry III (1574–89) embarked on a series of reforms of tax administration to raise revenue for his struggles with the Huguenots, the great nobles, and the provincial Estates. His overall objective was to centralize and standardize the tax system, bringing more of the kingdom under more direct royal control. In 1581, he combined the export and import duties into one farm, created a single *gabelle* for the north, and began centralizing the *aides*. This enlargement of the tax farms helped the king by improving the tax liens that secured loans from international bankers. Extending the reach of royal taxation, Henry III established new *généralités* and *élections* in areas where direct royal control had been absent or weak, eliminating, for example, the control of taxes by the Estates of Normandy.

These changes were often compromised by the exigencies of war that limited or rolled back reforms. More troubling for the long run was the sale of royal offices and the consequent growth of tax privileges, whittling away the tax base. The number of noble families rose sharply over time. The 283 percent increase between 1463 and 1666 took many potential taxpayers off the rolls (Gelabert, 1995). Gaining tax exemptions from the *taille* and *aides* on wine produced on their own estates, nobles, royal officers, and wealthy merchants gained a competitive advantage and purchased large quantities of agrarian land between 1550 and 1730 (Hoffman, 1986). As more productive activities escaped the fisc, revenue growth was further limited.

In spite of these difficulties, Henry III's efforts appear to have been reasonably successful. Between the 1560s and the 1580s, nominal royal tax receipts trebled. Real tax revenues climbed over 50 percent, as shown by the index of total tax receipts in Figure 3.1. This growth was the product of a rise in the average tax burden, as the index of per capita tax receipts rose by an equivalent amount. The civil war that brought Henry IV (1589–1610) to the throne caused royal tax revenues to plummet in the 1590s. The new king sought to strengthen the Crown and centralize power in the royal councils. The last ten years of his reign brought economic recovery and a regeneration of tax revenues.

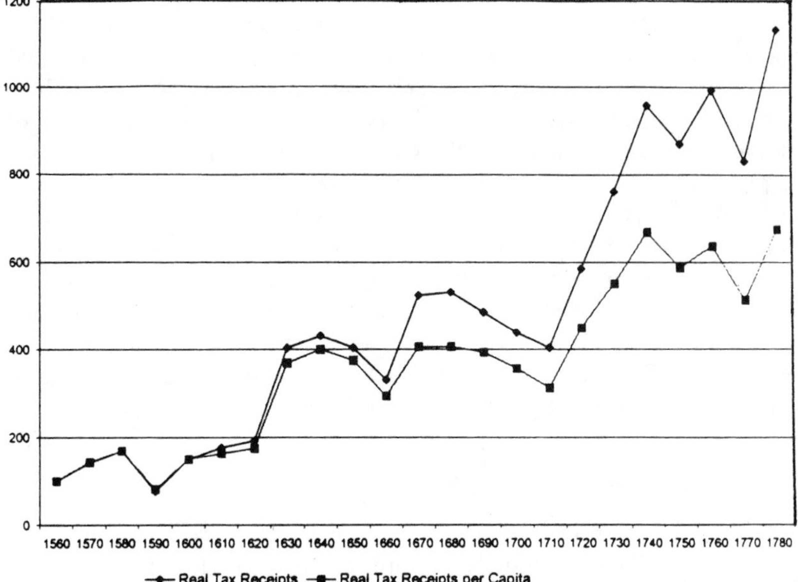

Figure 3.1 Indexes of total and per capita tax receipts.

Note: The data points represent averages for each decade of annual tax receipts converted into grain equivalents.
Source: Hoffman (1986, 1994).

Following his predecessor, Henry IV combined tax farms into larger units and reduced direct taxes, specifying more effective collection rules in the parishes.

Although troubled by revolts of nobles (1614–17), an internal war with Protestants (1621–9), peasant and urban revolts (1635–43), and France's entry into the Thirty Years' War in 1635, the Crown enjoyed a rise in tax revenue during the reign of Louis XIII (1610–43), as seen in Figure 3.1. Between the 1620s and the 1630s, nominal and real receipts more than doubled, due in large part to a rise in tax rates. Surtaxes were added, doubling direct taxes between 1625 and 1634. The king also tried to eliminate the greater fiscal independence of the *pays d'Etats*, but these changes occasioned rebellions in the provinces. In 1634, to gain more control of assessment and collection of taxes, the king introduced royal officials directly responsible to him, the *intendants*, into the *généralités*. The *intendants* were granted the key power to apportion taxes in 1642, but rebellion forced the king to retreat on this issue.

The period of rule by Cardinal Mazarin, beginning with the minority of Louis XIV (1643–51) and continuing until Mazarin's death in 1661, saw France slip into internal chaos. Real tax revenues began to decline during the war (1635–59) fought by France and Spain for hegemony in Europe. Throughout the conflict, both sides found it nearly impossible to raise enough money to finance the war. Attempts to raise taxes resulted in revolts throughout France. When the government attempted to reduce the *gages* of offices and eliminate the *paulette* in 1648, the Parlement of Paris and the venal officers of the Crown rebelled. These events fueled the provincial opposition to new taxes, beginning the revolt known as the Fronde. This civil war was joined the following year by the great nobility and lasted until 1653.

Overall, this period saw the beginning of the centralization of tax collections. Yet, the persistent domestic and foreign upheavals prevented more radical change. Consequently, the essential features of the tax system changed little, and the privileges granted by the Crown in times of weakness became more numerous and firmly entrenched.

3.4.2 Taxation Under Louis XIV

When Mazarin died in 1661, Louis XIV declared himself chief minister and reorganized royal councils, beginning a major fiscal reform. Sweeping away the existing network of officials, the king arrested the superintendent of finance, Nicholas Fouquet, and became his own chief minister. Obstructions were reduced when the *parlements* lost their right to registration and *remonstrances* in 1673 (Collins, 1995). As his head of royal finances, Louis selected Jean-Baptiste Colbert to design and oversee the reforms. For their efforts, Louis and Colbert were rewarded with not only a recovery in tax receipts from the nadir of the 1660s, but also a higher level. Nominal receipts rose steadily from the 1670s to the 1690s, although rising prices produced a slight decline in real revenues, as seen in Figure 3.1. This improvement was achieved by major changes in the organization of the tax system and improvements in its operation.

When Colbert assumed control of finances in 1661, he began a new effort to consolidate the tax farms. According to Matthews (1958), Colbert would have preferred *régies* to tax farms; but increasing the king's revenue quickly was of paramount importance, and for that he needed the skills of the tax farmers. Between 1663 and 1681, the finance minister slowly consolidated many of the single tax general farms into one all-encompassing Fermes Générales. Colbert moved to improve the monitoring of the *fermiers*. They were kept to a strict timing of payments, and their records were scrutinized. In 1681, he unified and clarified the legal code governing tax farming. The varied and scattered farms were organized into a single institution with a clear line of accountability to the Crown. Colbert achieved the crucial goal of raising revenue, driving hard bargains with the tax farmers. In 1661, the leases signed by his predecessor, Fouquet, yielded 36.9 million livres. Following Colbert's reforms, the leases on the tax farms in 1683 produced 65.8 million livres for the government. This increase was an impressive achievement. Between 1661 and 1683, prices appear to have been relatively stable (Labrousse, 1970); thus the increase is roughly a real increase. If the lease prices had grown at only the (presumably higher) rate of economic growth for the eighteenth century of 1 percent (O'Brien and Keyder, 1978), they would have totaled only 45.9 million livres. Instead, indirect tax revenues increased at an average annual rate of 2.7 percent.

Louis and Colbert also sought to raise more revenue from direct taxes, moving away from the exemption-riddled *taille*. Many influential critics attacked its inequities and promoted the principle that all subjects pay according to their ability (Bonney, 1995a). In 1699, a new tax, *capitation*, was levied on all lay people, from shepherds to the dauphin, and rates were fixed according to a table of 22 classes or occupations. While this was initially more equitable than the *taille*, the more influential managed eventually to secure exemptions from the *capitation* (Collins, 1995). When the tax was reinstated in 1701, it lacked the original progressivity. The War of the Spanish Succession drained the treasury, and a new tax, the *dixième*, was imposed. It was to be a temporary wartime levy of a 10 percent tax on all incomes. Yet, enforcement proved difficult. Contemporaries believed that declarations were far from accurate and were one-half of actual incomes, in spite of stiff penalties (Bonney, 1995c).

To reduce the opportunities for self-enrichment by venal officials, the *intendants* were given greater authority to monitor them. Directly responsible to the king, the *intendants* watched every aspect of the collection of direct taxes from naming of officials to assessments, demanding detailed economic data on the ability to pay of each jurisdiction.

The costly War of the Spanish Succession (1701–13) strained the system of taxation to the limit and saw a 20 percent drop in nominal tax receipts over the previous decade with a substantial fall in real revenue, depicted in Figure 3.1. The lease price of the Fermes Générales fell. When receipts declined because of the war, the farmers borrowed against future receipts to make good on their obligation to the Crown. In 1697, the six-year lease had a cumulative deficit of 50.7 million livres. As taxes declined, the government borrowed heavily against future taxes. Colbert's single tax farm began to fall apart as farmers, fearful of assuming the risk, refused the Crown's asking lease prices. Instead, many taxes were administered as *régies* from 1709 to 1714, with the farmers as *régisseurs* or commissioners accepting a fee (Matthews, 1958). Many of the tax reforms of Louis and his chief minister remained in place, even though they were compromised by more than a decade of war. Collections might have been more centralized and carefully monitored, yet the essential structure of the system remained largely unchanged.

Seen alone, France's tax reforms under Louis XIV appear to have been a major achievement, but they were quite modest in comparison with changes underway in Britain. Some aspects of the British tax system were initially similar – with the notable exceptions of French regionalism and tax exemptions.[9] The hearth tax, the excise, and the customs were farmed out. Between the Restoration of 1660 and the Glorious Revolution of 1688, the Treasury Board obtained complete control of all expenditures and a comprehensive knowledge of the state's fiscal activities. Willing to take the risk of varying but growing proceeds, the Crown canceled the customs farm in 1671, the excise farm in 1683, and the hearth tax farm in 1684.[10] This development contrasts with the continental fiscal systems, including those of the United Provinces and Prussia, where tax farming remained dominant and collection varied regionally. Although it took time to effect a complete transition, the British Treasury Board had control of revenue as well as expenditures. The Crown established standard procedures and customs, and excise commissioners began regular inspection circuits to monitor tax collectors. The result was a highly centralized, unified national tax system (Brewer, 1988). France did not begin to move in the same direction as Britain until a century later.

3.4.3 Taxation in the Eighteenth Century

By the end of the War of the Spanish Succession, the Crown was fiscally exhausted. Nominal tax receipts recovered from their wartime low but remained less than the level established in the 1690s. Rising prices pushed the real value of revenue below the prior decade's level. Louis XIV's death in 1715 placed the government in the hands of a regency during the minority of Louis XV. To establish his authority against Louis XIV's will, the regent, the Duc d'Orleans, restored the powers of registration and *remonstrance* to the *parlements*. Faced with huge war debts and low revenues, the regent was willing to experiment.

In 1716, the Duc de Noailles, in charge of the Crown's finances, sought to alter the character of the *taille*. Aware of complaints of the inequity of dividing a fixed tax among all taxpayers, he proposed a tax rate pro-

[9] While Britain was taxed, for the most part, as a unitary state, the Celtic regions, notably Scotland, evaded taxes, frustrating officials, efforts to ensure uniform payment (O'Brien, 1988).

[10] The hearth tax was replaced by a land tax soon after the Glorious Revolution.

portional to the declared income of each taxpayer. However, this project lost out to the plan of the Scot, John Law, who had the regent's ear (Touzery, 1994). Although a key objective of Law's "System" was to manage the debt, he wanted control of all government finance. In 1719 Law took over the lease of the Fermes Générales followed by control of the direct taxes. His plan to completely rationalize the combined direct and indirect tax collection was aborted when his System abruptly collapsed.

Law's successors were left with the task of resurrecting the tax system. They succeeded and, in spite of all the obstacles, brought about a significant rise in real revenue. Although this increase leveled off after the middle of the century, it appears an impressive achievement in comparison with the previous two centuries. One feature that Figure 3.1 highlights is the greater growth of total relative to per capita tax receipts, suggesting that beyond the 1740s revenues would have stagnated if the population had not continued to rise.

New direct taxes were raised in the eighteenth century. The *dixième* was used again between 1733–6 and 1741–50, during the Wars of the Polish and Austrian Successions, then abolished in 1751. Philibert Orry, the comptroller general, was concerned with how this tax was levied. An attempt to introduce a reformed direct tax on the basis of individual income faltered, as each *intendant* set different rates on property and income, increasing rather than decreasing the tax disparities. There was strong opposition from the Cours des Aides and the *élus*, who were threatened by the reform. This tax lost its progressive character and became a proportional supplement to the *taille* (Collins, 1995).

Orry's successor, Machault d'Arnouville, did not interfere with *intendants* who pursued this type of reform, but he directed his efforts to raising a new tax, the *vingtième*, and abolished the *dixième* in 1749. The *vingtième* or "twentieth" was intended to be a 5 percent tax on income. It was strongly resisted by the privileged, and the edict had to be forcibly registered by a *lit de justice*. Although, it was originally intended to cover all subjects, exemptions began to creep in. The clergy won exemption, and the provincial estates avoided the tax by offering lump sum payments. There was also considerable resistance to the declarations of income required for assessment (Mousnier, 1984). A second *vingtième* was added in 1756 for the duration of the Seven Years' War plus 10 years.

In 1759, the comptroller general, Etienne de Silhouette, planned to suspend the exemptions for the bourgeois and officers of the Crown for the duration of the war plus two years, impose a *subvention générale* without exemptions, and raise other tax rates. Bitter *remonstrances* to the king forced the minister's dismissal. Instead there was the imposition of a third *vingtième*, a doubling of the *capitation*, and an increase in postal fees, excises, and customs duties (Touzery, 1994). In 1761, the Crown proposed to make the second *vingtième* permanent and rescind the third. Again, this innovation was tempered by exemptions granted to the privileged classes and the *pays d'États*. The Crown attempted to ensure a proper valuation for the tax in 1763, but opposition from the *parlements* forced the government to retreat, and the yield from the two *vingtièmes* declined (Bonney, 1995c). Every major effort at reform was thus checked or compromised, from the introduction of the *capitation* to the employment of the *vingtième*.

The financial problems from the Seven Years' War did not disappear with the end of hostilities. There were selective defaults in 1763 and 1770. In the latter year, the *parlements* were suspended, giving the finance minister, the abbé Terray, an opportunity to make bigger changes. He made the first *vingtième* permanent and extended the second *vingtième* to 1781. A variety of tax exemptions were eliminated and expenditures were reduced, bringing the budget into balance (White, 1989). Terray attempted a revision in tax assessments, but resistance from the judicial establishment hampered this effort. Thus, between 1772 and 1782, only 4,902 parishes out of 22,508 in the *pays d'élections* had their rolls verified (Bonney, 1995c).

In its efforts to reform the tax system, the Crown waged a long struggle to reduce the influence of the *parlements*. In 1756, the two chambers of the Parlement de Paris were reduced to one. The Parlement de Pau was remodeled in 1764, and the following year the Parlement de Rennes was reorganized. Following the political coup in 1770, an overhaul of the legal system was engineered, abolishing four *parlements*, remodeling the remainder, and eliminating many venal offices (Doyle, 1996). Yet, this major political reform was reversed when Louis XVI arrived on the throne in 1774. Seeking good will, the new king recalled and reempowered the *parlements*.

Operating under these renewed constraints, Louis XVI's finance minister, Jacques Necker, managed the financing of the American War for Independence from 1776 to 1781 with considerable success and controversy. He proposed provincial assemblies to establish more representation and suppressed many venal offices. In 1777, Necker promulgated a decree to guarantee regular reassessment of lands subject to the *vingtièmes*. The Parlement de Paris responded with a *remonstrance* that regular reassessment was the equivalent of raising permanent taxes (Stone, 1981). Necker's successor, Jean-François Joly de Fleury, ended reform of the financial administration, although he gained a third *vingtième* for the duration of the war plus three years. When the monarchy's finances after the war continued to deteriorate, the minister,

Charles-Alexandre de Calonne, proposed a *subvention territoriale*, a tax in kind on all landed classes with no exemptions, organizing an Assembly of Notables in 1787 to circumvent the obstruction of the Parlement de Paris. The road to revolution began when these reforms were rejected by the hand-picked Assembly. The obstinate Parlement de Paris blocked any new taxation and proclaimed that only an Estates General could approve of new taxes. The Crown finally conceded defeat and in 1789 called for a meeting of the Estates General, which had not met since 1614.

The reign of Louis XVI, like that of many of his forefathers, saw a seesaw of reform, producing little change in the character of direct taxation. Similarly, indirect taxation was not substantially reformed, but slow improvements – like those in direct taxation – helped to drive up the yield from taxes. In the aftermath of the collapse of Law's System, the Crown attempted to revive the Fermes Générales. The tax farmers offered a very low lease price of 40 million livres, which was rejected by the government. In its place it set up a *régie* in 1721, paying the former farmers salaries and bonuses. The farmers apparently turned a huge profit as the Crown was unable to monitor its agents adequately. Desiring to return to the reliability of the Fermes Générales, Louis XV's chief minister, Cardinal Fleury, reestablished the institution in 1726, with an annual price of 80 million livres (Mathews, 1958).

After 1726, the form and structure of the Fermes Générales stabilized. In the 11 lease contracts signed between 1726 and 1786, the lease price gradually rose from 80 to 144 million livres. Although some of this increase in revenue may be attributed to economic growth, tax rates were increased. In 1705, a surtax of 10 percent was added, and this was doubled in 1715. In 1760, 5 percent was added, followed by another 5 percent on the *gabelles* and the entry taxes to Paris in 1763. This surtax was spread to all taxes in 1771, and 10 percent was added. Finally in 1781, another 10 percent was imposed and the rate made universal. Thus, between 1705 and 1781, the surtax rose from 10 to 50 percent (Matthews, 1954).

Over the course of the eighteenth century, the government began to move the farm away from a pure tax farm, intervening in such a way as to produce a slow but perceptible shift toward a government takeover, even though it never materialized. The government was more willing to accept risk and improved its ability to monitor the farmers, gaining the potential for higher revenues (White, 1997). By 1776, the farm was required to seek the finance minister's permission for all important decisions. In 1778, Minister Necker began to install Crown officials within the offices of the Fermes to audit its operations, thus improving the king's capacity to monitor. The 1774 lease required some sharing with the government of the profits. The 1780 lease was more demanding, setting a minimum price of 122.9 million livres. If revenues exceeded 126 million, the profits would be shared evenly between the farmers' syndicate and the Crown. Confident that it was moving in the right direction, the Crown placed the *aides* and the *domaines* in a *régie* in 1780 and the *traites* in a *régie* in 1783. Yet after 1783, the movement toward a salaried corps of tax collectors halted. The failure to continue in these changes reflected the successful opposition of the entrenched interests. If the government had been able to switch entirely to a *régie* and obtain most of the profits from the leases, one estimate (White, 1997) suggests that the Crown could have gained another 10 million livres of revenue.[11]

A comparison of the results of France's partial tax reforms in the eighteenth century with those in Great Britain is informative. While real total French revenues rose, they failed to keep pace with the growth of British revenues. Mathias and O'Brien (1976) find that indirect taxes were the engine that filled the coffers of the British king. For the whole of the eighteenth century, France seems to have increased direct and indirect taxes at about the same rate, keeping the proportion of their contribution to the French fisc roughly equal. At the beginning of the century, British government finance rested firmly on indirect taxation, with direct taxes representing approximately one-quarter of tax receipts. On the eve of the Revolutionary and Napoleonic wars, this had fallen to 20 percent, thanks to the growth in receipts from indirect taxes.[12] Looking more closely, customs duties provided on average about a quarter of all revenue. The principal sources of Britain's rich revenues were the excises and stamp taxes levied on domestic production and services. Standing at about 35 percent of all revenue, these taxes contributed over half of the tax revenue by mid-century (O'Brien, 1988). The British Exchequer successfully identified and taxed new goods and services, which the French Crown could barely consider given the parliamentary opposition.

The striking feature of the French tax system from its foundation in the Late Middle Ages to the end of the *ancien régime* is continuity. Reforming ministers and kings managed to centralize tax collections, unify the tax farms, and improve monitoring. Yet, vested interests prevented the elimination of the labyrinth of privileges and regional variation, changes in the basis of taxation, or a significant increase in the level. This inflexibility made deficit finance even more critical.

[11] At this time, the Crown's deficit stood at approximately 100 million livres.

[12] The reintroduction of the income tax in 1799 to meet the exceptional demand for revenue increased direct taxation's share of total receipts to over 30 percent in the early nineteenth century (O'Brien, 1988).

3.5 DEFICIT FINANCE

Financing frequent warfare was the central financial problem of the French monarchy. War helped form the nation states of Europe, and it challenged them to marshal their resources efficiently. From the sixteenth to the eighteenth centuries, deficits were primarily financed by debt rather than money; and France adhered to a specie standard, with one brief bout of paper money inflation in the early eighteenth century. By adopting a specie standard, France followed the best contemporary practice and avoided the distortions of inflationary finance. However, as with its instruments of taxation, France failed to modernize its instruments of borrowing. Britain had developed an efficient system of debt finance by the eighteenth century (Brewer, 1988). The consol, a simply priced and marketable homogeneous long-term security, was the principal instrument of debt finance. The transparency of the budget and debt policies made it clear to creditors that the debt was fully funded by future taxes. In the short term, a variety of unfunded debt instruments were employed with the Bank of England's discount operations, assisting with the management of this debt. The short-term debt was rolled over into consols and a sinking fund used to retire the long-term debt with the peacetime budget surpluses.

In contrast, France had many innovations but could not fully escape the origins of its system of debt finance. Even by the mid-eighteenth century, France's long-term debt consisted of numerous heterogeneous individual issues that were complexly priced and often difficult to transfer. Furthermore, much of the Crown's borrowing, especially its short-term borrowing, rested heavily on the venal royal officials. The notes of the *receveurs-généraux* and the *fermiers-généraux* provided much of its short-term credit. The Crown also pressured the privileged groups, like the regional Estates and the clergy, to provide loans, and it continued to rely on the sale of offices, particularly in crisis times. The characteristics of the debt and the added risk of default put a premium on French securities that raised the cost of deficit finance and lessened the optimality of French macroeconomic policy.

3.5.1 Deficit Finance and the Monetary System

Under a nineteenth-century classical gold or bimetallic standard, the price of specie was defined in terms of the currency and the price was fixed. The government abjured from any manipulation of the coinage, promising to keep the mint price of specie fixed through the purchase and sale of the specie in unlimited quantities. The mints converted bullion brought by the public into coin and sold coins freely to the public, allowing free export or conversion into bullion. Mints charged a fee in the form of mint charges to mint coin from bullion. The mint charges less the cost of production (*brassage*) produced seigniorage for the Crown. Britain was the first country, in 1694, to strictly abide by the rules of this standard (Bordo and Kydland, 1995). Before the nineteenth century, the French Crown and other states deviated from this prescription, debasing the coinage to gain higher seigniorage. Debasement could be achieved by lowering the fineness of coins, increasing the number of coins struck from a fixed weight of specie, or increasing coins' face value.

Debasement of the coinage was frequent in fourteenth- and early-fifteenth-century France. The Crown engaged in five major debasements: 1318–29, 1337–43, 1346–60, 1418–23, and 1426–9. Miskimin (1984) claims that debasement was an ineffective policy for generating revenue, undone by a rational public. However, the repeated use of the policy suggests that the Crown was successful in obtaining revenue from an inflation tax (Bordo, 1986). Examining the years 1418–23, Sussman (1993) found that the Crown dramatically raised the seigniorage rate and gained real revenues, even exceeding tax revenues. Like other rapid inflations, the adjustment of inflationary expectations eventually undermined this debasement policy. Nevertheless, this switch to inflationary finance was a rational response because the collection costs of taxes had soared with war and the invasion of French territory.

While these early debasements were driven by a need to generate substantial revenues for the government, debasements in the sixteenth and seventeenth centuries had a mixed character. Glassman and Redish (1988) and Sargent and Velde (forthcoming) have argued that debasement in these centuries was more often used to solve the technical problems of coinage than as a purely revenue-generating instrument. Coins of the period suffered heavily from wear and tear and illegal clipping. When these coins continued to circulate at their legal value, full-weight coins became undervalued and the latter circulated at a premium or were driven out of circulation. The solution was to raise the mint price to meet the market price. A similar problem occurred in bimetallism when the legal tender values of gold and silver coins departed from their relative market values, causing one metal to become undervalued. Debasement of the coinage was the technique selected by governments to correct for the undervaluation, with the objective of promoting the efficient operation of the monetary system. Many of the claims that debasements were for revenue (Bonney, 1981) appear to be adjustments to induce coin to flow back into France.

Under Colbert, there appears to have been no debasement of the currency.[13] After his death, finance ministers declared enhancements of the price of coin in 1689, 1693, 1701, 1704, and 1709. Although there are no recent studies of these changes, they were instituted during periods of serious wartime financial difficulties. In 1701, complaints were heard that the 8 percent reduction in the value of coins (the reduction was 10 percent in 1689) had eliminated the interest profits on short-term loans (Collins, 1995). It is not clear that this was different from earlier policy, as the changes in coin values were no larger than the reductions in the first half of the century. However, what may have caused more unrest after 1701 was the issue of coin certificates when the mint could not keep up with the pace of reminting. Initially, the quantity issued was small, 6.7 million livres in 1703. When the Crown realized that it could engage in a form of fractional reserve banking, it created a *caisse d'emprunts* or loan treasury in 1704, issuing notes bearing 6 to 10 percent interest, and the coin certificates began to carry interest. Reaching a total of 180 million livres in circulation in 1706, the certificates' market value fell by 60 to 70 percent of face value by 1707 (Bonney, 1995c). A new finance minister, Desmarets, created the Caisse Legendre, which pooled the resources of the 12 *receveurs-généraux* who issued interest-bearing notes collateralized by taxes. By the end of the War of the Spanish Succession, the *caisse* had issued 400 million livres, providing the government with substantial short-term credit (Collins, 1995).

John Law's efforts to reform the debt and tax system, described more fully subsequently, included a bank of issue, the Banque Royale. The expansion of banknotes to support securities prices produced inflation; the collapse of the "System" left a strong distaste for any paper money or any attempt to manipulate the value of the livre. This experiment helped to bind the Crown more firmly to a specie standard. In 1726, France returned to the bimetallic standard at a bimetallic ratio of 14.5. In this respect, France "caught up" to the best British monetary practice of strict adherence to a specie standard. Investors in French debt were guaranteed that their returns would not be reduced by a depreciation of the currency. This new French regime prevailed until the Revolution, with only a change in the bimetallic ratio to 15.5 in 1785 to adjust to the higher world price of gold. The abandonment of seigniorage reflects the rise in tax revenues, the product of reforms that lowered collection costs. Eschewing an inflation tax reduced distortions and improved the optimality of policy.

[13] In 1674, Colbert created the *caisse d'emprunts*, a type of bank. Individuals exchanged existing annuities for interest-bearing certificates at the *caisse* that were convertible to cash, subject to notice (Korner, 1995).

The failure of Law's Banque Royale also engendered a strong political aversion to chartering any institution with the tainted name of a bank. Consequently, the finances of the French state were hampered by the absence of a banking institution capable of providing the state with short-term liquidity to manage its debt, especially in wartime. In the next five decades, banking was almost exclusively private discount banking. After years of agitation from the financial industry, the Crown created the Caisse d'Escompte in 1776, modeled on the Bank of England – nearly 80 years after this important British innovation (Bigo, 1927). The Caisse was organized as a limited liability partnership with the right to discount bills of exchange and other commercial paper at a maximum interest rate of 4 percent and issue banknotes redeemable in coin. In the absence of other chartered banks, it had a de facto monopoly. Largely owned by members of the private banking houses, the Caisse was primarily a bankers' bank, offering credit to its members.

During the American War for Independence, the Caisse assisted with war finance by providing credit to the private bankers who helped to launch state loans. The Crown sold its loans to the private bankers, who resold them while drawing on short-term credit from the Caisse d'Escompte. After the war, in 1783, when the Crown exhausted its ability to float new securities, it demanded a secret loan from the Caisse d'Escompte. When it was rumored that note issue was rising, a run on the bank began. To the government's embarrassment, it was halted when the administrators of the Caisse made their accounts public and the Crown was forced to repay its loan. Afterward the stockholders reorganized the bank and increased its reserves to restore public confidence. As the state's problems grew worse, the new minister, Charles-Alexandre de Calonne, coerced the bank in 1785 to provide a 70 million-livre loan. Rising loans to the Crown and growing note issue forced a suspension of redemption in 1789, beginning the Revolutionary era of fiat money (Bigo, 1927).

3.5.2 The Origins of French Debt Finance

While taxes were raised during wartime and some revenue was occasionally gained from seigniorage, most war finance was paid for by borrowing. Debt finance, which permits a tax-smoothing policy, was potentially efficient. However, in the sixteenth and seventeenth centuries, France found it nearly impossible to follow this policy, as its tax revenues were rarely sufficient to cover the costs of servicing new war debts. Consequently, lenders understood that borrowing was contingent on favorable outcomes, and the anticipation of default added a premium to the cost of borrowing. Instead of paying down the wartime debt with peacetime surpluses, the monarchy defaulted after most wars.

France's approach to debt-financed deficit expenditure was formed in the early sixteenth century. One of the catalyzing events was the financial crisis of 1522–3. At this time, the *receveurs-généraux* dominated the fiscal system. With minimal accountability, they held and managed all tax receipts and handled the disbursement of funds with the king's private treasurer. These officials also served as the king's primary bankers, borrowing money in his name or their own. In the midst of a war with Charles V, Francis I was stung by a financial crisis. He responded by purging the *receveurs* and creating the central treasury to control the disbursement of funds.

The abysmal state of royal credit led to the creation of a new debt instrument, the *rentes sur l'Hotel de Ville de Paris*, loans collateralized by specific taxes. The king assigned a source of revenue to the Provost of the Merchants and Aldermen of Paris; in turn, the Hotel de Ville (city hall) created municipal *rentes* of equivalent value that were sold to the buyer. This structure provided a guarantee by a very influential group. Many merchants, aldermen, and members of the Parlement bought the *rentes*. Thus constituted, these loans carried a lower rate of interest than the rate demanded by financiers (Dent, 1973). *Rentes* were eventually issued against most tax revenues – *tailles*, the royal domain, *aides*, *gabelles*, and *traites*. When the Crown received contributions in the form of loans from the clergy and the regional Estates, they were often constituted using this system. Gradually, the *rentes* became an important form of borrowing by the Crown. By the end of the sixteenth century, the Crown had moved toward broader market debt. Yet, borrowing from the *receveurs* and *fermiers* provided much of the short-term credit, and the long-term debt was held by many powerful and wealthy individuals – the "bourgeois gentilshommes" including many royal officers (Collins, 1988).

Another key innovation by Francis I was the establishment of the *bureau des parties casuelles* (the bureau of casual parts) to collect nonrecurrent income. Most of this revenue came from the sales of royal offices that offered tax exemptions and other benefits. The sale of offices became a major financial instrument, with annual payments providing the interest on the loan, as well as an engine for generating tax privileges. Sales of offices were used intensively during times of greatest financial need, suggesting that the package of annual payments and other benefits made this the most costly form of borrowing. Financial entrepreneurs, *traitants* or *partisans*, proposed the sale of offices to the government and received commissions (Doyle, 1996).

At the same time as Francis I introduced these institutions, he executed a default accompanied by a *chambre de justice*. While the partial default reduced the king's outstanding debts, the concentration of the debt meant that it was aimed at the Crown's privileged creditors, many of whom appeared to take or actually took advantage of their position to earn enormous profits. Beginning in the fourteenth century, the king occasionally convened a special commission to uncover financial wrongdoing. A *chambre* typically swept through the fiscal system, netting many of the leading and well-connected financiers. The accused were heavily involved in the dual tasks of tax collection and lending to the government, either as royal officials or as *traitants* and *partisans*. Usually a pamphlet campaign blamed them for profiteering at the expense of the state and the people. The *chambre* had the power to impose penalties, ranging from modest fines to the death penalty. Some accused persons fled the country, while others battled the court. In most cases the sentences were never applied, and the accused "redeemed" themselves by paying a fine to the king for immunity or amnesty (Mousnier, 1984). The *chambres de justice* have been described as attempts to satisfy public opinion outraged by the financiers' immorality and abuses (Bosher, 1973), to free the king from control of a group of financiers (Mousnier, 1984), or as a fiscal device to raise revenue and curb excesses (Collins, 1988). They appear, however, to have been a strategic instrument to manage the debt during a default. The financial officers had profited during the hard times of war through short-term lending to the government. The Crown might be in debt to them currently, but they had already reaped substantial profits, unlike long-term lenders, who had been offered high interest rates and had the prospect of high future returns. A partial default on the longer-term debt shifted the risk of the bad outcome ex post to the longer-term lenders. A default might not strike the short-term lenders as severely. Consequently, their profits were adjusted ex post by a *chambre de justice*, imposing fines and lowering the returns to lending because of the bad state.

Like the creditors of the Crown, historians have found it difficult to discover the exact state of the Crown's deficit and debt, especially for the sixteenth and seventeenth centuries. The failure to adopt double-entry bookkeeping and the multiple and partial accounts render it a nearly impossible task. Guéry (1978) provides a table of revenues, expenses, and deficits; but his misreading of the accounts yields an improbable result with over a century of large deficits. Bonney (1981) offers a more careful reading of the documents that highlights the gaps and omissions, emphasizing the impossibility of producing any credible series. Nevertheless, the impression he provides reveals a pattern of wartime spending funded by borrowing, followed by default and a return to some semblance of fiscal balance.

Table 3.4. War, Defaults, and the Chambres de Justice

War	Years	Year of Default	Chambres de Justice
Last War of Religion	1585–98	1598	1597
War with Savoy	1600–1	1602	1601–2, 1605–7, 1607
Revolts by the nobility	1614–17		
Civil War with Protestants	1621–9		1624
Mantuan War	1629–30	1634	1635
France enters the Thirty Years' War	1635–48	1648	1643, 1645, 1648
The Fronde	1648–53	1652	
War with Spain	1650–9	1661–7	1656–7, 1661–5
Flemish War	1667–8		
Dutch War	1672–8		
War of the League of Augsburg	1688–97		
War of the Spanish Succession	1702–13	1716, 1720, 1726	1716
War of the Polish Succession	1733–8		
War of the Austrian Succession	1740–8		
Seven Years' War	1756–63	1759	
American War for Independence	1776–83	1770	

Note: Sources differ on the dates of the *chambres de justice*.

Sources: Richard Bonney in J. F. Bosher (1973), Dujarric (1981), Mousnier (1980), Collins (1988), and Collins (1995).

As the figures for the state of the budget and the debt are in such dispute for the sixteenth and seventeenth centuries, Table 3.4 is offered instead of dubious numbers. This table shows the major wars and revolts from the sixteenth to the eighteenth centuries, the defaults on the debt, and the *chambres de justice*. The first two defaults shown and the accompanying *chambres de justice* were part of the financial housekeeping that Henry IV and his minister, the Duke of Sully, carried out at the end of the wars of religion. In 1596–8, Sully estimated the debt at 296 million livres. Of this total outstanding, creditors, including the Swiss cantons, German princes, England, and The Netherlands, which held 147 million livres, were forced to accept a partial reduction in their claims (Collins, 1988). Further repudiations in 1602, with the *chambres de justice*, helped to make the Crown solvent again. By 1611, Sully had a projected surplus of 4.6 million livres with total expenses of 20.4 million (Bonney, 1981).

The assassination of Henry IV in 1610 began France's long descent into civil war, the revolt of the Fronde, entrance into the Thirty Years' War, and finally War with Spain. Once again, the budgetary figures for the years between 1610 and 1660 are notoriously difficult to interpret, but the chronic state of royal finances is clear. The Crown borrowed heavily and frequently failed to meet its obligations – accepting three major defaults, in 1634, 1648, and 1652, with the attendant *chambres de justice*. Often the monarchy borrowed at exorbitant rates. For example, in 1634, *rentes* paying 7.14 percent were sold for a yield of 33 percent or higher; and frequently payments were in arrears (Dent, 1973). At the end of the War with Spain, the Crown was paying over 25 percent interest on loans arranged by financiers, who collected large fees. In the 1620s and 1630s, the king also borrowed directly from his tax officers through the *droits aliénés*. These were rights to collect surtaxes on direct and indirect taxes, priced at 10 times the annual value of the right or *droit* (Collins, 1988). In 1634, the king defaulted by converting the surtaxes into annuities and reducing the effective interest payments on the capital from 10 percent to 4.16 percent. With desperate need for revenue, the sales of royal offices soared. The number of offices was increased by separating functions, creating and abolishing districts, and alternating years for holding offices. The sale of offices helped to spawn a large bureaucracy with a vested interest in protecting its privileges, including tax exemptions. Income from the *bureau de parties casuelles*, which had averaged about 10 percent of total ordinary royal income in the first decade of the century, rose to 50 percent in the 1620s and 1630s (Bonney, 1981). The *gages* became a heavy financial burden on the Crown. When Cardinal Richelieu surveyed the king's finances in 1639, he discovered that annual payments to officials had exceeded income from sales.[14]

A financial cleanup began in 1661 with Louis XIV's personal government and the nomination of Colbert as comptroller general in 1662. A *chambre de justice* swept away Nicolas Fouquet, the previous minister, and his financial network. Colbert estimated that the venal offices represented capital of 419 million livres, from which the king received a tax of 2 million livres and paid out *gages* of 8.3 million, and he began a suppression of offices. According to Colbert, 20,000 offices were suppressed, but the costs of the Dutch War (1672–8) induced the king to sell new offices to raise revenue (Doyle, 1996). The interest payments on the *rentes*, many of which had been sold with high yields, were also reduced. The end result of Colbert's work was an essentially solvent Crown at the beginning of the next round of wars. Colbert's accomplishment, even after the Dutch War, is seen in Table 3.5, where in 1683, the debt payment to revenue ratio was 18.5 percent. The Crown was now able to raise revenue without resort to bankruptcy or a *chambre de justice* until 1716.

[14] By comparison, while English kings had used the sale of offices and honors, this practice remained relatively modest because of the smaller involvement of Britain in the protracted military struggles on the Continent (Brewer, 1988).

Table 3.5. The Burden of the Debt

	Tax Revenues (million livres)	Debt Payments (million livres)	Debt to Revenue (percent)
1683	119	22	18.5
1699	145	48	33.1
1706	118	63	53.4
1713	131	90	68.7
1724	197	65	33.0
1740	211	57	27.0
1753	257	72	28.0
1764	322	124	38.5
1775	377	155	41.1
1788	472	292	61.9

Sources: Collins (1995), p. 163, gives debt payments for 1683–1713, and the tax revenue (decade averages) is from Hoffman (1986), Table 2. Marion (1914), pp. 120–1, provides the data for 1724, and Weir (1989), Table 2, for 1740–88.

Mousnier (1980) attributes this change to the reforms of Colbert that gave the government greater control over the tax system, presumably limiting the ability of the financiers to earn higher profits.

Beginning with the Flemish War and culminating with the War of the Spanish Succession, the military ventures of Louis XIV became more expensive. At the beginning, the Crown benefited from the steady rise in real tax revenues seen in Figure 3.1; but the mounting costs and steady, if not declining, real revenues made wartime borrowing increasingly expensive. On the eve of the Spanish War of Succession, the debt service to revenue ratio is already high, at 33 percent. Although measurement of the Crown's debt is a hazardous enterprise, it is clear that it rose considerably. Table 3.5 shows that debt payments grew much more rapidly than tax revenue, more than trebling in nominal terms between 1683 and 1713.

In this setting, a broadening of the market with new financial instruments was an important innovation. In 1689, the Crown issued the first tontines. The tontines pooled an issue of *rentes viagères* or life annuities, in which the annual payments accrued to the survivors. Both the tontines and life annuities tapped a larger pool of savings for public finance. In their first use, the tontines drew in 10,000 subscribers, who provided 6.5 million livres. To a considerable extent, these new instruments replaced the more costly borrowing by the sale of venal offices. In the War of the League of Augsburg, Louis XIV raised four times as much by the sale of *rentes* (Doyle, 1996).

Although the War of the Spanish Succession secured the throne of Spain for Louis XIV's claimant, it was a disastrously expensive endeavor.

It is generally thought that the debt contracted during the war amounted to about 1 billion livres (Collins, 1995). There is a wide range of estimates of the total debt at the end of the war. Bonney (1995b) believes that the interest-bearing public debt was 1,739 million livres in 1715. Clamageran (1876) prefers 1,936 million, while Riley (1986) sees a debt of 2,600 million livres in 1714. Usually excluded from these calculations is the value of the venal offices, which Doyle (1996) estimates to have been between 700 and 800 million livres in 1721. In spite of these uncertain figures, it is clear that the burden of the debt rose to an unsustainable level. Interest payments climbed from 33 percent of tax revenues in 1699 to 69 percent at the war's end.

At the death of Louis XIV, the regent was unable to meet interest payments. A *chambre de justice* and partial default began in 1716. The short-term debt was reduced, interest rates were cut, and the *chambre de justice* set fines of 219 million livres (Marion, 1914). Yet, these traditional drastic measures did not solve the Crown's financial dilemma. The regent turned to John Law, the Scots adventurer and financial advisor. In 1716, Law founded the Banque Générale, a joint stock bank of issue. Seeking a vehicle for debt management, Law established the Compagnie d'Occident in 1717 with monopoly rights to the exploitation of Louisiana. The public was invited to exchange depreciated debt for shares in the new company, which was presumably profitable because of its monopoly. Accepting the stock below face value, the company agreed to receive lower interest payments from the Crown. The public was pleased to obtain fixed-interest irredeemable debt for tradable variable-yield securities, and the Crown was eager to have its debt service cut. Adding more privileges, including trading companies, the tax farms and minting rights, Law's "System" gathered momentum with the issue of nonconvertible notes and loans by the renamed Banque Royale (Neal, 1990). Inflation induced by this banking expansion led Law to attempt to control stock prices, interest rates, and the specie value of the livre. The incompatibility of these goals produced a spectacular collapse of the "System" in 1720. The prices of shares and banknotes plunged. The value of the debt was not much reduced, standing at about 2.2 billion livres (Marion, 1914), but by 1724 interest payments were cut back to where they were in the early stages of the war, as seen in Table 3.5. The cleanup of Law's debacle took another six years and another default in 1726 until the state's debt service was lowered to a manageable level.

3.5.3 Debt Finance in the Eighteenth Century

Two important consequences of Law's failed experiment were the abandonment of paper money and strict adherence to a specie standard.

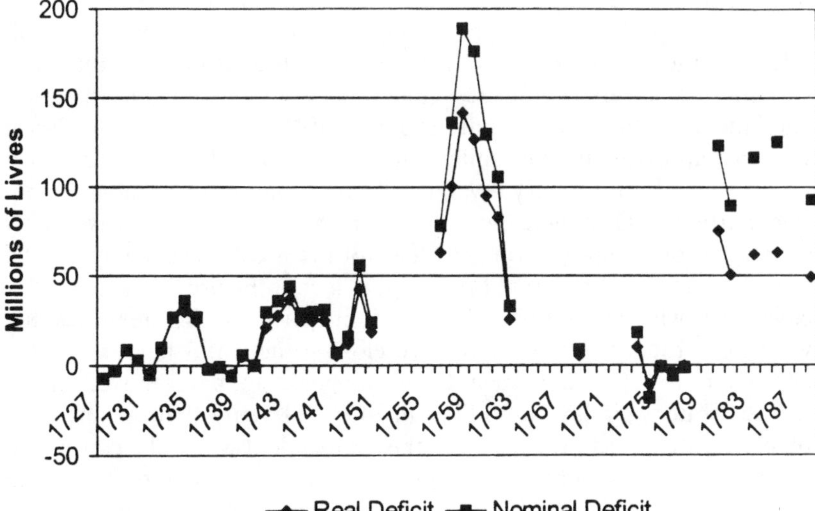

Figure 3.2 French government deficits.

Adherence to a bimetallic standard constrained France's macroeconomic choices; and policy focused on taxation and management of the debt, setting up a less distortionary macroeconomic policy regime. Fortunately, there are better statistics for the remainder of the *ancien régime* in the eighteenth century that allow a closer analysis of the Crown's policies.

The fiscal balance of the French Crown can be viewed in Figure 3.2. The data underlying this chart do not form consistent series and should be taken to show the general magnitudes rather than the precise fiscal state of the government.[15] Figure 3.2 shows that after John Law's debacle and the subsequent defaults, the budget was roughly in balance. During the War of the Polish Succession (1733–5), there was a budget deficit, but it disappeared afterward. The War of the Austrian Succession (1741–8) quickly sent the budget back into the red. In the absence of

[15] The deficits for the years 1773–88 were obtained from White (1989, Tables 1 and 3). For the period 1727–68, Riley (1987, Tables 1 and 2) provided the deficit information. To measure the size of the deficit, Riley's figures for credit items (borrowing) were subtracted from total revenue. For the years 1756–62, there was little information on total revenues and expenditures. Instead, credit items in the *affaires extraordinaires* were used as a proxy for borrowing. Actual borrowing may have been lower if there were reimbursements, or it may have been higher if there was borrowing recorded elsewhere. However, credit items appear to be the bulk of the borrowing. To measure the real deficit, Labrousse's price index (1970, Vol. II, p. 387) was used.

reliable data, what happened in the succeeding eight years of peace is unclear, although in two years of peace, 1749 and 1750, there was still a fairly large deficit. Yet, it seems clear that the Crown had managed two important wars without resorting to a default. Compared to earlier and later wars, these two required somewhat lower spending. The Polish war cost approximately 62 million livres or 21 million per year, which was 10 percent of ordinary revenues. The Austrian war was more expensive, perhaps 500 million livres, with an annual cost of approximately 25 percent of ordinary revenues.[16] Part of the fiscal success may also be attributed to the rise in real tax revenue, seen in Figure 3.1. The monarchy's borrowing capacity is evidenced in its pricing of life annuities that were age graded, at rates that were close to actuarial fairness (Velde and Weir, 1992). The French Crown appears to have moved closer to the strategy of tax smoothing in these 30 years than at any time before or afterward. Nevertheless, the French debt was still a contingent claim, with a real possibility of default. As seen in Figure 3.3, which reports the yields on consols or near-consol securities, the French Crown had to pay a substantial risk premium compared to Britain.[17] France took steps to improve its financial reputation. Service on long-term debt appears to have gradually declined from 67 million livres in 1722 to 60 million in 1734, 51 million in 1739, and 49 million in 1740 (Riley, 1986). After the Austrian war, the minister, Jean-Baptiste Machault d'Arnouville, established a sinking fund, the Caisse de Amortissement, in 1749. The proceeds of the new *vingtième* were assigned to this fund for the purpose of reducing the debt by repurchases, but it never became fully operational, as the tax revenues were diverted to pay the interest on the debt.

The Seven Years' War (1756–63) put an enormous strain on government finance. The unexpected duration and intensity of the war required much greater expenditure than the two previous wars. Riley (1986) estimated the cost of the war at 1,325 million livres, or about 190 million livres per year. Furthermore, the rapid increase in real tax revenues, shown in Figure 3.1, appears to have leveled off, and the annual cost was averaged over 70 percent of ordinary tax revenues. Only 30 percent of the cost was financed by tax increases. Thus, the deficit seen in Figure 3.2 was much larger during the Wars of the Polish and Austrian Successions. Yields increased on government securities (see Figure 3.3), as expected in the tax-smoothing model (Barro, 1987), to reallocate resources; but

[16] Calculated from Riley (1987).

[17] The source for France is Velde and Weir (1992), and for Britain it is Homer and Sylla (1996).

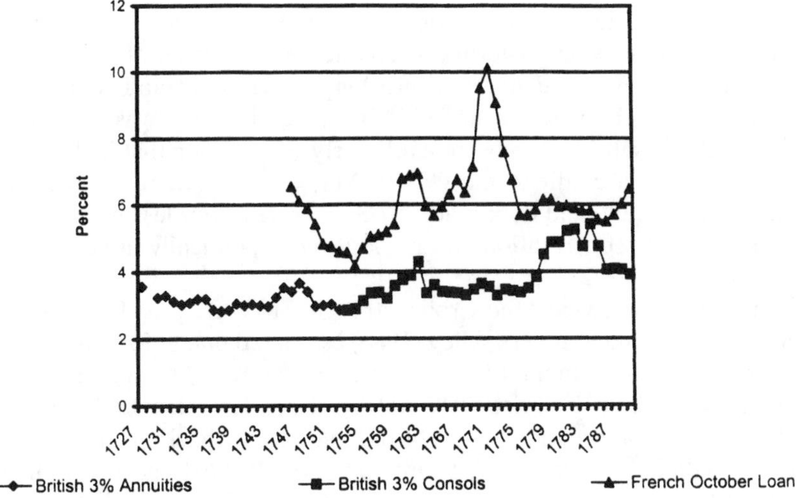

Figure 3.3 Yields on British and French securities.

the increase in France was greater than in Britain, suggesting greater borrowing requirements and perhaps a greater risk of default. One indication of increased financial stress is that in 1757, the Crown abandoned age-graded pricing of life annuities in favor of more costly and more attractive flat-rate pricing (Velde and Weir, 1992).

Financial innovation continued to broaden the market for government debt. During the War of the Polish Succession, 25,000 people contributed 26 million livres in the sales of tontines, and the same number contributed 30 million livres during the War of the Austrian Succession. Almost 50,000 contributors to one tontine produced 47 million livres for the Seven Years' War. Because tontines were issued in times of peak demand for war finance, the internal rates of return offered by both assets were attractive (Weir, 1989). In 1758, the government allowed the purchase of a life annuity on two lives, rather than one, with payments at a lower rate (Shakespeare, 1986). Apparently alarmed by the costs, in 1763 the Crown banned the issue of any tontines in the future. The multiple-life *rentes viagères* now proved popular, and in 1770 enterprising financiers hit upon the Genevan formula, in which life annuities were constituted on 20 young women who had survived smallpox and lived in the healthy city of Geneva. The annuities were pooled, and subscribers could receive a high return while reducing the risk. This form of *rentes* became a major source of financing during the American War.

The unexpected financial stress of the Seven Years' War led the Crown to conduct a selective partial default in 1759. Long-term loans were unaffected, but the short-term notes issued by the venal officers of the Crown were forcibly converted into longer-term debt and reimbursements of the debt were suspended.[18] This type of default was an "excusable" default, shifting the cost to a relatively select group that had earned high interest on credit to the Crown. Yet, it is important to note that the more broadly held debt made a *chambre de justice* less useful as an instrument of redistribution and made it more politically difficult for a default.

In the postwar years, the Crown struggled to correct its fiscal imbalance, without much success. Riley (1986) estimated that before the Seven Years' War, the debt in 1753 was approximately 1,200 million livres, requiring an annual service of 85 million livres. He calculated the debt by 1764 to be approximately 2,324 million livres – back to the level of 1714 – with a debt service of 196 million livres. In 1764, the government sought to revive the Caisse d'Amortissement (a sinking fund) to retire the debt, supplying it with new funds, and established a Caisse d'Arrérages to make interest payments on the *rentes viagères*, tontines, and *rentes perpétuelles* with the income from the two *vingtièmes*. However, this maneuvering did not permit any substantial reduction in the debt. Finally in 1770, the Crown was forced into a partial default. As in 1759, payments on short-term debt issued by the *receveurs* and *fermiers* were suspended and forcibly converted into long-term debt. But the default went further. Pensions were cut, and the tontines were forcibly converted to life annuities, lowering the future payments to the owners. The yields on other loans were lowered to 4 percent or less.[19] The result of this partial default was that the debt service was lowered to approximately 154 million livres per year, or about 40 percent of annual revenues (Vuhrer, 1886), still a very high charge on the budget. This default was broader and less selective, causing yields to soar. The partial default may have been "excusable," given the unexpectedly higher cost of the war, and it did not exclude the Crown from the market, but it seems to have stiffened resistance to any future defaults.[20]

The fiscal reforms (White, 1989) kept the Crown in rough balance once again until the outbreak of the American War (1778–83). After this

[18] In 1763, the Crown also reduced the reimbursable capital value of some loans sold during the war (Velde and Weir, 1992).

[19] In addition, the finance minister converted the tax on dividends, earmarked to pay for debt retirement, into a 10 percent tax on all interest payments.

[20] Considering the high yields paid on debt, Riley (1986) considers it a "pre-paid repudiation."

last *ancien régime* war, the Crown was never again able to come close to balancing its budget. The cost of the war has been estimated at 1,066 million livres, or slightly less than that of the Seven Years' War (Harris, 1976). Almost all of this amount – 997 million livres – was paid for with borrowing. Given the last default, the potential creditors-needed reassurance that default was not an inevitable outcome. The finance minister, Jacques Necker, apparently persuaded the public with his bold attempt to follow a tax-smoothing strategy (Bordo and White, 1991, 1994), but he was unable to secure the tax increases this required. Thus constrained, he sought to reduce the ordinary, nonwar expenditures of the Crown to fund the additional debt. Whether this strategy would have worked is the source of considerable controversy, but the failure to pursue tax reforms and manage the debt well subsequently proved fatal to the monarchy. By one estimate (Vuhrer, 1886), the service on the funded debt alone had reached 208 million livres, with a large unfunded debt outstanding. By the late 1780s, the Crown was in the position of borrowing to cover its debt service, beginning an explosive growth of the debt (White, 1989). Politically, default was inexcusable, and the Crown had to call for a new Estates-General, thereby setting the stage for the Revolution.

Like the tax system, the system of borrowing was never fully reformed. The critical needs of war financing led successive kings and finance ministers to continue their reliance on a system of privileged lenders that included the tax officials and the venal officeholders. Their importance was somewhat diminished over time, and new forms of debt were issued that drew on the national and international financial markets. Nevertheless, the monarchy was unable to depend completely on the open market. The inability to generate sufficient tax revenue and its frequent defaults made the government a risky borrower. Rather than incur even higher cost loans, it retreated to the old system. Instead of the more efficient tax-smoothing policy adopted by the British of paying down the last war's debt with peacetime surpluses, the French failed to raise taxes and built up the debt from one war to the next until default was necessary. High-cost, inefficient public finance was thereby guaranteed.

3.6 CONCLUSION

While France's failure to hold on to its American empire left it little legacy for the New World, its absence provides an important example of unsuccessful public finance. There were political constraints hampering reform and the development of a modern fiscal system. Privilege shaped French society and privilege shaped the fiscal system, with the vested interests it created blocking reform efforts. Varied and diverse tax privileges limited the growth of tax revenues and spawned hostility to their unfairness. Privilege created a venal class of government officials that controlled the tax system and dominated short-term borrowing. When the demands of war built up an unsustainable level of debt, partial defaults and *chambres de justice* punished these officials but never removed them. Even after the reforms of the eighteenth century, France remained shackled by macroeconomic institutions and policies that failed to provide the requisite revenue for the retention of New World colonies.

REFERENCES

Barro, Robert J. (1987). "Government Spending, Interest Rates, Prices and Budget Deficits in the United Kingdom," *Journal of Monetary Economics* 20 (September), pp. 221–48.

(1989). "The Neoclassical Approach to Fiscal Policy," in Robert J. Barro, ed., *Modern Business Cycle Theory* (Cambridge: Harvard University Press), pp. 236–64.

Bigo, Robert (1927). *La Caisse d'Escompte* (Paris).

Bonney, Richard (1973). "Chambres de justice in the French monarchy," in J. F. Bosher, ed., *French Government and Society, 1500–1850, Essays in Memory of Alfred Cobban* (London: The Athlone Press), pp. 19–40.

(1981). *The King's Debts: Finance and Politics in France, 1589–1661* (Oxford: Clarendon Press).

(1995a). "Early Modern Theories of State Finance," in Richard Bonney, ed., *Economic Systems and State Finance* (Oxford: Clarendon Press), pp. 163–230.

(1995b). "The Eighteenth Century. II. The Struggle for Great Power Status and the End of the Old Fiscal Regime," in Richard Bonney, ed., *Economic Systems and State Finance* (Oxford: Clarendon Press), pp. 315–92.

(1995c). "Revenues," in Richard Bonney, ed., *Economic Systems and State Finance* (Oxford: Clarendon Press), pp. 423–506.

Bordo, Michael D. (1986). "Money, Deflation, and Seigniorage in the Fifteenth Century: A Review Essay," *Journal of Monetary Economics* 18 (November), pp. 337–46.

Bordo, Michael D. and Finn E. Kydland (1995). "The Gold Standard As a Rule: An Essay in Exploration," *Explorations in Economic History* 32 (October), pp. 423–64.

Bordo, Michael D. and Carlos Vègh (1998). "What If Alexander Hamilton Had Been Argentinean? A Comparison of the Early Monetary Experiences of Argentina and the United States." National Bureau of Economic Research Working Paper 6862, December (Cambridge: NBER).

Bordo, Michael D. and Eugene N. White (1991). "Tale of Two Currencies: British and French Finance During the Napoleonic Wars," *Journal of Economic History* 51(2) (June), pp. 303–16.

(1994). "British and French Finance during the Napoleonic Wars," in Michael

D. Bordo and Forrest Capie, eds., *Monetary Regimes in Transition* (Cambridge: Cambridge University Press, NY), pp. 241–73.

Bouchary, Jean (1937). *Marché des changes de Paris a la fin du XVIIe siècle 1778–1800* (Paris: Paul Hartmann).

Brewer, John (1988). *Sinews of Power: War, Money and the English State, 1688–1783* (Cambridge, MA: Harvard University Press).

Bulow, Jeremy and Kenneth Rogoff (1989a). "A Constant Recontracting Model of Sovereign Debt," *Journal of Political Economy* 97 (February), pp. 155–78.

(1989b). "Sovereign Debt: Is to Forgive to Forget?" *American Economic Review* 79 (March), pp. 43–50.

Clamageran, J.-J. (1876). *Histoire de l'Impot en France* (Paris: Librarie de Guillaumin et Cie.).

Collins, James B. (1988). *Fiscal Limits of Absolutism: Direct Taxation in Early Seventeenth Century France* (Berkeley: University of California Press).

(1995). *The State in Early Modern France* (Cambridge: Cambridge University Press, NY).

Dent, Julian (1973). *Crisis in Finance: Crown, Financiers and Society in Seventeenth Century France* (Newton Abbot, U.K.: David and Charles).

Doyle, William (1974). *The Parlement of Bordeaux* (New York: St. Martin's Press).

(1996). *Venality: The Sale of Offices in Eighteenth Century France* (Oxford: Clarendon Press).

Dujarric, G. (1981). *Précis Chronologique d'Histoire de France* (Paris: Albin Michel).

Fritschy, Wantje (1990). "Taxation in Britain, France and the Netherlands in the Eighteenth Century," in P. Boomgard, series ed., *Economic and Social History of the Netherlands*, Vol. II (Amsterdam: NDHA), pp. 57–80.

Gelabert, Juan (1995). "The Fiscal Burden," in Richard Bonney, ed., *Economic Systems and State Finance* (Oxford: Clarendon Press), pp. 539–76.

Glassman, Debra and Angela Redish (1988). "Currency Depreciation in Early Modern England and France," *Explorations in Economic History* 25 (January), pp. 75–97.

Grossman, Herschel I. and John B. Van Huyck (1988). "Sovereign Debt as a Contingent Claim: Excusable Default, Repudiation, and Reputation," *American Economic Review* 78 (December), pp. 1088–97.

Guéry, A. (1978). "Les finances de la monarchie française sous l'ancien régime," *Annales Economies, Societes, et Civilisationes* 33(2), pp. 216–39.

Harris, Robert D. (1976). "French Finances and the American War, 1777–1783," *Journal of Modern History* 48 (June), pp. 233–58.

Hoffman, Philip T. (1986). "Taxes and Agrarian Life in Early Modern France: Land Sales, 1550–1730," *Journal of Economic History* 46, No. 1 (March), pp. 37–55.

(1994). "Early Modern France, 1450–1700," in Philip T. Hoffman and Kathryn Norberg, eds., *Fiscal Crises, Liberty, and Representative Government, 1450–1789* (Stanford, CA: Stanford University Press), pp. 226–52.

Homer, Sidney, and Richard Sylla (1996). *A History of Interest Rates*, 3rd ed. (New Brunswick, NJ: Rutgers University Press).

Korner, Martin (1995). "Public Credit," in Richard Bonney, ed., *Economic Systems and State Finance* (Oxford: Clarendon Press), pp. 507–38.

Labrousse, Ernest (1970). *Histoire Economique et Sociale de la France*, Vol. II (Paris: Presses Universitaires de France).

Lévy-Leboyer, Maurice and François Bourguignon (1985). *The French Economy in the Nineteenth Century* (Cambridge: Cambridge University Press, NY).

Mankiw, N. Gregory (1987). "The Optimal Collection of Seigniorage: Theory and Evidence," *Journal of Monetary Economics* 20, pp. 327–41.

Marion, Marcel (1914). *Histoire financière de la France depuis 1715* (Paris).

Mathias, Peter and Patrick O'Brien (1976). "Taxation in Britain and France, 1715–1810. A Comparison of the Social and Economic Incidence of Taxes Collected for the Central Governments," *Journal of European Economic History* 5, pp. 601–49.

Matthews, George T. (1958). *The Royal General Farms in Eighteenth Century France* (New York: Columbia University Press).

McCusker, John J. (1978). *Money and Exchange in Europe and America, 1600–1775: A Handbook* (Chapel Hill: University of North Carolina Press).

Miskimin, Harry A. (1984). *Money and Power in Fifteenth Century France* (New Haven, CT: Yale University Press).

Mousnier, Roland E. (1984). *The Institutions of France under the Absolute Monarchy, 1598–1789*, Vol. II (Chicago: University of Chicago Press).

Neal, Larry (1990). *The Rise of Financial Capitalism, International Capital Markets in the Age of Reason* (Cambridge: Cambridge University Press, NY).

North, Douglass and Barry Weingast (1989). "Constitutions and Commitment: Evolution of Institutions Governing Public Choice," *Journal of Economic History* (December), pp. 803–32.

O'Brien, Patrick (1988). "The Political Economy of British Taxation, 1660–1815," *Economic History Review* 41 (February), pp. 1–32.

O'Brien, Patrick, and Caglar Keyder (1978). *Economic Growth in Britain and France 1780–1914* (London: Allen and Unwin).

Ormrod, W. W. (1995). "The West European Monarchies in the Later Middle Ages," in Richard Bonney, ed., *Economic Systems and State Finance* (Oxford: Clarendon Press), pp. 123–60.

Price, Jacob (1973). *France and the Chesapeake* (Ann Arbor: University of Michigan Press).

Riley, James C. (1986). *The Seven Years War and the Old Regime in France: The Economic and Financial Toll* (Princeton, NJ: Princeton University Press).

(1987). "French Finances, 1727–1768," *Journal of Modern History* 59 (June), pp. 209–43.

Sargent, Thomas J. and François R. Velde (forthcoming). *The Evolution of Small Change: Beliefs, Experiments, and Technologies* (Princeton: Princeton University Press).

Shakespeare, Howard J. (1986). *France: The Royal Loans, 1689–1789* (Shrewsbury, U.K.: Squirrel Publications).

Stone, Bailey (1981). *The Parlement of Paris, 1774–1789* (Chapel Hill: University of North Carolina Press).

Sussman, Nathan (1993). "Debasements, Royal Revenues, and Inflation in France During the Hundred Years' War, 1415–1422," *Journal of Economic History* 53 (March), pp. 44–70.

Touzery, Mireille (1994). *L'invention de l'impot sur le revenu: La taille tarifée 1715–1789* (Paris: Comité pour l'Histoire Economique et Financière de la France).

Velde, François R. and David R. Weir (1992). "The Financial Market and Government Debt Policy in France, 1746–1793," *Journal of Economic History* 52 (March), pp. 1–40.

Vuhrer, A. (1886). *Histoire de la Dette Publique en France* (Paris: Gerger-Levrault et Cie.).

Weir, David R. (1989). "Tontines, Public Finance, and Revolution in France and England, 1688–1789," *Journal of Economic History* 49 (March), pp. 95–124.

White, Eugene N. (1989). "Was There a Solution to the Financial Crisis of the Ancien Regime?" *Journal of Economic History* (September), 49(3), pp. 545–68.

(1995). "The French Revolution and the Politics of Government Finance, 1770–1815," *Journal of Economic History* 55 (June), pp. 227–55.

(1997). "L'éfficacité de l'affermage de l'impôt: la Ferme Generale au XVIIIe siecle" in *L'administration des finances sous l'Ancien Régime* (Paris: Comité pour l'histoire économique et financière de la France), pp. 103–20.

4

The Netherlands in the New World

The Legacy of European Fiscal, Monetary, and Trading Institutions for New World Development from the Seventeenth to the Nineteenth Centuries

Jan de Vries

4.1 INTRODUCTION

The Dutch have not left many deep and enduring marks on the political and economic institutions of the New World; their presence as colonists, rulers, traders, and investors is not invisible (indeed, their presence as rulers is not yet over), but it hardly bears comparison with the transforming impact of an England or Spain, or even a Portugal or France. This negligible legacy was not the result of Dutch indifference. In fact, from the early days of the Dutch Republic an "Atlantic dream" – a New World redeemed from its Spanish/Catholic yoke, populated by Dutch settlers and Calvinist Indians, forming a productive and profitable part of a global trading economy – captured the imaginations of merchants, the House of Orange, and many Reformed clergymen and their followers.[1] In 1630 the new Dutch West India Company published a pamphlet with this bit of promotional verse:[2]

Westindjen kan syn Nederlands groot gewin
Verkleynt's vyands Macht brengt silver platen in.

[West India can become The Netherlands' great source of gain,
Diminishing the enemy's power as it garners silver plate.]

The "Atlantic reality" never came close to fulfilling the high hopes of the early promoters, but this was not for want of trying. The Netherlands

[1] Oliver A. Rink, *Holland on the Hudson* (Ithaca, New York, 1986), pp. 50–64; Cornelius Ch. Goslinga, *The Dutch in the Caribbean and on the Wild Coast, 1580–1680* (Assen/Gainesville, Florida, 1971), p. 87; C. Ligtenberg, *Willem Usselinx* (Utrecht, 1915); W. J. van Hoboken, "The Dutch West India Company; The Political Background of Its Rise and Decline," in J. S. Bromley and E. H. Kossmann, eds., *Britain and the Netherlands*, Vol. I (London, 1960), pp. 41–61.

[2] *Vrijheden by de Vergaderinghe van de Negenthiene vande Geoctoryeerde West-Indische Compagnie vergunt aen allen den gehenen die eenighe Colonien in Nieuw-Nederlandt sullen planten* (Amsterdam, 1630).

launched repeated efforts to achieve something in the New World:[3] It fought and worked to build an empire, indeed, to construct a *groot desseyn* (grand design) in the Western Hemisphere comparable to the inter-Asian trading network operated out of Batavia. When this failed, it sought to organize and dominate an international trading system that penetrated the plantation colonies of all the Atlantic powers. When this strategy was checked by the increasingly effective mercantilist policies of its rivals, the Dutch Republic set its sights on the construction of plantation economies. And, as these showed signs of failing, The Netherlands refocused its New World hopes on investment possibilities in the new American republics, especially the United States. These successive rounds of enterprise engaged The Netherlands and its advanced institutions with the developmental challenges of the Western Hemisphere. This engagement was filled with frustration and disappointment, and in the very long run it left precious little of an institutional legacy, but this is not to say that nothing was accomplished – and even frustrating experiences can prove instructive.

This chapter has twelve sections. Section 4.2 provides brief accounts of the early development of Dutch property rights and fiscal practices, which endowed the young Dutch Republic with efficient economic institutions. Section 4.3 reviews the Dutch fiscal system in the period 1579–1815, emphasizing the structure of taxation, the provision of public goods, and the Dutch state's exceptional resistance to bureaucratic centralization. Section 4.4 examines the rise and fate of the Dutch public debt and relates this to the emergence of the Amsterdam capital market. The Republic's money supply and associated institutions are also described in this section. With Section 4.5 we turn to the New World, and a discussion of Dutch colonizing institutions and practices. Sections 4.6 to 4.10 analyze successive Dutch strategies to produce commodities, trade, invest, and govern in the New World. Section 4.11 describes monetary policies in Dutch colonies, and Section 4.12 offers an assessment of Dutch financial and monetary institutions in their New World setting and speculates about "what might have been if . . . ."

4.2 PROPERTY RIGHTS AND FISCAL PRACTICES IN THE SIXTEENTH CENTURY

The Republic of the United Netherlands that emerged in the course of the 1580s from a protracted struggle against Spanish overlordship (a

[3] A detailed account of the successive phases of Dutch economic involvement in the New World is provided in Jan de Vries and Ad van der Woude, *The First Modern Economy. Success, Failure and Perseverance of the Dutch Economy, 1500–1815* (Cambridge, 1997), 396–402, 464–81.

struggle that would not end definitely until 1648) quickly claimed for itself a leading position in the economic life of Europe. It could do so, many have argued, because its war of liberation – the Dutch Revolt – constituted a "bourgeois revolution" that endowed the new state with institutions that secured the rights of private property, inaugurated a modern fiscal system, and established the conditions of trust and constitutional rule necessary to create a sound public debt. The new state did, indeed, establish several important new institutions crucial to its success as a commercial nation (to which we will turn presently), but its institutional foundations as a capitalist economy were not so much a product of the Revolt as they were a legacy of its "deviant" medieval past. These foundations included the emergence of free markets in land and labor, the development of constitutional controls over taxation, and the emergence of an uncoerced market in public debt instruments.

Conventions of historical discourse tend to link the establishment of free land and labor markets to the demise of *feudalism*, a set of institutions that recognized multiple claimants to the use of land, limited the right to alienate or reorganize the use of land, and tied labor to the land via nonmarket arrangements that institutionalized the power of a class of noble *surplus extractors*.

Feudal institutions were not unknown to the Low Countries, but throughout the maritime provinces that formed the economic heart of the Netherlands, they either had never taken root or had lost at an early date the power to inhibit the development of secure land titles and a mobile labor force. By the sixteenth century the region's seigneurialism was emasculated, having lost its role as a means of extraeconomic coercion. It had been transformed into a type of property right for its owners and a straightforward cost of doing business for those subject to its claims.

The weakness of serfdom and seigneurialism did not derive from a struggle against feudalism, but from institutional features of the region's early settlement history and early access to urban markets. The terms of settlement on the peat-bog frontier in the twelfth to thirteenth centuries,[4] the power given to livestock-raising peasants to escape seigneurial control,[5] the autonomous rights asserted by farmers united in drainage associations, and the avenues of escape offered by the urban and proto-urban settlements of the region all served to endow the maritime provinces with property rights and personal freedoms long before the

[4] On this theme see William H. Te Brake, *Medieval Frontier. Culture and Ecology in Rijnland* (College Station, Texas, 1985); H. van der Linden, *De cope* (Assen, 1956).

[5] See B. H. Slicher van Bath, "Boerenvrijheid," *Economisch-historisch herdrukken* (The Hague, 1964), 272–94.

emergence of a full-blown capitalist society. Or, to put it differently, the modernity of rural society derived from a deviant medieval heritage, not from a struggle to overthrow feudalism.[6]

The emergence of constitutional rule[7] in late medieval and early modern Europe generally was associated closely with the presence of cities and the existence of fragmented sovereignty. In short, a degree of competition needed to exist among potential sources of political leadership.

In the case of The Netherlands, the competitive condition is easily satisfied, for the region had been, ever since the division of the Carolingian Empire in the ninth century, a zone of contested political leadership. From the fleeting Kingdom of Lothar, through the Burgundian inheritance, to the ill-fated United Kingdom of the Netherlands of 1815–30, no strong, unified polity has long occupied the space of Europe's "middle kingdom" wedged between the French and the Germans, and between both of them and the English.

This competitive political space was filled at an early date with cities. These capital-rich entities and other, usually urban-based, corporate bodies were the political units that bargained with territorial rulers over issues of institutional change.

Charles Tilly, in *Cities and the Rise of States in Europe*, formulated the issue as follows:[8]

> The variable distribution of cities and systems of cities by region and era significantly and independently constrained the multiple paths of state transformation. . . . States, as repositories of armed force, grow differentially in different environments and . . . the character of the urban networks within such environments systematically affect the path of state transformation.

In Tilly's view, the more well endowed a territory was with capital-rich cities, the more state formation would assume a capital-intensive rather

[6] For general discussions of medieval developments in the northern Netherlands and the "transition" debate, see Jan de Vries, "On the Modernity of the Dutch Republic," *Journal of Economic History* 33 (1973), 191–202; Peter Hoppenbrouwers and Jan Luiten van Zanden, eds., *From Peasants to Farmers? The Transformation of the Rural Economy and Society in the Low Countries in the Light of the Brenner Debate* (Turnhout, Belgium, 2000).

[7] By *constitutional* rule I mean a government bound by clearly defined rules of governance, a functioning fiscal control exercised by a representative body, and a relatively broad base of representation in consultative bodies at the several levels of administration. *Democracy* would be an anachronistic term.

[8] Charles Tilly, "Entanglements of European Cities and States," in Charles Tilly and Wim P. Bockmans, eds., *Cities and the Rise of States in Europe, A.D. 1000 to 1800* (Boulder, Colorado, 1994), p. 6. See also his *Coercion, Capital, and European States, A.D. 990–1990* (Oxford, 1990).

than a coercion-intensive form – in short, the more the state will protect the interests of trade, industry, and finance in return for revenue.

Something like this scenario seems to be what North and North and Thomas had in mind for The Netherlands.[9] There, prospering cities predated the arrival of the Burgundian princes. These princes performed the valuable service of restraining the congenital tendency of towns to create local monopolies and feud among each other, while the towns, for their part, limited the arbitrary governance and confiscatory taxation to which princes naturally incline.

While this modus vivendi pertained to most provinces of the Burgundian Netherlands, the northern provinces that would later form the Dutch Republic possessed the added feature of numerous autonomous drainage authorities. These *local improvement associations* brought a form of corporate, even representative, life to the countryside as well as a durable vehicle for investment in land reclamation and soil improvement.

The final institutional achievement we will consider is the creation of a free market in public debt instruments. In early-sixteenth-century Europe the only credible issuers of long-term debt were cities. Territorial states lacked the secure sources of tax revenue and the constitutional checks on the policies of the ruler to attract funds from potential lenders on anything except a short-term basis and at very high interest rates.[10] The great financial innovation of the province of Holland in the period 1540–60 was to secure a steady stream of tax revenue and a reputation for fiscal probity that allowed it to attract funds voluntarily from a reasonably broad base of investors.[11] A key institution of municipal finance had been transplanted to the territorial level, giving Holland and other provinces an enormous fiscal power vis-à-vis the Habsburg central government, which remained beholden to costly short-term bank credit and the provinces themselves for funding.

4.3 THE DUTCH FISCAL REGIME, 1579–1815

The American revolutionaries of 1776, who clothed themselves in the garments of opponents of oppressive taxation, may well have taken their cue from the leaders of the Dutch revolt two centuries earlier, who held

[9] Douglass C. North and Robert P. Thomas, *The Rise of the Western World* (Cambridge, 1973), pp. 132–45; Douglass C. North, *Structure and Change in Economic History* (New York, 1981), pp. 151–7.

[10] Any number of works describe this predicament of Renaissance monarchs: John Munro, "Patterns of Trade, Money and Credit," in Thomas Brady, Heiko Oberman, and James Tracy, eds., *Handbook of European History, 1400–1600* (Leiden, 1994), pp. 147–85.

[11] James Tracy, *A Financial Revolution in the Habsburg Netherlands: "Renten" and "Renteniers" in the County of Holland, 1515–1565* (Berkeley and Los Angeles, 1985).

up the taxing policies of their Spanish overlords as a sure sign of Habsburg perfidy.[12] This issue (Philip II's regents sought to introduce a centrally administered 10 percent tax on commercial transactions) was second only to religious freedom as a driving force of the revolt. It can come as no surprise, therefore, that the fiscal regime of the new Republic was resolutely decentralized and so designed as to shelter commercial transactions from the considerable burdens of Dutch taxation.

The defensive needs of the Republic (which was at war with Spain almost continuously until 1648, then with England in three successive naval wars, and with France in land wars that stretched from 1672, with only brief interruptions, until 1713) were prodigious, and they were financed by taxes raised by the seven provinces in accordance with a quota that each province was required to meet in support of the central government's (chiefly military) budget. Holland, the leading province in every respect, paid 58 percent of this budget. We will focus on its tax system, which was broadly similar to those of the other provinces.

The central government was almost, but not entirely, without taxing authority. The only significant national tax was the customs duty levied on imports and exports. But tariffs were low (on average, perhaps 3–4 percent of the value of trade), and even here, collection was entrusted to the Republic's five regional admiralty boards. The justification for customs duties (the only significant levy on foreign trade) was the need to defray the convoy services provided by the admiralties to the merchant marine. It was hoped that these revenues would suffice to support the maintenance of a navy (a hope often denied by events).

Holland levied taxes on real property (a fixed percentage of the assessed valuation of land and structures – a valuation changed only twice in the Republic's history!) and collected various miscellaneous taxes, such as inheritance taxes on collateral heirs, stamp taxes, and occasional wealth levies. However, the cornerstone of Republican fiscalism was the excise tax. What had earlier been an exclusively urban tax could be introduced at the provincial level because of the thoroughgoing commercialization of the economy. Beginning with fixed levies on the sale of wine, beer, meat, peat, salt, soap, grain, woolen cloth, and spirits, and on the use of market scales, the excise was extended to an ever-widening

[12] The influence of the Dutch Revolt upon the American Revolution was perhaps chiefly evident in retrospect; the influence of the Dutch Republic's fiscal and banking institutions on the American Republic's first secretary of the treasury appears more direct and tangible. See E. J. Janse de Jonge, "Hollandse invloeden op de Amerikaanse overheidsfinanciën: Een analyse aan de hand van de opvattingen van Alexander Hamilton (1789–1795)," in W. Fritschy, J. K. T. Postma, and J. Roelevink, eds., *Doel en middel. Aspecten van financieel overheidsbeleid in de Nederlanden van de zestiende eeuw tot heden* (Amsterdam, 1995), pp. 115–32.

range of commodities and services in the course of the seventeenth century (candles, fish, cheese, butter, servants, funerals, tobacco, tea, coffee, chocolate, luxury coaches, private yachts). As the government added new taxes and adjusted the levy on existing ones, these indirect taxes proved to be a flexible source of revenue. By farming the tax collections out to hundreds of bidders in Holland's 18 tax districts, the state could count on a predictable inflow of funds, while taxpayer discontent was focused on the small-time operators who specialized in this line of work.

These excises, taken together, extracted just under 3 guilders per inhabitant of Holland when introduced in 1584, a figure that rose steadily to 10 guilders per head by the 1630s, when the excises accounted for two-thirds of Holland's total tax revenue. At that time, an average family of four would have paid excise taxes equivalent to 17 percent of the annual earnings of a fully employed unskilled laborer.[13]

This tax burden was substantial, and it was not often exceeded by much in later years. In search of new revenues, Holland experimented with income taxes, but none of its initiatives (in 1622, 1715, and 1742) proved workable. Wealth taxes proved to be more feasible, and they shifted from "extraordinary" (but very frequent) levies to annual impositions in 1722. By then the wealth tax was restricted to the value of bonds and other debt instruments.

Overall, Dutch provincial and central government tax revenues relied on real property taxes and customs collections in the Republic's first years. Revenues rose rapidly with the introduction and extension of indirect taxes – the excises – until these accounted, in the case of Holland, for over 60 percent of a much enlarged total revenue by the 1630s. Thereafter, and especially after the 1670s, further revenue increases depended on developing new direct taxes on income and wealth. By 1790 indirect taxes accounted for only about 40 percent of Holland's total revenues (Figure 4.1 and Table 4.1).

Besides provincial taxes, the Dutch taxpayer faced the demands – chiefly in the form of excise taxes and a wide range of fees – of urban governments (nearly half of all Dutchmen lived in cities). Rural dwellers did not escape additional taxation, for they were subject to the often substantial property taxes levied by drainage boards to defray the expenses of dike, windmill, and sluice maintenance. Finally, we can note the ubiquitous tolls for the use of roads, canals, locks, bridges, and harbors.

Public goods were hardly ever provided by the central government and rarely by the provincial governments. It was a principle of Republican statecraft that infrastructural investments and educational costs be

[13] De Vries and van der Woude, *First Modern Economy*, Table 4.6.

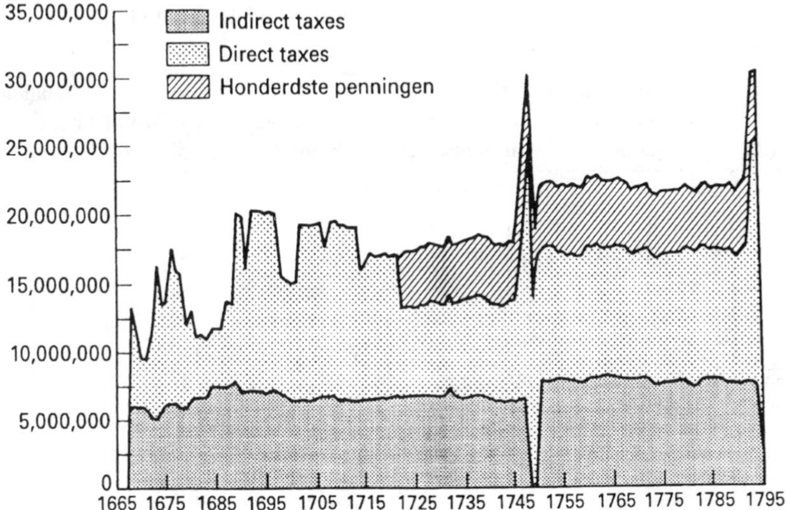

Figure 4.1 Public revenue in Holland, 1668–1794, by type: Indirect taxes, direct taxes, 1 percent wealth tax.

Source: Wantje Fritschy and René van der Voort, "From Fragmentation to Unification: Public Finance, 1700–1914," in Marjolein 't Hart, Joost Jonker, and Jan Luiten van Zanden, eds., *A Financial History of the Netherlands* (Cambridge University Press, 1997), p. 80.

devolved to the lowest possible unit of government, and be paid for as much as possible by the direct beneficiaries. Thus, intercity canals were built and maintained by the cities connected and supported by user fees; the costs of navigational aids at harbor entrances (lighthouses, buoys, channel dredging) were paid by levies on local shipping; schools were supported by fees and municipal subsidies; universities by their provinces; land drainage by the property owners within the polder.

In the eighteenth century it appeared to critics of this regime that the Republic suffered from underinvestment in such things as paved roads and channel dredging (from harbors to the open sea) because local economies could not justify expenditures that far exceeded what could be expected in short-run returns. No centralized state stood ready to subsidize grand uneconomic projects, since the central state had no significant independent taxing power.[14]

[14] The decentralized character of Dutch investment in transport infrastructure is discussed in more detail in Jan de Vries, "Transport en infrastructuur in het Noorden en Oosten van Nederland tijdens de Republiek," in J. N. H. Elerie and P. H. Pellenbarg, eds., *De welvarende periferie* (Groningen, 1998), pp. 11–22.

Table 4.1. Tax Revenue and Tax Burden Indicators for Holland (1552–1792) and the Republic (1720–1850)

Year(s)	Tax Revenue (in millions of guilders)	Estimated Population (in thousands)	Tax Burden per Capita (in guilders)	Tax Burden Deflated by Cost of Living Index (1624 = 100)
		Holland		
1552–60	0.34	360	0.94	26
1588	3.40	495	6.87	102
1599	4.60	550	8.36	88
1624	7.20	672	10.71	100
1635	10.50	718	14.62	119
1653	10.50	800	13.13	92
1669–71	11.40	880	12.95	108
1672–8	16.50	880	18.75	151
1679–87	13.20	880	15.00	142
1688–97	21.70	860	25.23	196
1701–13	19.40	845	22.96	195
1720–8	19.30	820	23.51	208
1740–5	20.80	790	26.33	217
1746–8	25.80	783	32.95	249
1749–54	22.00	783	28.10	240
1761–5	22.30	783	28.48	230
1788–92	24.90	783	31.80	221
		Republic (1720 = 100)		
1720	32	33	17.00	100
1750	37	41	19.50	114
1790	39	46	20.00	96
1806/7	45	50	22.20	80
1815	38.5	51	17.50	63
1850	54	68	17.50	91

Source: James D. Tracy, *A Financial Revolution in the Habsburg Netherlands* (Berkeley and Los Angeles, 1985), p. 203; E. H. M. Dormans, *Het tekort. Staatsschuld in de tijd der Republiek* (Amsterdam, 1991); M. 't Hart, *In Quest of Funds. Warfare and State Formation in the Netherlands, 1620–1650* (Leiden, 1989), pp. 48, 57; J. M. F. Fritschy, *De patriotten en de financiën van de Bataafse Republiek* (Hollandse Historische Reeks 10, 1988), pp. 36, 67; R. Liesker, "Tot zinkens toe bezwaard. De schuldenlast van het Zuiderkwartier van Holland, 1672–1794," in S. Groenveld et al., eds., *Bestuurders en geleerden* (Amsterdam, 1985), pp. 151–60. Revenue and expenditure data for the Republic as a whole are drawn from Wantje Fritschy and René van der Voort, "From Fragmentation to Unification: Public Finance, 1700–1914," in Marjolein 't Hart, Joost Jonker, and Jan Luiten van Zanden, eds., *A Financial History of the Netherlands* (Cambridge, 1997), p. 68.

Overall, Dutch taxation was broadly based (no one was exempt) and deeply penetrating (total taxes as a percentage of gross national product [GNP] were as high in 1713 as they would become in Great Britain by 1790).[15] But the Republic stands as a great exception to what appears to have been an iron law of European state development in that its developing fiscal system did not lead to a process of centralization of state institutions. The Republic remained resolutely decentralized and unbureaucratic until its end – indeed, until well after its demise. After the fall of the old Republic in 1795, it took 13 years of further political struggle to achieve a centralized fiscal system.[16]

4.4 THE DUTCH PUBLIC DEBT

Voluntary credit markets for public debt were pioneered by Europe's cities in the Middle Ages. Municipal practice was successfully transplanted to the provincial level in the Low Countries, most notably by Holland, in the mid-sixteenth century, and by the Dutch Republic as a whole after it achieved de facto independence from Spain in the 1580s. This adaptation of an urban/bourgeois practice to the larger stage of the territorial state is often seen as a key Dutch innovation, sustaining the provinces in their struggle for independence from Spain and fortifying them in the later wars against England and France.[17]

Provincial (and urban) borrowers issued three types of debt instrument. *Obligatien* were promissory notes intended to be short-term and, as bearer bonds, readily negotiable. More important were the longer-term debt instruments known as *losrenten* and *lijfrenten*. *Losrenten* were, strictly speaking, redeemable bonds, although they tended to become perpetual. Until the issuer redeemed them, the holder, whose name was recorded in a debt ledger, enjoyed an annual interest payment. *Lijfrenten* were life annuities, self-amortizing loans in which the issuer contracts to make annual payments to the buyer, or nominee, during his or her life. At death the principal of the loan is extinguished. In the 1570s *losrenten* paid the "twelfth penny" (i.e., 8.33 percent), while *lijfrenten* paid the "sixth penny" (16.67 percent); by 1609, the interest rates were the

[15] Compare Patrick O'Brien and Peter Mathias, "Taxation in Britain and France, 1715–1810," *Journal of European Economic History* 6 (1976), 601–50; J. M. F. Fritschy, *De patriotten en de financiën van de Bataafse Republiek* (The Hague, 1988), pp. 57–70; John Brewer, *The Sinews of Power* (New York, 1988), Ch. 4.

[16] The exceptional character of Dutch state development is explored in the work of Marjolein 't Hart. See her *The Making of the Bourgeois State. War, Politics and Finance During the Dutch Revolt* (Manchester, 1993). The struggle to centralize the Dutch fiscal regime is told with feeling in Simon Schama, *Patriots and Liberators. Revolution in the Netherlands, 1780–1813* (New York, 1977).

[17] See Tracy, *Financial Revolution*; 't Hart, *Making of the Bourgeois State*.

sixteenth penny (6.25 percent) and the "eighth penny" (12.5 percent), respectively.

As late as 1600, Holland's public debt was modest, no more than 5 million guilders. This was so in part because voluntary lenders were scarce. The reluctance to lend appears to have had less to do with the state's creditworthiness than with the numerous opportunities for higher returns in the commercial sector. The Twelve Years' Truce begun in 1609 reduced Holland's need to issue new bonds. Then, as in 1621, its debt stood at 23 million guilders (in addition, the Generality's debt was nearly 5 million). When war resumed in 1621, so did Holland's issuance of new bonds. By then the reluctance of investors to tie up capital in public debt had diminished substantially. From 1621 to the end of hostilities with Spain in 1647, Holland and the Generality borrowed 115 million guilders, over 4 million per year. This level of borrowing supplemented Holland's tax revenues by some 40 percent, which goes a long way to accounting for the generally stable tax burden of these decades. Of course, with a growing debt came steadily increasing interest payments. By 1640 the debt of some 95 million guilders required 6.5 million per year in debt service – itself about 60 percent of Holland's tax revenue.

In that year, confidence in Holland's public debt was such that the *losrenten* portion of the debt, mostly paying 6 percent, could be converted (i.e., the old bonds redeemed and new ones issued) to a 5 percent rate of interest. A second conversion in 1655 succeeded in reducing credit costs to 4 percent.

Lijfrenten, the life annuities, also received careful attention, and from no less than Johan de Witt, Holland's Grand Pensionary and effective head of government. He wrote the first treatise applying probability theory to compare the costs to the issuer of *lijfrenten* (where the age and life expectancy of the nominee determine the real interest rate) versus *losrenten*.[18] His findings exposed the high cost of *lijfrenten* issued without regard to the age of the nominee. Henceforth, when Holland issued *lijfrenten*, it should do so, De Witt argued, only at rates that varied with the nominee's age. In fact, the Republic made steadily diminishing use of *lijfrenten* as Dutch governments found they "were able to borrow by means of long-term redeemable (but in practice perpetual) annuities at rates equal to the lowest interest returns demanded in the private sector. The United Provinces had shifted to a program of credit exploitation that gave investors guarantees sufficient to convince them to accept interest-only lending formats."[19] This exploitation of the credit markets

[18] Johan de Witt, *Waerdije van lijfrenten naer proportie van losrenten* (The Hague, 1671).

[19] James C. Riley, *International Government Finance and the Amsterdam Capital Market, 1740–1815* (Cambridge, 1980), p. 104.

endowed the Republic with a spending ability that greatly exceeded its short-term ability to tax.

By converting bonds to lower interest rates and by stopping the issuing of expensive life annuities, Holland succeeded in reducing considerably its annual debt service. In 1668 Johan de Witt took satisfaction in the fact that he had managed to reduce annual debt service costs despite increasing the size of the debt by 30 million guilders.

A well-managed public debt offers timely increases in purchasing power to the state, as well as short-term tax moderation to taxpayers. But in the long run it has a substantial redistributive effect, channeling money from hundreds of thousands of taxpayers to a much smaller number of bondholders. Provincial bonds could be bought easily at the tax office in every significant city, and there is solid evidence that they were broadly held. Still, it is inevitable that such instruments will be substantially concentrated in the hands of the wealthy, and this tendency increased as bondholders of large portfolios reinvested their interest income in new bonds. This occurred on a large scale during the Republic's titanic struggle against Louis XIV's France in 1672–6 and 1689–1713. In this period the Republic was plunged into a fiscal nightmare. In the face of long-term price deflation and a stagnant domestic economy, the Republic doubled its public debt, placing an enormous strain on its fiscal regime. By 1713 the total debt probably exceeded 200 percent of gross domestic product (GDP), and service costs absorbed nearly the entire ordinary tax revenue of the provinces.

The story of how the Republic responded to this fiscal exhaustion cannot be told here. It must suffice to say that the regental families that both controlled the government and personally owned much of the debt were anxious to restore fiscal solvency but not eager to make radical changes in state institutions. They economized to the point of reducing the state to inaction and gradually redeemed a bit of the massive debt, until the revolutionary events of the 1780s and 1790s overwhelmed generations of cautious pruning (Figure 4.2).

More interesting for our purposes is the dilemma faced by the bondholders. Every year from 1714 to 1780 some 15 million guilders of after-tax interest income flowed into their hands, while the gradual redemption policy returned, after 1752, nearly 3 million per year to these same investors. They acquired the reputation of being great savers; the banker Henry Hope, who knew the richest of them well, estimated their savings rate to have been between 25 and 37.5 percent of their income, and modern studies of elite portfolios do not contradict this estimate. This high propensity to save may have derived from inherited Calvinist norms that militated against extravagance; however, the high income levels of many bondholders made it perfectly possible to wallow in luxury *and*

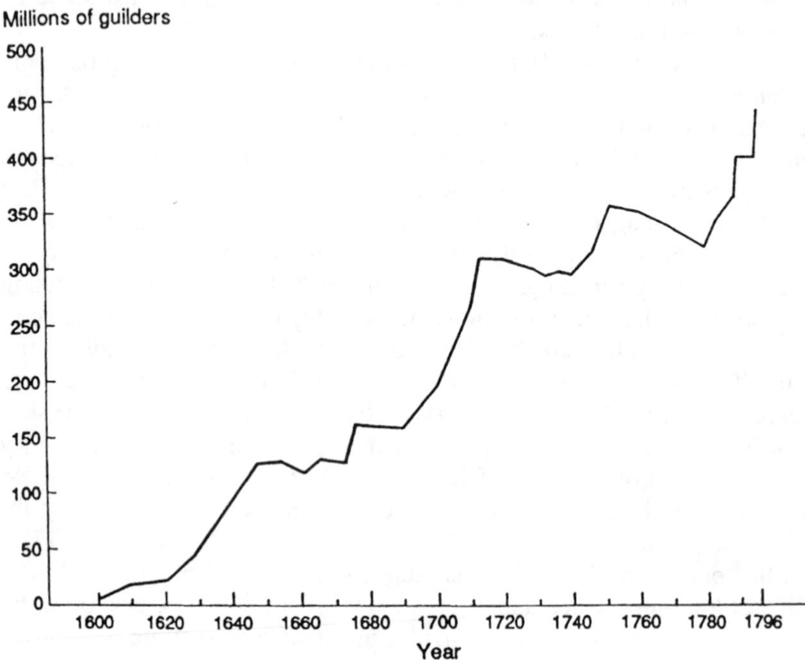

Figure 4.2 The public debt of Holland, 1599–1796.

Source: Jan de Vries and Ad van der Woude, *The First Modern Economy* (Cambridge University Press, 1997), p. 117. Data source: E. H. M. Dormans, *Het tekort. Staatsschuld in de tijd der Republiek* (Amsterdam, 1991).

reserve large sums for investment. A more important stimulus to saving, even in the face of low interest rates, would have been the fact that so much elite wealth consisted of domestic public debt. Such bonds are, in fact, a sort of interest-bearing money that holds the promise of future taxation needed to honor the claims represented by those very bonds. The classical economist David Ricardo explained (in his *equivalence theorem*) why such asset holders should save in anticipation of future taxation; eighteenth-century Dutch elites appear to have possessed an intuitive understanding of this insight (and, indeed, after the Republic's collapse in 1795 the bill began to come due).

This savings phenomenon is the essential backdrop for the major new economic initiative of the period: the emergence of Amsterdam as an international capital market. Rentiers with large holdings of domestic government bonds sought to place their interest earnings and redemptions in comparable debt instruments abroad. In the eighteenth-century context, where could one hope to place the colossal streams of income pouring into the pockets of the Republic's great bondholders? The capital markets did not offer many alternatives to foreign public debt, and gradually the number of creditworthy governments rose. But Dutch investors also kept an eye out for (riskier) alternatives, which came to include New World plantations, land speculations, and the public debt of newly independent states (about which, more later).

Table 4.2 presents a sketch of how the Dutch international capital market may have developed from the domestic government bond market in the course of the eighteenth century. "May have" because the table reflects assumptions that are plausible but not confirmed by extensive research: that bondholders tended to save a large fraction of their interest income and were inclined to reinvest their savings in comparable debt instruments. The purpose of this exercise is to discover the extent to which the capital market *could have been* financed on this "self-contained" basis.

Table 4.2 makes it clear that the rentiers of 1714 could easily have financed the entire growth of foreign lending to 1780, and much more besides, by reinvesting their bond redemptions plus about 25 percent of posttax interest earnings.

The Republic developed a sophisticated financial sector in the course of the eighteenth century. The merchant bankers, commercial lenders, private account holders (*kassiers*), and foreign exchange brokers at the Beurs supported nearly every type of financial transaction, foreign and domestic, possible at the time. But historians have faulted Dutch finance, variously, for being too cosmopolitan and too conservative. The first charge, that of the "Patriot" reformers of the late eighteenth century, held that the merchant bankers placed capital abroad to the neglect of the domestic economy. The charge of conservatism is based on the failure to develop either bank-note issuing or fractional reserve practices (the Amsterdam Exchange Bank was officially a bank of deposit and transfer).[20]

The Bank of Amsterdam was not (officially) a fractional reserve bank. If commercial banking was to evolve in the Republic, it would be from the cash management activities of the *kassiers*, comparable to London's goldsmiths. By the mid-eighteenth century these *kassiers* were treating their clients' cash balances as deposits from which they issued loans, and

[20] On the proforeign bias see Johan de Vries, *De economische achteruitgang der Republiek in de achttiende eeuw*, 2nd ed. (Leiden, 1968), p. 176; James C. Riley, *International Government Finance and the Amsterdam Capital Market*, pp. 224–40; De Vries and Van der Woude, *First Modern Economy*. The classic statement on Amsterdam's banking conservatism is Herman van der Wee, "Monetary, Credit and Banking Systems," in E. E. Rich and C. H. Wilson, eds., *Cambridge Economic History of Europe*, Vol. V., *The Economic Organization of Early Modern Europe* (Cambridge, 1977), p. 347.

Table 4.2. The Dutch Public Debt and the Money Market, 1600–1811 (All Figures, Millions of Guilders per Year)

		Average Annual Borrowing				Assumed Savings Rates		Added Financing Required[b]	
Period	Number of Years	Domestic Gov't	Foreign Gov'ts	Plantation Loans	Total Interest Income (After Tax)[a]	40%	25%	At 40%	At 25%
1600–19	20	2.09			2.12	0.85	0.53	1.24	1.56
1620–46	27	5.26			6.57	2.63	1.64	2.63	3.62
1647–71	25	1.20			9.38	3.75	2.35	–2.55	–1.15
1672–7	6	7.79			10.82	4.33	2.71	3.46	5.09
1678–89	12	0.07			11.91	4.76	2.98	–4.69	–2.91
1690–1713	24	10.84			13.72	5.49	3.43	5.35	7.41
1714–39	26	–0.95	4.00		18.82	7.53	4.71	–4.48	–1.66
1740–51	12	5.60	4.00		20.31	8.12	5.08	1.48	4.52
1752–62	11	–2.84	4.00	2.80	22.30	8.92	5.58	–4.96	–1.62
1763–79	17	–2.84	8.30	2.80	26.01	10.41	6.50	–2.15	1.76
1780–94	15	15.32	20.00		39.15	15.66	9.79	21.16	27.03
1795–1804	10	40.00	10.00		50.10	20.04	12.53	29.96	37.48
1805–11	7	12.40	10.00		51.20	20.48	12.80	1.92	9.60

[a] Includes all interest paid by Dutch provincial governments and foreign governments and dividends paid by the Dutch East India Company. The 37.5% tax on interest income from Holland bonds was levied in the eighteenth century. It is assumed that no interest was paid on plantation loans.

[b] These columns indicate the additional investments (beyond the assumed rate of reinvestment of existing bond income) needed to finance the new bond issues of the period. Negative figures (–) indicate periods in which the stream of saved interest income needed to seek placement in other spheres.

Source: For a more detailed account of these estimates and bibliographical references see De Vries and Van der Woude, *First Modern Economy* (Cambridge, 1997), Table 4.8, pp. 120–1.

their *kassierskwitanties* (*cashier's receipts*, or short-term bills in domestic commerce) certainly supplemented the specie-based money supply throughout the century. Still, their lending function did not evolve into development of large commercial banks, a failure that speaks more to the "perfection" of the money markets than to their imperfections. The large amounts of capital intermediated via the Beurs and merchant bankers prevented the emergence of an interest rate spread sufficient to sustain commercial bank lending.[21] Unable to pay (sufficient) interest on deposits, the *kassiers* could not attract a sufficient deposit base to evolve into commercial banks, institutions that did not emerge in Amsterdam until well into the nineteenth century.

Throughout this period, the Republic was awash in money. Bank notes were never issued on any scale until after 1815 – indeed, they did not become common until the 1840s – but this did not reflect a stubborn conservatism so much as it did the competition of bank deposit receipts, *kassiers*' promissory notes, bills of exchange, inland bills, and notarial credit instruments. From early in the seventeenth century, such instruments speeded the velocity of circulation of the overwhelmingly metallic money supply. That money supply appears to have grown over time to give the Netherlands a per capita money stock in the eighteenth century that stood substantially above that of neighboring countries. "Appears" is a required qualifier here because of the uncertainties that attach to any estimate of the money stock in a small open economy, in which coin from all over Europe circulated and whose mints produced many "trade coins" intended for export: the *leeuwendaalder* for trade with the Levant, the *rijksdaalder* for trade with the Baltic, and the *ducaat* for trade with Asia.[22] The estimates in Table 4.3 derive from minting records adjusted crudely for in- and outflows and checked by independent estimates of the money stock based on cash balances recorded in probate inventories.[23]

The Dutch guilder, much like the English pound sterling, was a paragon of stability from the early seventeenth century (after several debasements during the height of the price revolution) until 1936, when the guilder was (by a few hours) the last currency to abandon the gold standard.

[21] Joost Jonker, *Merchants, Bankers, Middlemen. The Amsterdam Money Market During the First Half of the Nineteenth Century* (Amsterdam, 1996), p. 247.

[22] M. S. Polak, *Historiografie en economie van de "muntchaos". De muntproductie van de Republiek, (1606–1795* (Amsterdam, NEHA Series III, 1998), emphasizes the export orientation of the Dutch mints. Consequently, he doubts that the Republic was always "awash in money."

[23] See De Vries and Van der Woude, *First Modern Economy*, Ch. 4.

Table 4.3. Estimates of the Money Supply in England, France, and the Dutch Republic, 1540–1790

	England	France	Republic
1540	£1.5 million	45 million l.t.	5 million guldens
1690	12 million	500 million	120 million
1790	25 million[a]	2,100 million	200 million
Per capita money supply, converted to guldens:			
1540	6.3 guldens	2.5 guldens	5 guldens
1690	29.4	18.5	60
1790	33.4[a]	35.4	100

[a] Coinage only; bank-note issue, which played a major role in eighteenth-century England, is not included in these estimates.

Source: N. J. Mayhew, "Population, Money Supply, and the Velocity of Circulation in England, 1300–1700," *Economic History Review* 48 (1995), 238–57; James C. Riley and John J. McCusker, "Money Supply, Economic Growth, and the Quantity Theory of Money: France, 1650–1788," *Explorations in Economic History* 20 (1983), 274–93; Debra Glassman and Angela Redish, "New Estimates of the Money Stock in France, 1493–1680," *Journal of Economic History* 45 (1985), 31–46; L. E. Challis, *The Tudor Coinage* (Manchester, 1978); De Vries and Van der Woude, *Nederland 1500–1815*, Table 4.2.

4.5 DUTCH INSTITUTIONS IN THE NEW WORLD

The first Dutch trading ventures beyond European waters – to the west coast of Africa, Asia, and the Caribbean – were all private initiatives taken by small partnerships of risk-taking merchants. Whether sailing to West Africa for gold, Southeast Asia for spices, or Punta de Araya (on the coast of Venezuela) for salt, the merchants made use of the commercial institutions already familiar for trade within European waters. They pooled their capital in *partenrederijen*, partnerships in which investors held shares such as one-eighth or one-sixteenth, and entrusted their capital to the active partner(s), usually for the duration of a voyage. The partnerships were contracted before notaries, who filed the documents and provided legal recourse in the event of problems. This flexible form of organization allowed merchants to distribute their capital among multiple ventures, thereby reducing their exposure to risk, and they could finance their voyages by contracting with private lenders, again, via notaries, for bottomry loans (*bodemerijbrieven*), loans secured by the hull of a ship, which served as collateral. The holders of these *bodemerijbrieven* had access to a secondary market, since they were traded at the Amsterdam Beurs.

These early ventures of the 1590s were risky and even audacious, in view of the monopoly claims of the Iberian colonial powers, but they were essentially trading ventures rather than colonizing projects. By

1600 discussions surfaced in both mercantile and governmental circles concerning the desirability of bundling the activities of the private merchants into monopoly trading companies. The benefits of such a move were partially economic: a reduction of competition among the rival partnerships of the numerous Dutch trading cities, a larger capitalization for these long-distance trades, and a reduction of risk through the internalization of protection costs. But the establishment of such consolidated enterprises was also seen as a more effective way to do battle against the Spanish enemy in distant lands and, ultimately, to secure colonial outposts necessary to conduct trade more securely.

In 1602 the States General of the Republic chartered a United East India Company (VOC) – united because it brought together the six merchant partnerships in as many cities already active in the trade with Asia. These merchants and many others, some 1,800 people in all, invested 6.4 million guilders to launch what would become for nearly two centuries the largest joint-stock firm in the world. The VOC quickly established itself as the dominant European trader in Asia. It augmented its large initial capitalization with short-term loans (5.6 million guilders between 1613 and 1620) and with plowed-back profits (it paid few cash dividends for its first 30 years of operation) to amass a working capital stock of tens of millions of guilders by the 1640s.[24] The company moved quickly to supplement its Europe-Asia trade in spices with an intra-Asian trade coordinated from its territorial base at Batavia, on Java. From there, it gradually secured strategic locations to enforce its control of Asian waters and territorial possessions to protect its access to Asian commodities. The Dutch empire in Asia was the possession of a company, not of the Dutch state.[25] The VOC was responsible for the defense and administration of its far-flung possessions, and was expected to pay for this overhead cost from its trading profits (and the tax revenue it could secure from its colonial subjects), and so it would remain until its final years.[26]

[24] Douglas Irwin, "Mercantilism as Strategic Trade Policy: The Anglo-Dutch Rivalry for the East India Trade," *Journal of Political Economy* 96 (1991), 1296–1314. This article argues that the VOC's initial charter provided an incentive lacking in its English rival for the directors to take a long-term view and accumulate capital rather than distribute profits.

[25] When the VOC was disbanded, control of its possessions passed to a government department. The appeal of a monopoly trading company did not fade, however, and in 1824 the Kingdom of the Netherlands established a firm with monopoly privileges in the Dutch East Indies, the Nederlandsche Handelsmaatschappij. Free access to the Asian colonies was not achieved until the 1870s.

[26] The best general survey of the history of the VOC is Femme Gaastra, *Geschiedenis van de VOC*, 2nd ed. (Zutphen, 1991). In English, one must still consult C. R. Boxer, *The Dutch Seaborne Empire, 1600–1800* (London, 1965).

The VOC had no dealings with the New World; its trading monopoly extended from the Cape of Good Hope eastward. But its dazzling success stood as a model for those urging the States General to charter a comparable monopoly company for the Atlantic zone. The government, which itself had pressed for the creation of the VOC in 1602, resisted a campaign to establish such a company in 1606 in anticipation of a hoped-for truce in the war with Spain – a truce secured in 1609. But when that truce expired in 1621, one of its first acts was to charter (15 precious years too late in the minds of the Republic's most ardent advocates of colonialism) the West India Company (WIC), with monopoly rights over all trade in West Africa and the New World (to the eastern tip of New Guinea).[27]

Although the new company's organizational structure closely resembled that of the VOC (five chambers and a governing board of 19 directors, compared to the VOC's six chambers and 17 directors), the similar outer forms masked significant internal differences. Just as the VOC bundled the energies of predecessor trading ventures, so did the WIC, but while the Asian ventures had all competed in the same basic trade, the WIC predecessors were all different. The New Netherlands Company was active in the Mohawk region's fur and pelt trade; various merchant consortia were active in the "Guinea" trade in West African gold and ivory; the merchants of Hoorn were committed to the Punta de Araya salt trade; and others, in alliance with Portuguese "New Christians" who had settled in the Netherlands, sought their fortunes in the Brazilian sugar trade. It would be the WIC's task to knit these disparate interests into a single, coherent commercial company.

To aid it in this task, the newly floated WIC hoped to draw upon the flourishing Republic's abundance of capital, efficient commercial institutions, and enormous seafaring sector. But the WIC initially found it difficult to gain access to these resources. It faced a reluctant investor community suspicious that the new company, whose most enthusiastic backers were conspicuously motivated by religious and patriotic sentiments, would undertake costly military ventures that would undermine commercial profitability. It took two years and a great deal of government "jawboning" to assemble the 7.1 million guilder initial capitalization (see Table 4.4).[28]

[27] Jonathan Israel, *Dutch Primacy in World Trade, 1585–1740* (Oxford, 1989), pp. 84–5.

[28] On the difficulty of raising capital, see P. J. van Winter, *De Westindische Compagnie ter kamer Stad en lande* (The Hague, 1978), pp. 12–18; Israel, *Dutch Primacy*, pp. 158–9. The reluctance of Amsterdam investors was compensated for by stimulating the interest of investors in nonseaport cities. These presumably less knowledgeable but fervently anti-Spanish investors committed as much capital as did the Amsterdam commercial community.

Table 4.4. Capital Invested in the West India Company, by Chamber

Chamber	Initial Capital	%	1629–39 Shares	1641–71 Bonds	Total	%
Amsterdam	f.2,846,585	40	6,984,885	3,104,754	12,936,224	54%
Zeeland	1,379,775	19	1,069,203	2,096,330	4,545,308	19
Maas	1,039,702	15	277,677	432,295	1,749,674	7
Noorderkwartier	505,627	7	782,683	618,370	1,906,680	8
Groningen	836,975	12	482,909	222,479	1,542,363	6
States General	500,000	7			500,000	2
Other cities			891,637		891,637	4
TOTAL	7,108,664		9,981,994	6,474,228	23,564,886	

Capitalization of the Second West India Company in 1674, by Chamber

	Shares	Bonds	Total	%
Amsterdam	1,608,466	931,426	2,539,892	56
Zeeland	367,346	628,899	996,245	22
Maas	197,606	129,688	327,294	7
Noorderkwartier	196,932	66,743	263,675	6
Groningen	193,246	185,511	378,757	8
TOTAL	2,563,596	1,942,267	4,505,863	

Source: Norbert H. Schneelock, *Actionäre der Westindischen Compagnie von 1674*, Beitrage zur Wirtschaftsgeschichte, Band 12, Stuttgart, 1982, pp. 28–37; Henk den Heijer, *Goud, ivoor en slaven. Scheepvaart en handel van de Tweede Westindische Compagnie op Afrika 1674–1740* (Zutphen, 1977), p. 47.

4.6 THE FIRST DUTCH ATLANTIC ECONOMY

In its first years, the new company found it difficult to set a clear course. Its first military ventures, attacks on Bahia, Brazil, and Saõ Jorge da Mina, on the Gold Coast of Africa, both failed. In these years the WIC sustained itself on the existing trades of the predecessor firms and on privateering. Then in 1628 the company hit the jackpot, achieving suddenly the greatest financial success of its history. Admiral Piet Heyn captured the entire Spanish silver fleet, carrying a cargo of at least 11.5 million guilders worth of silver. That great prize filled the company's coffers while also making possible the payment of a 50 percent dividend (the only substantial return its investors would ever receive). This event, in turn, drove WIC share prices up on the Amsterdam Beurs, allowing the company to issue new shares, borrow even more funds, and thereby finance a large fleet to set out upon the conquest of Brazil (see Table 4.4 for the new sums invested).

From 1630, with the conquest of Pernambuco (Recife) until the company was finally forced out of New Holland, as the Dutch preferred to call it, the New World enterprise was focused on Brazil and its sugar. The existing population of *moradores*, Portuguese settlers, mestizos and mulattos was quickly joined by WIC employees (some 10,000 at the peak in 1639) and by *vrijlieden*, former employees and immigrants, numbering 3,000 adult males by 1645. One-third of these settlers were Portuguese Jews, who had played a leading role in the Brazilian enterprise from the outset.[29] The WIC acted quickly to supplement its African trade in gold and ivory with a new trade in slaves in order to expand Brazilian plantation agriculture. In the 20 years after 1630 the company sent 31,533 slaves to Brazil. Meanwhile, the Dutch ports became Europe's leading centers of sugar refining. As all this enterprise took shape, the hope arose that the settlements on the Hudson River could supplement the fur trade with an expanded production of foodstuffs for the developing plantation economies.

This, then, was the grand design, but it was a design too large for the WIC to control and internalize. Unlike the VOC in Asia, the WIC in the Atlantic could enforce its monopoly privileges against neither foreign competitors nor Dutch private traders. The "leakage" of commercial benefits to private interests prevented the company from earning a satisfactory return on its capital, which meant that it continued to depend on the issue of shares and bonds to finance its activities. In contrast, the VOC could almost immediately begin to finance its expansion internally through retained profits.

In this setting, the WIC retreated from its comprehensive but unenforceable claims to monopoly rights. In 1638 it allowed its shareholders to trade privately in its Atlantic realm, hoping that this concession would at least help maintain the company's share prices on the Beurs. This did not satisfy the merchant community, 159 of whom petitioned the States General to allow free trade in the New World; by 1648 the WIC retreated further, allowing any Dutchman to trade in its New World territory upon payment of a recognition fee to the company.

The Portuguese *moradores*' revolt against Dutch rule in Brazil, begun in 1645, exposed the economic and political weakness of the company. It was unable to finance the defense of New Holland by itself (indeed, a withdrawal of WIC troops had occasioned the initial Portuguese attack), but the merchant community at home was dubious of any intervention that would jeopardize trade within Europe (i.e., Portuguese salt and

[29] Jan Lucassen, "Emigration to the Dutch Colonies and the USA," in Robin Cohen, ed., *The Cambridge Survey of World Migration* (Cambridge, NY, 1995), pp. 22–3. Only about one-quarter of the *vrijlieden* resided in Brazil with families.

wine).[30] At one point the Portuguese offered to return Brazil to the WIC in exchange for the restoration of Portuguese possessions in Asia. But in this the VOC showed even less interest than in a proposal to merge the two companies into a single Dutch colonial venture. To stop further talk of merger, the VOC paid the WIC a one-time subsidy of 1.5 million guilders in 1649. It could be generous in this way for, in fact, the struggle over Brazil was a godsend to the VOC: with the Portuguese fully occupied in the Americas, they were unable to defend their remaining Asian empire, which the VOC proceeded to pick apart. Meanwhile, the WIC, bereft of financial resources (its debt in 1649 stood at nearly 20 million guilders)[31] and lacking political support at home, had no choice but to abandon its last Brazilian foothold in 1654.

4.7 THE SECOND DUTCH ATLANTIC ECONOMY

In the aftermath of the Brazilian adventure, Dutch merchants stitched together a new Atlantic trading system. They made a virtue of necessity, exploiting the flexibility offered by the absence of a large territorial domain. This new Dutch Atlantic system integrated four key elements: (1) the WIC's monopoly trading function was now restricted to Africa's gold, ivory, and slave trades; (2) private Dutch merchants and planters encouraged sugar production by extending credit, establishing plantations (many developed by Sephardic Jewish planters who had left Brazil), and supplying manufactures to the Caribbean islands controlled by the British, French, and Spanish, as well as to the Chesapeake tobacco plantations; (3) the expansion of food production was encouraged in New Netherlands, especially to sustain Curaçao (the slave entrepôt); and (4) Dutch shipping handled the transport of Caribbean produce to the

[30] Opinions about the value of Brazil varied: Zeeland, heavily committed to the New World enterprise, was eager to commit public funds; Holland was more reluctant. Jonathan Israel notes that the Amsterdam merchants most committed to Brazil were Portuguese Jews. Indeed, many of the *moradores* who had risen in revolt were indebted to these Jews for purchases of slaves and commercial services. Under the circumstances, Israel reasons, many of Holland's Christian merchants doubted whether the benefits (to themsleves) of retaining Brazil could equal the costs. Israel, *Dutch Primacy*, pp. 168–70. E. van den Boogaart acknowledges the role of the Jews but emphasizes the large debts of these planters to the company itself – the 11 largest *senhores de engenho* owed nearly two million guilders on the eve of the revolt. E. van den Boogaart, "De Nederlandse expansie in het Atlantisch gebied, 1590–1674," *Algemene geschiedenis der Nederlanden*, Vol. 7 (Haarlem, 1980), pp. 237–8.

[31] Henk den Heijer, *Goud, ivoor en slaven. Scheepvaart en handel van de Tweede Westindische Compagnie op Africa 1674–1740* (Zutphen, 1997), p. 38. In 1649 the WIC had issued shares with a total face value of 17 million guilders, and bonds and short-term obligations totaling nearly 20 million guilders.

Netherlands, specifically to the sugar refineries of Amsterdam. In this way the ships, African slave depots, and Amsterdam sugar refineries were kept operating despite the absence of a substantial base of production on Dutch-controlled territory.

This more modest version of a Dutch Atlantic economy, one focused on the trading centers of Curaçao, Sint Eustatius, and Nieuw Amsterdam, proved to be more robust than the colorful but short-lived Brazilian escapade. As Dutch planters and merchants drifted away from Brazil, they directed their attention first to Barbados, speeding the transformation of that British possession from a tobacco farming to a sugar plantation economy.[32] Soon thereafter, the French island of Martinique was similarly developed.

Everywhere in the Caribbean, local planters tended to prefer Dutch commercial services to those of national monopolists, a preference reinforced by the Dutch hold over the slave trade. With Elmina (acquired in 1637), Luanda (1641), and some 20 other (formerly Portuguese) African forts under WIC control, the size of the Dutch slave trade was second only to the Portuguese until 1675. In the period 1650–74 the WIC shipped some 57,000 slaves, most destined for Curaçao to await sale to Spanish, French, and British planters. In the 1660s it looked for a time as though the buoyant French and British demand for slaves would revive the fortunes of the WIC, while Dutch private traders would prosper as (illicit but tolerated) providers of commercial services to the growing plantation economies. WIC shares, practically worthless in 1654, revived to 40 percent of par value by the end of 1664, and sugar shipments to the Republic stood at least at the level achieved during the Brazilian adventure. In 1660 the Republic's 66 sugar refineries, 50 of them in Amsterdam, supplied more than half of the refined sugar consumed in all of Europe.

This hardy commercialism functioned in an essentially hostile environment of mercantilism and could survive only by adapting to constraints that became steadily more restrictive. In the course of the 1660s, rival colonial powers gradually developed the economic and military instruments sufficient to enforce their monopoly claims, thereby shrinking inexorably the Dutch interloper's room for maneuver. The English

[32] The role of Dutch commerce as a catalyst in the transformation of Barbados – and in the creation of the "second Atlantic system" – remains a topic of debate. The strong version of the story points to the reduction by the Dutch of the prices of slaves, victuals, equipment, and sugar transport sufficient to make large-scale plantation-based sugar production possible. See Richard N. Bean and Robert P. Thomas, "The Adoption of Slave Labor in British America," in Henry A. Gemery and Jan S. Hogendorn, eds., *Uncommon Market: Essays in the Economic History of the Atlantic Slave Trade* (New York, 1979), pp. 390–8; V. T. Harlow, *A History of Barbados, 1625–1685* (Oxford, 1926).

Navigation Acts of 1651 were intended, among other things, to exclude the Dutch as suppliers of slaves and manufactures to, and buyers of sugar from, Barbados and other English islands. But these islands and the southern mainland colonies were Royalist nests eager to undermine the Commonwealth government of England. Consequently, Sint Eustatius flourished as a center of sugar smuggling, while Nieuw Amsterdam swept up Chesapeake tobacco.[33] By the mid-1660s, however, a restored monarchical England had conquered Nieuw Amsterdam, while the Navigation Acts were enforced on Barbados with sufficient vigor to cause the Dutch to shift their attention to the French island of Martinique. French trade ordinances of 1664 and 1673 had much the same intention as the Navigation Acts, of course, and Dutch traders responded by cultivating their long-standing interloper trade with Spanish possessions, especially Cuba and Puerto Rico. Moreover, by 1665 English slave traders could supply their own islands at competitive prices, and the establishment of the French Compagnie des Indes Occidentales (1664) and the English Royal African Company (1673) gradually marginalized the WIC's market position.[34]

The Republic's inability to deploy either diplomacy or sufficient naval power to break out of the mercantilist box being constructed by its neighbors had economic consequences that can be read directly from the fate of Amsterdam's sugar refiners. In 1668 only 34 of the 50 were in operation; by 1680, only 20. In addition, the combination of commercial losses and military expenditures overwhelmed the always fragile finances of the WIC, which was forced to reorganize in 1674.

The company survived – as the Second WIC – as an administrator of colonial possessions: the African trading outposts, six Caribbean islands, and its Wild Coast possessions, most notably Surinam. In addition, it retained its monopoly trading rights in Africa, including the slave trade, but this too was lost in 1734. From then until its dissolution in 1791, the WIC's only function was colonial administration and its only revenues came from user fees and local taxes.[35] Until the nineteenth century, the

[33] Jon Kepler, "Estimates of the Volume of Direct Shipments of Tobacco and Sugar from the Chief English Plantations to European Markets, 1620–1669," *Journal of European Economic History* 28 (1999), 116–18.

[34] Charles Wilson, *Profit and Power. A Study of England and the Dutch Wars* (London, 1957), p. 115.

[35] The fiscal regimes established by the WIC (and the colonization societies) were transparent in their operation and light in their burden. Colonists paid an *akkergeld* (land tax), a *hoofdgeld* (head tax per colonist and per slave), and *handelsrecognitiën* (trade fees) of 2.5 percent on the value of imports and exports. Until the mid-eighteenth century, taxes were usually paid in "commodity money," i.e., sugar. Henk den Heijer, *De geschiedenis van de WIC* (Zutphen, 1994), p. 181.

Dutch colonial empire was privately held (albeit subject to public pressure because of the periodic need to renew company charters).[36] With few exceptions, public funds did not directly support either the East or West Indian ventures, a fact that placed Dutch empire builders at a distinct disadvantage vis-à-vis their competitors.[37]

In view of the WIC's early financial debility, its unpopularity with the merchant community, and the early abandonment of Atlantic monopoly companies by England and France, it is a wonder that the Dutch persisted so long with an institutional form manifestly unsuited to the New World environment. The WIC's bankruptcy in 1674 was a good opportunity to be rid of this chartered monopoly company; instead, the States General pressured the holders of the worthless company paper to inject an additional 1.2 million guilders in order to float a Second WIC.[38] The Dutch state, where all but the most necessary – mainly military – functions were devolved to the provinces and cities, evidently found it difficult to assume direct control over its colonial possessions.[39]

Ironically, the inability of the Dutch to project military power in the Atlantic zone after 1674 offered them some advantages. Spain turned to the Dutch as suppliers of slaves and commercial services to its

[36] This exceedingly brief account cannot do justice to the history of the WIC. For more extended treatments, see Den Heijer, *De geschiedenis van de WIC*; Charles R. Boxer, *The Dutch in Brazil* (Oxford, 1957); Cornelis Ch. Goslinga, *The Dutch in the Caribbean and on the Wild Coast, 1580–1680* (Gainesville, Florida, 1971); Pieter C. Emmer, "The West India Company, 1621–1791: Dutch or Atlantic?," in L. Blussé and F. Gaastra, eds., *Companies and Trade. Essays on Overseas Trading Companies during the Ancien Régime* (Leiden, 1981). This article, plus several of Emmer's important articles on the Atlantic economy and the Dutch slave trade, are available in Pieter Emmer, *The Dutch in the Atlantic Economy, 1580–1880. Trade, Slavery, and Emancipation* (Aldershot, U.K., 1998).

[37] In the case of the Second WIC, the States General agreed in 1674 to provide a modest subsidy for military defense: the pay for 200 soldiers and the maintenance costs for fortifications. Altogether, this came to between 25,000 and 35,000 guilders annually.

[38] For an account of the debates leading to the decision to end the old company and establish a new WIC, see Henk den Heijer, *Goud, ivoor en slaven*, pp. 39–49. Holders of WIC shares received shares in the new company at the rate of 15 cents on the guilder on the condition that they inject new capital at the rate of 4 percent of the nominal value of the old shares. Bondholders were issued new bonds with a face value of 30 percent of that of the old bonds on condition that they pay in 8 percent of the nominal value of the old bonds.

[39] The Dutch colonial empire became "state property" only with the dissolution in bankruptcy of the WIC (1791) and VOC (1799). Even then, it took until 1806 before the then Batavian Republic established a Colonial Ministry. Institutional development is described in J. van Goor, *De Nederlandse koloniën, Geschiedenis van de Nederlandse expansie, 1600–1975* (The Hague, 1994), Ch. 5.

colonial empire. The WIC and its Curaçao trade center, its teeth having been drawn by British and French protectionism, prospered in the 1680s and 1690s as holder of the Spanish *asiento*, or slave supply contract, and as tolerated supplier of manufactured goods and shipping services to Spain's empire. This Spanish connection provided a relatively stable setting in which the Second WIC could actually pay some modest dividends (ranging between 2 and 8 percent; in 1687, 10 percent). But it usually paid nothing at all, and in 1713 even the possibility of participating in the Spanish *asiento* was lost as the Peace of Utrecht ending the War of the Spanish Succession awarded this lucrative concession to England's new South Sea Company. The Curaçao slave entrepôt collapsed, and with it the price of the Second WIC's shares. The general expansiveness of the eighteenth-century Atlantic economy was such as to provide Dutch Caribbean trading centers with occasional windfalls, usually the product of warfare among the major powers, but the idea that a second Dutch Atlantic economy based essentially on interloping could be a viable alternative to a colonial economy had been revealed much earlier to be wishful thinking. From the 1680s, a third Dutch Atlantic economy began to take shape, one based on the development of plantation economies in the Dutch territories of modern Surinam and Guyana.

4.8 DUTCH RULE

Besides the financial and trading presence of the Dutch in the New World, there is its political legacy to consider. Brazil was not long governed by the WIC, but while it was, it shared with New Netherlands, Surinam, Curaçao, and so on the general pattern of company rule. The company directors (Heren XIX) appointed a governor-general with broad authority to rule the possession. These administrators represented the trading interests of the company and of the Republic more generally; they frequently found themselves at odds with the interests of settlers. The several colonies varied in how these conflicts were handled. In Brazil a person of great independent stature, Count Johan Maurits of the House of Orange (the stadholder's cousin), became governor-general. He established a parliament with representatives of both the Dutch and Portuguese planter communities. These settler interests were also represented in the lower courts and in the administration of the orphan chambers (important institutions for the transmission of property).

In New Netherlands the successive governors instituted an advisory council that gave voice to settler interests, mainly in times of military danger. In 1653 Nieuw Amsterdam was granted a regular town charter, conferring burgher rights, and formed a regular town council. According to Donna Merwick: "It was the only seventeenth-century North American city that consciously strove to imitate a European city."[40]

In the Caribbean possessions, colonists were gradually admitted to the advisory councils (otherwise composed of high WIC officials) that supported the governors-general. The 1682 charter conferred by the States General for the WIC's governance of Surinam provided for a governor supported by a Policy Council and Council of Justice. The WIC-appointed governor selected the 10 members of the Policy Council from double lists of candidates nominated by all free inhabitants (including the colony's Jews, who formed 30–40 percent of the white population). This council advised the governor, but acquired the right on weighty matters to decide by majority vote. It also functioned as the criminal court. The Council of Justice – six members nominated by the Policy Council and elected by free men – heard civil cases.[41]

The brief rule of the Dutch in the colonies that, by their size, might have developed more complex governing structures makes it difficult to offer a confident assessment of the potential for representative government. After all, the English colonies before 1689 showed few signs that suggested their eighteenth-century development. But the Dutch colonies did distinguish themselves by upholding two traditions firmly rooted in the home country: freedom of conscience and free labor (for white settlers).

All of the Dutch colonial settlements (including the VOC's outpost at the Cape of Good Hope) were characterized by polyglot populations of Dutch, German, Huguenot, Jewish, and other European residents. While Roman Catholicism was not embraced in these communities (but not forbidden either), the various Protestant bodies and the Jews could worship freely – if not always openly – just as at home. While the English toyed for a time with theocracy, and while the Spaniards did not tolerate deviation from the Roman Catholic Church, the Dutch colonies had a distinctly "multicultural" character.

Dutch law, unlike English law in this period, did not recognize the legality of indentures.[42] People were not free to sell away their freedom,

[40] Donna Merwick, *Possessing Albany, 1630–1710. The Dutch and English Experiences* (Cambridge, 1990), p. 143.

[41] G. W. van der Meiden, "Governor Mauricius and the Political Rights of the Surinam Jews," in R. Cohen, ed., *The Jewish Nation in Surinam* (Amsterdam, 1982), pp. 49–50. The colony's governing documents are available in J. J. Hartsinck, *Beschrijving van Guiana* (Amsterdam, 1770).

[42] For a nuanced discussion of this blanket assertion, see Ernst van den Boogaart, "The Servant Migration to New Netherlands, 1624–1664," in P. C. Emmer, ed., *Colonialism and Migration; Indentured Labour Before and After Slavery* (Dordrecht, 1986), pp. 55–81. Servants who contracted to work in New Netherlands on multiyear contracts were not unknown, but their legal and economic position is readily distinguishable from that of English and French indentured servants.

let alone allow their labor contracts to be bought and sold; indeed, labor contracts in the Republic generally extended for no more than six months.[43] Nor was empressment legal in the Republic; the admiralties had to secure their sailors on the open market. Finally, it was not the Republic's habit to forcibly transport prisoners and charity cases to its colonies or to establish penal colonies abroad. Dutch penal institutions were then admired for their rehabilitative efforts! In sum, civil society for whites in Dutch colonies was uniquely free, even while public administration was in the hands of the companies.

It is in this context that the single most famous Dutch colonial institution should be discussed: the patroonship.

The patroonship was a device intended to enlist private capital in the settlement and administration of the WIC's possessions. In the absence of indentures, the financing of settlers in the New World was difficult to arrange and almost always involved subventions by the company. To reduce these costs in a difficult period, the company, after much debate, agreed to offer grants of land to private investors, patroons, in return for their commitment to furnish the colony with a minimum number of adult settlers (50 in the case of the New Netherlands patroonships) together with the necessary complement of farm capital and infrastructure. These settlers were free men and women, but to reduce the WIC's administrative costs, the patroons were granted the rights to administer "low and middle justice" on their lands and to tax colonists up to a fixed amount to defray the costs of defense and governance.

The first patroonships were established in the Caribbean (Berbice and Curaçao, 1627), followed by New Netherlands (1629). In the latter, five investors stepped forward to take advantage of the WIC's offer. Four of them formed a *partenrederij* (see Section 4.5), whereby each patroonship was divided into five shares. One patroon held two shares of the estate he would direct and one in each of the others. They thereby sought to pool the risks of the venture in accordance with maritime commercial practice. In the event, only one of the patroonships, that of Kiliaen van Rensselaer, became fully operational, but these colonizing efforts, so thoroughly capitalist in their inspiration and organization (they are similar to U.S. railroad land grants of the late nineteenth century), have

[43] The length of service contracts and the penalties for breaking them are good indicators of the practical freedom of "free labor." See David W. Galenson, "The Rise of Free Labor: Economic Change and the Enforcement of Service Contracts in England, 1351–1875," in John A. James and Mark Thomas, eds., *Capitalism in Context. Essays on Economic Development and Cultural Change in Honor of R. M. Hartwell* (Chicago, 1994), pp. 114–37. On the United States in the nineteenth century, see Gavin Wright, "The Origins and Economic Significance of Free Labor in America" (unpublished paper, Stanford University, 1995). Dutch practice seems to stand between the substantial contractual rigidity of England and the "anarchy" of the United States.

gone down in American historiography as attempts to transplant "feudalism" to the New World.

In 1846 E. B. O'Callaghan wrote that the patroonship provisions of the WIC "transplanted to the free soil of America the feudal tenure and feudal burdens of continental Europe."[44] He supposed that the patroonships were akin to the manors and seigneuries of the Old World, most likely because of the political functions given to the patroons – the administration of low and middle justice. This, indeed, was a typical prerogative of European seigneurs. In the New World setting, however, the patroon's court could rule on matters of no more than 50 guilders in value, and even such cases could be appealed. In other respects the settlers were tenants, not serfs or subjects, or, for that matter, indentured servants or slaves. Thus, O'Callaghan and the unending stream of American historians who have unthinkingly repeated this calumny (to this day, textbooks in U.S. history unfailingly refer to the patroonships as feudal or semifeudal) perpetuate a misconception that has its origins in Anglophile attempts to put a progressive face on the English conquest of New Netherlands.

In reality, the patroonship was a commercial proposition for all parties involved, designed to save the capital and reduce the expenses of the WIC, encourage private investment and settlement, and expand trade. The patroons (who, far from being feudal lords and aristocrats, included in their number Jews[45] and Amsterdam merchants) entered into risk-reducing partnerships as they would have in any other commercial venture of the time.

More to the point, the Hudson River Valley would have to wait for the arrival of the English to experience a regime in which land was

[44] E. B. O'Callaghan, *History of New Netherlands; or, New York under the Dutch* (New York, 1846), p. 120. Also influential in establishing this durable academic folk myth is John Romeyn Brodhead, *History of the State of New York* (New York, 1872). Even the otherwise alert and well-informed work of Oliver Rink cannot avoid saddling the patroonship with the predicate *feudal.* Oliver Rink, *Holland on the Hudson: An Economic and Social History of Dutch New York* (Ithaca and New York, 1986), p. 115.

[45] For example, in 1659 a patroonship was granted to David Nassy and coinvestors to establish a Jewish colony at Cayenne. The French took control of the area in 1664, whereupon they moved to neighboring Surinam, which came under Dutch control (from the British) in 1667. By 1694 Surinam had "92 Portuguese Jewish and 10 to 12 German Jewish families. . . . They were the owners of 40 sugar estates with a total of 9,000 slaves in that year." R. A. J. van Lier, "The Jewish Community in Surinam: A Historical Survey," in Cohen, ed., *The Jewish Nation in Surinam*, p. 19. Nassy's famous descendant, David de Isaac Cohen Nassy, wrote *Essai Historique sur la colonie de Surinam* (Paramaribo, 1788), a celebrated Enlightenment work advocating Jewish civil emancipation. G. J. van Grol, *De Grondpolitiek in het West-Indische Domein der Generalitieit* (Amsterdam, 1980), Part II, pp. 91–8.

distributed by privilege and by proximity to the throne. It would take English rule to convert the region to proprietary colonies ruled by true aristocrats and blanketed by great estates, to teach the conquered Dutch settlers "that land was the reward given for loyalty or service," and to encourage the cultivation of gentry life in the Hudson River Valley.[46] Indeed, the English conquest of New Netherlands, imposing the legal traditions of a more patriarchal and authoritarian society, gave rise to decades of legal friction between the new masters and the Dutch settlers.[47]

The patroonship's role as a settlement tool was brief and limited. The company later turned to the colonizing society – a chartered corporation to encourage settlement and, typically, plantation agriculture. These became active on the Wild Coast settlements after the 1680s. Here, again, the WIC was prepared to encourage subsidiary ventures, each with its own capital and balance sheet, to spread the costs associated with colonial administration. The largest was the Sociëteit van Suriname, founded in 1682, with shares equally divided between a Zeeland investor, the city of Amsterdam (which wanted to encourage sugar production to bolster its large refining industry), and the WIC itself.

4.9 THE THIRD DUTCH ATLANTIC ECONOMY: PLANTATIONS AND FINANCE

By the 1680s it had become apparent that the only course of action still open was to develop plantation economies on the Dutch territories of modern Surinam and Guyana. The data assembled in Table 4.5, sketchy though they are, show clearly that the plantation economy was a product of the 90 years after the 1680s and especially the 50 years before the 1770s. How was this new economy financed?

Until the 1750s the plantation economy was financed by a combination of private investment and commercial credit. The planters were a cosmopolitan crowd of Dutchmen, Huguenots, and Sephardic Jews, as well as various other nationalities. They usually financed the fixed capital investment privately, often relying on that old standby, the *partenrederij*. Alice Clare Carter describes the investments of the Belesaigne family, Amsterdam Huguenots, in their Berbice plantations. They participated in two partnerships, holding one-fifth shares in each. In addition, they participated in the ownership of ships (holding sixteen/thirty-second shares) that brought the colonial goods to Amsterdam, where the family

[46] Donna Merwick, "Dutch Townsmen and Land Use: A Spatial Perspective on Seventeenth-Century Albany, New York," *William and Mary Quarterly* 37 (1980), pp. 77–8.

[47] David E. Narrett, *Inheritance and Family Life in Colonial New York City* (Ithaca, New York, 1992), pp. 45–51.

Table 4.5. Wild Coast Plantations: Population and Commodity Exports

	Plantations	Slaves	European	Total Population[a]	Value of Exports (guilders)
			Surinam		
1668	23			3,000	
1684	80	4,300	811	5,100	
1704	128	9,000		c. 10,000	1.8 million
1737	370				
1750		51,100	2,133	53,800	5.8 million
1770	465	59,900	2,700	c. 65,000	12.0 million
1795	533	48,200	3,350	53,110	15.9 million
1830	576	48,800	2,023	55,900	
1862		36,500		52,900	
		Guyana (Berbice, Essequebo, and Demerary)			
1750		8,000	726	8,780	
1770	250	25,000		c. 27,000	

[a] Total includes free blacks. It does not include Indians and the *morannen*, escaped Africans.

Source: Stanley Engerman and B. W. Higman, "The Demographic Structure of the Caribbean Slave Societies in the Eighteenth and Nineteenth Centuries," in Franklin W. Knight, ed., *UNESCO General History of the Caribbean*, Vol. 3, *The Slave Societies of the Caribbean* (London, 1997); Alex van Stopriaan, *Surinaams contrast. Roofbouw en overleven in een Caraïbische plantage economie, 1750–1863* (Amsterdam, 1991), pp. 327–9; de Vries and van der Woude, *First Modern Economy*, p. 478.

operated a chocolate business.[48] We know nothing about how the Belesaigne family financed the acquisition of slaves, but other sources emphasize that the WIC, until 1734 the monopoly supplier, regularly sold slaves on credit. Credit was essential to the operation of this economy, and it was extended and managed by merchant bankers in the Republic.

Every planter maintained a long-term relationship with such a banker, who extended credit to the planter, accepted the planters' bills of exchange, and received the planters' commodities, which the merchant banker transported, insured, and sold for a commission. A 1755 sample of coffee and sugar planter accounts with Amsterdam bankers reveals that the average plantation debt stood at 32,000 guilders, between one-third and one-fourth of the assessed value of the plantations.[49]

[48] Alice Clare Carter, "The Family and Business of Belesaigne, Amsterdam, 1689–1809," in *Getting, Spending and Investing in Early Modern Times* (Assen, 1975), pp. 107–22.

[49] Alex van Stipriaan, *Surinaams Contrast. Roofbouw en overleven in een Caraïbische plantage economie, 1750–1863* (Amsterdam, 1991), p. 220.

This pattern of commercial relations, which differed little from plantation financing in British and French colonies, was disrupted by a major innovation in the 1750s. Willem Gideon Deutz, head of the merchant banking firm of W. G. en J. Deutz, introduced in 1753 the first *plantagelening*, or plantation loan. Also known as *negotiaties*, these were no longer short-term credits extended by the merchant banker, but long-term loans secured by the value of the plantations, with the funds provided by private investors. Deutz and later imitators pooled the mortgages of several plantations in a single unit trust, in which the investor bought shares. The value of the loan could be as much as five-eighths of the assessed valuation of the plantations (the bankers being rather more generous with other people's money than with their own). The investor received an interest rate usually of 6 percent (1 percent more than most foreign government bonds paid and nearly double the post-fisc return on domestic public debt issues). Most of these bundled mortgages were structured to initiate a gradual return of principal after 10 years. Presumably, by that time, the new productive facilities and the augmented slave labor forces financed by the loans would be fully operational.

This financial innovation stimulated a boom in the Dutch Caribbean. Amsterdam houses floated 241 unit trusts between 1753 and 1794 (when the practice came to a definitive end) with a total capitalization of about 80 million guilders. Half of this sum went to Surinam, a quarter to the Guyana settlements, and another quarter to foreign colonies, chiefly the Danish West Indies, where the Dutch were commercially dominant.[50]

The boom peaked in 1765–72, when nearly 6 million guilders per year was invested in *negotiaties*. The financial crisis of 1772–3 in Amsterdam was matched by trouble in the plantation colonies, as weather, declining coffee prices, and a revolt of the *morranen* (runaway slaves) conspired to plunge the planters into a liquidity crisis. As major banking houses suspended payments, the flow of credit on which the plantations depended began to dry up, precipitating the bankruptcy of many plantations, the collapse of the Dutch slave trade, and the loss to Dutch investors of at least three-quarters of the capital that had been sunk over the years into the plantation loans.

The issue of new loans did not end immediately. Investors remained prepared to supply capital to British planters on Tobago and Barbados (where hurricane damage sent them to the capital markets), and the

[50] Details on the plantation loans are drawn chiefly from J. P. van de Voort, *De Westindische plantages van 1720 tot 1795. Financiën en handel* (Eindhoven, 1973). See also Van Stipriaan, *Surinaams Contrast*, Ch. 7.

Danish islands also remained in favor.[51] But by 1777–80 new loans amounted to no more than a half million guilders per annum. In general, it appears that the plantation loan was a financial innovation that suited the immediate needs of cash-rich Dutch investors far more than it served the interests of the plantation economies. It took Surinam and Guyana a quarter century to overcome the structural financial crisis into which the easy money of the plantation loans had plunged them. Only after 1800 would they grow again as productive sugar exporters.[52]

4.10 A FOURTH DUTCH ATLANTIC ECONOMY?

The plantation loans display the curious combination of sophistication and naiveté that so often marks financial innovation. The Netherlands remained a land of abundant capital seeking placement, but neither the domestic economy nor the New World colonies now seemed to offer inviting prospects, and the Asian realm of the VOC was closed to private investors. In this context, foreign government bonds became, even more than before, the investment of choice for Dutch rentiers.

In 1780 the Amsterdam capital market had for many decades been the largest single investor in European government bonds. The value of Dutch holdings in foreign government debt was then at least 350 million guilders. More than half of this amount was invested in England, a country that declared war on the Dutch (for the fourth time) in 1780. In this context John Adams's embassy in search of loans was of special interest to many Dutchmen eager to support their enemy's enemy. The first Dutch loan to the American rebels, guaranteed by both France and the States General, was floated in 1781. The 5-million guilder loan raised in that year was followed by many more in the years thereafter. In 1787–93 the Amsterdam banker Pieter Stadnitski assembled 28 unit trusts in U.S. debt instruments; by 1803 Dutch investors held 22 percent of U.S. domestic debt, a total of 13.1 million U.S. dollars.[53]

Dutch investor interest was not limited to government paper. Six of Amsterdam's most prominent banking houses organized in 1792 the largest property development scheme then known, the Holland Land

[51] Charles Wilson, *Anglo-Dutch Commerce and Finance in the Eighteenth Century* (Cambridge, 1941), pp. 182–6; Stipriaan, *Surinaams Contrast*, p. 223; Van de Voort, *De Westindische plantages*, pp. 268–323.

[52] P. C. Emmer, "Capitalism Mistaken? The Economic Decline of Surinam and the Plantation Loans, 1773–1850; A Rehabilitation," *Itinerario* 20 (1996), 11–18.

[53] James Riley, *International Government Finance and the Amsterdam Capital Market* (Cambridge, 1980), p. 193. See also James Riley, "Foreign Credit and Fiscal Stability: Dutch Investment in the U.S., 1781–1794," *Journal of American History* 65 (1978), 654–78; Pieter J. van Winter, *American Finance and Dutch Investment, 1780–1805, with an Epilogue to 1840*, 2 vols. (New York, 1977).

Company.[54] This enterprise held title to 5 million acres of land in western New York and Pennsylvania. Dutch investors were also prominent in financing both the First and Second Banks of the United States.

The wave of defaults that swept through the Western world in the course of the Napoleonic Wars knocked the Netherlands from its place at the forefront of international investing. Two-thirds of the enormous Dutch public debt was effectively in default after 1811, and the market value of foreign assets fell by nearly half between 1800 and 1815. Yet, Dutch investors again showed a strong interest in foreign investing, especially once domestic debt redemptions became large after 1850. Amsterdam was now a secondary capital market, but it was usually second only to London in supplying capital to the U.S. federal government during the Civil War and to American railways during the post–Civil War construction booms. By 1895 Dutch foreign investment stood at a level 1.75 times its GNP, a level not exceeded by the United Kingdom, then the world's dominant capital exporter. Much Dutch capital then went to the East Indies, but the Dutch always remained important investors in the United States, which was the recipient of 30 percent of all Dutch capital invested abroad in the period 1875–1900.[55] By 1914, total Dutch foreign portfolio capital investment stood at about 2,000 million U.S. dollars, of which 40 percent was invested in the United States.[56]

The newly independent states of the Americas after 1820 did not succeed in attracting any comparable Dutch investor interest. Embassies and trade missions yielded little, except for an unhappy investment in the public debt of New Granada and a slightly better experience in Brazil. The historian of Dutch commercial life in Latin America and the Caribbean in the period 1780–1830 gave his book the title *The Contracting Horizon of the Dutch Merchant*.[57]

[54] James Riley, "Financial and Economic Ties. The First Century," in J. W. Schulte Nordholt and R. P. Swieringa, eds., *A Bilateral Bicentennial. A History of Dutch–American Relations, 1782–1982* (Amsterdam, 1982); Augustus J. Veenendaal, Jr., *Slow Train to Paradise. How Dutch Investment Helped Build American Railroads* (Stanford, California, 1996), pp. 8–13.

[55] Wybren Verstegen, "National Wealth and Income from Capital in the Netherlands, c. 1805–1910," *Economic and Social History of the Netherlands* 7 (1996), p. 100; K. D. Bosch, *De Nederlandse beleggingen in de Verenigde Staten* (Amsterdam and Brussels, 1948).

[56] These are the best estimates of Veenendaal, *Slow Train to Paradise*, pp. 174–5. In the 1990s the value of Dutch direct investment in the United States was good, second or third place among all foreign investors, behind only the United Kingdom and, sometimes, Japan. U.S. Bureau of Economic Analysis, *Survey of Current Business*, August 1998.

[57] Theo. P. M. de Jong, *De krimpende horizon van de Hollandse kooplieden. Hollands welvaren in het Caribisch Zeegebied (1780–1830)* (Assen, 1966).

4.11 MONETARY ARRANGEMENTS IN DUTCH COLONIES

As noted earlier, the Dutch Republic was well supplied – and, over time, increasingly well supplied – with circulating currency. The basic money stock was large by any standard, and financial instruments supplemented this significantly. The Republic was conservative to a fault in its avoidance of bank notes but evidently felt little need to be a leader in this area.[58]

Much of its coinage was designed for export, but all of the zones to which Dutch coin and specie flowed were to the east. This, of course, was the case in all trading nations. New World colonies that were not themselves centers of mining and minting suffered chronic monetary problems. McCusker and Menard's account of the money supply in the British American colonies on the eve of the Revolution emphasizes (1) the scarcity of small change, (2) the large role of Spanish and Portuguese coins, (3) the resort to paper issued by the colonies, and (4) the importance of "commodity money," where units of tobacco, sugar, and so on, "circulated" at fixed values.[59] Surinam and Curaçao, the two major Dutch colonial entities in the eighteenth century, can be described in precisely these same terms.

It was impossible to keep Dutch coin in circulation in the colonies. While in principle, it was not needed to trade with the home country (where bills of exchange and other credit instruments were available), it was needed for trade with North America, which supplied foodstuffs to the plantations. On Curaçao the Spanish piaster was the generally accepted unit of account, but this, too, tended to flow north and east, so that everywhere the money in local circulation consisted of false coins (the counterfeit gold Johannes minted on St. Thomas was notorious) and a miscellany of small, worn, and clipped coins. The *West Indisch Plakaatboek*, a compilation of the ordinances and regulations for Surinam and the islands, is littered with efforts to establish the fair value of the circulating Spanish coins and limit the permissible use of dubious coins. As an ordinance of 1741 observes, "if Spanish coins are forbidden, the inhabitants [of Surinam] have no small and few large coins, since little coin from Patria is brought to the colony" (no. 402).

The debased character of the circulating medium in the colonies caused the "Surinam" and "Curaçao" guilders to vary from the value of

[58] J. M. F. Fritschy, "De 'generale Beleenbank' en de financiële problemen in de beginjaren van de Bataafse Republiek," *Jaarboek voor de geschiedenis van bedrijf en techniek* 3 (1986), 109–34.

[59] John J. McCusker and Russell R. Menard, *The Economy of British America, 1607–1789* (Chapel Hill, North Carolina, 1985), pp. 337–41.

the guilder in Patria, since these were used only as units of account. The exchange rate tended to hover at around 1.25 Surinam guilders per Dutch guilder but could sink, as it did by 1811, to 4:1. In 1827 an effort to bring order to the colonial currency was made. The depreciated coin was taken out of circulation and replaced by a large shipment of Dutch coin. Two years later a "Particuliere West Indische Bank" was established (a state-backed institution despite its claim to be private) to provide exchange and credit facilities within the colonies. Until then, this had always been arranged via accounts kept in the Netherlands.

Indeed, the bill of exchange was the crucial credit instrument not only for trade between the colonies and Patria, but also for payments within the colonies. Before a bill was presented to the suppliers of European goods or slaves, the planters endorsed it for domestic payments made to colleagues. A protested bill, knowledge of which might take more than a year to reach the colony, created severe problems for the drawer, since a 25 percent penalty was attached to the renewal of such a bill. Here, too, the *Plakaatboek* offers abundant testimony to both the importance of and the chronic problems attached to the use of bills of exchange in domestic commerce.

The plantation loan boom after 1753 appears to have increased the credit facilities available to planters, reducing the need to have bills circulate domestically. The archive of the Middelburgsche Commercie Compagnie, a joint-stock company specialized in the slave trade, contains a collection of bills. In the seven years before 1753 only 31 percent of the bills were endorsed but once; the rest were endorsed two or more times. In the period 1765–71, fully 70 percent of bills were endorsed only once.[60]

This reduced use of bills in domestic circulation may also have been related to the introduction of paper money in the colonial economy. In Surinam this began in 1761, with the printing of *kaartengeld* (so called because the bank notes were printed on the backs of playing cards). The notes were issued against good bills of exchange at first and later against mortgages of houses in Paramaribo. These notes were originally issued in rather large denominations (3 guilders), suggesting that they were not intended for petty payments. In time, the notes in circulation reached prodigious levels: 1.1 million guilders issued in 1770–4, 5.6 million Surinam guilders in circulation in 1800, 6.5 million in 1811.[61] Even after discounting for the depreciation of the Surinam guilder, these were extraordinary stocks of money for a plantation economy with only a few

[60] Stipriaan, *Surinaams Contrast*, pp. 115–17.

[61] Stipriaan, *Surinaams Contrast*, pp. 258–64; J. A. Schiltkamp and J. Th. de Smidt, eds., *West Indisch Plakaatboek*, 2 vols. (Amsterdam, 1973), II: 1045–1137.

thousand free inhabitants. (Slaves in Surinam were not entirely excluded from the money economy; perhaps these findings suggest the need to reexamine assumptions about the circulation of currency in a slave society.) This monetary experiment run amok was brought to an end in 1813.

4.12 ASSESSMENT AND SPECULATION

The Dutch economic presence in the New World was not – is not – inconsiderable. When the early failure of the WIC and its grand design for the Western Hemisphere are placed beside the success of the VOC and its long reign as the dominant European power in Asia, one is inclined to depreciate too much the importance of the New World to the Dutch economy. In fact, Atlantic trade as a whole grew much faster than European trade with Asia. In the very long run (1510–1780), total European trade with Asia grew in volume by about 1 percent per annum, while European trade with the New World grew by over 2 percent per annum.[62] Even a gradually declining share of this dynamic trade could loom large in comparison to a large but stationary share of a more slowly growing trade. The small Dutch plantation sector of the 1680s was good for about 8 percent of total Caribbean commodity production. By the 1750s, the substantial growth of the Dutch plantations notwithstanding, its share had fallen to 6 percent of total output, and after the plantation loan boom, in 1775, the share had fallen further to under 5 percent of a vastly larger total output (30–32 million kilograms of sugar in the 1680s, 200 million kilograms in the 1770s).[63] Despite this steadily declining share, the total value of Dutch imports from the New World rose to approximately equal those from Asia by the 1770s.

The Dutch position was not negligible. But it was vulnerable because of the marginal character of the Dutch presence in the Caribbean of the eighteenth century. Under favorable circumstances (war between France and England, most obviously), the Dutch islands could become hotbeds of illicit trade. But this trade could disappear at the stroke of a pen, and if the Republic itself was involved in war (a prospect invited by its conspicuously evident military weakness), the consequences for its economic activity were serious indeed. Figure 4.3 reveals the volatile character of Dutch New World trade in the eighteenth century.

The marginalized political position of the Dutch, combined with the inherently volatile character of long-distance trade, exposed the Repub-

[62] Jan de Vries, "Connecting Europe and Asia: A Preliminary Consideration of the Factors Driving Long-Distance Trade in the Early Modern Period" (unpublished paper, University of California at Berkeley, 1998).

[63] De Vries and Van der Woude, *First Modern Economy*, p. 477.

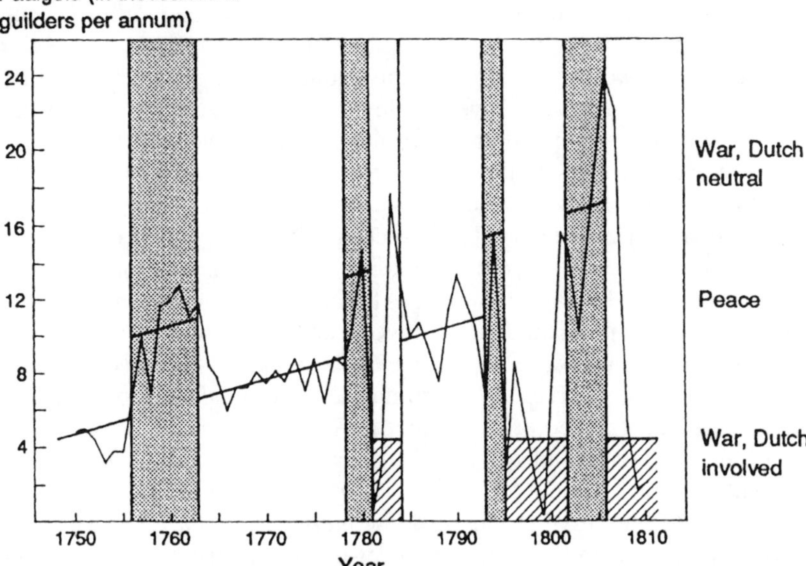

Figure 4.3 West Indies shipping in peace and war. An index of shipping volume entering Amsterdam from the Western Hemisphere. Based on *Paalgeld* revenue from ships entering the Zuider Zee, 1750–1810.

Source: Jan de Vries and Ad van der Woude, *The First Modern Economy* (Cambridge University Press, 1997), p. 479. Data source: W. G. Heeres, "Het paalgeld: een bijdrage tot de kennis van de Nederlandse handelsstatistiek in het verleden," *Economisch- en sociaal-historisch jaarboek* 45 (1982), 1–17.

lic fully to a highly risky economic environment. The Republic had well-developed institutions to manage risk at the micro level, but its decentralized state structure was not well suited to create a protected environment in which its institutions might take root in strange soils. Perhaps it was a recognition of this aspect of Dutch statecraft that inclined its leaders to embrace the joint-stock company as a colonizing agent. In the New World environment, where such a company could not be financially autonomous, this was the wrong choice; hence, the slightness of the Dutch institutional legacy in the New World.

The Dutch chauvinist (a rare species in this age) may enjoy speculating about how New World development might have proceeded had Dutch institutions sunk deeper roots – say, by a successful defense of New Holland and New Netherlands. By how much would Brazilian and U.S. well-being have been increased if these two nations had enjoyed more fully the beneficial ministrations of Dutch institutions, capital markets, and monetary arrangements? A brief visit to Surinam and

Curaçao, where the Dutch institutional legacy has indeed been substantial, might dissuade our chauvinist from dwelling too long on his visions of Brazilian Calvinists and well-scrubbed stoops and sidewalks in the Breestraat (Broadway) of Nieuw Amsterdam.[64] The thunder of falling ninepins in the Hudson River Valley should awaken our dreamer, and cause him to realize that institutions do not travel with less effort across space than they do through time. Even admirable institutions are inevitably reshaped by new environments and new external pressures.

The steadfast reliance on joint-stock trading companies to shoulder the financial burdens of empire building and the maintenance of free labor conditions (always excepting African slaves) placed the Netherlands at a severe political disadvantage in its competition with the other European colonial powers in the New World. Both of these conditions meant that market forces would dominate in colonial decision making. Attracting settlers required competition with the VOC's voracious appetite for men to sail to Asia. The superior returns available there guaranteed that the flow to the New World would never be more than a trickle. The potential settler in New Netherlands had to secure his passage and start-up financing; one ever-present alternative was to sign up with the VOC, which paid a signing bonus, monthly wages, maintenance while in company service, and the right to engage in a limited amount of private trading. The survivor could hope to return home with a significant nest egg. These hopes were not often realized, to be sure, but the ex ante calculation of costs and benefits seems to have made settlement in the New World uncompetitive.[65] The choices facing the poten-

[64] For a stimulating historical and contemporary survey of the Dutch Caribbean see Gert Oostindie, *Het paradijs overzee. De "Nederlandse" Caraïben en Nederland* (Amsterdam, 1997). Oostindie emphasizes the "negligent" character of Dutch colonialism in the Caribbean. After the early-seventeenth-century dreams of empire and wealth had faded, Dutch policy was icily instrumental. Language, culture, and religion were not imposed on the inhabitants in ways comparable to practices in the other colonial empires. Thus, today, Dutch is not the common language of the Caribbean islands; the Christian population is not primarily Calvinist; and neither high culture nor popular culture has a specifically Dutch stamp. While colonizers are usually faulted for cultural imperialism, Oostindie makes a good case for the long-term disadvantages (to the subject peoples) of colonial indifference.

[65] One of the very few eighteenth-century Dutch critiques of plantation slavery was written in response to news of a slave revolt in Berbice. Writing in *De Koopman*, Vol. 4, no. 32 (1773), "Colonius Agricola" argued that gentler treatment would bring such revolts to an end, since black slaves were no different than "we free Christians." He went on to ask why slavery was necessary in the first place: "Why not use free white workers? After all, are there not plenty of poor Germans?" ["Zijn er toch niet genoeg arme Duitsers?"] Indeed, the flow of German migrants to the Netherlands was large and continuous; the Netherlands came to be known as the "graveyard of Germany." But this labor supply moved east, not west. See Roelof van Gelder, *Het Oost-Indisch avontuur. Duitsers in dienst van de VOC* (Nijmegen, 1997).

tial migrant in the British Isles differed systematically, so that in the seventeenth century, when Britain sent approximately 370,000 persons to the New World and perhaps 100,000 to Asia (a significant minority of whom died while in EIC service), the Netherlands sent 15,000 settlers to the New World and 375,000 to Asia (of whom 215,000 died before their return).[66]

Similarly, financing the military power needed to secure and hold a New World empire required attracting funds on the private capital market. The same was true in Asia, but the sustained profitability of the VOC allowed it to draw on retained profits to finance its expansion plans. In the New World, the competitive commercial setting denied the WIC this option, and private capital markets rarely (after the 1630s) judged the prospects for gain superior to alternative opportunities in Europe.

So, the Dutch impact on the New World was greatest outside the context of state institutions, in the sphere of product and factor markets. "Prematurely" modern, the Dutch launched multinational enterprises before the age of mercantilism had ended. But their pioneering work in the development of international capital and commodity markets eventually had its effect on the other colonizers, so that today, the Netherlands is a minor state in a world of diminishing state power, but a major economy in a world of growing market power.[67]

[66] P. C. Emmer, ed., *Colonialism and Migration; Indentured Labour Before and After Slavery* (Dordrecht, 1986). Migration estimates are drawn from David Eltis, "Seventeenth Century Migration and the Slave Trade," in Jan Lucassen and Leo Lucassen, eds., *Migration, Migration History, and History: Old Paradigms and New Perspectives* (Dordrecht, 1995) and De Vries, "Connecting Europe and Asia."

[67] This theme is developed further in Jan de Vries, "Nederland in de wereld," in Frans Becker et al., eds., *Nederland in de wereld. Het zestiende jaarboek voor het democratisch socialisme* (Amsterdam, 1995), pp. 175–80.

5

Fiscal and Monetary Institutions in Spain (1600–1900)

Gabriel Tortella and Francisco Comín

5.1 INTRODUCTION

Long before abdicating, Charles V addressed the following prophetic words to his son and prospective heir, Prince Philip: "Financial matters will be left in such a state that you will have a lot of work."[1] The same could have been declared by every Spanish Habsburg monarch to his respective successor. It is said that Charles's abdication was motivated by financial troubles, and from then on, for more than a century, things became only worse.

The root cause of the financial problem was, as in most European nations of the time – and perhaps of all times – war. In peacetime the resources of the Spanish Crown were amply sufficient to cover expenses; the trouble was that peaceful years were the exception. At the end of Charles's reign, peacetime expenditure was only one half of ordinary revenue: even admitting that there was already a heavy burden of debt, a hypothetical budget would have been in balance. War upset all calculations. From the moment he spent a small borrowed fortune bribing the imperial electors, Emperor Charles was involved in wars on several fronts: against France over Italy in the 1520s, against the Turks in the Mediterranean in the 1530s, and then against the Protestants in Germany in the 1540s and 1550s. In spite of the wealth of his domains, ordinary revenue could not finance this continuous war effort, and he had to have recourse to credit. He became more and more indebted. This is why he forewarned his son about the intractability of financial problems.

In spite of all this, he had enormous resources at his command because his domains were vast and rich. Early in his reign, Italy and the Low Countries provided the largest part of imperial resources; in the long run, however, Spain (mostly Castile) became the main financial supporter of

[1] *Lo de la hazienda quedará tal que pasareys gran trabajo*. Cf. March (1941), II, p. 24.

the empire: this was probably the main reason why Charles established himself there. There are two main explanations of why Castile bore the brunt of imperial finance. In the first place, it was the richest and most populous of the Iberian kingdoms. At that time, Castile's economy was flourishing on the basis of sheepherding, wool exports, and woolen textiles. The building of the Spanish-American empire and its exploitation became Castile's crowning achievement and a new source of riches. In the second place, there were political reasons. Castile had a tradition of strong royal power, whereas Aragón-Catalonia had a "contractual" constitutional system that substantially reduced the taxing power of the monarch (Elliott, 1963, pp. 1–11, 45). The Aragonese[2] made full use of their political traditions to contribute only a very small part to overall expenditure. This issue came to a head in 1640.

5.2 THE TAX SYSTEM IN THE MID-SIXTEENTH CENTURY

Early in the reign of Philip II, around 1560, the royal accountants distinguished six kinds of revenue of the Crown of Castile: (1) ordinary revenues (*rentas ordinarias*), which contributed around 38 percent of total revenue; (2) American remittances (*remesas de Indias*), which contributed 23 percent; (3) church donations (*gracias eclesiásticas*), 13 percent; (4) extraordinary revenues (*rentas extraordinarias*), 11 percent; (5) additions (*aditamentos*), 10 percent; and (6) *maestrazgos* (mostly rents from the lands of the religious-military orders, of which the king of Spain was Grand Master – *Gran Maestre*), 5 percent (Ruiz Martín, 1968). We can also make a distinction between those revenues originating in the royal domain (rents and output of royal mines and lands), whose collection did not require agreement of the Cortes (the Spanish parliament), and those coming from taxes or the Church, which required consent of the Cortes or of the ecclesiastical authorities. The first set of revenues, the ones posing no political problems, amounted to about three fourths of the total.[3]

The most important group within the *ordinary revenues* was a curious pair, *tercias* and *alcabalas*, which together yielded 21 percent of total revenue (see Table 5.1). These two revenues were totally disparate, but bureaucratic inertia lumped them together, as they were collected jointly. The *tercias* were a subtraction of two ninths that the state made

[2] For our purposes, the Kingdom of Castile includes not only Old and New Castile, but also Galicia, Asturias, the Basque country, Navarre, Extremadura, Andalucia, and the Canary Islands; the Kingdom of Aragón includes Aragón proper, Catalonia, Valencia, and the Balearic Islands. (The people of Aragón and inland Valencia speak Castilian.)

[3] On Castilian sixteenth-century finance see Carande (1949), Ruiz Martín (1968), Fortea (1990), and Ulloa (1977); on the fifteenth century see Ladero (1973).

Table 5.1. Revenues of the Crown of Castile (1560) (Percentages)

	Revenue	*Situado*/Total
1. Ordinary Revenues	37.9	97.6
Tercias and *alcabalas*	21.2	61.9
Almojarifazgo mayor de Castilla	4.9	11.3
Almojarifazgo de Indias	1.8	4.4
Almojarifazgo of slaves	0.1	0.0
Diezmos de la mar (sea tithes)	0.9	0.2
Customs (*puertos secos*) between Castile and Aragón	1.6	4.1
Customs (*puertos secos*) between Castile and Portugal	0.9	1.9
Wool duties	2.0	3.9
Montazgo	1.0	2.7
Granada silk	1.6	3.4
Salines and others	1.8	3.7
2. Extraordinary Revenues	11.3	0.0
Ordinary and extraordinary from Castile	9.5	0.0
From the Cortes of Aragón	1.2	0.0
Moneda forera (seigniorage)	0.6	0.0
3. *Maestrazgos*	4.6	2.4
4. Church Donations	13.2	0.0
Cruzada (crusade bull)	8.0	0.0
Castile subsidy	4.1	0.0
Aragón subsidy	1.1	0.0
5. American Remittances	23.4	0.0
6. Additions	9.7	0.0
Penas de Cámara (royal fines and penalties)	0.1	0.0
Slaving permits	0.5	0.0
Almadén quicksilver	1.9	0.0
Mines	7.2	0.0
7. Total	100.0	100.0

Source: Ruiz Martín (1968).

upon the *tithe*. It was therefore a direct tax on agriculture, equivalent to 2.22 percent of gross output. The *alcabala* was a sales tax of Arabic origin that had been introduced by Alfonso X in 1269, although some authors put its origin even earlier in time.[4] The *alcabala* started out as 5 percent of the sale price; it was later increased, but never rose above 10 percent.

[4] *Al-qabala* means "the tax" or "the revenue" in Arabic. This is also the ethnological origin of the French *gabelle* (salt tax); in Spanish *gabela* means sales tax or excise. On the origins of the *alcabala* see Vicens Vives (1959), p. 261, Moxó (1963), and Bleiberg (1968).

Its burden varied with the product taxed; only grain and salt were exempted, and the percentage on meat was low. As a sales tax, it had few exemptions: as a rule the nobility had to pay it, but the clergy were exempted when the transaction was nonmercantile; the Basque country was exempted from it, and so were a few towns and institutions. Foreigners paid their own tax, poetically called *alcabala del viento* ("of the wind").

Alcabalas and *tercias* were collected by tax farmers until 1536. From then on, a new system was adopted, which would become a durable institution in Spanish fiscal custom: the *encabezamiento*. A tax was said to be *encabezado* (literally "headed") when the state assigned a quota to each territorial unit (city, town, or county) to be paid for the tax. Then it was the unit's business to collect it and deliver the predetermined lump sum to the state in due time. For the Spanish state at the time this system had a double advantage: it eliminated intermediaries' profits, and it minimized collection costs. It had one great drawback, however: as prices went up in the sixteenth century, the tax became "petrified," as the Cortes resisted the Crown's attempts to increase the nominal quotas. The clergy and the aristocracy, heavily represented in the Cortes, strove to shift the tax burden to other imposts from which these groups were exempted: the *servicios*. Another problem with the *encabezamiento* of the *alcabalas* was that, as inflation made them less productive, the local collectors tended to substitute other sources of income (poll taxes, concession charges, monopolies) to make up for the shortfalls. This led to administrative confusion and double taxation (Pulido, 1993, Ch. II).

The *commerce customs* were the second largest group within the ordinary revenues and yielded about 12 percent of the total. Of these, the tax on *wool exports* was of considerable importance since Castile was probably the largest exporter in Europe at the time. The general import and export customs duty was called at the time by the Arabic name of *almojarifazgo* (from *al-musrif*, "the inspector") and was charged in southern cities. Unsurprisingly, the *almojarifazgo* of Seville, which included the trade with the Indies, was the richest, as it produced 7 percent of total revenue (i.e., over half of the total commerce taxes). There were a series of other exactions on commercial traffic, such as the so-called sea tithe (*diezmo del mar*) and the dry-port taxes (*puertos secos*), levied on merchandise carried over land borders, that is, the Aragón–Castile border, and the Portugal–Castile border even after the annexation of Portugal in 1580. Another ordinary revenue was the tax on the silk industry (*renta de la seda*) of Granada. In general, the tax system of the Nasrid rulers of Granada had been respected by the

Christian kings after the conquest of this last Muslim kingdom in 1492. The rich silk industry of the city thus remained subject to specially heavy taxation, which alone yielded 1.6 percent of total revenue and which may have been the cause of the *morisco* rebellion in 1568 (Ulloa, 1977, pp. 359–73; Vincent, 1978). Another ordinary revenue was the *montazgo*, a tax paid by the Real Concejo de la Mesta, a powerful sheepowners' organization. In spite of the great wealth of the Mesta, the *montazgo* at that time yielded considerably less than the Granada silk industry (1 percent). Other ordinary revenues included the rents from the royal salt works, mines, and so on.

American remittances became a substantial fraction of total revenues after the mid-sixteenth century. On average, about one third of precious metal arrivals from America belonged to the Spanish Treasury. A large part of this was the *quinto*, the fifth of all mining production that belonged to the Crown by rights. Another part originated in royal mines, whose entire output belonged to the Crown. The bulk of the remainder originated in the payment of taxes and was the surplus of the imperial treasury after local expenditures were paid. To this must be added the occasional confiscation of private remittances, as was done in times of fiscal penury. While being a windfall for the Spanish state, American remittances ordinarily yielded less than the combined *tercias* and *alcabalas*: their contribution was between one fourth and one fifth of total revenue. They had one appreciable drawback: as they were dependent on the output of mines and local fiscal surpluses, and subject to the hazards of transatlantic travel, they were more volatile than other revenues (Flynn, 1980).

The *gracias eclesiásticas* were, as their name indicates, not proper taxes, but voluntary concessions agreed upon by the Church. In fact, the *tercias reales* ought to have been included here, but the traditional irrationalism of the Spanish administration grouped them with the sales taxes. Other *gracias* were the "crusade bull" (*bula de Cruzada*) and the ecclesiastical subsidy (*subsidio eclesiástico*). The crusade donation originated in the idea that the Spanish state carried out a constant war against the infidel, a sort of national crusade, for which it received help from the Church and all the faithful. Thus the bull was a mixture of alms and tax to which the commoners (*pecheros*) were strongly pressured to contribute with promises of salvation. The subsidy was paid directly by the Church by means of a sort of *encabezamiento* or *repartimiento* whereby the several bishoprics and parishes were adjudged a quota that they had to pay from their own means.[5]

[5] On the finances of the Inquisition see Martínez (1984).

Extraordinary revenues were even more confusing. Their main component was the *servicio*, which could be ordinary or extraordinary. The *servicio* was essentially an emergency tax, granted by the Cortes and typically intended to support a war effort. It was therefore paid only by the commoners, since the aristocracy was supposed to pay in deed, that is, to do military service. During the medieval *reconquista* (the Christian reconquest of Muslim Spain) the *servicio* became so common that it almost turned into an ordinary tax. This became legal under Charles V, who on top of the "ordinary service" started asking the Cortes for "extraordinary services," and even for "marriage services" in order to cover the expenditures of his weddings (Ulloa, 1977, p. 475). The *servicio* was intended to be paid for by local quotas, and then each commoner was assessed according to his wealth. The geographical distribution of this tax was uneven. Castile paid the bulk of it (in per capita terms, the differences were not all that large), but even within Castile some regions were exempt, such as the Basque country and Granada, although these were subject to other similar exactions. The individual incidence of the tax also was irregular because the wealth assessments, when they existed at all, were usually inaccurate. At most times and places the *servicios* were paid by means of the *sisa* (derived from *assize*), a sales tax that consisted in subtracting a fraction of the weight, typically one eighth, of the merchandise sold. In principle, the *sisa* was applied only on the articles sold to commoners, but this was difficult to put in practice. During the sixteenth century, as the *alcabalas* became petrified, the Cortes offered the *servicios* as a replacement, since the privileged classes, heavily represented in the Cortes, were exempt.

Extraordinary revenues reached their zenith under Philip II. After the defeat of the Armada in 1588, the king's debts were staggering and he asked the Cortes for an extraordinary service, which was so large that it became known as the *servicio de millones*. The losses of the Armada were estimated at 3,750 million maravedís, while the yearly ordinary revenues at that time were 3,250 million. The opposition to this new tax was so great that Philip had to spend a considerable amount to bribe the deputies; it was finally approved in 1590. The *servicio de millones* was supposed to be universally applied, but the nobility and the clergy fiercely resisted paying it. The mechanics of its collection were planned as follows: as usual, it was apportioned geographically by local quotas; then each city or village was supposed to gather the money by several alternative means: selling or leasing communal lands; drawing on the resources of the municipal mutual funds (*pósitos*); having recourse to poll or wealth taxes; or the *sisas*. In fact the *sisas* became the most common way of collecting the *millones*. Thus an impost that was intended to be a sort of wealth tax of universal application became a sales tax paid mostly by commoners. Even so, it became the single most important source of revenue in the seventeenth century.

The so-called *aditamentos* (additions) were mostly made up of income from the royal domain: mines and seigniorage, plus other dues from private mines. The most productive were the taxes from the Basque iron mines and the income from the Almadén mercury mines, which had accrued to the Crown with the *Maestrazgo* of the religious-military order of Calatrava. The Spanish *religious-military orders* paralleled the crusading orders like the Templars or the Hospitalers. They distinguished themselves in the *reconquista*, whence they became very rich by the acquisition of vast tracts of land. King Ferdinand of Aragón became grand master of the orders, and his grandson Charles V also secured the post and obtained from the pope the privilege of making it hereditary. Thus the Crown obtained the incomes of the orders, mostly in the form of land rents, leasing of pastures, and the output of some mines.

In addition to these six sources of regular income, the Spanish Crown had frequent recourse to more irregular sources, the so-called *arbitrios*, a word that can be loosely translated as "expedients." The most common kind of *arbitrio* was what we would today call privatization. The Crown had a variety of assets to sell, physical as well as institutional. The gradation was complex, because in many cases it was difficult to distinguish between selling and borrowing: by selling future assets and promissory notes, in fact, the Crown was just getting deeper into debt. Typical assets sold by the Crown in an emergency were lands and rights. *Baldíos*, or wastelands, owned by the Crown and largely unexploited, were sold in large amounts during the sixteenth century, especially after Philip II's first bankruptcy in 1557. Sales of offices, initiated by Charles V, were a lucrative source although unpopular with the citizens, who justifiedly protested that this expedient entailed a clear deterioration of government. Thus a certain bargaining developed whereby the king would be granted new taxes in exchange for a promise not to sell more offices. Other *arbitrios* were the sale of patents of nobility and *hidalguías* (*hidalgo* is the loose equivalent of "esquire"). These sales were also unpopular because nobles were exempt from most taxes, and this increased the tax burden of commoners. Other widely resented *arbitrios* were several methods of confiscation, from forced donations and loans to the sequestration of private specie cargoes. The Crown also sold rights, such as local feudal rights originally belonging to the king, or local taxes: the *alcabalas* of a certain county could be farmed out or sold outright. This also was an unpopular expedient because, as Adam Smith (1937, p. 854) wrote, "even a bad sovereign feels more compassion for his people than can ever be expected from the farmers of his revenue."

5.3 THE PUBLIC DEBT

The chronic insufficiency of all these sources to pay for the skyrocketing war expenditure caused the continuous growth of public debt, both short-term (*asientos*) and long-term (*juros*), until financial charges reached volumes similar to regular revenues. The *asientos* (literally, "settlements") were contracts between the Crown and bankers entailing the bankers' obligation to deliver a certain amount of money in a predetermined location (typically silver in Flanders) against short-term promissory notes or bills of exchange by the Crown. At the beginning, these notes or bills were payable at fairs (e.g., those of Medina del Campo, where the lucrative exports of wool were negotiated). But

> [t]he delicate mechanism of Fairs and merchant credit was not made for the enormous loans which the crown demanded: the governments asked for too much for too long. . . . Towards the end of the sixteenth century . . . changes were made. The *asientos* . . . were made directly repayable from a specific source of revenue instead of in a future Fair. . . . The *asiento* was thus essentially a short-term loan repayable from a specific revenue.[6]

This agreement, whereby a loan was assigned to a specific revenue, an assignment that served as collateral, was called a *situado* because the debt was "situated" upon that revenue. But the *asiento* could not raise floating credit forever. At a certain point all the available revenues for several years to come (say, up to five) were already assigned or situated to repay creditors; at this point, bankers would not regard a revenue five or more years ahead as safe collateral and would therefore refuse to extend more credit. This point was reached in 1557. In that situation the only choice for Philip II was to unilaterally convert *asientos* into *juros* (*juro* literally means "I swear"), which were long-term debt bonds with relatively low interest and also situated. There were several kinds of *juros*. The most important distinction is that between *juros perpetuos* (consolidated or irredeemable) and *juros al quitar* (which the debtor could redeem at will). Most *asientos* were converted into *juros al quitar*, of course, but in fact they became *perpetuos* (Toboso, 1987). There were also the *juros de resguardo*, which were issued to the *asentistas* (creditors) as an interest-yielding guarantee for their loans until the *situado* permitted definitive redemption. Unfortunately, the 1557 bankruptcy was only the first one. From then on, royal bankruptcies recurred with notable regularity, every 20 years or so until nearly the end of the seventeenth century. The *situado*, which was around one third of ordinary revenues at the beginning of the sixteenth century, reached more than

[6] Parker (1972), pp. 147–8.

100 percent at the time of the first bankruptcy. Then it hovered around that proportion for the rest of the sixteenth century and presumably (the figures are not available) during most of the seventeenth.

These fiscal policies were obviously deleterious to long-term economic development. Debt default and arbitrary confiscation made property rights patently insecure, weakened the credit of the Spanish state, and gravely hurt the banking system. But fiscal and monetary policies in the seventeenth century made matters infinitely worse.

5.4 THE SPANISH MONETARY SYSTEM IN THE GOLDEN AGE

In monetary stability – as in literature, art, and empire – Spain passed through her golden age in the sixteenth century, the only century that has not witnessed serious derangement of her coinage. But this golden age was literally followed by one of bronze.[7]

The monetary system – the set of monetary units – that Spain used through the early modern period well into the nineteenth century was created by Ferdinand and Isabella, the Catholic monarchs, at the close of the Middle Ages. As in many other matters, in matters monetary the Catholic monarchs marked the transition from the medieval to the early modern (period) in Spain. They put an end to political and economic confusion and set the basis of the national state. Not everything they did was successful (witness the Inquisition, mercantilism, and the imposition of religious and cultural uniformity), but many of the things they did left a deep imprint – for better or worse.

The Catholic monarchs found a chaotic monetary situation upon their joint assumption of the Crown, "one of the most deplorable our history registers," according to the authors of an official history.[8] Their monetary reform of 1497 established a trimetallic system whose main units were the excelente de Granada (or de la Granada, because it had stamped on it a pomegranate, the symbol of the recently conquered city of Granada), a gold coin; the real de plata, a silver coin; and the blanca, a *vellón* coin.[9] There was a medieval relic, however, that not even the Catholic monarchs could do away with, and this was the maravedí. Originally a gold coin – equivalent to the Arab dinar – used by the

[7] Hamilton (1947), p. 9. He liked this sentence so much that he used it in two books; cf. Hamilton (1934), p. 73.

[8] Anonymous (1862), p. 31.

[9] *Vellón* is a confusing word; it has two meanings: (1) tuft of hair or fleece of wool or (2) an alloy of copper and silver. The first meaning derives from *vello*, which means body hair, the second from the French *billon*, meaning "this alloy." Although the *blanca* was not as long-lived as other units, even today people use *estar sin blanca* for "not having a penny."

Almoravids, who invaded the Peninsula from Africa in the eleventh century, the maravedí underwent a series of metamorphoses: it was adopted by the Christian kingdoms, devalued, and changed into a silver coin, until finally it became a pure unit of account. The Catholic monarchs used it to establish the equivalences between their three basic monetary units: the excelente was worth 375 mrs, the real de plata 34 mrs, and the blanca 0.5 mrs. These coins changed names, but they remained the basic monetary units. The excelente was also called ducado, escudo, or doblón; the real de plata was later known as real de a ocho, peso duro, tálero, or dólar. Only the blanca disappeared in the long run and was confusingly replaced by the real de vellón, a new unit created by Charles II in 1686.

Although the Catholic monarchs probably hoped that their trimetallic system would be used throughout all of their kingdoms, in fact it worked almost exclusively in Castile; the Aragonese kingdoms maintained a silver system directly derived from the Carolingian division of the libra (pound) into 20 sueldos (*solidus*, shilling) or 240 dineros (*denarius*, penny). The Aragonese kingdoms also had gold ducats under different names. Their monetary systems converged slowly with that of Castile due mostly to Gresham's law, which operated at full speed in the seventeenth century. Navarra, although annexed by Ferdinand, originally king of Aragón, adopted the Castilian system early in the sixteenth century. The gold–silver relation established by the Catholic monarchs was 10.11 (i.e., 1 unit of gold was equivalent to 10.11 units of silver).[10]

As the preceding quotation from Hamilton implies, no great changes took place in the Spanish monetary system during the sixteenth century if we except the substantial inflow of silver and, to a lesser extent, of gold, especially during the second half, that is, the reign of Philip II. This entailed a gradual modification of the official gold–silver relation, which was about 12.1 by 1600 (Hamilton, 1948, p. 83). As is well known, Spain exported a large amount of the bullion it imported from the Americas in order to finance its European wars and its commercial deficit. In spite of this, and in spite of the three state bankruptcies under Philip II, however, the monetary system was not greatly affected, chiefly because Philip II made a point of not having recourse to debasement in spite of his fiscal tribulations.

[10] Throughout this chapter, we will describe the bimetallic ratio (units of silver per unit of gold) with a single figure, i.e., 10.5 instead of 10.5 to 1, for instance. As the price of silver goes down, the ratio seems to go up, but since we are taking gold as the standard of value and it is the denominator we are reflecting, the reverse is true, so that, for example, 15 is a lower ratio than 10.

5.5 THE BRONZE AGE: WAR, BANKRUPTCY AND INFLATION IN THE SEVENTEENTH CENTURY

Philip II inherited a troubled financial system; no wonder that his first bankruptcy was declared in 1557, a year after he assumed the scepter. His financial legacy, however, was even more troubled than what he received: his reign not only commenced but also ended in bankruptcy. He had to suspend payments in 1596, two years before his death. He had also suspended payments in 1575, when he reached a sort of forced agreement with his creditors under the name of *medio general*. Although it is said that the "prudent king," as Philip II was called, was not as fond of war as his father, in fact he was involved in military struggles throughout his reign. Of course, the best known and most ruinous of these wars was the "eighty-year war" against the Protestants in the Netherlands, which started in 1566 and lasted well into the next century. Connected to this was the ill-fated Armada expedition in 1588. Then there was the intermittent struggle against the French; the constant war against the Turks; the campaign for Portugal, which was annexed in 1580; and two serious internal conflicts: the Morisco rebellion in 1568 and the Aragón disturbances in 1590. This constant conflict explains the fact that in spite of a more than tripling (they multiplied by a factor of 3.5) of the Crown's ordinary revenues between 1555 and 1598, its indebtedness kept mounting; this is only natural, as expenditure in the same time span increased fourfold.

Philip III's reign (1598–1621) was marked by the legacy of his father but included a dangerous innovation: recourse to the debasement of coinage (the copper *vellón*) to finance the unmanageable deficit. There were few novelties in the field of taxes. Philip III had repeated recourse to the *millones* because ordinary revenues were all pledged several years in advance. The trouble was that even the *millones* (Philip II had asked the Cortes for a second *servicio de millones*, but the Cortes did not grant it until 1601) had been tied up in the last *medio general* of Philip II after the 1596 bankruptcy. So the new king resorted to all sorts of *arbitrios* and, already in 1599, to issuing copper *vellón* (also called "poor *vellón*," i.e., copper coins whose face value was higher than their intrinsic value because they lacked the silver component of the original currency, the "rich *vellón*"). In spite of the Cortes's protests, the issuing of copper coins went on; once debasement had taken place, there was no reason to even keep the face value of money near the value of its metallic content. In 1602 copper coins were minted with the same intrinsic characteristics as those of 1599, but with double denomination. Meanwhile the king was negotiating with the Cortes to suspend copper issues in exchange for a new *millones* service. He obtained it in 1607, but by then the fabulous sum of 22 million ducats' worth of copper coinage had been issued.[11] This did not prevent a new suspension of payments in 1606. It was the only one in Philip III's reign, perhaps thanks to debasements and to a fortunate event: the suspension of hostilities in the Netherlands in 1607, which led to the 12-year truce signed in 1609. This was perhaps the only wise decision in an otherwise infelicitous rule. A new mistake was made in 1609 with the expulsion of the remaining *moriscos*, which caused a serious economic crisis in Aragón and Valencia, the two regions where their population was densest; a typical oppressed minority, the *moriscos* were hard workers and steady taxpayers.

Although for a while he kept his promise not to debase, Philip III, alleging that the deficit was unsurmountable, asked the Cortes to relieve him of his promise in 1617. His plea was granted and new copper coin was issued until the Cortes again obtained a promise to suspend new copper coinage in exchange for a new *millones* service in 1619. But issuing new coin was not the king's only means of debasing the currency; another expedient was crying up (*resellar*) the money. This was done for the first time in 1603 and frequently repeated under Philip III and Philip IV. The operation was as follows: the people were ordered to take their copper coins to the mints; there the coins were restamped (*reselladas*) at double their face value. The owners were reimbursed with half of the coins (same face value as they had turned in), plus a little extra for the nuisance. The other near half was pure profit for the government, minus the cost of restamping. Of course, the profits would be higher if the crying up was done for higher face values. The advantage of the operation was that it made the buying of new copper bullion unnecessary; the disadvantage lay in the lack of public enthusiasm: smaller and smaller amounts were taken to be restamped every time. The situation was memorably described by Hamilton:[12]

> To bridge the gap between diminished revenues and swollen expenditures, the Crown resorted to unbridled coinage of vellon in the first quarter of the seventeenth century . . . ; but the large output of copper money by the best machinery then known . . . and crying up the coinage, when the king was too poor to buy copper, shook the foundations of Spanish life. . . . While universally envied because of her monopoly of the American gold and silver mines, Spain saw her precious metals driven out of circulation in the second quarter of the seventeenth century by a cumbersome and unstable medium of exchange . . . ; often the gold and silver that flowed in from the Indies never entered circulation in Spain. The private treasure was sequestered by the Crown for

[11] Hamilton (1948), esp. pp. 56, 70. According to Gelabert (1997), p. 29, ordinary and extraordinary resources combined were about 10 million ducats in 1598.

[12] Hamilton (1947), pp. 9–12, 36–7.

remittance abroad, along with the public treasure; and the owners were indemnified in vellon . . . ; several years' work with the contemporaneous account-books of municipalities, charity hospitals, convents, colleges, cathedrals, treasury officials, and the House of Trade (Casa de la Contratación) have given me the impression that vellon constituted at least 92 percent of the money spent in the 1650's. Apparently, the percentage rose to well above 95 during the next three decades of monetary disturbance and economic decline. . . . Not only were silver coins extremely scarce, but a significant portion of those available was degraded . . . and late in 1650 it was discovered that silver reals of defective fineness, coined in Peru . . . , were circulating in Castile. . . . And to aggravate the evil, unbridled inflation was generally followed by sharp deflation, mistakenly conceived as a remedy.

[. . . P]rogressive debasement and overissue of fractional coins drove the precious metals out of circulation, thereby forcing the mistresses of Mexico and Peru onto a cumbersome and unstable copper standard. The brusque alterations of monetary inflation and deflation – obviously far worse than either separately – . . . were at once a result and a fundamental cause of the economic decline.

The paradox of the mistresses of Zacatecas and Potosí being reduced to the almost exclusive circulation of copper coins is not difficult to explain. According to our calculations (Tortella, unpublished-2), Spain retained in minted form only 15 percent of gross silver imports. It retained all the gold it imported, but the value of gold imports was less than one tenth that of silver imports during the second half of the sixteenth century, when American remittances grew faster. We also know that these remittances leveled off and then decreased during the next century. The increase in the money supply that this inflow of precious metals brought about was offset by price increases, so that, in real terms, the money supply hardly grew at all in the reign of Philip II. The leveling off and then the fall in the importation of precious metals after 1595 left a gap in the money supply that was filled by *vellón* coinage. Prices also leveled off and even decreased during the first two decades of the seventeenth century as silver disappeared from circulation and was replaced by copper (Hamilton, 1934, Chs. 2, 8, and 9).

Tax revenues also faltered in the seventeenth century.[13] There were several causes for this. First of all, there was a series of self-defeating mechanisms in the Spanish fiscal system. The most important of those mechanisms probably was overtaxation, which ruined the Castilian economy.[14] This was understood by contemporaries and has been con-

[13] On seventeenth-century financial problems see Domínguez Ortiz (1960, 1984), Gelabert (1997), Pulido (1996), Ruiz Martín (1990), Sánchez Belén (1996), and Sureda (1949).

[14] According to García Sanz (1991), pp. 17–18, the tax burden in Castile went from 5 percent of income around 1500 to 10 percent around 1600 and then to 15 percent in the first half of the seventeenth century. Then it went down to around 5 percent in the eighteenth century. See also Bilbao (1990).

firmed by modern researchers such as Hamilton, Elliott, Ulloa, García Sanz, and Gelabert. The tax system, based on excises and apportioned by local quotas, was regressive and penalized the cities versus the countryside and commoners versus churchmen and nobles. Industry and trade, therefore, were discouraged. The flourishing sixteenth-century Castilian textile industry was taxed and regulated out of competitiveness (García Sanz, 1994, esp. p. 424). To this must be added the fact that tax farmers operated more efficiently in cities. Another self-defeating mechanism was the sale of patents of nobility and *hidalguías*, which reduced the number of taxpayers and thereby increased the tax burden on commoners; it has been estimated that about 1 million taxpayers "disappeared" in Castile between 1591 and 1631. A third perverse mechanism was the general insecurity of markets and property rights generated by the periodic bankruptcies and confiscations, compounded by the increasing uncertainty about the value of money as the seventeenth century progressed. To the self-defeating, antieconomic bias of the tax system must be added the ineptitude and corruption with which taxes were collected by bureaucrats and tax farmers. It has been calculated that as much as 40 percent of assessed taxes were lost in collection.[15]

The disaster climaxed under Philip IV, who succeeded his father in 1621. This was a bad year because it marked the end of the truce in the Netherlands. To strengthen his army, the new king immediately had recourse to all the means at his command. One of his *arbitrios* was the *crecimiento de los juros*, which in essence was a unilateral reduction of the interest owed on them (literally, "growth of the *juros*"; the expression is justified by the fact that, in order to obtain the same yield, the principal of the *juro* had to be increased). Another *arbitrio* was partial confiscation of private silver remittances, which were forcibly exchanged for *juros*. The king also had new recourse to bankers' *asientos*; but the easiest and cheapest expedient was to issue new inflated copper. During the 1621–6 period about 14 million ducats worth of debased coin were issued (Hamilton, 1948, pp. 60, 70). All in all, according to Hamilton, some 41 million ducats of copper were issued between 1599 and 1626. From then on, the new debasements were made by means of the *resello*. Philip IV had applied for a new *millones* service in 1623 and obtained it in 1626. Meanwhile he complemented his revenues with ever more imaginative *arbitrios*: sequestering the Almojarifazgos, selling the *asiento de negros* (the contract to sell slaves in the Americas), selling royal estates and vassals, confiscating American remittances, and issuing *juros* situated on the still hypothetical *millones* (Gelabert, 1997, pp. 73–5). In spite of all these expedients, the Crown's straits were such as to cause serious

[15] The Conde-Duque believed the proportion to be 70 percent: Elliott (1963), p. 307.

political difficulties; the king lacked the means to travel to Catalonia to swear the oath and receive homage from his vassals. As a consequence, the legitimacy of his rule in Catalonia was much in dispute there, and his person was unpopular, circumstances that contributed to open rebellion in 1640 (Elliott, 1963, esp. p. 154). On top of all this, or maybe as a consequence, the government suspended payments in 1627 and a new *medio general* was proclaimed. The irritation of the Genoese bankers was such that they threatened political reprisals. From that time on Portuguese bankers appeared on the scene, gradually replacing the Italians (Gelabert, 1997, pp. 76–7; Sanz Ayán, 1988, pp. 136–40).

In times of such difficulties the inequities in the distribution of the fiscal burden became glaring. It was evident that Castile paid a disproportionate share of the Crown's revenues, and the opinion became widespread in government circles that the imbalance ought to be redressed, not so much on ethical grounds as on those of necessity. Castile was exhausted and impoverished; the time had come for other kingdoms (Aragón, Portugal, the Basque provinces) to lend a hand. The champion of this idea was the prime minister of Philip IV, the Count-Duke of Olivares, who, since his basic aim was to strengthen common defence, called the project Union of Arms (*Unión de Armas*) (Elliott, 1986, Ch. VII). Of course, this was not a popular project outside Castile. To the other kingdoms, since Castile was the obvious leader, since political decisions were made in Madrid, and since Castile had kept the Indies and their remittances for itself, it was fair that Castile should bear the load of taxation. On ethical grounds, the discussion could be endless. On purely political grounds, it was obvious that Olivares was right. The grandiose imperial policies of the Habsburgs had ruined Castile and could not be carried on without additional support from the other kingdoms. Olivares, however, miscalculated the degree of interregional solidarity. The attempt to put the Union of Arms into practice provoked an explosion of unprecedented dimensions. In 1640 both Catalonia and Portugal rebelled and seceded from Castile. It took 12 years to subdue Catalonia; Portugal gained definitive independence.

The early 1640s marked the zenith of Castile's fiscal efforts and the end of its hegemonic ambitions. The treaties of Münster (1648, peace with the Netherlands) and the Pyrenees (1659, peace with France) sealed Castile's admission of defeat. But earlier, in a desperate effort to fight on all fronts, recourse was made to inflation again. In 1641 copper coins were restamped twice: the first time, their face value was doubled; the second time, it was tripled. Afraid of the widespread protests against inflation, the government then decided to cry down the money in 1642. The solution turned out to be even worse than the problem. It implied outright expropriation of the holders of coin. The government promised compensation, but this never arrived. Then, in 1642 also, silver was devalued or cried up: new coins were issued with 24 percent less weight for the same face value (Hamilton, 1948, pp. 64–5). All these expedients and many more were to no avail. After a frantic effort that increased the state's debt and exhausted all possible *arbitrios*, a new suspension of payments was declared in 1647. After this, many established bankers stopped extending credit to the Crown. From that time on, the feeling was widespread that the effort had been excessive, sails had to be trimmed, expectations lowered, and fiscal pressure diminished. Months after concluding the Peace of Münster, the king stated that he had signed it in order to "alleviate" Castilian taxpayers (Gelabert, 1997, p. 122), and the purpose of "reducing the services" was frequently proclaimed. One thing the Crown did was to start canceling the debts of many counties, towns, and villages whose arrears had been accumulating. But nothing more drastic could be done as long as wars went on.

Peace with Portugal was not signed until 1668. The last decades of the seventeenth century saw a clear retrenchment, but intermittent war with France prevented the fiscal rearrangement that writers and politicians thought essential. A series of moderate measures were taken, such as the creation of a Junta de Alivios (Council of Alleviations), which tried to limit expenditure and lower taxes. The state remained in arrears, however, to the extent that the queen mother conspired against the prime minister of her son, Charles II, because she held him responsible for the delays in the payment of her pension.

5.6 TIMID ENLIGHTENED REFORM IN THE EIGHTEENTH CENTURY

The Castilian tax system did not change substantially during the eighteenth century. It was still based upon indirect taxes. Some modifications, however, were introduced. Perhaps it would be best to start with one of these changes: a new classification of imposts that differed markedly from the one under the Habsburgs. State revenues were grouped under five main headings: (1) provincial revenues (*rentas provinciales*); (2) general revenues (*rentas generales*); (3) fiscal monopolies and concessions (*rentas estancadas*); (4) American remittances; and (5) tithes and other revenues (*rentas decimales y otras*).[16]

Provincial revenues, which on the average produced a little over 20 percent of total nonfinancial revenues (see Table 5.2), were mostly the old consumer and excise taxes, still collected by territorial quotas – hence their new name. There were grouped the *alcabalas* (there were several),

[16] On eighteenth-century finances see Artola (1982), Hernández Andreu (1972), Merino (1981), Pieper (1992), Tedde (1989), and Zafra (1991).

Table 5.2. Ordinary Revenues of the General Treasury of Spain (1753–1842) (Annual Averages; Percentages and Million Current Reales)

	1753–65	1763–1807	1815–20	1824–33	1834–42
1. Indies	20.0	13.7	0.0	0.0	8.4
2. Customs (general)	14.0	17.8	18.8	10.9	10.1
3. Provincial	20.0	22.5	11.5	22.1	16.8
4. Monopolies	22.0	21.8	16.0	26.1	22.2
5. (1 + 2 + 3 + 4)	76.0	75.8	46.4	59.2	57.5
6. Ordinary revenues	370.5	572.7	552.5	615.1	753.7
7. Total revenues	394.4	945.2	1,103.3	615.1	1,164.7

Source: Pieper (1992), Merino (1987), Comín (1990).

the *tercias reales*, the *servicios* (notably the *millones*), plus some new consumer taxes (meat, *cientos*, *fiel medidor*). The *millones* had become a regular tax that did not need express approval by the Cortes except in the Basque country, where approval by its councils was required.

In Catalonia, however, the tax system had been thoroughly overhauled after its defeat in the War of Succession.[17] The new Catalan system was called the *Equivalente*, because it was supposed to produce an average tax burden similar to that in Castile. The nature of the system, however, was totally different and much fairer, as it was based upon direct imposts. Its foundation was the *Catastro*, an inventory of real estate wealth, including factories, dwellings, and, of course, farms. Taxes were assessed on the estimated output of these assets. To this was added a personal *catastro*, exacted upon salaries, wages, and profits, excluding nobles and churchmen. In spite of these traditional exemptions, the *Equivalente* turned out to be a far superior system, and it is generally considered to have been one of the main factors in Catalonia's eighteenth-century economic recovery (Vicens Vives, 1959, p. 533).

General revenues were taxes on foreign trade, and contributed about 15 percent of total revenue during the second half of the eighteenth century, with an increasing trend. Included here are the *almojarifazgos*, *puertos secos*, and *diezmos del mar*, plus the general customs. The administration of general revenues was somewhat modernized during the eighteenth century. The *puertos secos* with Aragón were abolished in 1714,

[17] After Catalonia's first defeat in 1652, little was done to change its tax system, as the king, in order to mollify his rebellious subjects, had promised to respect Catalonia's institutions.

and later on most internal customs were removed except those with the Basque country. Another improvement was that external customs were gradually made uniform, a process culminating in 1770. At the same time, colonial trade was modernized: the monopoly by the Casa de Contratación (which was removed from Seville to Cádiz in 1717) was gradually abolished; the maze of regulations and prohibitions that constrained that trade was replaced by a modern tariff in 1778.

Fiscal monopolies provided incomes either from the direct state exploitation of a monopoly or from private concessionaires. These monopolies covered a varied list of products, the most important being tobacco and salt, but also including pepper, soda and *barrilla*, wood and rubber, official sealed paper (*papel sellado*), playing cards, liquor, and others. Most monopolies were established in the frenetic quest for extra income that took place during the first half of the seventeenth century. Tobacco (17 percent) and salt (5 percent) were the most remunerative monopolies. Spanish tobacco was manufactured in Seville in one of the largest factories of eighteenth-century Europe from the tobacco leaf imported from the Americas. Tobacco and salt monopolies were administered by the state; most of the others were initially given to concessionaries, but they reverted to state management with the administrative reforms of the eighteenth century.

American remittances were the most productive single item, yielding between 15 and 25 percent. After declining in the seventeenth century, the surpluses of the Mexico City, Lima, and Buenos Aires (after 1770) Treasuries grew in the eighteenth century, thanks chiefly to silver mining and administrative improvements, but their share of total revenue declined during the last third of the period.

Tithes (*tercias reales*) and other revenues contributed about 10 percent of total state income.

All in all, these five groups delivered nearly 90 percent of total government revenue. The rest came from what was called "extraordinary income" (*ingresos extraordinarios*) originating in the army treasuries, income from the royal estate, fines, deposits, and so on.

Although they fluctuated widely, total revenues showed a markedly positive trend during most of the century, due no doubt to relative peace, moderate but steady demographic and economic growth, and gradual commercial liberalization. In particular, the results of colonial trade liberalization were reflected in a spectacular growth of general revenues, especially after 1778. During the last decade of the century, however, war interrupted this healthy process, and practically all revenues fell while military expenditure, which had been growing steadily since 1776, shot up. In order to fund these end-of-century wars, increasing recourse was made to credit. The *vales reales* (a new type of public debt) were issued in the early 1880s, and they became the main instrument for deficit financing during this troubled period.

A lively debate has been going on recently (around the bicentennial of Charles III's death in 1788) about how "enlightened" the economic policies of Spain's enlightened despots were. It started when Barbier and Klein analyzed the structure of public expenditure under Charles III (usually identified as the incarnation of enlighted despotism in Spain) and showed that war was not only the main item but also the fastest growing item. Other authors have nuanced this opinion and uncovered some hard-to-detect public works expenses, but it remains undeniable that defense was by far the largest fraction of expenditure and also that in military emergencies all means were geared to warfare and civil enterprises postponed if necessary.[18]

It is also true, however, that Spanish enlightened rulers and their advisers made an unmistakable effort to reform the fiscal system, with several aims in mind: first, to increase revenue; second, to stimulate economic growth; and third, to ameliorate the distribution of the tax burden. All in all, however, enlightened reform failed, in fiscal as in other fields. The deficit persisted, although it was moderate until the last decades of the eighteenth century. Economic growth was so modest as to be almost imperceptible, and the tax burden remained very unfairly distributed, except in Catalonia.

The intermediate objectives of enlightened reform were centralization, unification, and simplification. Since the late seventeenth century, the tendency was to put all fiscal matters under a single tax comptroller, to shift collection from tax farmers to public servants, to create a single fiscal bureacracy for the whole country, and to make taxes universal and simple. One factor helped the reformers: the defeat of Catalonia and Valencia in the War of Succession permitted the Spanish Crown to do away with most local institutions in these two old kingdoms. But in the long run, inertia and the resistance of the privileged classes seriously limited the scope of reform.

Some innovations had been introduced in the late seventeenth century, when, in imitation of the French, the post of superintendent of finance was created, and then the posts of provincial *Intendentes*. This more agile schema gradually replaced the cumbersome Council of Finance (Consejo de Hacienda), a collective body in which local and estates interests were represented. The *Intendente* system was later on transplanted to the Americas.

[18] Barbier and Klein (1985); Merino (1987); Tedde (1989), pp. 140–7; Helguera (1986, 1991); Llombart (1994).

In 1721 the superintendent became in fact minister of finance (*Secretario del Despacho de Hacienda*), and a series of central offices (*contadurías*) were created to oversee several areas of fiscal administration. In 1749 a general ordinance regulating the *Intendentes* made them the backbone of the administrative and fiscal machinery. This permitted the "direct administration of revenues," which in theory was the total transfer of tax collection and management to the state bureaucracy, although in fact it involved only more direct supervision by civil servants. In large and medium-sized cities and seaports, state officials effectively carried out the functions; in more scattered settlements they just supervised. Although this was a marked improvement, centralization and unification had their limits: the Basque country, Navarre, and the Canary Islands kept their autonomy, as did the American colonies (*Hacienda Indiana*). Other autonomous centers (*cajas*) were the mints, the royal factories, some municipal bodies, and so on.

The most daring but in the end futile part of enlightened reform was the *contribución única* (single tax), an idea already mooted in the seventeenth century. In the eighteenth century the single tax was intended to do for Castile what the *Equivalente* had done for Catalonia. It was planned to be a direct tax replacing the *rentas provinciales*, which were justifiably considered to be muddled and unfair, and, like the Catalan *Equivalente*, to be based upon a *catastro*, to be levied not only on agricultural wealth, but on all sorts of assets. The champion of the single tax was the marquis of Ensenada, who in 1749 promoted the compilation of a detailed *catastro* of 22 Castilian provinces. In the end the *catastro* was all that was left of this ambitious project, but it must be said that it is a remarkable piece of work and an outstanding historical source. A watered-down version of the single tax was the *contribución de frutos civiles*, an impost on real estate that partially replaced some provincial revenues in 1786 (Anes, 1974, 1990). After the last old-style state bankruptcy in 1739, Spanish finances enjoyed some near-balance in the following decades, in spite of the emergencies of the Seven Years' War.

In monetary matters also, after the chaos of the seventeenth century, the eighteenth was one of relative stability. Philip V made several minor innovations. One of them was the introduction of a new gold coin, a new type of escudo commonly called *veintén* because it was valued at 20 *reales de vellón*. Another was lowering the bimetallic ratio to 16. Possibly the most important of these reforms was to establish a two-tier monetary system, much in line with what Motomura (1994) detected for the seventeenth century. Under Philip V the old gold and silver coins remained, but new, slightly debased versions were also issued. The distinction thus was made between "national money," used for international operations, and "provincial money," intended for day-to-day transactions. The gold and silver content of the provincial coins was lower, and this prevented their exportation. The Bourbons also introduced a certain discipline in the issuing of *vellón*, which contributed to price stability and to greater confidence in the monetary system.

Not all was well, however. The system remained seriously impaired by a number of factors. In the first place, while the two-tier system had its advantages, it also contributed to internal confusion, as two sets of coins with similar names and outward appearance but slightly different metallic contents circulated side by side. Furthermore, the War of Succession had left a considerable amount of foreign, mostly French, coins in Spain, which also circulated and added to the uncertainty. Furthermore, the habit of clipping and sweating the coins was prevalent, so that defective coins of indeterminate value (*macuquina*, *moneda cortada*) also were mixed with newer ones. To this must be added the circulation of coins from non-Castilian kingdoms (Valencia, Aragón, the Canary Islands), plus American coins. And to top it all off, *vellón* coins with varying proportions of silver (mostly pure copper) were the main circulating medium for petty transactions.

Things became problematic with the War of the American Revolution. Military expenditures increased, while revenues were gradually affected by conflicts at home and abroad. In 1780, under the inspiration of a French financial pundit, François Cabarrus, the government issued a novel type of public debt, the *vales reales*, which also was supposed to play the role of paper money. The first issue of the *vales* was moderately successful. In order to increase their acceptability, Cabarrus proposed the creation of a national bank. The proposal was accepted, and the Bank of Saint Charles was established in 1782.

The repeated bankruptcies of the Spanish state had ruined several generations of bankers and effectively destroyed whatever financial and credit system existed in early modern Spain.[19] The relative prosperity and orderly finances of the eighteenth century permitted the development of a modest private financial system, of which the best known firm was the Cinco Gremios Mayores de Madrid.[20] The covert bankruptcy of the Spanish state during the Napoleonic Wars again did away with this budding financial system. It also contributed mightily to the fall of its American empire after the Spanish authorities squeezed the colonial elites and the Church in a desperate effort to shore up the *vales reales* (Bazant, 1977, pp. 5–6).

[19] Tortella (1997); Schwartz (1996); Tedde (1988a, 1988b); Sanz Ayán (1988), esp. pp. 479–83.

[20] Matilla Tascón and Capella (1957), Tedde (1983), Maixé (1994).

5.7 THE NINETEENTH CENTURY: FISCAL TRANSITION AND REFORM (1800–1845)

The eighteenth-century wars with England and France were followed in the nineteenth century by the wars of independence of the Spanish American colonies, which did not end until 1824. Shortly afterward Spain had its own civil war (the Carlist War, 1833–9), between liberals and absolutists after the death of Fernando VII in 1833. It was during the Carlist War and the next decade (i.e., the period roughly from 1833 to 1850) that the so-called liberal revolution established a series of modernizing measures: a set of medieval institutions (the guilds, the tithe, the *Mesta*, feudal landownership, and internal customs) was abolished and a commerce code, disentailment, free trade, and a liberal tax system were put into place. With these measures, private property rights were established and public intervention in the market was reduced. Royal factories were sold, and the number of import prohibitions was reduced – although the tariff established in 1849 was quite protective. The most significant financial measure was the fiscal reform of 1845, commonly called the *Mon–Santillán reform* because it was carried out by Finance Minister Alejandro Mon with close advice from Ramón de Santillán, a financial expert best known as the first governor of the Bank of Spain and as a distinguished financial historian.

There were also changes in the monetary and banking systems, although the most durable of these changes, the establishment of the Bank of Spain as a central bank and monopolist of issue and of the decimal system in money, and introduction of the peseta as the monetary unit, were the result of protracted processes that lasted well into the twentieth century. We will first examine fiscal reform and then the evolution of the monetary and banking systems.

Between 1808 and 1845 the bases for a liberal public finance system were slowly laid down.[21] At the beginning of the 1840s, just prior to the tax reform of 1845, tax collection had little to do with the way in which it had been carried out at the beginning of the century; new, more modern taxes were introduced by Martín de Garay and Luis López Ballesteros under absolutism, and by the liberals during the "triennium" (1820–23) and the Carlist War, which improved upon what had been inherited from the eighteenth century. Some of these new taxes were direct (the *contribución de paja y utensilios* and a refurbished version of the *frutos civiles* taxed land and real estate and their incomes, although in a crude and cumbersome way; the *subsidio de comercio* taxed

[21] On nineteenth-century finances see Comín (1988, 1990, 1996), Fontana (1971, 1973, 1977), and Tortella (1994), Ch. VIII.

commercial and industrial profits, also crudely; in both cases the necessary statistical information was missing). Other taxes were indirect, such as the *contribución de puertas*, paid on goods brought to city markets, and excises on dried cod (*bacalao*) and liquor. The halting improvements of this transitional period paved the way for the reformers of 1845.

The basic piece of the fiscal reform by the Cortes de Cádiz (1810–14) was a new version of the *contribución única* that proclaimed equality before the law and simplified tax assessment and collection. It was anathema to the reactionaries who took power after Fernando VII's coup d'état in 1814, and they abolished it outright. During the triennium the liberals softened the radical program of the *doceañistas* (the men of the Cortes de Cádiz, so called because their Constitution was proclaimed in 1812), but even these watered-down reforms were unacceptable to Fernando VII after he was restored to absolute rule by the French in 1823. Going back to *ancien regime* taxes, however, proved very inefficient, and revenues plummeted. It was in order to increase revenues that López Ballesteros, Fernando's minister, modernized the Treasury as much as he could, which was little, in the 1820s.

Until the middle of the nineteenth century, tax revenues tended to fall after stagnating at the end of the eighteenth century. The fall was due mainly to the loss of the American colonies, the decrease in the volume of foreign trade, and the general disorder and administrative chaos existing during the wars and revolutions. The cessation of coin and bullion remittances from America, due to the colonial war, was the decisive factor for the ruin of the Spanish Treasury. In the last years of the empire, metal remittances from America, although smaller than in previous decades, were still a substantial source of revenue. But there were more adverse indirect effects of the colonial upheaval. On the one hand, remittances from the Americas, great or small, had been a guarantee that allowed the Spanish Treasury to obtain loans; on the other hand, the loss of the colonies affected colonial trade as well as entrepôt trade with Europe, and this also brought about a fall in receipts from customs duties.

The ability of the Spanish state to draw upon colonial revenue had permitted delay in introducing the necessary tax reforms, which had been planned since the middle of the eighteenth century but repeatedly postponed. In the medium term, the remittances from the colonies that had still not been lost – mainly from Cuba and the Philippines – were recovered. But there can be no doubt that this traditional dependence on resources from America led finance ministers into a series of bad habits, such as thinking that the problems would be solved in some way or other without the need to effect any kind of tax reform that could offend the powerful, and also that any increase in public expenditure would be only temporary and could be financed with "extraordinary resources," such as temporary taxes, voluntary loans, forced loans, public bonds (*vales reales*), and land sales (disentailment or *desamortización*).

The main reason for delaying tax reform until 1845 was domestic politics. The reform proposals made by the finance ministers of the absolutist regime met with the opposition of reactionary politicians who preferred to see the state fall into destitution rather than alter the social structure of the *ancien regime*, while the attempts at reform carried out during the liberal periods were as short-lived as the liberal regimes themselves. These alternations between absolutism and liberalism had a negative effect on tax revenues because they caused administrative disorder conducive to tax evasion, fraud, and smuggling; furthermore, war and uncertainty affected incomes and shrank the tax base.

The predicament of the Spanish state in the early nineteenth century can be readily appreciated in Table 5.2. Remittances from the Indies disappeared, but customs revenues replaced them to a certain extent because, although foreign trade fell, customs revenues did not fall as much as ordinary revenues. After the war against Napoleon the Spanish Treasury found that the share of its four traditional sources of income (the Indies, customs duties, provincial taxes, and monopolies) was reduced from 76 percent of ordinary revenues to 46 percent. The new sources of revenue established by Martin de Garay in 1817 did not raise sufficient income, and extraordinary expedients had to be used.

Partial reforms brought about increases in revenue later on. It is significant that the only one of the four traditional sources of revenue that increased between 1834 and 1842 was remittances from the colonies. This meant that the tax burden on Cuba and the Philippines had increased considerably. The liberals, faced with a fall in traditional sources of revenue and the insufficiency of what was raised from new sources, fell back on the remaining colonies, on disentailment, and on loans to finance the Carlist War. Loans could be obtained from the Banco de San Fernando, and advances (*anticipos*) could be raised with income from the overseas treasuries as a guarantee. Even after the 1845 reform, remittances from the colonies were about 5 percent of nonfinancial revenues until 1860, although their weight diminished radically afterward.

In summary, the main characteristics of this transitional fiscal system were as follows (see Table 5.2): (1) there was persistent recourse to public debt; (2) the provincial taxes (mainly the *alcabala*) and fiscal monopolies continued to provide the major portion of revenue: combined, they contributed about 40 percent; (3) the decline in trade and the increase in smuggling made customs receipts fall from 18 to 10 percent in the same period; (4) revenues from the Church fell from 13 to 7 percent; (5) remittances from the colonies fell from 14 to 8 percent; there was a certain rebound after they fell nearly to zero in 1815–33; and, (6) new taxes brought almost one fifth of the revenue. At the same time, taxes were made uniform for all citizens and all the different territories within the state (with the exceptions of the Canary Islands and the Basque country).

Modernization of *public spending* went hand in hand with the liberal revolution and became established after the Carlist War. The level of public expenditure followed a U-shaped curve during the first half of the nineteenth century: it reached a minimum in the early 1830s and then went up so that in the mid-1840s it reached a level similar to that at the beginning of the century. It would not appear that the level of spending was affected by the ideologies of the succeeding governments: there were other factors. Liberals and absolutists alike increased the level of spending in wartime and reduced it when funds were scarce. The containment of the level of spending during the second absolutist rule of Fernando VII (1823–33), for example, did not denote any ideological preference but rather a kind of imposed ceiling due to the fact that the regime was on the brink of financial collapse and refused to implement reforms that would have brought about greater revenues. Similarly, the growth in spending in the 1830s was more the result of a costly war than of the liberals' desire to expand state services.

From the latter years of the eighteenth century, the shortage of funds was such that many public obligations could not be met. The reduction in total spending meant that in the last years of the *ancien regime* sufficient resources could not be allocated to the Ministries of the Army and Navy in order to maintain the American colonies, to defend the country from the foreign invasions of 1808 and 1823, to prevent military coups and social unrest – in 1814 and 1820, or to put a rapid end to the civil war of 1833. The Spanish state of the first three decades of the nineteenth century – whether absolutist or liberal – could not even carry out the functions of defense and police, let alone justice. This inability to maintain order within, as well as to control national borders, had clear consequences for the Treasury. On the one hand, widespread smuggling heavily undermined the collection of customs duties. On the other, the shortage of funds was an obstacle to regular inspection and the collection of taxes.

Nevertheless, one can distinguish between the liberal and absolutist spending patterns. The absolutists' top priorities were the war machine and the royal family. They kept military expenditure very high even in times of peace, while the liberals paid more attention to government services such as public works, police, justice, education, and so on. The war-oriented nature of the budget was even greater than it seems because the costs and delayed payments of the War Ministry were channeled through the Ministry of Finance from 1798 on. Thus, in the early 1830s, military expenditures plus public debt payments gobbled up 82 percent of total spending; the royal household received an additional 12 percent, so that only 6 percent remained for other ministries. In the early 1840s, while military expenditures and public debt still amounted to 83 percent, royal expenditure had decreased to 3 percent, while other items saw their share expand to 14 percent.

While reducing military expenditure, in the 1840s the liberals also tried to reform the army so as to make it leaner and more professional. They succeeded only in part. As regards public debt, even though mismanagement persisted, the liberals made consistent efforts to improve its administration, but this was not achieved until the 1880s. The liberal outlook on civil spending was reflected in the creation of some new ministries: Interior, which appeared during the triennium, and largely replaced the army as domestic peacekeeper, and Public Works, established by the "moderate liberals" (*moderados*) in 1847. The liberal state also took over functions that had been carried out earlier, at least in part, by private individuals and the Church, such as the administration of local justice, education, custodial and administrative functions (archives, museums), and social assistance. Furthermore, after Church land and properties had been disentailed (*desamortización*) and its prerogative to receive the tithe (*diezmo*) had been abolished, the state assumed a steady subsidy to the Church as a compensation. In the long run, the state paid more in Church subsidy than it received from the sale of disentailed Church land.

Dwindling receipts and rigid expenditures produced chronic deficits, which oscillated between 20 percent of total spending in 1801–7 and 33 percent during the Carlist War (1833–9). Although budget deficits have been a constant in Spanish history, the situation grew markedly worse with the crisis of the *ancien regime* due to the causes we have examined: escalating war costs, rigid or decreasing tax receipts, mismanagement of the public debt. This was pointedly the case under Fernando VII, who fought the American Independence wars while obstinately refusing to reform the tax system and expecting to obtain or extort financial assistance from bankers while giving them little assurance that they would be repaid. As a consequence of these policies, the American colonies were lost and the Spanish state remained more in debt than ever. This was the situation the liberals inherited in 1833, with the addition of the Carlist War. No wonder *desamortización* appeared to them as the only solution to redress things promptly. Later on, thanks largely to the Mon–Santillán reform, they reduced the deficit, although they did not altogether do away with it. During the 1850–90 period, the average deficit was around 12.4 percent of total expenditure.

5.8 THE EFFECTS OF THE LOSS OF THE COLONIES ON THE SPANISH TREASURY

The repercussions of this loss on the Spanish economy have been assessed in different ways by economic historians. In Vicens Vives's view (1959), the loss of the colonies was the main cause of the financial crisis of the period and of the economic disasters that plagued Spain during the first half of the nineteenth century. According to one of his students, Josep Fontana (1971), with the loss of the colonial market, the Catalan bourgeoisie reoriented its production toward the domestic market and supported the bourgeois (liberal) revolution in order to stimulate domestic demand. Two fundamental sources of revenue were lost: remittances from the Americas and customs duties generated in transatlantic trade. Furthermore, the loss of remittances hurt the creditworthiness of the Spanish state.

Leandro Prados (1988, 1993) calculated that the loss of the colonies was not as catastrophic as Vicens and Fontana claimed. It did have certain negative effects in the short term, especially on the Treasury, and also deprived national industries of a protected market.[22] According to Prados (1988), the immediate impact was equivalent to a 3.9 percent reduction in national income, but in the medium term most sectors were able to adapt and the economy grew again, through a recovery of domestic demand and exports to Europe. Prados agrees with Fontana that the loss of the empire produced positive institutional effects because it favored the liberal or bourgeois revolution.

The long-term repercussions of the loss of the colonies on the Treasury, and on the Spanish economy as a whole, are difficult to assess, since they were amplified by two major factors: the French invasion (1808–14), and the latent civil war between absolutists and liberals, which became open in the 1830s. It is almost impossible to isolate the impact these factors had on the Spanish Treasury from those derived from the loss of the empire.

Furthermore, all the analyses of losses to the Treasury have only measured the reduction in revenues of the Tesorería General of Madrid, which was mostly limited to peninsular Spain. However, there was also an imperial Treasury with considerable autonomy, although ultimately administered from Madrid with considerable efficiency, as Carlos Marichal and Marcello Cormagni (Chapter 9 in this volume) have shown; its disappearance had added effects on Spain's finances. In addi-

[22] Although Prados maintains that the colonial markets had been lost before the end of the eighteenth century.

tion, when remittances from the mainland colonies faltered, Spain started to exploit Cuba and the Philippines fiscally.

To date, no study on the imperial Treasury as a whole has been undertaken (although this conference volume marks a significant step in that direction), but we know that the decisions regarding expenditure and revenue were always taken in the metropolis. The many and varied local *Cajas* and treasuries financed the spending of the different regions through the revenues they were able to raise. The treasuries with surpluses (*sobrantes*) made transfers to the others, mainly Madrid. Through the *situados*, the *Cajas* of New Spain and Peru were the main supporters of military spending in other colonies, as well as of the deficits of the Spanish Treasury. When the effects of the loss of the Mexican *situados* began to be felt, the tax systems within the colonies that were not lost were transformed so that, from usually being in deficit, they went on to produce regular surpluses. But although remittances from Cuba and the Philippines were still very high in the 1830s and helped to finance the war against the Carlists, those two colonies alone could not fill the gap left by the disappearance of the mainland revenues. So throughout the nineteenth century, finance ministers had to depend almost exclusively on tax revenues raised in mainland Spain. This was one of the reasons the tax system had to be reformed. The 1845 tax reform, therefore, was a long-term consequence of the loss of the empire.

While the tax system was being overhauled in Spain, however, it remained archaic in Cuba, Puerto Rico, and the Philippines, still based upon indirect taxes. Customs duties were the main source of revenue in Cuba and Puerto Rico, and the tobacco monopoly in the Philippines, to which was added the hated *tributo* (the poll tax paid by the natives) and some Church-related taxes, such as the tithe.

5.9 MONETARY CHAOS AND REFORM

The Spanish monetary system became seriously affected by the Peninsular War. Although the system was not legally modified during the conflict, it was greatly altered due to the vagaries of the struggle. The French invasion divided the country into two main areas, conquered and free, whose extensions varied. Furthermore, in the unconquered and liberated areas, several political units functioned at different times that tried to finance their war effort by issuing money and establishing new mints. In addition, in the French zone, French coins circulated freely in substantial amounts, and they tended to displace Spanish money by virtue of Gresham's law, since their silver content was less. Portuguese and English coins also circulated, although in lesser amounts. Portuguese coins, however, tended to stay in circulation because their silver content was also smaller.

These additions to the money supply did not imply a growth in the circulating medium, because they only partially compensated for the exportation of silver that went on as before, with the added problem that American remittances dwindled and then stopped. In these conditions the real problem was not that foreign coins caused inflation, but rather that they only partially compensated for the continuous hemorrhage of coined silver. In fact, there are indications that money was extremely scarce in the countryside: one of the causes of the failure of the liberal triennium was that its fiscal modernization required that the land tax be paid in coin, something that irked farmers, whose economy was largely a barter one.

As in fiscal matters, a distinction can be made between liberal and absolutist monetary policies. Absolutists, intent upon returning to the *ancien regime*, were loath to introduce changes in the monetary system. They did not want to admit that both the loss of the colonies and their eventual recovery required fiscal and monetary innovation. By and large, they expected to be able to borrow in the hope of recovering the lost colonies and going back to the days of steady silver inflows. The liberals also hoped to recover the empire, but they realized that the only way of winning the colonial wars was by backing the army with powerful financial means and also by offering the colonies a better deal than they had received before, which in practice would mean smaller silver remittances, if any. Both points implied that fiscal and monetary reforms were of the essence. But when the liberals finally were able to institute their reforms, the colonies had long been lost.

We have seen how slow the pace of fiscal reform was during the first half of the century. The difficulties with monetary reform ran largely parallel. The solution to the monetary problem, however, was simple. One of the long-term quandaries of the Spanish system was that silver was undervalued with respect to gold, according to the prices, official or otherwise, then prevailing in Europe. The Spanish bimetallic ratio was traditionally around 16 and even lower,[23] while in France it was around 15.5 and in England around 15. The result of this was, as we have seen, a steady outflow of silver. According to Sardá (1948, pp. 19–20), the Crown did not want to devalue gold because this would have implied lower seigniorage. As in the nineteenth and twentieth centuries, therefore, fiscal exigencies prevented the carrying out of an effective monetary policy by

[23] The 1772 reform had established a 15 ratio, but afraid that this might cause gold outflow, the king decreed a silver devaluation in 1779 that put it at 16. Further devaluation in 1786 lowered the ratio to 16.5.

the *ancien regime*. The liberal solution was to make the Treasury less dependent on seigniorage as a source of income by expanding the tax base while distributing the tax burden more fairly, and then to establish a bimetallic ratio close to the European average. An alternative policy would have been to maintain the bimetallic ratio but to lower seigniorage, thus making it more advantageous for private agents to carry specie to the mints for coinage. This is what the Cortes of the triennium tried to do in 1821 while forbidding the circulation of French coins. The return of absolutist rule in 1823 put an end to this experiment.

Fernando VII followed largely the same monetary principles during his two absolutist reigns (1814–20 and 1823–33). The old bimetallic ratio was maintained; in the old days this had produced steady exportation of silver, which was compensated for by American remittances. As these remittances now ceased or dwindled, the consequence was steady deflation. Coinage fell precipitously, and so did prices.[24] According to the *Hume theorem* this should have improved Spanish competitiveness and permitted balance of payments surpluses, which would eventually put an end to the exportation of silver. However, the Spanish economy at the time was too closed and near-subsistence for the Hume mechanism to function usefully. Fernando's solution was simpler: to borrow from bankers (most of them French) in order to fill the monetary gap and to finance the fiscal deficit all at once. This was an expensive solution, however. The colonies were lost, and the chances of repayment were rather dim; bankers, therefore, charged very high rates for their credit. According to Sardá (1948), of a total foreign debt outstanding of 4,460 million reales, only 1,000 effectively entered Spain during the "ominous decade" (1823–33). From a monetary standpoint, these amounts were a drop in the bucket. All in all, this was slightly over 1 percent of total gold and silver coinage during the period.

As to paper money, the circulation of the *vales reales* was very limited. It is true that in 1799, in an effort to improve their acceptability, they were declared to have full purchasing power. At that time, however, they were quoted at 5 percent of their face value, and it is very unlikely that they were in fact accepted in day-to-day transactions; even the state accepted them only in payment of some taxes at their market value. In 1818 they were demonetized, and this caused no problems because they were hardly used as money; it is doubtful that they were ever paid back in full by the government.

The Banco de San Carlos issued a few bank notes that had very limited circulation. Around 1803 some 58 million reales in bank notes were issued by the bank, but they were returned shortly afterward. They

[24] Tortella et al. (1970), Appendix 2, p. 287; Sardá (1947).

were accepted initially in exchange for the dreaded *vales reales* and immediately returned for conversion into specie. It is worth mentioning that, to the bank directors' surprise, more bank notes were returned than had been issued; obviously, some had been counterfeited.[25] Later on, the Banco de San Fernando, founded in 1829 to replace the defunct Bank of Saint Charles, also issued bank notes in Madrid, but the quantities were modest: about 24 million reales were in circulation around 1840 (Santillán, 1865, p. 221). The competition of a new bank, the Banco de Isabel II, founded in 1844, forced the San Fernando to increase its bank note circulation: by 1845 the joint fiduciary circulation of both banks was 110 million reales, still restricted to Madrid (Tortella, 1977, p. 54). In Barcelona the circulation of bank notes was even narrower in spite of the commercial and industrial character of the city: the Banco de Barcelona, its only chartered bank, had less than 20 million reales outstanding in 1846. So the total bank note circulation in Spain in the heady mid-1840s (it went down precipitously after 1847) was some 150 million reales, when by our own calculations, total gold and silver coinage amounted to some 2,240 million reales.[26]

Monetary reform arrived in the reformist 1840s. This was done by a decree of April 15, 1848, whose main novelties were the proclamation of the real as the official monetary unit, the establishment of the decimal system, and the maintenance of the bimetallic system with a new gold–silver ratio (15.77), which was almost immediately increased even further (to 15.6). The real had been the de facto monetary unit for centuries, but it was in 1848 that the maravedí, and the intricate system of accounting it implied, were abandoned. The total recoinage that the reform required, however, was never carried out. The problem at this time was that world gold output increased after 1850 due to the production of Californian and Australian mines. Before the authorities could complete the recoinage, Gresham's law got to work and gold started to displace silver from circulation. The Spanish authorities panicked and suspended gold coinage for a few years. The coinage in circulation remained heterogeneous, with eighteenth-century coins alongside French napoleons (five-franc silver pieces) and more modern Spanish coins.

5.10 THE MAIN FEATURES OF THE MON–SANTILLÁN SYSTEM

The new tax system, in spite of its virtues, had almost as much difficulty in balancing receipts and expenditures as had the *ancien regime*: Spanish

[25] Tortella (1997), Chs. 7–17, esp. Ch. 16.

[26] Tortella (unpublished-1), p. 19 (Table X). This does not include copper or *vellón*.

budgets were in deficit for all but four years in the nineteenth century after the reform was enacted (1876, 1882, 1893, and 1899). Let us now briefly examine the new tax and expenditure structure, as well as the main problems posed by the growing public debt.

The most important new tax was the *contribución territorial* (land tax), which supplied about 20 percent of ordinary income. It was collected in such a way that big landowners were undertaxed and small farmers overtaxed. The political clout of the landowning class and their opposition to statistical surveys prevented the formation of an accurate *Catastro*, so land tax assessments were based essentially on estimates by the landowners themselves. Furthermore, land taxes were assessed on the basis of local quotas (*cupos* or *repartimientos*): global tax payments were assigned to a given county and apportioned among taxpayers by the local officials; one can easily imagine that those with political power were not taxed heavily, and the burden was correspondingly shifted to smaller farmers. Thus, although the actual tax burden was not high, the clamor that was heard from many farmers about excessive taxation was not unjustified.

The *contribución industrial y de comercio*, a tax that fell upon industrial and commercial activities and that was also levied by a quota system, yielded about 5 percent of government revenue. It need not be said that if estimating the wealth in land and buildings was difficult, the difficulty of knowing the true taxable basis of commercial and industrial activities, where so many firms were small and informal, was even greater. These two direct taxes combined raised about 25 percent of total tax revenue; other direct taxes (on salaries and inheritances, and stamp duties) produced an additional 10 percent. Almost all of the rest came from indirect taxes, which were even more regressive. The mainstay of the system were the hated *consumos* (excises on food articles) and other consumer taxes, which included tobacco and salt taxes (in monopoly regime), and transport taxes (introduced later), plus foreign trade customs. All these combined yielded 40 percent. Of the remainder, the most important revenue was produced by *lotteries*, another monopoly, which yielded 8 percent, more than *disentailment* (6 percent) during the 1850–90 period. Other incomes worth mentioning came from state properties and franchises, from payments in lieu of military service, and from mint seigniorage. It is obvious that the tax system, even after the Mon–Santillán reform, was heavily regressive.

As to expenditures, about one third of the budget went to meet *debt payments and pensions*. Another third paid for *the military, the police, and the clergy*. Incidentally, the costs of maintaining the Church during those 40 years when incomes from disentail were at a maximum were actually higher than the amount earned from these sales. The economic ministries, *Finance* and *Public Works*, received another 27 percent of the budget. Three quarters of the Public Works budget was devoted to works proper, and 14 percent went to education. More than half of the finance budget was spent in the administration of lotteries and tobacco manufacture, and to reduce these high costs the tobacco monopoly was leased out in 1887. Among the remaining expenditures, 1.5 percent went to support the royal household, a considerable reduction from Fernando VII's days but a substantially higher proportion than today.

Perhaps the single most serious problem of budget administration during the second half of the nineteenth century was the gap between income and expenditure. The accumulated deficit from 1850 to 1890 rose to some 3,185 million pesetas, which implies an average yearly shortfall of 65 million (equivalent to 12.4 percent of expenditure, as we saw earlier). The result was a growing public debt. In turn, as we saw, a very large part of expenditure went to service this debt, imposing an enormous sacrifice on the country but still not large enough to cover total government commitments, so that the value of public bonds went down and rates of interest up. The long-term cause of this structural deficit is to be found in the breakdown of the balance established during the eighteenth century whereby the excess of expenditures over domestic income was offset by American remittances. The Spanish Treasury took almost a century to face the fiscal reality of the drastic fall in the colonial tax surplus. The great hope of the liberals in midcentury was that disentailment would replace American remittances, but, as we have seen, they were mistaken. Curiously enough, it was after the definitive liquidation of the empire in 1898 that a series of 10 successive budget surpluses was achieved for the first time in Spanish history.

5.11 TOWARD A MODERN FISCAL AND MONETARY SYSTEM

5.11.1 Fiscal and Monetary Problems of the Isabeline Period, 1850–68

During most of the century, the general tone of the debt problem and the solutions attempted followed, with little variation, the general pattern established during the reign of Fernando VII: continuous deficits, large accumulations of debt, and periodic "conversions" (*arreglos*), essentially partial repudiations more or less agreed upon with the creditors, who were frequently resigned to their fate and on many occasions taken advantage of. One can again make a distinction between the liberal and conservative positions toward the debt. The conservatives were much readier to resort to repudiation, whereas the liberals, more oriented toward development policies and laissez-faire economics, wanted to attract foreign capital and were therefore more in favor of fiscal responsibility. Their great panacea was land disentailment, which in addition to wresting power from the aristocrats and landowners (which it did not accomplish), increasing the area of cultivated land, and thereby production, and reducing food prices, was supposed to provide resources to fill the void that declining American remittances had left in the budget. Of the three missions the liberals assigned to it, disentailment accomplished only one: expanding acreage and food production.

The national debt increased during most of the nineteenth century, even though this growth was interrupted by various *arreglos*. In 1850 the total debt was about 3,900 million pesetas; by 1899 it surpassed 12,300 million, and it had reached higher levels in the 1870s. The three most important *arreglos* were those by Bravo Murillo (1851), Camacho (1882), and Fernández Villaverde (1899). Soon after the Mon–Santillán reform the new tax system showed its insufficiency, and interest payments on the debt were suspended because of the 1847–8 crisis; Bravo Murillo's settlement was an ill-camouflaged bankruptcy that unilaterally lowered both interest and principal on internal and external debts without in any way speeding up interest payments or capital redemptions. The indignation of English creditors was such that they managed to exclude Spanish securities from the London stock exchange. The debt was reduced slightly after 1854 thanks to the progressives' policy of using disentailment revenues to pay off bondholders, but this policy was later abandoned by the conservatives (*Moderados* and *Unionistas*), who preferred military adventures to meeting financial obligations. As a protest, the Paris stock market imitated London and excluded Spanish stock in 1861. From then on, the debt increased almost exponentially. The fiscal crisis in the late 1860s was one of the precipitating factors of the 1868 Glorious Revolution.

Monetary problems in the 1850s and 1860s stemmed largely from the difficulties derived from changes in the market bimetallic ratio and the lack of clear ideas on the matter on the part of the politicians. Silver outflows increased due to the fall in the market price of gold, which accentuated the undervaluation of the white metal in Spain in spite of the recent increase of the official bimetallic ratio by the 1848 reform. The first reaction of the Spanish authorities was to suspend gold coinage in 1851, which only made the problem worse because it caused deflation. This produced a further perturbation. Catalan token coin (calderilla), which was liberally manufactured by the Barcelona mint, invaded Castile in replacement of the vanishing silver. This calderilla was of the old nondecimal variety, only adding to the confusion in the circulating medium that was so characteristic of nineteenth-century Spain.[27]

Gold coinage was resumed in 1854 and the bimetallic ratio increased to 15.4, but the problems persisted. A new *monetary reform in 1864* attempted to alleviate these difficulties. The main idea of this new reform was to issue coin of rich *vellón* (or low-tenure silver) and token coin of bronze. It was thereby hoped that silver, thanks to its low alloy, would not be exported and that decimal bronze coins would replace the Catalan calderilla. Larger coins, however, would be of higher alloy. The new unit was the escudo, equivalent to 10 reales or to one half of a peso duro. The bimetallic ratio of 15.4 was maintained. The system may have worked, but it could not be put into practice, that is, a full recoinage could not be carried out, due to the onset of the 1860s crisis, which was especially severe in Spain.[28]

The problems of deflation were partially alleviated by a modest increase in banknote circulation. In January 1856 two laws framed a new banking system: the Banks of Issue Law admitted one of these per city; the Credit Companies Law gave wide latitude for the creation of industrial banks of the *crédit mobilier* type without any numerical limitation. In a few years some 20 banks of issue and more than 40 investment banks of very different sizes were established. This newfangled banking system was almost swept away by the mid-1860s crisis, but for 1865 the Spanish money supply has been estimated as shown in Table 5.4.

The figures are rounded because there is a degree of uncertainty. While we know fairly well the balance sheets of banks of issue, those of many investment banks are not available. We know that some of them issued "bonds" that circulated as bank notes, albeit probably within restricted circles. Although rough, therefore, Table 5.4 gives an acceptable picture of the situation at the time: silver had been reduced to one sixth of the money supply by constant outflows without the compensating American inflows of past centuries; bank money, however, provided a relative cushion by supplying one tenth of the total money stock. Sardá has written that this would have been the time for Spain to adopt the gold standard, since the yellow metal was then relatively plentiful. Things started to change soon afterward.

5.11.2 The Glorious Revolution: Monetary Reform and Financial Collapse, 1868–75

In September 1868 a military coup met with overwhelming popular support; Queen Isabel II abandoned Spain and later abdicated in favor

[27] Fernández Pulgar and Anes (1970), pp. 157–66; Sardá (1948), Ch. V.

[28] Sardá (1948), Ch. VI; Fernández Pulgar and Anes (1970), pp. 170–4; Tortella (1977), Ch. VII.

of her son. Thus opened a turbulent period in Spanish history, known as the *Revolutionary sexennium*, during which a provisional government, a regency, a monarchy under an Italian king, a republic, and a republican dictatorship succeeded each other, while Carlists in the north, anarchists in the south, and independentists in Cuba took up arms against the government. Finally, in the last days of 1874, Alfonso XII, the son of Isabel, was proclaimed king by another *pronunciamiento*. Thus was ushered in the long period known as the Restoration, which lasted well into the twentieth century.

After the 1868 Revolution the budgetary problem became intractable. The fiscal and general economic crisis caused by foreign and domestic factors (depression due to the fall in cotton prices at the end of the American Civil War, bankrupcy of Spanish railroads and the banking system, fiscal crisis, bad harvests) had contributed mightily to the political unrest that precipitated the Revolution. But the disorder that followed only helped to make matters worse. Taxes went largely unpaid: abolishing the *consumos* figured high in the revolutionaries' program, but how to replace them was left unsaid. Several experiments failed: yields plummeted while military expenditures soared due to increasing disorder and rebellion. As a result of all this, the public debt outstanding evolved as shown in Table 5.3.[29]

In the first years of the Revolution, governments found credit with some bankers and indebted themselves to pay arrears in the hope of being able to straighten things out in the future; but they could not, and after 1870 the situation got out of hand. While public debt outstanding went up, debt payments went down simply because the Treasury was unable to find the money. Budgets allocated smaller quantities to public debt payments each year, but the actual disbursements were far below the amounts allocated. In January 1874 a business weekly proclaimed: "The Spanish state is virtually bankrupt" (cited in Tortella, 1977, p. 542). In the face of such disaster the panaceas, the remedies, the agreements, the conversions, and the *arreglos* came tumbling one after another. In 1870 a lease contract for the Almadén quicksilver mines was made with the Rothschilds in return for a 42 million peseta loan. In 1872 the official Mortgage Bank (Banco Hipotecario) was chartered in exchange for a series of loans from the Banque de Paris et des Pays Bas, while the rate of interest paid on the debt was, once more, unilaterally reduced. In 1873 the Rio Tinto mines were leased out for 94 million pesetas. In 1874 the monopoly of bank note issue was granted to the Bank of Spain in return for a 125 million peseta indefinite loan. All in all, if the Revolution

[29] Prices were rather stable during the nineteenth century, although they increased from the mid-1850s to the mid-1860s and then went down gently until the mid-1890s. See Sardá (1948), pp. 299–315; Bustelo and Tortella (1976); Reher and Ballesteros (1993).

Table 5.3. Spanish Public Debt Outstanding, Selected Years (million current pesetas)

Year	Debt	Year	Debt	Year	Debt
1850	3,900	1868	6,138	1874	11,416
1857	3,482	1869	7,196	1875	11,574
1865	4,358	1870	7,289	1878	14,263

Source: Comín (1985), p. 130.

inherited a terrible fiscal situation in 1868, it bestowed an even worse conundrum on the Restoration in 1875.

The Revolution was more decisive in monetary matters. The first piece of revolutionary economic legislation was a decree in October 1868 on monetary reform whose avowed aims were (1) to break with the past and proceed to a general recoinage that would eliminate the symbols of the past regime and (2) to prepare Spain for eventually joining the Latin Monetary Union. To this end a new monetary unit was established, the peseta, a coin originated in Catalonia (*peçeta* in Catalan means "little piece") that had been circulating widely since the early eighteenth century and whose value was four reales or one fifth of a peso duro. It became the official unit simply because its value happened to be very close to that of a franc at the time. The franc was equivalent to 5.0 grams of silver; prior to October 1868 the peseta contained 5.19 grams. The October reform reduced the peseta's silver content to 5.0 grams, thus making it a "franc with a different name" and obviating the recourse to an entirely new unit. The system remained bimetallic, and the new ratio was as in France: 15.5.[30]

Spain never effectively joined the Latin Monetary Union, and it followed its own path on these matters. Recoinage proceeded apace, but the reversal of the market bimetallic ratio (due to the demonetization of silver in Germany, the general adoption of the gold standard, and increased world silver output – especially in the Nevada and Mexican mines)[31] again unbalanced the Spanish system. As the price of silver went down, Spain found itself in an entirely novel situation: silver flowed to its mints, while gold was exported. The Spanish authorities decided to suspend gold coinage in 1873, as had been done in 1851, but for the opposite reason: then it was estimated that there were too many gold coins around; now there were too few and in danger of being exported.

[30] Tortella (1977), pp. 512–14; Sardá (1948), Ch. VII; Fernández Pulgar and Anes (1970), pp. 181–6.

[31] See Flandreau (1996) on the causes of the demise of bimetallism.

Table 5.4. Spanish Money Stock and Money Supply Ca. 1865 and 1900 (million current pesetas)

	1865	1900
Bank notes	100	1,600
Deposits	60	960
Silver	250	1,300
Gold	1,100	395
MONEY STOCK		4,255
(Gold reserve)		(395)
(Silver and bank note reserve)		(610)
TOTAL RESERVE		−1,005
MONEY SUPPLY (M_1)	1,510	3,250

Source: Tortella (1977), Appendices E and F, and (1974), esp. p. 467, with minor modifications.

Another revolutionary novelty was the granting of the monopoly of issue to the Bank of Spain. This was a measure taken in a desperate effort to alleviate the fiscal problem. It was a stopgap decision but it had long-lasting effects on the monetary order because, although slowly at first, the Bank of Spain popularized bank notes and this changed the composition of the money supply. In order for the bank to be able to disburse its 125 million peseta loan, it was authorized to increase its bank note circulation; this was to be the pattern for many years to come (see Table 5.4).

5.11.3 The Restoration: Putting the House in Relative Order, 1875–1900

The Restoration inherited a financial system in shambles, and one whose situation was becoming worse every year, because as arrears accumulated, the deficit and the public debt grew. Among the emergency measures taken by Pedro Salaverría, the first finance minister of the Restoration, was an agreement he forced on the state's creditors that once again reduced interest payments. After reaching a century maximum in 1878, total debt outstanding started to inch down. In 1881–2, by means of the Camacho conversion, the interest and principal were drastically reduced through the creation of a new redeemable debt (*deuda amortizable*) at 4 percent. Juan Francisco Camacho, who had been finance minister during the revolutionary sexennium, had surely thought long and hard, from that time on, about how to resolve the crushing problem of the national debt, and he put his ideas into practice as soon as he returned to government eight years later.

The Camacho conversion was followed by a period of relative calm so far as the debt is concerned, thanks in part to the transformation of the monetary system, specifically the demonetization of gold. One of the outstanding features of the conversion was the guarantee that foreign holders of Spanish debt would be paid in Paris or London in francs or pounds sterling. These were the years when the peseta started to depreciate, a process that reached its peak at the century's end; under these circumstances, guaranteed payments in foreign money made the exterior debt very attractive, and many Spaniards invested in it to protect themselves from depreciation. The conversion was a success, but payments in foreign money involved a considerable export of gold, which combined with the commercial deficit and with speculative exports eventually nearly liquidated Spain's gold reserves by about 1890. From then on, punctuality in meeting payments on the debt once again became problematic. Since Spain probably did not have a steady basic balance of payments surplus at the time, the country again had to borrow to be able to keep paying interest on the debt. The situation was seriously aggravated by the beginning of the War of Cuban Independence in 1895, because financing the campaign produced a new growth in the debt, a steep rise in prices, and a major decline in the peseta on international markets. The disastrous outcome of the war necessitated yet another reform of the fiscal system, and this was achieved by the Villaverde stabilization. Among its measures were a new conversion of the debt and another settlement with the creditors entailing a further trimming of interest payments and other rights of bondholders. Furthermore, the so-called *affidavit* abolished payments in foreign currencies to debt holders who were either Spanish or domiciled in Spain. From then on, Spanish public debt was manageable and well managed. Raimundo Fernández Villaverde's reform included a wide fiscal overhaul whose most important novelty was the *contribución sobre las utilidades del capital mobiliario* (loosely translated as "tax on the yields of financial assets") which fell on salaries, debt bonds, securities yields, and company profits. Villaverde's reform was a great success on its own terms, and its most remarkable feat was a series of 10 budget surpluses.

The concession of the monopoly of bank note issue to the Bank of Spain could not, in the short run, save the country from financial chaos, but it did permit a drastic modification in the composition of the money supply. For one thing, the rapid expansion of bank notes and deposits popularized what we might call *bank money* at a rate that more than compensated for the disappearance of gold coins. For another, a passive policy stance in the face of rising gold prices during the 1870s, along with the abandonment in 1883 of the gold convertibility of Bank of Spain notes,[32] encouraged the disappearance of gold from circulation, and silver became the only metallic currency. In this way, within about 20 years the Spanish monetary system went from being a fully bimetallic one to being one of the few silver standards in Europe, precisely when the gold standard was being established throughout the world.

However, in spite of the adoption of a de facto silver standard that actually was a fiduciary standard, since the steady fall in the price of silver put the intrinsic value of coins far below their face value, prices remained relatively stable except for the years of the Cuban War (1895–8). There are various reasons for this stability: first, this was a period of falling prices in international markets; second, these were years of slow but steady growth for the Spanish economy, which brought with it an increase in the demand for money and credit; and third, in spite of having abandoned the discipline of the gold standard, and excepting the difficult years of the Cuban War, governments strived to maintain monetary restraint. If they were not even more restrictive with bank note circulation, this was due to the growing dependence of the Treasury on the Bank of Spain to finance the structural budget deficit. We find again that fiscal imperatives determined monetary policies.

In spite of the embarrassment of the monetary authorities toward the suspension of gold convertibility, this was probably the least bad solution. Rigid observance of the gold standard could have been an obstacle to growth. After all, Italy's frequent suspensions of gold convertibility did not prevent remarkable growth, while Portugal's adherence to it until 1891 does not seem to have been a stimulus to development.[33] The Spanish money supply grew slowly during the last quarter of the nineteenth century compared with other countries such as the United States, England, or France (Tortella, 1974, pp. 465–9), all on the gold standard legally or informally, by the way, but growth would have probably been even slower if the gold discipline had been maintained. In an underdeveloped country like Spain, the gold standard was an expensive luxury. The fiduciary standard had a serious drawback, however: it reinforced tariffs in increasing the degree of isolation of the Spanish economy.[34]

[32] The Bank was afraid that its gold would vanish if its bank notes were redeemed in the yellow metal at a time when the demand for gold was increasing due to the generalization of the gold standard and the payment of the Spanish foreign debt in gold-denominated foreign currency.

[33] Tattara (1995); Reis (1990); Braga de Macedo et al. (1996).

[34] For further discussion on the topic see Martín Aceña (1994) and Tortella (1974), pp. 480–1.

5.12 CONCLUSIONS

What was the meaning of the financial problem in the history of Spain? In other words, did the financial problem determine the course of Spanish history and could a different tax structure have made things different for Spain? Of course, only hypotheses and conjectures can be offered at the present time, but we submit them as a possible agenda for future research.

In spite of the serious shortcomings of the financial system of the Spanish Habsburgs, we would argue that they alone were not the root cause of the decline of Spain. In the first place, whatever the shortcomings of the tax structure and of the quality of debt management, the key problem was not one of quality but of quantity. In other words, the key problem was that Habsburg Spain overextended itself, and undertook a military effort that its subjects, no matter how fairly and efficiently taxed, would have been unable to pay for in any case. There was no conceivable tax reform within the *ancien regime* that could yield sufficient resources to support Spain's worldwide commitments and military enterprises. Furthermore, no matter how detestable, unfair, and incompetently managed Spanish finances were, they were not appreciably worse than French finances, and nevertheless in the end the French prevailed: there was no comparable decline of France, even though French finances were nearly as bankrupt and as incompetently managed as the Spanish (Crouzet, 1993; Dent, 1973; White, Chapter 3, this volume). Widely accepted comparisons of the English and French tax systems suggest that the burden of taxation was as unfairly distributed in England as in France, if not more so, and that while England's finances were more competently managed, the incidence of taxation was appreciably heavier in England (Mathias and O'Brien, 1976). Although this applies to the eighteenth century, it surely can be extended to the seventeenth. Britain's advantage, however, seems to have rested on the fact that the seventeenth-century revolution imposed a degree of respect for private property and citizens' rights, as well as a set of institutional innovations that were conspicuously absent in France and Spain (Capie, Chapter 2, this volume).

Where the Spanish experience seems to have been nearly unique is in monetary mismanagement. The dreadful *vellón* inflations and deflations in the seventeenth century constitute one of the most egregious examples of economic ineptitude in history, and this certainly helped to compound the blow that excessive taxation was inflicting on the Castilian economy. That this was clearly perceived by contemporaries is proven by the fact that Catalans and Portuguese rebelled when they believed that the Castilian tax burden and monetary system were going to be imposed on them (Elliott, 1963, Ch. XVII). It is also worth mentioning that, while Castile obtained a substantial and steady surplus from its American colonies, its overseas empire was spared the worst direct consequences of its seventeenth-century blunders.

However, the combination of an unfair and inefficient fiscal system, recurrent default on its public debt, frequent arbitrary confiscation of private citizens' property, and a notoriously incompetent monetary policy all contributed to the decline of Spain and its empire. As we argued earlier, it was not the fiscal shortcomings alone that caused the decline, but most crucially military overcommitment combined with grievous errors in general economic policy. Insofar as Spain's colonies inherited those policies and institutions, they were bound to have a painful transition to modernity. It took Spain a full century (the nineteenth) to reform and modernize its fiscal and monetary institutions. The Spanish-American cases studied in this volume seem to have a had a similarly long and tortuous passage.

Spanish fiscal and monetary policies, in turn, were strongly influenced by its colonial empire, not only while the grand empire existed, but even during the nineteenth century, when Spain was slow to adapt to the new realities in matters both fiscal and monetary. During most of the nineteenth century, Spain managed its economy and finances as though the empire were still standing: until the 1830s, its governments still nurtured the hope that the empire would be recovered and on these grounds refused to make radical reforms in the financial and monetary systems. Paradoxically, this lack of reform seriously hampered Spain's military effort in the Americas and thereby became self-defeating. When these reforms finally came in the 1840s, 1850s, and 1860s, with the imperial dream definitely abandoned, they were not sufficient to solve the problem of the structural deficit, and Spain remained entangled in its public debt quandary, which seriously hindered its monetary (and commercial) policies. Not until the definitive liquidation of the last remnants of the empire in 1898 was Spain able to balance its budget, substitute bank money for metallic currency, and start a sustained process of economic modernization.

REFERENCES

Anes, G. (1974). "La contribución de frutos civiles entre los proyectos de reforma tributaria en la España del siglo XVIII," *Hacienda Pública Española*, 27, pp. 21–45.

(1990). "La reforma de la Hacienda durante el reinado de Carlos III," *Hacienda Pública Española*, 2, pp. 7–12.

Anonymous (1862). "Breve reseña histórico-crítica de la moneda española y reducción de sus valores a los del sistema métrico vigente," in Gener (1862).

Artola, M. (1982). *La Hacienda del Antiguo Régimen*. Madrid: Alianza.

(1986). *La Hacienda del siglo XIX. Progresistas y moderados*. Madrid: Alianza.

ed. (1988). *Enciclopedia de Historia de España*, I. *Economía. Sociedad*. Madrid: Alianza.

Barbier, J. A. and H. S. Klein (1981). "Revolutionary Wars and Public Finance. The Madrid Treasury, 1784–1807," *The Journal of Economic History*, XLI, pp. 315–39.

(1985). "Las prioridades de un monarca ilustrado: el gasto público bajo el reinado de Carlos III." *Revista de Historia Económica*, III, pp. 473–95.

Bazant, J. (1977). *A Concise History of Mexico, from Hidalgo to Cárdenas, 1805–1940*. Cambridge: Cambridge University Press, NY.

Bilbao, L. M. (1990). "Ensayo de reconstrucción histórica de la presión fiscal en Castilla durante el siglo XVI," *Haciendas forales y Hacienda real. Homenaje a D. Miguel Artola y D. Felipe Ruiz Martín*. Bilbao: Diputación Foral de Vizcaya pp. 37–61.

Bleiberg, G. (1968). *Diccionario de Historia de España*, 3 vols. Madrid: Revista de Occidente.

Bordo, M. D. and F. Capie, eds. (1994). *Monetary Regimes in Transition*. Cambridge: Cambridge University Press, NY.

Braga de Macedo, J., B. Eichengreen, and J. Reis, eds. (1996). *Historical Perspectives in the Gold Standard: Portugal and the World*. London: Routledge.

Bustelo, F. and G. Tortella (1976). "Monetary Inflation in Spain, 1800–1970," *The Journal of European Economic History*, 5, pp. 141–50.

Carande, R. (1949). *Carlos V y sus banqueros*. Vol. 1, *La Hacienda Real de Castilla*. Madrid: Sociedad de Estudios y Publicaciones.

Comín, F. (1985). *Fuentes cuantitativos para el estudio del sector público en España*. Madrid: Instituto de Estudios Fiscales.

(1988). *Hacienda y economía en la España contemporánea (1800–1936)*, 2 vols. Madrid: Instituto de Estudios Fiscales.

(1990). *Las cuentas de la Hacienda preliberal en España (1801–1855)*. Madrid: Banco de España.

(1996). *Historia de la Hacienda pública, II, España (1808–1995)*. Barcelona: Crítica.

Comín, F. and P. Martín Aceña, eds. (1991). *Historia de la empresa pública en España*. Madrid: Espasa Calpe.

Crouzet, F. (1993). *La grande inflation. La monnaie en France de Louis XVI à Napoléon*. Paris: Fayard.

Dent, J. (1973). *Crisis in Finance: Crown, Financiers, and Society in Seventeenth-Century France*. New York: St. Martin's Press.

Dominguez Ortiz, A. (1960). *Política y Hacienda de Felipe IV*. Madrid: Revista de Derecho Privado.

(1984). *Política fiscal y cambio social en la España del siglo XVII*. Madrid: Instituto de Estudios Fiscales.

Elliott, J. H. (1963). *The Revolt of the Catalans. A Study in the Decline of Spain (1598–1640)*. Cambridge: Cambridge University Press, NY.

(1986). *The Count-Duke of Olivares. The Statesman in an Age of Decline*. New Haven and London: Yale University Press.

Fernández Pulgar, C. and R. Anes Álvarez (1970). "La creación de la peseta en la evolución del sistema monetario de 1847 a 1868," in Tortella et al. (1970), pp. 147–86.

Flandreau, M. (1996). "The French Crime of 1873: An Essay on the Emergence of the International Gold Standard," *The Journal of Economic History*, 56, 4, pp. 862–97.

Flynn, D. O. (1980). "La plata hispanoamericana y los mercados mundiales en el siglo XVI," *Moneda y Crédito*, 153, pp. 19–48.

(1982). "Fiscal Crisis and the Decline of Spain (Castile)," *The Journal of Economic History*, 42, pp. 139–47.

Fontana, J. (1971). *La quiebra de la monarquía absoluta, 1814–1820*. Barcelona: Ariel.

(1973). *Hacienda y Estado en la crisis final del Antiguo Régimen español: 1823–1833*, Madrid: Instituto de Estudios Fiscales.

(1977). *La Revolución Liberal (Política y Hacienda), 1833–1845*. Madrid: Instituto de Estudios Fiscales.

Fortea, J. I. (1990). *Monarquía y Cortes en la Corona de Castilla. Las ciudades ante la política fiscal de Felipe II*. Salamanca: Junta de Castilla y León.

García Sanz, A. (1991). "Repercusiones de la fiscalidad sobre la economía castellana de los siglos XVI y XVII," *Hacienda Pública Española. Monografías*, 1, pp. 15–24.

(1994). "Competitivos en lanas, pero no en paños: Lana para la exportación y lana para los telares nacionales en la España del Antiguo Régimen," *Revista de Historia Económica*, XII, 2, pp. 397–434.

Gelabert, J. (1997). *La bolsa del rey. Rey, reino y fisco en Castilla (1598–1648)*. Barcelona: Crítica.

Gener, J., ed. (1862). *Resumen de informes sobre la cuestión monetaria*. Madrid: Imprenta Nacional.

Hamilton, E. J. (1934). *American Treasure and the Price Revolution in Spain, 1501–1650*, Cambridge, Mass.: Harvard University Press.

(1947). *War and Prices in Spain, 1651–1800*. Cambridge, Mass.: Harvard University Press.

(1948). *El florecimiento del capitalismo y otros ensayos de Historia económica* (trans. A. Ullastres). Madrid: Revista de Occidente.

Helguera, J. (1986). *El Canal de Castilla*. Valladolid: Junta de Castilla y Leono.

(1991). "Las Reales fábricas," in Comín and Martín Aceña (1991), pp. 51–87.

Hernández Andreu, J. (1972). "Evolución histórica de la contribución directa en España desde 1700 a 1814," *Revista de Economía Política*, 61, pp. 31–90.

Ladero Quesada, M. A. (1973). *La Hacienda Real de Castilla en el siglo XV*. La Laguna: Universidad de La Laguna.

Llombart, V. (1994). "La política económica de Carlos III. Fiscalismo, cosmética o estímulo al crecimiento?" *Revista de Historia Económica*, 1, pp. 11–42.

Maixé Altés, Joan Carles (1994). *Comercio y banca en la Cataluña del siglo XVIII. La Compañía Bensi y Merizano de Barcelona (1724–1750)*. Coruña: Universidade da Coruña.

March, J. M. (1941). *Niñez y juventud de Felipe II*. Madrid: Fundación Universitaria Española.

Matilla Tascón, A. and M. Capella (1957). *Los Cincos Gremios Mayores de Madrid*. Madrid: Imprenta Sáez.

Martín Aceña, P. (1994). "Spain During the Classical Gold Standard Years, 1880–1914," in Bordo and Capie (1994), pp. 135–72.

Martínez, J. (1984). *La hacienda de la Inquisición (1478–1700)*. Madrid: Instituto de Estudios Fiscales.

Mathias, P. and P. K. O'Brein (1976). "Taxation in England and France 1715–1810." *Journal of European Economic History*, 5, pp. 601–50.

Merino, J. P. (1981). "La Hacienda de Carlos IV," *Hacienda Pública Española*, 69, Madrid.

(1987). *Las cuentas de la Administración central española, 1750–1820*. Madrid: Instituto de Estudios Fiscales.

Motomura, A. (1994). "The Best and Worst of Currencies: Seigniorage and Currency Policy in Spain, 1597–1650," *The Journal of Economic History*, 54, 1, pp. 104–27.

Moxó, S. (1963). *La alcabala. Sobre sus orígenes, concepto y naturaleza*. Madrid: Revista de Derecho Privado.

Otazu, A., ed. (1978). *Dinero y crédito (Siglos XVI al XIX)*. Madrid: Moneda y Crédito.

Parker, G. (1972). *The Army of Flanders and the Spanish Road, 1567–1659. The Logistics of Spanish Victory and Defeat in the Low Countries' Wars*. Cambridge: Cambridge University Press.

Pieper, R. (1992). *La Real Hacienda bajo Fernando VI y Carlos III (1753–1788)*. Madrid: Instituto de Estudios Fiscales.

Prados de la Escosura, L. (1988). *De imperio a nación*. Madrid: Alianza.

(1993). "La pérdida del imperio y sus consecuencias económicas," in Prados de la Escosura and Amaral (1993), pp. 253–300.

Prados de la Escosura, L. and Samuel Amaral, eds. (1993). *La independencia americana: consecuencias económicas*. Madrid: Alianza.

Pulido Bueno, I. (1996). *La Real Hacienda de Felipe III*. Huelva: Artes Gráficas Andaluzas.

Pulido Bueno, I. (1993). *Almojarifazgos y comercio exterior en Andalucía durante la época mercantilista (1526–1740)*. Huelva: Author.

Reher, D. and E. Ballesteros (1993). "Precios y salarios en Castilla la Nueva: construcción de un índice de salarios reales, 1501–1991," *Revista de Historia Económica*, XI, 1, pp. 101–51.

Reis, J. (1990). *A evoluçao da oferta monetária portuguesa, 1854–1912*. Lisbon: Banco de Portugal.

Ruiz Martín, F. (1968). "Las finanzas españolas durante el reinado de Felipe II," *Cuadernos de Historia, Revista Hispania*, 2, pp. 181–203.

(1990). *Las finanzas de la monarquía hispánica en tiempos de Felipe IV (1621–1665)*. Madrid: Real Academia de la Historia.

Sánchez Belén, J. A. (1996). *La política fiscal en Castilla durante el reinado de Carlos II*. Madrid: Siglo XXI.

Santillán, R. (1865). *Memoria histórica sobre los bancos Nacional de San Carlos, Español de San Fernando, Isabel II, Nuevo de San Fernando, y de España.* Madrid: Establecimiento Tipográfico de T. Fortanet.

Sanz Ayán, C. (1988). *Los banqueros de Carlos II.* Valladolid: Universidad de Valladolid.

Sardá, J. (1947). "Spanish Prices in the Nineteenth Century," *Quarterly Journal of Economics* (November), pp. 143–59.

(1948). *La Política Monetaria y las fluctuaciones de la Economía española en el siglo XIX.* Madrid: Consejo Superior de Investigaciones Científicas.

Schwartz Girón, P. (1996). "Juntar erarios y montes de piedad: un arbitrio barroco ante las Cortes de Castilla," *Revista de Historia Económica*, XIV, 1, pp. 53–90.

Smith, A. (1937). *An Inquiry Into the Nature and Causes of the Wealth of Nations.* New York: Modern Library (Edwin Cannan ed.) (orig. ed. 1776).

Sureda, J. L. (1949). *La hacienda castellana y los economistas del siglo XVII.* Madrid: Consejo Superior de Investigaciones Científicas.

Tattara, G. (1995). "Was Italy Ever on the Gold Standard?" Mimeo.

Tedde, P. (1983). "Comerciantes y banqueros madrileños al final del Antiguo Régimen," in Gonzalo Anes, Luis Angel Rujo, and Pedro Tedde, eds., *Historia económica y pensamiento social.* Madrid: Alianza/Banco de Esparia, pp. 301–31.

(1988a). *El Banco de San Carlos (1782–1829).* Madrid: Banco de España-Alianza.

(1988b). "El sector financiero," in Artola (1988), pp. 265–342.

(1989). "Política financiera y comercial en el reinado de Carlos III," in *Actas del Congreso Internacional sobre Carlos III y la Ilustración, Tomo III, Economía y Sociedad.* Madrid: Ministerio de Cultura.

Teichova, A., G. Kurgan-Van Hentenryk, and D. Ziegler, eds. (1997). *Banking, Trade and Industry. Europe, America and Asia from the Thirteenth to the Twentieth Century.* Cambridge: Cambridge University Press, NY.

Thompson, I. A. A. (1981). *Guerra y decadencia. Gobierno y administración en la España de los Austrias, 1560–1620.* Barcelona: Critica.

Toboso, P. (1987). *La deuda pública castellana durante el Antiguo Régimen. Los juros.* Madrid: Instituto de Estudios Fiscales.

Tortella, G. (1974). "Las magnitudes monetarias y sus determinantes," in Tortella, (1974), pp. 457–534.

(1997). "Banking and Economic Development in Spain," in Teichova et al. (1997), pp. 229–44.

(1977). *Banking, Railroads, and Industry in Spain, 1829–1874.* New York: Arno Press.

(1994). *El desarrollo de la España contemporánea. Historia económica de los siglos XIX y XX.* Madrid: Alianza.

(unpublished-1). "El Circulante Metálico en España a finales del siglo XVIII: Primeras aplicaciones de esta estimación para el cálculo de la Renta Nacional," mimeo.

(unpublished-2). "The Evolution of Spanish Money, 17–19th Centuries," paper presented at the preliminary session of the A Session on "The Legacy of Western European Fiscal and Monetary Institutions for the New World: The Seventeenth to the Nineteenth Century," Buenos Aires, Argentina (April).

ed. (1974). *La banca española en la Restauración. I. Política y finanzas*. Madrid: Banco de España.

Tortella, G., et al. (1970). *Ensayos sobre la economía española a mediados del siglo XIX*. Madrid: Banco de España.

Tortella, T. (1997). *Los primeros billetes españoles: las "cédulas" del Banco de San Carlos (1782–1829)*. Madrid: Banco de España.

Ulloa, M. (1977). *La Hacienda Real de Castilla en el reinado de Felipe II*. Madrid: Fundación Universitaria Española.

Vicens Vives, J. (1959). *Manual de Historia económica de España*. Barcelona: Teide.

Vincent, B. (1978). "Las rentas particulares del Reino de Granada en el siglo XVI: fardas, habices, hagüela," in Otazu (1978), pp. 249–78.

Zafra, J. (1991). *Fiscalidad y Antiguo Régimen. Las rentas provinciales del reino de Granada (1746–1780)*. Madrid: Instituto de Estudios Fiscales.

6

War, Taxes, and Gold

The Inheritance of the Real

Jorge Braga de Macedo, Álvaro Ferreira da Silva, and Rita Martins de Sousa

6.1 INTRODUCTION

6.1.1 Approach to the Currency Experience

War – and its implications for the expenditure side of the government budget – has always been associated with taxes. During most of the Portuguese monarchy, taxes included gold and other domain revenues coming from monopolies established on domestic and international trade. Together with silver and copper, gold was used as money, making its interaction with war and taxes central to the long-term pattern of economic growth and development.

The overview of Portuguese fiscal and monetary institutions from the seventeenth to the nineteenth centuries presented in this chapter is subtitled "The Inheritance of the Real" (plural réis), after the name of the national currency from 1435 until 1911.[1] To the extent that currency

We wish to honor the memory of Professor Teixeira Ribeiro, of Coimbra University and the Lisbon Academy of Sciences. Born in 1908, he influenced generations of Portuguese economists in the field of public finance and monetary economics (the latter is stressed in Macedo, 1980). He died on March 8, 1997, when we were finalizing the first draft of this chapter, which became *Nova Economics Working Paper No. 318* (henceforth MSS). We are grateful to Mike Bordo, Fernando Teixeira dos Santos, Nuno Valerio, and Eugenia Mata for comments received at a luncheon in Lisbon on the eve of the 12th International Economic History Congress in August 1998, where a summary of the paper was circulated. In his first presentation at the Lisbon Academy of Sciences on June 18, 1998, Macedo used the research available at the time, which he completed during a short stay at the National Bureau of Economic Research in late March 2000. He is now president of the Organization for Economic Cooperation and Development Centre, but the views cited here remain personal.

[1] There should be no confusion with the name of the Brazilian currency since 1994, even though Portugal and Brazil were politically united during most of the period, and the Portuguese monarchy ended only two decades after the Brazilian one.

experience is embedded in the overall evolution of fiscal and monetary systems, the legacy becomes a case study in institutional persistence and adjustment. In fact, the interaction of war, taxes, and gold implies a mix of fiscal, monetary, and exchange rate policies.[2]

Beginning in the sixteenth century, increasingly expensive warfare became a source of pressure for fiscal change. Times of war were also an auspicious context for the social legitimization of direct and indirect taxation capable of supplementing or replacing domain revenues. This legitimization linked taxation to private property rights in an almost "contractual" manner via the traditional representation of nobility, clergy, and towns in the Cortes. The custom that any new tax should be discussed there reinforced the financial freedom derived from the availability of a stable and convertible currency.

The inheritance of the real includes debates about the political and social legitimacy of taxes under changing military circumstances at home, in the overseas possessions, and in the European balance of powers. Due to the neutrality of Portugal during the Second World War, the link between war and taxes hardly involved the escudo (= 1,000 réis), but the growing level and changing composition of public expenditures brought back the need for national legitimization of taxes.[3]

Having stated the approach, this introduction proceeds with the outline of the chapter, provides a quantitative overview of the period 1555–1910 (Section 6.1.2), and explains the role of the Cortes in fiscal and monetary developments since the fourteenth century (Section 6.1.3). Section 6.2.1 emphasizes the role of domain revenues. Section 6.3.3 uses the structure of state revenue to reveal how the entrepreneurial domain state undermined the contractual basis of taxation, hindering reform and delaying economic development in the late eighteenth century.

The three following sections correspond roughly to the seventeenth, eighteenth, and nineteenth centuries. Guiding the analysis in the different subsections are changes in the monetary or fiscal regime, largely a reflection of the pressure coming from foreign invasions, as well as successive wars or revolutions at home. In Section 6.2, the pressure helps to explain the buildup against the union with Spain and the fiscal

[2] Standard open economy macroeconomic models of the exchange rate and of the balance of payments have been used in case studies of the performance of the classical gold standard in core countries in a volume edited by Bordo and Schwartz (1984). We are using them in even more remote institutional environments.

[3] After the euro succeeded the escudo in 1999, the mix between fiscal, monetary, and exchange rate policies reacquired some of the features of the gold standard, and of our interpretation of the interaction of war, taxes, and gold interaction. See Macedo (2000).

and monetary effects of the restoration war, respectively the early introduction of an income tax in 1641 (Section 6.2.2) and successive currency debasements until 1688 (Section 6.2.3). Section 6.3 presents the monetary and fiscal developments following the discovery of gold in Brazil, beginning with a characterization of the bimetallic monetary regime that preserved currency convertibility and stability until 1797 (Section 6.3.1). The drop in tax revenues from foreign and colonial trade and the risks of further involvement in the Seven Years' War led to a major reform of fiscal institutions in 1761 (Section 6.3.2).

The impact of the French invasions (1796–1808) on the tax system was most apparent in the efforts to overcome the tax immunities enjoyed by the nobility and clergy. The tax debate achieved almost the same salience as it did in pre-Revolutionary France. But it did not bring about an efficient, equitable, and simple tax system. Instead, mounting budget deficits resulted in the issuance of public internal debt. The transition to constitutional rule in 1820 was fraught with financial instability, including the first experience with inconvertibility followed by the transfer of the Crown to Brazil and currency devaluation. After the Brazilian declaration of independence in 1823, social unrest continued and led to a civil war (Section 6.4.1).

The redefinition of property rights and state functions is at the core of the political debates and actions attempting to build up a liberal state. Nevertheless, the establishment of representative institutions did not provide a new legitimacy for taxation. On the contrary, the liberal revolution was associated with the loss of social confidence and financial reputation, making the coexistence of political and financial freedom difficult, to the point where a major tax reform was introduced during civil war (Sections 6.4.2 and 6.4.3).

Up to the 1850s, many financial schemes designed to raise government revenue were tried, including debt issue, tax reform, forced debt, forced donations from the mercantile community, property confiscation, and privatization of state property. Eventually, there was a peaceful change in economic regime, involving compromises that softened political conflicts and maintained political and financial freedom for 40 years. Yet systematic resort to deferred taxation via external borrowing narrowed the domestic tax base and made the financing of public infrastructures unsustainable.

Domestic political instability returned, and the Baring crisis of 1891 was sufficient to force Portugal off the gold standard, keeping the real and then the escudo inconvertible for the next 100 years (Section 6.4.4). Section 6.5 concludes, stressing how forgetting the inheritance of the real may hurt Portugal's prospects in the eurozone.

Table 6.1. Income and Price Indicators for the Seventeenth to Nineteenth Centuries (percent per annum)

	Percentage of years $t = 356$	Growth rates				
		Pop (%)	GDP (%)	Deflator (%)	Money (%)	Gold Price (%)
1555–1640	24	0.3	0.5	5.3	n.a	0.2
1641–88	13	0.6	0.7	1.3	n.a	2.1
1689–1759	20	0.4	0.6	1.6	3.6	0.0
1760–97	11	0.4	0.5	1.7	0.9	0.0
1798–1834	10	0.5	0.4	–0.2	n.a	0.5
1835–54	6	0.6	–0.5	2.0	0.5	0.3
1855–90	10	0.7	2.6	1.1	3.5	—
1891–1910	6	0.8	1.7	0.6	0.7	0.7
Average	100	0.5	0.8	2.2	n.a	0.4

Source: See footnotes 4–7.

6.1.2 Overview of the Evidence

The empirical evidence that we have been able to assemble to back up our approach remains scanty, especially before the end of the civil war in 1834. The summary indicators reported in Table 6.1 should be interpreted accordingly.[4] Except for population, all series were collected from a variety of sources. Output data suffer from a serious break in 1834.[5] Price data link three different series in 1640, 1811, and 1867.[6] No money data exist before 1688 and between 1798 and 1833.[7]

[4] Annual data on prices in réis of gold, silver, and goods for the full sample period 1435–1910 and European convergence and fiscal indicators from 1834 to 1910 are reported in Appendix Tables 4 and 5 of Macedo, Silva and Sousa (2000).

[5] The series of population and gross domestic product (GDP) assembled by Angus Maddison for the OECD Development Centre, updating Maddison (1995) and forthcoming in Maddison (2000), include estimates for 1500, 1600, 1700, 1820, 1870, and 1913. They were interpolated to coincide with the periods recorded in Table 6.1. After 1834, the annual growth rates of GDP reported in Macedo (1995) were used instead (the Maddison rates would be 1.1 percent for 1835–54, 1.2 percent for 1855–90, and 1.3 percent for 1891–1910).

[6] The price indices assembled by Nuno Valerio and reported in Valerio (1997) were replaced by the estimates in Sousa (1999) for 1640–1810 and in Esteves and Marques (1994) for 1867–1910. The Valerio rates would be 6.8 percent for 1641–1688, 2.6 percent for 1689–1759, the same for 1760–97, .4 percent for 1798–1834, .5 percent for 1855–90, and .45 percent for 1891–1910.

[7] The money stock figures assembled in Sousa (1991) for 1834–90 were used instead of the ones reported in Neves (1994) for 1854–1910, but the average rate of growth for 1855–90 is the same. There are, nevertheless, disturbing differences in series attributed to Jaime Reis in Neves (1994, 249) and Mata and Valério (1994, 277), especially with respect to coins after 1890. The estimates in Sousa (1999) for money stock growth in 1689–1797

A quantitative monetary story based on trends in the velocity of circulation of money (obtained by dividing nominal income by the money stock) can be told only during one-half of our sample period. A downward trend can be attributed to increased monetization, lower interest rates, or a decline in hoarding.[8] Trends in the real price of gold can also be identified from Table 6.1, but English prices are not available before 1750, preventing a more accurate estimate of the real exchange rate.

Real exchange rate appreciation tends to cause a deficit in the current account of the balance of payments, which in principle will lead to an outflow of gold and in time bring about real exchange rate depreciation – completing the cycle. Changes in the nominal exchange rate may accelerate the process of real exchange rate adjustment if they do not generate the expectation of a continuously depreciating currency, which would wipe out the competitiveness gains through inflation.

This pattern of adjustment is seen over three century-long cycles of real appreciation and depreciation – 1555–1688, 1689–1834 and 1834–1910 – with varying exchange rate regimes within each of them. The upward trend in world prices during the first cycle dampens the rate of appreciation and magnifies the rate of depreciation relative to what can be calculated from Table 6.1. After the 1650s, the downward trend in world prices has the opposite effect until prices pick up in the late 1700s and become very volatile during the 1792–1813 period. Foreign deflation follows until the 1890s and inflation thereafter, magnifying again both relative price trends.

The nominal exchange rate remained fixed during most of the second cycle, with the resulting payments deficit being financed by outflows of gold. This allowed high private consumption growth and may justify the contention that "Portugal was one of the five richest countries in 1800."[9]

were used, including 1,378 contos in Castilian patacas in 1687 and then from 1702 and 1775 (without the deterioration factor of 1 percent assigned to domestic gold and silver coins). The required recoinage of foreign coins led the annual rate of money growth to fall by .5 percent during the first half of the eighteenth century. The gold price series is from Sousa (1999) until 1854; the sterling exchange rate from Mata and Valério (1996) is used thereafter.

8 Monetization and financial development would make the income elasticity of money greater than 1. Bordo and Schwartz (1984, p. 422) mention that in these cases money is like a "luxury good."

9 Bairoch (1976), who added that "it was amongst the three or four poorest in 1913." Divergence was most acute in the nineteenth century, even though, according to the data reported in Table 6.1, per capita income grew at an annual rate of only .1 percent in 1760–97. The quote is in Macedo (1995, note 3), where other convergence data are presented for the three subperiods in Table 6.1: –2.71 percent in 1834–54, 1.115 percent in 1855–90, and –0.15 percent in 1891–1910. See footnote 72.

Comparing Portugal to the Western European average, there is a slow convergence during the sixteenth century, from 70 percent to 74 percent, and then the per capita income ratio falls to under 40 percent in 1913.[10] This long divergence fits well with collective memories of "decadence" after the discoveries of the sixteenth century.

The unavailability of reliable national account data makes it difficult to establish the growth and development pattern for the nineteenth century. Even today, the monetary and fiscal overtones of decadence continue to be felt in collective memories. Still, with the distant horizon provided by Table 6.1, the alleged incompatibility between democracy and financial discipline disappears and the uneasy relationship between civil rights and financial freedom ceases to be grounded in the monetary history of Portugal.

Until further research leads to a satisfactory series of nominal income and the money stock, any assessment of the inheritance of the real will remain provisional. Nevertheless, the roots of the political and social legitimacy of taxes, sometimes called the *fiscal constitution*, will continue to be part of this inheritance.[11] For most of the the 200-year period between the Spanish and French invasions, the root was war. Table 6.2 shows the rising share of military expenditure, while the ratio of taxes to debt rises from 1588 to the 1760s.

Table 6.2 also shows the balance between revenues coming from domain sources and other revenues having their origin in taxes, the relative weight of indirect versus direct taxes, and the share of Lisbon.[12] These features of the fiscal constitution will be illustrated later, together

[10] The percentages were obtained using Maddison's (2000) data. The ratio rises to 41 percent in 1950 and 61 percent in 1973 and reaches the 1500 estimate of 70 percent in 1997. There is divergence even relative to world per capita income from 1820 (127 percent) until 1913 (85 percent). Similar evidence is reported in Macedo (1999) with a different source.

[11] This term is used in the political economy literature to describe relations between the state and the population involving both taxes and transfers. It includes the institutions enforcing the social contract and thus incorporates various exchange rate regimes, monetary standards, and state revenues: In particular, the existence of several redistributive revolutions during the twentieth century and the political instability observed during most of it did not change the fiscal constitution all that much, to the point that the resilience of public and private interest groups seeking transfers from the state and thereby holding on to the tax base still helped Macedo (1999) interpret Portugal's European integration. The complementarity of political and financial freedom is stressed in Macedo (1996) and footnote 50.

[12] Years when available information included all sources of state revenues were selected. The data for 1716 are seemingly incomplete, as the *décima* tax is not mentioned. In addition, revenues collected in the State of India and in the Atlantic empire were not considered, unless they were directed to mainland Portugal, as, for instance, the gold duties or the *donativo* tax. For more details see MSS, especially notes 12 and 13.

Table 6.2. Summary Fiscal Indicators: Seventeenth to Nineteenth Centuries

	1588	1619	1716	1762–76[a]	1801–3[a]
Military % of total expenditures	26			52	70[b]
Total revenues as % of debt	56			87	61
Total revenues in 1750 (1,000 contos)	1.3	1.8	5.1	4.9	3.6
Décima (% of total)	—	—	—	12	9
Customs and excises (% of total)	68	75	58	40	54
(% from Lisbon)	(54)	—	(60)	(68)	(76)
Domain revenues (% of total)	32	25	42	49	38

[a] Annual average.
[b] 1801.
Source: MSS, Appendix Table 1.

with the role of gold among domain revenues, rising in the 1700s, then falling and precipitating the financial crisis of the early 1800s.

6.1.3 The Cortes and the Fiscal Constitution

The threat of invasion from Spain existed throughout the Middle Ages and explains a fiscal constitution in which military expenditures had to be financed through innovative forms of taxation. It also helps to explain how the Cortes, a traditional form of representation of nobility, clergy, and towns, acquired such an important say in fiscal and monetary affairs.

In 1435, after several debasements, in order to finance the wars against Castile, the libra (the first national currency, created in 1253) was replaced by the real. One gram of gold was then worth 35 réis, but successive devaluations brought the price to 107 réis in the early 1500s. On the side of taxation the crucial date is 1387, when, for the same reason, the excise (*sisa*), previously a municipal tax, was transformed into a universal tax with a comprehensive base.[13] The late medieval states attempted to seize and tax new sources of wealth, mostly associated with the growing urban economy, in other European countries, such as Spain and France.[14]

The creation of the *sisa* was approved by the Cortes and, to that extent, the tax had a "contractual" origin. Moreover, its general character, its incidence, and its collection methods were extensively discussed in the Cortes of the 1400s and beyond. The fact that the Cortes approved the first general tax imprinted the fiscal constitution. Even though no

[13] On the *sisa* and on the pre-real (1 real = 35 libras) period, see MSS, note 2.
[14] Ormrod (1995) presents evidence on this historical trend.

written law existed on the fiscal relations between the Crown and the subjects, tradition and custom required that any new tax should be discussed in the Cortes.[15]

In spite of the remarkable innovation in tax design represented by the *sisa*, tax administration proved difficult. To make the collection of the excise on movable goods easier, the crown and each municipal corporation agreed in 1525 by contract that a fixed sum (*encabeçamento*) would be due. Municipal councils would be free to set tax parameters so as to raise the predefined amount (*cabeção*).

The only exception was the city of Lisbon, whose excise and *real d'água* (sales tax) were either directly collected by the Crown or tax farmed. The local self-taxation did provide a resolution to conflicts between taxpayers and Crown, but at the cost of a high degree of regional inequality in the distribution of the tax burden. In real estate transactions, municipalities requested a rate from nonresidents higher than that from residents. The tax began to be applied as a sort of toll on goods carried by outsiders into the towns, with negative effects on internal trade and economic specialization between different regions.

As a result of these attempts to tax primarily outsiders, inhabitants of a given municipality could be exempted from the payment of the excise on movable goods, since the *cabeção* was raised from the tolls or from the excise. As happened in Spain after the *encabezamiento general* of the excise in 1536, the change in the method of taxation caused revenue to stagnate. Furthermore, this transfer of tax responsibilities to municipalities reveals the incapacity of the Crown to build up an infrastructure for tax administration across the territory. Concentrating tax collection in the city of Lisbon made it easier to administer.

Portugal was also present in international credit markets, although to a lesser degree than Spain, well before the seventeenth century. Seeking better access to northern European financial markets, where Genoese and German bankers were most active, the Crown established the Feitoria da Flandres in 1508 and issued loans in Flanders through bills of exchange, payable in three months. Until the 1550s, the increase in these credits implied the renewal of the bills and accumulated interest. The bills of exchange were instruments of transfer and credit. The cargo of the spice fleets, namely pepper, served as collateral.

Creditors had accepted registered bonds, called *padrão de juro real*, paying a fixed rate of interest and carrying a variable price since the early 1500s. A public deed was necessary to sell these bonds, making them similar to real estate. In 1560, the Crown consolidated and transformed royal debt in *padrões de juro*, with interest of 5 percent, payable only in

[15] Cardim (1998) discusses this tradition and its practice throughout the seventeenth century.

the kingdom. This measure hurt foreign creditors who did not have a local residence and explains why the interest rate charged on external debt rose to 12–16 percent, much higher than the one set for domestic instruments.[16]

6.2 SPANISH RULE AND THE RESTORATION WAR

6.2.1 Domain Revenues

Seigneurial duties and other domain revenues are remnants of a time when it was thought that the sovereign was entitled to have enough land so as to be able to "live from his own means." They include any items that are part of the patrimony of the Crown and can be directly exploited, rented, or donated.[17] Revenues from trade in pepper, slaves, *pau brasil* (timber), or gold from Mina, in eastern Africa, must be considered as domain or patrimonial revenues too. They were a source of income for the Crown, associated with a royal trade monopoly whose importance is far greater than that of the traditional domain revenues: for instance, in 1587, these monopolies account for at least 207 contos (= million réis or thousand escudos, a unit still in use) net of the slave trade and sugar from Madeira, while the traditional "domain income" (rents from land and houses or seigneurial duties) was responsible for 45 contos. Nevertheless, monopoly revenues fell from one-third to one-fourth of the total between 1588 and 1619 due to difficulties in the pepper trade and to the low cargoes of gold coming from Eastern Africa.

Indirect taxes were the other main source of state revenues. There were taxes on internal circulation, transactions and consumption, and also custom taxes, which were responsible for over two-thirds of revenue in 1588 and three-quarters in 1619. Relative shares were reversed between the two years: The excise declined from 40 percent to 36 percent, while customs increased from 27 percent to 39 percent. In Lisbon, the sales tax *real d'agua* was collected in addition to the excise. Revenues increased to the point that, in 1588, Lisbon accounted for over

16 On the consequences of this measure, see Macedo, Silva and Sousa (2000) note 5. On the definition of public debt, see MSS note 6 and Appendix Table 1.

17 Domain revenues include rents from land and houses, seigneurial duties over farmers, and some other personal rights, which, in the taxonomy of state revenues proposed by Manuel Severim de Faria in the early 1600s, were labeled as *proprios*. They were mostly received in kind and in 1588 accounted for 6 percent of total revenue; this is the reason patrimonial revenues are sometimes claimed as "almost non-existent" in Hespanha (1986, p. 214). Scandinavian countries also based an important part of their revenue on domain duties or incomes from land, silver, and copper. Prussia, through the acquisition of new territory, which was incorporated in the patrimony of the king, is another example.

half of the revenues coming from the excise and other indirect taxes. Most of the duties on foreign trade were also collected at Lisbon's customs house, so that the rest of the country became less and less relevant to the Treasury.[18]

The financial importance of Lisbon throughout the seventeenth century is evident in another issue. During the union with Spain, the municipality of Lisbon served as guarantor of the consolidated debt emissions, with the local taxes on transactions (*real d'água* and *realete*) serving as collateral. In 1630, 120 contos were raised through this system, proving the apparent creditworthiness of municipal finances.[19] After the restoration of 1640 and until 1679, the Crown kept using this method to finance public expenditures.

6.2.2 The Income Tax

The tax burden rose during the last decades of the union with Spain. The end of the truce with the Netherlands in 1621 and the Spanish struggle in the international arena influenced Portuguese tax revenues in two ways. First, the Atlantic trade declined and with it revenues coming from customs and monopolies. Second, the Spanish Treasury needed a more substantial contribution from Portuguese taxpayers.

From 1621 to 1640, several administrative decisions were taken in order to raise taxes. Extraordinary levies (*serviços*) were imposed on the mercantile community of Lisbon and the municipalities of the kingdom; a new duty on salt was introduced in 1631; the *encabeçamentos* of the excise were increased in 1635; the *real d'agua* was extended to all the regions in 1635; and an income tax on officers and privileged people (*meias-anatas*) was introduced in 1631. Efforts were also made to require stamped paper (*papel selado*) on the appeals presented to the administration.

These attempts to increase taxes were responsible for the only tax revolts occurring before the constitutional regime. They eventually led to the overthrow of the Spanish rule and the foundation of a new dynasty (known as *restoration*) on December 1, 1640.[20] One of the first measures taken by the new government was to repeal any tax increase instituted during the union with Spain. Nevertheless, new taxes were needed to pay

18 Taxes on transactions and consumption in Lisbon rose between 1588 and 1619, but their share was 12 percent in both years, whereas the share of taxes collected across mainland Portugal dropped slightly. Unlike other indirect taxes, revenue from the excise declined from 1588 to 1619 (from 204 to 194 contos, as shown in Appendix Table 1 in MSS).

19 Hespanha (1993, 224–5) points out that selling *padrões de juros* continued to be a means of financing public expenditures.

20 References to the broad economic and social background are found in Mss, note 19.

for the war against Spain and for the claims on overseas possessions brought by the Dutch and the English. Selling *padrões de juro* or converting debts into these registered securities was another means to finance the independence effort.[21]

State revenues are not available for the early 1640s. However, the cost of an army with 20,000 men in infantry and 4,000 in cavalry was 65 percent higher than total revenue in 1619, when the financial situation was more favorable.[22] Access to financial resources was thus essential in order to pay for the military effort against Spain.

The creation of the first direct tax – the *décima* (tithe), in 1641 – should be seen in this light. As with the 1387 excise, a deliberation taken in the Cortes gave legitimacy to the tithe. The base is far broader than that of direct taxes collected in other European countries: Rents from real estate (the preferred form of wealth accumulation at the time), labor income, earnings from professional activities, profits from commercial or industrial activities, and even interest income were taxable.

The second statute of the *décima* (1654) introduced, for the first time, the procedures for a land and house survey in order to assess taxable value, as well as the registry of the occupational status of all the people living in each parish. The only exception to the incidence of this tax was the real estate held by the Catholic Church or welfare institutions. Nevertheless, land and houses belonging to the members of the clergy as personal property were taxable.[23]

The revenue of 200 contos recorded for 1660 and 1681 suggests that the *décima* accounted for 20 percent of revenues received, about the same as the excise collected in Lisbon. The *décima* then overtook the excise as a source of revenue to the Crown and ranked next to customs (366 contos). In addition, the excise and similar taxes collected in Lisbon amounted to 144 contos in 1660, almost 75 percent of the revenue coming from the excise across mainland Portugal. Revenue from the excise collected through the *encabeçamentos* paid by the municipalities stagnated throughout the 1600s.

After the end of the restoration war in 1668, the Cortes of 1697 asked for the withdrawal or at least a reduction of the tax. Through a decree of March 28, 1698, the Crown chose the second alternative. The participation of Portugal in the War of the Spanish Succession resulted in a

[21] Voluntary donations from the Catholic Church and from the mercantile community, together with individual contributions from leading Jewish merchants and financiers of Portuguese origin living in Amsterdam, helped the Treasury as well.

[22] According to Cardim (1998, p. 101), the cost was almost 1,700 contos.

[23] Silva (1988, 1993) presents the characteristics of this tax, methods of taxation, and interest to historical research. See also the references in Hespanha (1993, pp. 217–18).

decree of May 26, 1704, raising the *décima* from 4.5 percent to 10 percent, this time without any consent of the Cortes.[24] Conversely, the end of the war and the period of prosperity opened up by gold mining and commercial dynamism brought the tax rate to its earlier level.[25] Only the Seven Years' War, 50 years later, led to a new reform of the income tax (see Section 6.3.2).

6.2.3 A Hidden Tax: The Debasement of the Currency

In the 1500s, prices were rising but the currency was fairly stable. Until 1640, the real depreciated from 11 to 13 réis per gram (about 20 percent) in terms of silver and from 107 to 142 réis per gram (about 25 percent) in terms of gold. The absence of war threats and the discovery of precious metal in Africa and America helped maintain stability. But there were several devaluations, two of which were in double digits: against gold in 1555 and against silver in 1573. The real price of gold decreased at an average annual rate of 5 percent from 1555 to 1640, evident in Figure 6.1 (where the series are from MSS, the same as those used in Table 6.1).

Records of the inflows of precious metal by the Lisbon mint suggest that on the eve of the restoration, silver was the predominant specie in domestic circulation. Foreign money was used and accepted in domestic circulation, particularly Castilian dobrões (from 1643 to 1646), and patacas and meias patacas coined in the Spanish mints.

The increase in expenditure financed by the Treasury, mainly for the restoration war, was the justification for successive currency debasements. From 1641 to 1688, the nominal price of gold rose from 142 to 487 réis per gram (a price that would not be changed until 1822) and the price of silver from 16 to 31 réis per gram. These successive devaluations of the exchange rate had a fiscal objective, increasing revenue through seigniorage, in addition to stemming the outflow of domestic coins.[26] The resulting real devaluation rate from Table 6.1 comes to .8

[24] This is why the period after 1697 has been called *absolutism*.

[25] Decree of November 25, 1715, lowered the *décima* to 4.5 percent but revenues coming from this tax were not included in the 1716 list published by Santarém. See MSS Appendix Table 1.

[26] This devaluation policy was discussed at the time by the Conselho da Fazenda (Treasury Council), which was created in 1591 to rationalize and centralize a more archaic system, following the experience of Spain, and which became responsible for monetary affairs with the decree of February 13, 1642 (Peres, 1959). The details of minting operations do not include the precise timing of devaluations and of price rises. If prices rise immediately after the devaluation, there is no revenue gain from debasement, as pointed out by Bordo (1986). Godinho (1978) presents revenue figures for 1681 where the Lisbon mint represents 2.4 percent of total revenues. However, it was a year with other monetary changes, the revenue came only from the Lisbon mint, and other stamp houses were in operation, so no conclusion can be drawn.

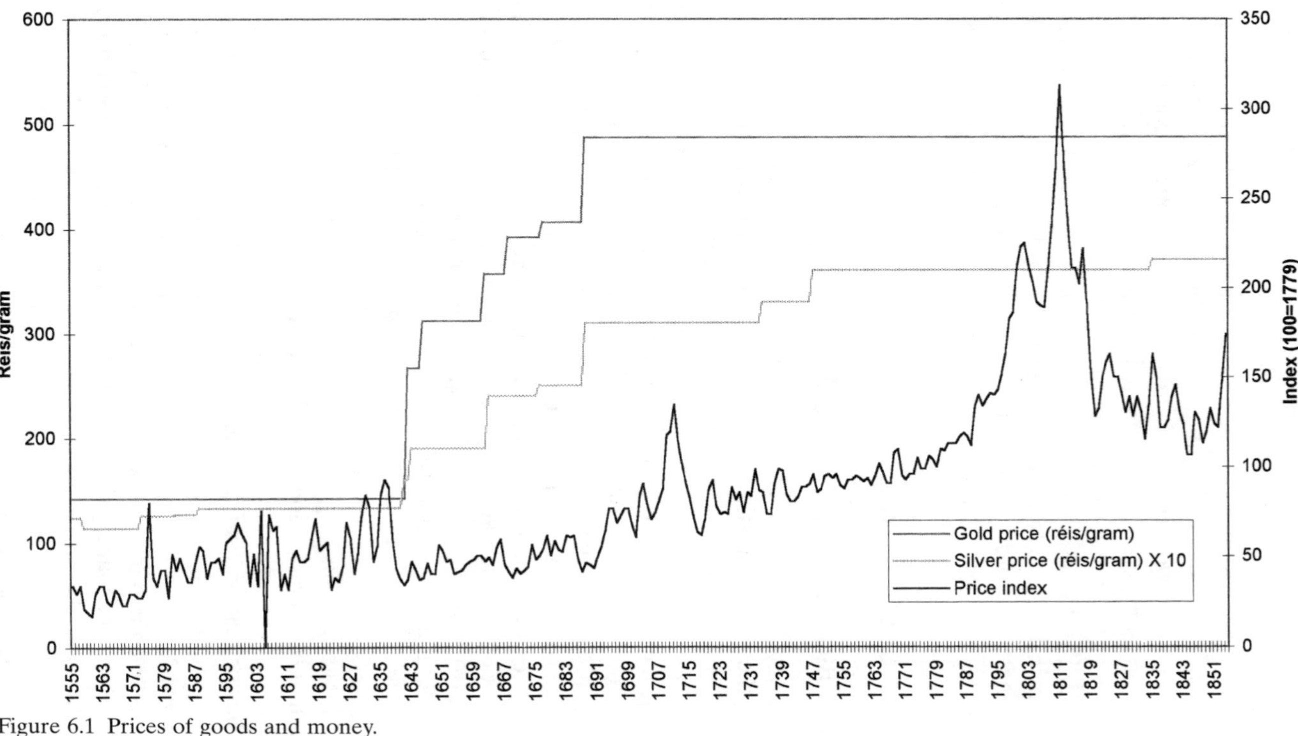

Figure 6.1 Prices of goods and money.

percent per annum, offsetting in part the real appreciation of the previous period.

There are frequent references to the shortage of coins, especially silver, explicitly acknowledging the outflow of precious metals, both in coins and as worked metal, to northern European countries. Portuguese coins, especially silver coins, had the best alloy, and debasing the currency was supposed to prevent gold and silver from flowing out of Portugal. The different valuation of precious metals among the countries with which Portugal traded was considered to be the primary cause of the monetary outflows but, in the 1680s and 1690s, the trade balance deficit began to be mentioned as a factor in the drainage of precious metals.

6.3 THE GOLDEN AGE

6.3.1 A Bimetalic Monetary Regime

In 1693, gold was discovered in the Caité area of Minas Gerais, Brazil. Part of the gold mined there was due to the Crown, through the so-called *quinto*, which from 1735 to 1750 was replaced by the *capitação*.[27] Taxes, revenues, and services were paid in bullion, coin, and even gold dust, in spite of legislative prohibitions registered in some periods, to the treasury of the Conselho Ultramarino (Overseas Council, created in 1642 to deal with empire questions except those connected with Africa).

Gold arrived not only in bullion and dust, but also in coins minted in Brazil, such as in the Rio de Janeiro mint (since 1702) and the Baía mint (since 1714). A significant share of gold was coined in these mints. Their existence must be justified as a way for the state to control precious metal at the source, thus reducing fraud on the journey to Portugal. Table 6.3 presents the amounts of gold coined, the percentage of coinage accounted for by private persons (as opposed to the Crown), the percentage of coins in gold (as opposed to silver and copper), and the percentage of gold coinage in the total arrivals of gold, mostly from Brazil.

The correlation coefficient between annual inflows and the amounts coined is quite low. The explanation lies in the great quantity of gold coins exported to Portugal, particularly after 1751. Between 1704 and 1789, gold coined in the Lisbon mint was only 61 percent of the coinage of the Rio mint, making the gold minted in Brazil decisive in Portuguese monetary circulation.[28]

[27] References in Macedo, Silva and Sousa (2000), notes 30 and 57.

[28] Sousa (1999, pp. 116, 226–9). Morrison (1999) uses chemical properties to identify the share of gold from Brazil in the French money stock.

Table 6.3. Coinage of Specie in the Lisbon Mint

Year	Gold (1,000 contos)	% Private	% Total	% Arrival
1688–1700	3.9	n.a.	73	n.a.
1701–10	9.5	95	84	106
1711–20	11.1	89	100	31
1721–30	12.8	49	100	19
1731–40	15.6	29	100	23
1741–50	20.9	52	97	34
1751–60	14.2	21	99	32
1761–70	9.4	14	91	26
1771–80	4.7	11	92	16
1781–90	2.2	18	66	20
1791–7	.9	49	37	n.a.

Source: Computed from annual data in MSS, Appendix Table 2.

In the entire period 1699–1788, gold minted in Lisbon was less than one-third of the arrivals of Brazilian gold. The coinage ratio rose before 1720 and in the 1740s and 1750s, while arrivals peaked in the 1730s and 1740s. Of course, the activity of the Rio and Baía mints was not exclusively directed to Portugal, but also to the internal circulation of the colony. The Lisbon mint also coined provincial silver and copper coins, mainly for Brazil, adding another overseas monetary connection.

On the fiscal side, the tax revenues included not only seigniorage, but also an additional due equal to 10 percent when the coinage was provincial.[29] Money was not evenly distributed across regions. Like any economy with strong export-oriented production, Brazil had more coin in circulation in the coastal regions that were directly dependent on international trade. In the mining region the circulation was in gold dust, the only local production, and in agricultural regions cattle served as a means to make transactions.[30]

Because Brazil was running a trade deficit, coins minted there arrived in Portugal together with exports of bullion. When the Rio mint began operations, most of the gold coins coming into Portugal belonged to private individuals. After the 1720s, they resorted less and less to the Lisbon mint to have their gold coined. This, in turn, implied a rising share of coinage for the Crown. Moreover, the creation of Brazilian mints provided the colony with monetary circulation that was not totally

[29] The intention to standardize the currency system throughout the empire documented in "Papel sobre a moeda por Bernardo Vieira Ravasco" in *Manuscritos Originais*, Ajuda Library (1687), never materialized, however.

[30] References in MSS, note 36.

dependent on the Lisbon mint. There was, accordingly, less of a tendency than in other new territories to issue paper money to carry out commercial operations with Brazil and within it.[31]

After 1714, however, the Porto mint ceased its activity and the Lisbon mint was the only center for coining money. As a consequence, individuals had to travel to the Lisbon mint in order to convert bullion into coins, and higher transaction costs were associated with the spread of money across the rest of the land. Such centralization of monetary issue was unusual at the time; the extent to which it implies restrictions on financial freedom depends on the alternatives offered to domestic wealth owners. In fact, Porto merchants received specie through the Brazilian fleets, which transported Portuguese gold, and they used Castilian coins. Overall, this centralized monetary structure hindered the monetary integration of mainland Portugal compared with countries like Holland or England.

From the 1688 devaluation to the introduction of fiat money in 1797, gold accounted for most of the coinage at the Lisbon mint, despite the increase in silver (in both absolute and relative terms) recorded in the 1770s and thereafter. Nevertheless, Castilian silver currency circulated in Portugal, without being recoined until 1785, so that bimetallism prevailed in practice.

The change in the legal value of silver in 1688 increased the coining of this metal in the 1688–90 triennium, to about 1,200 contos, mainly through reminting. This coinage, while continuing into the 1690s, dropped to about 240 contos (1691–9). From 1700 on, no silver was available for daily exchange in Portugal, and Spanish patacas remained in circulation (law of August 21, 1702).[32] This shortage changed the market value of silver, which resulted in the alteration of its legal value in 1734 (from 31 to 33 réis per gram) and in 1747 (to 36 réis per gram).[33]

In the meantime, patacas dominated circulation along the border with Spain and in the Algarve.[34] In the 1770s the external value of the Castil-

[31] There was only limited experience with the use of paper money for local transactions. Since 1771 bonds had seen issued in the Distrito Diamantino de Minas. The bonds of some trading companies had circulated as money since the 1750s.

[32] The shortage of silver is deduced from data of the Lisbon mint, but the Porto mint was also active between 1688 and 1714. This mint, originally authorized to coin silver, was granted permission to mint gold coins only in 1712. We do not know how much was coined because the books of the Porto mint disappeared. See Sousa (1999).

[33] The law was passed on August 7, 1747, the first coinage of this period being on August 22. See Sousa (1999, pp. 122–9, 306–8). The ratio between the two precious metals remained unchanged until 1822. The revaluation of silver against gold increased silver coinage, but there was no lasting effect since economic agents expected a higher revaluation of the metal, which continued to be in short supply.

[34] During the Pombal period, for example, bidding in the Algarve fishing auctions was carried out in pesos rather than in cruzados. See Sousa (1999, p. 264).

ian coins became higher than their internal value, and Spanish currency ceased to be legal tender in 1785. The refusal of transactions in Castilian specie explains the increased remintage of Castilian silver coins into national currency.

The state also controlled the destination of silver, especially during wars, because it was used to pay soldiers' wages. At the time of the War of the Spanish Succession, silver was delivered to the treasury of the Junta dos Três Estados for this purpose.[35] During the Seven Years, War, the Provedor of the mint was to buy all the silver delivered to domestic residents, so that it could be immediately transferred to the Treasury.[36]

There were three major gold minting periods: from 1703 to 1714, from the early 1720s until 1736, and from 1738 to 1763. Individuals could go directly to the Lisbon mint to coin the precious metal they received.[37] From 1702 to 1724, gold coined for the Crown amounted to less than 4 percent of total arrivals, but the state became the dominant recipient in the 1720s, as shown in Table 6.3. This was due to rising current and extraordinary expenditures, and it coincided with the closing of the Porto mint.

The Lisbon mint was the property of the Crown, which was also an important customer, making it a state reserve fund.[38] The abundance of gold made the resort to currency debasement unnecessary. Revenues that arrived in bullion or gold dust from Brazil became available to the Crown and were transformed into currency, which was used especially to finance war expenditures.

Gold mintage composition suggests that until the 1720s, coins of 4,800 réis prevailed, while between the 1720s and 1730s, small-value coins (480 and 800 réis) predominated. After 1735, precisely during the period when the state dominated gold mintage, coins of 6,400 réis, the highest face

[35] *Documentação Avulsa*, M. 1703–50, Lisbon Mint Archive. The Junta dos Três Estados was created in 1640 to supervise taxes used to finance the restoration war. However, after the 1650s, it took over the fiscal attributes of the Cortes (Cardim, 1998, pp. 102–3).

[36] Order sent *by Secretaria de Estado dos Negocios do Reino*, September 10, 1763. See *Entregas da prata das Americas no Real Erario* (1763–6), book 1604, Lisbon Mint Archive, which recorded these deliveries.

[37] In the Seville mint, societies of financiers were intermediaries between the individuals and the mint, at least until the 1710s; see Sindreu (1991, pp. 266–85).

[38] Some examples from requests found in the *Registo Geral* of the Lisbon Mint Archive confirm the role of the Lisbon mint as a state reserve fund. During the Seven Years' War, because no silver was being coined and the Rio de Janeiro fleet's sailing had been canceled, the Crown ordered the Lisbon mint to estimate the amount of gold in reserve and to coin all of it at once. In the 1730s, during a period of conflict in Colónia do Sacramento, several requests were made to the treasurer of the Lisbon mint to transfer currency to the Conselho Ultramarino to pay for uniforms, ammunition, powder, and various other war materials to be sent to Brazil.

value, dominated.[39] The bias of mintage composition toward higher denominations can be seen as another way of curtailing financial freedom. Because, with higher amounts to settle, coins of higher quality could be used, agricultural and industrial workers were averse to monthly, let alone daily, payments.[40] The annual amounts of copper coined were small when compared with the coinage of silver and gold. This also supports the higher quality of Portuguese monetary circulation allowed by gold coins of smaller value. This characteristic of mintage composition is probably not unique to the eighteenth century. It certainly explains the complaints by monetary authorities about shortages of coin for daily transactions.[41]

Gold arrivals helped to increase the Portuguese money supply at a rate six times greater than the domestic output in 1689–1759, yet with little effect on prices, certainly compared to the 1555–1640 period. In any event, gold was also applied to the redemption of public debt. A partial conversion of the debt was carried out in the 1740s, precisely the period of greater monetary issue to the state. This redemption included the decrease in interest charges and the reimbursement to creditors, who previously had not accepted a lower rate of interest.[42]

In the discussion of the long cycles of the real exchange rate revealed by Table 6.1, the outflow of gold, coupled with precautionary gold hoarding, exacerbated the shortage of coins in circulation and brought a risk of devaluation that eventually reversed the real appreciation.[43] One indication of this pressure may come from the difference between the value of gold and silver coins and their legal price, quite aside from the relative prices of the precious metals in circulation.[44]

[39] In terms of domestic circulation, other precious metals and copper were not absent from circulation and credit was a reality in Lisbon (Rocha, 1996). Copper was a metal for small daily transactions, because it could not be used in payments worth more than 100 réis (the law of September 25, 1800 increased the value of transactions to 5000 réis). Considering the behavior of copper coinage (see Appendix Table 2 in MSS), its continuity and quantity were greater between the 1730s and 1760s. From 1733 to 1766 the copper coinage was almost 275 contos, more than half the total coinage of this metal for the period 1688–1797.

[40] In the hinterland of Lisbon in the 1760s, permanent agricultural workers received annual wages of 20,000 réis on average (Silva, 1993, p. 144).

[41] More details are found in MSS, note 48.

[42] More details are found in MSS, note 53.

[43] Sousa (1999, pp. 257–62) claims that it is necessary to allow for substantial hoarding to explain the weak (and sometimes negative) relation between changes in money and prices. Morrison et al. (1999) claim that hoarding rises in time of war and is a major factor in the fall in velocity in France.

[44] Taking the ratio between the value and the quantity of gold coined and comparing it with the legal price of the gold, a "quality spread" is pictured in Figure 6.2 and Appendix Table 2 in MSS, together with spreads based on the legal tolerance in the weight of

According to Table 6.1, nominal income grew at an annual rate of 2.2 percent throughout the eighteenth century. Yet, from 1689 until 1759, money grew at over 3 percent per annum, but the rate fell to less than 1 percent per annum from 1760 until 1797, without any noticeable effect on either output growth or inflation. For convenience, the change is identified with Pombal's reforms beginning in 1760, a few years after an earthquake destroyed most of the capital city and the country prepared for its intervention in the Seven Years' War. The consequence is a fall and then a rise in the velocity of circulation of money at a rate about 1.4 percent per annum in each period.

With commerce and trade specialization, monetization increased, but it was not sufficient to prevent a persistent rise in prices and a sustained loss of competitiveness of Portuguese exports, a very high propensity to import, and a gradual loss of specie. When gold arrivals declined in the 1750s and thereafter, the capacity to import was curtailed and the same happened to state revenues. As foreign prices picked up, however, real appreciation was dampened.[45]

6.3.2 Pombal's Reforms

State revenue almost doubled at constant prices between 1681 and 1716. This rise in the financial capacity of the Crown was due mostly to two new sources of earnings for the Treasury: the king's monopolies over the extraction of gold and diamonds and over the sale of tobacco. Customs revenues also rose, and the excise and other consumption taxes paid in Lisbon more than doubled in value, following the general increase in state revenues and overtaking the revenues coming from the excise paid elsewhere on the mainland.

In the beginning of the 1760s, the Portuguese Crown was challenged on several fronts. The 1755 earthquake was responsible for serious losses of private property and wealth, and it demolished the royal palace and public buildings, such as the customs house and royal warehouses. In addition, the Atlantic traffic was confronted with a sharp drop in some staples (sugar, tobacco), which were sources of state revenues through monopoly or custom taxes. Moreover, gold mining was already on a downward trend, lowering the revenues associated with the monopoly

the coins. The upper band assumes that only the smallest currency denominations are available, whereas the lower band reflects the opposite case of largest denominations. Except in 1719, 1737, and 1778, the gold spread is within the legal values, confirming the high quality of Portuguese gold coins and explaining the preference for these coins in international payments. Sousa (1999) also presents spreads on silver coins.

45 English wholesale price inflation in 1760–97 was 1.2 percent, according to Mitchell (1978), so that the bilateral real appreciation is only .5 percent per annum.

enjoyed by the Crown (Table 6.3). Finally, the participation of Portugal in the Seven Years, War became imminent, with the inevitable rise in state expenditures.

The first measures were aimed at revising the regulations over the monopoly of gold mining and the payment of duties associated with it (decree of December 5, 1750), custom taxation (especially for sugar and tobacco, decrees of April 10 and May 20, 1756), and the prevention of smuggling (decree of November 14, 1757). The law became particularly severe against smuggling, since tax revenues were seen as crucial in a time of financial stringency. Also, a decree of December 22, 1761, created the Erário Régio (Royal Treasury) to centralize in one single department the collection of all taxes and state revenues.[46]

Another major initiative dealt with the regulation of the *décima*.[47] Its rate returned to 10 percent; all of its tax administration was centralized away from local officials; the methods used to assess wealth, survey and evaluate real property, and tax profits from loans were improved; and the universal character of the tax was reaffirmed. Its role in the Portuguese fiscal system was well understood by reformers.[48]

The importance of the revenues coming from the *décima* is clear from Table 6.2. On average it amounted to 11 percent of all the revenues for the period 1762–76, almost double the excise collected, except for the city of Lisbon. Even including Lisbon, and especially after 1765, the revenues are equivalent: an annual average of 663 contos for the *décima* against 700 contos for the excise.[49]

The structure of tax revenues did not change with this reform; customs retained its share, and that of Crown monopolies rose. Between 1716 and the period 1762–76, revenues from the monopolies over tobacco and Brazilian gold and diamonds rose by 60 percent in constant prices. Yet a countrywide tax administration was necessary in order to increase the share of the income tax in state revenues. After the difficulties of the

[46] Until then different revenues were directed to distinct offices subjected to a loose and distant control by the Conselho da Fazenda. This practice had been severely criticized by Manuel Severim de Faria a century earlier, when he disapproved of the existence of different financial departments, each with certain expenditures associated with the revenues it would receive. Therefore, state revenues involved a variety of small balances, which made the management of the Treasury difficult. The regulation of the new Royal Treasury also introduced double-entry bookkeeping, which was already the accounting norm in business practices. In 1591 the modernization of accounting was neglected, under the argument that similar practices were good for merchants but improper for a king (Hespanha, 1993, pp. 204–5).

[47] Decrees of September 26 and October 18, 1762.

[48] References in Macedo, Silva and Sousa (2000), note 61.

[49] Before 1765 the revenues coming through the collection of the *décima* were very low, demonstrating that its fiscal infrastructure had not yet been created.

Table 6.4. Comparative Tax Burden in 1763

Countries	State Revenues (million réis per person)
Netherlands	7.2
England and Wales	5.9
Portugal	3.5
France	2.4
Spain	2.4
Prussia	1.0

Sources: Described in MSS, Table 3.

1760s, renewed commercial affluence was reflected in increasing custom revenues and stabilizing revenues from royal monopolies, in which tobacco started to become more and more relevant. Therefore, improvements in income tax administration, which would increase the pressure on taxpayers across the country, became less pressing.

6.3.3 The Entrepreneurial Domain State

War gave legitimacy to new taxes and to system reform. In 1641 (as in 1387), the creation of a new tax was sanctioned by the Cortes, transforming the decision into that of a national response to the threats to autonomy. In the 1760s, in spite of the absence of the Cortes, the long preambles to the decrees gave an ideological and even historical justification for the reforms, urged by the threat of the Seven Years' War.

War was an exceptional situation that required extraordinary expenditures and exceptional means to finance them. Holland and England seemed to deal better with these challenges – and thus were able to assume a great power status in early modern Europe – because they combined political and financial freedom.[50] By contrast, the Portuguese Treasury obtained higher and higher revenues distinct from taxation, making it less dependent on increased contractual relations with other political or social entities. An inquiry into comparative state revenues in Europe, ordered by the French controller-general of finance, Bertin, summarized in Table 6.4, shows Portugal with higher state revenues per

[50] Their fiscal constitutions relied on representative institutions, controlling state finance, and allowed an extraordinarily high level of taxation. The ability to maintain high levels of public debt through a credible commitment of the government to uphold property rights is another difference, cited by Hoffman and Norberg (1994, pp. 299–310) and North and Weingast (1989). See also the references in footnote 10.

capita than France or Spain but a distant third relative to Netherlands and England.

Aside from gold and other domain revenues, another reason why the pressures for change did not seem to be particularly strong during this period was that Portugal did not play a major role in the European power struggle. Indeed, it severed its union with Spain, which under the Habsburgs did have such ambition.

The relevance of domain revenues was not a reminiscence of medieval times. Rather, they started to matter with overseas expansion and were based on an entrepreneurial attitude toward business opportunities and wealth accumulation. It was the monopoly assumed by the Crown over some trades and goods rather than the importance of taxes on overseas trade that set the Portuguese fiscal system apart from other European cases.[51]

This patrimonial relationship had evident advantages. Revenues that were easier to collect and based on the monopoly of a few goods allowed the Crown to lower the tax burden on mainland Portugal. As a result, peasant uprisings, as well as remonstrances by local elites, were avoided.

Moreover, royal control over gold production through the collection of the *quinto* and *capitação* established a close relationship not only between state revenues and monetary emission, but also between state expenditures and gold coinage. As mentioned, the mint served as a state reserve fund: a last resort when extraordinary expenditures found the Treasury short of means.

Indirect taxes on commercial transactions appealed to governments because the tax was hidden in the price of the product. Therefore, they were widespread across Europe. In Portugal, the excise had been the first general tax since 1387. It represented the social acceptance that the king could not live from his estate revenues alone, but had a public role and should be supported by the nation.

The contractual basis of taxation regressed in the mid-1500s, with the definition of a fixed amount for the excise to be paid by each municipality. The self-taxation by each community transformed the nature of the excise and represented a retreat in state formation, because tax administration failed to cover the entire country. The fiscal system became more concentrated in Lisbon, where the excise on movable goods maintained the nature of a transactions tax. As a result, the excise

[51] Godinho (1978, p. 72) coined the term *merchant state*. Yet this is not what differentiates the Portuguese case from other fiscal systems, but rather the patrimonial appropriation of the revenues from some trades. Indeed, Godinho's analysis stressed the importance of taxes for overseas trade, but the connection with the term was not immediate.

shaped power relationships between the center and periphery and indeed developed into a pathology of the Portuguese tax system that lasted well beyond this period.

This concentration in Lisbon of the tax system is also evident in the case of customs. As the capital city was the major port of the country, the national gate to the Atlantic commercial network, it concentrated most of the foreign trade.[52] Controlling this commercial gateway minimized the transaction costs of tax collection, explaining the importance of customs revenues.

Lower tax collection costs also explain efforts to collect the excise in Lisbon and to claim a proprietary relationship with some trades and goods that were highly valued in European markets. As a result, tax collections in Lisbon in 1766 accounted for 59 percent of the total.[53]

6.4 FROM FRENCH INVASIONS TO BRITISH ULTIMATUM

6.4.1 Political and Financial Crisis

Portugal's participation in European wars was a bad omen. French invasions followed, and then the opening of Brazilian ports to foreign trade in 1808. A brief respite in the 1820s led to constitutional rule, but the country experienced civil war from 1828 to 1834. The old financial system faced successive crises together with increased war expenditures. The impact of the war on state finance and monetary circulation might not have been very different from the experiences of other European countries, but the combination of the war and the loss of Brazil was uniquely grave.

In spite of new taxation and legislative efforts to overrule the tax immunities enjoyed by the nobility and the Church, the results were insufficient to overcome the financial problems of the state. In 1796 Church and nobility were required to pay the excise duties. The Church was also taxed in 1800 by an ecclesiastic *décima* and in 1809 was included in the exceptional defense contribution by an increase of the *décima*. In 1800 the *décima* was extended to the *comendas*.[54] These measures

[52] In the early 1800s, 75 percent of the Portuguese foreign trade was based in Lisbon (Justino, 1988–9, II, p. 151).

[53] This is the result of adding custom taxes collected in Lisbon's custom house, revenues of the Sete Casas (office where excises, *real d'água*, and similar taxes were collected) and the *décima* collected in Lisbon, and of comparing this total with the revenues coming from mainland Portugal. The share of Lisbon is based on data presented in Tomaz (1988), for custom and Sete Casas; the "*Livro de registo das contas correntes do rendimento da décima*," Arquivo do Tribunal de Contas, *Erário Régio*, 802, for the *décima* on the inhabitants of Lisbon. See Appendix Table 1 in MSS.

[54] This was a benefit given by the king to clergymen and members of military orders.

widened the tax base and lessened existing tax inequities, but the results were very modest.

State revenues, which increased in 1804 almost 37 percent, when compared with the average of the previous period, dropped again from 1804 to 1810 (see Appendix Table 1 in Macedo, Silva and Sousa (2000)). This decrease was explained by the behavior of the two structural state revenues: custom taxes and royal monopolies. Even though revenues from the *décima* doubled from 1797 to 1810 and increased 44 percent from 1804 to 1810, they could not offset the collapse of other state revenues. The behavior of custom taxes shows a decline of almost 50 percent from 1804 to 1810, explained by the French invasions and by the drop in colonial revenues as a consequence of the opening of the Brazilian ports to foreign trade in 1808. Looking to the revenues from monopolies, such revenues became much more dependent on tobacco.

The rise in the excise and other indirect taxes from the end of the eighteenth century to 1804, together with their reduction from 1804 to 1810, is due to the collections in Lisbon, emphasizing again the tax concentration there. Economic difficulties, as a consequence of French invasions, explain the drop of 36 percent in indirect taxes at the end of the 1810s. The weight of a financial structure centralized in Lisbon and fiscally concentrated in custom taxes and monopolies prevented the extension of the geographical domain of the tax base.

Therefore, the state needed to adopt other means to overcome the financial deficit, innovations in monetary and debt policy. While the sale of a *padrão de juro real* required registration through a public deed, an endorsable public debt instrument was offered for the first time in 1796. Then the March 13, 1797, loan increased the capital and the rate of interest, lowered the face value of the bonds, and stated that they could be used for some state payments. The lasting difficulties of the Treasury eventually led to the issuance of bonds with an even smaller face value than before, which could circulate as money at their nominal value and were to be accepted in any transaction. These smaller bonds created an inconvertible fiduciary means of payment, paper money, which, after 1797, was in circulation along with gold and silver coins.[55]

Other proposals to solve the financial problems through public debt were submitted in the last decade of the eighteenth century by authors linked to the Lisbon Academy of Science, created in 1779. Rodrigo de Sousa Coutinho, who had been president of the Erário Régio (1801–3)

[55] More details and references appear in Macedo, Silva and Sousa (2000), notes 70 through 73.

and minister, proposed the issue of internal public debt, with tax revenues serving as collateral along the lines of what was happening in England.[56] Realizing that the creation of new tax revenues required a more efficient tax administration, he suggested the creation of a bank capable of managing the public debt and issuing convertible bank notes. The objective was to place the control of debt and money in the hands of the financial community rather than in those of the Crown. The increase in tax revenues and the creation of an efficient public administration would then ensure that the higher volume of public debt would be serviced.

No such bank was created, and paper money remained an inconvertible fiduciary means of payment. Did the commercial and financial elite favor currency inconvertibility instead of the issue of convertible notes by a central bank? As paper money was either exchanged for specie or accepted as a means of payment with a discount, fiduciary circulation may have seemed profitable to wealth holders.[57] Yet, in 1796 the first public loan was a failure, making the issue of paper money in 1797 almost inevitable.

Wealth holders knew then that the Crown was unable to honor its debts due to the absence of an institutional control over financial matters. They understood therefore that Coutinho's reform proposals were not viable without a change in the fiscal constitution, involving expenditure control and improvements in tax administration, as well as tax design. After 1698 the Cortes had not been assembled to discuss fiscal issues and was therefore unable to play the role of a parliamentary institution. In a period of bitter financial crisis, this deprived the Crown of even this form of traditional representation.

Contemporaries already saw price fluctuations as a consequence of the discount of paper money. The price index in Figure 6.1 shows that after a period of moderate inflation during the second half of the eighteenth century, prices increased after the 1790s. From 1797 to 1813 prices more than doubled, dropping in the following two years. If this inflation can be explained by the devaluation of paper money, this was certainly not the only source. The Napoleonic Wars had disrupted production and distribution channels of grain. The consequence was scarcity in supply and higher prices across Europe. Table 6.1 reports deflation in the period 1798–1834, which, together with a devaluation of the real against gold by

[56] He distinguished the English experience from the French episode of the *assignats* and from the paper money issued during the war of American independence. On Coutinho's proposals and their interpretation, see MSS, notes 74 and 75.

[57] For this interpretation see Cardoso (1989, pp. 149–50) and Costa (1992, p. 291).

17 percent in 1822, brings about a slight depreciation in real terms against sterling.[58]

The circulation of paper money was considered a loss to the state, because it made expenditure in metal coins, namely by the army and navy, higher than it would otherwise have been: discount of paper money reached 60 percent during the French invasions. Paper money circulation was also limited to the cities of Porto and Lisbon.[59] Nevertheless, total gold and silver coinage from 1797 to 1807 was 25 percent of paper money issues.[60]

Estimates of public debt increased (gathered in Macedo, Silva and Sousa (2000), Appendix Table 1, Panel C) show a consolidated debt of about 6,000 *contos* from 1776 until 1817, plus a floating debt of over 10,000 *contos* beginning in 1801. Current and other debt also began to rise then, which is why the Crown decided to sell some of its properties in 1809. Between 1810 and 1820 the Crown did sell some lands, but the result was only 439 *contos*, a very small amount compared with the public debt. The Crown also resorted to external borrowing, but external debts cannot be blamed for the financial difficulties of the period, as they did not draw on internal resources. Foreign loans due to the French wars were paid by the indemnities of the Treaty of Vienna, and the foreign loans between 1815 and 1828 became Brazilian debt.

6.4.2 Revolution, Constitutional Rule, and Banking

Various attempts to redeem paper money were made after the 1820 revolution. It was in this context that the Bank of Lisbon, the first issuing

[58] Due to the linking of two different price indexes, the annual rates before and after 1810 show a real appreciation of .7 percent and a real depreciation of .2 percent after (4.1 percent and –2.5 percent, respectively, in Portugal and 3.4 percent and –2 percent in England respectively). Sterling was also inconvertible from 1797 to 1821, but it was not devalued. See footnote 76.

[59] See this representation in Pinto (1839, pp. 27–30). It is also interesting to note that the reasons given in this representation for the concentration of paper money circulation in Lisbon and Porto were the difficulties people outside the two largest Portuguese cities had in understanding that paper money without precious metal was nevertheless real money. Pinto also attributes inflation to paper money. Morrison et al. (1999, p. 52) claim that suspicion about fiat money prevailed in France throughout the eighteenth century and well into the nineteenth, to the point that Banque de France bills reached only 12 percent of the money stock in 1860.

[60] Estimated from *Estatística das moedas de ouro, prata, cobre e bronze, que se cunharam na Casa da Moeda de Lisboa desde o 1º de Janeiro de 1752 até 31 de Dezembro de 1871*, 1873. The three issues raised about 17,177 contos in paper money, the first one accounting for 97 percent of the total (Pinto, 1839, p. 21). It was thus much higher than the legal ceiling, illustrating the seriousness of the financial situation.

bank, was created in Portugal in 1821.[61] Only half of the intended capital was raised, thus preventing the redemption of paper money. Hence, in 1834 a decree tried to extinguish paper money, but two years later its amount still reached about 3,000 contos.

The liberal revolution reflected the difficulties suffered by the Portuguese state since the 1790s. The French invasions, the subsequent war, and departure of the Crown to Brazil had disruptive effects on a very fragile tax administration concentrated in Lisbon. Following the opening to foreign trade of the Brazilian ports, Lisbon became less important as a gateway to the Atlantic commercial network. Colonial trade also dropped, and revenues collapsed.

The monopolies of the Crown, which had accounted for most of the state's income, were dependent on colonial trade. Revenues from gold were decreasing and losses on the tobacco contract also occurred, even though tobacco remained a major source of revenue. Moreover, from 1811 to 1820, at a time when ordinary revenues were very low, the Portuguese government on the mainland territory incurred substantial debts in order to finance public administration and the army (Table 6.2 and MSS, Appendix Table 1, Panels B and C).

This period of difficulties made the peculiarities of the state's income more apparent. Just as the attempts to change the tax system and the resort to public credit from 1790 to 1808 were linked to reformist thought on these topics, reformist proposals resumed with the liberal revolution of 1820.[62] The experience was too short-lived to bring about lasting changes. Nevertheless, there were relevant decisions concerning public debt and monetary circulation. Plans were made to privatize properties of the Crown in order to pay the debt. The project to create a bank in Lisbon in order to control monetary circulation and to act as a privileged creditor of the state, which had been conceived in the late 1700s, was implemented just after the transfer of the kingdom's capital to

[61] This was like other banks created in Europe (Lains, 1995). Some months before the creation of the Bank of Lisbon, the minister of the Treasury estimated that the paper money issued since 1797 amounted to 17,000 contos de réis, at which fewer than 7,000 contos had been discounted until then. A related measure was the creation of the Committee to Retire Public Debt (*Comissão para liquidar a dívida pública*) on October 27, 1820, which resulted in the consolidation of the floating debt to officers, soldiers, and royal suppliers in 1821 and 1822. The assessment of the contribution of Manuel Fernandes Tomás, who chaired this committee is in Borges de Macedo (1995).

[62] Nevertheless, it is interesting to note that the petition movement starting in 1820 (similar to the French *cahiers de doléances*) and lasting until 1822 did not present many petitions against taxes. Only complaints about the excises and their variations among localities were relatively frequent. This may prove that the tax burden was not very high and that abuses in taxation were not perceived as distressing. Petitions on paper money were much more frequent, as well as complaints against seigneurial duties.

Rio de Janeiro. The first bank with these characteristics emerged there and then.

When the Bank of Lisbon was created in 1821, one of its functions was related to its contract with the state to redeem paper money, receiving the monopoly of note issuing. Due to this "public" function, the Bank of Lisbon started a long period of financial assistance to the state. The bank also engaged in commercial operations, discounting and issuing foreign bills of exchange, discounting government debt titles, accepting interest-paying deposits, and providing loans.

Banking operations did exist before the creation of the Bank of Lisbon, but they were mixed with other activities.[63] Both the privileges granted to the first bank and the instability following the first liberal revolution certainly prevented the emergence of other banks until 1835. It was then that the note-issuing privilege in the northern part of the country was granted to the Banco Comercial do Porto, breaking the monopoly enjoyed by the Bank of Lisbon. This rewarded the assistance given to the liberal party by the commercial interests associated in the Associação Comercial do Porto.

Tax administration was disrupted in the 1820s, customs revenues diminished, and the tobacco contract (accounting for almost 20 percent of state revenues) did not find contractors for the period 1824–6. At last, the contract was awarded, but with a drop of 28 percent when compared with the revenue for the period 1821–3. The 1822 budget presented a deficit of 1,607 contos (22 percent of the revenues), much higher than the deficit of 246 contos (only 3 percent of the revenues) in the 1821 budget.[64]

Furthermore, in 1821 and 1822, state revenues were almost 40 percent lower than in 1817 and almost 15 percent lower than in 1812, which had been a very difficult year for state finances, just after the end of the French invasions. The restrictions on financial and political freedom that followed the first constitutional experience were not a favorable context for reform

6.4.3 Tax and Monetary Reforms

The excise law of April 19, 1832, decreed by the new Treasury minister, Mouzinho da Silveira, reflected a new tax design. All the tax duties paid on transactions of movable goods were abolished, as well as toll taxes paid in some municipalities. The excise was maintained but only on real property transactions. Therefore, the old tax on consumption was completely transformed into a tax on property sales. The preamble of the

[63] References in MSS, notes 87 and 91.

[64] Details on tobacco revenues and the budget are in MSS, notes 93 through 96.

decree constituted a program of radical changes to the tax system. The enormous variety of taxes surviving from the slow accumulation of duties over centuries of fiscal history was to be rationalized and the fiscal system reduced to only two taxes: the custom tax on imports and the direct tax based on the old *décima*.[65]

The abolition of the taxes on transactions was not complete. The excise and similar taxes paid in Lisbon were maintained in Silveira's decree. This was the most complete acknowledgment of the importance of this tax as a source of state revenue. It was also an acknowledgment of the difficulties of tax collection across the country. In the mid-1850s, taxes on consumption were reintroduced as local taxes and became important sources of revenue for municipal councils. Municipalities retained the collection of local taxes on consumption, which had been abandoned by the central administration because they were difficult to impose and unpopular. Lisbon was the only place where the consumption taxes were maintained as central administration taxes until 1922. Therefore, the biases displayed by the structure of the revenues since the 1600s continued throughout the 1800s. State revenues remained concentrated in Lisbon (largely based on customs and consumption duties), and revenues from the tobacco contract maintained the past importance of trade monopolies to the Treasury.

Silveira's project was not implemented, and due to poor administration and the civil war, the revenue tax did not become relevant until much later. With the end of the civil war in 1834, more urgent matters required the attention of the government. In fact, the financial situation of the kingdom had not improved compared with the 1820s. Public debt had almost doubled since the beginning of the civil war in 1832. All this new debt was foreign. It rose from almost 30 percent of national income in 1832 to more than 55 percent in 1834.[66]

From 1834 on, excessive public debt was the primary policy challenge, together with the need to control the chaotic monetary circulation (a heterogeneous collection of paper money issued from 1797 to 1799; convertible notes from the Bank of Lisbon, which later became inconvertible; and a large variety of coins from different countries). Capital markets helped finance the public deficit throughout the period. As the deficit remained particularly high in the 1830s, the pressure due to the debt service increased.[67] Civil servants had their salaries reduced or were

[65] The law of June 30, 1832, abolishing the ecclesiastic tithe gives critical importance to the *décima* in the framework of the future tax system.

[66] Details are in Macedo, Silva and Sousa (2000), note 99.

[67] Data on public revenues and expenditures from 1819 to 1847 are available in Reis (1997, 37).

paid with bonds. State suppliers had their payments postponed and eventually converted into debt titles.[68] The violence and the illegitimacy of these means showed that the state was not capable of defending property rights. Suppliers and potential creditors abandoned contracts with the state or assessed them at a risk premium. The support of civil servants was also lost.

In order to cope with debt obligations, Church property was first nationalized and then sold to private bidders together with Crown estates. The sales were devised as a way to bring extraordinary revenues into the Treasury so as to redeem consolidated debt (either foreign or domestic) or as a way to accept state annuities as payment. The results were mediocre, even though the sale of Crown and Church estates did help retire public floating debt and paper money.[69]

There were no other sources of extraordinary revenues comparable to the nationalized estates. Incompressible budget deficits were financed through a variety of short-term debt instruments – bills, contracts, or promissory notes – which created a market for public debt titles. Like the paper money issued from 1797 to 1799, these titles were traded at a discount, which reflected the perceived sovereign default risk.

In 1842 a new government was formed, backed by a larger parliamentary majority. Financial stabilization coupled with the modernization of roads, railroads, and ports formed the program of the new administration of the Duke of Terceira, which was effectively led by Costa Cabral. To restore the financial credibility of the state, the new government tried to reduce expenditures, to increase revenue through land tax reform and new taxes, and to compress debt service through the conversion of the foreign debt to a fixed rate of interest of 4 percent. Furthermore, it tried to consolidate the floating debt through a long-term loan associated with the renewal of the tobacco monopoly in 1844.[70]

In order to give stronger incentives to private investment in the modernization of infrastructures, the state backed the projects, either by

[68] In 1837, the payment of interest was suspended and replaced by new debt titles that reinforced the lack of the confidence of investors in the Portuguese state (Mata, 1986, p. 8; Reis, 1997, pp. 49–51).

[69] This intention is clear from the law of May 30, 1834. However, only 11 percent of the amount of this operation was paid in cash, which means that the 726 contos received between 1835 and 1843 did not match the service of the foreign public debt in 1835 (interest alone was estimated at over 1,100 contos). In contrast, privatization helped to redeem public floating debt and paper money, as most of the 6,600 contos of the property sold were paid with various types of floating debt titles, including paper money.

[70] The winner of the public auction on the tobacco contract would pay an annual rent and would lend 4,000 contos to the state in order to redeem the floating debt.

granting rights that would secure amortization or by subsidizing the investments themselves. Better transportation was supposed to increase wealth and expand the tax base. Financial stabilization, in turn, would avoid the crowding-out effects of the public debt on private capital formation.

New banks were created, such as the Companhia União Comercial, created by alliances between Lisbon's capitalists in order to bid on the auction of the tobacco monopoly.[71] It not only participated in state finance, but also developed new activities in commercial banking and was a direct competitor to the Bank of Lisbon in the note-issuing business. The Companhia Confiança Nacional was another financial institution, established in 1844 to raise the 4,000 contos associated with the tobacco contract and to finance the business company created to carry out the modernization of the infrastructure.[72]

But the tax revolt in northwestern Portugal (known as *Maria da Fonte*) led to another civil war in 1846. The programs of financial stabilization and infrastructural modernization promoted by Costa Cabral resulted in the bankruptcy of the financial and public works enterprises used as vehicles for the projects. The lack of legitimacy of taxes was made worse by the absence of a credible monetary and exchange rate regime.

6.4.4 The Gold Standard and Afterward

The inconvertible notes of the Bank of Lisbon were gradually withdrawn (together with a multitude of foreign coins), paving the way for monetary reform, which occurred in 1854, when Portugal joined Great Britain on the gold standard. This decision marks the beginning of a virtuous cycle during which the real achieved nominal stability again. Independently of the output series used, between the 1850s and the early 1890s convergence was observed in terms of output growth and inflation in relation to the European average, the longest such episode to date under a democratic regime.[73]

Monetary stability followed the new political era that opened up in 1851 with the Regeneration movement: "a revolution to end all the revolutions," as it was then called. The different liberal factions reached an

[71] The Companhia União Comercial was created in the same year by Joaquim Pedro Quintela and Vicente Gonçalves Rio Tinto, who lost the tobacco contract to another group of capitalists.

[72] According to Reis (1997, pp. 143–51), its major financial innovation consisted in the project to create a network of provincial savings banks, which would form the basis of its lending business: to the state and to finance the Companhia das Obras Públicas.

[73] The acceleration of growth shown in Table 6.1 is also reflected in the data assembled by Maddison, but the rate falls to 1.2 percent, below that of the period 1891–1910 when 1.3 percent is reported. The average is computed with data supplied by Bordo and Schwartz (1996). See also footnote 9.

agreement about the political regime, which was sanctioned in 1852 by constitutional changes. The political scene was pacified, and a broad consensus about economic modernization and institutional reform emerged. A general awareness of the need to overcome the backwardness of the country led to the introduction of the metric system, new economic legislation, and a vast plan of public works.

Another feature of the monetary system established in 1854 was the competitive nature of note issue for most of the country, with eight joint stock banks issuing convertible paper money. These included the Bank of Portugal, which succeeded the Bank of Lisbon in 1846 and was granted the monopoly in the Lisbon district, which included the largest financial market.[74] The northwestern part of Portugal, where note-issuing banks were concentrated, was also the place of departure for most of the emigrants going to Brazil and other New World destinations. Even when they issued notes, however, banks provided remittance facilities and discounted and issued bills of exchange or foreign currency exchange, resulting overall in a lower concentration and more fragility.[75]

According to Table 6.1, after the instability cycle of 1798–1834, growing demand for money was associated with the acceleration of income growth and with greater monetization across the territory. The accession to the gold standard countered the negative consequences of the payments deficit, to the extent that it brought a "seal of approval" to the policies pursued in Portugal. This generated higher growth and inflation, however, whose negative effects on export competitiveness were exacerbated by world deflation.[76] In short, the program of public works was unsustainable, and difficulties in tax administration made a payments crisis inevitable. The lack of legitimacy of taxes was now associated with nonpublic expenditures, and political instability reemerged.

Figure 6.2 shows that full convertibility of the real into gold allowed higher financing of the government deficit in spite of rampant inflation-

[74] For details on the crisis affecting the Bank of Lisbon in the aftermath of the 1846 revolution see references in Macedo, Silva and Sousa (2000), note 107.

[75] In 1858 there existed 5 banks in Portugal and in 1865 there were 14, half of them chartered with note-issuing facilities. In 1875 the number rose to 51 (Justino, 1988–9, II, 212). The financial and banking crisis of 1876 meant the demise of some of these new banks, but it was the aftermath of the 1891 financial crisis that led to two important mergers in Porto banking establishments.

[76] Using data from 1872 to 1890 reported in Appendix Table 5 of Macedo, Silva and Sousa (2000), the rate of real appreciation comes to 1.4 percent per annum, while using only English price data for the entire subperiod brings the rate of appreciation to 1 percent per annum, less than the 1.8 percent recorded during the previous subperiod. See, however, footnote 58.

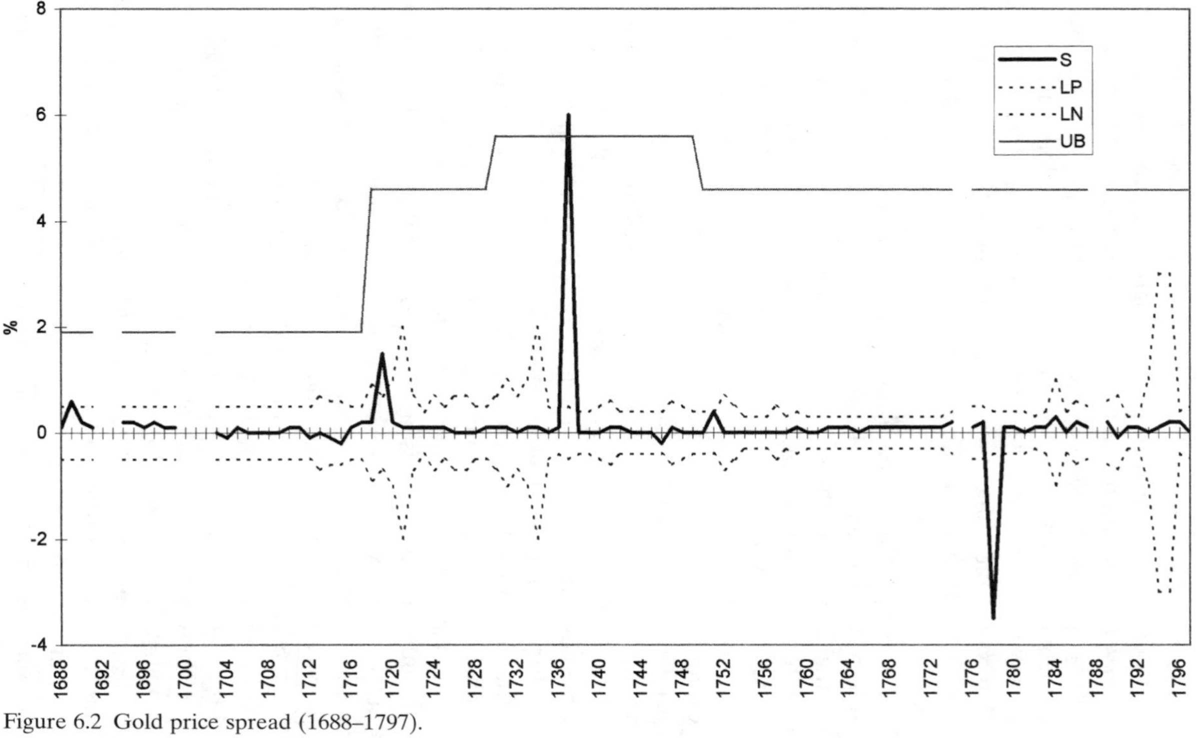

Figure 6.2 Gold price spread (1688–1797).

ary tendencies. Financial credibility of government policy was a crucial element in providing support for the program of public works outlined by the new Regeneration governments – whatever the motives invoked for joining the gold standard.[77] Indeed, the credibility effect of belonging to the gold standard created the external reputation that was essential to make Portuguese state securities attractive to foreign investors. The debt would then function as an anticipation of future state revenues, maximized by the positive effects of public investment in social overhead capital.

Due to the partial nature of the tax reforms of the mid-1800s, which failed to widen the tax base, however, tax returns did not cope with the substantial increase in the service of the public debt. Customs revenues and the tobacco contract (the latter surviving from the old monopolies) accounted for almost 50 percent of state income in 1890. In contrast, the share of direct taxes in total revenue fell throughout the period. In per capita terms they increased only 14 percent between 1864 and 1890 against 95 percent in custom taxes.

In territorial terms, most of the state revenues continued to originate in Lisbon. Adding the consumption taxes of Lisbon to the part of custom taxes paid over the imports through the port of the capital city, we obtain almost 40 percent of all state revenues. With the inclusion of direct taxes and other duties paid by the inhabitants of Lisbon, the proportion would certainly be more than 50 percent of the state revenues.[78]

These characteristics of the fiscal system were at the root of its structural insufficiency and represented a threat to future stability, which did not involve war expenditures but rather reflected the lower legitimacy to taxation in a period of civil strife. The return to higher deficits in the public accounts and deterioration of the domestic political situation, with republican agitation and a frustrated revolution in 1891, suggested a decline in the legitimacy of the monarchy itself.

Three other major events were responsible for putting an end to this period. These were the British ultimatum – enforced by the presence of two warships in the bay of Lisbon – in connection with Portugal's claim to the territories between Angola and Mozambique; the bankrupcy of Baring Brothers, the London banker of the Portuguese Crown; and the republican revolution in Brazil.

The suspension of convertibility in 1891 occurred well before the general movement away from the gold standard at the beginning of the First World War. Given the high trade deficit, the decline in emigrants'

[77] Thus Reis (1996, pp. 175–6) sees "no grounds for supposing that one of the motives for adopting the gold standard was the desire for easier access to the international capital market."

[78] References in Macedo, Silva and Sousa (2000), note 111.

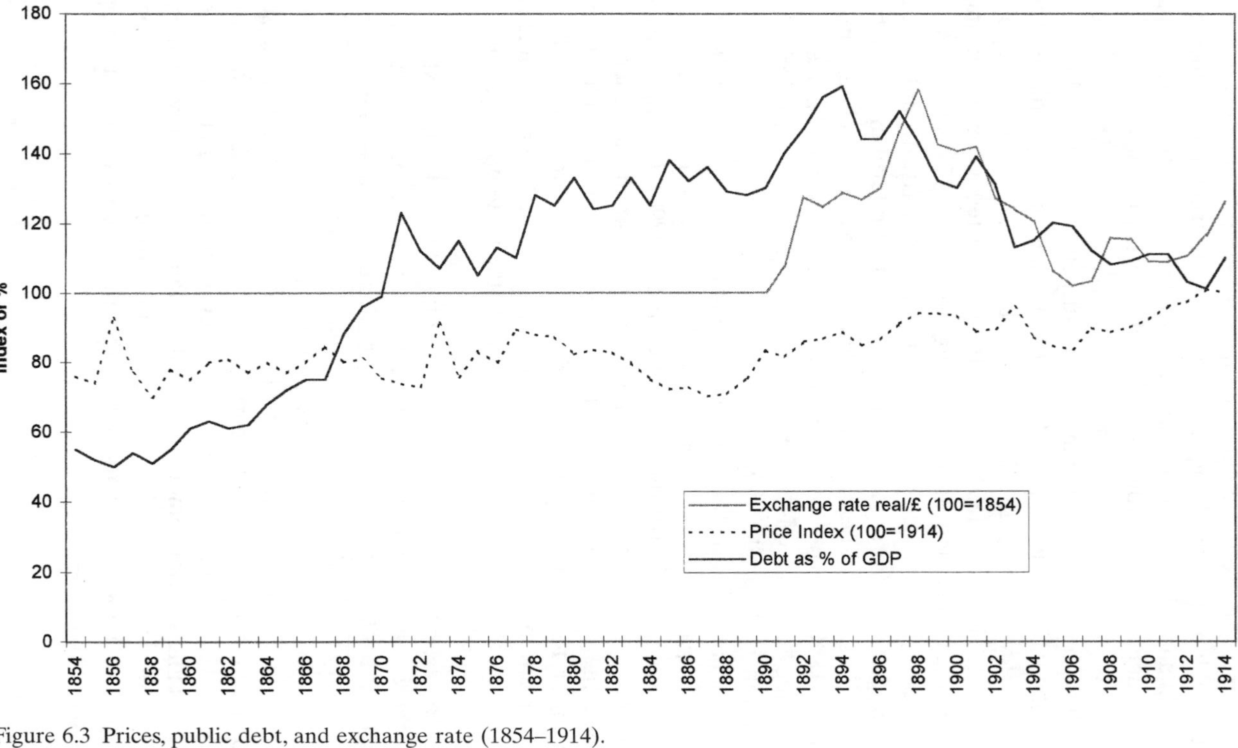

Figure 6.3 Prices, public debt, and exchange rate (1854–1914).

remittances shocked the external equilibrium and disturbed the expectation of long-term exchange rate stability. The structural insufficiency of state finance, exacerbated from 1888 to 1891 by exceptionally higher public deficits and the unavailability of external financing, precipitated the crisis.[79]

The monetary consequences of the suspension of the gold standard were two. First, due to the difficulties of other issuing banks and their bankruptcy in 1891, the Bank of Portugal gained the monopoly of bank notes issued in 1891. Second, the real started a continuous movement of depreciation against sterling until 1898. This movement was reversed with the increase in remittances from Brazil and increased demand for the Portuguese currency. In 1905 the level of the exchange rate prior to the suspension of the gold standard was reached. Throughout the 1891–1910 period, nominal depreciation reached .7 percent while domestic inflation was slightly lower at .6 percent but, given foreign deflation, real appreciation continued.

The financial and monetary crisis at the beginning of the 1890s had a strong impact on financial policy. The incentives for public investments in the country's infrastructure ended in the 1890s, leading to a more restrictive policy. In addition, the response to financial difficulties followed the same paths as it had before adherence to the gold standard. In order to reduce expenditures, the payment of foreign public debt amortization was suspended. The increase in state revenues came from increases in existing taxes, some of them temporary, but later permanent.[80]

Domestic and foreign creditors were taxed too. The interest received by the internal creditors was subject to a new tax of 30 percent after January 1892. Six months later, external creditors were also hit by the budgetary difficulties of the Portuguese state: from June 1892 the Portuguese government suspended the payment of two-thirds of its interest payments on the foreign debt. As the real was falling against the pound, payments in foreign currency became a greater burden to the budget. The reputation of the state fell even further, and the recourse to foreign loans became impossible until the Portuguese involvement in the First World War. The unilateral character of hidden or overt taxes on the interest on public debt made it clear that the state was unable to support property rights.[81]

[79] The public deficit increased about two-thirds between 1884–7 and 1888–91, from, respectively, an average of 8,000 contos to 13,500 contos (Mata, 1993; Mata and Valério, 1996).

[80] There were no tax changes, except for the urban estate tax created in 1899 (Mata, 1993).

[81] In spite of the increase in revenues coming from patrimonial sources, their share in revenues was much lower than in earlier times. Another interpretation is quoted in Macedo, Silva and Sousa (2000), note 114.

On October 5, 1910, a republican revolution ended the constitutional monarchy. Symbols like the flag, the national anthem, and the currency were changed by the new regime. On March 28, 1911, the real was replaced by the escudo, which (except for a few months in 1931) remained inconvertible until it joined the Exchange Rate Mechanism of the European Monetary System in 1992.[82]

6.5 CONCLUSION

In spite of growing financial globalization, the very concept of financial freedom has been ignored in Portugal and the legacy of financial stability forgotten. The reason may be that the real became inconvertible during the heyday of the gold standard, and the move remains associated with politically traumatic experiences. Instead, the inheritance of the real degenerated into a myth, which associated fiat money with human rights and, based on the civil wars of the early 1800s, held that democracy is biased toward budget deficits, hidden taxes, and an inconvertible currency. This association runs counter to the "contractual" experience of the Cortes, which provided social legitimization of new taxes – when needed to face war expenditures. After the turmoil of the early 1900s, a twin myth emerged: that only a conservative dictatorship could produce financial stability.[83]

This chapter has shown how the Crown had to preserve national sovereignty over borders defined in the thirteenth century in the face of external military threats. The social contract enforced by the Crown until 1797 relied on the ability to finance increasingly expensive warfare. The pressure to raise revenue became a motive for fiscal change since medieval times, as war provided social legitimacy for tax reform or currency depreciation. In the nineteenth century the contract broke down because foreign wars were replaced by domestic wars and revolutions, and the monarchy itself collapsed in 1910.

The political legitimacy of the monarchy influenced the monetary regime, the organization of expenditures and revenues, the technology of taxation and Treasury operations, and the patterns of deficit financing. Similarly, different military challenges to national legitimacy and the respective responses influenced the state's institution-building strategies and the protection of property rights. Several fiscal and administrative innovations were associated with the effects of war, and domain revenues

[82] The move completed a regime change initiated with the repeal of the constitutional ban of privatizations in 1989 but was initially misunderstood by public opinion, as described in Macedo (1995). Further evidence is cited in Macedo (1999, note 22).

[83] The inverse relationship between democracy and budgetary discipline was tested by Gomes and Tavares (1999) for the 1910–26 period.

became an obstacle to radical change and modernization of the tax system.

In 1387, when the main sources of revenue were still land properties and seigniorial rights, municipal excises (*sisas*) were transformed into a universal tax with a comprehensive base. The new tax was supposed to pay for the war with Spain. It had a contractual origin insofar as it was approved by the Cortes, which acted as guarantor of private property rights.

The fiscal and monetary institutions after 1580 and in the early seventeenth century reflect Spanish rule and the restoration of independence after 1640. Until 1688, successive debasements of gold and silver coins were required to pay for the restoration war. On the fiscal side, the *décima* was created in 1641 as a direct tax levied on income coming not only from real estate, as was the case in the rest of Europe, but also from labor, commercial and industrial activities, and interest on loans.

The contrast with England, a country presented as the paradigm of the evolution from the domain state to the tax state, is the continued dependence on revenues that were not based primarily on taxes to secure financial stability. In fact, taxes on domestic residents were lower and more poorly collected because of the importance of domain or patrimonial revenues.

Financial stability in peacetime was therefore accomplished with revenues coming from monopolies over trades and goods. The tax revenues coming from customs and the concentration of other taxes in Lisbon (as was the case with the excise) contributed to revenue stability. Revenues coming from the foreign trade and from the monopolies on colonial goods, which together represented more than 50 percent of the total, were more sensitive than domestic taxes to fluctuations in foreign trade.

The Portuguese case shows highly centralized fiscal and monetary institutions. Lisbon concentrated around 5 percent of the population, but more than 50 percent of the state revenues were collected in the capital city. Also, after 1714, monetary issuing was monopolized by the Lisbon mint while Brazilian mints remained in operation. This lopsided centralization of monetary and fiscal institutions was paired with slacker control of fiscal resources across the country, with the abandonment of indirect taxes on internal trade as a major source of state revenues and with the uneven distribution of money. It thus represented a regression in the fiscal constitution of the monarchy.

In contrast with the previous period, after 1688 and during the eighteenth century, monetary policy relied on a fixed exchange rate. The two adjustments in the legal price of silver, in 1734 and in 1747, were mere technical adjustments to bring silver to the market. Therefore, seigniorage was not increased to overcome financial problems. Some of the state requests to the mint to coin precious metals were justified by extraordinary public expenditures, namely, in war periods.

The importance of domain revenues also explains why institutional reforms did not develop as early as might be expected. The Crown was unable to deal with extraordinary expenditures by resorting to higher levels of consolidated public debt. Wealth holders did not support the modernization of state finance through the creation of a bank responsible for managing public debt and issuing convertible paper money because the government's commitment to uphold property rights was not credible.

In the late 1700s and early 1800s, the structure of state finance remained based on monopolies of overseas trades and on custom taxes. Accordingly, the French invasions and the fall in colonial commerce led to the abrupt contraction of state revenues. Meanwhile, expenditures were increasing due to the war. The dramatic coincidence of the increase in military expenditures as a result of the French invasions and the end of the trade monopoly with Brazil brought about a very large deficit.

Attempts to reform the tax system and to resort to government borrowing were unsuccessful. The introduction in 1797 of inconvertible paper money was responsible for a period of raging inflation lasting until the 1820s. This is how monetary disorder reversed one century of currency stability.

The financial crisis appears as a crucial motive for the liberal revolution of 1820. The first constitutional experience coincided with the creation of the Bank of Lisbon, suggesting the importance of broader institutional reforms in order to support sounder guarantees of stability to the wealthy elite and commercial interests. Nevertheless, the period that ended in 1851 did not have the political and constitutional stability needed to sustain financial stability.

The currency became convertible again only in the early 1850s, when money creation was subject to the well-defined rules of the gold standard. The constitutional agreement that pacified the country in 1852 and the globalization in the capital markets associated with the heyday of the classical gold standard helped to sustain this experience of real and nominal convergence under the constitutional monarchy. Monetary stability based on currency convertibility allowed a greater resort to debt, and it was coupled with rates of GDP growth higher than the average European performance, an unusual feat for Portugal.

Foreign-held public debt as a way to finance short-term deficits was a development strategy that assumed that in the long term the increase in tax revenues would take care of the debt service. But attempts to increase tax revenues led to strong social opposition and several tax revolts during the time when the threat of war brought legitimacy to taxes. Low tax rates hindered the sustainability of government budget accounts and the solvency of the country. At the end of the 1880s, budget deficits increased again and the political scene began to show signs of instability. In 1891, currency convertibility was suspended. It would not be restored until the escudo became part of the euro more than 100 years later.

REFERENCES

Bairoch, Paul (1976). "Europe's Gross National Product 1800–1975." *Journal of European Economic History*, vol. 5, no. 2, pp. 273–340.

Bonney, Richard, ed. (1995). *Economic Systems and State Finance*. Oxford: Clarendon Press.

Bordo, Michael (1986). "Money. Deflation and seignioriage in the fifteenth century – a review essay," *Journal of Monetary Economics*, 18, 337–46.

Bordo, Michael and Anna Schwartz, eds. (1984). *A Retrospective on the Classical Gold Standard 1821–1931*. Chicago: University of Chicago Press.

Bordo, Michael and Anna Schwartz (1996). "Fixed Exchange Rates as a Contingent Rule 1880–1990." In Macedo, Eichengreen, and Reis.

Cardim, P. (1998). *Cortes e cultura política no Portugal do Antigo Regime*. Lisboa: Cosmos.

Cardoso, Jose Luis (1989). *O pensamento económico em Portugal nos finais do século XVIII. 1780–1808*. Lisboa: Estampa.

Costa, F. D. (1992). *Crise Financeira, dívida pública e capitalistas*. Unpublished MA dissertation, UOR University at Lisboa.

Esteves, Paulo Soares and Carlos Robalo Marques (1994). "Portuguese GDP and its deflator before 1947: A revision of the data produced by Nunes, Mata and Valerio (1989)." Bank of Portugal Working Paper, May.

Godinho, Vitorino Magalhaes (1978). "Finanças públicas e estrutura do estado," in *Ensaios II*, 2nd ed. Lisboa: Ed. Presença.

Gomes, Miguel Costa and Jose Tavares (1999). "Democracy and business cycles: Evidence from Portuguese economic history," *European Review of Economic History*, 3, pp. 295–321.

Hespanha, A. M. (1986). *As vésperas de Leviathan. Instituições e poder político. Portugal – século XVII*. Lisboa: Author.

(1993). "A fazenda," in A. M. Hespanha (org.), *O Antigo Regime (1620–1807)*, in J. Mattoso (dir.), *História de Portugal*, vol. IV. Lisboa: Círculo dos Leitores.

Hoffman, P. T. and K. Norberg, eds. (1994). *Fiscal Crises, Liberty, and Representative Government, 1450–1789*. Stanford, CA: Stanford University Press.

Justino, David (1988–9). *A formação do espaço económico nacional. Portugal, 1810–1913*, 2 vols. Lisboa: Vega.

Lains, Pedro (1995). "Savings banks in Portuguese banking, 1880–1930: The role of Caixa Económica Portuguesa," in *Actas do Encontro História Empresarial em Portugal*. Évora: pp. 311–48.

Macedo, Jorge Borges de (1995). "Manuel Fernandes Tomás – do regional ao nacional," in *Amar, sentir e viver a história: estudos de homenagem a Joaquim Veríssimo Serrão*. Lisboa: Colibri.

Macedo, Jorge Braga de (1980). "Portuguese currency experience: An historical perspective," in *Estudos em Homenagem ao Prof. Doutor J. J. Teixeira Ribeiro*, vol. IV. Coimbra: Boletim da Faculdade de Direito.

(1995). "Convertibility and stability 1834–1894: Portuguese currency experience revisited," in *Ensaios de homenagem a Francisco Pereira de Moura*. Lisboa: ISEG.

(1996). "Europa e lusofonia, política e financeira: uma interpretação," in *Ensaios de homenagem a Manuel Jacinto Nunes*. Lisboa: ISEG.

(1999). "Portugal's European integration: The limits of external pressure." Nova Economics Working Paper 369, December.

(2000). "From the *real* to the euro, via the *escudo*." Lisbon: (mimer).

Macedo, Jorge Braga de, Alvaro Ferversa da Silva, and Rita Martins de Sousa (2000). "War Taxes and Gold: the Interface of the Real." *Working Paper No. 318.* Nova University of Lisboa.

Macedo, Jorge Braga de, Barry Eichengreen, and Jaime Reis (1996). *Currency Convertibility: The Gold Standard and Beyond*. London: Routledge.

Maddison, Angus (2001). *The World Economy: A Millenial Perspective.* Paris: OECD Development Center.

(1995). *Monitoring the World Economy, 1820–1992*. Paris: OCDE Development Center.

Mata, Eugénia (1986). "A dívida pública externa fundada de Portugal da guerra civil à Regeneração." *Revista de História Económica e Social*, 18, pp. 75–90.

(1993). *As finanças públicas portuguesas da Regeneração à primeira guerra mundial*. Lisboa: Banco de Portugal.

Mata, Eugénia and Nuno Valério (1991). "Foreign public debt and economic growth in Portugal, 1830–1985." *Estudos de Economia*, 11, pp. 419–32.

(1996). "Monetary stability, fiscal discipline and economic performance – the experience of Portugal since 1854," in Macedo, Eichengreen, and Reis.

Mata and Valério (1994). Historia Economica de Portugal uma Perspectiva Global, Lisboa: Editorial Presença.

Mitchell, Brian R. (1975). *European Historical Statistics 1750–1970*. London: Macmillan, 1978.

Morrisson, Christian, Jean Noel Barrandon, and Cécile Morrison (1999). *Brazilian Gold, Money and Economic Growth in France in the 18th Century*. Paris: CNRS.

Neves, João César das (1994). *The Portuguese Economy: A Picture in Figures: XIX and XX Centuries with Long Term Series*. Lisboa: UCP.

North, Douglass C. and Barry R. Weingast (1989). "Constitutions and commitment: The evolution of institutions governing public choice in seventeenth-century England." *The Journal of Economic History*, 4, pp. 803–32.

Omrod, W. M. (1995). "The west European monarchies in the Later Middle Ages," in Bonney.

Peres, Damião (1959). *Anais da Academia Portuguesa de História*, I série, vol. XIV. Lisboa: Academia das Ciencias.

Pinto, Agostinho Albano da Silveira (1839). *Dívida pública portuguesa. Sua história, progresso e estado actual.* Lisboa: Imprensa Nacional.

Reis, Jaime (1996). "First to join the gold standard, 1854," in Macedo, Eichengreen, and Reis.

(1997). *O Banco de Portugal das origens a 1914.* Lisboa: Banco de Portugal.

Rocha, Maria Manuela (1996). "Actividade creditícia em Lisboa (1770–1830)." *Análise Social*, pp. 136–7, 579–98.

Silva, Álvaro Ferreira da (1988). "Estruturas agrárias e relações sociais – fontes para o seu estudo (livros de décima e cartórios notariais)," in Maria José da Silva Leal and Miriam Halpern Pereira (coord.), *Arquivo e Historiografia. Colóquio sobre as Fontes da História Contemporânea Portuguesa.* Lisboa: Imprensa Nacional-Casa da Moeda.

(1993). *Propriedade, família e trabalho no "hinterland" de Lisboa. Oeiras, 1738–1811*. Lisboa: Ed. Cosmos.

Sindreu, Francisco de Paula Pérez (1991). *La Casa de la Moneda de Sevilla, su historia.* Sevilha: Fundacion Fundo de Culltura de Sevilla. Col. Focus.

Sousa, Rita Martins de (1991). "Money supply in Portugal, 1834–1891," *Estudos de Economia*, 12, pp. 19–32.

(1999). *Moeda e Metais Preciosos no Portugal Setecentista (1688–1797)*, Ph.D. dissertation. Institute of Economics and Management of the Technical University of Lisbon.

Tomaz, F. (1988). "As Finanças do Estado Pombalino, 1762–1776." *Estudos e Ensaios em Homenagem a Vitorino Magalhães Godinho.* Lisboa: Sá da Costa Editora.

Valério, Nuno (1991). "Periodização da História Monetária de Portugal." *Estudos de Economia*, 13, pp. 3–18.

(1997). "Um indicador da evolução dos preços em Portugal nos séculos XVI a XIX." *Working Paper No. 4. GHES.*

PART II

THE NEW WORLD

7

The United States

Financial Innovation and Adaptation

Richard Sylla

7.1 THEORETICAL CONSIDERATIONS

The United States in all likelihood was the most rapidly expanding economy in the world from the seventeenth through the nineteenth centuries. A high rate of growth of total product characterized both the colonial period before independence and the United States after 1776. All indications are that the rate of growth of total product for the two and a half centuries from 1650 to 1900 was a sustained 3.3 to 4 percent per year for most subperiods of, say, 20 to 30 years. The nature of the expansion, however, changed some time between 1776 and 1840. Before 1776, and probably for some time thereafter, the high rate of growth was mainly the result of a population that grew at about 3 percent per year along with a small increase, possibly 0.3–0.5 percent per year, in product per person. After 1840, population growth was slower – more like 2 percent per year – and product per person grew at 1.5–1.6 percent per year. The change between 1776 and 1840 marked the emergence of modern economic growth. Economic historians still debate its nature, timing, and causes.

The unusual character of American long-term economic expansion lies less in the modern growth since at least 1840 than in the high rates of the two centuries that came before the modern era. The high rate of American economic expansion before the start of the nineteenth century differed from experience elsewhere and, together with numerous wars the colonists fought, was bound to place stresses on public finances and monetary regimes, the foci of our comparative, collaborative research effort here. In the British North American colonies that became the United States, these stresses led to financial innovation as well as to revolution and independence. Financial innovation emerged more than three centuries ago in the colonial period of American history and became one of the continuing traditions of the United States.

Not long after independence, the Americans, demonstrating their already ingrained receptiveness toward financial innovation, replaced colonial and revolutionary-period financial and monetary institutions with new ones. It is of interest that in some respects the changes introduced were closer to European institutions than the old ones had been. One might expect that the New World would first import financial institutions and practices from the Old and then gradually diverge as those of the Old World were adjusted to New World conditions or even abandoned. On the other hand, we know from modern experience that there is also a tendency at work in history for financial systems to converge. Perhaps the U.S. innovations of two centuries ago constitute an early example of the historical tendency toward convergence. The U.S. experience raises a host of questions about why financial systems diverge and converge, and it provides materials for answers to some of them.

Just before the financial changes of two centuries ago, the Americans developed a unique federal system of government that divided responsibilities and revenue sources between the national government and state governments, each of which had sovereignty in its own sphere. The timing was not accidental. The new federal government established in 1789 under the authority of the Constitution became the spearhead for a modernized financial system. That government was dominated for a dozen years, 1789–1800, by the Federalist Party, led by a gifted finance minister, Alexander Hamilton, who as the first secretary of the Treasury planned and implemented financial modernization. The governmental system and the financial system the Hamiltonian Federalists sponsored, as they developed during the nineteenth century, proved remarkably stable in comparison to the experiences of most other countries. Yet they also proved to be flexible, adaptable, and innovative in ways that sustained, even increased, the high rate of economic expansion that had emerged in the colonial period. In the transition to modern economic growth that occurred in the United States between 1776 and 1840, financial change became one of the earliest and strongest underpinnings of economic change.

7.2 PUBLIC FINANCES

Local government was primal in the British North American colonies that became the United States. American government was constructed from the bottom up, unlike elsewhere in the world. Early in the colonial period, towns and then counties functioned as little republics, electing their own officers and levying their own taxes. As Tocqueville, wrote in his classic "Democracy in America", referring to New England in the early 1650s, "The colonies still recognized the supremacy of the mother country; monarchy was still the law of the state; but the republic was already established in every township."[1] The colonists established a strong tradition of self-government that in time, and as their numbers increased, enabled them to overthrow British monarchical and parliamentary rule over their country, and to replace it at state and national levels with long-familiar, home-grown republican institutions. These institutions divided taxing and spending functions between the states and the federal government. Relatively unchanged throughout the revolutionary upheavals were local governments, which continued to function after independence much as they had before 1776.

7.2.1 Revenues

Local governments in the colonies taxed property (mostly land or real property but also some forms of personal property) and polls (capitation levies). The mechanisms were straightforward. County and town officers (variously termed *justices*, *magistrates*, *commissioners*, *selectmen*, or *councilors*), or the people themselves in a town meeting, would call for a listing of property and polls, and then set rates of taxation designed to raise the amounts they thought necessary for public purposes. Another official, usually a sheriff, was assigned to collect the taxes and turn them over to a treasurer. Later, when ad valorem taxation came in, another official, an assessor, was needed, and if more than one assessor became necessary, a board of equalization came in to harmonize disparate assessments. No doubt the essentials of these mechanisms were brought by the colonists from the home country, England. The main difference, not a small one, is that in America citizens had more of a say in them, whereas in England they were handed down from higher levels of authority that were less democratic and republican.

Colonial governments (that is, the governments of the colonies that would later become states, as distinct from the county and town governments) could finance their minimal peacetime functions with imposts (import and export duties) and a colony property tax rate added to the local rates. An example will help to illustrate how minimal were these colony-level functions. Late in the colonial era, the New York colony's budgeted appropriations were but £4,645 in colonial pounds that were worth less than pounds sterling. Of this amount, £2,000 was for the crown-appointed governor, £1,100 for four judges, £500 for an agent to

[1] Alexis de Tocqueville, *Democracy in America* (New York: Alfred H. Knopf, 1946; 1st French ed. 1835), vol. 1, p. 40.

represent the colony in London, and £300 for the colony's treasurer, with the remainder for minor officers and supplies.[2]

Peacetime in colonial America, however, was as much the exception as the rule. Numerous wars with hostile native Americans (who often objected to their lands being grabbed) and non-English Europeans (for example, the French, Dutch, and Spanish, who also wanted to grab land) led to the innovation of *currency finance*. This was the issuance of fiat paper money or bills of credit, an important innovation of the Americans that was unknown in Europe. Bills of credit first appeared in 1690, during King William's War (1689–97), when an army of the Massachusetts colony returned from Quebec with neither the military nor the financial success they had hoped for by defeating and looting the French enemy. Demanding to be paid, the soldiers threatened mutiny. Because the colony's treasury was empty, the legislature authorized that the troops and their supplies be paid for with paper bills of credit issued in standardized form and round sums. The typical form read as follows:

> This indented Bill of Five shillings due from the Massachusetts Colony to the Possessor shall be in value equal to the money and shall be accordingly accepted by the Treasurer and Receivers subordinate to him in all public payments and for any Stock at any time in the Treasury.
>
> New England, February the Third, 1690. By order of the General Court.[3]

Massachusetts bills of credit were an innovation of fundamental historical importance. They were the first fiat paper money to appear in the Western world, they were widely imitated, and they became an important component of the American money stock during the century after 1690. Eventually, as we now know, the whole world copied them by abandoning paper monies convertible at fixed rates into precious metals.

Since bills of credit embodied a totally new concept of money, it is not surprising that they initially were greeted with skepticism and were received at discounts from specie. In 1691, the Massachusetts colony remedied this problem. It issued additional bills of credit to discharge its entire war debt and made the bills receivable in public payments at a 5 percent premium over their denominated value, and it promised taxes, to be collected a year or two later, to redeem, or *sink*, the bills. Bills of credit were then recognized as non interest-bearing

[2] Paul Studenski and Herman E. Krooss, *Financial History of the United States*, 2nd ed. (New York: McGraw-Hill, 1963), p. 19.

[3] See Arthur Nussbaum, *A History of the Dollar* (New York: Columbia University Press, 1957), p. 14.

public debt that also functioned as money; they rose to par in terms of specie and remained there for some two decades. During these years, the Massachusetts government discovered that it could meet most of its limited ordinary expenses by emitting bills of credit secured by pledges of future taxes.[4]

From Massachusetts the idea spread. The colony's notable financial innovation during King William's War was emulated by several other colonies during Queen Anne's War (1702–13), when the French and the Spanish, together with allied or otherwise hostile native Americans, seemed to threaten the English colonists from all sides. During the war, South Carolina (in 1703), New Hampshire, Connecticut, New York, New Jersey (all in 1709), Rhode Island (1710), and North Carolina (1712) began to issue bills of credit similar to those of Massachusetts.[5] Some issues bore interest and some were declared legal tender for all payments, not just for payments to the government. Virtually all promised redemption through taxes to be levied and collected later. And in virtually all cases the colonies discovered, as had Massachusetts, that they could go on meeting normal governmental expenses by issuing currency long after the war exigencies that had prompted the initial issues had passed. They also found that it was not necessary to pay interest on the bills or to receive them at a premium in public payments in order to keep bills acceptable as a paper currency.

Acceptance of bills of credit as currency set the stage for a related financial innovation with revenue implications for colonial governments, the *colonial loan office* or *land bank* or *loan bank*, as it is variously called. In this case, the South Carolina colony was the innovator. In 1712, nine years after the colony's first emission of bills of credit, South Carolina put out most of a new issue as loans on landed security to individual borrowers.[6] The private borrowers were to pay back 12 1/2 percent of their loans each year for 12 years, so that the colony would reap not only a return of principal but an interest yield of 8 1/3 percent amounting, over the life of the loan, to £50 interest for every £100 lent. Colonial loan office issues secured by pledges of private assets were standardized and issued in round sums just like the bills of credit secured by pledges of future tax revenues. Both were creations of government, and the two types of issues passed interchangeably as paper money in the issuing colonies.

[4] Andrew McFarland Davis, *Colonial Currency Reprints, 1682–1751* (New York: Augustus M. Kelley, 1964), vol. 1, p. 31.

[5] The most thorough general history of colonial currency issues is by Leslie V. Brock, *The Currency of the American Colonies, 1700–1764* (New York: Arno Press, 1975), but see also Edwin Perkins, *American Public Finance and Financial Services, 1700–1815* (Columbus: Ohio State University Press, 1994).

[6] See Brock, *Currency of American Colonies*, pp. 118–19.

Three functions were served: Citizens received loans from the loan office when other institutions for borrowing were primitive or nonexistent. The colony received an interest revenue that kept unpopular taxation low. And the expanding colonial economy received infusions of currency that facilitated economic expansion.

Like the Massachusetts bills of credit, South Carolina's loan office innovation quickly spread. In New England, Massachusetts implemented it in 1714, followed by Rhode Island (1715), New Hampshire (1717), and Connecticut (1733). In the Middle Colonies, Pennsylvania and Delaware signed on in 1723, followed by New Jersey (1724) and New York (1737). And in the South, South Carolina's example was followed by North Carolina (1729), Maryland (1733), and Georgia (1755). Of the 13 colonies that later revolted to form the United States, only Virginia did not implement the loan office innovation, although it did give it consideration when it issued its first bills of credit in 1755.

Bills of credit and loan office bills served as money in the American colonies, and as such will be discussed further in Section 7.3. But they also provided colonial governments with revenues from money printing (seigniorage) and interest on loans. Currency finance on the part of colonial governments created some problems, as might be expected, but it also solved many problems the rapidly growing colonial economies faced and was popular for that reason. It also represented a far cheaper means of providing a money supply than mining and coining precious metals. Is it any wonder, then, three centuries after the innovation of 1690, that in regard to fiat money the whole world has become like Massachusetts?

After the successful American Revolution of 1775–83, as before independence, local governments continued to finance their activities with property and poll taxes. Poll taxes declined relatively over time as a revenue source, but the property tax continued throughout the nineteenth century – indeed, continues to this day – as the mainstay of local tax revenue in the United States.[7] Other local revenues came from excises, licenses, and fees. Local governments during the nineteenth century also were enabled to borrow extensively on the American capital market, which developed rapidly after 1790 (see the later discussion).

The Constitution of 1787 had almost no direct impact on local governments, but it fundamentally altered the relationship between the states and the national government, that is, the new federal government the Constitution created. Under the Constitution, states lost the right to

[7] On the history of property taxation, see Glenn W. Fisher, *The Worst Tax? A History of the Property Tax in America* (Lawrence: University Press of Kansas, 1996).

practice currency finance and to tax imports and exports. The new federal government received the right to engage in currency finance (this was unmentioned in the Constitution but affirmed by later practice and judicial decisions), to tax imports, and to levy other indirect and direct taxes. At the same time, the Constitution lifted large financial burdens from the shoulders of the states by transferring their former defense and debt obligations to the federal government. For decades after 1789, the states, original and new, could finance their rather minimal fiscal needs with income from investments (which other changes of the postindependence era made possible – see the later discussion), from land sales, and from state tax rates applied to the local property tax base. New states, and later the old states as well, relied for tax revenue primarily on property taxes. Before the older states shifted to property taxation (after 1840), they supplemented and sometimes replaced revenues from investments with taxes on business.

Following colonial traditions, property taxes, local and state, were based on local assessments and collections by local officers either elected or appointed by elected officials. Since local assessment patterns varied, states eventually had to develop methods of equalizing local assessments to make tax burdens fair. There was a conflict between bureaucratic efficiency and uniformity of taxation, on the one hand, and local administration of the property tax, on the other. This tension over the property tax, America's oldest tax, persisted from the colonial era through the nineteenth century and down to the present day. Taxes on business in most instances were collected directly by state officers. By the early nineteenth century, the state governments – like local governments somewhat later – also began to avail themselves of the services of the capital market that grew up after 1790 by issuing debt to finance public improvements.

The new federal government relied primarily on customs duties for revenue, supplemented by land-sale revenues and at times by excise taxes. Given the rapid expansion of the American economy, which led to growing imports, customs duties were the reliable, if controversial, source of most federal revenue most of the time. Direct taxes were limited by the Constitution, which called for them to be apportioned among the states according to population. They were levied for war purposes twice in the early years, when war with France seemed imminent in 1798 and after war with Britain broke out in 1812. They were quickly abandoned when peace returned. Federal direct taxes were highly unpopular, in part because they invaded the tax bases that local and state governments considered their own.

By the late nineteenth century, federal excise taxes on alcoholic beverages and tobacco products together furnished in most years almost as much national revenue as customs duties. The Treasury Department under Hamilton in the early 1790s established a bureaucracy for collecting domestic excises and customs duties; it functioned with a high degree of efficiency. Income taxation, the mainstay of modern federal and, to a lesser extent, state public finance, was introduced several times during the nineteenth century, only to be abandoned when it ran afoul of constitutional strictures regarding direct taxation. These were overcome by amending the Constitution in 1913, the very end of the period of history dealt with here.

How large in the nineteenth century was the public sector of the United States, with all of its governments and layers of government? By modern standards, it was quite small: Today all governments in the United States absorb upward of a third of the nation's gross domestic product (GDP), but at the start of the twentieth century, it was only 8 percent of GDP, and as best we can tell, in the 1790s it was only about 4 percent. Nineteenth-century American government was also relatively small in comparison to European governments, in good measure because fewer wars and threats of war meant that Americans could spend a smaller proportion of their resources than Europeans on military establishments. Table 7.1, comparing U.S., U.K., and German government expenditures around the turn of the twentieth century, establishes this point. The two European governments committed larger percentages of their countries' GNPs to defense and debt charges (related in large part to past wars) than did the Americans. Despite such differences, the governmental share of GDP in the United States doubled between the 1790s and the 1900s, and since the GDP in real terms itself rose 100-fold in that period, the U.S. public sector was some 200 times larger in the early twentieth century than it was in the 1790s. In U.S. history, government was a "growth industry."

Within the public sector, during the 1790s the federal government, because it had assumed large debt and defense burdens, accounted for about 60 percent of total revenues and expenditures, the state governments about 10 percent, and local governments 30 percent. By the early 1900s, the federal share was some 25 percent, the state share about 15 percent, and the local share, largely as a result of rapid urbanization and the demands it generated for urban infrastructures, came to about 60 percent.[8] The twentieth-century "age of big government," declared by

[8] I discuss these data and other aspects of governmental revenues and spending during the nineteenth century in my chapter, "Experimental Federalism: The Economics of American Government, 1789–1914," in S. L. Engerman and R. E. Gallman, eds., *The Cambridge Economic History of the United States* (Cambridge: Cambridge University Press, NY), vol. 2, pp. 483–541.

Table 7.1. Government Expenditures by Functions as a Percentage of GNP (All Levels of Government)

				Civilian			
	Total (1)	Defense (2)	Public (3)	Law, Order, and Administration (4)	Economic and Environmental Services (5)	Social Services (6)	Total (4–6) (7)
United States							
1890	7.1	1.4	0.7	1.2	2.0	1.8	5.0
1902	7.9	1.5	0.5	1.1	2.1	1.9	5.1
1913	8.5	1.1	0.4	0.9	2.6	2.1	5.6
United Kingdom							
1890	8.9	2.4	1.6	1.7	1.3	1.9	4.9
1900	14.4	6.9	1.0	1.4	2.5	2.6	6.5
1913	12.4	3.7	0.8	1.6	2.2	2.2	7.9
Germany							
1891	13.2	2.5		n.a.	n.a.	n.a.	9.9
1901	14.9	3.3		n.a.	n.a.	n.a.	11.5
1913	14.8	3.3	0.7	2.4	2.2	5.1	9.7

Source: Richard A. Musgrave, *Fiscal Systems* (New Haven: Yale University Press, 1969), Table 4.1. Components may not add to totals because of omitted categories and rounding.

President Bill Clinton in the 1990s to be ending, would increase the federal share to two-thirds, with state and local governments accounting for roughly equal shares of the remaining one-third. The federal and state-plus-local shares of late-twentieth-century American government, it is of interest to note, were not very different from what they had been two centuries earlier, when all levels of government were far smaller in relation to the economy.

7.2.2 Expenditures

In colonial America, local governments established and protected property rights, constructed public buildings (county courthouses, town and city halls, jails), fostered public improvements such as roads, bridges, and port facilities, and provided basic education and poor relief. Some of these governmental functions were continuing, others sporadic. Typically, a tax rate was set for each purpose, making clear to citizens how the levies imposed were being spent.

At the colony level, elected assemblies made general laws under the guidance and supervision of Crown-appointed governors, established court systems, and, in cooperation with British authorities, provided for collective defense against external enemies. Only the last of these functions was costly, leading to the occasional overissues of bills of credit that later sound-money advocates would criticize. The colonial governments, as already noted, also furnished a paper money supply and provided loans to borrowers through land banks or loan offices.

In the tripartite federal system that emerged after independence and the Constitution, the federal government's chief functions were to provide for defense, conduct relations with other countries, and oversee foreign and interstate commerce as well as relations between states and citizens of different states. The last group of functions were the special province of a federal court system that Congress, the national legislature, established by provision of the Constitution. Most federal spending was for the army and the navy, for veterans of the army and navy and their families, for a postal service, and for servicing the national debt. The debt, born in the Revolution and mainly added to thereafter in wars, typically was paid down by consensus that this was good policy in times of peace. In the 1830s, the national debt was totally redeemed, an exceptional occurrence in world history and a tribute to the rapid growth that swelled customs duties and land-sale revenues. Some wanted the federal government to use its ample revenues directly by investing in economic infrastructure, but the politics of the era prevented such a role. Before the 1860s, attempts to involve the federal government in infrastructure

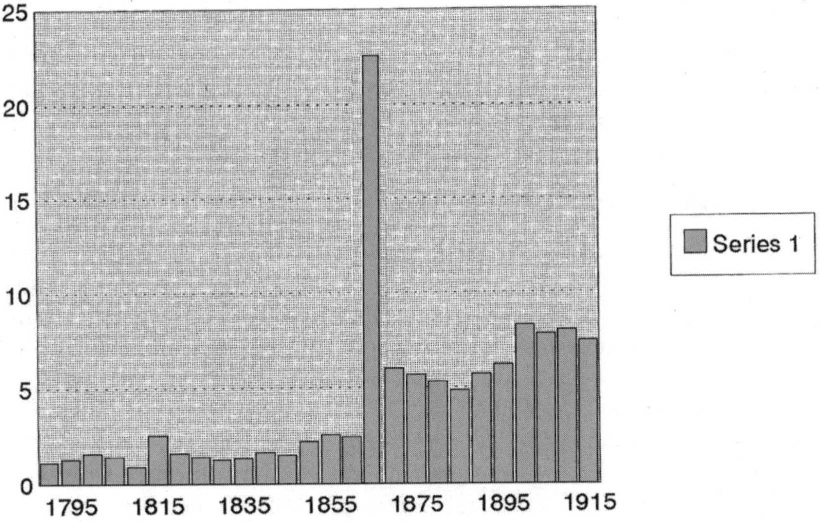

Figure 7.1 Real federal spending per capita, 1790–1915 (in 1915 dollars).

Source: derived from U.S. Bureau of the Census, *Historical Statistics of the United States, Colonial Times to 1970, Bicentennial Edition* (Washington, DC: Government Printing Office, 1975), Series A-7 and Y-336. Nominal data have been put into real terms using an unpublished consumer price index compiled and kindly furnished by Prof. Jack W. Wilson of North Carolina State University.

investments were undercut by state interests and the devotion of that era to the doctrine of states' rights.

The political climate changed when states' rights were weakened during and after the Civil War of 1861–5. The federal government then became more proactive, using its landed resources and the enlarged revenues from increased tariff rates and the alcohol and tobacco excises to aid transcontinental railroads, colleges, river and harbor improvements, the military, and – in initial forays into national welfare programs – continuing care for Civil War veterans and their widows and children. Figure 7.1, showing real federal spending per capita at five-year intervals from 1790 to 1915, captures one dimension of the change. After the fiscal exertions related to the Civil War (indicated in Figure 7.1 by the greatly enlarged per capita spending in 1865), spending did not return to prewar levels, as it had done after another war ended in 1815.

By the turn of the twentieth century, as a result of territorial expansion, immigration, and rapid economic growth, the United States was the largest economy and industrial power in the world. Its governmental system had subdued or eliminated all major threats to internal order.

Although government as a whole was small in relation to the American economy, compared either to Europe then or to the United States later, the American economy was so large as to make the U.S. government a great power.[9] The country had become the dominant nation of the Western Hemisphere and was preparing to play a leading role on the world geopolitical stage.

7.2.3 Financing Fiscal Deficits

An advantage developed by the United States in its earliest years was a sophisticated modern capital market and financial system. The appearance of this system was so sudden and its entrenchment as a part of the country's institutional base so quick and thorough that later observers did not fully appreciate the magnitude of the change it represented. Historians often seemed to assume that it had always existed in U.S. history. The last assumption is almost correct. The modern financial system was present from the time of the first federal administration of President George Washington. It facilitated, apart from the few major wars of U.S. history, the government's ability to finance deficits by borrowing rather than by printing money. This likely was a key difference between the United States and most other countries of the New World.

For the federal government, deficits arose mostly in wartime, when the Treasury issued bonds to finance war expenses. In two instances – the War of 1812 and the Civil War – it also had to resort to currency finance (see Section 7.3). The capital market made it easy to borrow to finance what small peacetime deficits there were, to take advantage of unusual opportunities (for example, the Louisiana Purchase, which overnight in 1803 doubled the size of the country), and to finance other land acquisitions. When the United States was not at war, however, the federal government's budget was typically in surplus, as rapid economic growth drew in imports subject to tariffs. Since, as noted, a major federal role in infrastructure was not allowed to develop for political reasons until the latter decades of the nineteenth century; surplus federal revenues were used to redeem federal debt. In other words, federal budget surpluses

[9] Such seeming paradoxes related to the size of the U.S. economy abound and lead to sources of confusion between Americans and others. An additional example is that, while international trade long was and to a lesser extent still is a small part of the U.S. economy, the country is nonetheless the largest trading nation in the world. While lecturing in Germany in 1996, I was asked by students why, given the great role of the United States in the world economy, there were few if any chapters on international trade and trade policies in U.S. economic history textbooks (including one, they noted, that I had coauthored). All I could say answer this unanticipated question was to invoke the paradox and say that for most American economic historians, international trade is a subtopic in chapters on domestic and foreign commerce. For Germans and others, it is a major topic.

were recycled through the nation's capital market to facilitate borrowing by other governments and the private sector.

New nations, especially those born of costly revolutions, do not soon become countries with pristine international credit and world-class financial systems. The United States is an exception to this rule. Another rule is that great economic institutions such as financial systems (as distinct, perhaps, from particular organizations such as banks, securities exchanges, and departments of government) seldom owe their origins mainly to the efforts of one person, however gifted. Again, the U.S. financial system is an exception. The person in this case was Alexander Hamilton (1757–1804), one of the Founding Fathers, who seemed to play a prominent role in most major events of U.S. history from the time he arrived as an immigrant from the West Indies in 1772 until he was killed by Aaron Burr (the sitting vice president of the United States) in a duel in 1804. During his career, Hamilton was many things including soldier, lawyer, and essayist, but most of all he was a statesman and public administrator equipped with uncommon financial insights and abilities.

When Hamilton arrived in colonial America, there were no banks and no securities markets as we now know them. There was no central bank, unless one counted the home country's Bank of England, on which Hamilton would make himself something of an expert. Indeed, there was no country, only colonies issuing fiat paper money and running government-sponsored loan offices that funded their lending with paper money printed for the purpose. After independence was declared, the national Congress and the state governments borrowed what they could from domestic and foreign supporters, but they had financed the Revolution mostly by printing money, that is, by currency finance, as had been the American practice for decades. The war was protracted. Fiat paper money was greatly overissued, and it depreciated toward worthlessness. All the while, Hamilton was in the Continental army, rising from captain of a New York artillery company in 1775 to lieutenant colonel and aide-de-camp to General Washington by 1777, and then a hero of the Yorktown victory of 1781 that effectively ended the war.

During military lulls, Hamilton mused on how financial chaos more than military deficiencies threatened the American cause. He studied economics and finance and began to formulate his vision of a future American financial system. In 1779, 1780, and 1781, still in his early twenties, he wrote three lengthy letters to national leaders in which he called for a great national bank based on specie and convertible bank notes to cure the obvious problems of fiat paper that he had observed. The last of these letters went to Robert Morris, shortly after he had been appointed Congress's superintendent of finance in 1781. Morris was thinking along similar lines, was encouraged by Hamilton's plan, and soon led the drive for the chartering of an institution more modest than the one Hamilton had sketched, the Bank of North America, which was the first American bank. Hamilton's letter to Morris also dealt with the war's legacy of debt:

> A national debt, if it is not excessive, will be to us a national blessing. It will be a powerful cement to our nation. It will also create a necessity for keeping up taxation to a degree which, without being oppressive, will be a spur to industry.[10]

Here we see the germ of the sweeping financial reforms that Hamilton, as the first secretary of the Treasury under the Constitution, would sprout not quite a decade later: a national bank issuing a bank note currency convertible into specie, and a national debt serviced by revenues from taxes (customs duties) that would at the same time give mild protection to domestic American industries.

We also can see in Hamilton the germ of American nationalism. Most people of the time were loyal to their states, the former colonies. Their country was seen as a loose league or confederation of states designed first and foremost to coordinate interstate efforts in the war of independence. (Analogies with today's European Union would not be strained, although Europe's union is more about keeping peace than waging war.) Hamilton, on the other hand, was an immigrant, in the country for less than a decade. He was not particularly attached to any state. Or to any Old World nation, since he was the illegitimate and orphaned offspring of a Scottish father and a French mother. Hamilton's only loyalties were to the new nation that was forming itself, and he perceived that state particularism and state loyalties were a barrier to forming the nation he envisioned.

After the letter to Morris, Hamilton distinguished himself militarily at Yorktown, studied and practiced law, and for a brief time was a receiver of national levies in New York State (a post in which he discovered the difficulties of getting states to pay Congress's requisitions under the Articles of Confederation, which had left the national government without tax powers). He served in the Confederation Congress and was instrumental in the founding of America's second bank, the Bank of New York, in 1784. In 1786, Hamilton was a New York delegate to the Annapolis convention that met to deal with trade disputes and tariffs between states, and he drafted that convention's report calling for the Constitutional Convention of 1787. At the Philadelphia convention

[10] H. Syrett and J. Cooke, eds., *The Papers of Alexander Hamilton*, 27 vols. (New York: Columbia University Press, 1961–1987), vol. 2, p. 635.

of 1787, Hamilton was again a New York delegate and a member of the small committee that drafted the Constitution. When the Constitution was submitted to the people for ratification, he recruited James Madison and John Jay to join him in explaining and defending it in *The Federalist* papers, writing the majority of the 85 classic essays himself. Then he led the successful fight for ratification in the New York state convention. The Constitution's supporters celebrated the feat by parading a float of a ship labeled "Hamilton" through the streets of New York City, and there was even a suggestion that the city be renamed Hamiltonia. Only 32 then, Hamilton had come a long way from his impoverished early years in the West Indies. But his greatest work, foreshadowed in the letters a decade earlier, was yet to come.

In 1789, President Washington named Hamilton treasury secretary. He set about organizing the department and its machinery for collecting the customs duties and internal excise revenues implemented by Congress. He also drafted his classic reports of 1790 and 1791 on converting the revolutionary debts into long-term federal securities, on a national bank, on a mint (defining the dollar and the monetary base), and on manufactures. The essential provisions of all but the last report were quickly adopted by Congress; many contained in the Report on Manufactures were adopted later. By the time of the Report on Manufactures in the fall of 1791, Hamilton's astonishing successes in organizing the finances of the new federal government and the nation's financial system had provoked an organized political opposition to Federalist policies. This was the Republican Party, led by Secretary of State Thomas Jefferson and James Madison, Hamilton's former ally by then a Virginia congressman, which defended the rights of states against what they saw as too much power in the federal government. The eternal cleavages and two-party system of U.S. political life were thus born of Hamilton's financial initiatives, and they became well established during President Washington's first term, 1789–93. Why the president, who like Jefferson and Madison was a slave-owning planter from Virginia, backed Hamilton virtually every step of the way is a question that still has not been answered by historians. But he did.

The key results of Hamilton's financial program, in addition to strengthened public finances, were a banking system based on bank liabilities convertible into a specie base and a capital market in which governments and private entities could raise funds by issuing bonds and stocks that were tradable in securities markets. The Bank of the United States chartered by Congress and organized in 1791 was the country's fourth bank and, capitalized at $10 million, was by far the largest. Hamilton modeled its charter on that of the Bank of England, and many provisions of the charter were subsequently adopted in the charters of banks organized under state laws. There were differences from the English model; the Bank of the United States was partly owned by the federal government, for example, and it could and did establish branches throughout the country. Neither was the case in England at the time. But like the Bank of England, it was a large corporation with a special relationship to the government and government finances, and it began to develop some of the functions that later would be known as functions of a central bank.

Hamilton's program for converting the revolutionary debts of Congress and the states into new U.S. bonds, with interest and eventually principal payable from federal revenues in specie (or specie-equivalent bank notes), created nearly $80 million of high-quality debt in 1790–2, and the Bank brought an additional $10 million of prime equity. Almost overnight, securities markets sprang up in major cities, with those of New York, Philadelphia, and Boston being the most active, liquid, and deep. The new bond and stock issues were regularly quoted and traded in each of the cities and became the nucleus of a national capital market. Newspapers in each city regularly published security price quotations from the local market and, with some delay, from the markets of the other cities. There is ample evidence of intermarket arbitrage from this interest in information, from surviving letters of market participants, and from the behavior of security prices. The new securities proved attractive to foreign investors as well, and many of the issues began to migrate to English and continental European markets, resulting in the capital inflow Hamilton had predicted in his reports. London quotations of U.S. security prices soon appeared in U.S. newspapers, but only sporadically. Since the information was about two months old by the time it reached the United States, it was not of much use to American market participants.

Local as well as national securities joined the newspaper quotation lists. Each city market soon had its local banks, insurance securities, and transportation securities, as well as state and local governmental debt issues to quote and trade. During the late eighteenth and early nineteenth centuries, the U.S. states were far more lenient than the British and other European governments in granting charters of incorporation to business enterprises. The U.S. corporate stock market, as a result, quickly became more integral to its economy than was the case in European nations.

As the nineteenth century unfolded, the federal, state and local governments were able in numerous ways to tap into the modern system created in the 1790s. So strong was the system that France in 1803 proved eager to give up the vast Louisiana territory in return for $11.25 million of newly issued U.S. securities that it could easily sell to Dutch, British, and even a few American buyers. Not long after, state governments were enabled by strong U.S. public credit and the capital market institutions that arose with it to borrow abroad and at home for infrastructure investments. The states were especially active in funding these road, canal, railroad, and bank investments from the 1820s to the 1840s. During that period the states issued for such purposes some $200 million of debt securities. Then, after a state-debt crisis in the early 1840s briefly tarnished American public credit in the world, U.S. local governments embarked on the same path. Local governmental debts increased from some $25 million in 1840 to $200 million in 1860 (when they equaled the level of state debt two decades earlier) and to at least $820 million in 1880 (according to Census data that were admitted to be incomplete).

An ability to incur long-term public and private debt, and to issue private equity, for infrastructure investments allowed the United States to create a huge internal transportation network and growing numbers of cities as the country developed and industrialized. But that was only one legacy of the new financial system. Under it, apart from the Bank of the United States, the state governments were left in charge of chartering banks. Since bank charters had value, the states could extract revenues from banks, as well as bank loans on favorable terms when it became necessary to finance temporary deficits. Initially, states invested in the stock of banks they chartered, benefiting public treasuries with dividends and capital appreciation. Such investments were made all the more attractive, of course, by liquid equity-trading markets.

Later, as doubts about the appropriateness of states participating as partners in private business enterprises arose, the states shifted to demanding one-time bonus payments in return for granting bank charters or to taxing banks in various ways on an ongoing basis. Or the states simply directed the banks they chartered, as conditions of their charters, to lend or invest in institutions deemed worthy of public support – schools, colleges, orphanages, water works, transportation enterprises, and other elements of infrastructure. The state legislatures in these ways encouraged a public role in development while keeping taxes lower than they otherwise would have been. The states in effect developed a powerful and lasting fiscal interest in the banks they chartered and, of course, an interest in the development of banking. It is hardly surprising, therefore, that there were some 30 state banks chartered by 1800, 100 by 1810, more than 300 by 1820, more than 700 by 1837, and upward of 1,500 by 1860.

Americans, of course, did not invent modern banking. In fact, they came to it rather late, after declaring their independence from Britain. But the proliferation of banks operating under governmental charters that were granted with increasing liberality in the early decades of the nineteenth century, and the close fiscal relationship of state governments to the banks they chartered, were without precedent. By 1825 the United States, with a population less than that of England and Wales, had more than twice as much capital invested in banks as did England and Wales.[11]

In the Old World, chartered banks then were few, and most of the banking business was in private, unincorporated institutions. In the United States, by contrast, incorporated banks proliferated, the privileges conferred by corporate charters attracting substantial investment in share (equity) capital. As a result, bank credit became widely diffused early in the country's history, very much under the aegis of government. Charters of incorporation for banks in the Old World had been a restricted privilege; in America by the middle of the nineteenth century they had become a democratic right. This, too, was a legacy of Hamilton, who was involved in the chartering of three of the first four U.S. banks and was ever the ardent advocate of governmental support for banking and other corporate initiatives.

Because the financial system made it possible for governments in the U.S. federal system to avail themselves of bank and capital-market credit, forced debt became a rarity in U.S. history. Forced debt had been common in the colonial period, when bills of credit were issued to finance numerous wars. It had also been the accepted method of American finance during the War of Independence. But forced loans were unusual thereafter. The only two examples from the nineteenth century were the printing of fiat money and the suspension of specie convertibility during major wars – the War of 1812 (1812–15, with suspension from 1814 to 1817) and the Civil War (1861–5, with suspension from 1862 to 1879). Prior to each of these wars, pro-states'-rights federal administrations had weakened the links of the federal government's finances to the nation's financial system. It was left to susequent administrations and congresses to restore them.

7.3 MONETARY REGIMES

In broad terms, the United States had two monetary regimes, pre-Constitution (colonial and Confederation periods) and post-Constitution, 1789 to the present. Each had to respond to the high

[11] See my paper, "U.S. Capital Markets and the Banking System, 1790–1840." Federal Reserve Bank of St. Louis *Review* 80 (May–June 1998), pp. 83–98.

rates of overall economic expansion that characterized the American economy.

7.3.1 The Pre-Constitution Regime

The colonial regime featured a variety of commodity moneys and the use of specie and foreign coins. Any hard-money system, however, proved difficult to maintain because of chronic trade deficits. Whatever English or European money the colonists brought with them or gained in other ways was spent to finance trade deficits almost as quickly as it came in. This necessitated considerable monetary experimentation and innovation simply to provide local media of exchange. The experiments included the adoption of wampum, the token shell money of the native Americans, as a medium of exchange. Various commodities – corn, rice, tobacco, and beaver pelts, for example – were also granted monetary status. As late as the early 1790s, just before the U.S. dollar came in, counties in Virginia still levied and collected county taxes in tobacco money. Precious metals gained mostly from trade with Latin America circulated in the English North American colonies, and some passing attempts were made to provide local coinages from inflows of bullion. Extensive use was also made of book credits, with settlements spread out over many months and even years. The crowning achievements of all this colonial monetary innovation, mentioned earlier, were the bills of credit, the Western world's first fiat paper money.

Colonial monetary innovations were likely demand induced, that is, called forth by the demands of a rapidly expanding economy for more means to facilitate exchanges of goods and services. A test of this hypothesis is whether innovation was greatest in those colonies that grew fastest. This seems to have been the case. Massachusetts was the second largest colony in terms of population and the most developed of all of them in its commerce. The colony made corn a legal tender in 1631, a practice that other colonies put into effect for different commodities.[12] Massachusetts also made wampum a legal tender in 1643 and again was followed by other colonies. But neither of these was a satisfactory solution to the money problem. Debtors would pay with inferior qualities of "eligible" commodities, and an officially rated monetary status for commodities also led to overproduction, in the sense that market prices fell below official ratings. Wampum was even counterfeited with bones and stones. Massachusetts therefore established a mint in 1652 for the purpose of coining silver. The most famous coin from that mint was the

[12] Nussbaum, *History of the Dollar*, p. 4.

so-called pinetree shilling.[13] The mint seems to have worked well enough for a time, for the colony ended the legal-tender status of wampum in 1661. In 1684, however, regulation overcame innovation when the English Crown ordered the mint shut down because it violated the royal prerogative of coinage. Six years later Massachusetts came up with its bills of credit, which quickly evolved into a fiat paper currency and then spread, as noted earlier, to all the other colonies.

The experiences of Massachusetts and the other colonies yielded numerous examples of monetary innovation in practice. The results of such innovations were sometimes quite inflationary, especially in New England, when bills of credit were overissued during the 1730s and 1740s. Innovations often have unpleasant side effects. But they also had the beneficial effect of removing what might otherwise have been a constraint on colonial economic growth. This point was missed by some later observers who saw the innovations as stopgap measures carried out at times of crisis and as ways by which debtor classes cheated creditors.

The decades before the American Revolution were marked by numerous wars and other crises as the English, the French, and the Spanish vied for control of North America. American colonial governments had to pay for much of these wars, and one of their ways of doing so was monetary innovation – fiat money printing usually followed by inflation. But politics and war are not the entire explanation of the innovations. In the Middle Colonies – New York, New Jersey, Pennsylvania, Delaware, and Maryland – colonial governments first issued paper money not to combat foreign enemies but to alleviate economic depressions. The governments of these colonies were rather successful in their antidepression monetary policies. Their paper money issues contributed to a half-century of relatively noninflationary economic growth before 1776.[14]

The worst inflationary excesses of the colonial period came in New England and the South. These were flank regions most exposed to territorial conflicts with the French and the Spanish. During King George's War from 1744 to 1748, Massachusetts bills of credit outstanding rose from £300 thousand to £2.1 million. By 1749 the price of silver measured in bills of credit was double what it had been before the war, in 1743.[15] This experience, along with those of the War of 1812 and the Civil War, provided nineteenth-century American writers with their prime exam-

[13] Nussbaum, *History of the Dollar*, pp. 6–7.

[14] See Richard Lester, *Monetary Experiments – Early American and Recent Scandinavian* (Princeton: Princeton University Press, 1939), chs. 3–5.

[15] Brock, *Currency of American Colonies*, pp. 33–4.

ples of the dangers of inconvertible paper money and governmental authority to sponsor it. From a twentieth-century perspective, of course, such doublings of the price level after a few years of war, or even during peacetime, do not seem quite so exceptional.

In the 1740s, however, such inflationary excesses were new and shocking. They seemed to expose the Achilles heel of paper money. The English Parliament reacted to them by passing the Currency Act of 1751, placing stringent limits on fiat paper issues in New England. In 1764, after another war financed by paper and attempts by colonists to pay British creditors with it, another Currency Act extended the limitations to the rest of the colonies. The colonies protested against this interference with their long-standing monetary practices – it was part of the rising revolutionary sentiment – and they secured some relaxation of the interference before the revolutionary crisis of the 1770s.

During the Revolution, the colonial innovation of paper money was carried to extremes. Within a week of the battle of Bunker Hill in 1775, the Continental Congress authorized an issue of $2 million in "Continental Currency," national bills of credit. By the end of 1779, 40 more issues swelled the total to more than $240 million. In addition, state paper money issues and loan certificates added to stocks of money and near-money. Soon the Continentals became worthless.

7.3.2 The Constitution's Regime

In the 1780s, after the Revolution was won, states resumed issuing paper money to combat postwar depressions, as the Middle Colonies had done with some success during the previous half-century. Then, however, there were attempts, particularly in Rhode Island when its state legislature was captured by agrarian debtor majorities, deliberately to cheat creditors by inflating the currency and declaring it legal tender for all debts. The British were no longer around to put a stop to such shenanigans. Such occurrences prompted nationalist leaders to ban state paper-money issues in the 1787 Constitution. Their preferred alternative – paper bank note and deposit liabilities issued by private-enterprise banks and convertible into specie on demand – had already been introduced to the United States by the first three U.S. banks founded during 1781–4. Convertible bank money became the chief component of the nineteenth-century monetary regime that replaced the fiat-paper regime operated by colonial and early state governments. It marked a step in the direction of Old World practice that had never caught on during the long colonial period.

The monetary clauses of the Constitution, as they took away the right of states to issue paper money, granted the federal Congress powers of monetary regulation. These were implemented following Hamilton's proposals of 1790–1. His report on a mint called for the United States to have a bimetallic specie standard, with the new U.S. dollar defined in terms of physical amounts of gold and silver. Specie became the monetary base, and the banking system, as discussed earlier, emerged quickly under both state and federal auspices to provide banknotes and deposits convertible into specie.

Apart from occasional suspensions of the specie standard in times of war or financial panic – the major instance coming during the Civil War era and lasting from 1862 to 1879 – the United States maintained the specie standard and enjoyed comparative long-run price stability: The price level of the early twentieth century was little changed from that of the late eighteenth century. Bimetallism never worked as Hamilton and others had hoped it would, but that was a minor inconvenience. For much of the nineteenth century, the United States in fact was a part of the international gold-standard regime led by Britain, the "in fact" becoming "in law" in 1900, after the greenback and populist/silver tamperings of the late nineteenth century demonstrated that a firmer commitment to gold would strengthen international confidence in the dollar.

Two early attempts to establish a national bank, one that likely would have grown into a full-fledged central bank on the evolving European model, failed when politics prevented their federal charters from being renewed when they expired in 1811 and 1836. These were Hamilton's First Bank of the United States, chartered in 1791, and its successor and larger replica (capitalization increased from \$10 to \$35 million), the Second Bank of the United States, chartered in 1816. The First Bank executed some central banking functions, but these were largely subordinated to Treasury functions of a similar nature under Hamilton and his immediate successors. The Second Bank, particularly under the leadership of Nicholas Biddle from 1823 to 1836, was more self-consciously a *central bank*, with the term itself arising for the first time (as far as this writer knows) in the American debates over the Bank's recharter during the early 1830s.

The two Banks of the United States, modeled as they were on the Bank of England, suffered from a design flaw that proved fatal to them in the rampant democracy of the country: They were profit-making corporations that both competed with and exercised central-bank control over the state-chartered banks that were growing in number and political influence through their ties to state governments. In less democratic England, this was not a problem (at least until the twentieth century), but in America it was poison. The First Bank failed to be rechartered by a single vote in the U.S. Senate, although the decision was reversed five years later after financial embarrassments during the War of 1812. The Second Bank in 1832 was rechartered by Congress, but the action was vetoed by President Andrew Jackson, an antibanking politician who nonetheless enjoyed the support of numerous state bankers, and Congress could not override his veto.

The United States therefore functioned without a true central bank until the Federal Reserve System appeared early in the twentieth century. Before this "Third Bank of the United States" came along, various public and private arrangements came in to substitute for a central bank. The U.S. Treasury was in a position to execute some central banking functions, and from time to time it did. In New England from the 1820s to the 1860s, the private Suffolk Bank of Boston cajoled country banks into keeping deposits with it in order to have their notes redeemed at par. Banks in a number of cities formed clearing houses, the first appearing in New York in 1853, and these organizations developed methods of extending the monetary base during episodic convertibility crises.

Under the National Banking System founded in 1863–4, during the Civil War, state bank notes were driven out of existence by taxation and the country for the first time had a uniform national currency issued under federal auspices. The system itself was essentially New York's free-banking system, introduced in 1838, as applied to the entire United States. Under both systems, banks were chartered administratively according to legislatively prescribed rules rather than by individual legislative acts. National banks were required by law to hold reserves that were set percentages of their note and deposit liabilities. Through a correspondent banking system that developed over time, the central reserves of the country came to be held in the large national banks of New York City, which therefore assumed in fact some of the roles of a central bank.

When the National Banking System came in, many regarded one of its key features to be the backing of bank notes with government bonds deposited with a new public authority, the comptroller of the currency in the Treasury Department. This provision was taken over from the 1838 New York State law and was a feature of all "American-style" free banking laws in other states before 1863. If a bank failed, the deposited bonds would be liquidated to compensate holders of its notes. The provision, however, looked backward, not forward, and was of limited significance. By the late nineteenth century, deposits became far more important than notes in the banking system's liability structure. Threats to the stability of individual banks as well as to the stability of the whole system resulted not from runs to convert notes to specie but rather to convert deposits to currency, which included specie, some fiat paper (U.S. notes, the Civil War greenbacks that were only partly retired after the war), and national bank notes.

Periodic financial panics and suspensions of convertibility (typically brief) pointed to problems in these arrangements. After the panic of 1907, Congress appointed a National Monetary Commission, the work of which resulted in the Federal Reserve Act of 1913. By making the Federal Reserve System the Third Bank of the United States, a nonprofit entity that controlled its member commercial banks but did not compete with them, Congress did not repeat a political mistake it had twice made decades earlier in chartering the First and Second Banks.

There were, as noted earlier, two lengthy suspensions of convertibility linked to wars. The War of 1812 led to a suspension from 1814 to 1817, but only in the part of the country outside of New England. In New England, the most commercial region of the country, which contained half of the country's banks and almost a third of its chartered bank capital, the conflict was unpopular. The region maintained specie convertibility, while bank notes from the rest of the country went to discounts as high as 30 percent. Government finance was instrumental in the suspension. The Treasury issued both long-term debt and short-term Treasury notes to pay its bills; the latter were essentially a fiat paper issue that banks treated as reserves. One of the first tasks of the Second Bank of the United States after it was chartered in 1816 was to restore convertibility. It did not handle the task very well; its initial expansion and then contraction of credit contributed to the financial panic of 1819. The episode contributed to its later unpopularity with the Jacksonian Democrats, who torpedoed its recharter by Congress.

The Civil War suspension lasted from 1862 to 1879. The U.S. price level and the price of gold roughly doubled during the war, as the government again borrowed extensively and issued the fiat-currency greenbacks. Soon after the war ended in 1865, attempts to bring about a quick resumption of specie convertibility by reducing the inflated money stock ran afoul of politics. Instead, the money stock was stabilized, and economic growth led to price-level deflation. By 1879, the pre–Civil War price level was reached and convertibility was restored. Throughout the suspension, remote and gold-rich California, like New England during the 1814–17 suspension, maintained convertibility.

One of the curiosities of nineteenth-century monetary policy is the commitment not just to restore price-level stability after wars, but to do so at prewar parities of the currency in terms of specie. Such policies necessitated deflation, which was usually accompanied by economic depression and both political and social unrest, albeit in the American case within the parameters of law and order established under the

Constitution. The twentieth-century approach to similar problems, at least after the U.K. experience in the 1920s, was different. It was to stabilize the price level after bouts of inflation, not to roll it back to earlier levels. The American tradition of decentralized – some would say fragmented – decision making in financial arrangements carried over from the colonial period into the nineteenth century. States developed state-chartered and "free" banking systems. These were supplemented throughout the nineteenth century by private, unchartered banks operating under common-law traditions. When the federal government reentered bank chartering with its National Banking System in 1863, it intended to supplant the old state-based chartering system. But that did not happen. State banking systems recovered after the federal onslaught of the 1860s, and the country continued with a dual banking system of federal and state chartering, resulting in tens of thousands of independent banks operating under numerous authorities. The best that can be said of these inelegant banking arrangements is that they were responsive to the needs of an economy expanding both structurally and geographically in ways that a more unified system might not have been. Banking in the United States remains one of the last bastions of states' rights in large measure because it was one of the first. The close ties of banks to state governments that developed early in the country's history, along with suspicions about too much federal power rooted in Jefferson's 1790s reactions to Hamilton's measures, were not easily overcome by later would-be financial reformers.

The U.S. diversity in commercial banking arrangements carried over into the rest of the financial system. Securities markets, brokers, and stock exchanges were organized in major cities at the end of the eighteenth century; gradually they were integrated into one national capital market. As New York City developed into the nation's financial center by the 1830s, the banking system and the securities markets became closely tied through bank reserves lent out on call at the New York Stock Exchange.

Insurance companies were among the first nonbank financial intermediaries, several dating to the eighteenth century. Over the course of the nineteenth century many other types of specialized financial intermediaries appeared. Investment bankers and savings banks were present by the decade of the 1810s. Mortgage banking and even mortgage securitization began a decade later, as did the trust company. By the 1830s a commercial paper market had emerged.

Decentralized decision making seemed conducive to continuation of the spirit of financial innovation established in colonial days. Yet the nature of the U.S. financial system as it emerged and developed from the 1790s to the 1830s was altogether different from pre-1789 financial arrangements. Commercial banks, bank money convertible to specie, a central bank, a funded national debt, securities markets and stock exchanges – these were not a part of the colonial American financial system. The orator and U.S. senator Daniel Webster (1782–1852) grew up with the new system and, speaking in the 1830s, he emphasized that Hamilton was the principal architect of the Federalist-era financial revolution that brought it into being:

> He smote the rock of the national resources, and abundant streams gushed forth. He touched the dead corpse of the public credit, and it sprung to its feet. The fabled birth of Minerva from the brain of Jove was hardly more sudden or more perfect than the financial system of the United States as it burst forth from the conception of Alexander Hamilton.[16]

Fine rhetoric. But what did Hamilton's system really accomplish? Before Hamilton, Americans were well off by the standards of that era, but their access to credit was limited and their assets lacked liquidity. Financial assets, moreover, were quite small in relation to real assets, and "cash," including precious metals in monetary form, was only a small part of what financial assets there were.[17] Hamilton's financial system changed all that. In doing so, it released the latent energies of Americans and their continent of resources, much as the steam engine at the same time released the latent energies of wood and coal. The modern economic growth that came to the United States during its first decades, as banking historian Bray Hammond was fond of saying, was based on steam and credit.[18]

7.4 LINKS OF MONETARY REGIMES AND PUBLIC FINANCE

As should be abundantly clear from the foregoing, throughout American history, the linkages of public finance to the monetary regime and to private finance in general were strong. The great innovation of the colonial era, fiat paper money, was government sponsored. It was introduced to solve pressing needs of public finance. Only after bills of credit appeared did colonial governments and private transactors make the pleasant discovery that they also met the continually growing demand for means of exchange. From there it was but a short step to the colonial loan office or land bank that provided additional paper means of exchange while at the same time expanding private credit facilities and

[16] Quoted by John Steele Gordon, *Hamilton's Blessing: The Extraordinary Life and Times of Our National Debt* (New York: Walker and Company, 1997), pp. 40–1.

[17] On American financial asset holdings on the eve of the Revolution, see Alice Hanson Jones, *Wealth of a Nation to Be* (New York: Columbia University Press, 1980), ch. 5.

[18] Bray Hammond, *Banks and Politics in America, from the Revolution to the Civil War* (Princeton: Princeton University Press, 1957).

giving its public sponsors an ongoing interest revenue. It should be remembered, however, that bills of credit were but a component of the colonial money stock. There were a variety of other components, ranging from specie to rated commodities to book credits. That is what has confounded attempts to demonstrate that colonial fiat paper money was inherently inflationary, or that it was not.

After independence, the federal government determined the monetary regime, and it essentially created the country's capital market as, under Hamilton's leadership, Revolutionary War debts were converted into high-grade bonds and a national bank was established. Motivated greatly by considerations of public finance, the states established their own state-chartered banking systems. Largely with similar motives the federal government, after losing its two national banks, set up during the Civil War a system of national banks modeled on state precedents. The federal and state governments always drew on banks for revenues and loans. Banks and other corporations, financial and nonfinancial, raised capital by issuing shares and debt in the capital markets that owed their origins to public finance. These markets, like the banking system, gave capital a liquidity it did not have in the colonial era.

7.5 OLD AND NEW WORLD HERITAGES

The U.S. heritage was mainly derived from the British heritage, but negatively as well as positively. From the start, that is, there were many deviations from British financial institutions and practices that owed their origins to regulatory stringencies of British colonial rule. Colonial financial innovation was undertaken in response to British regulations that prevented the colonies from duplicating home-country institutions, as well as to the high rate of economic growth the colonies experienced.

In a sense, the federal government after 1789 brought national public finance and the financial system closer to British institutions and practices than they had been when Britain ruled America. Nonetheless, U.S. banking for decades developed quite differently from Britain's system. From the start, U.S. banking was dominated by chartered corporations with limited liability, a system Britain would adopt much later. The U.S. monetary and banking systems also differed, due in part to bimetallism and the lack for extended periods of a central bank. The United States started in 1791 with a central bank similar to the Bank of England, abandoned it some four decades later, and then brought it back in a greatly altered form in 1913.

Still, the two countries were closely tied through trade, trade finance, and capital markets. U.S. federal debt securities and U.S. Bank stock were traded in London while Hamilton was Treasury secretary, and these transatlantic capital market linkages would facilitate the transfer of large amounts of foreign capital to the United States during the nineteenth century. There were obvious institutional and regime differences, but when the whole of the Old and New Worlds are compared, it is evident that the two countries were more similar than different in financial traditions. The twentieth century accordingly spoke of "Anglo-Saxon" finance and Anglo-American market-oriented financial systems, in contrast with continental European bank-based systems and hybrid Asian models. In this there is an element of irony. As separate nations, Britain and the United States furnish an example of financial-system convergence that was little evident before 1776, when the two were parts of the same empire.

8

The Legacy of French and English Fiscal and Monetary Institutions for Canada

Michael D. Bordo and Angela Redish

Canada is comprised of 10 provinces and 2 territories whose heritage derives from the (diverse) original peoples of the country and the institutions and cultures of the colonizing powers, as well as those of the equally diverse immigrants. To analyze the impact of imperial traditions on the development of fiscal and monetary institutions throughout the seventeenth to nineteenth centuries would require space and time that we do not have. We therefore focus our discussion on the role of British and French antecedents in the development of Canadian institutions by examining almost exclusively the experiences of Ontario and Quebec, the most populous colonies at the time of Confederation. We will present our data and analysis by breaking down the historical experience into three eras:

1. 1713–63: the French period – New France develops a sustainable economy
2. 1763–1867: the British colony period[1]
3. 1867–1914: the early postcolonial period

In 1713, after the Treaty of Utrecht, the economy along the St. Lawrence River experienced four decades of relatively peaceful development. The fur trading economy diversified with increasing agricultural settlement. Yet the economy also relied heavily on transfers from the imperial government to finance the civil service and the military presence. The population is estimated to have risen steadily from 23,000 in 1713 to the mid 50,000's in 1763 (Desbarats, 1996, 165).

After the Treaty of Paris in 1763, New France was ceded to Britain, and during the period 1763–92 the colony of Quebec was governed as a

[1] The colony was known as Quebec until 1791; then it split into two colonies – Upper and Lower Canada; in 1841 the colonies were united under one legislature, although there were two divisions: Canada West and Canada East.

single unit by administrative fiat from Britain.[2] The period includes the Quebec Act of 1774, the American Revolution, and the early years of the Loyalist emigration to Nova Scotia, the Eastern Townships of Quebec, and Ontario.

The influx of large numbers of Anglo immigrants led, in 1792, to the separation of the colonies of Upper and Lower Canada. Both colonies would be governed by a governor, advised by an Executive Council, and domestic legislation would be enacted by the bicameral house composed of an appointed Legislative Council and an elected Legislative Assembly. In 1841, following the Rebellion of 1837, the two colonies were reunited, although some functions were still administered separately in Canada East (Quebec today) and Canada West (Ontario). Finally, in 1846 the colonies were granted responsible government.

In 1867 the British North America (BNA) Act created the confederation of Canada from the colonies of Canada (East and West), New Brunswick, and Nova Scotia. Prince Edward Island (1873), Manitoba (1870), and British Columbia (1871) joined the Confederation soon afterward.[3] Confederation was motivated to a very large extent by economic forces: the overwhelming debts that had been incurred in the provinces to build canals and railroads, and the loss of preferential access to markets first in Britain and then in the United States. The BNA Act gave the federal government exclusive jurisdiction over money and banking, broad taxation authority, and residual powers.

Canadian fiscal and monetary institutions evolved through these regimes. Throughout the period under study, the monetary system developed with a backdrop of a specie standard, yet at no time did the colonies have their own mint, and the nominal anchor was created by the assignment of legal tender values to a variety of coins produced externally. The central tension for the monetary system lay between the "sound money" appeal of the specie standard and the fiscal benefits of a paper money issue. This experience echoes that of the 13 colonies to the south (Engerman and Gallman, 1996). Fiscal policies today bear a heavy imprint of British tradition, but the influences of environment and of the United States are also conspicuous. Except for the development of

[2] The boundaries of the area fluctuated: according to the Treaty of Paris, New France was divided into Quebec (basically the St. Lawrence Valley) and Indian territory; in 1774 the Quebec Act extended the boundary of Quebec to include much of old New France; in 1783 the Peace of Versailles set the southern boundary of Quebec in the middle of lakes Ontario and Erie, ceding a portion of the fur trade hinterland to the new United States.

[3] The Northwest Territories included the provinces of Alberta and Saskatchewan, which did not acquire provincial status until 1905. Newfoundland joined the confederation in 1949.

Table 8.1. Revenues (in Livres Tournois) of the Fermiers Generales

	Import Duties	Export Duties	Seigneurial	Total
1719	24,941.38	2,438.50	1,390.50	28,770.38
1720	25,363.50	1,580.50	90.95	27,034.95
1721	29,416.67	1,904.50	166.75	31,487.92
1722	21,080.25	2,679.50	111.17	23,870.92
1723	32,332.54	1,887.50	971.28	35,171.32
1724	30,070.83	1,161.00	614.48	31,846.31
1725	32,029.67	1,337.00	1,130.69	34,497.36
1726	36,698.17	1,107.00	746.68	38,551.85
1727	27,004.38	921.50	589.31	28,515.19
1728	42,257.70	1,493.50	514.08	44,265.28
1729	47,613.88	1,144.50	708.50	49,466.88
1730	51,856.08	919.00	3,989.98	56,764.06
1731	52,178.03	2,331.50	285.98	54,795.51
1732	49,993.10	1,138.00	1,874.82	53,005.92

Source: Nish (1975).

policies in the province of Quebec, the influence of French traditions is remarkably scant.

8.1 NEW FRANCE – THE FISCAL SYSTEM

The early fiscal regime following 1713 continued that of the period before the War of the Spanish Succession. Canada was part of the Domaine d'Occident, a tax farm that included France's West Indian territories.[4] The farm was held by the Fermiers Generales until 1732 and then by the Department of the Marine (Navy). The owner of the lease had the right to revenues from certain taxes and had certain obligations to provide public works. The former were comprised of import duties (primarily), export duties (however, not on beaver, whose market had already been satiated), and some seigniorial dues. The revenue to the French Crown reflected the lease payments.

Tables 8.1 to 8.3 summarize the available data. (Available data are not scarce – just available consistent data series!) Table 8.1 shows the revenues accruing to the holder of the tax farm in Canada from 1719 to 1732 (Nish, 1975). Total revenues grew gradually, with the import duty (primarily on alcohol) yielding considerably more than either seigniorial dues or export taxes. Table 8.2 shows the receipts of the Domaine d'Occident in Canada after it was taken over by the Department of

[4] A tax farm that was later integrated by John Law into the Compagnie des Indes.

Table 8.2. Receipts (in Livres Tournois) of the Domaine d'Occident in Canada

	Levies	Net Revenues	Supplementary Revenues
1733	116,064	37,772	
1734	n.a.	44,440	
1735	123,164	57,983	123,582
1736	104,712	22,074	68,793
1737	106,464	42,179	88,236
1738	105,829	64,871	59,698
1739	75,792	39,379	81,777
1740	78,310	32,948	79,521
1741	66,831	25,566	87,243
1742	53,364	8,547	90,000
1743	9,125	41,118	60,132
1744	64,168	n.a.	72,000

Source: Desbarats (1996), Table 5.8, p. 239.

Table 8.3. Expenditures (in Livres Tournois) of the French Intendant in New France

1719	430,804	1735	485,743
1720	382,499	1736	492,692
1721	577,932	1737	711,439
1722	406,158	1738	535,438
1723	412,093	1739	566,332
1724	383,671	1740	503,767
1725	393,594	1741	576,686
1726	398,150	1742	664,733
1727	416,897	1743	696,145
1728	750,803	1744	928,152
1729	464,510	1745	1,301,813
1730	494,217	1746	2,943,421
1731	420,554	1747	2,858,854
1732	482,447		
1733	457,045		
1734	439,387		

Note: For each year there is frequently more than one estimate of the expenditures, since intendants often constructed retrospective accounts. The primary problems were that final accounts might not arrive from Paris until several years later and that accounting within Canada was hampered by the distances involved. The conclusion that the French government spent far more in New France than it received in revenue is robust to the different estimates of the levels of government expenditure.

Source: Desbarats (1996), Table 4.1, pp. 131–20.

the Marine. Net revenues deduct the expenditure obligations of the lease holder from the gross revenues, and the supplementary column reflect additional expenditures by the navy to pay for the obligations of the lease holder. Table 8.3 shows the (other) spending by the French government in the colony (Desbarats, 1996, p. 131), which, as noted earlier, dwarfed any revenue the French obtained from the colony. At least one-third (and typically more) of the annual expenditure was attributed to fortifications and troop's pay, with another 20 percent being for food and merchandise, which, Desbarats argues, was equally a military expenditure.

Although the data are not great, at the aggregate level they tell a simple story. The bulk of French government expenditures were for military purposes, and these expenditures far outweighed taxes raised in Canada (i.e., the lease payments).[5] This raised two problems: solvency and liquidity. The solvency problem refers to how the French government borrowed or taxed in France to pay for its colonial expenditures; the liquidity problem (also known as the *transfer problem*) refers to how the transfer occurred. Both problems led recurrently to issues of fiat/fiduciary money in New France: the famous playing card currency discussed in the following section.

8.2 NEW FRANCE – THE MONETARY SYSTEM

The unit of account during the French period was the livre tournois, in which 12 deniers equal 1 sol and 20 sols equal 1 livre. The medium of exchange was, however, more complex. The underlying money was coins minted in France, such as the silver écu and the gold Louis d'or and silver dollars. As in many American colonies, there were frequent complaints of a shortage of currency.[6] Colonial officials responded by raising the value of the French coins by one-third, in the (perennially vain) hope that it would keep the specie in the colony.[7] However, in 1717, in recognition of the empirical and theoretical futility of such a policy, the overvaluation was abolished in Canada.

[5] The burden the colony imposed on French finances was not unnoticed at Versailles. In 1733 the king of France proposed increasing taxes on the colonists, but the Intendant in Quebec said that it would require 600 more troops to enforce such taxes (whether a poll tax or import or export duties). The king noted that the cost of the troops would be 140,000 livres per year, and the tax would raise 40,000 livres per year and left the taxes unchanged (Weaver, 1914, p. 748).

[6] Redish (1984) argues that the typical explanation for shortage of coin, an export drain, is an incomplete argument at best, since coin exports are endogenous to the monetary system.

[7] As did Massachusetts and other American colonies. There is some debate about the dates of such overvaluation. Shortt (1986, I, p. xli, 5) states that the first overvaluation occurred in October 1661. The overvaluation of one-third appears to have been in place from then until 1717. McCusker (1978, p. 282).

Other media of exchange arose as reflections of fiscal problems and the scarcity of specie. The most famous of these responses is the playing card currency.[8] The use of playing cards as a medium of exchange occurred first in the seventeenth century. In 1685 an anticipated shipment of specie from France to the colonial officials did not arrive. The colonial intendant (Jacques de Meulles) paid his bills by writing IOUs on playing cards, and insisted that they be accepted in payment of all debts in the colony, while promising to redeem them in the spring when the specie arrived on the first boat. The specie did in fact arrive, and the cards were redeemed.[9] Note issues continued intermittently until 1700, with the innovation that they were redeemed in bills of exchange drawn on the French Treasury in Paris rather than in silver.[10] During the War of the Spanish Succession far more cards were issued than were redeemed, and at the end of the war they were redeemed at 50 percent of par and future issues were banned.

Despite the capital losses accruing to past holders of playing cards at the beginning of the eighteenth century, there was a renewed issue of playing card currency in 1730. Prior to that, the colonial government had issued *ordonnances* that filled the same function as the initial playing card currency – a temporary substitute for payment in specie. The rationale for the new card issue is unclear. The governor wrote to the imperial administration and argued that the citizens were requesting that cards be issued again as a medium of exchange, and that in their absence merchants were issuing private notes that were accepted only at "usurious" discounts. The French government consented to the new card money but required that all issues be approved in France and that the quantity be strictly controlled. Issues were to be redeemed in bills of exchange drawn on the navy in France. The initial issue was for 400,000 livres, and 260,000 livres more were approved in the next three years. Further issues totaling 300,000 livres were made in 1742 and 1749.

[8] We draw on the work of Shortt (1986) and Zay (1892).

[9] This experience is comparable to that of the 13 colonies, where tax anticipation warrants and other bills of credit were issued by colonial governments, usually during wartime emergencies, on the promise of future taxes to be collected or specie to be remitted from Britain. See Smith (1985) and Michener (1987).

[10] The cards had the advantages that they could be used by illiterate people, who knew that the black cards were valued at 100 livres and the red ones at 50 livres. The cards were all imported from France; the first printing press did not arrive in Canada until 1749 (Zay, 1892, p. 132.) According to Shortt (1990) counterfeiting was a problem (although whether on smuggled cards is unclear): 1731–2 reference to the trial and punishment of a counterfeiter (pp. 627–9), and in July 1736 a man and his wife were executed for counterfeiting.

The cards circulated at or near par throughout the 1730s and occasionally rose to a premium over the motley collection of specie. However, war-induced fiscal problems again led to a depreciation in the 1740s, when the War of the Austrian Succession (1744–8) affected the budget of France and indirectly the colony. Although the volume of playing cards had increased, the expenses of war were mostly met by the issue of *ordonnances* by soldiers in the field. These were not limited by the need for approval from France, or even Quebec City, and expanded rapidly. By 1749 there were 40 million livres of paper money (including cards, *ordonnances*, and bills of exchange on the navy) that traded at a discount of more than 50 percent. The onset of the Seven Years' War (1756) led to further inflation, and after the French defeat in 1759 there was widespread fear that the cards were worthless. However, under the Treaty of Paris (1763), the French agreed to redeem the cards at 25 percent of their value.[11] (The redemption was in French bonds, which immediately traded at a discount.)[12]

8.3 BRITISH COLONIAL CANADA – THE FISCAL SYSTEM

The early period of British rule – after the end of the French period and before the Canada (1791) Act – was dominated by the U.S. War of Independence and resulting Loyalist immigration. Most of the Loyalists (an estimated 32,000 of 40,000) moved to Nova Scotia, and the remainder settled in the Eastern Townships and on the north shore of Lake Ontario. Early Anglo immigrants, the merchants who had moved to Quebec in 1763, had lobbied unsuccessfully for representative (of English settlers) government from the early days of British rule, but this had been thwarted by governors who advocated appeasing the French Canadians and then by the march of military events. The lobbying was increased by Loyalist settlements prompting the British to establish the two separate colonies. In 1791 the Canada Act split the colony into two and granted a form of representative government to both Upper (Ontario) and Lower (Quebec) Canada.

Perhaps the most surprising characteristic of fiscal policy in this period is the virtual absence of Canadian payments for British troops in the colony. From 1774 until the end of the War of 1812, Canada was under

[11] The bills of exchange were redeemed at 50 percent of their value and the *ordonnances* at 25 percent.

[12] The depreciation is sometimes suggested to have created an aversion to paper money among French Canadians, e.g., S. S. Carroll, "Canadian Paper Money," *Canadian Numismatic Journal*, Vol. 1, No. 4 (April 1956), pp. 70–4. Similarly, Shortt suggests that French Canadians preferred specie to paper money, and McIvor (writing in the 1950s) argues that "this characteristic of the French Canadian was undoubtedly an important factor contributing to the beginnings of banking in Canada" (p. 12).

Table 8.4. Population of Canada

	Upper Canada	Lower Canada	Canada
1720		27,666	
1754		55,000	
1763		65,000	
1791	[a]	161,311[a]	
1806	70,718	250,000	
1825	157,923	479,288	
1831	236,702	553,134	
1840	432,159	716,670	
1851	952,004	890,261	
1861	1,396,091	1,111,566	
1871[b]			3,689,257
1881			4,324,810
1891			4,833,239
1901			5,371,315
1911			7,206,643

[a] The population for the two Canadas was 161,311. In 1784 the population of Upper Canada (to be) was placed at 10,000.
[b] The numbers after 1871 are the population for Canada excluding Newfoundland.
Source: Census of Canada, 1931; *Historical Statistics of Canada* (Toronto: Macmillan, 1965); Desbarats (1996).

fairly constant threat of U.S. invasion, and the British authorities did not want to annoy the British subjects. Then, increasingly over the first half of the nineteenth century, Britain distanced itself from the Canadian colonies.

The colonial governments collected revenues, primarily from trade-based taxes, land revenues, and fees, to pay for the expanding costs of government. Those expenditures ranged from the legal system to the education system and, over time, increasingly toward the costs of infrastructure provision. The lack of a port in Upper Canada and the externalities from improvements to the St. Lawrence waterway led to protracted negotiations between the two colonies on the sharing of revenues and expenditures. The backdrop to these developments was the very rapid expansion of the population of both colonies shown in Table 8.4. The faster growth of the population of Upper Canada reflects the greater immigration to that province, while the growth of Lower Canada was somewhat slowed by net emigration.

For the period 1792–1841 the colonial government accounts of Upper and Lower Canada were kept separately. Figures 8.1 and 8.2 show

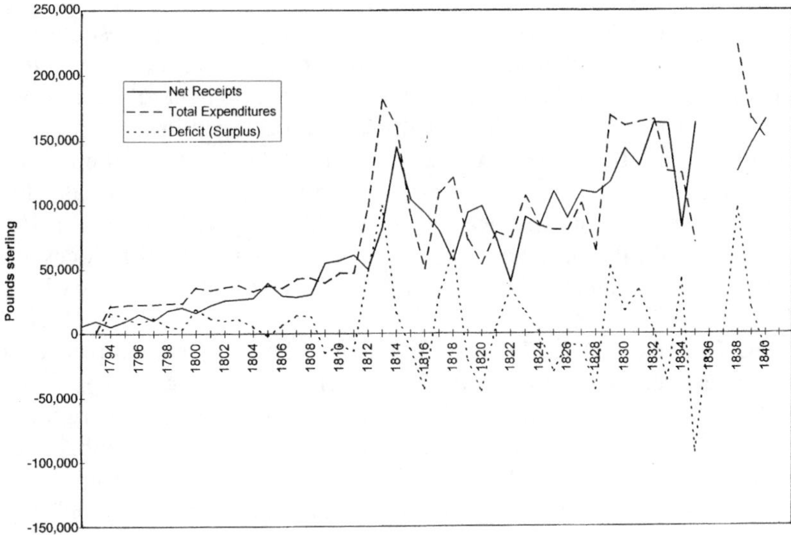

Figure 8.1 Fiscal conditions in Lower Canada.

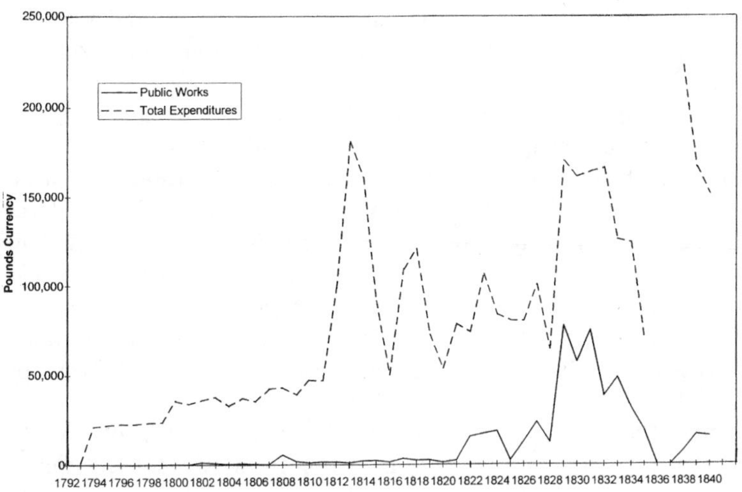

Figure 8.2 Public works expenditures in Lower Canada.

the fiscal history of Lower Canada.[13] The factors determining the fiscal status of the colony included the growth of the population, the War of

[13] An overview based on the annual revenue and expenditure accounts presented in Appendix K.K.K. of *Journals of the House of Assembly of United Canada*, 1847.

1812 and the Rebellion of 1837, and public works expenditures. In June 1812 the U.S. government declared war on Britain in response to a variety of perceived disagreements: naval interference on the Atlantic, British abetting of Indians in the Ohio territory, and general expansionism. The major clashes of the war in Canada occurred in 1812, and the Canadians held their territory as a result of (1) the loyalty of the French Canadians, (2) the superior training of British regular troops, and (3) the incompetence of American generals (McNaught, 1986, p. 71). The peace (the Treaty of Ghent) in 1815 reflected the British focus on France and Napoleon and did little more than restate the boundary lines of 1783.

The Rebellion of 1837 was an uprising of French Canadians against the legislature of Lower Canada. The lieutenant governor had appointed an Executive Council and a Legislative Council, which were both primarily Anglophone, while the elected Legislative Assembly was Francophone dominated. In the early 1830s the legislature ground to a standstill as the Upper and Lower Houses disagreed on every bill. The issues revolved around the relative political power of Anglophone merchants and Francophone farmers, the pull of democracy, and the poor harvests and economic depression of 1837. In November 1837, following rioting in Montreal, the British army fired on the *patriotes* and a number of skirmishes followed. By December the Rebellion had fizzled out (Lower, 1973, p. 92).[14]

The effect of population growth is seen in the secular growth of revenues, most of which were import duties and the similar growth of expenditures. The increase in the Casual and Territorial Revenues (which were predominantly land-derived revenues, including seigniorial revenues, timber fees, and land sales) in the late 1830s represented revenue from tolls on the Lachine Canal. The ordinary expenditures included allowances for the Civil List, the legislature, education, hospitals, and jails. These grew at the same rate as population, with the exception of expenditures on education, which increased from £2,000–3,000 per annum to £25,000 per annum after 1830.[15]

The first fiscal crisis in Lower Canada arose because of the War of 1812. Lower Canada's obligations arose from two sources: militia spending that accounted for the dramatic increase in expenditures in

[14] A rebellion in Upper Canada reflected the same concern with the power of a small elite and fizzled out as quickly. The major consequence of the rebellions was the appointment of Lord Durham to investigate their cause and his report leading to the Union of the Canadas.

[15] All sums are in pounds sterling. Dollars are rated at 4/6d.

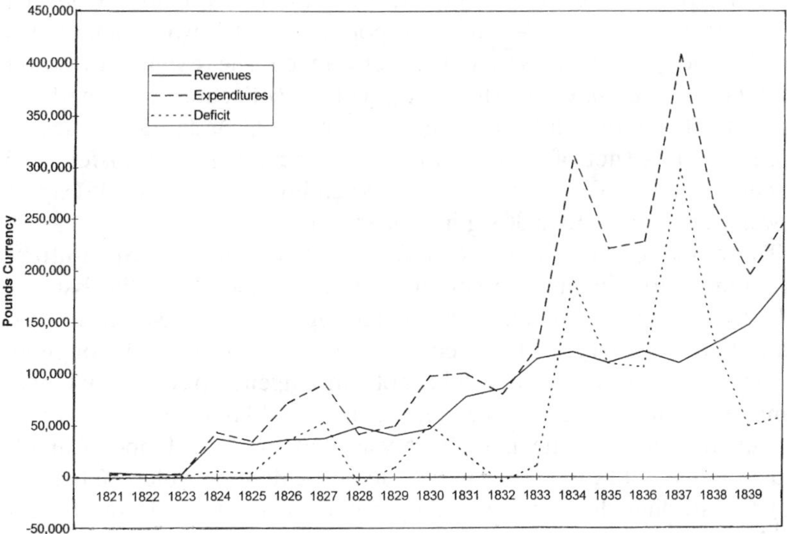

Figure 8.3 Fiscal conditions in Upper Canada.

1812–15 and the repayment of Army Bills that cost £45,777 in 1817.[16] In large part these expenditures were met by the imposition of duties (under Provincial Acts) that raised £27,965, £110,105, and £44,197 in 1813, 1814, and 1815, respectively. Total revenues in 1812 had been £49,730.

The high expenditures of 1829–31 reflect spending on public works (see Figure 8.2). In 1829 expenditures on the Lachine Canal exceeded £50,000 (33 percent of expenditures), while in 1830 and 1831 total expenses for "Internal Communications and Improvements" exceeded £95,000 – again about 30 percent of total expenditures. Unlike Upper Canada, Lower Canada raised relatively little money by issuing debentures, and the only debentures approved prior to the Rebellion were for £31,000 for improvements to the Montreal Harbor.[17]

The public accounts for Upper Canada are not as well preserved as those for Lower Canada. Comprehensive data start in 1822 and are summarized in Figure 8.3, which shows revenues (net of debenture sales), expenditures (gross of public works), and the deficit, which was financed by debenture sales. With respect to ordinary revenues and expenditures

[16] Expenditures were also unusually high in 1817 and 1818 because of payments "for the relief of distressed parishes."

[17] This exceeds expenditures on that line item, and presumably the funds were spent on the canals and other public works.

there are pronounced similarities between the two Canadas. Consider 1825 – an ordinary year – when the population of Lower Canada was almost exactly three times that of Upper Canada. The revenues of Lower Canada were £110,000 sterling (stg) net of collection costs and the transfer of import duty revenue to Upper Canada. Revenues in Upper Canada (net of collection costs but including the transfer from Lower Canada) were £28,364 stg.[18] Expenditures were £80,351 stg in Lower Canada and £31,636 stg in Upper Canada.

There is, however, a stark difference between the expenditures on public works in the two colonies and consequently in the issue of debentures. Upper Canada pursued an aggressive infrastructure program that was largely financed by the issue of debt. Throughout the 1830s the colony issued debt, both in currency payable in Upper Canada and in sterling payable in London, to build roads, canals, bridges, and even railroads. The net effect was that by 1841 Upper Canada had a funded debt of £1,179,949 (the domestic debt payable at 6 percent and the sterling debt at 5 percent), while Lower Canada owed only £96,748.[19]

In 1838 Lord Durham, sent by the Crown to report on the state of the colonies in the aftermath of the rebellions (especially of Lower Canada), recommended that the two colonies be united. The first governor-general was Lord Sydenham (Charles Poulett-Thompson), who brought with him the offer of an imperial guarantee for a loan of £1.5 million stg to refinance the existing provincial debt and to fund more public works.

The fiscal situation of Canada from 1841 to 1867 had two components: the growing debt of the colony and the use of commercial policy to promote economic growth and provide revenue. We have not yet built a detailed account of the state of the government's finances during the Union period, which are complicated by a change in the fiscal year, a change in the unit of account, and changes in accounting practices. The data in Figure 8.4 show the deterioration in Canada's finances between 1851 and 1866. In the early 1850s the province encouraged infrastructure investment (primarily in railroads) and guaranteed loans issued to finance the expenditures. The recession in 1857 led issuers to default, and the indirect obligation of the province became direct debt.

[18] The accounts presented in Appendix KKK are in round currency (£cy) and list the revenues as £31,513. The exchange rate is £1.11 cy = £1 stg. Expenditures were listed as £35,116 cy.

[19] The interest payments for Upper Canada in 1836–8 were about 10 percent of ordinary revenues and expenditures.

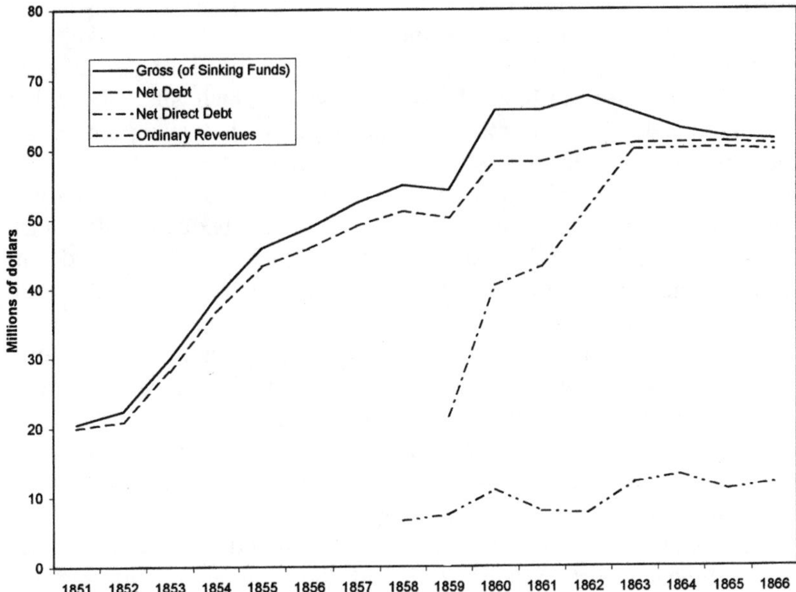

Figure 8.4 Canada's debt, 1851–66.

British abandonment of preferential access for colonial products motivated changes in Canadian commercial policy, abolition of timber preferences (1842) and of the Corn Laws (1846) being the most damaging for the Canadian economy. Canadians (with British assistance) negotiated duty-free access to U.S. markets for primary products. The Reciprocity Treaty of 1854 permitted Canadian raw materials access to U.S. markets in return for the same access to U.S. goods in Canada.[20] The impact of this legislation on the economy is debatable, but the impact on the government's revenue was unambiguously negative. The treaty was abrogated by the United States in 1865, providing a further impetus for Confederation.

8.4 BRITISH COLONIAL CANADA – THE MONETARY SYSTEM

When Britain took over the colony of New France, the monetary system was in disarray. The British government introduced legislation in 1764, effective January 1, 1765, to mandate the use of the British unit of account and to value coins according to Queen Anne's proclamation. This proclamation effectively created a new unit of account for the

[20] In addition, there were benefits to the United States in terms of access to the St. Lawrence waterway and to fishing rights off Nova Scotia.

British American colonies denoted the *pound currency* (£cy), in contrast with the pound sterling (£stg), and denoted by £x/-/-d (whereby £1 equaled 20 shillings [20/-], each of which comprised 12 pence). The proclamation rated the Spanish dollar at 6/- cy, which, since the dollar was valued at 4/6d sterling, made the exchange rate between pounds currency and pounds sterling £1 stg = £1.33 cy. The proclamation made gold coins from Portugal, Germany, England, France, and Spain and silver coins from France and England, as well as the Mexican dollar, legal tender.[21] McCusker (1978) states that Montreal typically used this "lawful money" (£133.33 cy per £100 stg) and Quebec City used a third unit of account, Halifax currency, with an exchange rate of £111.11 cy per £100 stg. In 1777 Halifax currency was adopted throughout the colony, implying that the dollar was rated at 5/- and other coins in proportion. Both the 1764 and 1777 acts (and indeed the amendments in 1796, 1808, and 1809) undervalued gold coin and some of the silver coins, with the result that the medium of exchange comprised French silver coins and pistareens – the most overvalued coins.[22]

The monetary system of the Canadas continued the "multi-coin" standard of the early postconquest years, with the legal tender ratings of the coins being altered intermittently by the colonial legislature. Until 1841 the unit of account, the Halifax currency equaled $4 ($1 = 5/–), and dollars were used frequently both as a medium of exchange and as a unit of account. In 1841, at imperial insistence, the dollar was rated at 5/1d, and the resulting dislocation of trade with the United States led to provincial legislation to make the dollar the unit of account. The Colonial Office did not easily allow this transition from the British system. In 1850 the Coinage Act revaluing the dollar was disallowed, but this simply prompted the provincial legislature to pass more encompassing legislation. In 1853 the provincial government, in concert with the legislatures in the other British North American colonies, passed legislation adopting the decimal dollar system and making gold the sole unlimited legal tender.[23] The introduction of token subsidiary silver coins in the United States, new faces in the House of Lords, and the unanimity of the North American colonies combined to lead to acceptance of the bill. By 1867 Canada had a dollar unit of account, and the eagle at $10 and the sovereign at $4.8666 were full legal tender. We turn now to issues of paper money and the introduction of banking.

[21] Chalmers (1893, pp. 178–9). Copper coins were also made legal tender, but in 1777 the legal tender was limited to amounts of less than one shilling.

[22] The effects of overvaluation are discussed in Rolnick and Weber (1986), Redish (1984), and Greenfield and Rockoff (1996).

[23] See Shortt (1986) for references.

The first paper money issues were those of the British Commissariat used to finance the War of 1812. The United States declared war on Canada on June 29, 1812, and commenced an invasion of Upper Canada a month later. (British) General Isaac Brock commenced issue of "Army Bills" at York (now Toronto) in July 1812, an issue that was regularized by an act of the House of Assembly of Lower Canada in August 1812.

The legislation authorized the issue of two types of bills: large bills (denominations of $25 and above) that bore 6 percent per annum interest and were redeemable in bills of exchange drawn on the British government in London, and non interest-bearing small bills (denominations between $1 and $20) payable in specie on demand. The bills (large and small) were made legal tender, and both types apparently circulated freely (Stevenson, 1892). The provincial government committed itself to paying the interest on the bills and to redeeming in specie any bills unpaid after five years. The exchange rate for bills was to be announced fortnightly.[24]

By February 1813 fiscal pressures led to expansion of the amount of permissible issues to £500,000. However, the extending legislation did not commit the provincial government to further interest or principal liabilities. The legislation was further extended in January 1814, when the limit was raised to £1.5 million. Under this third extension, between £200,000 and £500,000 had to be in small bills, which were now redeemable in bills of exchange on London, or in large denomination Army Bills, but not in specie.

However, in December 1814 a peace treaty was signed between the United States and Britain, and the military need for Army Bills disappeared. The amount of Army Bills outstanding declined from £1,249,996 in March 1815 to £396,778 by December. In November 1815 the commander of British forces (Sir Gordon Drummond) stated that Army Bills could be redeemed in cash and would stop bearing interest after two weeks. After several extensions the Army Bill office was finally closed on December 24, 1820.

In contrast to the playing card money, Army Bills were redeemed in full at the end of the war. The issues are often credited for both the success of the British military efforts and increased prosperity during the war. In contrast with the United States, where the issue of Treasury notes was clearly inflationary, evidence on the inflationary consequences of the Army Bills is hard to find. In part this reflects the limited price data for

[24] The exchange rate was typically at a discount reflecting the premium on gold in London. That is, the Canadian currency stayed at par with gold, so £100 stg bought in London might cost only £80 in Canada.

the period and in part the fact that Canada's major trading partner – Britain – was simultaneously undergoing inflation. Ouellet (1980) argues that the Army Bills were inflationary, and his data on the price of such nontradables as eggs, straw, and firewood show averages 50 percent higher in 1810–14 than in 1805–9 (p. 176). Yet he argues that the Army Bills facilitated British spending in Canada and raised provincial revenues through the increase in imports.

The success of the Army Bills and the vacuum created by their departure are widely believed to have been influential in the introduction of banking into the Canadas.[25] In 1817 merchants in Toronto and Montreal petitioned their respective legislatures for bank charters, which were granted and received royal assent in 1822. The charters allowed the banks to issue circulating notes that were redeemable in specie on demand. The banks could make loans (on "real bills"), take deposits, deal in foreign exchange, and establish branches. Liabilities were limited to three times the paid-in capital stock, and the banks were, of course, bound by the usury laws of the colonies. In the 1830s, when legislation to grant new bank charters or to increase the capital of existing banks was considered, imperial officials attempted to tighten the regulations on the banking sector. These attempts were largely unsuccessful in the 1830s but were incorporated into bank charter legislation in the 1840s.

By 1841 bank charters, which had initially been rather idiosyncratic, were relatively uniform. In response to Colonial Office pressure, charters typically required bank note issues to be limited to less than paid-in capital; shareholders faced double liability; banks were required to make twice yearly balance sheet statements to the legislature; banks that suspended convertibility of their notes were required to suspend discounting; and if the suspension lasted for more than 60 days, the bank charter was forfeit.

The only general suspension of convertibility occurred in 1837–9, during the period of both international financial distress and domestic political turmoil (the Rebellions in both Upper Canada and, more seriously, Lower Canada). On hearing of the suspension of convertibility in New York, Montreal bankers met and agreed that they too would suspend. Quebec City banks quickly followed suit (Redish, 1982, p. 75). Specie immediately rose to a premium, 12 percent above par, but the suspension allowed the banks to continue discounting. Ironically, the Rebellion in Lower Canada eased the resumption of specie payments in May

[25] See Shortt (1986), Breckenridge (1894), and Redish (1982).

1838 since it led to an infusion of military spending and British cash. (The banks suspended again in November 1838 after a second, smaller rebellion and resumed in June 1839.)

In Upper Canada, suspension of convertibility required approval of the legislature and the lieutenant governor, who argued that "commercial faith and national honor" required the maintenance of convertibility.[26] In July 1838 the lieutenant governor assented to legislation permitting suspension; however, by then the panic had passed, and the Commercial Bank (one of the three chartered banks in Upper Canada), which applied for permission to suspend, was deterred by the lieutenant governor's threat not to accept its notes in government payments. Finally in September the Commercial Bank suspended. The other two Upper Canadian chartered banks had suspended in March 1838 after amendments to the Suspension Act that extended the deadline for resumption of convertibility from May 1838 to May 1839, and allowed suspended banks to trade in specie and to issue notes up to twice the value of their paid-in capital.[27] In April 1839 the banks applied for a renewal of the act and it was extended for six months, leading one local paper to note that the Family Compact (the mercantile elite) "have his Excellency bound hand and foot." All three banks resumed in November 1839.

During the suspension, the note issues of the banks rose significantly (at their peak to 60 percent above the presuspension peak). However, bank notes were at a discount of only 1–2 percent after June 1838, and the prices of bills of exchange on London did not rise perceptibly.[28]

The arrival of Lord Sydenham (Charles Poulett-Thompson, a Currency School advocate) led to an attempt to establish a government note issue. Sydenham proposed removing the right of note issue from the chartered banks and creating a Bank of Issue. His proposal was largely

[26] He also argued that suspension would affect the value of Upper Canadian bonds in London, a factor that would not have affected Lower Canada since, as noted, the Lower Canadian legislature had not raised any funds in London (Redish, 1982, p. 96).

[27] Strangely, the influx of British troops and money has been used to explain both the Lower Canadian banks' resumption of convertibility and the Upper Canadian banks' resumption of convertibility. The issue is whether the incoming funds were specie (as in Lower Canada) or bills of exchange (as in Upper Canada). In July 1838 a new lieutenant governor arrived in Upper Canada and wrote to the banks urging resumption and arguing that there was no longer a need for resumption. The Bank of Upper Canada refused.

[28] Bordo and Redish (1993) argue that this reflects expectations of resumption at par and the increase in economic activity caused by the British military presence after the rebellion.

motivated by the potential seignorage. He estimated the bank note circulation to be £1 million, and if 25 percent reserves were held, the interest saving on the residual would be about £35,000 per annum. Sydenham had been "one of the most ardent supporters" of the Currency School in England and believed that, in addition to the potential revenue benefits, a provincial bank would provide a more sound currency (Davoud, 1937, p. 105). With the enthusiastic support of the banks, the act introduced on August 20, 1841, was shelved on August 31, despite Sydenham's view that it was "a measure which I would rather carry and make perfect than anything I have ever done" (cited in Davoud, 1937, p. 105).

The legislature did, however, manage to get some seignorage revenue. In 1841 they introduced a 1 percent tax on all note issues in excess of specie holdings (McIvor, 1958, p. 48). In the 1850s, bank charters were amended so that a minimum of 10 percent of paid-in capital was held in the form of provincial securities (McIvor, 1958, p. 50). In 1860 the finance minister, Alexander Galt, again broached the possibility of a provincial bank of issue, which again failed. However, in 1865, when the government's accounts were in desperate shape, he had greater success. Although his proposal for a bank of issue failed, legislation was passed allowing the province to issue notes. Provincial notes were to be secured by 20 percent specie reserves and the remainder by government bonds. While other banks would retain their right to issue notes, the Bank of Montreal, the largest bank and the government's bank, agreed to surrender its note issue in return for being the government's note-issuing agent.

At the time of Confederation then, the Province of Canada had 19 banks with the power to branch and to issue notes. The system had evolved in part in reaction to Canadian needs – the particularly large seasonal variations in money demand indicating that the payoff to an "elastic" currency was high (see Champ, Smith, and Williamson, 1996) – and in part to pressures from the Colonial Office, which perhaps offset the political power of the banking elite in Canada.

8.5 POSTCOLONIAL CANADA – THE FISCAL SYSTEM

As noted at the beginning of the chapter, one of the motivations for Confederation was the debt burden in the Maritimes and the Canadas. In 1867 the debt inherited by the new country was $70 million, which grew in the early years as the Confederation expanded and took on the debt of the incoming provinces. In addition the country experienced annual deficits in the 1870s as tax revenue, which was predominantly (86 percent) customs and excise tax revenue, stagnated in the depression and its aftermath.

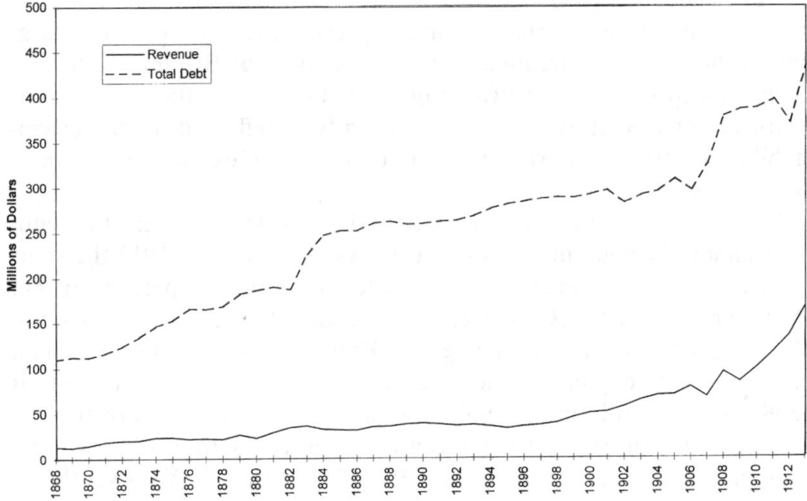

Figure 8.5 Canada's debt, 1868–1912.

The need for increased revenues was one reason for the National Policy tariff of 1879, the major fiscal policy change of the postcolonial period. However, the tariff increases were also explicitly introduced to promote manufacturing industry in Canada. As shown in Figure 8.5, revenues did rise substantially between 1880 and 1885, but thereafter they again stagnated. The legislation raised tariff rates on clothing and iron and steel by between 10 and 15 percent and in general raised tariffs from 17.5 percent to over 20 percent.[29]

The effects of the tariff have been one of the most widely debated issues in Canadian economic history. Theory is consistent with increasing or decreasing real income (for example, the new learning-by-doing and imperfect competition models predict an increase in income); and with increased extensive growth or not; and with expansion or stagnation of the industrial sector. All of these positions have been held by Canadian economic historians, with the issue not resolved today.[30]

The other major change in late-nineteenth-century fiscal policy was the debt resulting from federal government subsidization of the construction of the Canadian Pacific Railway. Debt per capita rose from $31 in 1868 to $43 by 1880 and then to $55 in 1885 as a result of the railway

[29] Tariff rates from Harris and Lewis (1995).

[30] See, for example, Dales (1966); Easton, Gibson, and Reed (1988); Eastman and Stykolt (1967); and Harris and Lewis (1995).

subsidies between 1880 and 1885. It basically remained at that level and was $56 per capita in 1913.[31] As in the preconfederation period, a large part of the infrastructure investment was financed by Britain, and foreign capital inflows were a critical source of funding for the government, as for the private sector. These inflows, in turn, reflected the underlying stability of the fiscal regime and implicit and explicit government guarantees.[32]

Customs and excise duties remained the principal sources of revenue for Canada throughout the pre–World War I period. By 1913 the share of these duties in total revenue had fallen only from 86 percent in 1868 to 80 percent in 1913 (Gillespie, 1991). As discussed in the next section, the federal government took over the Provincial Note issues of Canada and gradually expanded the uncovered issue from $4.3 million in 1868 to $18.8 million in 1907. The increases were not erratic, and on occasion contributed significantly (5 percent) to revenues – for example, in 1868–73, 1878–82, and 1904–7 (2 percent). Yet overall, the government continued the sound money or orthodox policies of the colonial era.

8.6 POSTCOLONIAL CANADA – THE MONETARY SYSTEM

The nature of both the monetary and banking systems in Canada in the post-Confederation period was determined by the structures put in place during the colonial period. The Canadian government established the same gold standard, with sovereigns and American eagles being legal tender. It was not until 1908 that a branch of the Royal Mint was established in Ottawa, and in 1912 it began to issue Canadian gold $5 and $10 coins (which had gold content identical to that of eagles and their halves). The federal government also took over the provincial note issues of the Canadas and renamed them *Dominion notes*. The Dominion Notes Act of 1870 prohibited the issue of chartered bank notes in denominations less than $5, giving the government a monopoly on the issue of $1, $2, and $4 notes. Dominion notes were partially (20 percent) backed by gold up to a limit that began at $9 million and rose to $50 million in 1914. Issues in excess of the limit were required to be backed 100 percent by gold.

The banking system evolved over the postcolonial period, but in ways consistent with the colonial experience. The defining characteristics of the system – branch banking, chartered banking, issue of bank notes

[31] The ratio stayed at $55 until 1900 and then declined to $48 in 1906 before rising again in the wake of the economic crisis of 1907.

[32] Guarantees that are clearly illustrated for the pre-Confederation period in Carlos and Lewis (1995).

secured only by general assets of the bank, and absence of a central bank – were maintained.[33] Changes to the system included increasing concentration in the banking sector and greater coordination amongst banks. The former occurred primarily through mergers: Between 1900 and 1920 the number of banks fell from 35 to 18.

In 1890 the Canadian Banker's Association was formed, which operated a nationwide clearing house and also represented the chartered banks in matters of mutual concern. Two legislative changes provided greater protection to note holders in the event of a bankruptcy: firstly, notes were made a first charge against a bank's assets in case of default; secondly, the Bank Circulation Redemption Fund reimbursed note holders immediately (and would then be reimbursed, in turn, by the receivers of a bankrupt bank) in the event of default.[34] Other legislation allowed banks to issue notes in excess of their paid-in capital if they either paid a tax (after 1908) or deposited gold or Dominion notes in the Central Gold Reserves (established 1913).

8.7 CONCLUSIONS

What was the fiscal and monetary legacy to Canada from its imperial home countries, France and England? From France very little endured. The basic fiscal and monetary institutions that endured into the nineteenth and twentieth centuries were not from the *ancien régime* (although Quebec did adopt the Napoleonic Code for its civil law, which did impact on commercial and financial dealings).

Canada inherited British monetary and financial institutions, which it adapted to Canada's special needs: the development of infrastructure, the imperative of overcoming vast distances, and protection against the threat of invasion from the United States. Canada adopted British fiscal orthodoxy based on the norm of a peacetime balance between government expenditures and receipts, with wartime deficits financed in part by borrowing and by transfers from the home country. Canada also raised most of its revenues from indirect taxes. A limited institutional adaptation of the British model, however, was the use of bond-financed infrastructure expenditure by Upper Canada.

Canada also inherited stable monetary institutions from Britain: virtually continuous adherence to the gold standard and the creation of a sound nationwide branch banking system based on the real bills doctrine. However, Canada did not establish a formal central bank until 1934.

[33] These "defining" characteristics were modified in the twentieth century by the introduction of a discount window after 1914 and by the establishment of the Bank of Canada in 1934 (see Bordo and Redish, 1987).

[34] See Bordo, Redish, and Rockoff (1994, 1996).

The Canadian experience can be thought of as having three components: a uniquely Canadian component, a North American component, and an American component. The Canadian experience was unique among all the former New World colonies in that its fiscal and monetary institutions have always been very conservative. In comparison to the U.S. experience, there was much less monetary experimentation (with the exception of playing card money in New France). Use of the inflation tax in wartime was also very limited compared to the U.S. experience and to that of Latin America. Also in comparison to the United States and some Latin American countries, Canada did not establish a national bank of issue like the First and Second Banks of the United States.

An additional way in which Canada differed from the other New World colonies was in its chronic dependence on fiscal transfers from the home country. This was the case under both France and Britain. This is in comparison with the British North American colonies in the eighteenth century, which had considerable fiscal autonomy. However, the extensive British transfers in the early nineteenth century in large part reflected concern over losing all of its northern possessions to the United States. The legacy of Canada's dependence on its imperial benefactors continued after Confederation, with the federal government acting as a surrogate for London. The government has always played a much more extensive role in the Canadian economy than is the case in the United States.

Yet there were similarities between Canada and the United States. Both countries had, in overall terms, a record of stable and conservative fiscal and monetary experience, which stands in stark contrast to the experience of the former Latin American colonies. Perhaps as a result, both were fortunate in their receipt of continuous and massive capital inflows in the latter part of the nineteenth century (Bordo and Rockoff, 1996).

Finally, while Canada differed from the rest of the New World in terms of stability and conservatism, and also in its dependence on the home country, it also shared many similarities. First was the imposition of military expenditure in wartime, which led to paper money issues by New France and extensive deficit financing of the War of 1812. Second was the need for capital to develop infrastructure, which led to bond-financed peacetime deficits in Upper Canada and then the creation of a national debt after Confederation.

Canada's stable and conservative fiscal and monetary experience must explain both the differences between North and South America (that is, Canada's common experience with the United States), and the uniquely Canadian aspects of its experience. A key question is, did Canada adopt sound money and conservative fiscal policy because the shocks that it faced were considerably smaller than those faced by Latin America (far fewer wars and smaller, less frequent terms of trade shocks), because of the legacy of British political stability embedded in its inherited institutions (the rule of law, well-defined property rights, and parliamentary democracy), or because of greater income equality (which may, in turn, reflect a different resource endowment)?[35]

REFERENCES

Bordo, M. and A. Redish (1987). "Why Did the Bank of Canada Emerge in 1935?" *Journal of Economic History* 47: 405–18.

(1993). "Maximizing Seignorage Revenue during Temporary Suspensions of Convertibility: A Note," *Oxford Economic Papers* 45: 157–68.

Bordo, M., A. Redish, and H. Rockoff (1994). "The U.S. Banking System from a Northern Exposure: Stability versus Efficiency," *Journal of Economic History* 54(2): 325–41.

(1996). "A Comparison of the Stability and Efficiency of the Canadian and American Banking Systems, 1870–1925," *Financial History Review* 3: 49–68.

Bordo, M. and H. Rockoff (1996). "The Gold Standard as a Good Housekeeping Seal of Approval," *Journal of Economic History* 56: 389–428.

Bordo, M. and C. Vegh (1996). "If Only Alexander Hamilton Had Been Argentinean: A Comparison of the Inflationary Experiences of the U.S. and Argentina in the 19th Century," NBER working paper.

Breckenridge, R. M. (1895). *The Canadian Banking System 1817–1890*. New York: American Economic Association.

Carlos, A. and F. Lewis (1995). "The Creative Financing of an Unprofitable Enterprise: The Grand Trunk Railway of Canada, 1853–81," *Explorations in Economic History* 32(3): 273–301.

Carroll, S. S. (1956). "Canadian Paper Money," *Canadian Numismatic Journal* 1: 70–4.

Chalmers, R. (1893). *A History of Currency in the British Colonies*. London: Eyre and Spottiswood.

Champ, B., B. Smith, and S. Williamson (1996). "Currency Elasticity and Banking Panics: Theory and Evidence," *Canadian Journal of Economics* 29: 828–64.

Dales, J. (1966). *The Protective Tariff in Canada's Development*. Toronto: University of Toronto Press.

Davoud, H. T. (1937–8). "Lord Sydenham's Proposal for a Provincial Bank of Issue," reprinted in E. P. Neufeld, ed., *Money and Banking in Canada*. Ottawa: Carleton University Press (1964): 95–105.

[35] On the importance of parliamentary democracy see North and Weingast (1989), and on the role of factor endowments and income distribution see Engerman and Sokoloff (1994).

Desbarats, C. (1996). "Colonial Government Finance in New France, 1700–1750." Ph.D. thesis, McGill University.

Eastman, H. C. and S. Stykolt (1967). *The Tariff and Competition in Canada.* Toronto: Macmillan.

Easton, S., W. Gibson, and C. Reed (1988). "Tariffs and Growth: The Dales Hypothesis," *Explorations in Economic History* 25: 147–63.

Engerman, S. and R. Gallman (1996). *The Cambridge Economic History of the United States*, Vol. 1, *The Colonial Period*. New York: Cambridge University Press.

Engerman, S. and K. Sokoloff (1994). "Factor Endowments, Institutions, and Differential Paths of Growth among New World Economies: A View from Economic Historians of the United States," NBER Working Papers Series on Historical Factors.

Gillespie, W. Irwin (1991). *Tax, Borrow and Spend: Financing Federal Spending in Canada, 1867–1990*. Ottawa: Carleton University Press.

Greenfield, L. and H. Rockoff (1996) "Law in Nineteenth Century America," *Journal of Money, Credit and Banking* 27(4): 1086–98.

Harris, R. and F. Lewis (1995). "The Impact of the National Policy on Canadian Manufacturing, 1880–1920," mimeo, Queens University.

Lower, A. (1973). *Canada: An Outline History*. Toronto: McGraw-Hill Ryerson.

McCusker, J. (1978). *Money and Exchange in Europe and America, 1600–1775, A Handbook*. Chapel Hill: University of North Carolina Press.

McIvor, R. Craig (1958). *Canadian Monetary Banking and Fiscal Development*. Toronto: Macmillan.

McNaught, K. (1986). *The Pelican History of Canada*. Toronto: Penguin Books.

Michener, R. (1987). "Fixed Exchange Rates and the Quantity Theory in Colonial America," *Carnegie Rochester Conference Series on Public Policy* 27: 277–307.

Nish, C. (1975). *François-Etienne Cugnet, 1719–51: entrepreneur et enterprises en Nouvelle-France*. Montreal: Fides.

North, D. and S. Weingast (1989). "Constitutions and Commitment: The Evolution of Institutions Governing Public Choice in 17th Century England," *Journal of Economic History* 49: 803–32.

Ouellet, F. (1980). *Economic and Social History of Quebec, 1760–1850*. Ottawa: Carleton University Press.

Redish, A. (1982). "The Optimal Supply of Bank Money: Upper Canada's Experience," Ph.D. thesis, University of Western Ontario.

(1984). "Why Was Specie Scarce in Colonial Economies? An Analysis of the Canadian Currency 1796–1830," *Journal of Economic History* 44: 713–28.

Rolnick, A. and W. Weber (1986). "Gresham's Law or Gresham's Fallacy," *Journal of Political Economy* 94(1): 185–99.

Shortt, A. (1986). *Adam Shortt's History of Canadian Currency and Banking 1600–1880*. Toronto: Canadian Banker's Association.

Smith, B. (1985). "Some Colonial Evidence on Two Theories of Money: Maryland and the Carolinas," *Journal of Political Economy* 93: 1178–1211.

Stevenson, James (1892). *The War of 1812, in Connection with the Army Bill Act*. Montreal: Foster Brown and, Co.

Timberlake, R. (1993). *Monetary Policy in the United States*. Chicago: University of Chicago Press.

Urquhart, M. and W. Buckley (1965). *Historical Statistics of Canada*. Toronto: Macmillan.

Weaver, R. (1914). "Taxation in New France," *Journal of Political Economy* 23: 736–55.

Zay, E. (1892). *Histoire Monétaire des Colonies Françaises*. Paris: Typographiede J. Montorier.

9

Mexico

From Colonial Fiscal Regime to Liberal Financial Order, 1750–1912

Carlos Marichal and Marcello Carmagnani

In 1776, on publishing his famous work, *The Wealth of Nations*, Adam Smith was convinced that the fiscal structure of the Spanish Empire in Central and South America was more efficient than that of the crumbling British colonial administration in North America. A quarter of a century later, in 1803, on his prolonged visit to Mexico, Alexander von Humboldt obtained a similar impression, which he registered in his widely read *Political Essay on the Kingdom of New Spain*, underlining the fact that the Mexican fiscal system was an extraordinarily successful tax machine.[1] On the other hand, by the mid-nineteenth century, both domestic and foreign observers expressed a gloomy and pessimistic view of the finances of the independent Mexican republic, a fact ratified by its incapacity to defend its territory adequately against foreign invasion forces, whether from the United States or from Europe.[2]

These contrasting historical views are testimony to a singular and still unexplained transition of Mexico from rich colony to poor nation, at least from the point of view of state finance. This striking shift is particularly surprising given the fact that Mexico was the largest silver producer and exporter in the world in the late eighteenth century. The Mexican silver peso circulated everywhere – throughout the islands of the Caribbean, in Europe (generally being reminted or restamped), and

The coauthors of this chapter wish to indicate that Carlos Marichal is responsible for the text dealing with the period 1750–1857, while Marcello Carmagnani has covered the period 1857–1912.

[1] Humboldt (1991), in particular, book 6, chaps. 13 and 14. The first edition of this six-volume work was published in Paris between 1807 and 1811.

[2] On the finances of the Mexican early republic and its observers see Tenenbaum (1987), which also covers the financial/military problems provoked by the U.S. invasion of Mexico in 1847. For an overview of Mexican finance during the French occupation of Mexico (1863–7) the classic work is still Payno (1868).

as far away as China and India, where it had been used for centuries. Indeed, the Mexican peso was the original prototype for the American dollar (more specifically, the silver dollar) and therefore has won a singular place in monetary history. After independence, Mexico continued to export pesos in considerable quantities, but in less important proportions, and, certainly, the financial reputation of the new republic was not comparable to that of the old viceroyalty of New Spain.

While independence did not bring prosperity but rather poverty to the new state, leading to the loss of half of its territory in the war with the United States (1847), by midcentury Mexican elites began to carry out a series of political and economic reforms that would lead to the construction of a new political consensus and eventually to the modernization of the fiscal and administrative structure of the government of the republic, as well as a growing convergence with the international economy. By the end of the nineteenth century, the Mexican state displayed many of the features of a modern liberal regime with respect to fiscal debt and monetary policies as well as practice.

A key question for comparative history is, what is an adequate analytical framework to explain the dramatic shifts in the management of the public economy of Mexico over more than a century? Evidently, the first point to emphasize is the close relation between changes in fiscal regimes and political and institutional change (whether as the result of war, revolution, or reforms). In this regard, it is possible to identify *three historical models* of fiscal structure and dynamics in the period covered in this chapter. The first corresponds to the colonial fiscal structure of Bourbon Mexico, which included a combination of patrimonial taxes with a complex set of indirect taxes and state monopolies. This old but efficient fiscal regime had the singular advantage of suffering no deficits; indeed, it produced regular surpluses, which were transferred to the metropolis and to other territories under the aegis of the Spanish Crown. The organization and logic of the colonial fisc were therefore determined by the Spanish imperial state, which also had sovereignty over what we could denominate the largest monetary union in the eighteenth-century world, stretching from Spain to Spanish America and thence to the Philippines.

The second fiscal model was the one that resulted from the wars of independence. The tax structure of the nascent Mexican republic was based on a combination of several surviving taxes of the colonial regime plus customs duties, which provided the bulk of the revenues of the federal government. In this regard, it would appear that the Mexican case can be analyzed in the light of Hinrich's interpretive model of a fiscal transition that moved from a traditional tax state (quite strongly patrimonial, albeit in the Spanish imperial mold) toward a transitional tax state that depended heavily on indirect taxes.[3] However, the new government was plagued by so many political, military, and institutional obstacles that this transition can only be qualified as a failure.

It was only in the mid-1850s, and particularly with the ratification of the Constitution of 1857, that a new sociopolitical pact of profound consequences was established, laying down the institutional foundation for the subsequent construction of the liberal state in Mexico. From this perspective, it is possible to speak of the beginning of a process of convergence between the Mexican and Western European experiences with respect to fiscal policy, financial organization, and the monetary regime, which would gather strength from 1867 and culminate at the turn of the twentieth century. Tax reforms were accompanied by institutional innovations of considerable importance that reinforced property rights and allowed for greater accuracy and transparency in terms of economic information. Tax collection was improved, and budgetary deficits were eventually replaced by regular surpluses by the end of the century. Finally, Mexico moved from its secular silver standard to a gold standard in 1905, marking the most advanced stage of its convergence with the fiscal and monetary practices then current in Europe and the United States.

Section 9.1 of this chapter deals with the unsuccessful transition from colonial regime to independence. Section 9.2 deals with the impact of liberal reforms from 1857 to the early twentieth century.

9.1 FROM COLONIAL FISCAL ORDER TO INDEPENDENT DISORDER

9.1.1 The Revenue System of Colonial Government in Bourbon Mexico

The revenue system of colonial Mexico was an extremely complex structure constructed over a period of three centuries, with especially important changes carried out in the second half of the eighteenth century. The latter, which are commonly known as the *Bourbon reforms* – being implemented throughout the Spanish Empire from the 1760s – spurred a notable increase in the income of the viceregal administration that was able not only to cover all local administrative and military expenditures but also to export a growing volume of fiscal revenues to other parts of the Spanish Empire. In fact, as we argue later, the government of the viceroyalty of New Spain assumed the functions of a virtual submetrop-

[3] Hinrichs (1966) describes three stages in the evolution of tax systems, from traditional tax regimes heavily based on patrimonial taxes, to a transitional regime, and then to a modern tax system.

olis that helped, in key ways, to sustain what was the oldest and most extensive of the European empires of the eighteenth century.

The multiplication of wars among the European powers in the second half of the eighteenth century – particularly between England, France, and Spain – led to a marked increase in the costs of sustaining their respective colonial and naval administrations.[4] There was, however, a striking contrast between the failure of England and France to compel their American colonies to finance the great surge in military expenditures and the accomplishments of the more archaic Spanish monarchy, which reaped greater fiscal benefits from its American possessions than ever before in the second half of the eighteenth century.[5]

The principal explanation of this surprising Spanish success story is to be found in the efficiency (in terms of extraction capacity and routine operation) of the tax machinery in the Spanish American colonies, especially in New Spain. According to Herbert Klein, by 1800 residents of Bourbon Mexico paid 70 percent more taxes per capita than Spaniards in the metropolis.[6] While this is somewhat of an overstatement, according to our new estimates, which put the figure closer to 40 percent, there is no doubt that the colonists were making a striking contribution to the imperial administration.[7]

Four sources provided the bulk of income to the royal treasury in New Spain (Table 9.1). The most archaic and sui generis of the colonial fiscal exactions was the tribute tax (*tributo*) levied on all heads of households in the Indian towns (the so-called Indian republics or communities).[8] The rate was approximately two silver pesos (two dollars), to be paid yearly by every *tributario*, levied uniformly on Indian peasants who lived and cultivated their own land but only occasionally on peasants who worked on haciendas or plantations. As Table 9.1 shows, the annual income generated from this source was slightly over 1 million pesos, making up

[4] The great surge in colonial and naval expenditures of the competing European powers came particularly as a result of the Seven Years' War (1756–63). For a perceptive analysis of the financial impact of this war on one major power see Riley (1980).

[5] Marichal (1997b) estimates the costs and benefits of Mexican fiscal remittances to the metropolis and other parts of the Spanish Empire during this period.

[6] Klein (1985), p. 598.

[7] Marichal (1997b, 1999) provides the new estimates. The figures indicate that Mexicans paid more taxes than Frenchmen per capita but less than Englishmen, using data from Mathias and O'Brien (1976) and Bonney (1995); however, an accurate comparison would require comparison of real per capita income in each country.

[8] This tax was derived from the tribute paid to the Aztec emperors by all subject peoples and therefore can be considered to be an "American" tax with no European legacy. For detailed information on the institutional description of each of the taxes, see the multivolume work by the functionaries of the colonial treasury (Fonseca and Urrutia, 1845–51), a work originally written in the late 1780s.

Table 9.1. Income of the Different Branches of the Royal Treasury in New Spain, 1795–9 (annual average, in silver pesos)

	Values in Pesos		
Branches	**Gross Income**	**Collection Costs**	**Net Income**
Mining taxes	4,512,191	524,096	3,988,095
Trade taxes	4,174,124	444,086	3,730,038
Indian tribute	1,247,861	87,910	1,159,951
State monopolies	8,852,943	4,033,311	4,819,632
Church fiscal transfers	688,186	29,932	658,254
Administrative income	94,476	2,861	91,615
Other income	233,778	8,939	224,839
Forced loans	652,625	300	652,325
TOTAL	20,456,184	5,131,435	15,324,749

	Percentage Values		
Branches	**Gross Income**	**Collection Costs**	**Net Income**
Mining taxes	22.06%	10.21%	26.02%
Trade taxes	20.41%	8.65%	24.34%
Indian tribute	6.10%	1.71%	7.57%
State monopolies	43.28%	78.60%	31.45%
Church fiscal transfers	3.36%	0.58%	4.30%
Administrative income	0.46%	0.06%	0.60%
Other income	1.14%	0.17%	1.47%
Forced loans	3.19%	0.01%	4.26%
TOTAL	100.00%	100.00%	100.00%

	Collection Costs as Percentage of Gross Income		
Branches	**Gross Income**	**Collection Costs**	**Net Income**
Mining taxes	100.00%	11.62%	88.38%
Trade taxes	100.00%	10.64%	89.36%
Indian tribute	100.00%	7.04%	92.96%
State monopolies	100.00%	45.56%	54.44%
Church fiscal transfers	100.00%	4.35%	95.65%
Administrative income	100.00%	3.03%	96.97%
Other income	100.00%	3.82%	96.18%
Forced loans	100.00%	0.05%	99.95%
TOTAL	100.00%	25.09%	74.91%

Note: In the case of the state tobacco monopoly, collection costs include the payment of sums to tobacco leaf producers, to workers in the state factory, and for other costs of production.

Source: Memoria instructiva y documentada del estado comparativo de los productos de la Real Hacienda desde el año de 1809 (Mexico, 1813), Ms. 1282, Biblioteca Nacional (Mexico).

approximately 7.6 percent of the net income of the viceregal government in the 1790s.

The second traditional revenue source for the colonial administration was mining taxes, the most important being the *diezmo minero*, a 10 percent duty levied on all silver produced. This tax was charged at the Mexico City mint, where all silver from the viceroyalty was brought to be coined. The importance of this mint for world economic history was registered by Humboldt on his visit there in 1803:

> It is impossible to visit this building . . . without recalling that from it have come more than two billion pesos over the course of less than 300 years . . . and without reflecting on the powerful influence that these treasures have had on the destiny of the peoples of Europe.[9]

While the direct tax on mine production was the single most important item among the varied list of exactions that fell upon Mexican silver, a close runner-up was income derived from seigniorage, as the data on minting revenues indicate (*amonedación de oro y plata*). Additional income was derived from the sale of the products of the state-owned mercury monopoly, an essential ingredient for colonial silver refining processes, but the bulk of the income thus generated was used to buy more mercury and shipped off to Spain. The net revenue obtained from mining taxes – directly and indirectly – was close to 4 million pesos in the 1790s, approximately 26 percent of the total net income of the viceregal government.[10]

A third source of income was taxes on trade, most of which were duties on internal commerce (*alcabalas*) and on native alcoholic beverages (*pulques*), producing 24 percent of net receipts.[11] According to the detailed studies of Garavaglia and Grosso, the products of internal trade taxes increased systematically until the 1790s in part

[9] Humboldt (1991), p. 457. For estimates of the total flows of silver and gold from the Americas to Europe from the sixteenth to the eighteenth centuries, see the relatively recent but already classic work by Morineau (1985), which has made obligatory a reevaluation of all of Earl Hamilton's estimates.

[10] These calculations are substantially higher than the relevant percentages offered by Klein (1995), but it should be noted that Klein did not use consolidated accounts, nor did he discount the costs of fiscal administration or take into account seigniorage of the mint. In Table 9.1, a slight reduction should be calculated in terms of the income derived from silver mining because the total costs of the mercury monopoly are not included.

[11] While there were specific taxes on foreign trade, such as the *almojarifazgo* duty, port customs were not of great importance. But imported goods, like domestic goods, were subject to the *alcabala* at rates that ranged from 6 percent in the 1770s to 8 percent in the 1780s to 6 percent in the 1790s, rising subsequently during the wars of independence (1810–20) to 15 percent.

because of increased commercialization but also as a result of the increasing pressure exerted by collectors.[12] It should be added that the *alcabalas* were a European fiscal instrument introduced into Spanish America and operated in form identical to their counterparts in Spain and France.[13]

Another European, more specifically Bourbon, fiscal innovation was the tobacco monopoly, established in New Spain in 1767, which by the end of the colonial period had become the single largest source of public revenues, providing almost 30 percent of the government's net income. The state-owned tobacco factory in Mexico City employed over 8,000 workers by 1800, but this was only a part of the total number of people who depended on the monopoly for their livelihood: among these must be included some 2,000 administrative and commercial employees and several thousand tobacco farmers. But this great enterprise was not autonomous, as it maintained close financial, commercial, and productive links to the tobacco monopolies in Cuba, Louisiana, and Spain. Indeed, this enormous state-owned firm was a vast multiregional enterprise, perhaps the largest of its kind in the eighteenth-century world.[14]

Other fiscal contributions to the colonial government of New Spain included a variety of sources, some of them relatively independent of the central administrative management. For instance, there were several categories of Catholic Church income that were collected by ecclesiastical functionaries and then transferred to the state.[15] In any case, as recent research has demonstrated, the tax machinery of the viceroyalty was a well-organized money-extraction mechanism that provided a growing stream of income to the local administration, to other colonies, and to the Spanish Crown.[16] It is to this subject that we now turn.

9.1.2 Expenditure Trends: The Viceroyalty of New Spain as a Submetropolis

A review of the allocation of funds received by the colonial administration of Bourbon Mexico indicates that it is necessary to adopt a methodological approach that is somewhat at variance with the approach of

[12] On *alcabala* trends see Garavaglia and Grosso (1985, 1987). On *pulque* collections see Hernández Palomo (1980).

[13] In Spain they were known as *consumos*, but they figured under the categories of general income as *rentas provinciales*; see Merino (1981) and Fontana (1971).

[14] Deans-Smith (1992) has published an excellent study of the Mexican tobacco monopoly.

[15] For details see Marichal (1989a).

[16] Again, Klein (1995) is a basic source, but Jaúregui (1994) and Garner (1993), chap. 5, also provide important overviews.

those studies on European tax systems that focus mainly on the gradual construction of a "national" tax administration.[17] In this case, the imperial logic went far beyond a restricted "national" logic of fiscal and financial administration. For, indeed, the viceroyalty of New Spain was a key part of a *well-integrated transatlantic fiscal machine*. Each part of the tax administration of the Spanish Empire was connected to the other parts to a greater or lesser degree.

In this regard, it should be observed that recent detailed research on the finances of the Spanish Empire suggests that a profound revision is necessary of the relatively simple scheme of metropoli-colony to explain the fiscal dynamics of empires. More attention must be devoted in the case of the Spanish universal monarchy of the *ancien regime* to the complex functioning of its *three-tiered* system of management of imperial finance.

The dynamics of this system can be explained by the operation of basic principles that determined the disbursement of state monies in accord with the expenditure requirements of the multiple treasuries and administrative units of the empire and the vicroyalty. A first, basic, and secular principle (applied since the sixteenth century) was that the largest number of expenses should be covered in situ by local tax income, collected on a regional level and accumulated in a local *caja real* (treasury).[18] However, when a local treasury office produced a fiscal surplus, this would normally be transferred to another regional *caja* that had a deficit. But these remittances were not necessarily limited to the viceroyalty; they were also shipped abroad to different points of the empire, as we will see.

In the case of New Spain, we can observe a *first level* of this tridimensional fiscal system in the transferences realized among the 24 different regional treasury offices of the viceroyalty, in most cases to cover military expenditures. For example, certain regional treasuries such as those of Veracruz and Yucatán (that habitually accumulated fiscal surpluses) were responsible for the payment of a substantial part of military expenses of regional *cajas* that had scarce tax income such as the military garrison in Campeche, strategically located in the Gulf of Mexico. Similarly, the military presidios of northern Mexico – which had limited revenues – depended heavily on the remittances of funds that had been collected in the the more proximate regional treasuries of Guadalajara and Bolaños, which accumulated a regular

[17] The literature is vast, some of it summarized in the essay by Finer in Tilly (1975). A seminal modern example is Bonney (1989).

[18] Merino (1987), pp. 11–28, offers a preliminary scheme of this principle in operation in the Spanish treasury administration.

surplus of monies from taxes on local silver production as well as on trade.

A *second level* of expenditures was the transfer of surplus fiscal funds from one colony to another, which were known as *situados*, those from New Spain being directed principally to the Greater Caribbean – including Cuba, Santo Domingo, Puerto Rico, Florida, Louisiana, and Trinidad. These constituted a broad network of *intraimperial transferences* the quantitative importance of which suggests that historians should rethink some fundamental aspects of the way that imperial finance operated in Spanish America.[19] In addition, it should be noted that the viceroyalty of New Spain also provided regular fiscal subsidies for the Philippines and more occasional sums for Guatemala and Central America, especially in times of emergency.

Finally, on the *third level*, Bourbon Mexico also proved to be a source of revenues for the metropolitan Treasury.[20] During the greater part of the eighteenth century, the fiscal funds transferred from Mexico to Spain were on a lesser scale than those sent to other Spanish colonies in the Carribean, but in the 1790s the monies sent to the home country reached the huge sum of almost 50 million pesos, for an annual average sum of almost 5 million pesos.

These diverse and considerable remittances help explain why contemporary observers like Adam Smith were impressed with the capacity of Mexico and the South American colonies to help support the Spanish Empire. The contrast with the Anglo-American colonies was stark, for when British authorities demanded much smaller sums from their overseas subjects in the 13 colonies (in the 1760s), the response was entirely different, to the extent that it is often argued that fiscal rebellion was a leading cause of the War of Independence that began in 1775.[21]

9.1.3 The Accumulation of Public Debt at the End of the Colonial Period

During most of the eighteenth century, the colonial government of New Spain did not have recourse to debt for a simple reason: it did not suffer from deficits. On the contrary, as we have argued, the administration of

[19] In the latter half of the eighteenth century, New Spain covered about 75 percent of the administrative and military costs of the government of Cuba and a large portion of these costs of the other Caribbean colonies mentioned. For detailed information see Marichal and Souto (1994) and Marichal (1999), chap. 1.

[20] The fiscal remittances from the Americas in the second half of the eighteenth century provided an average of approximately 20 percent of ordinary revenues of the *tesorería general* in Spain, the central exchequer. For estimates see Marichal (1997b, 1999).

[21] Thomas (1965) provides estimates of the tax burden in the Anglo-American colonies.

Bourbon Mexico enjoyed considerable fiscal surpluses. But by the end of the century, external demands increased so rapidly that, according to the consolidated accounts of the Treasury, expenditures began to surpass ordinary income.[22]

What caused these new and surprising deficits in the accounts of the viceregal government? Evidently, the imbalance in the accounts was not caused by inability to generate sufficient tax income to pay internal costs, which were covered quite satisfactorily. The problem lay in the external costs that the viceroyalty was supposed to meet. What actually occurred was that the metropolis and other parts of the empire were *transferring their deficits to New Spain*, which, in turn, was expected (and forced) to satisfy these extraordinary demands with its own monies.

By the mid-1790s the regular tax resources of Bourbon Mexico were found to be inadequate for this increased task. As a result, the successive viceroys, of Revillagigedo (1791–4), Branciforte (1796–7), Azanza (1798–1802), and Iturrigary (1803–8), began requesting a combination of voluntary and forced loans from the population of New Spain. At this point, there emerged for the first time a large and eventually permanent colonial debt.

Some of the extraordinary funds extracted from the Mexican population were not voluntary and did not figure as debt. Among these, the most important were a series of so-called donations (*donativos*) that obliged every resident of the viceroyalty to pay a kind of head tax. The rates were fixed according to a racial or ethnic distinction. Each Spanish or white Mexican head of household was to pay two pesos, while Indians and persons of mixed blood paid one peso or sometimes a bit less. This was clearly an archaic form of raising funds in times of extraordinary need and had been introduced by the Spanish government into the Americas in the early seventeenth century.[23] The *donativos* were usually called for during wars and, not infrequently, in times of agrarian crisis and plague. However, their application was intensified at the end of the eighteenth century as a result of the various international wars in which the Spanish Crown became involved.[24]

Nonetheless, the bulk of extraordinary income after the 1780s tended to come in the shape of voluntary loans that offered relatively attractive interest rates and were guaranteed by the mortgage of fiscal branches such as tobacco. The debt service on these loans was covered regularly,

[22] In the 1790s these nominal deficits were running at a rate of 2 million pesos per year. See Marichal (1999) for details.

[23] Artola (1982) suggests that the *donativos* were first introduced in Spain under Philip II in the sixteenth century, but it would appear that they had a more ancient origin.

[24] Marichal (1990) provides the details.

making them desirable investment instruments, particularly for the richer members of the colony. The bulk of the funds were raised through two corporations, the extremely powerful mercantile guild, the Consulado de Comercio de México, and the mining guild, the Tribunal de Minería.[25]

Some of the individual sums placed by colonial entrepreneurs and rentiers in these loans were quite remarkable. The wealthiest merchants suscribed heavily, some of them, like Antonio Bassocco, placing over 1 million silver pesos (1 million dollars) over a period of 15 years; it may be added that it is doubtful that any individual merchant in the Europe of the same period would have had the liquid capital to invest a similar sum in public securities. All in all, subscriptions ranged from smallish contributions of 5,000 pesos to a maximum of 200,000 pesos on the approximately 10 major loans issued between 1793 and 1810.[26]

The Mexican Catholic Church was also heavily involved in most of the state credit operations, as convents and monasteries, bishops and cathedral councils, and even the fiscal branch of the Inquisition placed funds at 5 percent interest in state loans. By 1804, however, the demands of the Madrid government for extra funds reached a fever pitch and, as a result, the Finance Ministry introduced a radical financial measure in the American colonies: the government ordered a large part of Church monies that had been lent out as mortgage loans to a vast number of urban and rural proprietors transferred to the royal treasuries in each region.[27] In exchange, the Church would receive debt certificates and would be paid 3 percent interest annually, but these apparent benefits were not sufficient to counterbalance the frankly expropriatory character of the decree. In fact, the public remonstrances against this policy were so extensive and bitter that historians have found in them a significant reflection of the social discontent that would lead to the outbreak of the widespread insurrections in Mexico in 1810.[28]

[25] On the Consulado see the detailed financial study by Guillermina del Valle Pavón (1997), and on the mining Tribunal see the classic study by Howe (1949).

[26] Details are presented in Marichal (1999).

[27] The sums received from the Church were then to be sent on to Mexico City and thence to the port of Veracruz, where they were to be shipped to Europe. In fact, these monies (close to 10 million silver pesos) were sent (between 1806 and 1808) via Amsterdam to the Napoleonic treasury to pay off the subsidy King Carlos IV had been obliged to pay the French emperor since 1803. See Marichal (1999), chap. 5, and Buist (1974), chap. 4, for details.

[28] The policy was known as the *Consolidación de vales reales*, and was carried out in the Americas between 1804 and 1808. For details on the revenues obtained throughout the American colonies, see Liehr (1980); on the implementation in New Spain, see Sugawara (1976) and Marichal (1989a).

By early 1810, the indebtedeness of the colonial government in Mexico had reached close to 30 million pesos and had begun to weigh heavily on the local exchequer. The largest debts were due to the Church (a total of almost 15 million pesos) and to private individuals (approximately 12 million pesos), plus additional sums due to a variety of institutions.[29] But once again, it should be emphasized that these colonial debts were not established to pay local expenses but rather to cover metropolitan deficits and financial expenses.

For the reasons mentioned previously, we suggest that a revision of certain concepts and terminology used to describe the nature of the *state* in Bourbon Mexico is well overdue. Over the last 20 years, many historical essays have used the term *colonial state* to describe the royal administration of New Spain, but without adequate justification. If used indiscriminately, this concept poses a large number of historical and theoretical problems, for it suggests a degree of fiscal and/or financial autonomy that did not exist. Indeed, the viceroyalty was a very important part of the Spanish Empire (and played on occasion the role of a fiscal submetropolis because of the surplus funds it accumulated), but it was not a state within a state. Rather, it was a key part of an old but still extensive imperial state, which was run from the center and was actually able to strengthen the fiscal integration of its quite different and distant parts.[30]

9.1.4 The Fiscal Impact of the Revolutionary Wars, 1810–20

The outbreak of insurrectionary movements in various regions of central Mexico in 1810 quickly led to a profound fiscal crisis in the viceroyalty. During the decade 1810–1820 – which was marked by a persistent civil war that pitted the viceregal administration and its army against a ramshackle collection of rebel forces – the fiscal situation progressively worsened. Three major factors caused a gradual weakening and disintegration of the complex colonial treasury system. The first was the extraordinary rise in internal military expenditures. The second was the growing tendency to rely heavily on forced loans, a circumstance aggravated by the old outstanding colonial debts on which service began to be suspended. The third was the trend toward increasing fiscal autonomy of local treasuries, which reduced the transfer of funds from the regions to the capital, seat of the viceregal government.

[29] The debts of private individuals were almost all administered by the corporations of the Consulado de Comercio and the Tribunal de Minería, which operated as financial intermediaries. See details in Valle Pavón (1997) and Marichal (1999).

[30] A penetrating view of the nature of the Spanish monarchy is that of Elliott (1992); a more specific argument on the role of the viceroyalty within the empire in the late eighteenth century can be found in Marichal (1997a).

Centralization thus gradually gave way to an ad hoc process of federalization of the territory and the fiscal administration of New Spain. The colonial fiscal system, which had operated as a well-integrated network of 24 regional treasuries (which transferred surplus funds among each other to cover local deficits, as well as to the central *caja* in Mexico City), began to break down.[31] Not surprisingly, the former remittances of fiscal monies from the viceroyalty to Spain and/or to the Spanish colonies in the Caribbean were suspended, and thus the principal links to the imperial fiscal and financial machine were cut off. At the same time, the accounts of the fiscal administration became increasingly chaotic, making it difficult to follow tax trends with precision.

The war had a powerful impact not only on the fiscal system but also on the monetary system in Mexico. Local military commanders found it necessary to hoard local resources in order to finance regional armies and to defend their positions against the insurgents. Furthermore, in order to control and obtain greater income from the increasingly depressed mining sector, regional military and civilian chieftains decided to establish local mints. As a result, the old monopoly of the Mexico City mint was broken, and the coining of silver became increasingly decentralized.

Furthermore, as the economy deteriorated, local credit markets progressively disintegrated. In a country with an unequal distribution of income as extreme as that of Bourbon Mexico, the lack of confidence of a small circle of very wealthy actors (large merchants, miners, and rentiers) in the future stability of the state and economy became an additional source of havoc, and capital flight intensified with remarkable speed.

Finally, in 1820, on receiving news of the downfall of the absolute monarchy in Spain, the Mexican military and political elite resolved to reach a consensus and declare independence from the home country. The most prominent royalist general, Agustín de Iturbide, assumed power as head of state and proceeded to initiate a series of half-baked reforms that were intended to conserve the social status quo and to allow him personally to occupy the throne of what would be a short-lived independent Mexican imperial government.[32]

9.1.5 Independence and Chronic Deficits: The Failure of Fiscal Reforms in Mexico from the 1820s to Midcentury

While independence wrought dramatic transformations in Mexican society and polity, many aspects of the colonial administrative apparatus

[31] The most penetrating analysis is that of TePaske (1989).

[32] For details see Tenenbaum (1989) and Anna (1981).

were subsumed into the new national state that emerged in the 1820s. Much of the central bureaucratic and military structure was passed on, albeit with a number of significant changes.[33] At the same time, many of the colonial fiscal bureaucrats continued to exercise their functions after 1820.[34] In addition, a significant part of the tax structure was conserved, but with several major adjustments due to the new political/administrative divisions derived from the creation of a federal republic.[35] Finally, certain more specific elements of the colonial financial legacy – such as the inherited public debts – were retained on the ledgers of the financial accounts of the new state and on the agenda of political debate but were never satisfactorily resolved.

That aspects of the colonial administration were incorporated into the new independent government, nonetheless, should not make us overlook fundamental contrasts in sovereignty, political organization, and administrative reform. The new institutional framework that served as an underpinning to the post independence fiscal and financial systems was established by the federalist Constitution of 1824, following the overthrow of General Iturbide, who had fled the country a year before. Under the new political jurisdiction, the federal government of Mexico was to coexist with local state governments, following the example of the United States.

The new fiscal structure ratified in 1824 was federalist but proved to be a fountain of conflict and controversy for half a century.[36] The first contradictory aspect of the Mexican institutional framework in the 1820s was the superimposition of a U.S. federalist model upon the old colonial Spanish system of government, which had been characterized by a high degree of centralism modified by a certain flexibility with respect to distribution of tax funds among the regional treasuries. The new tax system, instead of allowing for flexibility, proved to be rigid, inefficient, and prone to intensify bitter rivalry among federal and state fiscal bureaucrats for the appropriation of revenues.[37]

The second source of conflict arose from the weakening of the old colonial bureaucracy, which despite its faults had managed to be effective in collecting taxes and maintaining accurate accounts on an incredibly complex range of sources of state income. The dilution of the tax

[33] See Jaúregui (1997), chap. 6, and Arnold (1991).

[34] See the charts on personnel in Arnold (1991).

[35] See Carmagnani (1983, 1984) and, for a case study of the the Estado de México, see Marichal, Miño, and Riguzzi (1994), vol. 1.

[36] An excellent recent compilation on the federalist structure of the Mexican fiscal system is Jaúregui and Serrano (1997), which includes case studies of many states and more general overviews by a dozen leading specialists in the field.

[37] For analysis of bureaucratic infighting, see Arnold (1991) and Tenenbaum (1987).

administration and increasing subordination of fiscal employees to local political chieftains and clans made revenue collection increasingly anarchic after independence, and accounting methods suffered notably. As a result, no one in government or the army had a real grasp of how much money would be available, nor did they have a precise idea of how it was being spent. Indeed, the contrast with the extraordinarily detailed fiscal reports of the late eighteenth century is still a cause for surprise among historians.

In the third place, prolonged economic recession affected the income of the states, in particular, and thus implicitly weakened the federalist model. Political and fiscal sovereignty were thus challenged constantly, and added to the instability and weakness of the new republic.[38] The causes of the long depression of the Mexican economy, which extended from the end of the 1820s to the 1850s, are the subject of an intense historical debate protagonized by the provocative (although not yet substantiated) hypotheses put forward by economic historians Enrique Cárdenas and John Coatsworth.[39] In any case, it would certainly appear that while some of the tax reforms may have had positive effects (for instance, the elimination of most taxes on silver mines), the inefficiency in collection of income of the federal government and the increase of contraband contributed to unstable and low revenues, undermining state finance and confidence in both polity and economy.

A review of the major categories of tax income can perhaps shed some light on a few of the major problems confronted by the Mexican government in these early decades. First, it should be noted that as a result of the wars and the reforms of the early 1820s, the colonial tax structure was radically revamped. To begin with, two major sources of income – the tribute tax and mining taxes – were abolished. This implied a nominal reduction in the potential income of the state by almost 30 percent – at the levels current in the late colonial period.

In the case of the tribute tax on Indian communities, collection had been suspended during the better part of the war period (1810–20), and it appeared politically counterproductive to attempt to reimpose this archaic exaction, as well as being contradictory in terms of the elite's effort to establish a new liberal institutional framework for the emerging republic.[40] In the case of the taxes on silver production, it must be

[38] Carmagnani (1983, 1984) has produced the seminal studies on the relation between political and fiscal sovereignty in early republican Mexico.

[39] Cárdenas (1984) and Coatsworth (1978, 1990).

[40] Nonetheless, after a short period, at the state level it proved feasible to reintroduce (a somewhat reduced) tribute tax under new names, as occurred in the state governments of Yucatán, Oaxaca, and Chiapas. A modified version was also reimplanted in the state of Mexico, although here municipal and state officials vied for its control. For details see Marichal, Miño, and Riguzzi (1994), vol. 1, pp. 122–3.

remembered that during the wars, mining production had fallen steeply and recovery was slow. To maintain the old heavy state mining taxes was therefore unthinkable unless the political elite wished to risk deterring both national and foreign investors from investing in the mines that had long been the most dynamic sector of the economy.

The new, federal government also lost other colonial taxes, several of which were transferred to the state governments on the basis of the political pact among regional elites that led to the ratification of the Constitution of 1824. The most important of these were the taxes on internal trade (*alcabalas* and *pulques*), which became the backbone of most state governments for almost half a century. Unfortunately, the collection of these sales taxes by local administrations had negative consequences for interstate commerce, as regional military commanders and tax functionaries charged extortionate rates on much of the trade. Thus, federalization of these taxes did contribute to economic modernization rather than the reverse, tending to limit mercantile activity and accentuating the fragmentation of markets.

Because of the tax reforms and transfers, from 1824 the federal government was relatively hard put to find sufficient resources to cover all of its considerable expenditures. Fortunately, it had retained taxes on foreign trade, which provided an average of over 6 million pesos per year to the central exchequer. As may be noted in Table 9.2, this represented almost 50 percent of total federal income in the late 1820s, a proportion that remained fairly consistent throughout the nineteenth century. In other words, the dependence of the central treasury upon foreign trade was extreme, and abrupt fluctuations in commerce tended to generate fiscal havoc.

Finally, it should be noted that the federal government also depended upon a series of subsidies – fiscal transfers known as *contingentes* – from the state governments. A quota system was arranged by which the most heavily populated and richest states were to provide the largest sums.[41] Initially, the federal authorities had some success in obtaining these sums on a regular basis, as can be observed from the average of over 1 million pesos transferred yearly to the federal treasury from the state exchequers in the late 1820s (Table 9.3). But in the early 1830s the *contingente* payments fell sharply, and the system began to fall apart. This development inevitably doomed the early federalist experiment (1824–35), which was replaced by what was, from the fiscal perspective, an equally unsuccessful centralist regime (1835–45).

During the centralist administration – headed at various times by the less than virtuous General Santa Anna – a systematic attempt was

[41] For a brief discussion of the *contingente* system see Marichal, Miño, and Riguzzi (1994), vol. 1, pp. 49–53.

Table 9.2. Revenues of the Mexican Federal Government, 1826–31 (in silver pesos)

Revenue Sources	1826–7	1827–8	1828–9	1829–30	1830–1	1826–31	%
Foreign trade taxes							
Aduanas marítimas	7,828,208	5,692,026	6,497,288	4,815,418	8,287,082	6,624,004	48.62%
Anticipación por derechos marítimos				684,265	2,046,059	546,065	4.01%
Avería	646,195	377,210	18,431	3,714	1,889	209,488	1.54%
Aduanas de frontera		5,315	1,098	118	30,531	7,412	0.05%
Derecho de almacenaje					3,589	718	0.01%
Internal trade taxes							
Aduanas de los territorios y D. F.	645,476	792,092	768,294	787,870	1,474,567	893,660	6.56%
Pulques	160,087	166,267	143,330	136,619		121,261	0.89%
Aduanas interiores	55,936	24,437	4,639	22,705	232,185	67,980	0.50%
Peajes	64,441	26,120	18,037	19,155	24,514	30,453	0.22%
Taxes on silver and mints							
Dos % de platas	99,642	95,533	73,190	84,815		70,636	0.52%
Casa de Moneda de México	3,862			29,651	135,480	33,799	0.25%
Derecho del 2% de circulación de moneda					74,912	14,982	0.11%
Derechos de plata y oro	15,001	12,954	11,106	8,078	17,413	12,910	0.09%
Fiscal transfers from states							
Contingente de los Estados	979,145	1,381,412	1,435,970	1,398,432	1,356,563	1,310,304	9.62%
Señalamiento extraordinario a los estados			185,109	562,441		149,510	1.10%
State monopolies							
Tabaco	914,947	1,212,462	1,013,159	841,374	934,663	983,321	7.22%
Correos	143,977	146,160	114,201	85,256	230,683	144,055	1.06%
Salinas	63,516	49,552	62,452	65,671	66,505	61,539	0.45%
Pólvora	114,112		102,071	39,219		51,080	0.37%
Lotería	45,511	49,483	32,196	41,258	41,260	41,942	0.31%
Other sources of income	2,411,763	1,611,600	3,334,425	2,573,946	2,317,517	2,249,850	16.51%
TOTALS	14,191,819	11,642,623	12,814,996	12,200,005	17,275,412	13,624,971	100.00%

Source: *Memorias de Hacienda*, 1827–32.

Table 9.3. **Expenditures of the Mexican Federal Government, 1826–31 (in silver pesos)**

Expenditures by Branch	**1826–7**	**1827–8**	**1828–9**	**1829–30**	**1830–1**
Legislative branch	477	374	398	266	462
Executivo branch		42	24	42	25
Secretaria of Relaciones	222	374	322	303	609
Secretaria of Justicia	147	164	197	141	299
Secretaria of Guerra y Marina	10,156	8,822	7,496	7,693	8,341
Secretaria of Hacienda	2,537	1,029	3,720	3,461	6,730
Other administrative expenses	2,825	2,004	1,778	1,904	1,135
SUBTOTAL	16,364	12,809	13,935	13,810	17,601
Debt service		168	82	19	
Reserves	527	428	576	275	791
Others	126	240			
TOTAL	17,017	13,645	14,593	14,104	18,392

Distribution of Expenditures of the National Treasury, 1826–31 (in pesos)

BRANCHES	**1826–7**	**1827–8**	**1828–9**	**1829–30**	**1830–1**
Secretaría de Guerra y Marina	10,155,878	8,822,569	7,496,287	7,692,632	8,340,659
Secretaría de Hacienda	2,536,810	1,028,977	3,719,632	3,461,165	6,729,988
Others	3,671,530	3,130,546	2,801,059	2,674,694	2,530,642
TOTAL	16,364,218	12,982,092	14,016,978	13,828,491	17,601,289

Distribution of Expenditures of the National Treasury, 1826–31 (in percentages)

BRANCHES	**1826–7**	**1827–8**	**1828–9**	**1829–30**	**1830–1**
Secretaría de Guerra y Marina	62.06%	67.96%	53.48%	55.63%	47.39%
Secretaría de Hacienda	15.50%	7.93%	26.54%	25.03%	38.24%
Others	22.44%	24.11%	19.98%	19.34%	14.38%
TOTAL	100.00%	100.00%	100.00%	100.00%	100.00%

Source: Tenenbaum (1987), Chart B, pp. 213–14; *Memorias de Hacienda, 1827–32*.

made to require the state governments to submit complete accounts of their income to the central treasury and to transfer as large a portion as possible of any existing fiscal surpluses to the capital. The model for reforms was basically Napoleonic: the leaders of the Centralist Party had much sympathy with the reforms carried out by the French emperor, which had allowed the establishment of a more modern and uniform administration.

Nonetheless, in Mexico in the 1830s and 1840s, uniformity and modernization were two objectives at odds with political, social, and economic reality. Internal political discord, repeated foreign military interventions, skyrocketing debts, a surge in contraband, and extreme laxness in public and military administration were the more characteristic features of the period.[42]

Finally, it may be noted that throughout this period Mexico remained on a pure silver standard, a fact not surprising since it remained the world leader in production and export of silver. The bulk of the Mexican monetary system was composed of silver metallic circulation, with a relatively small portion of copper coins for retail transactions. The predominance of silver, however, did not prove a true boon; on the contrary, it had a number of inconveniences. During the colonial era, the silver riches of Mexico led Spain to attempt to extract as much silver coinage from the viceroyalty as possible, creating a number of severe problems that have already been underlined, leading to the export of huge volumes of fiscal resources abroad without compensation. After independence, both local and foreign silver merchants developed a complex transport and commercial network to extract silver from Mexico illegally: perhaps as much as 50 percent of Mexican silver left the country between 1820 and 1860 without being registered. Despite the effects of these extractions on the local monetary system, Mexicans remained unwilling to accept other monetary instruments such as paper money. This contributed to the late development of the Mexican commercial banking system, which did not begin to consolidate until the late 1880s.

Additional problems were created by a sharp rise in contraband of imported goods, in particular textiles and tobacco, largely provoked by the high indirect taxes levied by both the federal and state governments. As a result, fiscal income remained depressed for a good four decades. The Mexican post independent experience therefore was a notorious example of how a country with an apparently strong monetary system suffered from severe financial problems (in both the public and private

[42] An interesting view of the travails of Mexico can be found in contemporary travelers' accounts: see, for example, Brantz Meyer (1844) or Calderón de la Barca (1866). The basic historical monograph on finance in the period is Tenenbaum (1987).

sectors) as a result of an inadequate fiscal system that was plagued by unstable tax revenues, high military and debt service costs, and, inevitably, chronic deficits.

In fact, it would only be with the political and fiscal reforms initiated after midcentury (begining with the Constitution of 1857) that the Mexican state would be able to begin to recover from the traumatic and complex impact of the transition from a colonial regime to the new modern world of liberal and national states.

9.2 TOWARD A NEW FINANCIAL ORDER, 1857–1912

9.2.1 Federal Finances: The Institutional Framework

The development of a new liberal and federal order in Mexico after midcentury was complex and in many ways signaled a whole new era in the country's history. The economic convergence between Mexico and Europe began during the 1857–67 decade and continued until 1912. It was during this period that the modern institutional framework of the Mexican state was established and a new financial and fiscal order was built.

The new institutional order set forth in the 1857 Constitution contains some features that are significant for this study. For the first time in the history of Mexico, the key factors that encouraged Mexico's linkage to the international economy were redefined so that the rule of law would prevail between economic partners. Furthermore, the reform and expansion of constitutional law provided for a whole set of new rules that allowed for active interdependence between institutions and public finances.

Under the Constitution of 1857, attention was given to the sound development of international relations. For the first time in Mexico's history, constitutional guarantees were offered to Mexican citizens and foreigners alike in matters such as private property, freedom of trade inside and outside the country, freedom of association, and legal equality for all persons involved in the economy, irrespective of their nationality.

Interdependence between institutions and finance was also established through new codes of rules and laws that dealt with the spheres of economic activity. A broad range of civil, mercantile, mining, and administrative laws began to be enacted in the 1850s, aimed at regulating economic relations between individuals and the government. These long overdue reforms helped trigger a new liberal fiscal relationship under which taxpayers were expected to contribute to sustain the state according to their personal income, which was measured in terms of each individual's level of consumption. In return, the government would compensate taxpayers by providing a series of public goods, such as education, transportation, security, and so on. Beginning in the decade 1857–67, these new regulations drew together different domestic and international economic and fiscal dimensions, creating a whole new set of dynamics within a new institutional framework.[43]

The convergence of Mexican fiscal and monetary systems with European ones was based on two fundamental principles, both already present in the European experience. The first one pertained to property and information rights, which were the basis for the establishment of the new economic constitution. The second related to the separation of powers, which, in the case of Mexican public finances, meant the dual power of the executive and congress at the federal level, as well as increased coordination between federal and states finances.

Given the limited scope of this chapter, it is not possible to develop these two principles in detail or to establish in full the nature of the convergence with practices that prevailed in Europe. This task would require a much more comprehensive examination that goes far beyond the purpose of this chapter.[44] Thus, we will focus on those factors that shed light on the interaction between fiscal and institutional dimensions.

First of all, one must take into account that the new property rights encountered obstacles, particularly in rural areas. Unlike what took place in the European countries, in Mexico (as in most Latin American nations) no agrarian law guaranteed private ownership of agricultural land. There is no doubt that, in this sense, in Mexico the weight of customary law in rural areas was greater than in European countries such as Spain, France, and Germany. This was probably so because of the legacy of a series of traditions in Mexican agrarian communities rooted in three centuries of colonial experience.[45] In spite of the force of tradition, the new liberal rights did slow down the informal process of land, water, and forestry appropriation and enabled the government to take control of untitled natural resources. By restoring state command over natural resources, the government was able to sell them and thus generate new federal income.[46]

Property and information rights facilitated the formulation of the state's new institutional guidelines. In contrast to what had occurred

[43] On constitutionalism see Sinkin (1979).

[44] Discussions of economic institutions are found in Armstrong (1987), pp. 37–40 and Carmagnani (1994), pp. 25–55.

[45] For Mexican customary law see Molina Enríquez (1979) and McBride (1927).

[46] Between 1881 and 1896, the government sold 96.3 million hectares of land, realizing 173.5 million pesos (more than 150 million dollars): cf. Carmagnani (1994), pp. 256–9. For general information on privatization of public lands see Holden (1994).

during the first half of the nineteenth century, the government was subsequently obliged to provide equal guarantees for all legitimate interest groups in the new economic order. European and Mexican liberalism understood interest groups to be economic operators who proceeded according to the standards set by institutions. Within this context, the idea that an essential function of the state was to promote the incorporation of new social actors into the economic system was based on the assumption that greater economic dynamism would increase fiscal revenues.[47] A quick glance at the regulations that were ratified by the Mexican governments during the 1868–1912 period confirms that governments concentrated their efforts on stimulating entrepreneurship by offering clearer regulations in the area of public finance and guarantees that no punitive taxes or measures would be imposed on productive or commercial activities.[48]

While the reorganization of economic institutions was the basic condition for strong federal finances, the separate powers of government allowed for the development of liberal finances. In this regard, it was the duty of the executive power, both the president of the Republic and his appointee, the secretary of the Treasury, to define public expenditure and identify the sources of its finance, as well as to exercise the budget and receive taxes and fees. On the other hand, it was the sole duty of the legislative branch, particularly the House of Representatives, to approve and control the budget, in addition to endorsing taxes, fees, and loans to cover public expenditure.

Until very recently, it was held that this liberal principle, which underlies all Western budgets, did not function in Mexico given what was presumed to be the all-embracing power of the president over parliamentary life. But in a recent study, I have shown that during the second half of the nineteenth century there was intense parliamentary activity in Mexico, that the budget was approved following formidable debates and spent accordingly. In sum, there was a constant struggle between the power of the president and the powers of Congress.[49] The general trend of the period 1868–1912 was that the budget bill sent by the president would be continually amended, first by the Budget Committee and then on the floor of the House of Representatives. On

[47] In the absence of modern studies, see Pablo Macedo (1905). The most recent edition is that of UNAM, México (1989).

[48] Carmagnani (1994), passim.

[49] See Carmagnani (1994), pp. 101–65. A good synthesis on Mexican presidentialism in the nineteenth century is Alicia Hernández Chávez, "La parábola del presidencialismo mexicano, in Hernández Chávez" (1994), pp. 17–39. The dynamics of Mexico's budget were quite similar to those of the United States; see Stewart (1989).

only one occasion was the budget approved without amendentments by the Committee, for changes were almost always introduced by one or both houses of Congress. This process is highly significant because it underscores the fact that budgetary approval was not a mere formality, subject to the president's will. The Mexican Congress played an important role from 1867 on in interpreting and introducing reforms that responded to the demands of different interest groups represented in Congress.

In summary, it is possible to identify a permanent twofold conflict between government and Congress: the first between the government and the Budget Committee and the second between the government and Congress as a whole. The tension between government and the Committee gradually diminished in matters such as federal powers over administrative, economic, and war expenses. Yet tension between the executive and Congress increased when issues such as expenditure for federal management and economic development were at stake, reaching its maximum intensity when expenditure on war and foreign affairs was involved.[50]

9.2.2 Fiscal Aspects of Economic Convergence

During the second half of the nineteenth century, as Mexico entered the mainstream of Western economic development, its federal finances tended to converge with European financial systems. This convergence becomes highly visible in the attempts made to achieve a balanced budget and the constant political and economic importance attached to the matter by those responsible for Mexican economic policy. Before 1867 – the year that marked the beginning of a new liberal fiscal era – all budgets had shown deficits, unlike the following period of 1867–1911, when only 25 budgets (56.8 percent) were negative. This Mexican trend toward balanced budgets was part of a more general tendency that

[50] The following table describes the interaction between the president and Congress, as well as that in Congress, for all budgets between 1868–9 and 1910–11:

	No Change	Increase	Decrease
Bill vs. Committee	1	15	26
Bill vs. Congress	0	11	33
Committee vs. Congress	3	3	36
	No Diff. (%)	**Increase (%)**	**Decrease (%)**
Bill vs. Committee	2.4	35.7	61.9
Bill vs. Congress	0	25.0	75.0
Committee vs. Congress	7.1	7.1	85.8

Source: Carmagnani (1994), p. 124.

gained ground in the leading European countries: Great Britain, during the same 1867–1911 period, had only 5 negative budgets (11.4 percent), while France had 24 (54.5 percent).[51]

The quest for balanced budgets reflected the prevailing international inclination, which we interpret as a general demand for responsible state management of fiscal policy to promote real growth in the economy. This was a common historical trend in leading countries as well as in followers with regard to public finance, indicating a common economic culture among those responsible for designing economic and fiscal policies. It also suggests the existence of a public opinion that demanded responsible management of public resources.

One reason for focusing on the budget as one mechanism capable of promoting convergence is that it responded to the need for more fluid capital movements. In other words, since there was no institutionalized economic collaboration in the nineteenth century, international financial coordination was possible only through standards of conduct recognized and valid for all countries, independent of their rank in the world economy. Budgetary discipline was thus one of the basic instruments for collaboration and convergence on an international level. This is so because a balanced budget limits government excess expenditure, which in turn reduces the pressure to rely on international capital markets and improves conditions for investment, both by companies and by entrepreneurs.

This explains why a follower nation, like Mexico, set a high value on budgetary discipline: it allowed for economic linkage to leading countries well before the government decided to adopt the gold standard. One has to bear in mind that up to the 1890s, leading countries acknowledged that Latin American and other follower countries could have monetary standards different from the gold standard so long as they maintained a parameter of convergence, that is, a balance between public expenditure and revenue. This meant that budgetary discipline was, so to speak, the domestic aspect of the rules of the games that enabled the international economy to grow in the nineteenth century.

The evolution of federal expenditures and revenues helps us understand how Mexican finances managed to come close to the ideal of convergence that was behind all public finance during the second half of the nineteenth century. Table 9.4 shows that this was due to the fact that expenditures increased at a slower rate than revenues. This trend lasted for half a century and was the outcome of a particularly success-

[51] See Peacock and Wiseman (1967); Hicks (1954); Levy-Leboyer and Casanova (1991); and the recent review of the history of European public finance in Comín (1996).

Table 9.4. Federal Expenditure and Revenues in Mexico (%)[a]

	A Expenditures	B Revenues	A – B Exp – Rev
1867–8/1881–2	5.1	5.6	–0.5
1881–2/1895–6	4.4	2.5	+2.0
1895–6/1910–11	5.8	6.3	–0.5
1867–8/1910–11	5.1	4.8	+0.3

[a] Average annual growth rates.
Source: Carmagnani (1994), passim.

Table 9.5. Annual Growth of Federal Expenditure, 1867–8/1881–2 (%)[a]

TOTAL	3.5
Education	7.1
Justice	5.8
Post and telegraphs	22.0
Economic transfers	14.4

[a] Average annual growth rates.
Source: Carmagnani (1994), passim.

ful fiscal maneuver adopted between 1868–9 and 1881–2.[52] This relationship between federal revenues and expenditures was established by a profound restructuring of federal expenditure, as can be seen in Table 9.5.

The restructuring of federal expenditures was achieved basically by reducing and restricting current expenses. Within a few years (to be exact, between 1867–8 and 1881–2), current expenses dropped from 80.3 percent to 42.2 percent of total expenditure. Thus, an additional 2.1 million pesos became available to the Treasury on a yearly basis, the equivalent of 0.6 percent of the gross domestic product (GDP). These funds were earmarked for service of the public debt and to promote conditions that would encourage companies via subsidies to invest in the modernizing of communications (railways, harbors, steamship lines). Two facts underscore this new trend: between 1867 and 1881 total public debt

[52] In this period, federal revenues and expenditures had a highly positive correlation (r = 0.968) and, therefore, a positive regression (R = 79076 + 0.9333). Both coefficients indicate that after almost half a century of highly disruptive budgets, a correlation between expenditure and revenue was established, in which increases in federal expenditure depended essentially on increases in federal revenue.

Table 9.6. Growth Rates of Federal Revenues, 1867–8/1881–2 (%)[a]

Total federal revenues	5.6
Patrimonial or state revenues	21.5
Public services revenues	9.0
Indirect taxes	
Imports	10.0
Exports	–6.1
Excise (stamp tax)	18.0
Direct taxes	0.1

[a] Average annual growth rates.

Source: Carmagnani (1994), passim.

decreased from 32.7 percent to 24.6 percent of the GDP, whereas new subsidies for economic activities by the beginning of the 1880s came to represent 1.3 percent of the GDP.

Federal expenditure followed federal revenues once the latter had regained their course, attaining an annual growth rate of 5.6 percent in the 1867–82 period, all within a growing context of liberalization of international trade. While progressively fewer taxes were paid on exports, and although there were tax reductions on imports, the new budget equilibrium was the result of an increase in domestic taxes on consumption (stamp tax), as well as fees paid on the new public utility services and on the sale of public lands (patrimonial or state revenues).

As can be observed in Table 9.6, revenues were restructured by liberalization and by introducing indirect taxes on consumption. Free trade led to reduced income from exports, a consequence of the gradual elimination of taxes, but it brought a growth of revenues derived from imports, which flourished through the combined effect of reduced customs duties and improved performance in domestic production and markets. The stamp tax on consumption reflected the new fiscal policy, which was based on the assumption that the resources necessary to sustain any increase in federal expenditure should come from an increase in consumption, which, in turn, indirectly reflected the country's economic growth. Trade liberalization and the new relationship between consumption and federal revenues were the novel aspects of the recent fiscal regime that led to the convergence of the Mexican experience with the European one.

In addition to the changes in tax revenues, the new fiscal regime set a price on income obtained from the sale of natural resources, such as land, mines, water resources, and so on. As happened in Europe and in all American countries, Mexican federal revenues from patrimonial alienation (sale of state property) grew at a very high rate: 21.5 percent annually between 1867–8 and 1881–2. As can be seen in Table 9.6, this rate was four times faster than that of total government income. In the Mexican case, these revenues came from three sources: from the sale of unexploited national patrimony that was not generating any monetary income; from confiscation of the property that belonged to the Church; and, finally, from the sale of some public urban services (urban streetcars and trains).

The idea behind the sale of federal property is closely related to the political desire to use public resources in order to obtain monetary resources that could be used for promotion of a long-needed modern transportation system (railroad, roads, ports) and other public services such as education, postal, and telegraphic facilities. During the 1881–5 period, the federal transfer of funds to private enterprise in the areas of railroads, roads, and ports represented around 2 percent of the GDP.

The Mexican experience indicates that during this period of formation of a new federal finance system, the country followed the same path as Western European countries. After nearly half a century of abnormal fiscal and economic policies in Mexico, a different economic, fiscal, and monetary culture gradually developed, gaining ground with entrepreneurs and politicians. This new conception was founded on the idea that the fiscal regime was the main component and requirement for a stable economy and continued growth. Along with the reorganization of Mexican federal finances came the process of convergence with Western fiscal and monetary standards, which was to bear fruit from the 1890s on. In effect, strict fiscal discipline was observed between 1895 and 1911, when no further deficit budgets were registered.[53]

If we accept this definition of a balanced budget, we will attempt to verify its validity through the calculations in Table 9.7. It is important to note that the rate of growth of total revenues in the 1895–6 to 1910–11 period was less than that of federal expenditure, which was 6.3 percent annually. This different pace of growth indicated that an increase in revenues led to a balanced budget, which was reinforced by increases in

[53] Moreover, the relationship between federal expenditure and revenues remained high since an increase in each new unit of income led to a matching increase of 0.85 units of new public expenditure. In this way, a balanced budget (P*) depended on an increase in income (I); on the productivity of public expenditure (Gp) (that is, on the marginal utility obtained through the investment of a unit of expenditure); and on the productivity of public credit (CPp) (defined as the marginal utility due to each new unit of credit obtained by the government and invested in new federal expenditure), excluding what finally would be earmarked for consolidating or exchanging the preexisting debt.

Table 9.7. Federal Revenues and Expenditures, 1896–7 to 1910–11 (%)[a]

	Revenues	Expenditures
1895–6/1910–11	5.3	6.3
1895–6/1901–2	4.2	4.1
1901–2/1906–7	11.1	11.1
1906–7/1910–11	–0.2	3.3
1895–6/1899–1910	5.1	—
1896–7/1900–1	—	5.8
1900–1/1904–5	7.7	—
1902–3/1906–7	—	11.4
1905–6/1909–10	3.2	—
1907–8/1910–11	—	3.7

[a] The growth rate of the various periods has been estimated according to the criterion used by the Treasury (Secretaria de Hacienda), which estimated average revenues during the previous five-year period. We have extended our calculation to federal expenditure using the five-year-period criterion from the Treasury and the hypothesis that the positive effects on federal expenditure should be looked at a year after the five-year average increase in current revenues.

Source: Carmagnani (1994), pp. 298–9.

federal expenditure and productivity. Due to the growing productivity of federal expenditure, the private economy was also strengthened, both at the entrepreneurial level and at the firm level. All this generated adequate conditions for the expansion of federal revenues. Five-year movements show that an increase in revenues preceded an increase in federal expenditure, while during the second phase, greater productivity in federal expenditure led to an acceleration in public revenues.

The benefits of the convergence of Mexican public finances with international parameters can be seen in the positive relationship between federal expenditure and GDP.[54] Between 1895–6 and 1910–11 federal expenditure per capita went from 2 to 4 current dollars, while public expenditure as a percentage of GDP remained constant at 4.5 percent.

If we concentrate our analysis solely on federal transfers to private enterprise in the area of public utilities (railroads, transportation, ports, mail, telegraph and telephone services), we will see that between 1895 and 1900 they represented 5.8 percent of the new GDP generated during this five-year period (424 million pesos), and between 1905 and 1910 they

[54] The federal expenditure–GDP correlation coefficient was 0.884, with a very low standard deviation (0.00117).

Table 9.8. Mexican Public Debt, 1867–1911 (current U.S. million dollars)

	Domestic Debt	Foreign Debt	Total Debt	Debt/ Revenues[a]
1868	75.3	67.0	142.3	9.4
1880	51.3	76.2	127.5	4.9
1885	81.0	60.1	141.1	4.9
1890	86.0	55.0	141.1	3.9
1895	65.5	87.8	153.3	5.7
1900	61.7	112.4	174.2	5.5
1905	65.8	155.2	221.0	4.3
1910	67.6	149.9	217.5	3.9

[a] Number of annual federal revenues necessary to cover the total federal debt.

Source: Carmagnani (1994), passim.

rose to 10.1 percent of the new GDP generated over that five-year period (827 million pesos). This means that the main goal of public expenditure consisted basically in promoting economic activity while maintaining low levels of spending in the social, educational, and judicial sectors. In fact, this explains why the correlation between federal expenditure and the GDP did not increase. Mexican convergence with European fiscal and budgetary parameters thus represented a fundamental economic stabilization mechanism between 1867 and 1885 and enabled the country to attain a faster economic growth rate from the 1890s on.

9.2.3 Financial Convergence in Public Debt and the Monetary Systems

While Mexico shared important features with contemporary European fiscal experience, a number of differing factors show that the convergence was not total. One of the main differences was the Mexican monetary system, which restrained Mexico's convergence with the international financial system. The negative factors (Table 9.8) are better understood if we bear in mind that the process of fiscal convergence during the decade of the 1880s went hand in hand with trade liberalization and the inception of a modern public credit system.

The interdependence between the fiscal system and public credit led to a whole series of links. The new public credit regime was founded on explicit recognition of the legitimacy of the bulk of internal and external debt accumulated from the time of independence on. Thus the different administrations were required to service the debt through payments on capital and interest, with full legal equality for all creditors, independent of their nationality. It was also held (previous acceptance by the government and by the bondholders) that the debt could be freely bought and sold. Freedom to enter into these transactions implied acceptance that the prices of bonds would be set by the market. This, in turn, allowed the development of a national monetary market linked to international markets.

The evolution of the Mexican public debt shows that there was a drop in domestic debt (that is, the debt payable in silver), which remained fairly constant while the external public gold debt rose, especially after 1895. It can also be observed that unlike the trend in federal revenues and expenditure, the first attempts to make the public debt converge with international parameters (carried out between the 1860s and the 1880s) proved insufficient. Between 1868 and 1880 the debt/revenue ratio did drop from 9.4 to 4.9, but during the following decade, between 1890 and 1900, a new and marked episode of divergence increased the volume of federal revenues necessary to cover the total debt, with the debt/revenue ratio rising from 3.9 to 5.7. It was only at the turn of the twentieth century that the second convergence took place, returning to levels similar to those of the 1880s.

The debt/revenue ratio illustrates the difficulties encountered by Mexico in following international financial parameters, since monetary convergence was far more complex than simply modifying fiscal trends. In fact, the financial convergence of a country like Mexico required the ability to put in place new and very efficient mechanisms both in the domestic monetary market and in its connections with the monetary markets of the leading economies, that is, those of London, Paris, and Berlin. To begin with, Mexico did not have a strong banking system. Prior to the passage of the banking law of 1896, banking business was done only through a few firms: the Bank of London and Mexico founded in 1864; the National Bank of Mexico established in 1881; a mortgage bank, the Banco Hipotecario, established in 1882, the old Monte de Piedad (a pawnbroker institution established in the 18th century); a handful of local banks in the states of Chihuahua, Nuevo León, Durango, Zacatecas, Puebla, and Yucatán. Moreover, the development of banking and of capital markets was associated with the construction of railways and the financial needs of entrepreneurs that had to negotiate the subsidies given to them by the government in Treasury notes in silver pesos.[55]

[55] Capital markets and the banking system in Mexico have been studied by Carlos Marichal (1997c) and by Stephen Haber, "Financial Markets and Industrial Development: A Comparative Study of Governmental Regulation, Financial Innovation, and Industrial Structure in Brazil and Mexico, 1840–1930," in Haber (1997). See also Carmagnani (1994), p. 339, and Riguzzi (1996), pp. 31–98. For a good contemporary description of the Mexican banking system, see Bureau of Foreign Commerce, Department of State, *Commercial Relations of United States with Foreign Countries, 1898*, vol. I, Washington, D.C., 1899, pp. 512–21.

During the 1860s and 1870s, all things considered, Mexico was favored by the international economic context (in which bimetallic standards were common) because it was one of the major producers of silver in the world. Silver enjoyed its last auspicious moment precisely during the 1860–70 period due to the discovery of gold in California and Australia (1849–66) and also to an increase in the demand for silver for trade with Asia. The result was that the price of gold dropped below the traditional parity of 1:15.5 in the years prior to 1866, but once again moved up and reached parity between 1866 and 1876.[56] Hence, if we take into account the international monetary context before 1876, we can say that promoting convergence of Mexican public credit policies with those of Europe was not exceedingly difficult or burdensome. It was sufficient to take advantage of the circumstances, as was done by Mexican financial officers.

Nonetheless, after 1876 the world context changed and posed completely different problems. Due to the effects of the rapid changes in the international monetary environment, and the rapid and generalized acceptance of the gold standard, the first movement toward convergence came under threat. Internal factors had led to a new spiral of federal overspending, which, in turn, spurred a considerable volume of floating debt. At the same time, silver currency swiftly lost value: the market ratio of silver to gold increased quickly, reaching 22.10 in 1889 and 31.57 in 1895.[57] During the five-year period from 1881 to 1885, federal expenditure in current U.S. dollars increased 8 percent annually, while federal revenues in current U.S. dollars were reduced by 1.9 percent annually.

As can be seen, over the course of the decade 1885–95, two conditions were now moving the Mexican economy toward a new episode of divergence from European fiscal and monetary parameters. The first consisted in increasing fiscal deficits and the second in maintenance of the silver standard despite the worldwide trend toward adoption of the gold standard. While fiscal tools did exist to allow for a quick correction of a budget deficit, there were no monetary instruments for a corrective measure if the value of silver dropped, a fact of special importance if we take into account that Mexico did not have a bimetallic monetary system, but rather a pure silver standard one. Thus the monetary imbalance between Mexico and the European countries, especially Great Britain, was very high.

Mexican elites were slow to attempt changes in monetary policies because demonetization of silver on an international level hurt silver

[56] On bimetallism see Redish (1994) and Oppers (1995).

[57] On silver depreciation and its impact on foreign trade see Zabludowsky (1992), pp. 290–326.

producers' income, although it did not affect federal revenues in the same proportion. In fact, due to the total liberalization of trade, silver was tax-free, and federal revenues derived from imports and consumption were scarcely touched because the drop in the purchasing power of Mexican exports did not surpass 0.2 percent per annum between 1889 and 1896.[58] The restructuring of the public debt before 1890 was not a complicated matter because essentially it was an internal debt with a nominal value of 75.3 million pesos, the market value of which did not exceed 50.7 million pesos. The enormous difference between nominal and market values provided ample opportunity for the Treasury's amortization of 24.6 million pesos in bonds by investing at most some 9 million pesos in 10 years. On the other hand, the deterioration of monetary conditions and the new spiral of budgetary deficits did have repercussions on the gold public debt; in fact, budgetary deficits generated some 45–50 million dollars of new floating debt in less than a decade.

In spite of the efforts made by bankers and Mexican financial bureaucrats to facilitate access to international capital markets, the difficulties in achieving consolidation of the public debt in 1885–6 illustrate some of the obstacles to such a strategy. In effect, this consolidation was partially unsuccessful due to the continuing growth of liabilities in the budget. Some 185 million pesos of internal and external public debt were exchanged for new bonds with a nominal value of 138 million pesos, but the floating debt continued to grow, reaching 78 million pesos in 1890. In other words, while consolidation reduced the long-term public debt by 47 million pesos (25.4 percent), deficits increased the short-term public debt by 78 million pesos (39.2 percent).[59]

The authorities responsible for fiscal and monetary policy thus learned to evaluate the importance of controlling the monetary situation and other conditioning factors, especially internal productive growth and increases in exports. We should not forget that during the 1877–1910 period, the value of Mexican exports in dollars grew at a rate of 6.9 percent, similar to the growth rate of the volume of exports. Thus, we see that the growth rate for Mexican exports was higher that those of other follower economies with exports similar to Mexico's. Learning through trial and error at a time when Mexican foreign trade grew and became more diversified sometimes led Mexico's economic policy makers to overlook the fact that the continuation of the silver standard made monetary reform particularly difficult, in spite of their awareness of the definitive primacy of the gold standard.

[58] Ibid. [59] Carmagnani (1994), pp. 279–84.

The Mexican financial system suffered from structural weakness throughout the period 1880–95 at both the banking and stock exchange levels, as well as in the management of the monetary system. At the beginning, the National Bank of Mexico and the London and Mexico Bank were the only banks authorized to issue bank notes against current metallic currency. Under such conditions, banking operations depended on the amount of fiduciary coin placed in circulation, guaranteed by metallic reserves, basically silver coins on deposit or public debt securities equivalent to one-third of the value of the banknotes.

The money supply was not greatly changed by the issue of these bank notes. In 1882, 2 million pesos were in circulation and by 1890 there were 21.6 million pesos, but 17.5 million pesos were held as currency reserves in the banks. The estimate of silver currency held by the public was around 46.3 million pesos. By 1900 the amount of bank notes in circulation was 55.2 million pesos, currency reserves amounted to 51.8 million pesos, and silver coins held by the public amounted to 73.2 million pesos. During the 1890–1900 period, the rate of growth of silver coins held by the public was low (5.8 percent), banknotes increased at a rate of 10.8 percent, and bank reserves at a rate of 11.4 percent.

Thus, one can observe that the transformation from a money supply based on silver coins to a combination of coins and bank notes did occur. This change was an absolute requirement in order to develop a financial intermediation through new banking institutions, that is, a central bank, a clearing system, and a stock exchange market. Nonetheless, what strikes any scholar is the scarce attention paid by the Ministry of Finance (the sole financial authority until the 1920s) to the structural weakness of the Mexican financial institutions and the need for modernization.

Some modern features are to be found in the new banking law of 1897. On the one hand, this law banned the use of public bonds as short-term bank reserves. On the other hand, it established that the amount of bank notes issued could not double the bank's reserves; in addition, the maximum expiration term for commercial paper was set at six months. We now know that, in practice, the maturity of commercial paper was extended to a year, but this meant that the money supply increased constantly through the increase in commercial paper. In fact, between 1900 and 1910, the bank notes in circulation increased from 55 to 109 million pesos, that is, at an annual growth rate of 5.7 percent, whereas currency reserves went from 51 to 99 million pesos, an annual rate of 7.6 percent. Moreover, in spite of the fact that the new banking law authorized an interest rate on deposits, an increase in short- and long-term deposits was not registered. During the 1897–1904 period, short-term deposits increased from 1.7 to 2.5 million pesos, whereas other deposits went from

2.1 to 8.4 million pesos. Our conclusion is that the Mexican financial system was unable to develop a dynamic money market and thus forge a strong linkage with the international market.[60]

It was not until the beginning of the twentieth century that Mexico's fiscal officers drew up a medium-term scheme in order to achieve a more solid fiscal and monetary convergence between Mexico and the international economy. The new convergence stemmed from a strategy that we can term flexible because it did not attempt to block the production of silver or substitute for it totally with other types of production. It was a strategy that first attempted to establish the right conditions to overcome the country's monometallic dependence on silver through the introduction of a somewhat shaky bimetallism whereby gold functioned as a general equivalent exclusively for trade and financial relations with other countries. After this first step, new measures were taken to allow for a flexible gold system, that is, a gold exchange standard, whereby silver coinage had unlimited legal tender but a fixed gold value at the same time that gold became the general equivalent for internal and external trade, as well as financial and monetary transactions.[61]

Once the pure silver standard was abandoned between 1895 and 1901, the need to minimize the effects of the persistent devaluation of silver grew. The effect of this was to open a big gap between federal revenues and expenditures expressed in pesos, which grew at a rate of 4.2 percent and 4.1 percent, respectively, whereas that expressed in dollars barely grew at 1.6 percent and 1.5 percent, respectively. The attempt to achieve balanced budgets required strict discipline with regard to government spending. Thus, Mexico's fiscal and financial positions led to considerable internal and external risks. The risks were even greater if we take into account that a considerable part of the public debt – 109 million dollars – was in gold, of which a good share had been taken in the late nineteenth century, when the Mexican peso was worth much more in terms of gold.

The devaluation of silver had an impact on two variables: amortization and interest on the gold debt, especially that contracted in European financial markets, which increased in direct proportion to the devaluation of silver. At the same time, federal revenues dropped since

[60] There is a notable lack of studies on the financial system; a still useful reference is Conant (1910). The best monetary statistics are found in Cerda (1992) Tables 1–8. See also the essays by Marichal and Haber in Haber (1997).

[61] Kemmerer (1916) is still useful. The political debate on the gold standard has been studied by William Schell Jr., "Money as Commodity: Mexico's Conversion to the Gold Standard," *Mexican Studies/Estudios Mexicanos* (1996), n. 1, pp. 67–89.

all interest rates and taxes were charged in silver pesos. To make matters worse, silver devaluation reduced foreign export-purchasing power since silver remained Mexico's main export product. Under such circumstances, the fiscal situation and international debts once again threatened to separate Mexico from the international financial markets, unless the effects of the silver devaluation were neutralized by increasing and diversifying exports and/or by establishing a positive relation between import capacity and the purchasing power of exports.

Between 1895 and 1902, exports, expressed in gold, increased at a 6.4 percent annual rate and imports at a 6.3 percent rate. This shows that import capacity did not diminish, nor did the purchasing power of exports. Another positive indicator that favored the new fiscal and monetary convergence was the smaller share of silver in exports, dropping from 50.6 percent to 35.5 percent. At the same time, there was an improvement in the ratio between the prices of Mexican exports and imports, which increased annually at a rate of 2.7 percent between 1892 and 1908. Finally, interest rates and payments of the foreign debt in gold did not increase during this period.

Exchange uncertainty and the precarious relationship between Mexico and the gold standard between 1890 and 1902 explain why the ratio between debt and its service did not increase, remaining at a third of overall expenditure. Nonetheless, the measures adopted in order to achieve greater fiscal and monetary convergence limited Mexico's access to international capital markets.

The financial stability attained by the beginning of the twentieth century allowed for another step toward international monetary convergence. Once the negative conditioning factors were neutralized, federal revenue was partially indexed to gold, especially that derived from imports. In 1903 a new mechanism went into effect that allowed import duties to be charged on the basis of the New York exchange rate parity of 220 percent (1 gold dollar = 2.2 silver pesos). The reasons for indexing import duties to gold were to prevent exchange rate fluctuations from affecting the service of public debt and to stabilize foreign debt in gold. We can readily see the importance of this decision. Because customs duties on imports were now linked to gold, for the fiscal year 1903–4 revenue from import duties went up to 14.8 million dollars, whereas servicing of the debt reached 9.4 million dollars. With customs duties anchored to imported goods, the fluctuations in total revenues (which had risen to 40.2 percent in a year) and income rose by 36.8 million dollars in 1902–4. Additional advantages were achieved as a result of the stability in the consolidated world exchange rate. For Mexico, favorable conditions would prevail in the international financial market once European authorities and financial operators knew that the Mexican government was not incurring excessive debt. Such was the case between 1903 and 1906, when the external debt went up from 111.3 to 155.2 million dollars, a sign that fiscal and financial convergence had been achieved.

Financial convergence meant that the Mexican monetary system could finally step into the prevailing international mainstream, which was, at the time, the gold standard. In 1905, Mexico finally adopted the gold exchange standard; in other words, gold took on the role of a general equivalent, while silver was demonetized without being taken out of circulation completely.

The gold exchange standard included the monetary and fiscal ideas in vogue internationally, which were adopted willingly by the Mexican political elite. They were convinced that by adopting the gold standard, they could protect domestic production from exchange rate fluctuations, facilitate foreign investment, normalize foreign trade, and provide the government with an additional instrument for preserving a balanced budget while at the same time allowing for prudent regulation of banking transactions.

One must also realize that the prevailing economic thought was constantly repeated in essays and newspapers. At home or abroad, when discussing the gold standard, Mexican representatives heard again and again the benefits of the system: everywhere in Europe, in London, Paris, and Berlin, and, after 1900, in New York, financial elites spoke of nothing but its merits. It was thus made clear that Mexico's convergence with the gold standard symbolized its becoming part of the concert of civilized nations.

9.2.4 Conclusion

The Mexican case shows us that the adoption of the gold standard eventually became a prerequisite for the internationalization of the economy. Our analysis of the Mexican fiscal and monetary experience sheds light on why convergence with the other Western economies was necessary. For instance, economic policy makers in follower countries, that is, in countries that exported raw materials and agricultural products, were particularly interested in promoting greater integration of their respective countries with the international fiscal, financial, and monetary systems. They were aware of the fact that convergence would improve their ability to profit from the decline in interest rates in capital markets, improve the credibility of national bonds and securities in international stock markets, and also give greater confidence to foreign investors. In other words, improving economic performance was not just a matter of improving exports but also a financial matter.[62]

In our analysis, we have contrasted, or rather refuted, traditional ideas that continue to be repeated in some good international financial history textbooks, in which Latin American countries, and Mexico in particular, are presented as lacking any budgetary, fiscal, and monetary discipline. The alleged lack of discipline is attributed to the political monopoly exercised over economic policy by the large agricultural landholders in the respective countries. From this view follows the idea that these groups avoided the establishment of a modern fiscal system in an effort to exempt themselves from taxation, and at the same time that they withheld support for any reform in the monetary regime in order to profit from the continuous depreciation of their national currency.

Our argument follows a different trajectory. First, it demonstrates the interest of entrepreneurs, politicians, and Mexican financial officers alike in reforming and using fiscal and monetary instruments to their best advantage in order to avoid budgetary deficits. All were fully aware of the fact that these deficits affected not only the country's economic growth but their income as well. This is why we have insisted that Mexican fiscal and monetary convergence with European parameters was not a mere formality, but rather one that had real and concrete motives. The value that politicians and public opinion attributed to Mexico's inclusion in the concert of civilized nations points to the importance given to joining the international monetary system and the gold standard. The behavior of a follower country like Mexico in search of convergence was hence not very different from the experience of other countries, especially European nations like Spain and Italy.

A general and final conclusion is that the historical evidence of the late nineteenth century indicates a clear need for any economy to achieve close coordination between monetary and fiscal policies. This implied – at the time – a positive correlation between fiscal discipline and participation in the gold standard, which is also to say that balanced budgets and sound public credit were two basic conditions for participation in the contemporary international monetary and financial systems. In this regard, one must also keep in mind that the gold standard bears not only on monetary policy and on the price system but also, in a fundamental way, on fiscal policies and therefore on the political system as a whole. The interactions between economy and politics are

[62] On this subject see Michael D. Bordo and Finn E. Kydland, "The Gold Standard as a Rule," in Eichengreen and Flandreau (1995), pp. 98–128; Michael D. Bordo and Finn E. Kydland, "The Gold Standard as a Commitment Mechanism," in Bayoumi, Eichengreen, and Taylor, (1996), pp. 55–100; and Bordo and Rockoff (1996).

constantly present in any form of cooperation necessary to maintain an active economic convergence between countries.[63]

REFERENCES

Alamán, Lucas (1985). *Historia de México*, 5 vols. Mexico: Fondo de Cultura Económica/Instituo Cultural Helénico (facsimile of the first edition of 1849–52).

Anna, Timothy (1981). *La caída del gobierno español en la ciudad de México*. Mexico: Fondo de Cultura Económica.

Armstrong, George M., Jr. (1987). *Law and Market Society in Mexico*. New York: Praeger.

Arnold, Linda (1991). *Burocracia y burcratas en México, 1742–1835*. Mexico: Consejo para la Cultura y las Artes.

Artola, Miguel (1982). *La hacienda del antiguo régimen*. Madrid: Alianza.

Barbier, Jacques and Herbert Klein (1981). "Revolutionary Wars and Public Finance: The Madrid Treasury, 1784–1807," *Journal of Economic History*, 41, no. 2, pp. 315–39.

Bayoumi, Tamim, Barry Eichengreen, and Mark P. Taylor, eds. (1996). *Modern Perspectives on the Gold Standard*. Cambridge: Cambridge University Press.

Bonney, Richard, ed. (1995). *Economic Systems and State Finance*. Oxford: Oxford University Press/The European Science Foundation.

Bordo, Michael D. and Finn E. Kydland (1996). "The Gold Standard as a Commitment Mechanism," in Bayoumi, Eichengreen, and Taylor, pp. 55–100.

Bordo, Michael D. and Hugh Rockoff (1996). "The Gold Standard as a Good Housekeeping Seal of Approval," *Journal of Economic History*, n. 2, pp. 389–428.

Bordo, Michael and Eugene Nelson White (1991). "A Tale of Two Currencies: British and French During the Napoleonic Wars," *Journal of Economic History*, 51, 2, 303–16.

Brading, David (1975). *Mineros y comerciantes en el México borbónico, 1763–1810*. Mexico: Fondo de Cultura Económica.

(1985). "Facts and Figments in Bourbon Mexico," *Bulletin of Latin American Research*, 4, 1, pp. 61–4.

Brewer, John (1989). *The Sinews of Power: War, Money and the English State, 1688–1783*. London: Unwin Hyman.

Buist, Marten G. (1974). *At Spes Non Fracta: Hope and Company, 1770–1815: Merchant Bankers and Diplomats at Work*. La Haya: Martinus Nijhoff.

Canga Arguelles, José Antonio (1833–4). *Diccionario de Hacienda*, 2 vols. (Facsimile edition by the Instituto de Estudios Fiscales, Madrid, 1984.)

Cárdenas, Enrique (1984). "Algunas cuestiones sobre la depresión mexicana del siglo XIX," *HISLA, Revista Latinoamericana de Historia Económica y Social*, 3, pp. 3–22.

[63] A good study of the interaction between economics and politics is to be found in Gallarotti (1995). See also Hefeker (1995).

Carmagnani, Marcello (1983). "Finanzas y estado en México, 1820–1880," *Ibero-Amerikanisches Archiv*, neue folge, 9, 3/4, pp. 279–317.

(1984). "Territorialidad y federalismo en la formación del estado mexicano," in I. Bensson, G. Kahle, H. Konig, and H. Pietschmann, eds., *Problemas de la formación del estado y la nación en Hispanoamérica*. Koln and Wien: Bohlau Verlag, pp. 289–304.

(1994). *Estado y mercado. La economía pública del liberalismo mexicano, 1850–1911*. Mexico: Fondo de Cultura Económica.

Cerda, Luis (1992). "Exchange-Rate and Monetary Policies in Mexico from Bimetallism to the Gold Standard: 1890–1999, *Documentos de Trabajo ITAM*, México.

Cerutti, Mario (1983). *Economía de guerra y poder regional en el siglo XIX: gastos militares, aduanas y comerciantes en años de Vidaurri (1855–1864)*. Monterrey: Archivo General del Estado de Nuevo León.

Chowning, Margaret (1992). "The Contours of the Post-1810 Depression in Mexico: A Reappraisal from a Regional Perspective," *Latin American Research Riview*, 27, 2, pp. 119–50.

Coatsworth, John (1978). "Obstacles to Economic Growth in Nineteenth Century Mexico," *American Historical Review*, 83, 1, pp. 80–100.

(1990). *Los origenes del atraso*. Mexico: Alianza Mexicana.

Comín, Francisco (1996). *Historia de la hacienda pública*, 2 vols. Barcelona: Crítica.

Conant, A. (1910). *The Banking System of Mexico*. Washington, D.C.: National Monetary Commission.

Deans Smith, Susan (1992). *Bureaucrats, Planters and Workers: The Making of the Tobacco Monopoly in Bourbon Mexico*. Austin: University of Texas Press.

Dickson, P. G. M. (1967). *The Financial Revolution in England: A Study in the Development of Public Credit, 1688–1756*. London: Oxford University Press.

Eichengreen, Barry and Marc Flandreau, eds. (1995). *The Gold Standard in Theory and History*. London: Routledge.

Elliott, John H. (1992). "A Europe of Composite Monarchies," *Past and Present*, no. 137, pp. 48–71.

Fishlow, Albert (1985). "Lessons from the Past: Capital Markets during the Nineteenth Century and Interwar Period," *International Organization*, 39, 3 (Summer), pp. 420–60.

Fonseca, Fabián de y Carlos de Urrutia (1845–51). *Historia general de la Real Hacienda*, 6 vols. Mexico: Vicente G. Torres.

Fontana, Josep (1971). *La quiebra de la monarquía absoluta, 1814–1820: la crisis del Antiguo régimen en España*. Barcelona: Ariel.

(1981). "La financiación de la guerra de la independencia," *Hacienda Pública Española*, no. 69, pp. 209–17.

Gallarotti, Giulio, M. (1995). *The Anatomy of an International Monetary Regime. The Classical Gold Standard, 1880–1914*. New York: Oxford University Press.

Gamboa, Ricardo (1994). "Las finanzas muncipales de la ciudad México, 1800–1850." Mexico: Instituto Mora.

Garavaglia, Juan Carlos and Juan Carlos Grosso (1987). *Las alcabalas novohispanas, 1776–1821*. Mexico: AGN.

Garner, Richard (1993). *Economic Growth and Change in Bourbon Mexico*. Gainesville: University of Florida Press.

Haber, Stephen, ed. (1997). *How Latin America Fell Behind. Essays in the Economic Histories of Brazil and Mexico, 1800–1914*. Stanford, Calif.: Stanford Unviversity Press.

Hefeker, Carsten (1995). "Interest Groups, Coalitions and Monetary Integration in the XIXth Century," *Journal of European Economic Review*, no. 3, pp. 489–535.

Hernández Chavez, Alicia, ed. (1994). *Presidencialismo y sistema político. México y los Estados Unidos*. Mexico: Fondo de Cultura Económica.

Hernández Palomo, José Jesus (1980). *La renta del pulque en Nueva España, 1663–1810*. Sevilla: Escuela de Estudios Hispanoamericanos.

Hicks, Ursula K. (1954). *British Public Finances. Their Structure and Development, 1880–1952*. London: Oxford University Press.

Hinrichs, H. H. (1966). *A General Theory of Tax Structure Change During Economic Development*. Cambridge, Mass.: Harvard Law School.

Holden, Robert H. (1994). *Mexico and the Survey of Public Lands*. De Kalb: Northern Illinois University Press.

Howe, Walter (1949). *The Mining Guild of New Spain and Its Tribunal General, 1770–1821*. Cambridge, Mass.: Harvard University Press.

Humboldt, Alejandro (1991). *Ensayo político sobre el reino de la Nueva España*. Mexico: Ed. Porrúa. (Original edition published in Paris, 1807–11.)

Jackson, John Alexander (1978). "The Mexican Silver Schemes: Finance and Profiteering in the Napoleonic Era, 1796–1811." Ph.D. thesis, University of North Carolina, Raleigh, NC.

Jaúregui, Luis Antonio (1994). "La anatomía del fisco colonial: la real hacienda de la Nueva España, 1784–1821." Tesis doctoral, El Colegio de México.

Jaúregui, Luis Antonio and José Antonio Serrano, eds. (1997). *Finanzas y Estado en la Primera República Federal Mexicana, 1824–1835*. Mexico: Instituto Mora/El Colegio de México.

Kemmerer, Edwin Walter (1916). *Modern Currency Reforms in India, Puerto Rico, Philippine Islands, Straits Settlements and Mexico*. New York: Macmillan.

Klein, Herbert (1985). "La economía de la Nueva España, 1680–1809: Un análisis a partir de las cajas reales," *Historia Mexicana*, 34, no. 136, pp. 561–609.

(1988). "Recent Trends in the Study of Spanish American Colonial Public Finance," *Latin American Research Review*, 23, 1, pp. 35–62.

(1995). *Las finanzas americanas del imperio español, 1680–1809*. Mexico: Instituto Mora, Universidad Autónoma Metropolitana.

Klein, Herbert and John TePaske (1987–9). *Ingresos y egresos de la Real Hacienda de Nueva España*, 2 vols. Mexico: Instituto Nacional de Antropología e Historia, Colección Fuentes.

Levy-Leboyer, Maurice and Jean-Claude Casanova (1991). *Entre l'Etat et le marché. L'economie fran aise des années 1880 à nos jours*. Paris: Gallimard.

Liehr, Reinhart (1980). "Statsverschuldung und privatkredit: die "consolidación de vales reales in Hispanoamerika," *Ibero-Amerikanishes Archiv*, N.F. Jg. 6, no. 2, pp. 150–83.

Macedo, Pablo (1905). *La Evolución mercantil; Colunicaciones y Obras públicas; La Hacienda Pública*. Mexico: UNAM.

Marichal, Carlos (1989b). "El tratado de subsidios con Napoleón y las finanzas novohispanas, 1803–1808," *Revista de Ciencia Sociales y Humanidades*, Universidad Autónoma Metropolitana, 9, no. 27, pp. 41–54.

(1990). "Las guerras imperiales y los préstamos novohispanos, 1781–1804," *Historia Mexicana*, 39:4, 156, 881–907.

(1995). "La Iglesia y la Corona: la bancarrota del gobierno de Carlos IV y la consolidación de Vales Reales en la Nueva España," in Pilar Martínez López-Cano, ed., *Iglesia, estado y economía, siglos xvi ald xix*. Mexico: UNAM, pp. 241–62.

(1997a) (ed.). *De colonia a nación: el tránsito fiscal, 1750–1850*. Mexico: El Colegio de México.

(1997b). "Costos y beneficios fiscales del colonialismo: Nueva España y España, 1790–1810," *Revista de Historia Económica*.

(1997c). "Obstacles to the Development of Capital Markets in Nineteenth Century Mexico," in Stephen Haber, ed., *How Latin America Fell Behind*. Stanford, Calif.: Stanford University Press, pp. 118–45.

(1999). *La bancarrota del virreinato: la Nueva España y las finanzas del imperio español, 1780–1810*. Mexico: El Colegio de México.

Marichal, Carlos, Manuel Miño, and Paolo Riguzzi (1994). *Historia de la Hacienda Pública del Estado de México*, 4 vols. Toluca.

Marichal, Carlos and Matilde Souto (1994). "Silver and *Situados*: New Spain and the Financing of the Spanish Empire in the Caribbean in the Eighteenth Century," *Hispanic American Historical Review*, 74, 4 (1997a), pp. 587–613.

Mathias, Peter and Patrick O'Brien (1976). "Taxation in England and France, 1715–1810," *Journal of European Economic History*.

McBride, George M. (1927). *The Land Systems of Mexico*. New York: American Geographic Society.

Merino Navarro, José Patricio (1981). "La Hacienda de Carlos IV," *Hacienda Pública Española*, no. 69, pp. 139–81.

(1987). *Las cuentas de la Administración central española, 1750–1820*. Madrid: Instituto de Estudios Fiscales.

Molina Enríquez, Andrés (1979). *Los grandes problemas nacionales*. Mexico: Era. (Originally published 1909.)

Morineau, Michel (1985). *Incroyables gazettes et fabuleux métaux: les retours des trésors americains d'après les gazettes hollandaises, xvie–xviiie siècles* París and London: University of Cambridge Press/Maison des Sciences de l'Homme.

Neal, Larry (1990). *The Rise of Financial Capitalism: International Capital Markets in the Age of Reason*. Cambridge: Cambridge University Press, NY.

Oppers, Stefan E. (1995). "Recent Development in Bimetallic Theory," in Jaime Reis, ed., *International Monetary Systems in Historical Perspective*. London: Macmillan, pp. 47–70.

Payno, Manuel (1868). *Cuentas, gastos acreedores y otros asuntos del tiempo de la intervención francesa y del imperio*. Mexico.

Peacock, Alan T. and Jack Wiseman (1967). *The Growth of Public Expenditure in the United Kingdom*. London: Allen & Unwin.

Redish, Angela (1994). "The Latin Monetary Union and the Emergence of the International Gold Standard," in Michael D. Bordo and Forrest Capie, eds., *Monetary Regimes in Transition*. Cambridge: Cambridge University Press, pp. 68–86.

Riguzzi, Paolo (1996). "Los caminos del atraso: tecnología, instituciones e inversión en los ferrocarriles mexicanos, 1850–1900," in Sandra Kunz Ficker and Paolo Riguzzi, eds., *Ferrocarriles y vida económica en México (1850–1950)*. Mexico: El Colegio Mexiquense-UAM, pp. 31–98.

Riley, James C. (1980). *International Government Finance and the Amsterdam Capital Market, 1740–1815*. Cambridge University Press.

Salvucci, Richard (1994a). "Economic Growth and Change in Bourbon Mexico: A Review Essay," *The Americas*, 51, 2, pp. 219–31.

(1994b). "The Real Exchange Rate of the Mexican Peso, 1762–1812: A Research Note and Estimate," *Journal of European Economic History*, 23, 1, pp. 131–40.

Sinkin, Richard N. (1979). *The Mexican Reform, 1855–1876. A Study in Liberal Nation Building*. Austin: University of Texas Press.

Stewart, Charles H. (1989). *Budget Reform Politics in the House of Representatives 1865–1921*. Cambridge: Cambridge University Press.

Sugawara, Masae (1976). *La deuda pública de España y la economía novohispana*. Mexico: Colección Científica INAH, no. 28.

Tedde, Pedro (1988). *El Banco de San Carlos, 1782–1829*. Madrid: Alianza-Banco de España.

(1989). "Política financiera y política comercial en el reinado de Carlos III," *Actas del Congreso Internacional sobre Carlos III y la Ilustración*, vol. 2. Madrid: Ministerio de Cultura, pp. 139–217.

Téllez, Francisco and Elvia Brito (1990). "La hacienda municipal de Puebla en el siglo XIX," *Historia Mexicana*, 39, 4, pp. 951–78.

Tenenbaum, Barbara (1987). *The Politics of Penury: Debts and Taxes in Mexico, 1821–1856*. Albuquerque: University of New Mexico Press.

(1989). "Taxation and Tyranny: Public Finance during the Iturbide Regime, 1821–1823," in J. Rodríguez, ed., *The Independence of Mexico and the Creation of the New Nation*. Los Angeles: University of California Press, pp. 201–13.

TePaske, John (1983). "New World Silver, Castile and the Far East (1590–1750)," in John. F. Richards, eds., *Precious Metals in the Later Medieval and Early Modern Worlds*. Durham, N.C.: Duke University Press, pp. 425–45.

(1989). "The Financial Disintegration of the Royal Government of Mexico during the Epoch of Independence," in J. Rodríguez, ed., *The Independence of Mexico and the Creation of the New Nation*. Los Angeles: University of California Press, pp. 63–84.

TePaske, John and Hebert Klein (1983). *The Royal Treasuries of the Spanish Empire in America*, 3 vols. Durham, N.C.: Duke University Press.

Thomas, Robert Paul (1965). "A Quantitative Approach to the Study of the Effects of British Imperial Policy Upon Colonial Welfare," *Journal of Economic History*, 25, 4, pp. 615–38.

Tilly, Charles, ed. (1975). *The Formation of Nation States in Western Europe*. Princeton, N.J.: Princeton University Press.

Valle Pavón, Guillermina del (1997). "El Consulado de Comercio de la Ciudad de México y las deudas novohispanas (Siglo XVIII)." Tesis doctoral, El Colegio de México.

Velde, Francois R. and David R. Weir (1992). "The Financial Market and Government Debt Policy in France, 1746–1793," *Journal of Economic History*, 52, 1, pp. 1–39.

Walker, David (1986). *Kinship, Business and Politics: The Martínez del Rio Family in Mexico, 1824–1867*. Austin: Univeristy of Texas Press.

White, Eugene N. (1989). "Was There a Solution to the Ancien Regime's Financial Dilemma?" *Journal of Economic History*, 49, 3, pp. 545–68.

Zabludowski, Jaime Enrique (1992). *La depreciación de la plata y las exportaciones*, in Enrique Cárdenas, ed., *Historia económica de México*. México: Fondo de Cultura Económica.

10

Property Rights and the Fiscal and Financial Systems in Brazil

Colonial Heritage and the Imperial Period

Marcelo de Paiva Abreu and Luiz A. Corrêa do Lago

10.1 PROPERTY RIGHTS IN A LONG-TERM PERSPECTIVE

Rent-extraction activities traditionally have played an important role in Brazil since colonial times; witness the central role played by farmed-out monopolies and tax contracts and the many restrictions affecting economic activities. Much has been written about property rights in imperial Brazil (1822–89), but most of it has dealt with either land property rights or slave-owning during the transition to a free-labor regime. Labor policies played a major role in Brazil from colonial times as the government underlined permanently the dominance of the objective of maintaining low manpower costs throughout the period. Requiring net slave imports, the Brazilian economy was particularly vulnerable to an interruption of the slave trade. Thus, the commitment to cease slave imports in 1830 was openly disregarded for 20 years, and enforcement came only as a direct result of British pressure through the Royal Navy, especially in the second half of the 1840s.

As the final abolition of slavery only took place – without compensation to owners – in 1888, the transition to free labor remained one of the important economic issues during the empire. As free labor was attracted to Brazil, land legislation became a crucial element of wage determination for free labor. In spite of land legislation in the first half of the 1850s that would have allowed land ownership by immigrants, actual control of the land (*posse*) and the ability to preserve this control were the crucial factors. Land ownership on the agricultural frontier was to be defined by continuous occupation and was consequently beyond the reach of most immigrants. Land was available in theory, but mostly to the powerful large-scale squatter occupying the agricultural frontier and not to the immigrant. Otherwise, wages would increase and could affect the long-term profitability of plantation agriculture, as would be expected from the *Domar hypothesis*. The legalization of land ownership was a protracted process, and one in which political power and outward violence at the local level played a decisive role. As Dean (1971) puts it: "*Posse* [actual control of the land] fundamentally denied the authority of the state. The Crown had to be able to maintain its rights over public lands and – even more important – it had to establish a legitimate means of alienating them. If most of the lands in private hands was [sic] illegally acquired, then how was the state to guarantee any individual's property rights?"[1] There was thus no clear long-term definition of property rights concerning two of the most important nonfinancial assets in imperial Brazil: land and slaves. In both cases, government action could (and in the case of slaves did) disregard individual and legally registered private property rights.

Both the question of labor supply, involving slavery and European immigration, and the process of occupation of new lands in the nineteenth century have been the object of numerous studies. However, practically nothing has been written on property rights and on fiscal and financial matters in imperial Brazil. It is thus important to underline from the start the exploratory nature of this chapter. North and Weingast (1989) stress the importance of constitutional developments brought about by the Glorious Revolution of 1688 in England a powerful factor, in the development of the capital markets due to the inducement to lend made possible by an improvement in property rights. The question at issue was the protection of private property "from the depredations of the sovereign,"[2] which was made possible by the greater strength of Parliament and the increased independence of common-law courts. North and Weingast's analysis has been complemented in certain aspects, and especially so in relation to the role of indirect debt by the sovereign through joint stock companies.[3] But the essential link between strengthening of property rights and consolidation of financial markets remains the main focus of interest.

In discussing Brazil, the conventional analysis has to suffer significant adjustments. The idea of an evolutionary long-term strengthening of property rights, going hand in hand with the shift of political power from

[1] Dean (1971), p. 610. See also Lago (1988). In the south of Brazil, because of specific government settlement policies, immigrants had access to land ownership. This area was, however, distant from the plantation zones. In those zones, as a foreign observer noted in 1889, "title to land cannot legally be acquired by mere occupancy unless commenced previous to [1850] though in practice squatters cannot be removed and everyone takes and keeps what he wants, unless a stronger man comes and takes it from him." See Wyndham (1889), p. 41.

[2] Turnor (1674), quoted by Carruthers (1996).

[3] See Carruthers (1996), chapter 5.

the Crown to Parliament, is much less clear than in more advanced economies.

In that context, it is important to define what is meant by property rights for the purposes of this chapter. Clearly, what is being examined is not the existence or absence of legislation involving private law and defining the right of individuals to own private property and to dispose of it or the security of private contracts. The notion of private property or property rights in that sense, and rules to make them enforceable in courts of law, had clearly been established to some extent in sixteenth-century Portugal and had been inherited by colonial Brazil, where houses, slaves, cattle, plantations, and various types of assets and merchandise were the object of inheritance as well as of private contracts of purchase and sale, while bills of exchange were used in commercial transactions.

What is the main concern of this study is how the government on specific occasions might infringe those rights by undermining the value of financial assets held by individuals (in Brazil or abroad) through its fiscal or financial policies or through actions similar to outright confiscation, akin to "the depredations of the sovereign."

In that broader view, several more advanced economies were not immune to infringement of property rights by their governments in the nineteenth century through such actions as repudiation of the public debt, debasement of the metallic currency or the forced circulation of paper money, and extraordinary taxation and creation of an inflationary environment or of political instability, which actually corroded the real values of assets, in spite of the existence of well-defined private ownership and the theoretical legal security of private contracts.

In contrast with former colonies of Great Britain, Brazil could never look at Portugal, and particularly at Portuguese financial institutions, as paradigms to be closely followed. Although Portugal was a metropolitan power, it remained a rather underdeveloped economy facing difficulties of financial consolidation akin to those faced by its former colony, in spite of some episodes of financial creativity. The paradigm was Britain, even if the institutional inheritance was strongly Portuguese. The whole institutional context including the strong powers of the king could fail, as already mentioned, to provide protection from government action affecting real assets such as land and slaves in real practice, even though in theory the prevailing legal system, based on Roman law, clearly allowed such assets to be legally registered under the names of their owners. Property rights were fragile and constantly undermined in the colonial period, and part of that fragility filtered into the nineteenth century. This chapter is a preliminary investigation concentrating only on the projections of such characteristics on the fiscal and financial systems developed in Brazil during the empire.

After this introduction, Section 10.2 considers the colonial heritage from the perspective of fiscal and monetary regimes. Section 10.3 briefly sketches the direct and indirect costs of independence from a financial point of view. The next two sections consider in sucession fiscal policies and monetary aspects of Brazilian finance during the empire. Aspects related to revenue, expenditure, public debt, and the political economy of public finance are examined in Section 10.4. The next section covers monetary issues: changing monetary standards, the several versions of a Banco do Brasil, the alternation of restrictive and lax monetary regimes, and changes of policy affecting the note issuing rights of private banks. Section 10.6 presents the provisional conclusions.

10.2 THE COLONIAL HERITAGE

Production of sugar was the first economic activity in Brazil in the sixteenth century, leading to permanent settlement of the colony and giving rise to its first fiscal apparatus. The establishment of a royal government in Bahia in 1549 resulted in the appointment of a *provedor-mor da fazenda*, the main fiscal Crown official in the colony, who reported directly to Lisbon. The main principles and regulations of the *regimentos* of the *provedor-mor* and of the partial *provedores* of the royal Treasury were maintained, with slight changes, during the whole colonial period. The *provedor-mor* was to establish a customs house (*alfândega*), with the appropriate books of revenues and expenditures, the updated regulations, and provisions for the levy of rights. He also had to organize a house for the royal treasury business (*casa de contos*), having with that objective "all the books necessary, one to register revenues and their titles, another of *forais* and *regimentos*, provisions, salaries, contracts, rents, and so on." His duties also included the organization of customs and *contos* houses such as those in Bahia in all the captaincies. He had to separate revenues according to branches and auction their contracts, demanding guarantees from the contractors, following the treasury *regimento* enforced in Portugal. He was also to demand that the *provedores* in each captaincy present annual accounts of revenues and expenditures and require them to send the balance to the treasurer resident in Bahia. The staff of the *provedor-mor* was to constitute the first fiscal and financial bureaucracy in Brazil, and it reflected, at an early date, the objective of the Portuguese Crown of guaranteeing rent extraction from Brazil.[4]

[4] Garcia (1975), pp. 101–3.

The initial revenues to the Crown from the colony originated from brazilwood in the early sixteenth century. The cutting and exportation of that dyewood was successively the object of a monopoly contract, temporary free exploitation, and again a monopoly farmed out to contractors. However, the principal economic activity developed in Brazil in the second half of the sixteenth century was sugar production. "From 1580 to 1680, Brazil [was] the world's largest producer and exporter of sugar."[5] Thus, in addition to the already existing income from brazilwood, the "most important tax [was] constituted by the *dízimo*, the tenth of the [sugar] crop that the *senhor de engenho* [had] to pay to the Order of Christ, whose estate [was] administered by the crown. Generally paid in sugar as it would come out of the [sugar] purging house (*casa de purgar*), it was farmed out, the price of the contract varying with the crops or expected crops."[6] Thus taxation was mainly on production, not on trade.

The principle of farming out tax collection in the colony through periodical auctions was established at an early date. Figures for tax farming contracts exist for given years both for Brazil as a whole and for specific captaincies from the sixteenth to the eighteenth centuries, when that practice would continue to be maintained. The incidence of the *dízimo* (tithe of 10 percent on all products) was indeed comprehensive (including all types of products besides sugar, such as "manioc, bananas, potatoes, sheep, goats, chickens," etc.).[7] The frequently close relationship of the contractors with local public officials would be a constant cause of concern of the metropolis.[8]

Though the *dízimo* (tithe) was for a long time the only tax paid within the colony, there were also taxes on the entry and sale of Brazilian products in Portugal. In the late 1500s, those products were supposed to pay 10 percent of customs duties (*dízima*) and 10 percent of *sisa* (sales tax), or a total of 20 percent upon entry in the metropolis, though sugar mill owners, who shipped their own sugar, could obtain exemptions for a number of years.

After the union of the two Iberian crowns in 1580, a new tax, the *consulado* of 3 percent, was created in the 1590s, supposedly to fund the construction of warships to protect the ships trading between Brazil and Portugal. The same pretext was later used for the imposition of another tax, the *averia*. After 1630, the war with the Dutch led to an increase in taxation to finance the recovery of the northeast, as well as the new fleet

[5] Schwartz (1987), p. 67. [6] Mauro (1983), p. 259.

[7] Johnson (1987), pp. 37–8. For the eighteenth century, see Maxwell (1973), p. 261.

[8] Azevedo (1973), pp. 251–2.

system created in 1649. In Portugal, the right of *meias-anatas*, a contribution paid by all holders of public office such as judges and notary publics, was also created. The definitive peace with Holland in 1661 led to the payment of a war indemnity, as well as indemnities to persons who had suffered expropriation in Pernambuco by the Portuguese in 1654, including the Jews who had left Brazil,[9] part of which was borne by Brazilian colonists. The dowry of a Portuguese princess was also a pretext for additional temporary taxes, and some municipal taxes – normally excises (*subsídios*) on certain imported or local consumer goods – were levied in some cities of Brazil, even though municipalities would never have the same importance as in Spanish America.[10]

Agriculture was the basis of economic taxation in Brazil, but Crown monopolies on certain products were also renewed or created in the early seventeenth century to try to bolster the crown's revenues. "A new royal monopoly on brazilwood was established in 1605.... Similar monopolies were established on whaling and salt while an *estanque*, or monopoly, on tobacco sales in Portugal would be created in the 1630s."[11] In all cases, the contracts were also farmed out to private contractors through a system of auctions held periodically.

The growing need for labor in the colony was met by increasing imports of African slaves into Brazil. Those slaves were taxed by the Portuguese Crown on embarkation in African ports, increasing their final price in Brazil, even though they were often purchased in exchange for sugar cane, brandy, tobacco, and other Brazilian goods. "The slave trade was open to all Portuguese on payment of a due. The collection of dues was farmed out, by means of an *asiento* (contract) to a *contratador*, who delivered the *avenças* (agreements) to the traffickers."[12]

The direct tax represented by the *dízimo* (raised in kind as a withholding tax) was borne by Brazilian producers. It is difficult to discuss the actual incidence of the taxes imposed on Brazilian products upon entry in Portugal and to what extent these taxes affected the prices received by Brazilian producers or were borne by the final European consumers. On the other hand, the taxes charged on the embarkation of goods to Brazil, also normally on the order of 20 percent (plus 3 percent of *consulado* and 3 percent of the *averia*), were clearly a burden on the colony's inhabitants.

The generalized system of credit granted by metropolitan and local merchants to the colonists, involving the use of letters of exchange since the late sixteenth century, with balances being only periodically settled

[9] See Wolff (1991) for a list of the beneficiaries.

[10] Alden (1968), pp. 304–6. [11] Schwartz (1987), pp. 98, 103.

[12] Mauro (1987), p. 52.

in currency instead of paid in kind, as was most frequently done, coincided with a limited circulation of coins in the colony. In fact, during the sixteenth century, barter was frequent and even the payment of pensions and salaries by the general government was often in kind, apparently as an adaptation to the scarcity of currency.[13]

The colonists were also on several occasions and from an early date subject to the negative impact of manipulations of the face value of Portuguese coins – for instance, in 1568, when copper coins were devalued; in 1642 and 1663, when silver coins of previous reigns were countermarked in the metropolis to increase their nominal value by 20 and 25 percent, respectively; and in 1688, when both silver and gold coins had their nominal value increased by 20 percent, again with their intrinsic value unchanged. In Brazil, Spanish American silver coins were countermarked in 1643 to increase their value by 50 percent (the colonists of Bahia being given one month and those of the hinterland two months to present their coins to be substituted), and new countermarks were applied in 1663 and 1679, the silver 8 reales of unchanged intrinsic value being respectively valued at 480, 600, and 640 réis. In most occasions, there is evidence of complaints of the colonists against the *levantamento* of the currency, which was a clear infringement of their property rights to the extent that nominal prices for their products did not automatically increase.[14]

The acute shortage of coins and the use of other goods for transactions, as well as the payment of wages, pensions, and other state obligations in kind (which was favored by the tithe system), are widely documented for the seventeenth century as well. However, the Portuguese currency was the standard of value to which all goods were referred in the case of payments in kind, and Brazil was clearly a "monetary economy."[15]

Only in 1694 was the first mint[16] finally authorized in Bahia to issue coins for local use (and with circulation forbidden in the metropolis). The law of March of that year stipulated a seigniorage of 6.66 percent on the coinage of gold and silver, the same observed in Portugal, supposedly to cover production costs.[17] The mint was later temporarily moved to Rio

[13] Varnhagem (1962), tome 1, p. 343.

[14] Varnhagem (1962), tome 1, pp. 342–3; Sombra (1938), p. 74; Calógeras (1960), pp. 7–8; Boxer (1962), p. 28; Prober (1966), pp. 25–8; Coimbra (1958), tome II, pp. 136–40.

[15] See Lago (1973).

[16] The Dutch had made small emergency issues of silver and gold coins denominated in florins in 1645–6 and in 1654 in Pernambuco but did not establish a mint. *Ordenanças*, or paper bills issued in 1640 and 1643, also had had forced circulation in Recife for short periods. See, respectively, Prober (1966), p. 23; Calógeras (1960), p. 6; Lissa (1987), p. 13; and Trigueiros (1987), pp. 65–6, who refers to *ordens de pagamento*.

[17] Coimbra (1959), vol. III, pp. 66–7.

de Janeiro and then to Pernambuco before returning permanently to Rio in 1703. Copper coins were also issued in Oporto between 1694 and 1699 for exclusive circulation in Brazil. The difference of 10 percent in the value of the colonial coinage locally as opposed to its value in the metropolis, to hinder the export of coins, which was observed in other American colonies, also prevailed initially in Brazil.[18] However, after 1702, the coinage of gold Portuguese or "national" coins was also allowed in the colony, most being exported to Portugal. In 1714, a second mint was created in Bahia. In Minas Gerais a third mint issued only gold coins from 1724 to 1734.

The discovery of significant quantities of gold, turning Brazil into the world's largest producer, would entail new regulations and fiscal controls in the gold mining regions, while the previously existing taxes were maintained in other regions of the colony. The increase in production would permit a significant increase in Brazilian coinage of gold and, to a much lesser extent, of silver (after 1695) and copper (after 1729), and in spite of prohibitions and the concern of the Portuguese authorities about contraband, gold dust would also circulate widely. Barter and payments in kind would also continue in certain regions well into the nineteenth century. Juntas da Fazenda, independent of the *provedor-mor*, were created after 1761 in the mining captaincies to deal with fiscal affairs, and a special silver coinage with circulation restricted to Minas Gerais was issued in Rio de Janeiro and Bahia from 1752 and 1774 after another special copper issue in 1722. The issue of both colonial and national gold coins continued throughout the century and there are clear indications that both types of coins circulated within the colony despite efforts of the colonial authorities to prevent it.

Gold production was taxed on the basis of different systems at different times, and the selling price of gold was set by the Crown and not through market mechanisms, which was always a source of complaint of the miners. "Different forms of collection [of the *quinto* (fifth) on production] . . . fell into two general categories: collection by a form of capitation tax or collection in foundry houses . . . [where gold was cast into stamped gold bars or transformed into coin.] . . . In the space of 30 years the search for the perfect method led the crown in Minas Gerais to go from a quota based on a form of capitation to a foundry house (1725), to capitation (1735) and back to foundry houses (1751). Evidence of royal frustration was the proposal floated in 1730 and again in 1752 to examine tax farming as an alternative to direct collection by the crown, but this was never adopted. The advantage of foundry houses (from the crown's perspective) was ease and speed of collection, whereas collec-

[18] McCusker (1978), pp. 118, 282, 301; Calógeras (1960), pp. 9–10.

tion by capitation could result in delays of two or three years. As for the colonists, they were as adamant as they were inconsistent in their public opposition to one or the other method."[19]

Different systems were also adopted for diamond mining after the 1720s, when Brazilian production flooded the world market and reduced the price of the stones. The capitation tax levied on each slave employed after 1739 was changed in 1753, when two separate contracts were adopted, with little success. After 1771, a General Inspectorate of the diamonds was created to administer directly the royal monopoly of mining and sale of the diamonds. But "the oppressive system of totally isolating" the diamond areas ceased. The government monopoly would, however, last until 1845.[20]

As gold production faltered after mid-century, revenues of the *quinto*, after exceeding 100 *arrobas* in the 1750s,[21] fell to an average of 86 *arrobas* in the 1760s and to 68 *arrobas* between 1774 and 1785, and arrears on the annual revenue target of 100 *arrobas* developed.[22] In parallel, as gold production declined, the capacity to import goods from abroad and from other captaincies was also reduced, and the *entradas*, the taxes levied on slaves and goods entering or leaving the gold-producing region, also declined. These taxes, contrary to the collection of taxes on gold, were also farmed out to contractors, and arrears also developed. For fear of contraband, the reaction of the Crown included the prohibition of the goldsmith craft in Brazil in 1766.

The supply of gold coins, especially the "Johannes" or "Joe" or *peça* of 4 escudos, equivalent to 6,400 réis, led that coin, which was minted both in Portugal and in Brazil, to become by mid-century a "universal coin of the Atlantic World," whose purity was admired and which was often locally countermarked in the Caribbean.[23]

By the late 1780s, it was estimated that the arrears of the gold taxes had reached 538 *arrobas*. The mechanism of the *derrama*, through which

[19] Russell-Wood (1987), p. 227. Boxer (1962), p. 199, mentions that "the capitation tax proved highly unpopular" and that farmers and cultivators paying *dízimo* on their crops and *quinto* on their slaves were "being liable in effect to double taxation."

[20] Silva (1987), pp. 262–3, 276; Castello and Dodsworth (1940), pp. 4–8, 11–13.

[21] An *arroba* equaled 14.69 kilograms.

[22] Maxwell (1973) pp. 47–8, stresses the consequent "fall-off . . . of gold coin entering into circulation."

[23] McCusker (1978), pp. 300–1. The exchange rate of the Portuguese gold coin against sterling in London did not vary significantly from 1698 to 1775. In Brazil, the "weak" provincial coins were issued at 1,760 réis per *oitava* from 1695 to 1702 and at 1777.66 réis per *oitava* from 1749 to 1822. The "strong" system of Portuguese national currency, including the 6,400 réis, was issued at 1,600 réis per *oitava*. The "Joe" was issued from 1727 to 1822, basically in the two mints of Rio de Janeiro and Bahia. The fineness of all coins was 22 *quilates* (0.91666 fineness). See Prober (1966), p. 18.

a capitation tax would be levied in each municipality of the mining regions, to be added to the *quinto* to complete the 100 *arrobas* expected by the Crown, and which had been proposed by the municipalities themselves in the 1750s, was never demanded by the Junta da Fazenda, which supervised tax collection in the mining region, and which was aware of the decline in gold production. The threat of a *derrama* in early 1789 in Minas Gerais helped to obtain the support of affluent people and tax farmers in arrears for a conspiracy that failed, but that was supposed to separate Brazil from Portugal and create a republic (which, in turn, was expected to be initially supported by the *quinto*). The raising of the *derrama* as a capitation tax on the population at large, and not only on gold producers, would have represented an infringement of property rights and an unfair burden on the population as a whole, but given the 1789 conspiracy, the *derrama* was never implemented.

By that time, coins were already comparatively scarce in the colony, and the certificates issued by the General Inspectorate of Diamonds (*bilhetes de extração*) became in practice the first paper money in Brazil. They were complemented in 1803 by the *bilhetes de permuta* of the foundry houses, issued against the Juntas da Fazenda and the Treasury, which also circulated as currency.[24] Once the government ceased to honor the commitments represented by those certificates, they began trading at a discount, involving losses to their holders.

Through taxes, prohibitions, and monopolies, as well as through the fleet system implemented in 1649 and maintained until 1765, the Portuguese Crown restricted economic freedom within the colony and its commerce, as well as a full exercise of property rights of the colonists. An edict of 1785 also prohibited more sophisticated textile manufacturing in workshops, allowing only rough cotton to clothe the slaves.

But government action through legal instruments on certain occasions also favored some groups to the detriment of others within the colony, interfering in private contracts. "The planters' habit of buying necessary equipment on credit for 20–30 percent above the Lisbon price by mortgaging the next harvest at a set price below its market value was the cause of endless acrimony and remonstrance to the crown. In 1663, and periodically thereafter, planters managed to stop engenhos and canefields from being sold piecemeal to satisfy debts, but the mercantile interest was always strong enough to prevent the realization of the planters' dream – a complete moratorium on debts."[25] This "right" was later extended to the *lavradores de cana* (sugar cane planters without a sugar mill), as confirmed by legal rulings in the 1720s, and would result in

[24] Simonsen (1967), pp. 408–9; Calógeras (1960), pp. 27–8; Trigueiros (1987), pp. 66–8.

[25] Schwartz (1987), p. 133.

legislation protecting the sugar mills from seizure well into the nineteenth century.

On the other hand, while new regular taxes on production besides the *quinto* were not implemented in the eighteenth century, additional fiscal exactions took the form of extraordinary taxes such as the aids asked from Brazilian municipalities for the reconstruction of Lisbon, destroyed by an earthquake in 1755. This resulted in increases in the already existing municipal taxes.[26]

Exactions also resulted from the attacks of foreign powers, as exemplified by British privateers in the late sixteenth century and the expropriations carried on by the Dutch in northeast Brazil. An eighteenth-century episode was the attack on Rio de Janeiro by the Breton corsair Duguay-Trouin in 1711. Nicknamed the "parfait gentilhomme," he found considerable booty in the abandoned city and received a substantial sum in coins, sugar, and cattle, as ransom for the city and the forts that he threatened to level to the ground. The money was taken from the fifth, the mint, and a forced and substantial contribution by the wealthiest citizens.[27]

The arrival of the Portuguese court in Brazil in 1808, fleeing Napoleon's armies, would change the nature of taxation in the colony, as the ports of Brazil were opened to direct foreign trade with other nations and as some taxes raised in the home country were transplanted to the colony. The landing of the court resulted in a clear infringement of the rights of urban property owners in Rio de Janeiro, as in order to accommodate the thousands of courtiers and civil servants who had accompanied the royal family, the government requisitioned many private houses for their use.

[26] See Alden (1968), pp. 305–7. See also pp. 279–352 for an extensive discussion of fiscal matters in eighteenth-century Brazil, including the reorganization of the royal fisc, Portuguese revenues from the colony, government expenditures, local government debt, and the expropriation of the "extensive urban and rural properties of the Society of Jesus," expelled from Brazil in 1759–60. Among other taxes, Alden mentions the creation of a *quinto* (fifth) on cattle hides at the end of the seventeenth century, the collection of a 10 percent ad valorem tax on imports between 1699 and 1719 established by maritime municipalities to support local military garrisons, and a guard tax levied by the municipality of Rio de Janeiro for the "maintenance of the guard ship off the Brazilian littoral." He also gives details on the *entradas* established between 1710 and 1714 and levied on goods entering Minas Gerais, as well as on the interior customs stations (*registros*) raising transit tolls (*passagens*) along the trails between various captaincies and the mining region. These interior taxes, however, would never have the same relative importance as *alcabalas* in Spanish America. On "local dues levied by town councils for the upkeep of roads and bridges and other municipal services"and on taxation in general, see Boxer (1962), pp. 187–91. For contracts of the royal *dízimos* and tolls in the eighteenth century see Boxer (1962), pp. 347–50.

[27] See Boxer (1962), pp. 93–101.

By the second decade of the nineteenth century, when the Brazilian colony was elevated to the status of United Kingdom with Portugal (1816), the main existing taxes in Brazil were the *dízimo*; export duties differentiated by ports; import duties; transit taxes between captaincies; the royal *quinto* on gold production; the royal or national subsidy, levied on meat, hides, sugar cane, brandy, and rough woollens manufactured in the country; the literary subsidy to fund schools, charged on heads of cattle in slaughter houses, brandy, or *charque* (jerked beef); a tax on most shops and on carriages to fund the Banco do Brasil; a tax on each sugar mill or distillery; a tenth of the income of urban rented property; the *sisa* of 10 percent on the sale of houses and other urban property; the *meia-sisa* of 5 percent levied on the sale of slaves with a profession; and the so-called *novos direitos*, a 10 percent tax on the salaries of employees of the Finance and Justice departments (as the Portuguese *meia-anata*). Several other taxes and levies including the stamp tax, chancery rights, salt, and port taxes were also charged on certain transactions.

Some of these taxes would remain in force during part of the nineteenth century, though the *dízimo* was finally abolished in 1821. Tax farming of the salt tax and of the tax on whale fishing was definitively abolished in 1801.[28]

The immediate revenue needs of the court had led to the opening of Brazilian ports in 1808 and to the levying of tariffs on imported goods, which were initially regulated in the Treaty of 1810 with Britain. From then on, the road to political independence was open and the practice of basing government revenues on the taxation of international trade (rather than on production through the *dízimo*) was firmly established.

The end of the colonial period was marked by further manipulation of the currency. In the 1790s, copper coins of reduced module and copper content were issued for circulation in the mining region. The so-called *escudete* countermark was applied to the existing copper coins in 1809, doubling their value, and to the previous century special silver coinage for Minas Gerais, increasing its value by 15 percent.[29] Spanish American silver pieces of 8 reales were acquired in large quantities by the Portuguese Treasury in Brazil for a value around 800 réis, and countermarked or recoined with the value of 960 réis after 1809 and until the 1820s.[30] Soon the little gold that remained in circulation disappeared. A

[28] Varnhagem (1962), tome V, pp. 102–3; Simonsen (1967), pp. 413–15; Viana (1922), p. 192; Calógeras (1960), p. 31.

[29] See Coimbra (1959), tome III, pp. 159–60.

[30] See, for instance, Walsh (1830), vol. I, p. 456 and Coimbra (1959), tome III, pp. 158–66. Silver coins had been previously issued at 7,600 réis per mark (or 229.450 grams) from 1695 to 1758 (and in Bahia from 1799 to 1810, but only the 640-réis coin) and at 8,250

final blow to the circulation of precious metals was the emptying of the Treasury coffers by the Portuguese King D. João VI when he returned to the metropolis in 1821.[31] By then, circulation of copper and paper money (the notes issued by the first Banco do Brasil, created in 1808) was already predominant.

10.3 THE COSTS OF INDEPENDENCE

In 1822, Crown Prince D. Pedro, the older son of the Portuguese king, declared the independence of Brazil as the *cortes* of the metropolis were trying to reestablish the colonial status and economic and political subjection of Brazil to Portugal. In this he was assisted by some Brazilian politicians with Portuguese university educations such as José Bonifacio de Andrada, but there was no group of thinkers with a strong background in political economy to assist the new government in formulating the new country's economic policy.

José da Silva Lisboa, Viscount of Cairú, who had read Adam Smith and supported the liberal trade policy inevitably adopted after 1808, was not succeeded by knowledgeable civil servants and certainly not by figures of the stature of Hamilton in the United States. The conduct of government matters would therefore suffer no abrupt change from Portuguese practices.[32] The new Emperor Pedro I (1822–31) also took power in a country with an extremely high illiteracy rate (probably 85–90 percent in a population of some 4 million), which unfavorably affected the spread of information, the adoption of new practices, innovations, and institutional change.

Independence was a costly process in Brazil. Recognition by Portugal with the intermediation of Britain involved important concessions to both countries. In the case of Portugal, this involved payment of indemnities basically through the transfer of responsibility for the service of foreign loans contracted in Britain. D. João VI, on leaving Brazil in 1821, as a parting gesture indicating the stance of the Portuguese Crown on property rights, not only paid no more than lip service to the need to

réis per mark from 1768 to 1802, with a 0.91666 fineness. From 1809 to 1834 they would be issued at 8,192 réis per mark. However, the fineness of the 8-reales pieces on which the 960-réis (pieces were recoined was 0.903 or 0.896, as opposed to the 11 *dinheiros*) silver (0.91666 fineness) used in the other Brazilian colonial coins. See Prober (1966), p. 17.

31 Viana (1922), pp. 185 and 195–205; Calógeras (1960), pp. 22, 26–7, 35; Coimbra (1959), tome III, pp. 158–60. The royal *quinto* had declined from 70 arrobas of gold in 1777 to 24 in 1811, 12 in 1818, and only 2 in 1820, according to Eschwege (1899), p. 752, reducing substantially the supply of metal to the Bahia and Rio de Janeiro mints.

32 The most striking illustration of how slow changes could be in the former colony is the observation of the minister of finance in his report of 1828 that customs houses were still regulated by a *foral* of 1587. See Veiga Filho (1898), p. 113.

protect the Banco do Brasil from the cash drain provoked by the decision to return to Portugal, but took over assets held by the bank, as already mentioned.[33]

But much more important in the long term was the renewal by Brazil of treaty obligations between Portugal and Britain concerning both the slave trade and Brazilian commercial policy. By a convention of 1827, Brazil agreed to discontinue the importation of African slaves within three years. While this commitment remained a dead letter until the 1840s, it provided a sound legal basis for the British onslaught on slave trade activities that culminated with Brazilian legislation finally outlawing the trade in 1850 and leading to its definitive interruption. More immediately important was the renewal in 1827 for 15 years of the commitment by Portugal with Britain that the Brazilian import tariff would not exceed 15 percent ad valorem.[34] Due to the lack of alternative sources of revenue in a primarily exporting economy, and given the increased expenditure generated by the many regional political troubles from independence to the early 1840s, such a decision was tantamount to a situation of persistent fiscal imbalance, and led to large fluctuations of the exchange rate that plagued the regency government during the minority of the new Emperor D. Pedro II (1831–89) and persisted for a few years after he finally took power directly in 1840. The return of the freedom to tax after some British procrastination, and the consequent increase in the share of import duties in total revenue, led to a marked improvement in public finances and to a less unstable exchange rate regime from the mid-1840s. So much for the alleged lack of involvement of the British Foreign Office with business interests in Latin America.[35]

10.4 FISCAL ISSUES IN THE IMPERIAL PERIOD (1822–89)

The basic elements of the fiscal apparatus inherited from colonial times were preserved during the first years of the imperial period. The Public or National Treasury, which had been established as "Erário

[33] See Franco (1979), chapter IV. See also Viana (1922), pp. 195–205, on the report of the commission created to study the reorganization of the Treasury and the debt and currency problems created by D. João VI's departure and the "independence loan."

[34] See Manchester (1933), chapter 8. This rate was extended to other nations in 1828. See Fontoura (1921), p. 29, who presents a detailed description of tariff legislation and of all the changes in import duties and exemptions in the imperial period, as well as the contemporary justifications for those changes.

[35] Brazil is a major counterexample for most of the points raised in Platt (1968) about the stance of the British government in Latin America. See pp. 312–16. Platt also repeats the often raised but never proved point about the damaging impact of the 1827 Commercial Treaty on Brazilian "manufactures." Its much more important fiscal impact is disregarded.

Régio" in 1808, continued to be subject to the instructions of the Lisbon Erário dating from 1789, until a decree was issued with new instructions in 1829. The Juntas da Fazenda, established in some captaincies after 1761, were also in most cases maintained in the newly created provinces, also using regulations of the past until 1831, when Tesourarias da Fazenda were created (which would last until 1891). The law of October 4, 1831, containing instructions to the provincial Tesourarias, still referred to the practice and responsibilities involved in the farming out of taxes through auctions, but given the changes in the nature of taxation, with the elimination of the *dízimo* and the growing relative importance of taxes on foreign trade, tax farming tended inevitably to lose its importance.[36]

The monopoly of brazilwood was maintained well into the second empire and that of diamond production until 1845. The taxation of gold according to a fraction of production also continued in the 1830s. A law of October 8, 1833, created a new tax on urban slaves, excluding those below 12 years of age. There was thus substantial continuity in the fiscal area and even the organization of the *alfândegas*, in spite of their accrued importance, did not initially undergo any significant changes.[37]

Central government revenue in the early 1830s relied heavily on duties collected on foreign trade: import duties, export duties, and related taxes such as those relative to docking and lighthouse. This was so in spite of the constraints imposed by the British treaty. From the point of view of collection costs, this is in line with predictions based on marked differences between taxes on trade and internal taxes.[38] These costs are much lower for taxes on trade, especially if waterborne. The much higher internal tax collection costs lead to tax monopolies, while taxes on trade are rarely farmed out. The political resistance of landowners to taxation of land, which in many cases they occupied rather than owned, was well known. The so-called interior taxes and duties affected many transactions not directly related to foreign trade, such as the transfer of real estate, contracts, inheritances, and property of urban slaves. From the mid-1840s, freedom to tax imports at more than 15 percent ad valorem was recovered, and there was some increase in import duties. There were no significant changes in the structure of revenue until the end of the

[36] See Almeida (1922), pp. 8, 14, 18–20, 33.

[37] Showing a recovery with respect to the *quinto* in the late 1810s, the 25 percent tax levied on the gold produced with more advanced technology by the British mining company of Gongo Soco yielded some 128 *arrobas* between 1828 and 1834, according to a table of the Contadoria de Fazenda of Minas Gerais, reproduced in *Revista do Arquivo Público Mineiro*, IV, 1899, p. 293. In the 1830s, import duties were levied by the Alfândegas and export duties by Mesas do Consulado, which were reformed in 1836–7.

[38] See North and Thomas (1973).

empire. A slave emancipation fund was created so that, together with legislation ending slavery for newborn children of slaves (1871), the slave population could be gradually reduced. By the 1880s some new interior taxes had been created, but revenue still depended basically on the taxation of foreign trade.[39] See Table 10.1 for a breakdown of central government revenue by types of duties and taxes.

The share of import duties in ordinary revenue after 1833 was always above 50 percent. It rose to nearly 60 percent in the late 1830s and to almost 70 percent in the mid-1850s; then it fell. But it remained around 50–60 percent for the rest of the empire. Export duties collected by the central government corresponded to slightly more than 5 percent of ordinary revenue in the early 1830s. Their share then rose rapidly to almost 25 percent, fell to 12 percent in the 1850s, and stabilized at 15–17 percent for most of the last years of the empire. By the late 1880s it was back to 12–13 percent. Interior taxes made up 25 percent of revenues in the early 1830s and, after declining to almost 10 percent in the early 1840s, rose to stabilize at around 22–29 percent in the last decades of the empire.[40]

The level of import duties showed an increasing trend during the empire. The average tariff, measured by the ratio between collected duties and the value of imports, remained around 17 percent in the 10 years before 1843. It then increased rapidly, reaching 30 percent in 1848–9, remaining roughly between 25 and 30 percent until the late 1860s. It then was increased to 35–40 percent, until further rises in the late 1880s to almost 50 percent.

Brazilian preeminence as a coffee supplier to the world market[41] had important consequences from the point of view of tax incidence, especially since the price elasticity of demand for coffee was low. It was recognized in the nineteenth century that taxation of coffee exports was likely to result in increased world coffee prices.[42] Moreover, Abreu and Bevilaqua (2000) have shown that, due to the country's dominant position in the world coffee market, there is an optimal tariff mechanism at work in Brazil, with increased production costs caused by increased protection being transmitted to world coffee prices. The foreign consumers ended by paying, through higher coffee prices, the increased costs of coffee production. This argument, of course, applies only to coffee. Taxes

[39] See Carreira (1980), passim. New taxes included those on railway tickets and on the consumption of tobacco. See Mello (1984), p. 249, and Veiga Filho (1898), p. 90.

[40] Raw data from Carreira (1980), passim.

[41] In the six decades or so after independence, the value of coffee exports increased at the rate of 3 percent a year and the share of coffee exports in total exports rose to more than 60 percent.

[42] See Ridings (1994), p. 195, quoting *Relatório do Ministério da Fazenda*, 1872, p. 75, and 1879, Anexo B, pp. 5–6.

Table 10.1. Brazil: Revenue Structure, 1833–4 to 1888, Percent of Total Revenue

	Import Duties	Export Duties	Interior Taxes	Maritime Taxes
1833–4[a]	53.4	6.4	38.0	2.1
1834–5	50.7	5.7	41.7	1.9
1835–6	52.9	6.4	38.8	1.9
1836–7	61.5	17.6	18.4	2.5
1837–8	59.6	19.6	17.2	3.6
1838–9	60.5	20.1	15.3	4.1
1839–40	54.6	24.8	17.2	3.5
1840–1	65.3	19.0	11.9	3.8
1841–2	66.5	18.4	11.4	3.7
1842–3	59.5	19.6	17.0	3.9
1843–4	60.4	17.8	17.7	4.0
1844–5	60.6	16.8	20.0	2.7
1845–6	59.8	19.3	18.7	2.3
1846–7	60.2	17.6	20.0	2.1
1847–8	57.2	20.4	19.8	2.5
1848–9	61.7	15.3	20.7	2.3
1849–50	65.3	14.3	18.3	2.1
1850–1	65.7	15.1	17.5	1.7
1851–2	72.2	13.2	13.0	1.6
1852–3	69.1	13.9	16.4	0.6
1853–4	69.6	11.3	18.5	0.6
1854–5	68.4	12.9	17.9	0.7
1855–6	67.0	12.3	20.1	0.7
1856–7	67.6	14.2	17.7	0.5
1857–8	66.0	13.6	19.8	0.5
1858–9	62.7	15.9	20.7	0.6
1859–60	63.1	12.9	23.4	0.7
1860–1	61.1	14.8	23.6	0.4
1861–2	61.0	16.0	22.4	0.5
1862–3	58.3	17.7	23.4	0.6
1863–4	59.5	17.6	22.4	0.5
1864–5	61.9	17.3	20.3	0.5
1865–6	59.6	19.6	20.3	0.5
1866–7	60.3	17.2	22.0	0.5
1867–8	52.2	22.4	25.0	0.4
1868–9	54.2	22.2	23.1	0.5
1869–70	56.4	19.2	24.0	0.5
1870–1	57.8	16.3	25.5	0.5
1871–2	59.3	17.4	22.8	0.5
1872–3	57.1	18.3	24.1	0.5
1873–4	56.5	17.4	25.5	0.6

(continued)

Table 10.1 *(continued)*

	Import Duties	Export Duties	Interior Taxes	Maritime Taxes
1874–5	54.3	18.4	26.9	0.4
1875–6	56.0	16.6	27.2	0.3
1876–7	55.7	16.8	27.4	0.1
1877–8	55.9	16.1	27.9	0.1
1878–9	54.2	16.6	29.1	0.1
1879–80	55.1	15.8	28.9	0.2
1880–1	54.3	16.3	29.1	0.3
1881–2	56.9	15.3	27.5	0.3
1882–3	58.2	13.1	28.4	0.3
1883–4	61.2	12.8	25.6	0.4
1884–5	55.5	14.2	29.9	0.4
1885–6	58.0	12.3	29.4	0.3
1886–7[b]	59.4	13.4	26.9	0.3
1888	63.2	10.4	26.1	0.3

[a] Fiscal year beginning July 1.
[b] Three semesters.
Source: Raw data from Carreira (1980).

on foreign trade unfavorably affected the income of exporters outside the core of coffee-producing regions. The effect of high export and import taxes on regions outside the coffee core was to reduce the competitiveness of Brazilian noncoffee exports and reduce their shares of the world markets in the long term (see Table 10.2 for the share of different commodities in total exports).

Provincial taxation was important: fragmentary and inadequate data on provincial and municipal finance indicate that such revenues were roughly 25 percent of central government revenues from the mid-1840s to the mid-1880s.[43] Due to the lower collection costs, provinces also relied on taxes on trade, including foreign trade. Though provincial taxation of foreign imports was illegal according to the 1824 Constitution, changes in legislation in the 1830s and various subterfuges created in the following decades resulted in its widespread adoption.

According to the 1824 Constitution, it was the duty of the legislative chambers to "annually establish the amount of public expenditures and to distribute the direct contribution . . . to authorize the government to contract loans . . . to establish the adequate means for the payment of the public debt . . . to regulate and administer the "bens nacionais" [basically, property expropriated from the Jesuit order in the eighteenth

[43] See Carreira (1980) and Straten-Ponthoz (1854).

Table 10.2. Brazil: Commodity Export Shares of Total Exports, 1850–9 to 1880–9 (percent)[a]

	Coffee	Sugar	Cotton	Rubber	Total
1850–9	48.7	21.3	6.3	2.2	78.6
1860–9	45.9	12.3	17.7	3.1	79.0
1870–9	56.3	11.8	9.7	5.5	83.3
1880–9	60.5	10.6	4.4	7.6	83.1

[a] Ten-year average of yearly shares; 1850–1 to 1887–8: fiscal years.
Source: Computed from *Anuário Estatístico do Brasil*, 1939–40, p. 1380.

century] . . . [and] to determine the weight, value, inscription, type and denomination of coinage, as well as the standard of weights and measures. . . . " The Chamber of Deputies had the exclusive power to take the "initiative regarding taxes."

However, the "Additional Act" of 1834 allowed provincial legislative assemblies to legislate on the "establishment of the municipal and provincial expenses, and the taxes necessary to meet them, provided they do not harm the general impositions [taxes] of the Central Government."[44] Consequently, the initially exclusive constitutional power of the Chamber of Deputies of the empire to create taxes was circumvented, and what taxes would not negatively affect the revenues of the central government became a matter subject to interpretation.

As a nineteenth-century observer noted, article 12 of the "Additional Act," by "forbidding [explicitly] the provinces to decree import taxes 'a contrario sensu' seemed to concede [implicitly] that faculty relatively to export taxes."[45] However, it was apparently clearly perceived in the provinces of the northeast that "in face of the competition suffered by [their] sugar and cotton [exports] in international markets, taxes on exports could not be raised [without a negative impact on production] contrary to the situation in the coffee provinces which, in view of the dominant position of Brazilian production, could transfer to the foreign consumer the burden of the increase in export taxes on coffee."[46]

On the other hand, the word *importation* in the same article was itself the object of discussion as to whether it included "merchandise from one province which entered another province," which led to a clarification by the Council of State in 1861 forbidding the taxation of interprovincial imports. But even this was not an absolute ruling as, when the political

[44] Nogueira (1987), pp. 64–5 and 86–8.
[45] Veiga Filho (1898), p. 112. [46] Melo (1984), p. 250.

issue of the transfer of slaves from the northeast and other areas to the coffee regions became more serious in the early 1860s, the interprovincial slave trade was burdened with both provincial export and import taxes.

Early in the imperial period, from 1837–8 to 1850, in view of the insufficient revenues of many provinces,[47] the central government granted them special aids (*suprimentos*). The imperial government also assumed some local expenditures, such as those related to lower courts and the clergy. "The Imperial government thus posed as the magnanimous and understanding father" of the prodigal provinces, when actually it was the main beneficiary of a system that deprived the provinces of revenues that, in the view of many, belonged to them. It should not be surprising, therefore, that given their budgetary difficulties, some provinces resorted to "consumption taxes which in reality increased the taxation on imports, either coming from abroad and from other provinces." Since the 1840s, this expedient was adopted "at first infrequently and timidly" by Pernambuco and other provinces, mainly in the northeast, with the understanding that there were constraints on provincial taxation of exports.

"In view of the favorable overall economic situation in the 1850s and 1860s, especially for cotton, provincial import taxes remained unnoticed, except for occasional consultations to the Council of State or in one or another *aviso* of the Ministry of Finance. Things would change during the recession in the 1870s [when the price of cotton fell abruptly] and complaints against [provincial import] taxes would increase, culminating with the 1882 episode [when, after a "strike" of the local merchant community, Pernambuco was forbidden by the head of the Cabinet in Rio to levy import taxes]."

The imperial and provincial taxes levied in the northeast declined 30 percent in the 1870s. Several provinces had serious problems in meeting their current expenses and were unsuccessful in floating internal loans. The decline in the international price of cotton and sugar prompted those provinces to reduce or eliminate export taxes on those products. Among other provinces, "Paraíba had to create a series of new [local] taxes, the heavy incidence of which on the free population of the interior created the climate of popular revolt which [would] explode in the revolt of the *Quebra-Quilos*." In such a context, interprovincial trade of both imported and Brazilian products was also taxed in the provinces of the northeast, at rates varying from 3 to 30 percent, and creative names such as *disembarkation tax* were imagined to legitimize that practice.

[47] See Veiga Filho (1898), pp. 112–13, who lists the few local taxes left to the provinces and municipalities, the scope of which was further reduced when the central government adopted the "Tax on Industries and Professions" in 1867.

In the early 1880s, in spite of lengthy discussions in the legislative chambers, the central government did not establish a new criterion of distribution, in favor of the provinces, of the general taxes raised by the empire. Therefore, from 1885 to 1889, ignoring its previous firm statements as to their illegality, "the Imperial government closed its eyes, as it had done until 1882, and accepted provincial import taxes as a lesser evil." In the early 1880s, these unconstitutional import taxes corresponded to about one-third of the provincial revenues in Pernambuco and Alagoas, slightly less in Rio Grande do Norte, one-fourth in Ceará, and slightly less than one-fifth in Bahia.[48]

Given those developments, the question remains to what extent the solvency of the central government was maintained, at the cost of a fiscal imbalance in the provinces, through the government's persistent refusal to allow the provinces greater participation of the provinces in the revenues raised as general taxes by the imperial government in the various regions.

The imperial export tax, after fluctuating between 5 and 7 percent in the 1850s and early 1860s, rose to 9 percent during the Paraguay War and returned to 7 percent in the mid-1870s.[49] Provincial export taxation was rather heavy in some provinces, reaching 13 percent on rubber in Pará. Export taxation by coffee-producing provinces was much lower, typically 4 percent,[50] but in 1888 provincial taxes added to the tax charged by the central government resulted in total export duties of 13 percent. In Rio Grande do Sul, in that same year, exporters of meat and hides paid 4 percent to the provincial government and 9 percent to the central government.[51]

The following comments of the British secretary of legation, referring to the decline in cotton exports of the northeast in 1874, illustrate how

[48] Melo (1984), respectively, pp. 249–50, 258–60, and 278–81. On p. 267, he notes that the coffee provinces did not impose consumption taxes.

[49] The provincial export tax was often added to the imperial export tax. Thus, according to the British consul in Rio, in 1869, "the export duty on cotton amounts to 13 percent and 40 réis . . . per arroba . . . at Rio de Janeiro; at Pernambuco 14 percent and 20 réis per arroba; coffee pays 13 percent and 40 réis per bag. Sugar pays 13 percent plus 90 réis additional at Pernambuco. Minor articles also pay heavy export duties. These duties are calculated on the market prices of the respective articles at the port of shipment, so that the planter is also taxed 13 percent on the cost of the conveyance of his product to the market." See Report by Mr. Consul Lennon Hunt on the Trade and Commerce of Rio de Janeiro during the Year 1869, in British Parliamentary Papers (from now on referred to as PP), 1870, Vol. 64, p. 232. In the early decades of the empire, export taxes were specific, that is, defined as fixed sums in milréis per unit of weight or length, also differentiated per product and per province. For several examples, see Onody (1953), p. 62.

[50] See Ridings (1994), p. 197. [51] Wyndham (1889), pp. 18–19, 59.

the taxation of exports could harm exports other than coffee: "this great reduction arises from prices realized leaving no margin to the planters, as more than half the value is absorbed in the expense of carriage, provincial duties and storage and export duty of 9 percent."[52] More than two decades later, also illustrating the combined negative impact of local taxation and Imperial and provincial export taxes, "a deputy for Pará complained [in 1888] . . . of the heavy export duties to which his constituents [were] subject, namely 9 percent on the value of the rubber as a state tax, 13 percent as a provincial tax, and 2 percent as a municipal tax, making together 24 percent of export tax on its value, besides the cost of packing, freight, insurance and commission."[53]

The characteristics of the Brazilian coffee export economy ensured that the income of coffee growers was relatively unaffected by increased import duties, but these increased duties had quite a regressive effect on the income of the urban population that depended on the supply of imports. The effects of exchange rate devaluation that generally followed downturns in the world economy were partly absorbed by the coffee growers. Devaluation involved an increase in costs of production denominated in domestic currency and thus a rise in world coffee prices in the long run. In the short run, there was a weakening of world coffee prices, as coffee stocks tended to be dumped in the market following devaluation. There was still on balance a significant increase in the income of coffee growers in domestic currency.[54]

[52] See Report by Mr. Drummond on the Trade of Rio de Janeiro, PP 1875, Vol. 74, Part III, p. 205.

[53] Wyndham (1889), p. 18. The same report contains the following information on export duties: "the state export duty on sugar, which produced £80,000 a year, has lately been abolished [1887], but 9 percent is charged on india-rubber, cacao, Brazil nuts, hides, hair, spirits, tobacco, timber and Brazilwood, 7 percent on coffee and 5 percent on other things not enumerated. The export duties gave the State £885,400 during the first half of 1887; £561,900 in the first months of 1888, of which 60 percent from coffee, 16 percent from india-rubber and 4 percent from tobacco. 5 percent has for three years been charged over and above other export taxes to promote emancipation but Senator Christiano Ottoni stated on October 27, 1888, that not one slave had been emancipated with the money so received.

In addition to this, the individual provinces raise considerable export duties on the identical articles which pay the State export duties; for instance, Santa Catarina is now raising export duties on Mandioca flour 6 percent; prepared mate, sugar, coffee & c 4 percent; beans, maize and tapioca 8 percent; rice 10 percent." Subterfuges were also used by some provinces to raise disguised import duties, which, as the British diplomat recalls, were illegal. Examples included "200 réis per ton on sailing ships and steamers" entering the port of Sergipe and an import duty of 3 percent established in Pernambuco in 1885 "on the officially-declared values of imports under the name of '*giro comercial*'." Ibid.

[54] See Abreu and Bevilaqua (1996), passim.

While it is clear that the political role of the planters' class as a whole was absolutely predominant during the empire, there were regional cleavages associated with different agricultural specialization and economic interests, notably between the northeast (which produced sugar, cotton, and tobacco) and the coffee regions. This issue became particularly clear when, after the interruption of the African slave trade, export of slaves from the northeast to the coffee provinces increased considerably. Christie, the British minister in Rio de Janeiro, in a report of 1862, emphasized a speech of Senator Silveira da Motta in 1861, who mentioned the dangers of secession associated with the interprovincial slave trade.[55] After some tension, the issue was gradually solved through the imposition by the coffee provinces of prohibitively high taxes on the importation of slaves.

In general, however, the political class and "the deputies shared a common social background," with converging interests, and represented the landed interests, which strongly opposed ideas such as a land tax.[56] A common objective of politicians was the patronage of local chiefs and control over positions of authority. As noted in a recent work, "even if the revenues from which local appointments were paid went first to the central government before returning, that would not disturb the local boss, whose power did not depend on a constituency politically unhappy with the level of taxation (which fell mainly on imports anyway). As long as he could name his clients to all the posts in the public service and there was no rival font of placement, he did not demand an increase in positions and thus an increase in revenue. Moreover, he and many of his clients were interested in such positions more because of the authority they conferred than because of the salaries they brought."[57] Thus, there does not seem to have been large-scale embezzlement of local revenues or widespread corruption to the detriment of a majority of the population.[58]

The annual "net income" required to qualify as a voter was relatively high, excluding a large part of the population, particularly the poor, from direct participation in political affairs. This was not a particularly atypical situation in the nineteenth century. In 1881, with some 12 million

[55] See Christie to Lord Russell, Rio, Sept. 30, 1862, in PP 1863, Vol. 71, pp. 115–16. See also Lago (1988), pp. 345–7, on the speech of Silveira da Motta and for partial data on the interprovincial trade from 1850 to 1880.

[56] A land tax was included in the 1843 project of a Land Law but was rejected when it was finally passed in 1850. It was adopted in 1880 by the Chamber of Deputies, only to be rejected by the Senate. See Veiga Filho (1898), p. 99.

[57] Graham (1990), p. 180.

[58] There are, however, references to "more corruption than in any part of the world" in the Rio customs house in the late 1820s in Walsh (1830), vol. I, p. 447.

inhabitants, Brazil had 150,000 electors and some 200,000 in 1889. In 1848 France, with a population almost three times larger, had fewer than 250,000 electors before the Revolution in that year, which established universal male suffrage and resulted in 9 million voters.[59]

A rare manifestation of nonconformity and protest of the free poor occurred in 1874–5 in the northeast, the so-called revolt of the Quebra-Quilos, which occurred "when a new tax imposed on the foodstuffs that peasants sold on market day, their still present fear that the national census was designed to enslave free men of color, and the use by merchants of the newly adopted metric system to cheat them of their due, sparked a major revolt that lasted several months."[60]

A major exception to the general lack of emphasis on policies directed to the free poor was the attention given by the central government to the northeast when a prolonged drought caused a public calamity after the mid-1870s. The number of casualties may have reached 200,000. Thus, between 1877 and 1880 the government spent almost 74,000 contos (of which 50,000 were spent in 1878–9) to alleviate the effects of the drought (30,000 contos were spent in Ceará alone). In that situation, the population of the country as a whole contributed to the relief of a region.[61]

In regard to legislation concerning the urban poor, another rare occurrence was the consideration by the imperial government of tax concessions to companies willing to construct "reasonably priced, sanitary worker housing in Rio de Janeiro." After detailed proposals for houses called *evaneas*, "the imperial government approved proposals . . . in the 1870s and 1880s, and granted concessions [but] no projects were completed during the empire."[62]

The government was more generous in giving subsidies, advantages, and tax exemptions, especially after the 1840s, to manufacturing establishments of various types, as listed in reports of the Ministry of Finance, and which, in the case of Mauá's Ponta de Areia large foundry and shipyard, included both import tax exemptions and

[59] Nogueira (1987), p. 37.

[60] See Graham (1990), p. 38 and pp. 103–5, on qualifications for voting.

[61] Figures from a table in the report of Minister of Finance José Antonio Saraiva of 1880, reproduced in Bahia (1978), p. 265. According to a British secretary of legation, "during 1877 to 1879 tens of thousands of inhabitants died or disappeared [in Ceará] and £6,000,000 was lost – i.e to say the public exchequer granted £400,000 for their succour soon after the commencement of the calamity." See Wyndham (1989), p. 31.

[62] See Hahner (1986), pp. 132–3.

Table 10.3. Brazil: Financing the Paraguay War, 1864–72 (in contos de réis)[a]

	Foreign Loans	Domestic Gold Loans	Domestic Paper Loans	Paper Currency Emission	Other	Total
1864–6	35,219	0	15,154	3,017	0	53,390
1866–7	0	0	36,433	22,677	2	59,112
1867–8	0	0	22,782	53,911	7	76,700
1868–9	0	27,000	27,288	17,910	0	72,198
1869–70	0	0	44,031	5,480	180	49,691
1870–1	26,522	0	26,146	10,220	700	63,588
1871–2	0	0	21	0	1,225	1,246
TOTAL	61,741	27,000	171,855	113,215	2,114	375,925

[a] One conto de réis equals (1 million) réis. The monetary standard was the milréis, which was written 1$000. One conto de réis was written 1:000$000. The parity of 1846 was 27 pence per 1$000.

Source: Carreira (1980), p. 469.

government orders. The importation of machinery during the imperial period was often exempted from payment of tax or subject to reduced rates.[63]

It was internal and external warfare that defined the basic features of central government expenditure under the Brazilian Empire.[64] First, there were the hostilities related to independence in the early to mid-1820s. Then came the Cisplatina wars in the late 1820s for control of what was to become Uruguay as a British-designed compromise with Argentina. Separatist movements trying to exploit the weakness of the central government led to civil war in the south in the 1830s and in the core of the economy in the southeast in the early 1840s. Expenditures of the War and Navy Departments, which reached 65 percent of total expenditure in 1823, were approximately 50 percent in the late 1820s and still higher in the late 1830s. They were never below 35 percent in the more peaceful 20 years from 1845. During the 1865–70 Paraguay War, such expenditures were back to 65 percent of the total (see Table 10.3 for the official Brazilian version of the "costs" of the war). It was only after 1870 that military expenditure fell to less than 20 percent of total

[63] See Lago et al. (1979), especially pp. 7–18. For an extensive list of "factories" receiving government incentives and exemptions during the imperial period, see Distrito Federal (1908).

[64] For data and details see Carreira (1980), especially pp. 627ff.

Table 10.4. Brazil: Deficit as a Share of Total Expenditure and Structure of Expenditure by Selected Secretaries in Total Expenditure, 1833–88 (percent)[a]

	Deficit as a Share of Total Expenditure[b]	War and Navy	Finance	Agriculture	Other
1833–4	–8.8	41.1	47.1	0	11.8
1834–5	–14.8	36.5	49.1	0	14.4
1835–6	1.4	33.3	32.4	0	34.2
1836–7	3.6	34.9	40.0	0	25.1
1837–8	33.0	42.4	44.2	0	13.4
1838–9	17.4	44.5	42.1	0	13.4
1839–40	36.1	55.6	32.1	0	12.3
1840–1	28.4	48.6	35.4	0	16.0
1841–2	40.6	48.9	36.7	0	14.4
1842–3	46.8	46.0	37.0	0	17.0
1843–4	17.7	42.0	40.2	0	17.9
1844–5	16.1	41.0	39.1	0	20.0
1845–6	9.5	40.4	38.8	0	20.8
1846–7	7.5	40.0	38.3	0	21.7
1847–8	17.6	38.7	39.6	0	21.8
1848–9	7.5	41.6	37.7	0	20.7
1849–50	2.6	39.3	37.1	0	23.6
1850–1	1.6	42.9	35.6	0	21.5
1851–2	16.3	47.8	32.7	0	19.5
1852–3	–15.0	35.1	31.6	0	33.3
1853–4	4.7	39.9	36.3	0	23.9
1854–5	4.5	n.a.	n.a.	0	n.a.
1855–6	4.0	40.3	31.1	0	28.6
1856–7	–21.8	40.0	33.7	0	26.3
1857–8	3.9	47.7	25.9	0	26.4
1858–9	11.0	41.9	28.5	0	29.5
1859–60	16.7	42.3	28.1	0	29.7
1860–1	4.4	37.1	30.9	0	32.1
1861–2	1.1	35.6	35.0	14.3	15.1
1862–3	14.7	34.7	37.3	13.3	14.8
1863–4	3.0	37.5	34.7	13.7	14.1
1864–5	31.6	48.7	24.0	12.6	14.6
1865–6	52.0	65.9	18.4	7.0	8.7
1866–7	46.4	59.6	23.6	9.5	7.3
1867–8	57.1	59.5	27.1	7.5	5.8
1868–9	42.0	53.9	32.4	8.5	5.2
1869–70	33.0	54.3	30.2	9.7	5.8
1870–1	2.3	32.0	40.2	18.3	9.4
1871–2	–3.5	22.3	39.3	12.8	5.6

	Deficit as a Share of Total Expenditure[b]	War and Navy	Finance	Agriculture	Other
1872–3	8.0	34.5	34.6	20.8	10.1
1873–4	13.6	32.4	35.0	21.5	11.1
1874–5	15.4	32.1	35.0	21.1	11.9
1875–6	18.4	21.1	35.5	14.5	29.0
1876–7	25.6	26.3	35.8	24.6	13.3
1877–8	32.8	18.8	33.7	27.8	19.7
1878–9	35.8	13.2	29.6	26.2	31.0
1879–80	19.6	16.1	41.2	27.8	14.9
1880–1	5.3	17.9	43.8	26.6	11.7
1881–2	5.4	41.9	41.2	26.8	11.7
1882–3	15.3	20.6	40.2	28.3	10.9
1883–4	12.8	20.0	38.2	31.0	10.7
1884–5	21.7	21.5	51.5	40.4	11.2
1885–6	15.2	20.6	51.1	33.1	11.1
1886–7	2.9	16.8	42.5	29.8	10.9
1888	–20.7	18.4	44.5	24.3	12.8

[a] Other ministries were Empire, Justice, and Foreign Affairs.
[b] Negative signs mean superavits.
Source: Raw data from Carreira (1980).

central government expenditure (see Table 10.4 for a breakdown of central government expenditures).

The ratio between deficit and central government expenditure reflected such developments, peaking with military expenditure. It was 40 percent in the late 1820s and also in the late 1830s (see Table 10.4). It exceeded 45 percent in the early 1840s and reached 60 percent during the Paraguay War. In the second half of the 1870s the cumulative effect of the financial crisis of 1875 and the already mentioned severe drought in the northeast generally kept the deficit above 20 percent of expenditure, reaching more than 35 percent in 1878–9.

Even in the late imperial years, central government expenditures in São Paulo, the core of the new coffee-producing region, were extremely low, less than 2 percent of total central government expenditure. Revenue raised in the province was more than 7 percent of total imperial revenue but lower than that in rubber-booming Pará and in the economically declining provinces of Bahia and Pernambuco. Important recipients of development-related resources distributed in the late 1880s included Pernambuco, Rio Grande do Sul, and, to a lesser extent, Bahia. Military expenditures were concentrated in the southern and western provinces along the Parana and Paraguay rivers: Rio Grande do Sul, Santa Catarina, Paraná, and Mato Grosso.[65]

Throughout the review of the empire, the fact that the geographical destination of general government expenditures did not coincide with the general revenues generated in the various regions, the so-called problem of provincial balances, was the object of keen discussion. In fact, in many states of the northeast (and later also in Pará), the balances transferred to the imperial government far exceeded the expenditures of the imperial government in those provinces. (One of the leaders of the Praieira Revolution in 1848 in Pernambuco would list as one of the motives of the insurrection "to [ensure] that the money raised in the province would stay" in Pernambuco.) Examining the imperial budget of 1869–70, the journalist and politician Tavares Bastos "concluded that of the 36,000 contos levied [as imperial taxes by the central government in the northeast and the north], only 1/3 had been the object of general expenditures in those regions, leaving a favorable balance of 24,000 contos. After deducting from that total the expenditures relating to interest and railways, subventions to shipping companies serving those northern regions, and the proportional quota of those provinces in the obligations of the central government, there was still a balance of 6,600 contos."[66]

The question of the net balances of the north-northeast was a reality in spite of the fact that the south, including the Corte (the Capital city of Rio and suburbs), contributed two-thirds of the total general revenues and the north-northeast the remaining one-third. It was not a question of which provinces generated more resources but rather of which ones transferred larger net balances. In the south, only the coffee provinces of São Paulo and Rio de Janeiro generated net balances. The south as a whole was a region representing permanent deficits to the imperial government since the general revenues raised by the central government in its provinces corresponded to only one-third of the general expenditures incurred in the region.

In fact, in several southern provinces the central government faced deficits, notably as a result of general expenditures for European immigration and military expenditures. There was undoubtedly a transfer of resources from some provinces to others, associated with the strong centralization of taxes and expenditures by the imperial govern-

[65] Data for 1885–6 from Carreira (1980), Vol. II, pp. 658–9.

[66] Melo (1984), pp. 251–2. The author relies on calculations of Tavares Bastos and politicians, but those estimates are open to debate. According to national censuses, Brazil had 9.93 million inhabitants in 1872 and 14.33 million in 1890. The populations of the *Norte* (north and northeast) were, respectively, 4.97 million (50.1 percent) and 6.48 million (45.2 percent) in those same years.

ment, but the actual "balance" of specific provinces is very difficult to determine.

The secretary of the empire was responsible for the imperial household, as well as for expenditures by the legislative power, transfers to the Catholic Church, health, education, and eventual relief expenditures such as those for the alleviation of the effects of the droughts in the late 1870s. This explains the high share of other secretaries of state in Table 10.4.

Expenditures by the Ministry of Agriculture were concentrated in the payment of guarantees to foreign investors in Brazil. Expenditure on government railways, harbors, subsidies to steamship companies, and urban infrastructure also increased significantly in the last imperial years. In fact, the secretary of agriculture was responsible for expenditures related to transportation systems, harbors, and telegraphs, and also for immigration. Immigration subsidies in the late 1880s amounted to more than 20 percent of the Ministry of Agriculture's budget. Contracts guaranteeing the remuneration of foreign direct investment were very common in imperial Brazil, especially in connection with the development of the railway system and the central sugar mills in the northeast. Frequently such contracts entailed both imperial and provincial guarantees. All such central government guarantees were redeemed in the early 1900s. There were in principle no financial losses to guarantee holders, who were in fact able to reap the differential between risk-free interest rates on British consols and the high interest rate guaranteed by such contracts.[67] The total failure of the central sugar mills in the 1880s in spite of guarantees was due to one of the most famous episodes of entrepreneurial incompetence rather than to the government stance on guarantees.[68]

Cases of incompetence could also be found in railway management. An interesting counterexample to the idea that guaranteed contracts might be totally risk-free is an episode mentioned in a British consular report. It concerns the Natal and Nova Cruz Railway in Rio Grande do Norte, whose operating deficit (working expenses), totaling £74,600 from 1881 to 1887, spurred a legal action against the company in London for the recovery of those losses. The capital being £549,600 and the guaranteed interest 7 percent, "in consequence of this guarantee the State paid up to the end of 1887 a total of £343,227." While the Brazilian minister of finance sympathized with the idea that "the shareholders gave their money in the understanding that they were to get 7 percent whereas they

[67] See Graham (1968), pp. 149–59, and Rodrigues (1902). Monteiro (1993) has shown the shortcomings of the negotiations that led to the redemption of such guarantees.

[68] See Eisenberg (1974), chapter 5.

receive nothing of the sort . . . [t]he Minister of Agriculture at once replied that they had no reason whatever in this complaint and that they ought to have found out before the line was made what it could produce independently of the government guarantee." The conclusion of the British diplomat is surprisingly favorable to Brazilian interests: "British investors in these concerns have lost sight of the fact that investments cannot be expected to combine complete security with 7 percent. If they want complete security, anyone doing business in Brazil can tell them of railway debentures here which will be always sure to pay a small percentage in gold." Thus it is clearly debatable if in this episode the property rights of the shareholders were or not respected. What also emerges is the credibility of the Brazilian railway debentures.[69]

The Ministry of Finance's budget included expenditures for pensions and retirement payments and, most important of all, service on the domestic and foreign debt. In the initial years of independence, public debt was mainly foreign debt (see Table 10.5), but the share of foreign debt in total debt fell continuously to about 50 percent in the 1850s and early 1860s. There was a recovery during the Paraguay War but the declining trend was resumed afterward, and by the early 1880s the share was below 30 percent. It returned to a level near 40 percent in the late 1880s as big foreign loans were floated, taking advantage of Brazil's extremely favorable credit ratings. The central government faced difficulties in placing public loans denominated in domestic currency as inflation accelerated in the 1850s and 1860s. It resorted to internal loans whose service was indexed to the foreign exchange rate. Gold internal loans were floated in 1869 and 1881. Both interest and amortization were payable in gold or in domestic currency at the parity exchange rate of 27 pence per milréis.[70] This increased the share of public debt indexed to the foreign exchange rate by a further 5 to 15 percent, depending on the year (see Table 10.5). Debt-export ratios reflect the economic vicissitudes already commented on. It is once again important to note that an initially high foreign (and internal gold) debt-export ratio was gradually reduced but rose again toward the end of the empire. Trends in the ratio of debt service to total expenditure followed the pattern of debt-export ratios. Initially high values in the 1820s, on the order of nearly 25 percent,

[69] See Wyndham (1889), pp. 53–4. He added that "a representative of certain notable German capitalists had recently offered to buy up or redeem the railways on which 7 percent and 6 percent were guaranteed, on the sole condition that the State would guarantee 5 percent to be actually received by the shareholders, even should the lines not pay working expenses. This makes the question clear as his Excellency [the late minister of finance] did not accept the offer of those German capitalists."

[70] See Pacheco (1979), pp. 145–6, for a description of the conditions attached to the 1879 internal loan.

Table 10.5. Brazil: Internal and External Debt, 1823–89[a]

	Imperial External Debt (in £1,000)[b]	Imperial Internal Debt (in £1,000)	Imperial Debt (in £1,000)	Average Exchange Rate (pence per milréis)[b]	Share of External Debt in Total Debt (%)	Share of Exchange Rate Indexed Debt in Total Debt (%)	Total Exports (in £1,000)[c]	Debt-Export Ratio (%)	Exchange Rate Indexed Debt-Export Ratio (%)
1824	1,333	n.a.	n.a.	48.2	n.a.	n.a.	3,851	n.a.	n.a.
1825	5,086	n.a.	n.a.	51.9	n.a.	n.a.	4,622	n.a.	n.a.
1826	4,976	n.a.	n.a.	48.1	n.a.	n.a.	3,319	n.a.	n.a.
1827	4,866	735	5,601	35.2	86.9	86.9	3,662	1.53	1.33
1828 (Je)	4,806	1,121	5,927	31.1	81.1	81.1	4,142	1.43	1.16
1829 (Je)	5,519	1,245	6,764	24.6	81.6	81.6	3,441	1.97	1.60
1830 (Je)	5,332	1,324	6,656	22.8	80.1	80.1	3,348	1.99	1.59
1831 (Je)	5,332	1,544	6,876	25.0	77.5	77.5	3,373	2.04	1.58
1832 (Ap)	5,332	2,498	7,830	38.1	68.1	68.1	3,263	2.40	1.63
1833 (Je)	5,332	2,795	8,127	37.4	65.6	65.6	5,632	1.44	0.95
1834 (Je)	5,332	2,972	8,304	38.7	64.1	64.1	5,328	1.56	1.00
1835	5,332	3,253	8,585	39.2	62.1	62.1	6,776	1.27	0.79
1836	5,367	3,134	8,501	38.4	63.1	63.1	5,476	1.55	0.98
1837	5,257	2,470	7,727	29.6	68.0	68.0	4,129	1.87	1.27
1838 (Je)	5,207	2,549	7,756	28.1	67.1	67.1	4,863	1.59	1.07
1839 (Je)	5,580	3,526	9,106	31.6	61.3	61.3	5,688	1.60	0.98
1840 (Je)	5,580	3,432	9,012	31.0	61.9	61.9	5,384	1.67	1.04
1841	5,580	3,739	9,319	30.0	59.9	59.9	4,936	1.89	1.13
1842 (D)	5,580	4,111	9,691	26.8	57.6	57.6	4,584	2.11	1.22
1843 (D)	6,187	4,256	10,443	25.8	59.2	59.2	4,708	2.22	1.31
1844	6,187	4,455	10,642	25.2	58.1	58.1	4,941	2.15	1.25
1845	6,187	4,828	11,015	25.4	56.2	56.2	5,685	1.94	1.09
1846	6,187	5,396	11,583	26.9	53.4	53.4	5,885	1.97	1.05
1847	6,187	5,643	11,830	28.0	52.3	52.3	6,760	1.75	0.92
1848	6,187	5,061	11,248	25.0	55.0	55.0	5,865	1.92	1.06
1849 (S)	6,187	5,527	11,714	25.9	52.8	52.8	5,932	1.97	1.04
1850	6,183	6,283	12,466	28.7	49.6	49.6	8,121	1.54	0.76
1851	6,010	6,456	12,466	29.1	48.2	48.2	8,083	1.54	0.74

(continued)

Table 10.5. ***(continued)***

	Imperial External Debt (in £1,000)[b]	Imperial Internal Debt (in £1,000)	Imperial Debt (in £1,000)	Average Exchange Rate (pence per milréis)[b]	Share of External Debt in Total Debt (%)	Share of Exchange Rate Indexed Debt in Total Debt (%)	Total Exports (in £1,000)[c]	Debt-Export Ratio (%)	Exchange Rate Indexed Debt-Export Ratio (%)
1852 (Ap)	6,979	6,571	13,550	27.4	51.5	51.5	8,418	1.61	0.83
1853	5,872	6,827	12,699	28.5	46.2	46.2	9,121	1.39	0.64
1854 (D)	5,824	6,644	12,468	27.6	46.7	46.7	10,439	1.19	0.56
1855 (D)	5,636	6,630	12,266	27.6	45.9	45.9	10,841	1.13	0.52
1856 (D)	5,493	6,631	12,124	27.6	45.3	45.3	13,150	0.92	0.42
1857 (D)	5,345	6,405	11,750	26.6	45.5	45.5	10,669	1.10	0.50
1858 (D)	6,719	6,151	12,870	25.6	52.2	52.2	11,372	1.13	0.59
1859 (D)	6,484	6,031	12,515	25.1	51.8	51.8	11,793	1.06	0.55
1861	7,655	7,254	14,909	25.8	51.3	51.3	13,241	1.13	0.58
1861 (D)	7,432	7,308	14,740	25.6	50.4	50.4	12,857	1.15	0.58
1862 (D)	7,205	7,636	14,841	26.3	48.5	48.5	13,424	1.11	0.54
1863	10,820	8,313	19,133	27.2	56.5	56.5	14,892	1.28	0.73
1864	7,947	8,558	16,505	26.7	48.2	48.2	15,733	1.05	0.51
1865	14,735	8,373	23,108	25.0	63.8	63.8	16,370	1.41	0.90
1866	14,417	9,138	23,555	24.2	61.2	61.2	15,786	1.49	0.91
1867	14,069	9,949	24,018	22.4	58.6	58.6	17,326	1.39	0.81
1868	13,697	8,869	22,566	17.0	60.7	60.7	14,351	1.57	0.95
1869	13,064	15,999	29,063	18.8	45.0	56.5	15,453	1.88	1.06
1870	12,721	22,123	34,844	22.1	36.5	46.1	15,439	2.26	1.04
1871	15,826	28,384	44,210	24.0	35.8	43.3	19,089	2.32	1.00
1872	15,463	29,724	45,187	25.0	34.2	41.5	22,392	2.02	0.84
1873	15,053	30,801	45,854	26.1	32.8	39.9	20,620	2.22	0.89
1874	14,630	30,674	45,304	25.8	32.3	39.3	22,392	2.02	0.80
1875	19,488	32,129	51,617	27.2	37.8	43.8	20,820	2.48	1.09
1876 (Oc)	19,037	30,851	49,888	25.3	38.2	44.3	20,573	2.42	1.07
1877 (Ap)	18,501	30,889	49,390	24.6	37.5	43.0	19,063	2.59	1.11
1878 (Oc)	17,929	30,224	48,153	22.3	37.2	43.3	19,508	2.47	1.07
1879	17,154	32,649	49,803	21.4	34.4	40.3	19,789	2.52	1.01
1880	16,554	33,188	49,742	22.1	33.3	38.7	21,249	2.34	0.91

	Imperial External Debt (in £1,000)[b]	Imperial Internal Debt (in £1,000)	Imperial Debt (in £1,000)	Average Exchange Rate (pence per milréis)[b]	Share of External Debt in Total Debt (%)	Share of Exchange Rate Indexed Debt in Total debt (%)	Total Exports (in £1,000)[c]	Debt-Export Ratio (%)	Exchange Rate Indexed Debt-Export Ratio (%)
1881 (S)	15,871	38,239	54,110	21.9	29.3	44.1	19,138	2.83	1.25
1882	15,002	37,204	52,206	21.2	28.7	44.1	17,378	3.00	1.32
1883	19,036	37,654	56,690	21.6	33.6	47.5	19,493	2.91	1.38
1884	18,420	36,124	54,544	20.7	33.8	47.7	19,504	2.80	1.33
1885	17,827	32,942	50,769	18.6	35.1	50.0	15,110	3.36	1.68
1886 (Ap)	23,554	36,888	60,442	18.7	39.0	51.0	20,502	2.95	1.50
1887[d]	22,952	42,298	65,250	22.4	35.2	45.3	23,406	2.79	1.26
1888	28,568	46,415	74,983	25.2	38.1	46.5	21,714	3.45	1.61
1889	30,351	48,023	78,374	26.4	38.7	46.4	28,552	2.74	1.27

[a] Abbreviations in the column for dates refer to the end of the month for which internal debt stock information is available: Je (June), Ap (April), D (December), S (September), Oc (October). No reference means the end of March.
[b] Calendar years.
[c] From 1833–4 to 1886–7, the fiscal year starting July 1.
[d] Doubled second-semester exports for 1887.
Source: Levy (1995) and Fundação Instituto de Geografia e Estatística (several years).

fell gradually, to reach 16–17 percent in the 1850s and 1860s and still remained below 20 percent in the 1870s, only to rise above 30 percent in the late years of the empire (see Table 10.6).

Incomplete and fragmentary data indicate that the funded and floating debt of the provinces in the mid-1880s was not very important: about 7 percent of total (foreign and domestic) central government debt.[71] According to a British consular report, in 1887 the funded debt of the provinces was £4,174,146 and the floating debt £1,951,674, totaling £6,125,820, "though according to another almost equally good, though not as in the first case, parliamentary authority, the total is £5,299,202." These figures were compared to the central government debt of £72,097,230 on December 31, 1888, including £28,598,400 of external debt and £43,498,830 of funded internal debt (figures that are somewhat different from those presented in Table 10.5) and a "total debt" of the central government estimated by the minister of agriculture in October 1888 at £90 million. Still, according to the same report, "it was in the latter part of 1888 that the provinces for

[71] See Carreira (1980) for the provincial debt in 1885.

Table 10.6. Brazil: Public Debt Service, 1824–88

	Quotation 5% Loans	Foreign Debt Service (in £1,000)	Internal Debt Service (in £1,000)	Total Debt Service (in £1,000)	Share of Service in Total Expenditure (%)
1824	98	22	n.a.	n.a.	n.a.
1825	85	119	n.a.	n.a.	n.a.
1826	59	303	n.a.	n.a.	n.a.
1827	60	402	52	454	26.1
1828	64	294	80	374	20.8
1829	73	307	96	403	21.6
1830	55	432	98	530	28.2
1831	44	267	108	375	n.a.
1832	48	267	141	408	n.a.
1833	67	267	210	477	26.7
1834	79	267	230	497	23.8
1835	84	267	322	589	25.1
1836	84	291	262	553	24.7
1837	74	315	245	560	24.0
1838	77	312	199	511	24.1
1839	71	316	202	518	15.7
1840	71	279	244	523	17.8
1841	64	279	247	526	15.3
1842	71	279	259	538	16.5
1843	73	435	253	688	24.7
1844	90	309	270	579	21.5
1845	81	309	286	595	22.9
1846	88	309	308	617	21.8
1847	81	309	327	636	21.5
1848	75	309	329	638	21.7
1849	88	309	327	636	20.4
1850	88	314	346	660	16.6
1851	95	461	381	842	16.2
1852	103	382	408	790	21.8
1853	98	1,410	396	1,806	42.0
1854	99	328	402	730	16.4
1855	100	445	395	840	18.2
1856	101	396	395	791	17.1
1857	99	393	382	775	13.5
1858	102	432	367	799	14.2
1859	100	963	360	1,323	24.1
1860	99	526	432	958	17.0
1861	99	552	436	988	17.5
1862	101	548	456	1,004	16.1

	Quotation 5% Loans	Foreign Debt Service (in £1,000)	Internal Debt Service (in £1,000)	Total Debt Service (in £1,000)	Share of Service in Total Expenditure (%)
1863	100	579	484	1,063	16.6
1864	101	2,911	518	3,429	36.9
1865	74	616	548	1,164	9.2
1866	74	977	559	1,536	12.6
1867	75	997	631	1,628	10.5
1868	79	1,001	658	1,659	15.5
1869	88	1,233	832	2,065	18.6
1870	92	929	1,196	2,125	23.1
1871	97	1,070	1,634	2,704	26.6
1872	97	1,088	1,784	2,872	22.6
1873	98	1,114	1,857	2,971	22.5
1874	100	1,107	1,929	3,036	22.5
1875	98	1,357	1,935	3,292	22.9
1876	94	1,357	2,090	3,447	24.0
1877	93	1,411	1,854	3,265	21.1
1878	92	1,446	2,082	3,528	20.9
1879	95	1,532	1,976	3,508	26.2
1880	98	1,382	2,307	3,689	28.9
1881	101	1,426	2,589	4,015	31.5
1882	101	1,546	2,099	3,645	27.0
1883	100	1,452	2,150	3,602	26.0
1884	98	1,481	2,382	3,863	28.3
1885	99	1,431	2,162	3,593	30.8
1886	100	1,504	2,050	3,554	30.0
1887	100	1,707	2,176	3,883	27.3
1888	101	1,892	2,411	4,303	33.8

Source: Debt service data from Levy (1995).

the first time began to issue foreign loans, notably São Paulo, Bahia, and Pernambuco."[72]

Several property rights issues arise from questions related to the Brazilian public foreign debt. When the service of these loans was contractually defined in terms of foreign currency there were, in principle, barring default, no property rights difficulties. However, quotation of

[72] See Wyndham (1889), p. 9. He also notes that answering a senator's question on "whether constitutionally they had the right to do so . . . the Prime Minister answered that 'though caution was needed, yet such necessity did not lessen the right of the provinces to contract within or without the empire such loans as they might desire'." Only in the

Brazilian bonds depended to a degree on the market evaluation of how economic policy was being conducted. Low quotations, especially in relation to loans floated at par value, could badly affect the rate of return on specific loans. Although quotations of Brazilian sterling loans fluctuated significantly during imperial years, the end-of-year quotation of Brazilian 5 percents in London in 1831, the worst year during the empire, was 44. But during certain periods, such as the late 1850s and early 1860s, as well as the 1880s, credit standing was very high, exceeding 100.[73] The Brazilian Empire was thought to have "unlimited access" to the London financial market.[74] If the deteriorating debt-export ratios and falling exchange rates as well as the continued fiscal disequilibria are taken into account, it is somewhat surprising that quotations in the 1880s remained so high.

Much of the literature on long-term debt suggests that Brazil had a worse record of payment of its foreign debt service than most other debtor countries. But most of these evaluations are not relevant and are even misleading when the focus of the analysis is the imperial period, that is, the period from 1822 to 1889. Some of this work seeks only to evaluate the record concerning dollar loans, which were floated only after the First World War.[75] Others analyze behavior in the long term, starting in 1850 and ending in 1970.[76] However, the initial period from the 1820s to 1850, which is excluded, was marked by the default of many borrowers but not of Brazil.

Preliminary results of a research project on this issue show that while the counterfactual rates of return for consols remained at around 3.1–3.2 percent yearly, actual rates of return on Brazilian bonds floated during the empire between 1824 and 1875 varied between 4 percent and 10.3 percent yearly. It is, of course, true that the variance in yearly rates of return was much higher for Brazilian bonds than for consols, but for most of the imperial loans this has to be set against the significantly higher rates of return of Brazilian bonds.

Holders of internal loans floated without indexation faced potential losses due to higher inflation in Brazil than in the rest of the world. Inter-

republican period would the external debt of the states become important. According to Veiga Filho (1898), p. 269, the São Paulo 1888 loan amounted to £714,000 and the Bahia 1888 loan to £800,000.

73 Brazil, in contrast to most Latin American countries, did not technically default on its sovereign central government debt before 1937. In the late 1880s, Brazil converted all its 5 percent foreign loans floated between 1865 and 1886 to 4 percent. See Marichal (1989), p. 49, and Abreu (1988), passim.

74 Dutot (1857), pp. 71–2. In the early 1870s, Brazilian bonds normally traded in London above par. See Mulhall (1873), pp. 7–9.

75 Such as Eichengreen and Portes (1989) or Jorgensen and Sachs (1989).

76 Lindert and Morton (1989).

nal loans not indexed to the foreign exchange rate carried a differential interest rate of 1–1.5 percent over the interest rate on indexed loans of 4–5 percent.

Fluctuations of the exchange rate were significant during the empire. First, there was a continuous devaluation from independence until the early 1840s, when the average yearly exchange rate was maintained between 25 and 29 pence per milréis. During the Paraguay War it devalued sharply to reach a minimum of 17 pence in 1868, but in 1872–76 it was back to 25–7 pence. Following the difficulties in the second half of the 1870s, the milréis slowly devalued, to reach a level below 19 pence in 1885–86 and only recovered in the last years of the empire, when it again approached legal parity.

Inflation rates were relatively low if compared to the Republican experience but high if compared to inflation rates in developed economies, or rather, deflation rates in most major economies.[77] The very unreliable price indices available for the earlier period suggest yearly inflation rates of 0.9 percent in the 1830s, 0.4 percent in the 1840s, 3.6 percent in the 1850s, and 2.8 percent in the 1860s.[78] More reliable wholesale price indices show yearly rates of –1.3 percent in the 1870s and 0.3 percent in the 1880s.[79] This indicates that domestic prices roughly doubled between 1830 and 1889, in line with exchange rate depreciation from 50 to 27 pence per milréis.

In such a situation, holders of internal debt denominated in milréis faced losses, which, however, were not a direct result of conscious action of the central government, except to the extent that it engaged in foreign wars and public spending, which were not unrelated to inflation.

10.5 MONETARY REGIMES AND BANKING DURING THE EMPIRE

After independence in 1822, the Banco do Brasil continued to issue notes that would constitute a substantial fraction of the currency in circulation until 1829. However, in 1827, given the large quantity of counterfeit copper coins in Bahia, the central government allowed the issue of *cédulas* for recalling those coins, and those became known as *provincial money*. This measure was to be extended to other provinces of the empire according to a law of October 3, 1833, which determined that all copper coins should be recalled by the provincial Tesourarias. In the

[77] Between 1830 and 1889 the U.S. wholesale price index (Bureau of Labor Statistics) fell by about 10 percent and the Rousseaux price index for Britain by more than 30 percent. See U.S. Department of Commerce, (1975), p. 201, and Mitchell and Deane (1971), pp. 471–2.

[78] See Goldsmith (1986) and Buescu (1986).

[79] See Catão (1992).

meantime, several provinces (besides Bahia and the Rio de Janeiro mints) had issued copper coins, including Goiás, Mato Grosso, São Paulo, and Minas Gerais, all subject to counterfeiting as the imperial copper issues.

For the enforcement of the 1833 Law, the National Treasury issued *cédulas para o troco da moeda de cobre*, which, in contrast to those issued for Bahia, were legal tender and had forced circulation as paper money until 1837. They were to be exchanged for the nominal value of copper coins, less 5 percent that would revert to the Treasury. In 1834 and 1835, countermarks were applied by some provincial governments to copper coins to reduce their value by one-half (Ceará and Pará) and even to one-fourth (Maranhão) to try to obstruct their exit from the provinces.[80]

Given those complications involving the copper coins in circulation and extensive counterfeiting, the imperial government issued the Law of October 6, 1835, meant to reestablish the credibility of the copper currency. All copper coins were to be presented for countermarking, the false coins would be confiscated and destroyed, and the copper coins of 80, 40, and 20 réis would be countermarked with half of their value. This process was never completed, and countermarked and old coins circulated in parallel for decades. This confused situation of the copper currency in the early empire cannot be dissociated from the unfavorable fiscal situation in the period. The repetition of colonial practices regarding the currency, which infringed on property rights, would, however, cease after the late 1840s.

In contrast to the vicissitudes associated with copper coinage, the new imperial government did not debase the limited gold coinage issued until 1833, preserving the weights and fineness of the late colonial period. But initially it retained the previous habit of issuing a "strong" and a "weak" coinage. The 6,400 réis of 4 oitavas at 1,600 réis per oitava corresponded to a parity of 67.5 pence per milréis. The 4,000 réis of 2.25 oitavas at approximately 1,777 réis per oitava corresponded to a parity of 60.75 pence. The silver 960 réis continued to be issued at an overrated nominal value, and the rare silver coins of other denominations also preserved the late colonial standard (of 128 réis per oitava).[81]

However, the issue of precious metals was insufficient to meet the demand for money, and by a decree of June 1, 1833, the government

[80] See Trigueiros (1987), pp. 68–74.

[81] According to the 1833 report of the Ministry of Finance, the seigniorage on coins was 6.66 percent for the 6,400 réis, 18.5 percent for the 4,000 réis, and 15 percent for the silver coins. The legal relation between gold and silver was approximately 1 to 13.5 when the market ratio was 1 to 16. The exchange rate parity of the 960 réis was only 54 pence, while the commercial par was around 60 pence. See Viana (1922), pp. 184–5.

decided to have a uniform currency and ordered Treasury notes to be stamped in England, initiating a monopoly of note issue by the Treasury initially from 1825 to 1838 and again from 1866 to 1889.[82] Actually, by keeping a legal relation between gold and silver coins different from the world market relation, the government fostered a substantial drain of gold coin from the country.

The second monetary system of the empire, involving debasement of the metallic currency, lasted in principle from 1833 to 1846 (but actually 1848 in view of the delay in the implementation of the new laws). Gold pieces of 10,000 réis were issued at 2,500 réis per oitava, and the so-called series of silver *cruzados* (including coins of 1,200, 800, 400, 200, and 100 réis) were still issued in silver of 11 *dinheiros* (0.91666 fineness) but at the rate of 160 réis per oitava. In the late 1840s, new legislation established new standards for gold (4,000 réis per oitava) and silver (281.6 réis per oitava), which would be basically maintained from 1849 to 1889.[83]

As regards the par exchange rate, the Brazilian legal monetary standard had been broken in 1833 from the preindependence legal tender parity of 67.5 pence per milréis to 43.5 per milréis.[84] New legislation in 1846[85] further broke parity from 43.5 pence to 27 pence per milréis.[86] While the legal definition of the milréis remained unchanged until the

[82] On coinage in the early empire, see Coimbra (1960), tome IV. For a summary of note issue, see Lissa (1987), pp. 13–14. For a more extended discussion, see Calógeras (1960), chapters IV and V.

[83] See Coimbra (1960), tome IV, chapter XVI; Prober (1966), pp. 17–18; Trigueiros (1987), pp. 56–7; Calógeras (1960), chapters V and VI. Calógeras presents annual figures on coinage and note circulation between 1809 and 1853. Between 1809 and 1821, 9,192 contos in gold, 13,215 contos in silver, and 1,004 contos in copper had been issued, as opposed to 8,070 contos in notes of the first Banco do Brasil. Betwen 1822 and 1830, total coinage was some 555 contos in gold, 2,749 contos in silver, and 12,124 contos in copper, while in 1830 notes in circulation included 1,490 contos of Treasury notes and 18,860 contos of notes of the Banco do Brasil. From 1831 to 1835, gold coin issues totaled some 406 contos and silver issues only 19 contos, while copper issues reached 1,456 contos. In 1835, the value of the copper coins countermarked by the central government was 20,000 contos, replacing previous issues, while the new Treasury note issue was 30,702 contos. From 1836 to 1848, gold coinage was limited to 551 contos and silver issues to 71 contos, while note circulation in 1848 included 47,802 contos in Treasury notes and 1,515 contos in private bank notes. From 1849 to 1853, already under the new monetary standard, gold issues totaled 16,374 contos and silver issues 2,385 contos, as opposed to a note circulation of 46,693 contos in Treasury notes and 5,569 contos in bank notes in 1853. See Calógeras (1960), p. 80. Wyndham (1889), p. 14, quoting contemporary official sources, advances the coinage figures of 8,114 contos in gold and 16,038 contos in silver from 1810 to 1829 and of 951 contos in gold and 67 contos in silver between 1830 and 1849 (possibly 1848), which are roughly in line with Calógeras's figures.

[84] Law 59 of October 8, 1833. [85] Law of September 11, 1846.

[86] See Calógeras (1960), chapter 5.

end of the empire, the Brazilian foreign exchange rate fluctuated significantly, as mentioned in the previous section.[87]

This was not unrelated to the characteristics of monetary circulation in independent Brazil, which, as already seen, was mostly based on paper currency after the end of the 1820s. The 1830s were marked by the scarcity of money as Gresham's law stimulated in succession the expulsion from circulation of gold, silver, and copper that became debased. Only in the late 1840s was metallic circulation again important.[88]

A government-controlled Banco do Brasil with some features of a central bank had been created when the Portuguese court moved to Rio de Janeiro in 1808 and was liquidated in 1829 mainly in a reaction against an experience that was thought to have been marred by gross mismanagement. Since the Treasury was heavily indebted to the bank due to advances, its shareholders were paid at 90 percent.[89] A second Banco do Brasil planned in 1833 was never launched. There were no significant private banks before the early 1850s. Some small banks were created, first in the provinces, then in Rio. Some financial services for coffee growers in the southeast were provided by *comissários*, which acted as purchasing and selling agents in the main urban centers and provided advances on future crops.[90] The share of banking deposits in the means of payment rose continuously from less than 10 percent in 1850 to around 60 percent in 1889, but the ratio of means of payment to GNP was perhaps around 20 percent both in the late 1820s and in the late 1880s.[91]

[87] The new legal relation between gold and silver was 1 to 15 5/8, and a law of July 26, 1849, established in practice a gold monometallic system by limiting the obligation of receiving payments in silver coins to 20 milréis, and keeping the limits previously established for payments in copper coins. In the following year, the demonetization of the old coins and the requirement to have them recoined was also established.

[88] See Carvalho (1858), p. 42.

[89] Calógeras (1960), chapters III and IV, makes this the centerpiece of his strong criticism of the decision to liquidate the bank.

[90] See Laerne (1885), chapter 5, for a very good description of the role of the *comissários* or the excellent Stein (1957), chapter 4.

[91] See Goldsmith (1986), pp. 36, 44. These figures are very approximate, as no data on GNP exist. Starting from a series of nominal GDP based on money supply (M2), wages paid, exports plus imports, and government expenditures, and on an average price index based on price series precarious from both a statistical and a methodogical point of view, Goldsmith computed the following per capita real GDP growth rates: 1851–60: 1.34 percent; 1861–70: 0.91 percent; 1871–80: –0.24 percent, and 1881–9: –0.58 percent and the average of 0.34 percent for 1850–89, corresponding to a growth rate of total real GDP of 2.04 percent. Allowing for changes in the terms of trade, the per capita growth rate for the whole period would increase to 0.7 percent. Goldsmith also quotes the estimates, also based on indirect methods, of Buescu of an average rate of 0.3 to 0.4 percent for the period 1850–89 and of Furtado, a weighted average of 1 percent based on regional estimates for the whole second half of the nineteenth century. Coatsworth (1997), p. 13,

The 1850 Commercial Code, by making possible the establishment of joint stock companies, stimulated the creation of new private banks. The Banco do Brasil of Mauá & Co. was established and eventually transformed into a new government-controlled Banco do Brasil in 1853. The 1850s and early 1860s were marked by the increasing role of banks in issuing paper currency: whereas by 1850–1 notes issued by banks were 2 percent of total paper currency in circulation, this participation rose to a peak near 80 percent in 1865–6.[92] The Banco do Brasil acquired through takeovers the monopoly of issue in Rio de Janeiro in the mid-1850s. The consequences of successive liquidity crises led to a reappraisal of the emission rights legislation. In 1860 issuing rights of private banks were curtailed. In 1866 the emission privileges of the Banco do Brasil were withdrawn and the issuing monopoly returned to the Treasury. The gradual withdrawal of Banco do Brasil notes in exchange for bonds was provided for.[93] The issue of Treasury notes, which had more credibility, was particularly important in view of the banking crisis of 1864 and the Paraguay War, as financial uncertainty and "the requirements of the government on . . . account [of the war] resulted in the disappearance of almost the last ounce of specie from the country."[94]

The Banco do Brasil played an important role in alleviating the impact of successive financial crises such as those of 1857 and 1864, during which the government eased its issuing constraints. But there are suggestions that these stances were politically motivated, as shown by the reluctance to weather the consequences of the 1875 crisis. This crisis led in the end to the failure of Banco Mauá, which had had, though on a much smaller scale, a role similar to that played in France by the Crédit Mobilier.[95]

At the end of the 1880s, in another round of the confrontation between *papelistas* and *metalistas* – the Brazilian versions of the Banking

based on Bulmer-Thomas, records that Brazilian exports per capita in current dollars would have increased from US$5 in 1850 to US$8.6 in 1870 and to US$9.6 in 1890. On p. 4, the same author reproduces 1994 estimates by Maddison that suggest that in 1890 Brazil's per capita income corresponded to 21 percent of that of the United States, while the corresponding figures for Argentina, Chile, and Mexico were, respectively, 49 percent, 35 percent, and 25 percent. On the basis of an estimate by Coatsworth of a ratio of 36 percent for Brazil in 1800, which he acknowledges to be possibly underestimated, it would appear that Brazil's position in relation to the United States suffered a significant deterioration during the imperial period.

92 Calógeras (1960), passim.

93 Law of September 12, 1866. On bank issues between 1836 and 1889, see Trigueiros (1987), pp. 87–9.

94 See the already quoted report of Consul Lennon Hunt on the Trade . . . of Rio de Janeiro . . . in 1869, p. 239.

95 See Pradez (1872), p. 164.

and Currency schools – legislation was passed providing for a return to multiple emission, which had no practical importance before the end of the empire. The very expansionary monetary policies adopted in the first two years of the Republican regime were partly based on this imperial attempt to cope with the increased monetization related to the abolition of slavery. But while the bullionists had been able to have some influence in 1888 and prevented a clear victory of the *papelistas* the position was sharply different in 1890. New legislation made possible a massive increase of inconvertible currency and led to very high inflation. It would take a decade to bring economic policy under control.[96]

Foreign banks had an important role to play from the early 1860s. N. M. Rothschild & Sons of London had the monopoly in the flotation of foreign loans for the central government of Brazil from the mid-1850s to the early twentieth century. It also acted as a paying and purchasing agent for the Brazilian government. Foreign banks were first installed in the early 1860s: the London and Brazilian Bank in 1862 and the Brazilian and Portuguese Bank, later renamed the English Bank of Rio de Janeiro, in 1863. The Brasilianische Bank für Deutschland was created just before the end of the empire. Foreign banks became particularly important during the Republic and reached the peak of their influence just before the First World War.[97]

While the volume of paper money issues during the second empire is reasonably well known, and there exist records of the mintage of imperial coins, these figures are not sufficient to measure accurately the supply of currency in Brazil during the period, especially the supply of metallic currency. It has been shown that the export and import of Brazilian and foreign coins were included in the trade statistics, and coins from various countries were used in Brazil in domestic transactions from the 1850s to the 1880s. For instance, a decree of October 24, 1857, established a fixed rate in milréis for sovereigns and half-sovereigns to be received by government departments. The Finance Ministry report relative to that year justified this measure, stating that it "supplied our markets with a perfect money, well-known and admitted by the commercial world, while saving

[96] See Franco (1983). The early years of the Republic were also characterized by the formation of many joint stock companies and by active speculation in the Rio Stock Exchange, favored by the expansion of credit and by inflation. Many companies went rapidly bankrupt, and this period has been since then referred to as that of the *Encilhamento*, literally the "act of harnessing a horse."

[97] See Joslin (1963). See also the Report of Mr. Consul Westwood on the Trade of Rio de Janeiro for the Year 1863, PP 1865, Vol. 53, p. 72. This diplomat records that "the London and Brazilian Bank . . . direction in London, capital £1,500,000 . . . does a very important business" and registers the recent foundation of the "Brazilian and Portuguese Bank . . . direction in London, capital £1,100,000."

the expense of having it recoined." In fact, 59.5 percent of the 35,000 contos issued in gold coins of the new milréis standard between 1849 and 1859 corresponded to foreign coins transformed into Brazilian coin, while only 32 percent of the issues of silver coins in the same period corresponded to "old national coins," the remaining fraction corresponding to imported silver coins and silver bars. The "precautionary demand" for money seems to have often been met by foreign gold and silver coins in view of the lack of confidence in the paper money of the Treasury. In the 1880s, this trend was reinforced by European immigration, as confirmed by a British consular report that states that immigrants working in coffee plantations asked to be paid and also saved in sovereigns. On April, 21, 1889, the imperial government issued a new circular confirming the authorization of the use of sovereigns in all "public and private transactions."[98]

To the extent that the imperial coinage did not represent a significant fraction of the total money supply, the government's opportunities for seigniorage or to resort to debasement of the coinage were limited. By the late 1880s, shortly before the imperial government authorized new private bank note issues based on metallic reserves, a report suggested an increase in the seigniorage rate applied to silver coins by the Brazilian mint, but this apparently was not implemented.[99] There was also no government attempt to manipulate the precious metal content of coins in circulation through debasement. In order to supply small change, in the 1870s, nickel and bronze coins of smaller denominations

[98] For the quotations in the text, see Lago (1982), pp. 502–3. Table 5, on p. 504, shows the various foreign coins circulating in Rio Grande do Sul in 1860 and their value in milréis according to the local British consul. Between 1846–7 and 1867–8 the "gross" imports of coins into Brazil included in merchandise trade totaled £18.8 million. The data on "gross" exports of coins are more fragmentary. Calógeras (1960), pp. 77–8, mentions the circulation of British sovereigns in the 1850s at the rate of 8,890 réis per sovereign, later legally extended in 1875. See also Wyndham (1889), p. 12, on the habit of hoarding large sums outside the banks and (p. 15) on Italian immigrants asking for sovereigns in December 1888, distrusting Treasury notes. In the same report it is stated that in 1889, besides the sovereign being legal tender at the fixed rate of 8,890 réis, "other foreign gold coins [were] also accepted at the Custom House, but merely at the exchange of the day."

[99] Azeredo Coutinho, Necessidade de Aumento da Senhoriagem na Moeda de Prata do Brasil, 1887, quoted by Coimbra (1959), tome III, p. 67. Coutinho was for some time *provedor* of the *Casa da Moeda* (mint). On seigniorage rates in mid-century and the 1860s, see Calógeras (1960), pp. 76, 81, 82, who mentions the rate of 14.22 percent for silver in 1857. There were also taxes of *afinação*, *fundição*, and *moedagem*. According to an already quoted British consular report, "by law anyone can have gold or silver coined for them at the mint, the legal fineness of each being 0.917. The mint charge to private persons for coining gold is $2^1/_2$ percent, for silver it is 9.86 percent." See Wyndham (1889), p. 14.

were introduced, as no copper coins had been minted since the 1830s.[100] In summary, there was no infringement of property rights in the area of metallic currency after 1849, and this may again be related to more balanced government accounts, to which a greater capacity to tax foreign trade after 1844 gave a significant contribution. On the other hand, as in other countries, such as the United States during the Civil War, the issue of inconvertible currency by the Treasury, notably during the Paraguay War, in an inflationary context, did represent the imposition of an "inflationary tax" that reverted fully to the government in the periods of Treasury monopoly of note issue.

Given the limitations of the scope of this chapter, it is not possible to deal adequately with the question of how property rights were affected by the imperfection and laxity of government regulations concerning the rights of emission of banks, the banks' imprudent behavior, and government rescue, generally through the generous discount windows of the Banco do Brasil. While it does not seem that there was any important direct use of taxpayers' money, there were macroeconomic consequences linked to the accommodating monetary policies adopted by the government. Moreover, at the microeconomic level, defective regulation in 1857 and 1864 made possible the overextension of financial houses, which went bankrupt.[101] This was not, of course, something that happened only

[100] The accumulated coinage between 1854 and February 1889 was approximately 28,280 contos in gold, 17,245 contos in silver, 3,805 contos in nickel, and 3,799 contos in bronze. In the whole period 1849–89 some 44,654 contos in gold, 19,630 contos in silver, 3,805 contos in nickel, and 3,799 contos in bronze would have been coined in Brazil. See Calógeras (1960), pp. 80 and 88, for the raw annual data. Wyndham (1889), p. 15, presents totals of gold and silver coinage between 1849 and 1859 of, respectively, 37,230 contos and 8,182 contos, and of 8,411 contos in gold and 10,787 in silver between 1859 and 1887. Still, according to Calógeras, in 1888 the total note issues of the Treasury and banks in circulation reached 205,288 contos, of which 188,869 were Treasury notes. An idea of the drain that the supply of metallic currency could suffer in given years through exports, and elements of comparison with the preceding figures, are provided by the following data based on raw figures from a consular report: the total official value of exports in the fiscal year 1876–7 of 101,047 contos included exports of 5,833 contos of gold and silver coin, and between 1879–80 and 1881–2, out of a total official value of exports of 315,769 contos, 5,135 contos corresponded to gold and silver coin and 522 contos to paper money. See Report by Mr. Sandford on the Commerce of Brazil during the last 15 years, pp. 1884–5, vol. 76, part IV, Commercial no. 40 (1884), pp. 368–9.

[101] At least since the early 1850s, financial houses engaged in various banking activities, including commercial discounts and loans, while investing heavily in real estate and other illiquid assets. On the other hand, many accepted deposit accounts that were actually demand accounts that could be drawn at short notice, leaving them very exposed in case of a panic. In 1857, the crisis was of a commercial nature and occurred mainly in Rio de Janeiro, as a reflection of the crises in Europe and North America, which affected Brazil's foreign trade. Several financial houses in Rio de Janeiro suffered heavy

in Brazil, such financial crises being ripples of financial crises at the center of the world financial system. But the total net losses entailed by bankruptcies in Brazil were equivalent to 50 percent of the means of payment in 1864. The liabilities of A. J. A. Souto & Cia in 1864 were about £4 million, not too different from the £5 million of Overend, Gurney of London two years later.[102]

10.6 CONCLUSIONS

Based on the analysis presented in the previous sections on public finance and the monetary regime during the Brazilian Empire, it would seem that, if account is taken of the property rights record in relation to nonfinancial assets (land, but especially the emancipation of some 600,000 slaves without compensation), the record concerning financial assets was rather good.

Periods of lax monetary and financial regime policy were in general politically determined: the long crisis of independence; war in the River Plate and the Regency before D. Pedro II's coronation; the Paraguay War; and the difficult years during and following the big drought in the late 1870s. It is not difficult to detect similar periods in the financial history of mature metropolitan economies as well.

It would seem that most of the criticisms that could be leveled against particular aspects of fiscal, monetary, and financial policies could be somewhat blunted by the recognition of the structural limitations of decision-making processes in an economy geared to commodity exports using cheap labor. Otherwise, a full counterfactual exercise of how the Brazilian economy would have behaved if, say, the constraint on slave imports had become really binding in 1830, or if land policies had been similar to those adopted in other economies unconstrained by land availability, would be needed.

losses but continued to operate, postponing the recognition of their negative results. Some of them, such as A. J. A. Souto & Cia, survived with the active support of the Banco do Brasil. By 1863, some of these financial houses had taken additional risks in order to expand their operations, and besides renewing bad loans, they extended excessive credits to recently created unhealthy companies, often based on bonds and titles issued by these companies. Those operations temporarily masked certain abuses and losses. A general loss of confidence associated with the bankruptcy of companies in several sectors of activity resulted in the crisis of 1864, which affected many financial houses, the total liabilities of which reached 110,500 contos. Since liquidation only permitted them to cover 35 percent to 40 percent of the outstanding commitments, losses amounted to 65,000 to 70,000 contos, around £7.3 to £8 million. See Calógeras (1960), pp. 141–8.

[102] See Calógeras (1960), p. 145; Goldsmith (1986); p. 44; Clapham (1966), p. 263.

It was thus as a direct consequence of the political power of landowners that taxation relied mostly on duties on foreign trade. That the increased production costs of coffee due to high protection as well as export taxes could be shifted to coffee consumers probably delayed the introduction of significant internal taxation such as excise and income taxes, which had to wait until World War One. The financial record of the empire was extremely good, especially under D. Pedro II (1831–89). This applied to public foreign debt as well as to the high rates of return also guaranteed to direct foreign investment. While this latter treatment may have been overgenerous, the policy must be put into perspective by the serious frictions between government and foreign suppliers of public services in the context of foreign exchange devaluation during the Republican regime. It was also during the Republic in the twentieth century that unilateral moratoria on the foreign debt would be declared by Brazil (1930s and 1987).

A strong conclusion that comes out of this preliminary stocktaking of the imperial period, as compared to monetary, fiscal, and financial developments since 1889, is that any idea of a gradual and evolutionary consolidation of the respect of property rights by the central government in regard to financial assets or less discriminatory taxation must be ruled out. With all the imperfections of government policies during the empire, and in spite of a strengthening of private law and of the judicial system in the twentieth century, as well as a better definition and registration of landed property, developments without any precedent have since then unfavorably affected property rights from the perspective of this study. A short list of such developments would have to include government interference in the distribution of foreign exchange cover, default of foreign debt service, increased restrictions on the right of establishment of foreign firms including financial intermediaries, compulsory sales of government "loans," and highly inflationary government financing. Finally, there were recent (1990) episodes of freezing of financial assets in the context of failed stabilization attempts that were indeed akin, in their treatment of property rights, to what the colonial *derrama* might have represented.

REFERENCES

Abreu, M. de Paiva (1988). "On the Memory of Bankers: Brazilian Foreign Debt, 1824–1943," *Political Economy* 4 (1), pp. 45–81.

Abreu, M. de Paiva and A. S. Bevilaqua (2000). "Brazil as an Export Economy, 1830–1930," in E. Cardenas, J. A. Ocampo, and R. Thorp, eds., *An Economic History of Twentieth-Century Latin America*, Volume 1: *The Export Age*. Basingstoke, UK.: Palgrave, 428.

Alden, D. (1968). *Royal Government in Colonial Brazil.* Berkeley: University of California Press.

Almeida, J. Bellens de (1922). *História das Tesourarias da Fazenda e Delegacias Fiscais*. Rio de Janeiro: Imprensa Nacional.

Andrada, A. C. R. de (1923). *Bancos de Emissão no Brasil.* Rio de Janeiro: Leite Ribeiro.

Azevedo, J. Lucio de (1973). *Épocas de Portugal Econômico*. Lisboa: Livraria Clássica Editora (reprint of the 1928 edition).

Bahia, Governo do Estado, Secretaria de Planejamento Ciência e Tecnologia (1978). *A Inserção da Bahia na Evolução Nacional*, Volume 4: *First Etapa 1850–1889*. Salvador: Fundação de Pesquisas CPE.

Bethell, L. (ed.) (1987). *Colonial Brazil.* Cambridge: Cambridge University Press, NY.

Boxer, C. R. (1962). *The Golden Age of Brazil, 1695–1750.* Berkeley and Los Angeles: University of California Press.

Buescu, M. (1996). "A Inflação Brasileira durante o Império: um Enfoque Histórico," *Carta Mensal*, Confederação Nacional de Comércio, 42, 500.

Calógeras, J. P. (1960). *La Politique Monétaire du Brésil.* (translated into Portuguese as *A Política Monetária do Brasil*). São Paulo: Companhia Editora Nacional.

Carreira, L. de Castro (1980). *História financeira e monetária do Império do Brasil*, 2 vols. Brasília: Senado Federal (1st edition, 1889).

Carruthers, B. G. (1996). *City of Capital. Politics and Markets in the English Industrial Revolution.* Princeton: Princeton University Press.

Carvalho, H. (1858). *Études sur le Brésil au Point de Vue de l'Emigration et du Commerce Français*. Paris: Garnier Frères.

Castello, A. de Vianna do and J. Dodsworth (1940). *Produção e Comércio de Diamantes no Brasil.* Rio de Janeiro: Tipografia Baptista de Souza.

Catão, L. A. V. (1992). "A New Wholesale Price Index for Brazil during the Period 1870–1913," *Revista Brasileira de Economia*, pp. 519–33.

Clapham, J. (1966). *The Bank of England. A History, Vol. II.* Cambridge: Cambridge University Press, NY.

Coatsworth, J. H. (1997). "Economic and Institutional Trajectories in Pre-Modern Latin America," presented at the conference on Latin America and the World Economy in the Nineteenth and Twentieth Century, Bellagio, June 30 to July 4.

Coimbra, A. da Veiga. *Noções de Numismática.* Tome II, 1958; tome III, 1959; tome IV, 1960. São Paulo: Coleção da Revista de História.

Dean, W. (1971). "Latifundia and Land-policy in Nineteenth-Century Brazil," *Hispanic American Historical Review*, pp. 606–25.

Distrito Federal (1908). *Notícia do Desenvolvimento da Indústria Fabril no Distrito Federal* (official publication). Rio de Janeiro.

Dutot, S. (1857). *France et Brésil.* Paris: Guillaumin & Cie.

Eichengreen, B. and R. Portes (1989). "After the Deluge: Default, Negotiation and Readjustment during the Interwar Years," in B. Eichengreen and

P. H. Lindert, eds., *The International Debt Crisis in Historical Perspective.* Cambridge, Mass.: MIT Press, pp. 12–47.

Eisenberg, P. L. (1974). *The Sugar Industry in Pernambuco. Modernization without Change, 1840–1910.* Berkeley: University of California Press.

Eschwege, G. (1899). Notícias e Reflexões Estadísticas da Provincia de Minas Gerais. *Revista do Arquivo Público Mineiro*, Ano IV.

Fontoura, J. Carneiro da (1921). *Documentação para a História das Tarifas Aduaneiras no Brasil, 1808–1889.* Rio de Janeiro: Livraria J. Leite.

Franco, A. A. de M. (1979). *História do Banco do Brasil (Primeira Fase – 1808–1835).* Brasília: Banco do Brasil.

Franco, G. H. B. (1983). *Reforma Monetária e Instabilidade Durante a Transição Republicana.* Rio de Janeiro: BNDES.

(1991). *A Década Republicana: O Brasil e a Economia Internacional – 1888/1900.* Rio de Janeiro: IPEA.

Fundação Instituto Brasileiro de Geografia e Estatística (several years). *Anuário Estatístico do Brasil.* Rio de Janeiro.

(several years). *O Brasil em Números.* Rio de Janeiro.

Garcia, R. (1975). *Ensaio sobre a História Política e Administrativa do Brasil, 1500–1810.* Rio de Janeiro: José Olympio.

Goldsmith, R. W. (1986). *Brasil 1850–1984: Desenvolvimento Financeiro sob um Século de Inflação.* São Paulo: Harper and Row.

Graham, R. (1968). *Britain and the Onset of Modernization in Brazil 1850–1914.* Cambridge: Cambridge University Press, NY.

(1990). *Patronage and Politics in Nineteenth-Century Brazil.* Stanford, Calif.: Stanford University Press.

Hahner, J. E. (1986). *Poverty and Politics: The Urban Poor in Brazil, 1870–1920.* Albuquerque: University of New Mexico Press.

Johnson, H. B. (1987). "Portuguese Settlement, 1500–1580," in Bethell, pp. 1–38.

Jorgensen, E. and Sachs, J. (1989). "Default and Renegotiation of Latin American Foreign Bonds in the Interwar Years," in B. Eichengreen and P. H. Lindert, eds., *The International Debt Crisis in International Perspective.* Cambridge, Mass.: MIT Press, pp. 48–85.

Joslin, D. (1963). *A Century of Banking in Latin America to Commemorate the Centenary in 1962 of The Bank of London & South America Limited.* London: Oxford University Press.

Laerne, C. F. van Delden (1885). *Brazil and Java. Report on Coffee-Culture in America. Asia and Africa.* London: W. H. Allen.

Lago, L. A. Corrêa do (1973). "The Rise and Decline of the Brazilian Sugar Economy, A 'Monetary' or 'Exchange' Economy?" Unpublished paper, Department of Economics, Harvard University.

(1982). "Balança Comercial, Balanço de Pagamentos e Meio Circulante no Brasil no Segundo Império: uma Nota para uma Revisão," *Revista Brasileira de Economia*, 42 (4), pp. 317–69.

(1988). "O Surgimento da Escravidão e a Transição para o Trabalho Livre no Brasil: um Modelo Teórico Simples e uma Visão de Longo Prazo," *Revista Brasileira de Economia*, 36 (4), pp. 489–508.

Lago, L. A. Corrêa do, F. Lopes de Almeida, and B. M. F. de Lima (1979). *A Indústria Brasileira de Bens de Capital*. Rio de Janeiro: Editora da Fundação Getúlio Vargas.

Levy, M. B. (1994). "El Sector Financiero y el Desarrollo Bancario en Río de Janeiro," in P. Tedde and C. Marichal, eds., *La Formación de los Bancos Centrales en España y América Latina (Siglos XIX y XX). Vol. II: Suramérica y el Caribe*, pp. 61–84, Banco de España (Madrid): Estudios de Historia Económica no. 30.

(1995). "The Brazilian Public Debt – Domestic and Foreign, 1824–1913," in R. Liehr, ed., *The Public Debt in Latin America in Historical Perspective*. Vervuert Iberoamericana, pp. 209–54.

Lindert, P. H. and Morton, P. J. (1989). "How Sovereign Debt Has Worked," in J. D. Sachs, ed., *Developing Country Debt and Economic Performance*, Volume 1: *The International Financial System*. Chicago: University of Chicago Press, pp. 39–106.

Lissa, V. I. (1987). *Católogo do Papel-Moeda do Brasilo* Brasília: Editora.

Manchester, A. K. (1933). *British Preëminence in Brazil. Its Rise and Decline. A Study in European Expansion*. Chapel Hill: University of North Carolina Press.

Marichal, C. (1989). *A Century of Debt Crises in Latin America: From Independence to the Great Depression 1820–1930*. Princeton: Princeton University Press.

Mauro, F. (1983). *Le Portugal, Le Brésil et l'Atlantique au XVIIe Siècle (1570–1670)*. Paris: Fondation Calouste Gulbenkian, Centre Culturel Portugais.

(1987). "Political and Economic Structures of Empire, 1580–1750," in Bethell, pp. 39–66.

Maxwell, K. R. (1973). *Conflicts and Conspiracies: Brazil & Portugal 1750–1808*. Cambridge: Cambridge University Press.

McCusker, J. J. (1978). *Money and Exchange in Europe and America, 1600–1775: A Handbook*. London: Macmillan.

Melo, E. Cabral de (1984). *O Norte Agrário e o Império*. Rio de Janeiro: Nova Fronteira/INL.

Mitchell, B. R. with the collaboration of P. Deane (1971). *Abstract of British Historical Statistics*. Cambridge: Cambridge University Press.

Monteiro, R. M. (1993). As Garantias Ferroviárias no Brasil: Uma análise dos *Rescission* Bonds e do resgate das estradas de ferro. Rio de Janeiro: Monografia de Final de Curso, Departamento de Economia, PUC.

Mulhall, M. G. (1873). *Rio Grande do Sul and its German Colonies*. London: Longmans, Green & Co.

Nogueira, O. (1987). *A Constituição de 1824*. Brasília: Centro de Ènsino à Distância.

North, D. C. and B. R. Weingast (1989). "Constitutions and Commitment: The Evolution of Institutions Governing Public Choice in Seventeenth-Century England," *The Journal of Economic History*, 49 (4), pp. 803–32.

North, D. C. and R. P. Thomas (1973). *The Rise of the Western World. A New Economics*. Cambridge: Cambridge University Press.

Onody, O. (1953). "História do Imposto de Exportação no Brasil," *Revista de História da Economia Brasileira*, Ano I, no. 1, pp. 51–64.

Pacheco, C. (1979). *História do Banco do Brasil (História Financeira do Brasil desde 1808 até 1951)*, Vol. III. Rio de Janeiro.

Pelaez, C. M. and W. Suzigan (1976). *História Monetária do Brasil: Análise da Política, Comportamento e Instituições Monetárias*. Rio de Janeiro: IPEA.

Platt, D. C. M. (1968). *Finance, Trade and Politics in British Foreign Policy 1815–1914*. Oxford: Clarendon Press.

Pradez, C. (1872). *Nouvelles Études sur le Brésil*. Paris: Ernest Thorin.

Prober, K. (1966). *Catálogo das Moedas Brasileiras*. São Paulo: Private edition.

Reybaud, C. (1856). *Le Brésil*. Paris: Guilhaumin et Cie.

Ridings, E. (1994). *Business Interest Groups in Nineteenth-Century Brazil*. Cambridge: Cambridge University Press, NY.

Rodrigues, J. C. (1902). *Resgate das Estradas de Ferro do Recife a S. Francisco e de Outras que Gozavam da Garantia de Juros. Relatório apresentado ao Exm. Sr. Dr Joaquim Murtinho, Ministro da Fazenda* . . . , Rio de Janeiro: Imprensa Nacional.

Russell-Wood, A. J. R. (1987). "The Gold Cycle, c.1690–1750," in Bethell, pp. 190–243.

Schwartz, S. B. (1987). "Plantations and Peripheries, c.1580–c.1750," in Bethell, pp. 67–194.

Silva, A. Mansuy-Diniz (1987). "Imperial Re-organization 1750–1808," in Bethell, pp. 244–83.

Simonsen, R. C. (1967). *História Econômica do Brasil (1500/1820)*. São Paulo: Companhia Editora Nacional (1st edition, 1937).

Sombra, S. (1938). *História Monetária do Brasil Colonial*. Rio de Janeiro: Laemmert.

Stein, S. J. (1957). *Vassouras. A Brazilian Coffee County, 1850–1900*, Cambridge, Mass.: Harvard University Press.

Straten-Ponthoz, A. van der (1854). *Le Budget du Brésil ou Recherches sur les Ressources de cet Empire dans leurs Rapports avec les Intérêts Européens du Commerce et de l' Émigration*, Tome premier. Paris: Librairie d'Amyot.

Trigueiros, F. dos Santos (1987). *Dinheiro no Brasil*. Rio de Janeiro: Léo Christiano Editorial.

Turnor, T. (1674). *The Case of the Bankers and Their Creditors Stated and Examined*. London.

U.S. Department of Commerce. Bureau of the Census (1975). *Bicentennial Edition. Historical Statistics of the United States. Colonial Times to 1970*, Washington, D.C.: Government Printing Office.

Varnhagem, F. A. de (1962). *História Geral do Brasil*. São Paulo: Melhoramentos.

Veiga Filho, J. P. da (1898). *Manual da Sciencia das Finanças*. São Paulo: Typ. da Companhia Industrial de São Paulo.

Viana, V. (1922). *Histórico da Formação Econômica do Brasil*. Rio de Janeiro: Imprensa Nacional.

Walsh, R. (1830). *Notices of Brazil in 1828 and 1829*. London: Frederick Westley and A. H. Davis.

Wolff, E. and F. Wolf (1991). *Quantos Judeus estiveram no Brasil Holandês? e outros Ensaios*. Rio de Janeiro: Private edition.

Wyndham, H. (1889). Reports on the Finances, Commerce and Agriculture of Brazil for the years 1887 and 1888 (compiled by Mr. Gough). *British Parliamentary Papers*, vol. 78, no. 504. London.

11

Argentina: From Colony to Nation

Fiscal and Monetary Experience of the Eighteenth and Nineteenth Centuries

Roberto Cortés Conde and George T. McCandless

11.1 INTRODUCTION

The development of economic institutions in Argentina was driven both by factors particular to the conditions of the region and to the structure of the viceroyalty from which Argentina grew and by economic pressures of a larger scale. For this reason, our chapter contains two parts comprising Sections 11.2 to 11.8. The first is a detailed discussion of the conflicts and pressures inherent in the economic structures and institutions of the colonial administration and of the attempts by the new nation, Argentina, to mold these institutions into, or replace them by, something more consistent with the emerging realities. The sources of these new institutions are of primary interest. The second, consisting of Section 11.9, presents a formalized dynamic economic/political model that is intended to highlight some of the claims of the first part. In particular, the importance of distance and the ability of the government to collect and utilize taxes and to deliver services are shown to be sufficient to generate outcomes that mimic the main flow of much of Argentina's economic history.

11.2 THE IMPERIAL ADMINISTRATION (1620–1776)

The Spanish brought to America the institutions they knew from Castilla, which they had developed over the centuries of the Reconquest. In the vast New World, these institutions changed as a result of a variety of circumstances, important among which were those that resulted from the nature of the resources that the Spanish encountered.

The Spanish colonization of America had traits distinct from that of the other European powers. While the political, religious, and cultural

Roberto Cortés Conde is responsible for Sections 11.1 to 11.8 and George T. McCandless for Section 9.

traditions of Spain undoubtedly left their stamp on the institutional structure of the colonies, possibly more important was the peculiar geographical characteristics of the natural resources of the region. The population settlements, the location of economic activity and of urban centers, and the administrative and fiscal policies were all conditioned on the exploitation of the silver deposits of Nueva España (Mexico) and Alto Peru (Bolivia). The discovery of the world's richest silver deposits (in an epoch when silver served as specie) determined that economic activity would center on the locations where these deposits were found, almost independent of the inconveniences that these locations presented. Since the deposits were found in locations far from coasts and ports – in the Mexican central mesas and the Bolivian altiplano – the Spanish were forced to construct an extended transport network and, along with it, a system of cities to serve both as waypoints on the long journeys[1] and as production centers to provision the mining areas and to supply transport and commerce.

The natural resources and rights to Indian labor were legally the property of the Crown. In addition, the Crown controlled the international trading monopoly. The Crown never did exploit these directly, but conceded rights to intermediaries in exchange for tax payments to the Crown (at various times a tenth or a fifth of output in the case of silver). The Crown was forced to construct an administrative mechanism to ensure the accurate collection and delivery of the mining tax revenue, Indian labor, and the flow of international trade and its accompanying tax revenues.

The Spanish established a system in America that, although it had been designed at the time of the Reconquista, was shaped by the enormous distances they encountered there. The Spanish vocation for centralized policy making did not fit in well with the distances and difficulties of communication and transport presented by the New World.

Over time, the empire that was created to provide wealth for the Crown generated increasing costs of administration. The colonial bureaucracy (different from that of English America) did not receive its income from the metropolis, but was expected to find it from the areas it administered. It is not surprising that the revenue that was left over after expenses and was passed on to the Crown declined over time (the most notorious case was that of the Rio de la Plata). This decline in revenues was one of the main reasons behind the Bourbon reforms of the eighteenth century.

Only the fantastic richness of mineral resources such as silver permitted the continued existence from the sixteenth to the eighteenth

[1] Cortés Conde (1982).

centuries, in the conditions that existed then, of such vast administrative entities. The government was not created to administer for a colony of farmers, but rather to exploit, supply, and defend the world's richest silver mines.

11.3 THE EMPIRE'S PERIPHERY: THE VICEROYALTY OF THE RIO DE LA PLATA (1776–1810)

Types of Taxes

Founded in 1776, the Viceroyalty of the Rio de la Plata was established to stop the expansion of the Portuguese on the east bank of the Rio de la Plata[2] and included the ancient *intendencias* of Buenos Aires, Cordoba, Tucuman, Alto Peru, and Cuyo.[3] It had many characteristics of the rest of the colonial administration, but some particular ones as well. This new entity embraced regions with fiscal resources of different origins. In the mountain region (the north), income came mainly from mining and from coining money. In the lowlands (the littoral and the south), most income came from taxes on commerce (the *almojarifazgos* and *alcabalas*). The lack of agricultural development in the southern part of America meant that income from this source was very poor. Smaller, but still important, were the taxes (direct tribute and labor) paid by the indigenous populations. The principal sources of income were:

1. the tenth. This was originally a fifth that was paid to the Crown for the silver mine concessions. In response to the labor shortage that began in the seventeenth century and increased costs, the fifth was reduced to a tenth, *el diezmo*. Since much of the earlier labor was forced indigenous labor (the *mita*), some fraction of the fifth should be considered a payment by the mine concessionaires for the use of the indigenous labor and, as such, a tax paid by the native populations to the Crown through labor service. The Crown received additional revenue through seigniorage gained from the coining of money in the Casa de Moneda in Potosi.
2. tribute from the indigenous populations. A head tax assigned to each member of a village or tribe and paid either individually or communally.
3. *alcabalas*. This tax has had long-lasting consequences in the Rio de la Plata. Its origin is from Castilla in Spain. It is a tax that the Crown did not need to have approved by the Spanish Parliament. In principle, it was treated as a sales tax and, as a consequence,

[2] Lynch (1958). [3] Lynch (1958).

should have been paid where the sale took place. This was not, in fact, the case. The practice, and the at times contradictory colonial rules, converted the *alcabala* into a tax on the entry and exit of merchandise.[4] The ad valorem tax varied with time. Repeated payments at the frontiers of the viceroyalty and at the towns where trades took place resulted in very high prices, contraband, and multiple protests and conflicts, especially when the tax rate was increased.[5] They were, as Levene argued, notoriously damaging.[6] The *alcabala* not only permanently raised the specie price of commodities – which is a classic characteristic of mining economies – but also helped sustain, along with the great distances and the high costs of transportation, the existence of segmented markets. That the *alcabala* lasted so long demonstrates that there were few income alternatives in a society where agriculture was practically absent, where livestock raising was quite primitive, and where the principal economic activity consisted of trading between the mining centers and the ports. In Potosi, the main sources of government revenues were the silver tax and indigenous tribute. In Salta, there was tribute, but the revenues from the *alcabala* were much more important. In Cordoba, there was only the *alcabala*. In the south in Buenos Aires, mining revenue and tribute were unimportant; instead, the main revenue sources were import duties on external trade.

Local government revenues in Potosi came mainly from mining and, in Buenos Aires, from the taxes on external trade. Local government in the rest of the Viceroyalty of the Rio de la Plata depended on the *alcabala* for its sustenance and to pay its officials.

4. *almojarifazgo*. This was a tax on imports that Buenos Aires collected along with the *alcabala*. There existed other taxes similar to those in Spain, such as the sale of public offices and ecclesiastical charges, which were much less important than the three mentioned previously. In addition, there was a set of lesser taxes charged by the municipalities. The government also obtained

[4] Santos Martinez (1961). [5] Levene (1940).

[6] "The tax of *alcabalas*, contrary to what was clamored for in Spain, had disastrous effects on America," noting that the interpretation of the decree of 1877 that had abolished the tax had resulted in the opposite: instead of getting 3 percent of the tax collected in Buenos Aires when the goods were intended for the interior, the *Superintendente de la Real Hacienda* determined that the Customs House of Buenos Aires should meet the 3 percent of the tax of first sale (without the sale having occurred), and if the goods were transported to the interior, it should collect a 4 percent *alcabala* in the frontier provinces and 6 percent in the rest.

income, but nothing substantial, from the sale of monopolies: tobacco, playing cards, gunpowder, and so on.

In general, the annual income of the Viceroyalty of the Rio de la Plata was less than that of New Spain and similar to that of Peru.

11.3.1 The Administration of Taxes

The organization of the colonial administration had characteristics that had enduring consequences for the Rio de la Plata region. The Ordenanza de Intendentes divided the fiscal administration into *intendances* with principal and subordinate offices. These offices collected taxes to be remitted to the Crown and, at the same time, to pay for their own expenses and those of local functionaries (principally the military). Once the local expenses were covered, the rest was forwarded to a central office, which first paid its own expenses and forwarded what remained to the Crown. Although these treasury offices did not have authority to spend without approval of the Crown, given the distances and local needs, it is probable that they were able to have more autonomy than was prescribed in the regulations. They had this autonomy because they did not depend on funds sent from Spain, but rather on funds that they raised themselves. Given such local autonomy, the fraction of the revenues that were spent locally grew over time.

It was the *alcabala* and the possibility of collecting and spending the revenues raised by it that gave autonomy to local authorities. Later, it was the *alcabala* that served as the fiscal base for the provincial governments. Once they gained independence from Spain, the local authorities maintained the *alcabala*, which they called import and export taxes, and it was this tax that constituted the fiscal foundations of the federalist system.

11.3.2 Buenos Aires, a Government Subsidized from Outside the Region

The two main treasury offices (*cajas*) were in Potosi and Buenos Aires, and at the end of the eighteenth century they had similar levels of income (over 1 million pesos). However, the expenses of Buenos Aires were greater than its income, so that even before the creation of the Viceroyalty of the Rio de la Plata, it received *subsidios* (transfers) from the Caja de Potosi. In both areas, the principal government expenditures were for the bureaucracy, and in the Rio de la Plata most of these bureaucratic expenses were military. These additional expenses came from the need to defend the frontiers of the Banda Oriental against the

Portuguese and in the south against the indians. During the period of the viceroyalty, the lowlands ran permanent deficits relative to the mountain region.[7]

Those living in the highland regions of Upper Peru in the north did not see themselves benefiting directly from the military expenditures of the Buenos Aires region. While the highland region did receive many benefits from the Spanish imperial system, mainly in subsidized mercury, indian labor, and a transit system that protected the flow of goods both to and from Spain, these were not generally perceived as coming from Buenos Aires. While the defense of the Buenos Aires area from the Portuguese was part of the larger imperial strategy, it brought no clear, direct benefits to those paying the taxes in Potosi. This conflict between taxes and perceived benefits was to become one of the main reasons for the breakup at independence of the viceroyalty.

The southern lowlands lived mainly by trade, and the system of consumption taxes and *alcabala* fell heavily on them, so they fought against these taxes and the trade monopolies and argued for free trade. The Upper Peru highlands, including the cities of western Argentina that lived by supplying the city and mines of Potosi, opposed freer international or internal trade as a threat to their revenues and production.

When the Napoleonic invasions cut off governmental services from the Spanish Empire and provoked the crisis of monarchal allegiance, the two regions responded differently. The Rio de la Plata opted for independence. The highlands, which were still more attached to the ancient viceroyalty of Peru and the production system it provided, stayed loyal.[8]

In his excellent study of the finances of the Viceroyalty of the Rio de la Plata, Klein concluded that although it was second in importance to New Spain, the viceroyalty of the Rio de la Plata did not generate significant profits for the Royal Treasury in Madrid. However, since the viceroyalty did not run deficits, the Crown was able to maintain its control of the south of the continent without drawing on resources from the metropolis.

Nonetheless, he added, the viceroyalty at the end of the eighteenth century did not present itself as a united country. When "a proportion

[7] There were repeated accusations of corruption, generated in part by a very imperfect system of accounts, by the variety and diversity of taxes, by the great distances, and by the excessive fiscal burden of a system with multiple and repeated taxes. As the needs of the public treasury translated into a tax burden, which became more and more insupportable, the opportunity costs of violating the laws declined. As smuggling became common, the costs fell even more.

[8] Alvarez (1936).

so high of its income was assigned to pay for the coastal defenses and fortifications against the indians, one can conclude that Upper Peru was being taxed beyond reason, for the lower regions. Upper Peru needed neither the coastal installations nor the port, could trade through Lima, and had its own Audiencia and Casa de Moneda." In this case, Klein concluded, "one can argue that the cost of being a part of the Viceroyalty was excessive for Upper Peru given the minimum defense it received."[9]

The preceding conflicts led to the breakup of the viceroyalty of the Rio de la Plata once the Spanish authority was removed. Not only that, they contributed greatly to the fiscal and political problems of the emerging nation of Argentina.

11.3.3 The Monetary Regime

Alvarez says that "in the epoch of the Viceroyalty, similar to what had occurred since the discovery and conquest, there were in use coins and money of account, but the last had lost the importance that they had when an almost absolute lack of a numeraire forced people to make transactions measured in terms of common goods: yards of linen, iron wedges, etc. Coins, which were characterized as today by weight and by law, had as their basic standard the mark and the half-pound (230.0465 grams) and the doubloon. The doubloon was divided into 24 quilates of gold and 12 dineros for silver."[10] The most common gold coins were the ounce or doubloon of eight (later pelucona) that was equal to $17.08 of gold, although later the Crown reduced the gold content to $16.03. Silver coins were the principal circulating medium in America, "since these could be produced from the production of its mines."[11] The most common silver coins were the real and its multiples: the real of two (the peseta), real of four (the half peso), and real of eight (the peso, an ounce of silver). Fluctuating over time, between 16 and 17 silver pesos were equivalent to one gold peso (one ounce of gold).

Alvarez says that "neither copper coins nor the paper money that circulated in Spain under the name of *vales reales* found popular acceptance in the Rio de la Plata."[12] One of the major differences between the American colonies of Great Britain and the Rio de la Plata (and, for that matter, the rest of Spanish America) was the lack of paper money issued either by the government or by banks in the latter. The monetary regime was bimetallic, but the money in common use was the peso, the money of eight reales of silver.

[9] Klein (1973). [10] Alvarez (1940), p. 235.
[11] Juan Alvarez, "Monedas, pesas y medidas," p. 238.
[12] Juan Alvarez, "Monedas, pesas y medidas," p. 243.

In the early years of the conquest and in various regions isolated from commercial traffic during much of the colonial period, money of the earth (*moneda de la tierra*) was used popularly. *Moneda de la tierra* consisted of goods in common use that served as units of account: yards of linen, for example.

11.4 FROM COLONY TO NATION: THE DECADE OF REVOLUTION (1810–20)

From the end of the eighteenth century, the Spanish regime in South America underwent repeated crises. During the rebellion of Tupac Amaru, Buenos Aires did not receive any subsidies from Upper Peru and had to learn to survive without them. The government at Buenos Aires made successive concessions liberalizing commerce and permitting trade with various neutral powers. These concessions produced a notable increase in tariff revenues that themselves suffered from the fortunes of the war that the European powers waged on the high seas. Extraordinary expenses, such as those associated with the English invasion, put pressure on a fiscal regime that the authorities could not bring into balance under the new events. Their victory at Trafalgar left the British in control of the Atlantic and, accordingly, reduced commercial traffic with metropolitan Spain. Afflicted by these circumstances, Viceroy Baltasar Hidalgo de Cisneros, in 1809, authorized commerce with Great Britain, which by then had become an ally of the revolutionary authorities of Spain that were resisting the Napoleonic occupation.

In May 1810, Buenos Aires broke away from what remained of this government and set up its own. This rupture had diverse consequences. From the very beginning, various regions of the old viceroyalty did not accept the authority of Buenos Aires. Among these were the Banda Oriental de Uruguay, Paraguay, and, most important of all, Upper Peru, with its mines at Potosi. Except for a brief occupation by part of the army of Buenos Aires, the separation from Upper Peru was definitive. Buenos Aires had lost its income from the mines. The revolutionary government (*junta*) authorized free trade in Buenos Aires with ships flying any flag and this increased tariff revenues, although the increase was not enough to compensate for the loss of Potosi. As an expression of its liberal ideals, the government at Buenos Aires abolished the indian tributes. On the other hand, it maintained its colonial privilege on the monopoly of international trade and its right to tax this trade.

The separation of Upper Peru resulted in a severe monetary contraction. This contraction was aggravated, in some years, by the war with the royal forces, which impeded the flow of commerce with Upper Peru and Chile that normally produced significant inflows of silver. The revolutionary government was forced to raise armies in the north, in Paraguay, and in the Banda Oriental. They could not cover these military expenditures with the income from trade taxes and looked for other sources of revenue. They resorted to loans – some voluntary, most forced – and to the confiscation of the property of enemies (mainly Spanish merchants). The debt issues took on, at times, the characteristics of quasi-money and circulated, although by all accounts in a very limited fashion.

In spite of its enormous difficulties, the government did not resort to inflationary financing (as had the revolutionary governments of the United States and France). There were no significant changes in the administration of tax, although the Treasury at Buenos Aires became the National Treasury, to which were attached, with functions of taxing and disbursement, the Customs House of Buenos Aires (increasingly charged with paying the public debt), the armies on campaign, and the provincial treasuries.

11.4.1 The Provincial Treasuries

Although little is known about the functioning of the provincial treasuries in the decade of the revolution (Maeder has written about the treasury of Corrientes),[13] it is probable that they continued providing the support for local functionaries (those who did not depend on the income of the Cabildos) and of the military forces.

While the central government (*junta*) in Buenos Aires was supported by the income from foreign trade, the authorities of the interior lived off the income from the *alcabalas* on incoming and outgoing merchandise. These *alcabalas* (not municipal taxes) were the main sources of income for the provincial governments that developed from each major interior city.[14]

The bureaucracies of the interior defended these sources of income, from which they had subsisted since colonial times. In the following decade, after the failure of some attempts (such as that in San Juan) to replace these taxes with a property tax, not only was the *alcabala* on domestic trade reaffirmed, but since it did not raise sufficient funds, the provinces called for participation in the income of the Customs House at Buenos Aires. The centralized structure of the viceroyalty had left open the opportunity for the local bureaucracies to sustain themselves with the revenue from the taxes on interior trade.

In a country with little agricultural development and a ranching industry that was difficult to evaluate and tax, but with considerable commercial activity based on supplying the mining activities of Upper Peru, taxes on internal trade were probably very efficient. While the

[13] Maeder (1981). [14] Zorraquín Becú (1953).

revenue these taxes generated was minuscule relative to the revenues earned from external trade, it was indispensable for the survival of the local bureaucracies. From this need arose the later battles over sources of fiscal revenues.

A regime based on the collection of taxes on mining and on internal commerce (*alcabalas*) restricted, in the following periods, the formation of markets and the economic development of the country.

11.4.2 The Monetary Regime

The war in the north not only resulted in loss of control of the revenues of the mines of Potosi, but also produced a general shortage of money. The governments of what had been the Viceroyalty of the Rio de la Plata tried a number of isolated, failed attempts to coin money and, in a few instances and with limited acceptance, circulated debased or fraudulent coins (the peso of Guemes, for example).[15] When the war was truly ended and trade connections were reestablished, the money in common usage was again silver, mainly the boliviano of eight reales. There was also limited circulation of quasi-monies: bonds of the government and of the Caja de Fondos de Sud America.[16] Proper banks did not exist.

11.5 THE CONFEDERATION OF THE PROVINCES (1820–52)

11.5.1 The Province of Buenos Aires in Five Years of Progress (1820–5)

In 1820 the national government collapsed, and Buenos Aires had to confront the problems that arose from its defeat and to form a provincial government. Although the Army of the North, which Juan Bautista Bustos had led into rebellion and which had followed him to his province of Cordoba, had disappeared, military expenses were still heavy. The period from 1820 to 1825 was the longest period of peace during the turbulent years just after independence. This peace permitted the authorities to bring some order to the fiscal accounts and to implement some important reforms. For the first time, the government produced an income and expenditure budget. Taxes on international trade were the most important source of revenue, and although the tax rates were lowered, in spite of fiscal necessities and pressure from protectionist interests, the tax on imports ranged from 15 to 30 percent, with goods that competed directly with those produced in the country taxed at 25 percent.

A new property tax was implemented, but this encountered serious opposition from landowners and raised insignificant amounts of revenue,

[15] Segreti (1975). [16] Amaral (1988).

chiefly because a good land assessment did not exist and turned out to be very difficult to implement.

One important innovation was the organization of the public debt through the institution of the office of Crédito Público, which was designed on the basis of the English experience of the seventeenth century. The Province of Buenos Aires assumed the obligations that the national government had contracted before 1820 and guaranteed these and future issues. It also created the Caja de Amortizacion to pay off this debt and assigned it the income from a variety of sources.

One important commercial innovation was the opening of the Banco de Buenos Aires, a bank of deposits and discounts on which the government bestowed a monopoly on the issue of bank notes and various fiscal privileges. This bank, although private, served as the financial agent for the government. The government deposited the funds from the Barings loan of 1824 in the coffers of this bank and used them to discount commercial paper. The first Argentine monetary expansion did not come about from government financing practices, but rather from credit issued to the private sector. Only in the latter part of this inflationary period did the government increase its operations with the bank. In January 1826, the government withdrew all of its metallic reserves from the bank, decreed its bank notes inconvertible, guaranteed those notes, and absorbed the bank into the new Banco Nacional.

11.5.2 The War with Brazil and the Internal Wars (1826–8)

The war with Brazil initiated a period of terrible fiscal disorder. It produced an extraordinary increase in expenditures and a dramatic fall in income from the Customs House (see Figure 11.1). The expenses increased because of the formation of an army that was much bigger than any that had existed during the War of Independence and that had to be supplied outside of the national territory. On the other hand, the successful Brazilian blockade of the port of Buenos Aires in 1826 caused tariff revenues for that year to virtually disappear.

The government used funds from the Barings loan, which had originally been designated for the construction of the port at Buenos Aires, appropriated the reserves of the Banco de Buenos Aires, made use of the inconvertible bank notes, and, after 1826, used issues of the newly created Banco Nacional (with which it had replaced the Banco de Buenos Aires) that acted as its treasury. These note issues, along with forced loans, provided the necessary funds. So began a long period of inflationary financing in the province.[17]

[17] Amaral (1988).

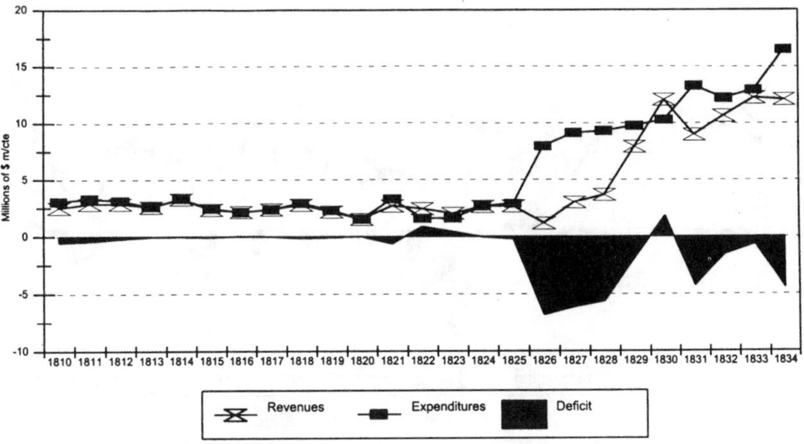

Figure 11.1 National Treasury and Buenos Aires, 1810–34.

Sources: Amaral (1988); Miron Burgin, *Aspectos económicos del Federalismo Argentino* (Buenos Aires: Hachette, 1960); *Extracto Estadístico de la República Argentina correspondiente al año 1915* (Buenos Aires: Compañía Sudamericana, 1916); Tulio Halperin Donghi, *Guerra y Finanzas en los orígenes del estado argentino (1791–1850)* (Buenos Aires: Editorial de Belgrano, 1982); Juan Carlos Nicolau, *La reforma económico-financiera de la Provincia de Buenos Aires (1821–1825) liberalismo y economía* (Buenos Aires: Fundación Banco Provincia de Buenos Aires, 1988); *Registros Estadísticos del Estado de Buenos Aires, Republica Argentina* (Direccíon General de Estadística de la Nación); Adolfo Saldías, *Historia dela Confederación Argentina*, vol. 4 (Buenos Aires: La Facultad, 1911).

The great innovation was the appearance of bank notes. The convertible bank notes issued by the Banco de Descuento or Banco de Buenos Aires circulated in the territory of the province. In the interior, Bolivian and Chilean silver coins continued to circulate.

11.5.3 The Finances of Rosas (1830–52)

The status of the provincial finances was critical in 1830 when Juan Manuel de Rosas first became governor. There had been attempts to organize the public debt and, under his predecessor, Juan José Viamonte, in 1829, there had been a failed attempt to return to convertibility (in a way that would have caused serious deflation and, for that reason, was resisted). Up to 1831, Buenos Aires was at war with a coalition of interior provinces. In 1832 and 1833, the deficit declined and the exchange rate stabilized. In 1835, Rosas returned to power as governor of the province, promising an orderly administration. At least in principle, he seems to have fulfilled this promise, for there was a surplus during 1835 and 1836, though not in the years that followed. In 1837, a new conflict began, this time with Bolivia, and the negative consequences of this

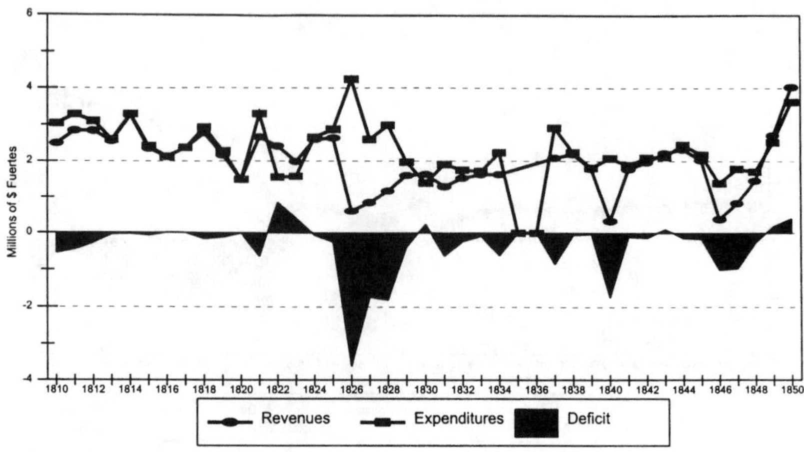

Figure 11.2 National Treasury and Buenos Aires, 1815–50. Pesos Fuertes.

Source: See Figure 11.1.

war on the budget were aggravated by the French blockade and Juan Lavalle's military uprising against Governor Rosas. It was, above all, the blockade that caused the new drop in income from the Customs House. So began the distinctly inflationary period of Rosas's administration. From here on, the deficits of the treasury were covered by note issues of the Casa de Moneda (see Figure 11.2).

11.5.4 The Relations between Rosas and the Provinces of the Interior

There were repeated proposals for organizing the country and the division between the provinces of the income of the Customs House of Buenos Aires (which had been nationalized briefly during the presidency of Bernardino Rivadavia in 1825 but which had then returned to the control of the province). These proposals were obstinately resisted by Rosas, who would not think of giving up these revenues. Rosas formed alliances with some of the poor provincial governments, not only because of his superior military power, but also because some of these governments were dependent on subsidies from Buenos Aires. Although these alliances were offered with extreme prudence, they did save some governments from extremely embarrassing situations. Perhaps the most severely dependent province was Santa Fe, which served as a pivot for control of the littoral and the center of the country. This technique, as seen from the results of three decades, was probably less costly for Buenos Aires than giving up control of the income from the Customs House and allowing the local governments a greater level

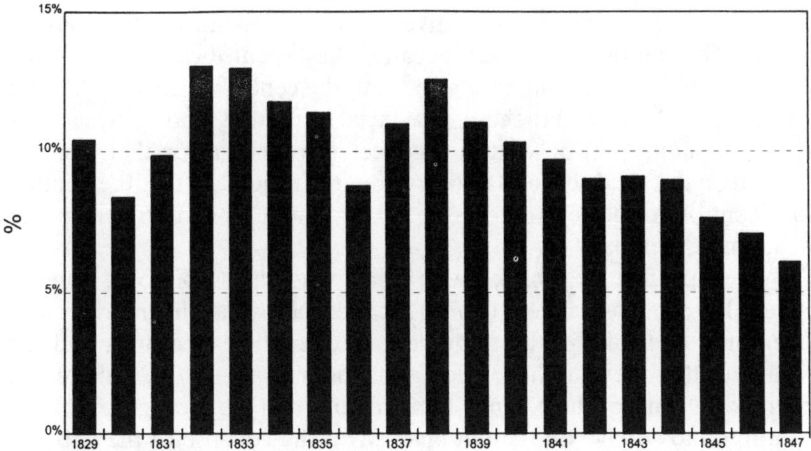

Figure 11.3 Interest rates, 1829–49.

Source: Miron Burgin, *Aspectos económicos del Federalismo Argentino* (Buenos Aires: Hachette, 1960).

of autonomy (although they would always be subordinate to Buenos Aires).

The government used the Casa de Moneda as a treasury and, with legislative authorization (which was not difficult to get for those who had essentially dictatorial power), ordered it to issue legal paper money anytime it was needed to cover a fiscal deficit. These issues were highly correlated with the decline of income that resulted from the blockades.

The note issues of the Casa de Moneda occurred in the period 1837–40 and especially in 1846, so that by the end of 1846, the issue totaled 125 million pesos corrientes compared to a total issue of 14 million pesos corrientes in 1836. This produced an enormous depreciation in paper money so that, compared to the old exchange rate, in which one paper peso equaled one of silver, by 1846 one paper peso equaled five centavos of silver.

As noted in Figure 11.3, from 1829 to 1840, the very high rate of interest implied a return on provincial public debt that reflected a very high rate of risk. This must have had a negative effect on investment and economic activity.

11.5.5 The Consolidation of the Autonomous Provinces

The rise of the provinces, out of the principal colonial cities and the regions that surrounded them, which took place with the rupture of the legitimate monarchy that had kept the Viceroyalty of the Rio de la Plata together, was nothing more than the continuation of fiscal administrations that had already been relatively autonomous during the colonial period. That autonomy existed because they spent locally most of the revenues that they should have sent on to the central government. Klein and Maeder[18] show that these provincial treasuries and subtreasuries spent the major part of what they collected from taxes on their personnel and on the local civil and military administrations, so that the net that they sent on to the central treasury was insignificant (5 to 6 percent for Salta and Cordoba).

When in 1820 they broke with Spain and the Cabildo of Buenos Aires elected a government (*junta*) for the viceroyalty, the interior cities attempted to maintain the same control over their treasuries and the resources that they had had, by default, under Spain. By 1820, there had been no reforms of the colonial fiscal regime, and the local governments continued to survive on the old taxes. With the collapse of the national government in that year, various provinces proclaimed their right to autonomy and assumed control of government, the war, and the management of their own finances.

At the beginning of the 1820s there were various financial reforms. The provinces could not impose taxes on property or income (direct taxes) given the rudimentary nature of their economies, which comprised basically ranching with scattered agriculture. In agriculture, where the population is sedentary and works the whole year on the same piece of land, evaluation of that land and collection of taxes are relatively easy. In an economy of rudimentary and nomadic ranching, resources are more difficult to find, to measure, and to tax. Confronted with these problems, provincial governments maintained the taxes on the entrance and exit of goods. In reality, they merely continued the ancient *alcabala*.

Centers of tax collection, originally headquarters of the colonial *intendantes*, multiplied at each city with a subtreasury that claimed autonomy, in spite of the fact that their revenues were very different. Some provinces, such as Cordoba and Corrientes, had moderate levels of income. Others, such as Santa Fe, were chronically poor. However, the sum total of the income of all the other provinces did not reach the level of that of Buenos Aires (see Figure 11.4).

The geography of the country, which in colonial times had been Mediterranean and had looked to Potosi, changed at independence and condemned all the other cities to be subordinate to the one with the port to the high seas on the estuary of the Rio de la Plata. The distances, the high costs of the rustic forms of transport, and the diverse interests

[18] Klein (1973) and Maeder (1981).

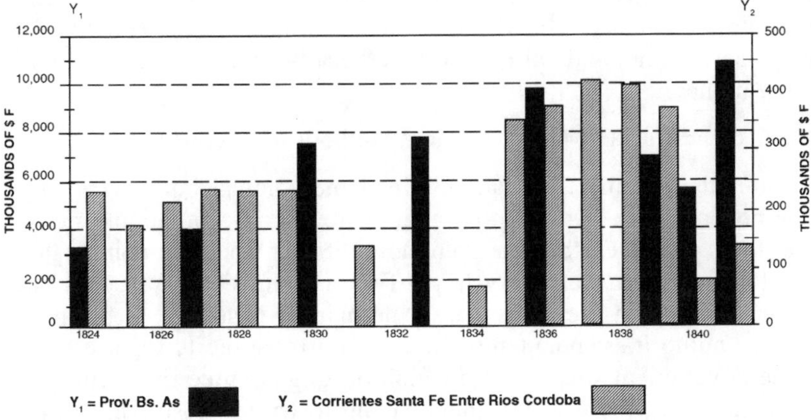

Figure 11.4 Provincial revenues, 1824–40.

Source: See Figure 11.1.

provoked political and fiscal fragmentation. The internal customs duties further raised the costs of goods already burdened by huge transportation costs and helped keep provincial markets small and fragmented. All these problems speeded up the decline of the interior of the country with respect to Buenos Aires, which had access to international markets.

This fragmentation was the source of the numerous conflicts that poverty made interminable, given that no one had sufficient power or ability to swing the balance of power definitely to his side. The war was a permanent source of expenditures that were sometimes covered by tax revenues, other times by debt issue, a few times by domestic currency but mostly by hard currencies, and finally by that anachronistic tax, confiscation. In addition, the interior provinces did not have access to inflationary financing. On the one hand, although the scarcity of cash was general, there did exist fractional silver money from positive trade balances with neighboring countries such as Bolivia and Chile that occurred any time the civil war moved elsewhere. On the other hand, the lack of confidence and the general weakness of the provincial governments led to failure any time they attempted to issue paper money (the Banco Hipotecario of the Coalición del Norte, for example), although there were in circulation debased coins that had been produced by various provincial governments.[19] These restrictions obliged the provincial governments of the interior to resort to

[19] Segreti (1975).

obsolete methods. The fiscal accounts of the provincial governments were better balanced, on the one hand, because they accounted for loans as income and, on the other, because they could not issue paper money.

11.5.6 *Caudillos* and Their Obsolete Methods of Financing

Without the income that had sustained the colonial bureaucracy, the new governments were in no condition to exercise monopoly power over their provinces; this was even more difficult when the regions they had to administer were very large. The enormous empty spaces and distances between the cities were a permanent challenge to the post-colonial authorities and a temptation, often irresistible, to replace them. If the government was not in a condition to guarantee the security of the inhabitants, there were others willing to try to do so. These were strongmen, local *caudillos*, who, within a limited sphere of influence, provided the functions of government and for which they extracted other forms of payment. For the centralized authorities, the costs of providing security were so high that in practice they were ineffective. The breakup of the viceroyalty that followed independence produced division and ambiguities about the locations of frontiers. Internal and external conflicts followed in succession almost without interruption, and the expenses of war absorbed most of the budgets. The *caudillos* appeared almost inevitable when survival of the government depended on them. They faced no restrictions when the opportunity cost they offered was complete submission or loss of life. It is probable that those who helped or financed the various sides of the conflicts expected high returns on their expenditures given the risks that they were running. While the conflicts continued, confidence in the ability of the government to survive was in doubt, and this had predictable effects on the government's ability to collect taxes and to issue debt. These circumstances made forms of government such as that of the *caudillo*, with reduced dimensions, low costs of exercising effective power, and the lowest costs of social decision making the most viable. In economies that had turned predominantly rural, with minimal circulation of money, it was much more difficult to pay taxes. Here one returns to the situation where taxes were paid in kind and where a *caudillo* formed an army, almost private, from the workers of his ranch, mounted on his own horses and fed from his own livestock. This made the authority of the *caudillos* even more effective. These were rural chiefs who pillaged these resources but who, as has often been the case in centralized governments, confused the public budget with that of their own household.

11.6 THE PACT OF SAN NICOLAS (1853–61)

With the fall of Rosas, the Pact of San Nicolas introduced fundamental reforms in the finances of the nation and the provinces that made the nation-state viable. The external customs houses became the property of the nation, and the *alcabalas*, the internal customs on which the provincial governments had depended, were abolished. The Constitution of 1853 (Article 4) confirmed these points.

11.6.1 The Confederation and Buenos Aires

The formula worked out at San Nicolas and recorded in the Constitution of 1853 (Article 4) was intended to solve the problem of the fiscal organization of the Argentine nation. The province of Buenos Aires was not satisfied with this formula, which converted its capital city and port into a separate federal district and the capital of the Republic. Buenos Aires rebelled against the central government, refused to accept the Constitution of 1853, and for almost 10 years remained separated from the rest of the nation, continuing successfully its control over the Customs House. For this reason, except for the years 1859 and 1861, when armed conflict broke out, the administration of the Customs House was relatively orderly.

The federal government moved to Parana in Entre Rios and went through difficult times. Under the constitution, it was left with the income of the customs from river trade and from the foreign trade of land at Cuyo (Mendoza) and in the north,[20] which were far from producing income of the magnitude of Buenos Aires.

According to Marichal, the total tax income of the Confederation between 1854 and 1857 ranged from 1.5 million to 2.3 million silver pesos. Buenos Aires alone (the city and the province were one) had annual tax income between 1856 and 1860 of around 3 million pesos fuertes (equal to 1 million pesos of silver).[21]

The fiscal regime of San Nicolas was even more difficult for many of the interior provinces. The direct taxes on property and profits were not able to compensate for the loss of income from the *alcabalas*. Many of these provincial economies were still too rudimentary for these taxes to earn much revenue. In spite of its own difficulties, the federal government attempted to aid some of these provinces.

The government of the Confederation tried to compensate for the lack of tax income by borrowing through banks such as the branch of

[20] Marichal (1995). [21] Marichal (1995).

the Brazilian Mauá Bank, or through financial agents like Bushenthal, selling bonds, with little success to the public or trying to charter a bank of issue, a project that also failed.

11.6.2 The Monetary Regime

In the interior, the principal circulating money consisted of Bolivian silver coins that were used as the unit of account for the sporadic issues of bank notes that some provinces attempted. Still, the unit of account in official use was the silver peso, equal to the ancient peso of eight reals and the hard peso (peso fuerte) of Buenos Aires.

In Buenos Aires, a number of distinct money issues circulated, all with legal tender. In 1854, Buenos Aires opened a bank of the state, the Banco de la Provincia de Buenos Aires, which accepted deposits and discounted notes but which did not initially issue bank notes, a facility it obtained in 1866 during the war with Paraguay when the National government accepted its metallic notes.

Still, to help pay for the expenses of the war with the Confederation, between 1859 and 1861, the provincial government resorted to a number of note issues that raised the total circulation to 300 million pesos corrientes and produced a dramatic depreciation in the paper peso. Its larger tax base and its ability to resort to inflationary financing gave Buenos Aires an advantage against the Confederation, which was permanently on the edge of bankruptcy, and was one of the reasons for its success in the conflict.[22]

11.7 NATIONAL ORGANIZATION (1862–80)

Still, it was the triumph of the Confederation in 1859 and the Pact of San Jose de Flores that in 1860 drove Buenos Aires to accept the Constitution of 1853, with modifications that designated the central government of Buenos Aires as the capital but did pass the customs revenues to the national government.

A true national government was established in 1862, which exercised authority over the entire country. The national government paid five years of annual subsidies of 2 million pesos fuertes (Marichal, 1995) to the province of Buenos Aires in exchange for the right to customs duties. The province reduced its expenses because it no longer needed to support the army, which was now supported by the national government, maintain representation in foreign countries, or administer such a wide range of taxes. Both Buenos Aires and the Confederation had incurred

[22] Alvarez (1946).

enormous expenses during their confrontation; the Confederation financed most of these with debt and Buenos Aires with note issue. The national government assumed these obligations, agreeing to amortize the issues of Buenos Aires of 1859 and 1860 and making payments to the province from 1865 on of 5 million pesos fuertes in public bonds. Later, the national government took charge of the debt of the Confederation, paying off the debtors with 7 million pesos fuertes of public bonds. Taking into account that in 1864 total tax revenues of the national government were a bit more than 6 million pesos fuertes, this indicates the importance that the government gave to assuming these debts. As a result, Customs House revenues were ceded to the nation and the long political struggle between the interior provinces and Buenos Aires finally came to an end.

At any rate, the income from the Customs House formed a solid base for the financing of the national government, and during the first administration of Mitre it achieved, for the first time in many decades, a surplus. However, the balanced budgets did not last long. The war with Paraguay and internal conflicts produced huge expenditures that, along with the debts already accumulated, generated even worse budget deficits. The expenditures on war during the administration of Bartolomé Mitre represented some 42 percent of total expenditures, and during the administration of Domingo F. Sarmiento they represented 30 percent. The situation seems even worse if these expenses are compared to tax revenues, of which they represented 51 and 42 percent, respectively. The central government had committed half of its income to activities on which its own existence depended. This all seems even more difficult if one adds the government's obligations on its consolidated debt. The sum of debt payments and payments for the wars represented, during the administration of Mitre, 58 percent of expenditures and 70 percent of income; during the administration of Sarmiento, 38 percent of expenditures and 55 percent of income; and, during the administration of Nicolas Avellaneda, 42 percent of expenditures and 53 percent of income. One can see that for the first presidents of the nation, two-thirds of national income was precommitted and, for the next two, about half of the government's income was already committed. Since what remained could not cover the rest of its expenses, the government could not find a solution other than contracting additional debt. The right to collect Customs House duties, which had been the source of political dispute for so many years, could not guarantee meeting the expenditures of the new national administration. Although the country grew, it did not grow as fast as did central government expenditures. With limited and precommitted income, the first governments relapsed into continuous deficits.

11.7.1 The Monetary Regime, Bank Notes, and Financing of the Deficit

After various decades of inflationary financing in the province of Buenos Aires, the national government was not given the power to issue paper money directly. The government continued to have the right to produce coins, but the right to issue paper money, in the form of convertible notes, was left to banks of issue (authorized by the government once they had provided the appropriate guarantees) in order to provide for good development of business. Note issue was not to be used to cover deficits of the government. Consequently, except for two cases, in 1867 and 1876, government deficits were not monetized. In the two cases where they were, it was done by issuing bank notes in exchange for debt obligations of the government. In this way, the note issue did not result in seigniorage for the government, but rather in extra profits for the banks that received interest-paying assets (the government bonds) in exchange for non-interest-paying debts (the bank notes).

In spite of a federal constitutional prohibition, a provincial constitutional prohibition, and the law of 1863 to the same effect, the Banco Provincial kept issuing metallic notes that circulated at the same time as the notes of the offices of exchange until 1876. After that year, both circulated as legal tender paper money. Without being able to appeal to issuing money, the national government fell back on debt. The government purchased some goods and services directly with bonds issued at par, but given the steep discounts at which the government bonds traded, these suppliers must have overcharged (at least nominally) to cover the discounts. (See Figure 11.5 for a history of interest rates.)

As the gap between tax income and expenditures widened, the debt increased and, in each period that followed, required more debt servicing (see Figure 11.6). Throughout the presidency of Mitre, the difference between income and expenditures was greater than 9 million pesos fuertes (55.93 million $F of expenditures and only 46.23 million $F in tax revenue), mainly because of the war with Paraguay. Under Sarmiento, the deficit took an enormous jump, and from this arose the tremendous problems that Avellaneda had to confront. The difference rose to almost 40 million $F (126 million $F in expenditures and 88 million $F in tax revenue). In the administration of Avellaneda, the difference was reduced through a fall in expenditures, although tax revenues did not grow. Expenditures were 108.83 million $F against 86.49 million $F, so the difference was now 22 million $F. How dramatic was the administrative control of Avellaneda can be understood only if one takes into account that in 1875 expenditures were 49 million $F and by 1877 they were only 14.69 million $F. The payments for debt service between 1875

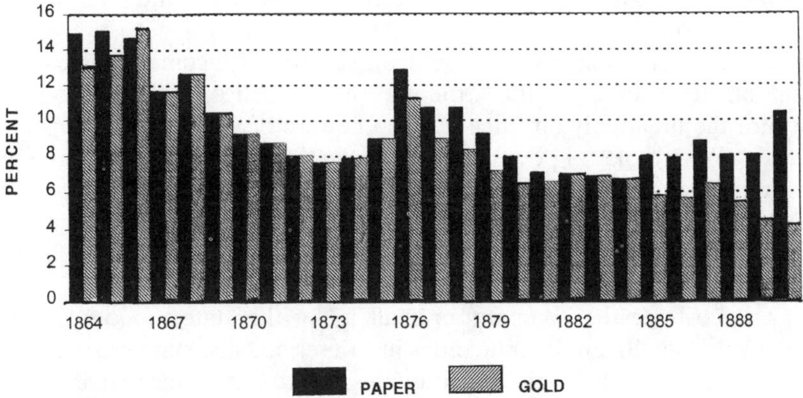

Figure 11.5 Interest rates, 1864–90.

Source: Roberto Cortés-Conde, *Dinero, Deuda y Crisis. Evolución fiscal y monetaria en la Argentina* (Buenos Aires: Editorial Sudamericana, 1989).

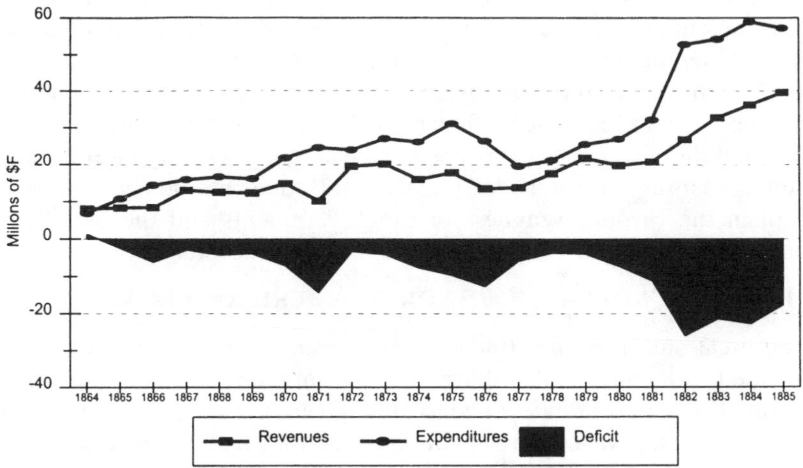

Figure 11.6 National Treasury, 1864–85.

Source: See Figure 11.1.

and 1879 totaled 42.6 million $F, some 7 million $F a year. Annual tax income was steady over this period at about 15 million $F. Debt payments were equal to about 50 percent of tax income.

The rate of growth of public debt, although high, was less than one might expect given the traditionally exaggerated estimates. From 1864 to 1880, it rose 140 percent, for an annual growth rate of 6 percent. The problem was that expenditures during that period rose by 180 percent, for an annual growth rate of 7 percent (in both cases, the data are in constant prices).

Governments that cannot count on sources of income sufficient to support their bureaucratic structure (fiscal, justice, and military) to secure the monopoly on force need to beware of the recurring appearance of other poles of power that challenge their authority and compete for their monopoly. The appearance of these alternative sources of power worsens the situation because they increase expenditure and widen the fiscal deficit, causing a huge increase in the debt, which makes the financial administration of the state practically impossible.

The cost for the competitors challenging the state monopoly was relatively low. Given the difficulties just described, the state was already weak, far away, and with few resources to mobilize. Since challengers raised armed forces with troops and horses from their own establishments, which didn't require money salaries and which lived off the land, their costs were not onerous. In addition, these challenges frequently ended with a compromise solution in which neither side won completely and one of the conditions for the precarious peace was that the national government covered the expenses of its contender. The weight of these obligations was another factor that led to later conflicts.

The enormous territory over which the government claimed the monopoly on the exercise of power, the difficulties of transportation, and regional differences so diverse as to reduce the possibility of efficiency and consensus and to make the national administration very costly, explain the chronic weakness of the governments and the persistent political instability during most of the nineteenth century.

11.8 THE EUROPEAN AND NORTH AMERICAN LEGACY

The fiscal and monetary traditions of the *ancien regime español* were adapted with important modifications in what today is Argentina. Later, during the period of independence, the government tried to adapt, in a pretty chaotic environment, institutions that they had observed in Great Britain and the United States. Systems that had relative success in other locations (the tax collections – those of the Customs House were easy to implement – or bank notes, either under a monopoly regime, as in England, or under a system with multiple banks, as in the United States) were implemented with such distortions that they did not result in orderly public finances or efficient monetary regimes. The poverty of the administration, after the loss of Potosi, condemned it to an almost permanent war against whoever contested its power, forcing these governments to use all the tools available to them to obtain resources. Institutions were established that did not impede access to these resources and were modified whenever it was necessary to obtain more.

The priority of their own immediate survival caused these government to create for themselves problems of intertemporal credibility.

The consolidation of fiscal and monetary institutions, through a complicated and difficult evolution, took almost a century.

The colonial administrative system, before and after the Bourbon reforms, consisted in administrative units of enormous dimensions with a network of urban centers, connecting the resources (the mines) with the port, surrounded by desert. The distances made the costs of administration very high and, for that reason, gave relative financial and administrative autonomy to the administration of the various cities and regions.

The defense of the southern frontiers placed such heavy financial burdens on the mining regions of the north that they were considered illegitimate under the unified monarchy. When the monarchy disappeared, the local authorities decided to control their own resources. The colonial tax system help encourage this separation.

In the north, fiscal resources came from taxes on mining production (the *quinto*, later the *décimo*), on seigniorage, and on the indian tribute. In Buenos Aires, fiscal resources came from taxes on international trade and from a sales tax (the *alcabala*). The *alcabala* was paid not only where the sale was made, but also where the goods entered the viceroyalty, making the tax doubly heavy.[23]

Local subtreasuries (secondary offices) collected the *alcabala*, and although they should have sent it to the central government, they deducted their own expenses, those of the local governmental administration, and those for local military defense. It should not be surprising that an increasingly large percentage of these taxes remained in local hands, and after Buenos Aires separated from Spain, the local administrations (which became the provinces) wanted to take control of all of the funds that they raised. This is the source of the increasing fragmentation of the ancient colonial administrations and of the obstinate effort of each new government to take control of these tax resources, which, poor as they were, constituted their sole source of survival.

Later, in the period from independence until national organization (1810–62), the sources of income were taxes on foreign trade (Buenos Aires being the richest port) and internal trade (in each province where the *alcabala* continued as internal customs duties), later modified to taxes on imports and exports, sales, and goods in transit. Goods were taxed several times, so that along with high costs of transport, internal markets remained segmented for five decades.

Under the Pact of San Nicolas in 1852 and the national Constitution of 1853, the internal customs were suppressed and, in 1862, the Customs

[23] In addition, there was the *almojarifazgo*.

House of Buenos Aires passed to the national government. Under the new constitutional regime, the provinces were left with direct taxes, on wealth and on production (ranching, capital, etc.), that were difficult to collect and generated no little resistance. Under the period of the Confederation, the central government recognized numerous exceptions to the new regime, and the provinces – including Buenos Aires – looked for different forms of *subsidios* to overcome the loss of taxes from the interior customs houses. The new regime (fiscal pact) that divided the functions of the federal and provincial governments permitted the consolidation of the Argentine state beginning in 1862, which still had to resolve other difficulties before settling down in 1880. This order was maintained with relative success until the 1930s, when new important reforms were introduced.

The colonial monetary regime consisted of a bimetallic standard, although in practice it was really a silver standard. There were no paper monies, but in some regions and periods money of the earth (*monedas de la tierra*) was important.

The same monetary standard was in effect during the first decade after independence, but the separation of the north, with the mines of Potosi, and the war produced a severe contraction of the supply of silver and a generalized money shortage. The income from the Customs House in Buenos Aires compensated, but only in part, for the loss of income from Potosi, yet the revolutionary government did not resort to money issue to finance the expenditures of the war. However, they began to utilize some types of quasi-money with limited circulation.

By the early 1820s the country was already divided, and Buenos Aires established the first bank with the right to issue bank notes. This was an important innovation that, as was the case in Great Britain, attempted to end a shortage of fractional currency or coins in a province that traded internationally primarily in gold (unlike the rest of the country, which traded primarily in silver). This adaptation of British institutions might well have been successful and provided a numeraire and a channel for savings. Unfortunately, the fiscal needs of a state confronted with a war with Brazil led the government to absorb this bank as an arm of the state, to convert its bank notes into inconvertible legal tender, and to begin a long period of inflationary financing of public expenditures. In 1836, Rosas abolished the bank. From this time until 1867, Buenos Aires went over to a regime of inconvertible legal tender notes issued by the treasury (Casa de Moneda) and frustrated for several decades the development of institutions of financial intermediation. In the interior, silver coins from neighboring countries (mainly bolivianos) continued to circulate, and the development of banks had to wait until the middle of the century.

In the second half of the century, during its confrontations with the Confederation, the government of Buenos Aires (with the Banco de la Provincia de Buenos Aires) and later on, once it was organized, the national government (with the Banco Nacional) returned to using banks of issue to cover deficit financing. Institutions such as the Office of Exchange (Oficina de Cambios), originally thought of as a Caja de Conversion (currency board), failed and, with them, convertibility when the government did not strictly follow the rules of the gold standard. The idea of adopting the system of national banks from the United States failed because the Bancos Garantidos, rather than being a system of private banks with the right to issue bank notes under a set of strict rules, developed into a system of agencies dedicated to financing the deficits and debts of the provincial governments.

Each time it adapted one of the institutions from Great Britain or the United States, Argentina did so in such a way as to leave the governments with a substantial degree of discretion, a degree of discretion that these governments were quick to use whenever they started to feel pinched by a lack of tax revenues. This was the reason for the repeated failures and the increasing lack of public confidence in government policies and for the inefficiency in the fiscal and monetary institutions. This also caused the public to hide their savings (via hoarding), reducing capital available for investment and raising interest rates to the point where it retarded economic growth.

After the severe crisis of 1890, the country began a period of more mature institutional building that culminated with the monetary reforms of 1899, which, until 1930, prevented the government from issuing money. The reforms introduced in the fiscal regime and a judiciary framework that, along with the Constitution of 1953, protected property rights were preconditions for the massive entry of capital and workers that permitted the growth of markets and of the economy, and produced a new base of resources from which to sustain the administrative structure of the state.

11.9 A MODEL OF LATIN AMERICAN STATE FORMATION

The preceding analysis illustrates how the history of Argentina, especially in the nineteenth century, was determined by its physical dimensions and by the difficulties encountered in collecting and distributing tax revenue and in providing public services (especially defense). We believe that these difficulties have been a very important factor in the development of Argentine economic history and, following a fairly standard practice in economics, provide a model that contains most of these elements and in which, it can be argued, simulated time paths can approximate that of Argentina.

We want a simple model that will capture some of the aspects of the history of Argentina (and of the Americas) from the period of the Spanish Empire to the present. Among the features of this history that we wish the model to partially explain are the dissolution of the Spanish Empire, the rise of *caudillos*, and the formation of nation-states. One of our objectives is to illustrate the importance of a government entity's ability to produce public goods, and the importance of transportation costs and changes in the technology of transportation in describing the breakup and conflicts of the early independence period and the following national consolidation. This model demonstrates one of the reasons that federal governments interested in national consolidation invested so heavily in transportation infrastructure (in the case of Argentina, in railroads). The model points out why it is not an accident that stabilization of the political situation in Argentina occurred at the same time as massive railroad investments (in the 1860s).

In our model, we construct potential government entities that can produce a composite public good. Different locations have different abilities to produce this public good (representing the notion that some locations have natural characteristics that make them better centers of administration than others). In the general model, the good is produced with decreasing returns to scale technology.[24] Transport of public goods is costly, so locations farther from the center of government do not receive as much utility from each unit of the public good as do those closer in. If one thinks of the provision of security from internal and external threats as an important public good, the farther one is from the center that is providing this security, the more costly it is to have the service delivered. We include learning in the model in the sense that the longer one has resided at a particular governmental location, the better one knows how to acquire the public good and the more utility one gets from any given quantity of public good produced at that administrative center. This assumption is intended to capture the idea that learning to deal with any particular bureaucracy has investment costs and that the longer one has been in a given system, the better one knows how to deal with it. Locations can join the government of other locations, contribute taxes to the production of the public good by that government, and consume what remains of the public good after transportation costs are deducted. Any location can join any bordering government or can become independent and produce its own public goods. Locations are allowed to remain members of a government they

[24] The model gets substantially the same results if linear or increasing returns to scale production are used. Decreasing returns were used for the simulations.

belonged to in the previous period even if some intervening locations have chosen to leave that government.

We begin the simulations of the model with a single empire, representing that of Spain. All locations are members of the same government, which has only moderate ability to produce the public good. Parameter values are restricted to those that generate an equilibrium that is dynamically stable in the sense that none of the members wishes to leave the empire at its initial productivity level and initial size. At some date, the productivity of this site of government declines sufficiently so that at least some members wish to leave. Those locations that leave the empire first become independent and then generally group to form larger government units. The process continues until a new stable equilibrium (in the previously described sense) is reached.

In the second stage of the experiment, once a dynamically stable equilibrium is obtained, the cost of transportation is lowered. This is meant to reflect changes in the technology of transportation or in the ability to provide public services. The standard result (if the decline in costs is sufficiently large) is that some locations choose to leave the government they are with and join the government of their neighbor. As this process continues, the number of states declines and the size of most of the remaining states grows. The formation of states is path dependent in the sense that if we arrive at some configuration of parameters (specifically, transportation costs), the number and size of states depend on the values of the coefficients in previous periods. It is not always the case that the most efficient producers of public goods are the centers of governments, although it is almost never the case that a relatively bad producer of public goods is the center of government.

The first part of this chapter pointed to a number of key factors in the development of Argentine institutions. The long distances, the population low density, high costs of transportation, the main source of imperial revenue located in the mines in Upper Peru, the fragmentation of the tax collection and delivery system, the different incomes and expenditure requirements of Upper and Lower Rio de la Plata, and the post independence taxing advantage of the port in Buenos Aires were all mentioned as local conditions that led to the breakup and national conflict after the loss of the centralizing authority of the Spanish Crown. With various minor adjustments, this model can incorporate all of these details (and does include some important ones in the current version). The power of the model is that it can, without many of these details, mimic the experience of Argentina with the breakup at independence, with some sectors of the old viceroyalty of the Rio de la Plata remaining with the Crown longer than others, with the rise of *caudillos* and the development of the provinces, and with the later national consolidation.

11.9.1 The Model

The model we use is a dynamic version of one developed by Alesina and Tabellini (1996). The economy is a circle of circumference N. One individual (or potential government entity) lives at each integer location, so there are N individuals in the economy. Each location is a potential site for the production center of a government. In each period, individuals choose to belong to a center of government. They can be their own center, they can stay with the center they currently belong to, or they can join the center to which either of their neighbors belongs. Since the economy is a circle, each location has exactly two neighbors. At the beginning of each period, each individual gets to make a choice about which government to belong to out of the set of permitted governments.

The quantity of public goods that can be produced at location y, $q(y)$ is given by

$$q(y) = f(s(y), e(y))$$

where $s(y)$ is the total amount of tax revenue paid by individuals who are members of the government at location y and $e(y)$ measures the efficiency of site y in producing the public good. We assume that the function $f(,)$ is linear in $e(y)$ and displays decreasing returns to scale in $s(y)$. Different locations can have different abilities to produce public goods. The idea behind this is that some sites are naturally better locations for being governments than others based on their geographic location or for some other real reason. For the simulations, efficiency is uniformly randomly distributed and, except for one location, does not change through time. One location is chosen at the beginning of the simulation to be the center of an empire. The efficiency at this location is chosen to be sufficiently large to guarantee a dynamically stable initial empire equilibrium. The simulations of the model begin when this value is exogenously lowered sufficiently to cause the empire, at least partially, to break up.

The government at site y has $s(y)$ individuals who are members. Each individual who belongs to this government contributes one unit of income to the government as tax revenue. Every government charges the same tax to its members, so there is no preference over governments based upon the level of taxes. The government centered at y produces public goods that are consumed by all individuals who belong to that government and who pay taxes to that government. The government at location y has an income of $s(y)$ and uses all of this income to produce public goods.

Each individual belongs to a government. Consider the case of individual x, who belongs to government y and has belonged to that government for $t(x, y)$ periods. This individual x lives at a distance, $d(x, y)$,

$$d(x, y) = min|x - y|_{\text{mod } ulusN}$$

from the government at point y. Our economy is a circle and the distance measure is the shorter of the two distances between points x and y. The utility that individual x gets from being a member of government y is equal to

$$u_x(f(s(y), e(y), t(x, y), d(x, y)))$$

This utility depends positively on the quantity of public goods produced, $f(s(y), e(y))$, positively on the length of time that this individual has belonged to this government, $t(x, y)$, and negatively on the distance that the individual is from the government $d(x, y)$. While the same quantity of public goods is available to all members of the government, the farther an individual is from the government center, the less that individual is able to access these public goods because transportation of the public good is costly. The longer an individual has belonged to a particular government, the more able that individual is to take advantage of the public goods that the government is producing. Including $t(x, y)$ in the utility function represents the existence of a learning curve for gaining access to public goods.

Individuals choose to enter or leave a government based on the utility that the government provides them and the utility provided by a subset of alternative governments. Individuals are only allowed to remain with their current government, to choose to join the governments of which the two individuals who border them are members, or to have a government of their own. Because individuals can leave a government and be on their own, the utility that individual x receives from any government he continues to belong to is bounded below by $u_x(f(1, e(x), 0, 0))$.

In other words, individual x will never remain in or join a government if the utility he receives falls below what he would receive in the first period during which he is his own government and uses his one unit of income to produce his own public good.

Individuals have limited information about what others will be doing at time t. Therefore, they decide to enter a neighboring government at time t if the utility they would receive from that government as it is constituted at time t, but with themselves included, is greater than the utility they will have from staying with the government to which they belong as it currently is.[25] They estimate their utility from joining the government at time t (which they will not benefit from until time $t + 1$) as

$$\overline{u}_x^{t+1} = u_x(f(s^t(y)+1, e(y), 0, d(x, y))$$

if x was not a member of the country based at y at date t and as

$$u_x^{t+1} = u_x(f(s^t(y), e(y), t(x, y), +1, d(x, y))$$

if x was a member. If $\overline{u}_x^{t+1}$ is greater than u_x^{t+1}, then individual x changes governments.

11.9.2 Results of the Simulation

Figure 11.7 shows an example of a run of this model.[26] On the horizontal axis are the 100 locations of the economy; remember that location 100 is the neighbor of location 1 because we are wrapping the line to a circle. The model begins with all locations belonging to the government located at location 2.[27] In period 2, as with the fall of the Spanish monarchy after the French occupation of Spain, the ability of that location to provide government services drops sharply (in the example economy, to zero). The thick horizontal segments at time 2 represent all of those locations that declare independence. Those locations that are white at time 2 still remain in the empire (in the example, some locations near 2 still belong to the empire). By the time dynamic stability is achieved (by time 14), the empire has broken up into a large number of fairly small elements. The size of each political entity is the space between the vertical lines.

What has happened is that the decline in the ability of the center of the empire to provide services has caused the utility of belonging to the empire to fall below the utility of being on one's own. In time 2, those locations that are better off being on their own become independent and in later time periods (3 through 14) combine with their neighbors to form

[25] This assumption is made to make the solution process simpler. An alternative, more rational expectations type of assumption would be to have individuals calculate the value of belonging to a government as it would be construed if all those who wished to join it actually did so. This equilibrium is much more complicated to find. While the particular equilibrium is path dependent, once some dynamically stable equilibrium is reached, it is a rational expectations equilibrium in the preceding sense.

[26] Parameter values were chosen to illustrate our claims about South American state formation. Other choices of parameter values can result in, among other possibilities, the empire remaining whole, the empire partly dissolving and then reforming, a new empire being formed around another location, and every location remaining independent.

[27] Because of some programming idiosyncracies of the computed program employed, Matlab, using location 1 for the home of the empire generates some very strange errors. Any other location works fine.

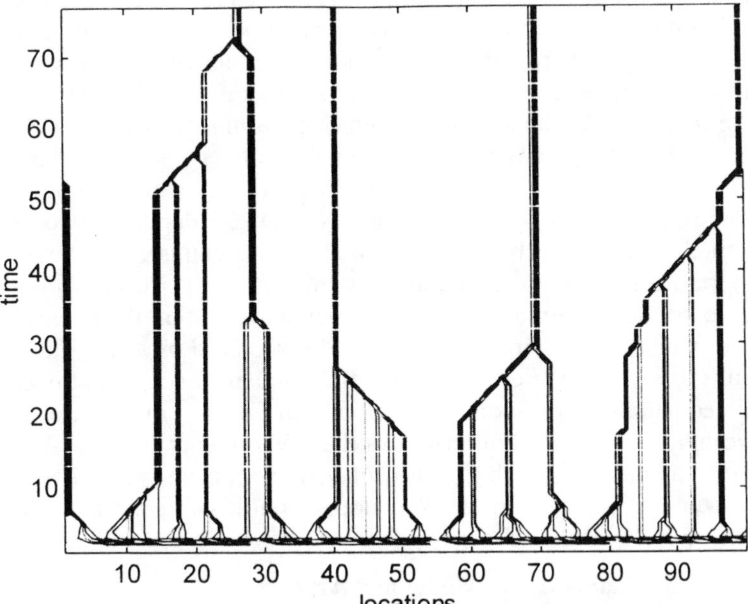

Figure 11.7 A simulation of the model. The vertical lines show the borders of the various governmental regions. The horizontal lines are Nash equilibria. This is the Windows bitmat version of the graph.

larger units. As these units grow, they absorb some of the neighboring locations that may have stayed with the empire for the first few periods and those of their neighbors who have less ability to produce the public good. A location that is not the global best at producing the public good may dominate the economy if its neighbors are sufficiently poor at producing the public good that they join up with this location early on. Because of the substantial amount of public good that it is producing, this location can quickly become the center of a large nation and even the center of a new empire.

Each thin horizontal line represents a point where dynamic stability has been achieved and where the cost of transport is reduced anew. At each stage in this example, transport costs are reduced by about 17 percent. As the costs of transport decline over time, the size of political entities grows until, after six declines in costs, where these costs are only 33 percent of the initial costs, there are only five states. Note that during the passage of time (and the reduction in transport costs), some states formed and grew and were then later absorbed by other neighboring states.

The exact size and center of governments formed as outcomes of this model are quite sensitive to the values of certain parameters. One parameter that generates surprisingly large changes in the results as a result of fairly small changes in the value of the parameter is the value to which $E(2)$, the coefficient of the ability to produce government services of the empire, drops when we begin the simulations. Not surprisingly, a fairly small drop in this value means that the empire stays intact. Larger changes result in some of the locations becoming independent for a period of time but later being reabsorbed by the empire. Still larger changes result in the empire's continuing in some of the locations but with some locations maintaining their independence. Within the range of values for which the empire terminates and is replaced by other states, the results are widely varied, not just in the number of states that exist after 15 reductions in transport costs, but also in the site of the center of the government and in the boundaries of the governments that exist. The results display more than a bit of the *butterfly effect* from chaos theory, where very small changes in an exogenous variable can generate very different types of equilibria.

11.9.3 This Simulation of the Model and Argentina

While the preceding example is only one of many possible outcomes, the main characteristics occur over a fairly wide set of parameter values. The center of the empire does not need to be very good at providing governmental services (relative to other locations) as long as a large enough set of locations belongs to it to give it enough revenues to dominate any other site that is on its own. It must be big enough to provide, for example, enough military power at any member site to prevent the locals from declaring their independence. While the Spanish Empire in the region of the Rio de la Plata was not terribly efficient, it survived until the Napoleonic invasion of Spain severely reduced Spain's ability to provide public services. The old cities of the viceroyalty of the Rio de la Plata were initially substantially autonomous and combined mainly to fight against common enemies. The long distances and high costs of transport prevented Buenos Aires from effectively imposing its control over the old viceroyalty. As in the model, the viceroyalty split up into small areas, each managed by a local *caudillo*. Some of these autonomous areas later came together into temporary or more permanent units such as Bolivia and the League of the North. As transport improved and external threats declined, the provinces came together into a number of national governments. These national states have been comparatively stable (as happens in the model) in the face of a wide range of continued declines in transport (or public service delivery) costs.

One important characteristic of the history of Argentina that the model does not directly include is the difficulties that the provinces experienced in collecting taxes. However, the greater ability of a local *caudillo* to provide and pay for the public services (mainly defense) compared to that of a more distant government (Buenos Aires) can be considered one of the costs of distance. The improvement of local tax collection and the nationalization of the import tax revenue from the port of Buenos Aires can be thought of as two features reducing the costs to a national government of administering public services to the more distant provinces. In the model, as in nineteenth-century Argentina, these cost reductions lead to nation formation.

One of the very early acts of the new Argentine national government was the encouragement and subsidy of the construction of a national railroad network (with the work mainly done by British firms). Much of this network can be rationalized by purely economic arguments: the productivity of the soils near the lines would soon permit high output of goods to be transported by these railroads. However, many lines connecting Buenos Aires with cities of the interior could not be easily defended by purely economic arguments and were justified with more political arguments. Such political arguments reflect exactly the kind of cost reduction in transporting public services that this model assumes. Not only in Argentina, but also in Mexico and the United States, the railroads were major contributors to the formation of the nation-state. Other countries, such as Brazil, benefited from a structure whereby cheap water transport permitted one central government to exercise substantial control over the nation's territory. Even today in Colombia the terrain imposes such high transportation costs that the national government is unable to exercise its authority over the whole country.

The simple circle version of the economy is enough to display the main ideas of this model. More difficult, but perhaps more realistic, would be to develop a version on a plane and where the transportation costs are not uniform. At the limit, one might even model a land mass similar to South America where waterways are represented by a matrix of low transportation costs between certain areas and mountains by higher costs. These physical features should predict (as a glance at a map suggests) how the nation-states are shaped and why they persist for so long in essentially the same shape. An additional step toward realism would be to give some areas higher tax revenue potential (like the mining areas).

For all its simplicity, this simulation of the model matches well the general pattern of state development that was observed in what was the viceroyalty of the Rio de la Plata. We believe that it provides additional support and an organizing framework for the detailed historical discussion of the earlier sections of this chapter.

NOTE

The monetary units used in this chapter and in the figures are defined as follows:

$F (unit of account) = peso fuerte; equals the old Spanish silver peso of 8 reales = 1 U.S. dollar.

$ m/cte (medium of exchange) = peso moneda corriente; originally was at par with the silver peso. It was devalued in 1867 so that 25$m/cte = 1$F.

$Gold (unit of account) = peso gold; 1.033 $gold = 1$F.

REFERENCES

Alesina, Alberto and Guido Tabellini (1996). "On the Number and Size of Nations," working paper, Harvard University.

Alvarez, Juan (1936). *Las Guerras Civiles Argentinas y el problema de Buenos Aires en la República*. Buenos Aires: La Facultad.

(1940). "Monedas, pesas y medidas," in *Historia de la Nación Argentina*, vol. 4. Buenos Aires: Academia Nacional de la Historia, pp. 235–49.

(1946). "Guerra económica entre la Confederación y Buenos Aires (1852–1861)," in *Historia de la Nación Argentina*, vol. 8. Buenos Aires: Academia Nacional de la Historia, pp. 167–206.

Amaral, Samuel (1988). "El descubrimiento de la financiación inflacionaria: Buenos Aires, 1790–1930," *in Separata de Investigaciones y Ensayos*, no. 37. Buenos Aires: Academia Nacional de la Historia, pp. 379–418.

Cortés Conde, Roberto (1982). "Aspectos económicos en la fundación de ciudades en América Latina," in *De Historia e Historiadores. Homenaje a José Luis Romero*. Buenos Aires: Siglo XXI, pp. 345–55.

Klein, Herbert (1973). "Las Finanzas de Virreinato del Río de la Plata en 1790," *Desarrollo Económico, Revista de Ciencias Sociales*, vol. 13, p. 396.

Levene, Ricardo (1940). "Riqueza, Industria, y Comercio durante el Virreynato," in *Historia de la Nación Argentina*, vol. IV. Buenos Aires: Academia Nacional de la Historia, Ed. El Ateneo, p. 291.

Lynch, John (1958). *Spanish Colonial Administration, 1782–1810. The Intendant System in the Viceroyalty of the Rio de la Plata*. London: Athlone Press.

Maeder, Ernesto J. A. (1981). *Historia Económica de Corrientes en el Período Virreinal: 1776–1810*. Buenos Aires: Academia Nacional de Historia.

Marichal, Carlos (1995). "Liberalismo y Política fiscal: La paradoja argentina, 1820–1862," in Anuario IEHS, Tandil.

Santos Martinez, Pedro (1961). *Historia Económica de Mendoza durante el Virreinato, 1776–1810*. Madrid: Consejo Superior de Investigaciones Científicas.

Segreti, Carlos S. A. (1975). *Moneda y Política en la Primera Mitad del siglo XIX (Contribución al estudio de la Historia de la Moneda Argentina)*. Tucumán: Fundación Banco Comercial del Norte.

Zorraquín Becú, Ricardo (1953). *El Federalismo Argentino*. Buenos Aires: Ed. La Facultad.

12

Continuities and Discontinuities in the Fiscal and Monetary Institutions of New Granada, 1783–1850

Jaime U. Jaramillo, Adolfo R. Meisel, and Miguel M. Urrutia

12.1 INTRODUCTION

In this chapter we study the structure of the fiscal system of the Viceroyalty of New Granada toward the end of the colonial period. Then we discuss how the tax system inherited from the Spanish Empire evolved over the period 1821–50.

The conclusion that emerges from the review of the evidence is that the new republic was successful in improving the tax regime it had received from Spain. By 1850, the Republic of New Granada possessed a fiscal system that was much more fair, efficient, and neutral than it had been in 1810.

In 1717 the Captaincy-General of New Granada was raised to the status of viceroyalty. However, six years later New Granada was again declared to be a Captaincy-General. Finally, in 1739 the Viceroyalty of New Granada was reestablished. The viceroyalty included basically the territory of what is now the Republic of Colombia plus Panamá; the Captaincy-General of Venezuela, over which it had very little control; and the Presidency of Quito. In this chapter, when we refer to the Viceroyalty of New Granada we only include the territory of the present republics of Colombia and Panamá.

In the 1810s, when most of the Spanish American colonies achieved their independence, the former territories of the Viceroyalty of New Granada formed the Republic of Colombia, comprising modern Venezuela, Colombia, Panamá, and Ecuador. However, by 1831 it had broken up into three separate republics: Venezuela, Ecuador, and New Granada. The last republic changed its name in 1863 to the Republic of Colombia.[1]

The authors acknowledge comments by Michael Bordo, Roberto Cortés – Conde, Maurice Brungardt, Malcolm Deas, Hermes Tovar, and Gustavo Bell.

[1] For an introduction to the history of Colombia see Bushnell (1993).

12.2 STRUCTURE OF ROYAL FINANCE IN THE VICEROYALTY OF NEW GRANADA

12.2.1 The Economy of the Viceroyalty of New Granada in the Eighteenth Century

Throughout the colonial period New Granada was among the less dynamic domains of Spain in the New World. The basis of its foreign trade was gold, but on a scale that was not comparable to that of silver in Mexico or Peru. Thus, during the three centuries of Spanish rule, New Granada remained a backwater, with regions that were clearly differentiated and had limited economic interactions among themselves due to the very rugged topography of the country.

In the census of 1778, the only countrywide census of the colonial period, New Granada had a population of 739,759.[2] The largest group was composed of people of mixed races (*mestizos, mulatos, and zambos*) and the free blacks, who together represented 49 percent of the population. The next largest group was the white population, with 25.4 percent of the total. The indian population contributed 19 percent of the total and the black slaves 6.2 percent.

The main cities were Santa Fe de Bogota, the capital of the viceroyalty, with a population of 20,000, and Cartagena, a fortified port in the Caribbean, with a population of 13,000.[3]

New Granada experienced two cycles of gold production during the colonial period. The first cycle extended from 1550 to about 1620 and the second from 1680 to 1820.[4] The period from 1620 to 1680 was characterized by a deep crisis in the mining sector of the viceroyalty, with a severe reduction in gold production.

The first gold cycle (1550–1620) was concentrated in central Colombia (Santa Fe de Bogota, Tunja, Velez, and Pamplona), Popayán, and Antioquia. Both in central Colombia and in Popayán the main source of labor for the exploitation of gold was the indian population.

The second gold cycle (1680–1820) was centered initially in Choco and later in the Antioqueño region. In Choco the main source of labor was black slaves. In contrast, in Antioquia mining was primarily an activity of small independent miners.[5]

New Granada was always a colony of second rank within the Spanish American empire. However, in the eighteenth century it was far from stagnant. Gold production, as calculated from the fiscal records of

[2] Urrutia and Arrubla (1970), p. 19. [3] McFarlane (1993), p. 32.
[4] Colmenares (1978), pp. 239–40. [5] Twinam (1985), p. 80.

Table 12.1. Gold Production in the Principal Mining Regions of New Granada (thousands of pesos)

Period	Popayán	Barbacoas	Novita	Citara	Antioquia	Total
1700–4	638					638
1705–9	821					821
1710–14	1,069					1,069
1715–19	1,039	275		716	176	2,206
1720–4	1,308	163		943		2,414
1725–9	1,452		1,134	367		2,953
1730–4	1,270		992	863		3,125
1735–9	1,391	613	1,293	1,073	256	4,626
1740–1	1,124	317	1,466	857	348	4,112
1745–9	792	326	1,460	852	316	3,746
1750–4	564	243	1,159	588	544	3,098
1755–9	944	461	854	644	559	3,462
1760–4	1,020	921	966	721	820	4,448
1765–9	1,055	952	884	794	751	4,436
1770–4	1,483	995	1,189	619	1,125	5,411
1775–9	1,360	893	1,051	588	1,684	5,576
1780–4	1,908	1,361	1,323	617	1,987	7,196
1785–9	1,731	1,688	1,253	905	2,655	8,232
1790–4	1,616	1,767	1,450	1,217	3,281	9,331
1795–9	1,541	1,783	1,391	1,190	3,662	9,567

Source: Melo (1979), p. 68.

the royal treasury, increased throughout the century. The production statistics presented in Table 12.1 were calculated from the revenues of the *quinto*, a tax of around 5 percent on the value of gold produced.[6] As the production statistics in Table 12.1 show, except for a drop in total production from 1739 to 1759, output increased steadily. The average annual rate of growth from 1700–4 to 1795–9 was 2.3 percent (see Figure 12.1). This was above the rate of population expansion, which was probably around 1.5 percent annually.[7]

In spite of the dynamism of the gold mining sector (up to 1780, gold was practically the only export product of the viceroyalty and in

[6] Melo (1979), p. 66. Since 1777 the *quinto* tax had been consolidated with other taxes on gold mining, and a global tax of 3 percent was established.

[7] Since there was only one complete population census in the colonial period, it is not possible to estimate the rate of growth of the population of New Granada in the eighteenth century. However, we know that from 1777 to 1851, the rate of population growth was 1.5 percent. Thus, and as a first approximation, this last rate is indicative of what was probably happening to the population in the late eighteenth century.

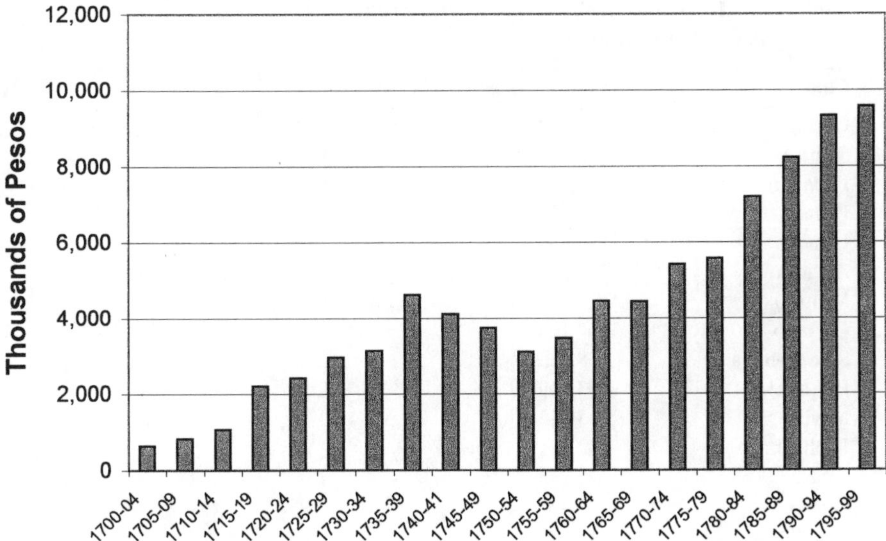

Figure 12.1 Gold production in the Viceroyalty of New Granada (1700–99).

Source: Table 12.1.

the final decades of the century represented no less than 90 percent of total exports), tax collection in New Granada remained practically stagnant. Based on unpublished research, Jaime Jaramillo Uribe argues that "The general evolution of the economy of New Granada throughout the eighteenth century reveals a remarkably static development. The graph of total fiscal revenues of the royal treasury shows an almost horizontal curve up to 1780. After that date there were some increases in export trade and in incomes such as tobacco, liquor, and alcabalas. The rest, some twenty items, have only very slight variations."[8]

What do these tax figures reveal, the economic weakness of New Granada or a less abusive and exploitable colonial structure? Perhaps both, since undoubtedly New Granada had a less strong economy than the viceroyalties of Peru, Mexico, or Buenos Aires, but it was also characterized by a limited degree of bureaucratic control on the part of the colonial authorities.[9] The absence of pre-Columbian structures of long standing, in contrast to New Spain and Peru, plus a very rugged topography, seems to have resulted in an inability of the state to control the economy of New Granada. Thus, as we shall discuss in the next section

[8] Jaramillo Uribe (1993), p. 92.

[9] This discussion is based on the comments and suggestions of Maurice Brungardt.

Table 12.2. Revenues of the Cajas Reales of the Viceroyalty of New Granada (1783)

Caja	Revenues (pesos)	%
Cartagena	651,742	29.32
Santa Fe	438,899	19.75
Popayán	208,082	9.36
Panamá	206,233	9.28
Honda	146,060	6.57
Antioquia	121,929	5.49
Mompox	112,178	5.05
Cartago	67,106	3.02
Santa Marta	58,563	2.63
Portobelo	53,039	2.39
Novita	33,913	1.53
Riohacha	32,371	1.46
Citara	23,793	1.07
Ocaña	21,467	0.97
Pamplona	18,503	0.83
Remedios	16,208	0.73
Neiva	12,431	0.56
Girón	10,610	0.48
TOTAL	**2,222,517**	**100.00**

Source: Mora de Tovar (1983), pp. 305–15.

when we study the Comunero Revolt of 1781, Crown officials encountered enormous difficulties in tax production in the Viceroyalty of New Granada.

12.2.2 Structure of Royal Incomes: 1783 and 1808–9

In 1783, the Viceroyalty of New Granada had a net fiscal income that amounted to $2,233,127 silver pesos. The major *cajas* (regional treasuries) by income were those of Cartagena (29.19 percent), Santa Fe de Bogota (19.65 percent), Popayán (9.32 percent), Panamá (9.24 percent), and Honda (6.54 percent). Together these five treasuries received 73.94 percent of the total income paid to the royal treasury in New Granada (see Table 12.2).

Cartagena had the highest fiscal revenues as a result of its importance as the main port of New Granada in the Caribbean. The most important tax in this city in 1783 was the *almojarifazgo*, a tax on foreign trade. The other two important revenues were the royal monopolies on liquor (*aguardiente*) and tobacco. Together these three accounts represented 89 percent of all revenues received by the *caja* of Cartagena in 1783.[10]

Although Cartagena received significant revenues from the foreign trade taxes and the royal monopolies, its expenses were generally higher than its income due to the enormous costs of building and maintaining its fortification and paying for a permanent army. In 1778, for example, its veteran troops numbered about 500 men.[11] A report of the same year estimated the expenses of the city at around 500,000 pesos, while its revenues were only 220,000 pesos. Since in the eighteenth century these deficits were almost permanent, the city had to be subsidized through transfers from other royal treasuries. These subsidies, called *situados*, were common throughout the Spanish Empire. For example, New Spain subsidized the military defenses in the Caribbean, particularly in Havana.[12]

Between 1761 and 1802, the treasury of Cartagena received annual *situados* that amounted to 14,349,451 pesos, that is, an annual average of 337,739 pesos.[13] These transfers came mostly from Santa Fe de Bogota and other treasuries of what is now Colombia. The presidency of Quito contributed only 2.4 percent of the transfers.

The population of New Granada in 1783 was close to 800,000. Thus, in that year, the per capita revenues of the Treasury in this viceroyalty were slightly less than three silver pesos.[14] In contrast, in the 1790s, the taxes per capita paid by the inhabitants of New Spain were approximately eight pesos a year.[15] This sharp difference in the level of per capita tax revenues highlights what we stated previously: that throughout the colonial period New Granada remained a relatively poor backwater with scant control of the economy on the part of government officials.

It should also be mentioned that in contrast with the almost 3 silver pesos per capita in taxes paid in New Granada, in the 1790s in the Iberian Peninsula the Spanish Crown collected about 4.8 silver pesos per person.[16]

As we shall see, the economic weakness and the rather lax bureaucratic control of New Granada were reflected not only in the level of per capita revenues, but also in the structure of those revenues. In other

[10] Mora de Tovar (1983), p. 313.

[11] "Copia del plan de defensa formado por Real Orden por el Brigadier Roon Agustin Crane" (1778), Tome 41, fls. 405–18.

[12] In the 1780s it also subsidized the coast guard of Cartagena. Ibid, f. 406.

[13] Jara (1994), p. 155.

[14] If we assume that between 1778 and 1783 the rate of population growth was 1 percent, per capita revenues in 1783 were 2.9 silver pesos.

[15] Klein (1995). [16] Ibid.

colonies of the Spanish Crown, such as New Spain and Buenos Aires, taxes on mining, together with taxes on trade, represented the main source of income. For example, in 1790 in the Viceroyalty of Buenos Aires, mining taxes represented 32.1 percent of all revenues, and trade and production taxes another 21.8 percent.[17] The other important tax was the head tax on the indian population, which in Buenos Aires in 1790 amounted to 16.4 percent of all revenues. The sum of the taxes on mining, trade, and tribute on indians represented 70.3 percent of the total.

In contrast with the predominance in the Viceroyalty of Buenos Aires of the taxes on mining, commerce and production, and tribute on indians, in 1783 in New Granada the sum of these three types of taxes was 36.3 percent of total revenues (see Table 12.3). For example, taxes on mining were only 9.8 percent of total revenues. This was a very different situation from that of Mexico, where throughout most of the eighteenth century taxes on mining fluctuated between 20 percent and 27 percent of total tax collection.

The distinctive feature of the structure of royal income in the Viceroyalty of New Granada in the final decades of the colonial period was the enormous importance of state monopolies, especially on liquor and tobacco. In 1783 state monopolies accounted for 59.3 percent of the total fiscal revenues of New Granada. This situation was in sharp contrast with that of most other Spanish American colonies, where state monopolies (excluding the mercury monopoly, which was closely linked to mining production) rarely achieved such prominence and generally accounted for only 5 percent to 10 percent of total revenues.[18]

Why did royal monopolies play such a central role in the fiscal incomes of the Viceroyalty of New Granada? One reason could be that to the extent that it had a very static economy, with exports per capita that were much lower than those of Cuba, Mexico, Peru, or Buenos Aires, the participation of the gold-producing mining sector in the economy of New Granada was smaller than that of the export sector in the previously mentioned colonies.[19] Thus, taxes on the mining and commerce sectors could not be increased very easily.

An additional circumstance that must be taken into consideration in order to find out why mining taxes were such a small proportion of total revenues in New Granada was the very significant presence of

[17] Klein (1973), p. 445.

[18] Klein and Barbier (1988), p. 46.

[19] In 1792 the exports of New Granada represented only 4.5 percent of total exports from Spanish America. From 1782 to 1796 exports of New Granada to Spain were only 3.2 percent of the total of Spanish America; see Palacios (1993), p. 120, and Fisher (1990), p. 153.

Table 12.3. Revenues of the *Cajas Reales* of New Granada (1783)

Category and Type of Tax	Value (pesos)		%
1. Mining		**219,050**	**9.83**
Quintos de oro and *plata*	44,933		
Fundición and *ensaye*	3,950		
Rescates and *amonedado*	170,167		
2. Taxes on commerce and production		**199,895**	**8.97**
Alcabala	153,550		
Reales novenos	31,168		
Sisa	15,177		
3. Indian Tribute		**63,333**	**2.84**
4. Taxes on royal bureaucratic salaries and sales of offices		**39,827**	**1.79**
a. Civil			
Media anatas	15,219		
Oficios vendibles	9,076		
SUBTOTAL	24,295		
b. Ecclesiastical			
Espolios	4,973		
Vacantes menores	7,500		
Media anatas eclesiásticas	1,122		
Mesadas eclesiásticas	1,937		
SUBTOTAL	15,532		
5. Monopolies of the state		**1,323,034**	**59.37**
Tobacco	597,000		
Aguardiente	596,023		
Salinas	62,618		
Papel sellado	16,795		
Cruzada	41,495		
Pólvora	4,370		
Naipes	4,733		
6. Miscellaneous income		**54,788**	**2.46**
Fletes and *pisos*	2,110		
Salarios de ministros	710		
Vacantes de novenos	619		
Oficios vendibles	9,076		
Tierras de escobilla	799		
Registros de minas	4		
Esmeraldas	1,600		
Bienes monstrencos	12		
Composición de tierras	4,181		
Reales bodegas	3,699		
Juegos de gallos	136		
Azogues	133		
Penas de cámara	2,712		
Aprovechamientos	28,997		
7. Taxes on foreign trade		**328,496**	**14.74**
Almotarifazgo	300,948		
Avería	27,548		
TOTAL		**2,228,423**	**100.00**

Note: The accounts have been classified following Klein (1973).

Source: Mora de Tovar (1983), pp. 305–15.

contraband trade. As has been amply documented, smuggling was intense in the Caribbean provinces of New Granada (Cartagena, Santa Marta, and Riohacha). According to the historian Lance R. Grahn, in New Granada contraband developed more fully than in any other Spanish American colony.[20] In 1737 the lieutenant general of Cartagena, Blas de Lezo, calculated that three-fourths of the viceroyalty's gold production, about 1,250,000 silver pesos per year, were illegally exported through Cartagena.[21]

At the end of the colonial period, Jose Ignacio de Pombo calculated the annual value of contraband trade to be 3,000,000 pesos of foreign products imported and a similar value of gold exported illegally to pay for those imports.[22]

The combined effect of a very small and not very dynamic export sector and the widespread evasion of taxes on mining and foreign trade through contraband was that New Granada had a peculiar structure of royal revenues in which incomes from state monopolies amounted to 59.3 percent of total revenues in 1783.

The most productive state monopolies were tobacco, liquor, and salt. To the extent that these three monopolies taxed articles of popular consumption, their effect on income distribution must have been very regressive. Thus, it seems understandable that the fiscal reforms of 1781, which were designed to raise revenues, particularly from the tobacco and liquor monopolies, led to one of the two major uprisings that occurred in Spanish America in the eighteenth century: the Revolt of the Comuneros.[23]

The overhaul of the fiscal system of New Granada was initiated in 1778 with the arrival of the Crown official Juan Francisco Gutierrez de Piñeres. He had been assigned as a priority the task of augmenting royal revenues in New Granada. Among the reforms he undertook was the reorganization of the tobacco monopoly. Five regional administrations were set up under the central direction of Bogota. Detailed instructions were set forth, and a special force to eradicate illegal cultivation was established.[24] Numerous towns and regions were excluded from the cultivation of tobacco as a result of Piñeres's reforms. The outcome was a rise in the price of tobacco and increasing resentment, which resulted in

[20] Grahn (1985), p. 125.

[21] Ibid., p. 138. The illegal export of gold was facilitated by the fact that in New Granada gold was not produced in large mines but mainly by small independent miners. Additionally, the available technology permitted the conversion of the mined gold into small nuggets of large value that were easy to transport, an ideal product for smugglers.

[22] Pombo (1986), p. 62.

[23] The other major revolt was the Tupac Amaru Indian revolt in Peru; see Phelan (1980).

[24] McFarlane (1993), p. 212.

the Comunero Revolt of 1781. The revolt began in the towns of Socorro and San Gil, located in Santander, a region particularly affected by the new fiscal measures since it was a tobacco-producing center. It soon spread to other towns, where the offices of the tobacco and liquor monopolies were sacked and the stocks of liquor and tobacco sold among the population. By May 1781 the rebels had assembled in the town of Zipaquira a force of 20,000 that was ready to march on the capital. With only a small force in Santa Fe de Bogota to resist, the colonial authorities accepted all the demands of the rebels for dismantling the fiscal reforms. After these negotiations the rebels dispersed. In 1782 the colonial authorities renounced the fiscal concessions they had agreed upon with the Comuneros, and the leaders were arrested and executed.[25] Although it ended in final defeat, this open challenge to the reforms intended to raise tax revenues in the viceroyalty helps us to understand how the tensions generated by the imperial fiscal regime provided one of the principal motivations for the independence movement.

The critique of the fiscal system was an important element in the anticolonial discourse of the leaders of the struggle against the Spanish Empire. In 1804 the main economic commentator of the Viceroyalty of New Granada in the years inmediately preceding independence, the merchant Jose Ignacio de Pombo, called for "a moderation in the fiscal laws: the end of the tobacco and liquor monopoly, particularly in the maritime provinces of Riohacha, Santa Marta, Cartagena, Panama, Barbacoas, Choco, and the tribute on the Indian population, that maintains it in a state of primitive barbarism."[26]

Antonio Nariño, one of the principal leaders of the independence movement, argued that the colonial fiscal system so distorted the economic incentives that the result was an overall reduction in output. He also believed that "There are some taxes that are more negative because of the obstacles they create for the contributors, than because of the amounts collected by the Royal Treasury."[27] Among the taxes that Nariño considered to have this characteristic were the *alcabala* (a tax on all commercial transactions) and the monopolies on tobacco and liquor. Undoubtedly, the stifling effect on economic activity of the imperial tax system was one of the main antecedents of the anticolonialism of the local elite in New Granada in the opening years of the nineteenth century.

In Table 12.4, we present the structure of the tax revenues of the viceroyalty of New Granada for the years 1808 and 1809. It must be

[25] For a detailed account on the Comunero revolt see Phelan (1980).

[26] Pombo (1986), p. 57.

[27] Cruz Santos (1965), Tomo I (1965), p. 231.

Table 12.4. Revenues of the *Cajas Reales* of New Granada (1808 and 1809)

Category and Type of Tax	Value (pesos)		%
1. Mining		**283,213**	**6.64**
Quintos de oro y plata	149,277		
Fundición	2,386		
Amonedación	131,550		
2. Taxes on commerce and production		**584,270**	**13.71**
Alcabala	447,516		
Reales novenos	114,510		
Sisa	22,244		
3. Indian tribute		**766,716**	**17.99**
4. Taxes on royal bureaucratic salaries and sales of offices		**42,092**	**0.99**
Media anatas	21,176		
Oficios vendibles	20,916		
5. Monopolies of the state		**1,797,857**	**42.18**
Tobacco	953,043		
Aguardiente	371,114		
Salinas	242,949		
Papel sellado	110,965		
Pólvora	119,786		
6. Miscellaneous income		**390,660**	**9.16**
Pasos de ríos	13,191		
Herencias trasversales	3,823		
Composición de tierras	6,656		
Composición de pulperías	11,325		
Protectoría	1,558		
Temporalidades	95,017		
Subsidio eclesiástico	42,613		
Diversos	216,477		
7. Taxes on foreign trade		**398,034**	**9.34**
TOTAL		**4,262,842**	**100.00**

Note: The accounts have been classified following Klein (1973) and subtracting "Hacienda en Comun."

Source: Galindo (1978), p. 225.

emphasized that between 1783 and 1808–9 no major changes occurred in the structure of tax receipts, with one exception: the apparently enormous increase between those dates in the head tax on the indian population. The tribute on indian heads of households increased from 2.8 percent of total revenues in 1783 to 18 percent in 1808–9. However, an increase of this extent probably did not occur, and reflects problems in the data.

The increase in the collection of the indian tribute in the eighteenth century occurred throughout Spanish America. By the 1790s, the indian tribute was the largest single source of revenue for the royal treasury in both Peru and Alto Peru.[28] To a large extent, this increase in the collection of the indian tribute was the result of the eighteenth-century expansion of the indian population, which occurred in most of the viceroyalties. However, it is highly unlikely that an increase of the magnitude reported in Table 12.4 actually occurred. However, since we have only one year of observation, 1783, it is difficult to draw a conclusion.

12.3 EVOLUTION OF THE FISCAL SYSTEM IN THE REPUBLIC OF NEW GRANADA, 1831–50

12.3.1 Initial Reforms and Counterreforms, 1821–30

Because of the chaos that occurred during the bloody war against Spain, there is an almost complete absence of published fiscal records for the decade 1810–20. Anibal Galindo, a prominent economic commentator on the nineteenth century, expressed this situation very clearly: "The period from 1810 to 1821, when the Republic of Colombia was created, has no fiscal history."[29]

With the creation in 1821 of the Republic of Colombia, which comprised the territory of present Ecuador, Colombia, Panamá, and Venezuela, a period of fiscal system reform began. This is hardly surprising since the tax system was one of the aspects of the Spanish colonial empire that the patriots most resented. The Congress of 1821 abolished the following taxes:[30]

1. The tribute on indian heads of households.
2. *Alcabalas* on all sales of domestic production.
3. The liquor monopoly.
4. The exports of coffee, cotton, sugar, liquor, and woods for construction were exempted from export taxes for 10 years. In addition, exporters of hides, cacao, and indigo had to pay only 10 percent ad valorem; mules and horses were taxed 15 pesos per head and cattle 12 1/2 pesos per head.

In the following years more taxes were abolished[31]:

[28] Klein (1995).

[29] Galindo (1978), p. 136. In the Archivo Historico Nacional de Colombia, there are fiscal records for most of the years from 1810 to 1830. However, they have not been reconstructed, in part because the information is disseminated and much of it has not been catalogued.

[30] Secretario de Hacienda, *Memoria al congreso* (1823).

[31] Nieto Arteta (1983), pp. 60–1.

5. A law of March 13, 1826, exempted from export taxes quinine, rice, and corn.
6. A law of May 19, 1824, exempted from the *diezmo* (a tax on agricultural production) all new plantations of several crops.
7. A law of May 28, 1825, eliminated the *media anata* tax.

The initial impulse to eliminate the taxes inherited from the colonial system lost momentum and even suffered some setbacks in the early 1830s. Why? The Marxist economic historian Luis Eduardo Nieto Arteta has argued that these setbacks were the result of a reactionary class alliance that became dominant after 1830. Furthermore, he maintains that "the colonialist reaction was integrated by the landlords, the clergy, and some members of the army that had a caste mentality, because they had been formed as such within a colonial economy."[32]

After 1828 many of the taxes that had been abolished after independence were reestablished. For example, in 1828 the liquor monopoly and the *media anata* (a tax on the salaries of public officials) were reintroduced. This setback led Nieto Arteta to argue in his very influential economic history of nineteenth-century Colombia that "The Revolution of Independence did not modify the colonial tax system, nor the organization that Spain created in New Granada."[33]

Nieto's interpretation coincides with the views of the principal exponents of economic liberalism in Colombia in the nineteenth century, who were very influential in the 1840s and 1850s: Salvador Camacho Roldan, Miguel Samper, Manuel Murillo Toro, and Florentino Gonzalez. For example, Salvador Camacho wrote in 1850: "The great Revolution of 1810 that transformed immediately our political system, almost in nothing touched our fiscal system, leaving among a people living in democracy the monopolies, the abuses, and the inequities of the [colonial] tax system."[34]

Most contemporary Colombian historians accept the idea that the tax system of the colonial period survived almost intact until the liberal economic reforms initiated in 1848 by the secretary of finance, Florentino Gonzalez. For example, in an article included in the most influential textbook on Colombian economic history, Jorge Orlando Melo, referring to the economic reforms of the 1850s, maintains that "Until that moment the [tax] system continued to be essentially the same one that had existed during the colony."[35]

In the next section we will demonstrate that the traditional interpretation that claims that the tax system of the Spanish Crown

[32] Op. cit., p. 58. [33] Ibid., p. 91.
[34] Camacho Roldan (1976), p. 19. [35] Melo (1987), p. 147.

survived almost without changes until 1850 is completly at odds with the facts. As we shall see, ideological factors help to explain why this false interpretation has become so deeply entrenched in Colombian historiography.

12.3.2 The Structure of Fiscal Incomes in 1831–2 and the Accomplishments of the Tax Reforms by 1836

In Table 12.5 we present the structure of tax revenues for the recently created Republic of New Granada during the fiscal year from July 1, 1831, to June 30, 1832.[36] It constitutes the first report of the incomes of the new nation 21 years after it declared its independence from Spain.

Several things must be highlighted about the structure of tax revenues in 1831–2, which show that there were already significant differences from the tax system that existed during the period of Spanish domination. In the first place, the revenues from the head tax on the indian population amounted to only 0.4 percent of total revenues. The drop was the result of the final abolition of this tax in March 1832. When it was eliminated, the secretary of finance expressed his satisfaction: "This was a horrible tax that marked the slavery of the Indian population. I would like to express the wish that at no time, nor by any type of authority or person it be reestablished in the territory of New Granada."[37]

A second element to be highlighted is that, in contrast with the situation in the final decades of the colonial period, taxes on foreign trade were now the main source of income after the state monopolies. For example, in 1808–9 taxes on foreign trade represented only 9.3 percent of all revenues. In contrast, by 1831–2 they had increased to 33.1 percent. As we shall see in more detail in the next section, the fundamental characteristic of the tax system that emerged with the republic was its dependence on foreign trade taxes.

A third characteristic of the emerging republican tax structure was that most of the revenues collected from foreign trade corresponded to taxes on imports. In effect, in 1831–2, of the total fiscal revenues from foreign trade, only 3.2 percent resulted from export taxes.

The rapid increase in the share of taxes on foreign imports and the reduction in taxes on exports were part of the explicit objectives of the first secretary of finance of the Republic of Colombia, Jose Maria del Castillo y Rada. In his report to the Congress in 1823, Del Castillo set out the orientation of the fiscal authorities with respect to foreign trade

[36] The Republic of New Granada comprised the territories of what are currently Colombia and Panamá.

[37] Secretario de Hacienda, *Informe al Congreso* (1833), p. 28.

Table 12.5. Tax Revenues of the Republic of New Granada (July 1, 1831–June 30, 1832)

Category and Type of Tax	Value (pesos)		%
1. Mining		**149,923**	**6.44**
Quintos and *fundición de oro and plata*	24,619		
Casa de moneda	125,304		
2. Taxes on commerce and production		**294,345**	**12.65**
Alcabala	247,789		
Novenos del Estado	43,788		
Alcabalas de finca raíz	2,768		
3. Indian tribute		**10,208**	**0.44**
4. Taxes on royal bureaucratic salaries and sales of offices		**35,057**	**1.51**
a. Civil			
Monte Pio Ministerio	12		
b. Ecclesiastical			
Espolios	27,154		
Vacantes menores and *mayores*	6,159		
Mesadas eclesiásticas	1,732		
5. Monopolies of the state		**875,975**	**37.65**
Tobacco	488,771		
Aguardiente	115,968		
Salinas	265,789		
Papel sellado	5,447		
6. Miscellaneous income		**190,255**	**8.18**
Correos	73,080		
Productos de imprenta	16		
Hospital de San Lázaro	463		
Aprovechamientos	8,417		
Hospitales sin destinos	2,077		
Seminario de nobles de Madrid	2,076		
Caja indígena de Nemocón	401		
Temporalidades	26		
Arrendamiento de tierras	103		
Crédito público	50,459		
Multas	7,796		
Conventos suprimidos	66		
Efectos and *fincas del Estado*	2,671		
Noveno de consolidación	23,568		
Derecho de hipoteca and *registro*	1,187		
Hacienda en común	9,232		
Bodegas del Estado	97		
Diez por ciento de rentas municipales	1,332		
Comisos	1,230		

Category and Type of Tax	Value (pesos)		%
Secuestros	3,449		
Derechos de cargas sobre efectos extranjeros que transitan el río Magdalena	1,907		
Mandas forzosas	132		
Bienes de difuntos	470		
7. Taxes on foreign trade		**770,958**	**33.13**
Importación	497,643		
Exportación	24,885		
Extracción presunta	95,940		
Consulado	107,499		
Alcabala	16,395		
Otros	28,596		
TOTAL		**2,326,721**	**100.00**

Note: The accounts have been classified following Klein (1973).
Source: Secretario de Hacienda, *Informe al Congreso* (1832).

taxes: "Customs are the source of one of the most productive taxes; and forgetting about its intrinsic advantages or disadvantages, the legislators should seek to increase its revenues, for the benefit of national wealth. Moderate import duties; extreme supervision in the ports; well selected employees, benefits for those that detect fraud; liberty to export domestic products without duties; . . . such should be the policies that are set in place, and that before could not be established, so that this tax be of great help for the necessities of the nation."[38]

Thus, already in 1831–2, significant changes could be observed in the structure of tax revenues as a result of the reforms that had been introduced under the very difficult circumstances created by a costly and prolonged war.[39]

In Table 12.6 we calculate the revenues produced in 1801 by the taxes that had already been abolished by the republican governments by 1836. The total in 1801 of the 15 taxes abolished by 1836 was 25.4 percent of all revenues. This was an enormous achievement, especially

[38] Secretario de Hacienda, *Informe al Congreso* (1823), p. 8.

[39] In 1841 there was a drop in total revenues per capita to only 47 pesos of 1840 as a result of the civil war known as the War of the Supremes, which lasted from 1839 to 1842 but was most intense in 1841. In that year the war affected the Caribbean coast provinces. The rebel forces seized the main ports on the Caribbean coast in order to have access to the custom revenues. As a result, the government suffered a drop in its tax collections. Secretario de Hacienda, *Memoria al Congreso* (1842), p. 4.

Table 12.6. Taxes That Existed in New Granada in 1801 and Had Been Abolished by 1836

Tax	Value of Revenue in 1801 (pesos)	Percent of Total Revenues in 1801
Alcabala	97,762	14.65
Tributo indígena	14,424	2.16
Protecturía	904	0.14
Inválidos	3,223	0.48
Medias anatas	4,394	0.66
Tierras	7,974	1.20
Pólvora	1,381	0.21
Arriendo de gallos	370	0.06
Imposiciones a censo	24,155	3.62
Oficios vendibles	2,196	0.33
Real subsidio	245	0.04
Bulas de cruzadas	5,863	0.88
Bulas de carnes	777	0.12
Naipes	440	0.07
Camellón	5,248	0.79
TOTAL	**169,356**	**25.39**

Note: The participation is with respect to total revenues, which were classified by type of tax.
Source: *Memorias de Hacienda* (1826–36).

if we take into consideration that in the period 1810–50 there was a drop in exports and real income per capita in New Granada.[40]

12.3.3 Overall Evolution of Fiscal Revenues, 1831–50

In the period 1831–50, fiscal revenues in the Republic of New Granada went through two clearly identifiable subperiods. The first one extends from 1831 to 1842, when total revenues per capita tended to fall (see Figure 12.2 and Table 12.7). In fact, total revenues per capita dropped from 1.44 pesos of 1840 in 1832 to 0.87 pesos of 1840 in 1842, a decrease of 38 percent.

After 1843 total revenues per capita tended to increase and by 1850 they had already increased by 17 percent.[41] We have been able to

[40] Jose Antonio Ocampo calculated that in 1846–50, exports per capita in real terms were 42 percent below the level in 1802–4. Ocampo (1984), p. 89.

[41] The quality of the only price index available for Colombia in the nineteenth century has been, at least for this particular period, questioned. Although his methodology is not very explicit, it seems that in some years Alberto Pardo used as a price index the level

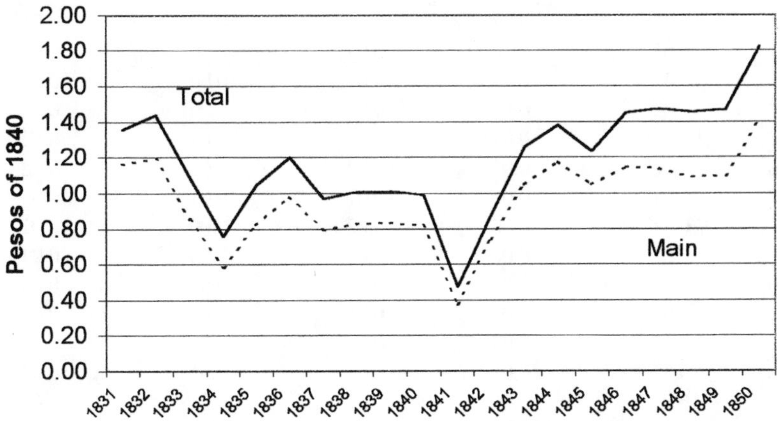

Figure 12.2 Evolution of real revenues per capita (1831–50). Note: "Total" refers to the total tax revenues per capita in real terms of Table 12.7. "Main" refers to the sum of the real revenues per capita of the tobacco, salt, and customs taxes.

Source: Table 12.7.

construct a series from 1831 to 1850 of the nine principal tax revenues. Together these taxes represented about 90 percent or more of total revenues (see Table 12.8). For example, in 1842–3 they amounted to 89.3 percent of total revenues in that fiscal year.[42] The sum of these taxes is what we use as total taxes collected in Figure 12.3 and Table 12.7.

It must be emphasized that the overall evolution of the nine taxes presented in Figure 12.2 and Table 12.7 is dominated by the behavior of only three of them: the tobacco, salt, and foreign trade taxes. In effect, the correlation coefficient between the sum of these three taxes and the sum of the nine taxes we are discussing is .98.

of expenditures from a convent in Bogotá and did not construct a price index since he did not have individual prices (Pardo, 1972, p. 229). Because this difficulty and because of the absence of any other price index, we have decided to deflate the nominal figures by a five-year moving average of the Rousseaux Price Index for Great Britain (Mitchell, 1962, p. 471). Although the use of the British price index might seem a completely inadequate solution, further analysis shows that the results are consistent with different alternatives. For example, the results are almost equivalent if the U.S. wholesale price index is used. This is hardly surprising since the parallelism of the price levels of countries under the gold standard has been widely discussed, for example, by McCloskey and Zecher (1980).

It is perhaps more surprising that Alberto Pardo's strongly questioned price index leads to results that are almost identical to those obtained with the British price index. In fact, the correlation coefficient of the real revenues per capita constructed with the British price index and the one calculated with Pardo's index is .86, and they have exactly the same overall pattern.

[42] Secretario de Hacienda, *Informe al Congreso* (1844).

Table 12.7. Revenues Per Capita in Nine Tax Categories (pesos of 1840)

	Customs	Liquor	*Diezmo*	Mortgages	Paper
1831	0.64	0.08	0.04	0.00	0.01
1832	0.67	0.10	0.04	0.00	0.01
1833	0.37	0.10	0.05	0.00	0.02
1834	0.23	0.06	0.03	0.00	0.02
1835	0.34	0.07	0.04	0.00	0.02
1836	0.48	0.07	0.04	0.00	0.02
1837	0.34	0.06	0.01	0.01	0.03
1838	0.37	0.06	0.02	0.00	0.02
1839	0.35	0.06	0.02	0.00	0.02
1840	0.34	0.06	0.03	0.00	0.02
1841	0.05	0.02	0.01	0.00	0.01
1842	0.32	0.04	0.01	0.01	0.03
1843	0.54	0.08	0.02	0.01	0.04
1844	0.53	0.09	0.02	0.01	0.04
1845	0.39	0.08	0.01	0.01	0.03
1846	0.44	0.09	0.12	0.01	NA
1847	0.39	0.09	0.10	0.01	0.04
1848	0.32	0.09	0.13	0.01	0.05
1849	0.31	0.10	0.12	0.01	0.04
1850	0.41	0.10	0.14	0.01	0.05

	Mining	Salt	Tobacco	Mail	Total
1831	0.02	0.15	0.38	0.04	1.36
1832	0.02	0.22	0.30	0.06	1.44
1833	0.02	0.15	0.33	0.06	1.10
1834	0.02	0.11	0.25	0.04	0.76
1835	0.04	0.14	0.34	0.05	1.05
1836	0.03	0.12	0.39	0.05	1.20
1837	0.03	0.12	0.33	0.04	0.97
1838	0.03	0.12	0.33	0.04	1.01
1839	0.03	0.13	0.34	0.04	1.01
1840	0.02	0.13	0.35	0.04	0.99
1841	0.02	0.11	0.21	0.04	0.47
1842	0.03	0.13	0.29	0.02	0.87
1843	0.02	0.14	0.37	0.04	1.26
1844	0.02	0.26	0.39	0.04	1.38
1845	0.02	0.25	0.41	0.03	1.24
1846	0.08	0.26	0.44	NA	1.45
1847	0.06	0.27	0.48	0.03	1.47
1848	0.06	0.27	0.51	0.04	1.45
1849	0.05	0.28	0.51	0.04	1.47
1850	0.04	0.28	0.72	0.07	1.82

Note: The total refers to the sum of the nine tax categories presented. For a discussion of the price index used, see footnote 41.

Source: Galindo (1874), Tables 1–12.

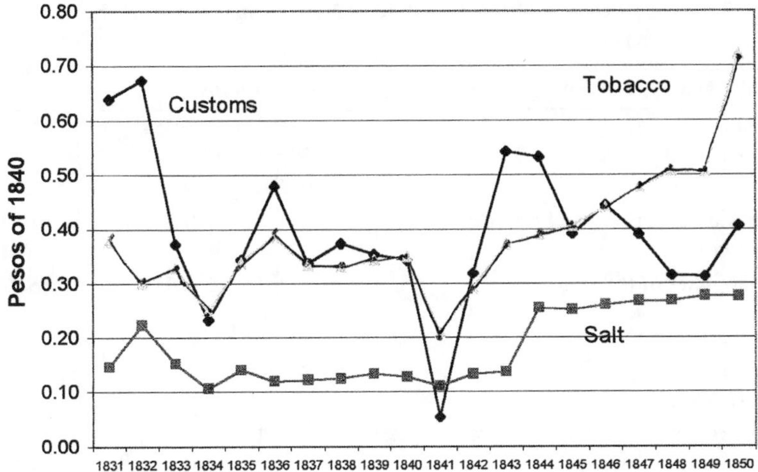

Figure 12.3 Evolution of the real revenues per capita of the customs, salt, and tobacco taxes (1831–50).

Source: Table 12.7.

Undoubtedly, the main sources of revenue throughout the period were the taxes on foreign trade, which were mostly collected on imports. Although after 1847 the gross revenues from the tobacco monopoly were higher than from foreign trade, in net revenues the latter were larger.[43] In effect, customs taxes were highly efficient since the expenditures to collect them amounted to only a small proportion of gross revenues. For example, in 1849 expenditures required to collect customs taxes were only 5.1 percent of gross revenues (see Table 12.9); in the case of the salt monopoly, expenditures were 27.9 percent of gross revenues, and for the tobacco monopoly this proportion increased to 64.2 percent. Thus, although the tobacco monopoly contributed the most to gross revenues, in net revenues it was behind the customs and salt taxes.

Several things helped to make possible the consolidation of the taxes on foreign trade, which fell basically on imports, as the most important republican tax. In the first place, with the elimination of the virtual monopoly on foreign trade that the Spanish products and merchants had in the colonial era, the main source of imports became Great Britain. Imports of textiles represented more than 80 percent of total imports by the Republic of New Granada. The drastic fall in real terms in the prices of British exports of cotton textiles permitted an enormous increase in

[43] The drop in foreign trade taxes after 1847 was the result of a law of June 14, 1847, that reformed the customs taxes. Secretario de Hacienda, *Memoria al Congreso* (1850), p. 70.

Table 12.8. Tax Revenues of the Republic of New Granada (September 1, 1842–August 31, 1843)

Category and Type of Tax	Value (pesos)		%
1. Mining		**226,351**	**7.61**
Quintos and *Fundición*	59,509		
Amonedación	166,842		
2. Taxes on commerce and production		**41,185**	**1.39**
Diezmos			
3. Monopolies of the state		**1,339,712**	**45.07**
Tobacco	784,695		
Aguardiente	172,840		
Salinas	288,562		
Papel sellado	79,539		
Hipotecas and *registros*	14,076		
4. Miscellaneous income		**231,194**	**7.78**
Exportación de mineral concentrado	579		
Derecho de internación	5,599		
Derecho de sello de títulos and *patentes*	312		
Correos	80,681		
Multas	6,789		
Empréstitos	25,679		
Donativos	928		
Venta de cal	888		
Ramos diversos	109,739		
5. Taxes on foreign trade		**1,134,107**	**38.15**
TOTAL		**2,972,549**	**100.00**

Note: The accounts have been classified following Klein (1973).
Source: Secretario de Hacienda, *Informe al Congreso* (1844).

Table 12.9. Gross and Net Tax Revenues in the Republic of New Granada (1849)

Tax	Gross Revenues (pesos)	Expenditures (pesos)	Net Revenues (pesos)	Expenditures as a Proportion of Gross Revenues
Customs	540,239	27,466	512,773	5.1
Tobacco	873,705	560,694	313,011	64.2
Salt	479,064	133,419	345,645	27.8

Source: Galindo (1874) and calculations of the authors.

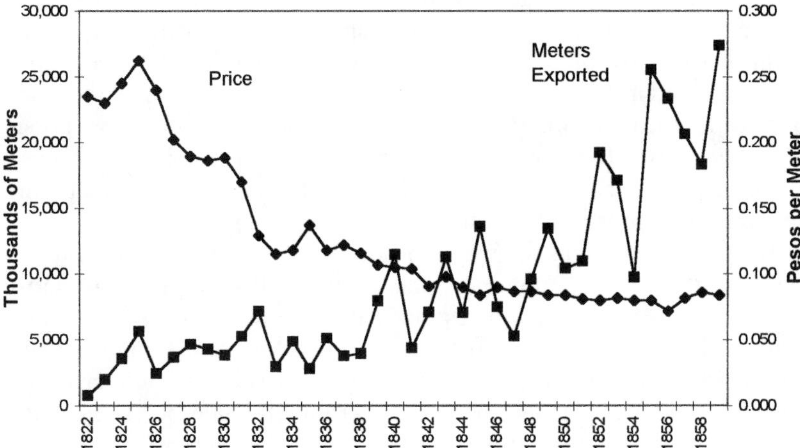

Figure 12.4 Exports of cotton textiles from Great Britain to Colombia (1822–50).

Source: Palacios (1993), p. 114.

the importation of this product. Between 1822 and 1850 the annual rate of growth of cotton textile imports into New Granada from England was 6.9 percent (see Figure 12.4).[44] This rapid increase in cotton imports was reflected the drop in real terms of the price of this product as a result of the Industrial Revolution. The possibilities created by independence for fully exploiting the benefits of freer trade are tangible in this specific case.

What domestic consumers in New Granada were observing was that, year after year, they were paying lower prices (in 1850 the price of one meter of British cotton imported into New Granada was just 55 percent of what it had been, in real terms, in 1831). Thus, the increase in the level of customs taxes was not perceived by the consumers.[45]

After the late 1830s, the most controversial tax was the tobacco monopoly. In terms of gross revenues it was the main tax. But perhaps even more important than its quantitative impact is the fact that since the 1830s there were several relatively successful, although limited, attempts to export tobacco to European markets.[46] Thus, there was increasing pressure on the government to abolish the monopoly. However, it had not been eliminated for purely pragmatic reasons: it played a central role in financing the government, and there were no

[44] Palacios (1993), p. 114.

[45] Ibid., p. 114, and calculations of the authors. The proportion between customs taxes and the value of imports increased from 15.2 percent in 1835 to 21.9 percent in 1844.

[46] Harrison (1951), p. 117.

good alternatives for regaining the income that would be lost if it were eliminated. Even William Wills, an influential British merchant established in Colombia since 1826, who generally defended free markets, stated in 1831: "even though the general application of the principles of political economy should be put into practice whenever possible, the end of the tobacco monopoly should not be precipitated, because under the present circumstances instead of obtaining positive results, this measure could produce a disaster."[47]

An additional reason why the government was reluctant to eliminate the tobacco monopoly was its belief that depending almost exclusively on the customs taxes made it very vulnerable. In 1837, due to an incident with Great Britain, the ports of New Granada were blockaded by the British Navy. As a result, President Francisco de Paula Santander concluded that the government would be at great risk if it did not have alternative sources of revenue, such as the tobacco monopoly.[48]

The salt monopoly was, in net revenues, the second most productive tax. However, it was considerd very inconvenient for reasons of equity. The secretary of finance, Manuel Murillo Toro, was especially forceful in his critique of the salt monopoly. In his report to the Congress in 1850 he argued that "This tax is, without doubt, one of the most productive and well administered that the national treasury has, but it has the defect that it taxes considerably an article of absolute necessity, and it does it with much inequality. The inhabitants of the provinces of Panama, Cartagena, Santa Marta, Riohacha, Mompox, Antioquia, Choco, and Barbacoas do not pay for this contribution; other provinces pay very little; and even those where there are salt mines pay different amounts. In Popayan the quintal of salt is sold for 74 reales, while in Mompox it can be bought for 8, in Santa Marta for 4; in Mariquita for 48 and in Bogota for 32."[49]

The other principal taxes were not comparable to the revenues generated by the salt and tobacco monopolies and the customs tax. All the other taxes produced in per capita terms revenues that were generally below 10 cents of 1840 (see Figures 12.5 and 12.6). The *diezmo* revenue increased drastically after 1846 because, up to 1845, only the portion corresponding to the state had been reported. Thus, the revenues before and after 1846 are not directly comparable.

In 1850 the structure of tax revenues in existence was the result of three decades of republican reforms (see Table 12.10). Some of the most unpopular taxes of the colonial period had been abolished (such as the head tax on indians and the *alcabala*). However, other colonial

[47] Deas (1996), p. 25. [48] Bell (1997), p. 115.

[49] Secretario de Hacienda, *Informe al Congreso* (1850), p. 8.

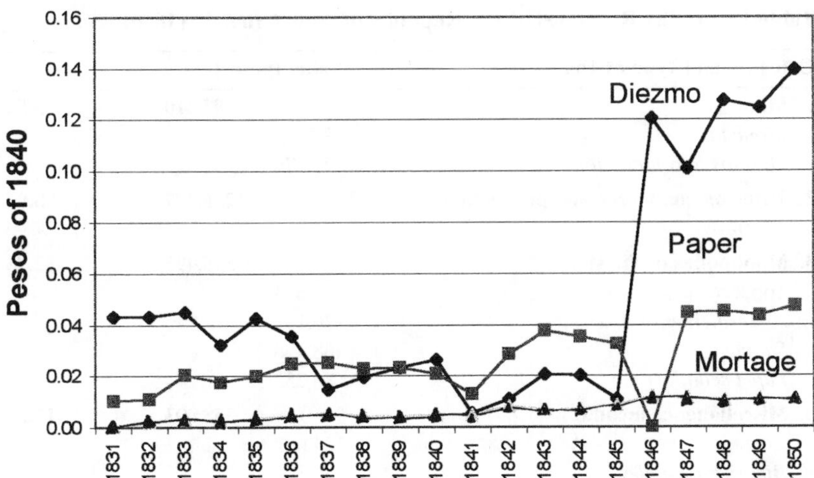

Figure 12.5 Evolution of the real revenues per capita of paper, *diezmo*, and mortgage taxes (1831–50).

Source: Table 12.7.

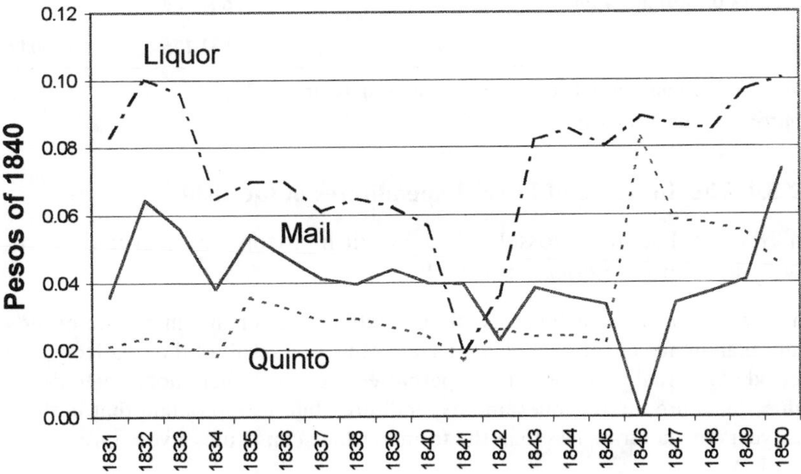

Figure 12.6 Evolution of the real revenues per capita of the liquor, mail, and *quinto* taxes (1831–50).

Source: Table 12.7.

taxes remained: *diezmos*, *quintos*, the tobacco monopoly, the salt monopoly, and the liquor monopoly. The first three were eliminated in the reforms of the 1850s. However, the salt and liquor monopolies survived well into the twentieth century as essential features of the Colombian tax system.

Table 12.10. Tax Revenues of the Republic of New Granada (1850)

Category and Type of Tax	Value (pesos)		%
1. Mining		**103,210**	**3.52**
Monedas	27,831		
Quintos and *fundición*	75,379		
2. Taxes on commerce and production		**236,427**	**8.07**
Diezmos			
3. Monopolies of the state		**1,545,495**	**52.73**
Tobacco	826,644		
Aguardiente	170,141		
Salinas	468,458		
Papel sellado	80,252		
4. Miscellaneous income		**358,093**	**12.22**
Correos	124,082		
Bienes nacionales	56,370		
Peajes and *pontazgos*	22,367		
Censos, alquileres, and *premios*	18,868		
Internación de sales and *mercancías*	4,200		
Impuestos de rentas varias	132,206		
5. Taxes on foreign trade		**687,950**	**23.47**
TOTAL		**2,931,175**	**100.00**

Note: The accounts have been classified following Klein (1973).
Source: Camacho Roldan (1999), p. 151.

12.3.4 The Structure of Fiscal Expenditures in the 1830s

In 1838 Carl August Gosselman, a Swedish citizen who traveled extensively in South America, observed:

> In New Granada public finances are in a better situation and in a more orderly state than in any of the republics I have visited, as a result of the relatively long period of internal peace, which has permitted the government not only to determine which are the revenues and expenditures, but also to obtain that in these last years the latter be less than the former, which constitutes a very rare case in South America.[50]

Information on the expenditures of the central government of New Granada is available only for the eight years from 1832 to 1840 and for a few years in the 1840s. All the evidence shows that except for 1841–2, when revenues dropped drastically as a result of the civil war known as the War of the Supremes, fiscal deficits were small or nonexistent, as Gosselman had commented. For example, from December 1, 1832, to

[50] Gosselman (1962), p. 120.

August 31, 1840, the central government had revenues that amounted to $18,973,983, while in the same period expenditures amounted to $17,955,320, that is, revenues were 5.7 percent above expenditures.[51]

For the 1840s data on government expenditures are not as complete as they are for the 1830s. However, for the four years between 1847 and 1850 we know that in two of them (1847 and 1848) there was a surplus and in two of them a deficit (1849 and 1850). Thus, it seems that overall there was a relative balance in the budget of the government in New Granada in this period. The main reason seems to have been that there was only one civil war in the period 1831–50. Also, New Granada did not engage in any foreign war throughout the nineteenth century. This was certainly not the case in many other Latin American countries. For example, Argentina in 1826–30 was engaged in war with Brazil and was affected by internal conflicts. The result was a period of fiscal disorder that led to a period of inflationary finance.[52]

In Table 12.11 we present the expenditures of the central government from 1832 to 1840. It is evident that salaries represented the main obligation of the government, especially the salaries of navy and army personnel, which together amounted to 41.4 percent of all expenditures. The other important outlay was for the tobacco monopoly, which represented 15.1 percent of the total.

It is important to emphasize that payments of public debt represented only 5 percent of total outlays. The small outlay for this category reflects two situations. In the first place, the foreign debt was not being paid. During the war of independence, the Republic of Colombia (Venezuela, Ecuador, New Granada) had obtained loans in London to pay for the expenses of the war. When the Republic of Colombia broke up, a process of negotiations for the division of the debt began. Finally, in 1839, New Granada accepted the responsibility for 50 percent of the debt. In the meantime, no payments were made.[53] In 1845 New Granada renegotiated its debt, and met the established payments between 1846 and 1849. After the later date, payments were suspended. What this reflects is the absence of foreign loans in the period 1831–50 as a possible source of finance for the government of New Granada.

The second point is that in an impoverished economy, as was New Granada in the period immediately following independence, the possibility of raising loans by the government in the local credit market was very limited. Under these conditions, and with little chance to appeal to the inflation tax due to the limited development of the banking and

[51] Secretario de Hacienda, *Memoria al Congreso* (1843), Cuadro 11.

[52] Cortes-Conde and McCandless (chapter 11, this volume).

[53] Junguito (1945), pp. 59–98.

Table 12.11. Expenditures of the Government of the Republic of New Granada (December 1, 1832–August 31, 1840)

Expenditures	Value (pesos)		%
1. Salaries and expenditures		**12,331,339**	**68.67**
Civiles	2,649,122		
Hacienda	2,196,227		
Guerra	6,823,698		
Marina	616,033		
Legación Romana	46,259		
2. Expenditures		**4,392,160**	**24.46**
Plaza	41,156		
Fortificación	56,900		
Hospitales	288,604		
Tobacco	2,709,200		
Correos	255,894		
Generales	1,040,406		
3. Payments of public debt		**893,836**	**4.98**
Payment of interest on the consolidated debt	149,955		
Amortization of the consolidated debt	9,984		
Floating debt	371,147		
Debt assigned to the treasury by law of April 30, 1835	156,842		
Sent to England	205,908		
4. Pensions		**72,186**	**0.40**
5. Miscellaneous expenditures		**266,785**	**1.49**
Devolutions from import taxes	70,129		
Devolutions from *alcabala*	33,867		
Devolutions from liquor	24,185		
Devolutions from salaries and pensions	16		
Devolutions from fines	301		
Supplements to the Casa de Moneda	10,000		
Remitted for coinage	23,667		
Mermas de fundición	6,607		
Premios de Exportación	73,185		
Payments for registration rights	8		
Payments for *comisos*	32		
Payments for *bienes embargados*	1,982		
Returns from *censos*	7,991		
Exchange of coins	11,023		
Freights and insurance	3,792		
TOTAL		**17,956,306**	**100.00**

Note: The sum of the different items does not coincide exactly with the total since we have eliminated the reales.

Source: Secretario de Hacienda, *Memoria al Congreso* (1843), Cuadro II.

financial institutions, the government was forced to manage its finances with austerity and prudence.

12.4 THE MONETARY SYSTEM: FROM THE CHAOS CREATED BY THE WAR OF INDEPENDENCE TO THE REFORMS OF MID-CENTURY

12.4.1 The Monetary Chaos Produced by the War of Independence

During the colonial period there were two minting houses in New Granada, one in Santa Fe de Bogotá and one in Popayán. The monetary unit of the Spanish colonies was the silver peso of eight reales, with a standard of purity of .902 2/3.[54] However, during the eighteenth century in New Granada, coins with different standards of purity were minted: gold coins with purities of .916$^1/_2$, .901, and .875 and silver coins with purities of .902 and .901. Toward the end of the colonial period, there was also circulation of the macuquina, a silver coin of irregular shape whose standard of purity fluctuated between .908 and .916. It had been minted in Mexico and Peru during the Habsburg era and had arrived in New Granada through the subsidies that were sent from the treasuries of New Spain and Peru to cover the local deficit.[55] Because the shape of the macuquina was irregular, it was relatively easy to falsify or cut in its edges.

The years of the struggle for independence from Spain (1810–19) left the newly created nations with a chaotic situation with respect to circulating coins. In the first place, there was a proliferation of coins of low quality, which were used to finance the expenditures of the war. The first minting of these low-quality coins was ordered in 1811 by the Patriotic Junta of Cartagena.[56] These coins were made of copper, they had a nominal value of half a real and two reales and were minted in 1815. In the Casa de la Moneda of Santa Fe de Bogotá the patriots minted a coin known as provincial or china, of which three types were issued.

The Constitutional Congress of 1821 decreed that all the coins of gold and silver minted after that date had to conform to the same specification that had been used under the Spanish Empire. However, as the historian Jose Manuel Restrepo commented about this law: "It was impossible to follow it in the state of disarray and misery which characterized fiscal revenues. The law was eluded by minting coins of poor quality and stamping them with a date previous to the prohibition. This

[54] Torres Garcia (1980), p. 20. The standard of purity of a coin was the percentage of higher-quality metal it contained. For example, a gold coin with a standard of purity of .900 had 90 percent gold and 10 percent metals of lesser value.

[55] Safford (1965), p. 115. [56] Barriga (1969), Tomo II, p. 127.

was done following reserved orders of the President, while General Santander was in charge."[57]

During the years of the war of independence the Spaniards also contributed to the monetary chaos. When they briefly reestablished control of New Granada, Viceroy Montalvo ordered the minting of coins in Santa Marta and Cartagena. These silver coins did not have a fixed weight or fixed specifications. As a result, it was very easy to falsify them.[58] The army of Pablo Morillo also introduced wherever it went a coin of very poor quality known as the caraqueña.

12.4.2 First Attempts to Reestablish Monetary Stability

As we have seen, when the war of independence concluded in New Granada, there was in circulation a wide array of coins of gold, silver, and copper with different weights, qualities, and specifications. This monetary chaos created difficulties for internal trade and increased transaction costs. To put an end to this situation, the Constitutional Congress of 1821 decided that the solution was to return to the monetary system weights and specifications that had existed under the Spanish domination, and to retire from circulation all the coins of poor quality and inferior specifications. For this reason, the copper coins of Santa Marta and Cartagena, the caraqueña, the macuquina, and all the coins with a low content of silver were to be eradicated. Although this was the intention of the government, these coins were not retired from circulation due to lack of funds. In fact, and as has been mentioned, the government continued to issue coins with a standard of purity of .538, violating the prohibition of the Constitutional Congress of 1821.

After 1821 an effort was made to unify the qualities and specifications of the coins in circulation. This was, however, a very slow and partial process. A law of March 13, 1826, established the specifications for the new gold and silver coins. Additionally, in 1826 the recall of the macuquina was ordered, and it was to be reminted as a silver coin with a standard of purity of .666$^1/_2$. However, according to the historians Henao and Arrubla, "This operation could not be carried out rapidly because the machines of the Casa de la Moneda in Bogota and Popayan were already deteriorated, and the great quantity of older coins in circulation were gradually displacing the new ones, which emigrated to Venezuela and Ecuador; thus, in 1846 the re-minted coins had almost disappeared and in the province of Bogota the macuquina was circulating widely."[59] Even worse, apparently the circulation of macuquinas

[57] Restrepo (1860), p. 14. [58] Ibid., p. 13.
[59] Henao and Arrubla (1912), Tomo II, p. 514.

increased, because it was profitable to import them from the Antilles. For example, in 1838, macuquinas imported from Jamaica produced a gain of 25 percent in the operation.[60]

Additionally, there seems to have been extensive falsification of the macuquina. In 1831 the counterfeiters benefited from a decree that ordered that the macuquina be accepted temporarily, "[e]ven though it were clipped and without specifications clearly legible for its nominal value."[61] Legislation that requires the acceptance of any type of money considered to be of inferior quality leads to the operation of Gresham's law: bad money displaces good money. It should be made clear that in this context good money is the one that has a higher intrinsic value (in gold, for example) than other types of money that have the same nominal value.

The law of May 31, 1838, authorized the government to retire the macuquina and clipped coins from circulation. That year, in his report to the Congress, the secretary of finance commented: "The law of May 14, 1826, ordered the amortization of the macuquina and clipped coins. The past turmoils and the situation of the Treasury have not permitted the realization of that law and in the meantime the problem grows. The evil every day increases in intensity and it is necessary to proceed with firmness and determination to the operation of the amortization."[62] However, as with previous attempts to amortize the macuquina and clipped coins, the one ordered by the government in 1838 was not carried through.

It is important to mention that up to 1870, when the first successful commercial bank was established in Colombia, the money supply consisted of metallic coins.[63] The relative balance of government finances in the first half of the nineteenth century, as a result of a period of political stability, implied that the government did not have to appeal to an inflationary tax to pay for its expenditures.

Before the appearance of commercial banks in the 1870's, the credit market had been controlled by the Catholic Church. Since the colonial period the Church had a virtual monopoly of the credit market through a type of mortgage loan known as "censoo". The liberal reforms of the 1850's and 1860's reduced the influence of the church in the economy and opened the way for the establishment of commercial banks.[64]

[60] Safford (1965), p. 116. [61] Barriga (1969), Tomo III, p. 27.

[62] Torres (1980), p. 26.

[63] There were some limited and rather unsuccessful attempts to issue paper money during independence and in the 1850s (Ibañez, 1990).

[64] Meisel (1990).

12.4.3 The Monetary Reform of Tomas Cipriano de Mosquera

Toward the mid-1840s the monetary situation of New Granada was chaotic. All attempts at monetary reform had failed and in some cases had even made the situation worse.

The existing legislation contributed to the monetary chaos because it made equivalent, in nominal terms, coins with different intrinsic value (that is, in metallic content). A contemporary economic commentator summarized the situation found by the government of General Tomas Cipriano de Mosquera as follows: "The monetary laws persisted in trying to force the owners of gold ounces to exchange an ounce of gold for 16 pesos that contain 245 grams of silver, as they exchanged it for 16 Spanish pesos, which contained 382 grams of silver."[65] As a result of this situation, by the mid-1840s many observers spoke of what they considered was a scarcity of money, and which in reality was the operation of Gresham's law: and the disappearance of good money.[66] If money had been scarce, prices should have been falling, but instead price stability was observed. Thus, there was no shortage in the total amount of money, but rather in the amount of money of good quality.[67]

As a result of these difficulties the government of General Mosquera carried through in 1846 and 1847 an extensive monetary reform, led by the influential Secretaries of Finance Lino de Pombo and Florentino Gonzalez. The reform established that all coins would have 90 percent of pure metal and 10 percent of lower-grade metals (a standard of purity of .900). As a result, no more coins of low quality would be minted and those already in circulation, such as the macuquina, would be collected and reminted.

The efforts of the Mosquera administration to retire the macuquina from circulation were successful. At the end of 1848 almost all of these coins had been collected. By the beginning of 1849, 380,620 pesos of macuquina coins had been retired, with a total cost to the government of 53,000 pesos.[68]

Why was the Mosquera administration successful in reforming the monetary regime and retiring the macuquina when all previous governments had failed? Undoubtedly, the Mosquera government faced a much

[65] Galindo (1978), p. 161.

[66] For a discussion about the alleged scarcity of money see Meisel (1990).

[67] In a study on colonial Canada, Angela Redish concluded that although most of the contemporary observers spoke about a scarcity of money, the problem was the poor quality of the specie in circulation as a result of Gresham's law (Redish, 1984).

[68] Helguera (1958), p. 348. The expenditures for retiring the macuquina amounted to about 10 percent of the revenues from customs taxes and to less than 5 percent of total revenues.

better fiscal situation than its predecessors. As we saw in the previous section, after 1843 a relatively sustained increase in the revenues per capita, in constant pesos, of the government began. This improvement in fiscal conditions permitted the monetary reform of 1846–7, and the tax reforms of 1848–50.

12.5 CONCLUSIONS

In this chapter, we have discussed the basic structure of the tax revenues of the treasuries in the Viceroyalty of New Granada toward the end of colonial rule (1783 and 1808–9). In that structure, several of the main features of the economy of New Granada in the eighteenth century can be observed: (1) it is clear that even in the context of the Spanish American Empire, it was a poor economy; (2) the mining sector, and therefore the export sector, was relatively small; (3) it was not a very dynamic economy compared to the viceroyalties of New Spain or Buenos Aires.

In the anticolonial reaction that finally led to the declaration of independence from Spain, the tax system was one of the principal catalysts. For the ideologues of the movement for national liberation, the fiscal regime that Spain had imposed upon its colonies was characterized by inequity, inefficiency, and negative effects on the growth of output. To rapidly put an end to this system was the main objective of the first finance secretaries of the new republic, beginning with Jose Maria del Castillo y Rada in the 1820s. However, the overall economic contraction that affected New Granada after independence made the task of transforming the fiscal system extremely difficult, and some taxes that had been abolished had to be reestablished, at least temporarily, like the indian tribute. Other taxes, like the tobacco monopoly, were abolished only in the late 1840s.

The difficulties encountered by the finance secretaries in the 1830s and 1840s led the liberal ideologues of the 1850s to minimize the achievements of transforming the tax system of the period 1821–50. This negative assessment has been shared by most Colombian historians, for whom the colonial fiscal regime survived until 1850.

As we have seen in this chapter, it is not true at all that in the Republic of New Granada the colonial tax system was intact by the middle of the nineteenth century. In fact, by that date the young republic had a much better fiscal system than the one it had inherited from Spain. In the first place, it was a much fairer system. The extreme inequities, such as the head tax on indians and the taxes on public employees, had already been eliminated. Also, the regime was much more efficient since the most important sources of revenues had become the taxes on foreign imports, and their collection was very efficient since the expenditures required were only about 5 percent of gross revenues. Finally, many of the colonial taxes that distorted the efficient allocation of resources had been abolished by 1850, such as the *alcabala* and the export taxes. These achievements occurred in the face of an economic contraction and a reduction in exports per capita. By 1850 New Granada was one of the poorest countries of Latin America, with exports per capita of 1.9 U.S. dollars, well below the Latin American average of 5.2 U.S. dollars.[69]

After the administration of Tomas Cipriano de Mosquera (1845–9), the movement toward liberal economic reforms gained influence. In 1848 the end of the tobacco monopoly was approved by the Congress (however, an export tax on this product was established). By 1850 the production and export of tobacco were completely liberated. Under a cycle of increasing international prices, exports grew rapidly during the 1850s and 1860s, and tobacco became the country's leading export product.

In 1850 the other important reform of the tax system was the decentralization of incomes and expenditures, by which the finances of the regional states were strengthened. The principal taxes transferred to the regional governments were the *diezmo*, the *quinto*, and the liquor monopoly. The *diezmo* tax was rapidly abolished in the 1850s by the provincial governments. Almost half of the provinces eliminated the liquor monopoly, and Antioquia, the main producer of gold, abolished the *quinto*.[70]

To replace the revenues lost from the taxes eliminated, most provinces tried to establish a direct tax of 10 percent of total income. However, the revenues collected were never very high and there were always many difficulties, especially in obtaining reliable information on personal incomes. However, even with these difficulties, in 1873 the revenues from the income tax represented 16.9 percent of the total revenues of the nine provincial governments.[71]

However revolutionary the fiscal reforms of the 1850s may seem, when seen from a longer-term perspective the changes introduced were not so dramatic. For example, if we compare the structure of the tax revenues in 1850 with what existed in the early twentieth century, it can be seen that in many respects they were quite similar. For example, in 1906 three taxes that in 1850 amounted to 43.7 percent of all revenues (customs, the salt monopoly, and mail) represented 60.7 percent of total

[69] Bulmer-Thomas (1994), p. 38. In 1850 the only Latin American countries with fewer exports per capita were Paraguay and Guatemala.

[70] Melo (1987), p. 148. [71] Deas (1993), p. 82.

revenues.[72] Even more, these three taxes continued to be the basis of the tax system until the late 1930s, when the income tax started to play an important role.[73]

If in the period 1831–50 the advances in reforming the tax system inherited from Spain were so significant, and the reforms of the 1850s were not as profound as they are generally believed to be, why has the consensus view among Colombian economic historians been that the Spanish fiscal regime survived until 1850? We think that this is an example of intellectual history in which Albert O. Hirschman's notion of *fracasomania* is especially helpful. Hirschman coined the term *fracasomania* to refer to a trait often found among Latin American policymaking elites, consisting in: "the insistence on [the] part of each new set of policymakers to decry as utter failure everything that has been done before."[74]

Hirschman attributes this trait to the consequences of a protracted intellectual dependence. Intellectual dependence leads policymakers and intellectuals to look abroad for solutions and orientations rather than to carefully evaluate domestic experiences. The way to justify the lack of attention to what has been done by previous generations is to declare that everything that has been done before is a complete failure.

Florentino Gonzalez, the main ideologue of the liberal reforms of the late 1840s and early 1850s, had lived in France and England from 1841 to 1845 before he became secretary of finance in 1846. Not surprisingly, he was one of the persons who contributed most to the thesis of the complete failure of the fiscal reforms in the period 1821–50. However, when all the evidence is carefully analyzed, it is clear that there was no *fracaso*.

REFERENCES

Barriga, Villalba, A. M.(1969). *Historia de la Casa de Moneda*. Bogotá: Banco de la Republica.

Bell, Gustavo (1997). "Regional Politics and the Formation of the National State: The Caribbean Coast of Colombia in the First Years of Independence, 1810–1860," D. Phil. Thesis in Modern History, Oxford University.

Bernal, Joaquin (1984). "Las finanzas del sector público central en los años veinte treinta," *Coyuntura Económica*. Vol. 4 No. 2, p. 131.

Bulmer-Thomas, Victor (1984). *Economic History of Latin America Since Independence*. Cambridge: Cambridge University Press.

Bushnell, David (1993). *The Making of Modern Colombia: A Nation in Spite of Itself*. Los Angeles: University of California Press.

[72] Diaz (1996), Table 20. [73] Bernal (1984), p. 131. [74] Hirschman (1981).

Camacho Roldan, Salvador (1900). *Memorias*. Bogotá: Editorial Bedout.

(1976). *Escritos sobre economía y política*. Bogotá: Colcultura.

Colmenares, Germán (1978). "La economía y la sociedad coloniales, 1550–1800," in Jaime Jaramillo Uribe (ed.), *Manual de Historia de Colombia*, Tomo I. Bogotá: Biblioteca Colombiana de Cultura.

(Dec. 29, 1778). "Copia del plan de defensa formado por Real Orden por el Brigadier don Agustín Crane." Cartagena: *Archivo Histórico Nacional de Colombia, Colonia, Milicias y Marina*, Tomo 41.

Cruz Santos, Abel (1965). *Economía y hacienda pública*. Bogotá: Ediciones Lerner.

Deas, Malcom (1993). *Del poder y la gramatica*. Bogotá: Tercer Mundo Editores.

(1996). *Vida y opiniones de Mr. Williams Wills*. Bogotá: Banco de la República.

De Pombo, José Ignacio (1986). *Comercio y Contrabando en Cartagena de Indias*. Bogotá: Nueva Biblioteca Colombiana de Cultura.

Diaz, Silvia (1996). "Finanzas públicas del gobierno central en Colombia, 1905-1925." Trabajo de Grado, Facultad de Economía, Universidad de los Andes.

Fisher, John (1990). "The Effects of Comercio Libre on the Economies of Colombia and Perú: A Comparison," in John R. Fisher, Allan J. Kuethe, and Anthony McFarlane, *Reforms and Insurrection in Bourbon New Granada and Peru*. Baton Rouge: Louisiana State University Press.

Galindo, Anibal (1874). *Hacienda éconómica y estadistica de la Hacienda Nacional*. Bogotá: Imprenta de Nicolas Ponton.

(1978). *Estudios económicos y fiscales*. Bogotá: Colcultura.

Gosselman, Carl August (1962). *Informe sobre los Estados Sud-americanos en los Años de 1837 y 1838*. Estocolmo: Biblioteca e Instituto de Estudios Ibero-Americanos.

Grahn, Lance R. (1985). "Contraband, Commerce, and Society in New Granada, 1713–1763," Ph.D. dissertation, Duke University.

Harrison, John Parker (1951). "The Colombian Tobacco Industry, From Government Monopoly to Free Trade, 1778–1876," Ph.D. dissertation, University of California.

Helguera, Leon J. (1958). "The First Mosquera Administration in New Granada, 1845–1849," Ph.D. dissertation, University of North Carolina.

Henao and Arrubla (1912). *Historia de Colombia*. Bogotá: Escuela Tipográfica Salesiana.

Hirschman, Albert O. (1981). *Essays in Trespassing, Economics to Politics and Beyond*. Cambridge University Press, NY.

Ibañez, Jorge Enrique (1990). "La emisión de billetes en el siglo XIX," in *El Banco de la República: Antecedentes, Evolucion y Estructura*. Bogotá: Banco de la República.

Jara, Alvaro (1994). "El financiamiento de la defensa en Cartagena de Indias: los excedntes de las cajas de Bogotá y de Quito, 1761–1802," *Historia*, Vol. 28, p. 155.

Jaramillo Uribe, Jaime (1993). *De la Sociología a la historia*. Bogotá: Ediciones Uniandes.

Junguito, Roberto (1985). *La deuda externa en el siglo XIX, cien años de incumplimiento*. Bogotá: Tercer Mundo Editores.

Klein, Herbert (1973). "Structure and Profitability of the Royal Finance in the Viceroyalty of the Rio de la Plata in 1790," *Hispanic American Historical Review*, Vol. 53, No. 3, pp. 440–69.

(1995). "The Great Shift: The Rise of Mexico and The Decline of Perú in the Spanish American Colonial Empire, 1680–1809," *Revista de historia económica*, Vol. 23, No. 1, pp. 35–61.

Klein, Herbert, and Barbier, Jacques A. (1988). "Recent Trends in the Study of Spanish American Colonial Public Finance," *Latin American Research Review*, Vol. 23, No. 1, pp. 35–62.

McCloskey, Donald and Zecher, Richard (1980). "How the Gold Standard Worked, 1810–1913," in H. Frenkel and H. Johnson (eds.), *The Monetary Approach to the Balance of Payments*. London: George Allen and Unwin.

McFarlane, Anthony (1993). *Colombia Before Independence: Economy, Society, and Politics Under Bourbon Rule*. Cambridge: Cambridge University Press, NY.

Meisel R., Adolfo (1990a). "El patrón metálico, 1821–1879," in *El Banco de la República: Antecedentes, Evolución y Estructura*. Bogotá: Banco de la República.

(1990b). "Los bancos comerciales en la era de la banca libre, 1871–1923," in *El Banco de la República: Antecedentes, Evolución y Estructura*. Bogotá: Banco de la República.

Melo, Jorge Orlando (1979). *Sobre historia y política*. Bogotá: La Carreta.

(1987). "Las vicisitudes del modelo liberal, 1850–1899," in José Antonio Ocampo (ed.), *Historia Económica de Colombia*. Bogotá: Siglo Veintiuno Editores.

Mitchell, B. R. (1962). *Abstract of British Historical Statistics*. Cambridge: Cambridge University Press, NY.

Mora de Tovar, Gilma (1983). "Las cuentas de la Real Hacienda y la política fiscal en el Nuevo Reino de Granada," *Anuario de historia social y de la cultura*, No. 11, pp. 305–15.

Nieto Arteta, Luis Eduardo (1983). *Economía y cultura en la historia de Colombia*. Bogotá El Ancora.

Ocampo, José Antonio (1984). *Colombia y la economia mundial, 1830–1910*. Bogotá: Siglo Veintiuno Editores.

Palacios, Marco (1993). "Las consecuencias económicas de la Independencia en Colombia: sobre los origenes del subdesarrollo," in Leandro Prados de la Escosura and Samuel Amaral (eds.), *La Independencia Americana: Consecuencias Económicas*. Madrid. Alianza Editorial.

Pardo, Alberto (1972). *Geografia económica y humana de Colombia*. Bogotá: Ediciones Tercer Mundo.

Parker Harrison, John (1951). "The Colombian Tobacco Industry, From Government Monopoly to Free Trade, 1778–1876," Ph.D. dissertation, University of California.

Phelan, John Leddy (1980). *El Pueblo y el Rey, la Revolución Comunera en Colombia 1781*. Bogotá: Carlos Valencia Editores.

Redish, Angela (1984). "Why Was Specie Scarce in Colonial Economies? An Analysis of the Canadian Currency, 1796–1830," *Journal of Economic History*, Vol. 12, No. 3, pp. 713–28.

Restrepo, Jose Manuel (1860). *Memoria sobre la amonedación de oro y plata en la Nueva Granada*. Bogotá: Imprenta de la Nación.

Safford, Frank (1965). "Commerce and Enterprise in Central Colombia, 1821–1870," Ph.D. dissertation, Columbia University.

Secretario de Hacienda (various years). *Informe al Congreso*. Bogotá.

(various years). *Memorias de la Hacienda*. Bogotá.

Torres Garcia, Guillermo (1980). *Historia de la Moneda en Colombia*. Medellín: FAES.

Twinam, Ann (1985). *Mineros, comerciantes y labradores: las raices del espiritu empresarial en Antioquia 1763–1810*. Medellín: FAES.

Urrutia, Miguel and Arrubla, Mario (1970). *Compendio de Estadísticas Históricas de Colombia*. Bogotá: Universidad Nacional.

PART III

COMMENTARIES

13

The State in Economic History

Herschel I. Grossman

Each of the contributions to this volume on fiscal and monetary institutions attempts in one way or another to describe and to interpret the historical role of the state in promoting economic development. Not surprisingly, the volume exhibits a tension between alternative characterizations of the state and between two associated ways to think about economic policy. Both of these characterizations are prominent in current research in positive political economy.

One characterization views the state as an agent of its citizens – specifically, the agent to which the citizenry assigns the task of effectuating collective choices about resource allocation and income distribution. In this characterization, the power to tax serves as the state's essential method of enforcing collective choices. Taxation is the means by which the state prevents free riding on the provision of nonexcludable public goods.

In characterizing the state as an agent of its citizens, we implicitly define the citizenry to be the politically enfranchised subset of those people who are under the dominion of the state. In other words, the citizens are those subjects of the state who have political power. Given the characterization of the state as an agent of its citizens, basic problems for understanding the historical role of the state in promoting economic development are to identify the subset of subjects who comprise the citizenry and to explain the determination of this subset.

Once the citizenry has been identified, the next problem is to understand how the citizenry exercises its political power – that is, to understand the relation between the citizenry as principal and the state as agent. A central part of this problem is to explore how the political

Revised version of comments prepared for the Twelfth International Economic History Congress, Session A4: The Legacy of Western European Fiscal and Monetary Institutions for the New World: The Seventeenth to Nineteenth Centuries, Madrid, August 25th, 1998.

system aggregates and reconciles the interests of different groups within the citizenry in order to effectuate collective choices. A further problem is to evaluate these collective choices according to various criteria of efficiency. The effectuation and evaluation of collective choices is the subject of a large literature in positive political economy.[1]

The objection to this research program is that viewing the state as an agent of its citizens involves a paradox. In order for the state to enforce collective choices about resource allocation and income distribution, the citizenry must subject itself to the state's power to tax and to spend. The paradox is that with these sovereign powers in hand, the state can exploit its citizens by taxing and spending for its own purposes.[2]

This observation leads to the alternative characterization of the state as the instrument of a ruling elite. *Ruling elite* is a generic name for whatever group appropriates the net revenues of the state.[3] Actual historical examples of ruling elites include a monarch and the royal court, the members of a ruling party, the military, the professional politicians, the bureaucrats, and, in contemporary American local government, the public employees' unions.[4] Both theory and observation suggest that in

[1] David Austen-Smith and Jeffrey Banks (1999) provide a comprehensive treatment of the theory of preference aggregation for collective choices.

[2] The resulting dilemma was recognized even in biblical times. In First Samuel 8:4–22, the people of Israel are of one mind in requesting that the prophet Samuel "make us a king . . . [who] may judge us, and fight our battles," but Samuel warns the people that a king will impose heavy taxes for his own purposes and cause them "to cry out in that day because of your king whom ye shall have chosen you." Despite Samuel's apt warning of the potential for abuse of sovereign power, the Israelites decided that having a king would be better than not having a king. Indeed, almost all societies that have made the transition from hunting and gathering to settled agriculture and industry seem to have reached the same conclusion. This observation suggests that the citizenry typically finds itself to be better off with a state than without a state, even though the state can tax and spend for its own purposes.

This result is especially likely to obtain if each group of people takes as given the decisions of other groups of people to form states. Historically, as Michael Taylor (1982) points out (p. 130), "The formation of states in most societies has been the direct or indirect result, in least in part, of the presence nearby of already existing states. . . . Societies without a state are subjugated, colonised or absorbed by states." As noted, in the biblical story, one of the reasons that the Israelites give for wanting a king is to "fight our battles." Nevertheless, it is possible that the formation of states is globally inefficient and that a hypothetical anarchic world without states would be Pareto superior to a Cournot–Nash equilibrium with states.

[3] The characterization of the state as the instrument of the ruling elite is independent of the historical origin of the state. In the biblical story, even though the state was formed at the initiative of the citizenry, having subjected themselves to the state's sovereign power to tax and to spend, the citizenry cannot prevent the king from imposing heavy taxes for his own purposes.

[4] The present discussion assumes that the citizenry and the ruling elite are distinct groups. Martin McGuire and Mancur Olson (1996) relax this assumption. They assume that the

stable democracies the ruling elite typically includes a political establishment that is an implicit coalition of ostensible political opponents.[5] As the *Wall Street Journal* (October 24, 1990) has observed about the American federal government, "Republicans and Democrats have forged a political class to divvy up the profits, fighting only over precisely how to pick pockets." The apt term *proprietary state* emphasizes the analogies between the ruling elite and the owners of a private enterprise and between the characterization of the state as maximizing the wealth of a ruling elite and the standard economic model of a private enterprise.[6]

Even if characterizing the state as the instrument of the ruling elite is descriptively accurate, economic historians still might ask the following question: Would it be a productive research strategy to abstract from this reality and to characterize the state instead as an agent of its citizens? In other words, does characterizing the state as an agent of its citizens provide a useful "as if" framework for positive analysis of economic policy? Or can we understand economic policy only by explicitly characterizing the state as proprietary?

13.1 THE CONSTRAINED PROPRIETARY STATE

Like profit-maximizing private enterprises, the proprietary state must solve a constrained maximization problem. One constraint on the proprietary state derives from the ability of its subjects to avoid or to evade taxation. The Laffer curve summarizes this constraint.[7] Another constraint on the proprietary state derives from the need for the state's policies to be credible. A third constraint on the proprietary state results from the possibility that a maltreated citizenry would depose the incumbent ruling elite, either by legal or extralegal means. In this context, the

ruling elite, in addition to appropriating the net revenues of the state, also pays taxes and utilizes public goods. McGuire and Olson show that the distinction between the state as an agent of its citizens and the state as the instrument of a ruling elite depends on the assumption that the state's economic policies affect the citizenry and the ruling elite differently.

5 Alberto Alesina (1988) provides a seminal treatment of the theory of political collusion.

6 Some authors call the proprietary state *predatory*, but it is not clear why the state warrants this pejorative term, which is not usually applied to profit-maximizing private enterprises. A referee suggests that if a proprietary state makes some people worse off than they would be under anarchy, then it would be appropriate to call the state predatory. But in general, the existence of a proprietary state need not make anybody worse off. In other words, a proprietary state can be a Pareto improvement over anarchy.

7 Focusing on the Laffer curve, Grossman (1998) rationalizes the biblical request "Make us a king" by deriving within a general equilibrium model of production and predation sufficient conditions under which, in an isolated economy, a proprietary state that maximizes the wealth of the ruling elite is a Pareto improvement over anarchy.

ability to depose the incumbent ruling elite is a critical component of political power and, hence, is a distinguishing feature of the subset of subjects who comprise the citizenry.[8]

Pursuing the analogy between the proprietary state and a private enterprise, Herschel Grossman and Suk Jae Noh (1990, 1994) take the objective of maximizing the wealth of the ruling elite to be a generic property of the state. They show that, this objective notwithstanding, any configuration of policy choices is possible, depending on the constraints that the state faces. Most important, Grossman and Noh show how, under appropriate conditions, the possibility that maltreated citizens would depose the incumbent ruling elite can cause the proprietary state, in maximizing the wealth of a ruling elite, to act as if it were an agent of its citizens. In other words, Grossman and Noh show that Adam Smith's metaphor of a self-interested individual being led by an "invisible hand" to promote the interest of the society can also be applicable to the proprietary state.

This analysis does not depend on the process by which maltreated citizens would depose the incumbent ruling elite. It is not necessary to distinguish elections from revolutions or other extralegal actions. In applying the theory, however, it is necessary to distinguish deposition of the incumbent ruling elite from more common political changes in which the incumbent ruling elite merely replaces its own leadership, whether through an election or a coup d'etat.[9] Furthermore, the possibility that

[8] Political theorists sometimes argue that constitutional devices can limit possible abuses of sovereign power and also can mitigate credibility problems. But as students of constitutional political economy themselves recognize, this literature has not settled the issue of the viability of constitutional rules. To quote Geoffrey Brennan and James Buchanan (1980), "our whole construction is based on the belief, or faith, that constitutions can work, and that tax rules imposed within a constitution will prevail" (p. 10). Similarly, Kenneth Rogoff (1985) suggests that the state could mitigate the credibility problem associated with monetary policy by delegating power to a person whose own conservative preferences are such that this agent opportunistically chooses the same policy that the state would choose if the state could make binding policy commitments. But Rogoff does not explain how the state commits itself not to revoke the authority of this agent. The analysis sketched out here focuses on the preferences and constraints that underlie the political–economic equilibrium. It abstracts from the institutional question of whether or not this equilibrium is embodied in a formal constitution.

[9] Bradford DeLong and Andrei Shleifer (1993) claim that prior to the Industrial Revolution, "Most European thrones were insecure." As supporting evidence, they offer the following facts about the throne of England between 1066 and 1702.

> The succession of eighteen out of thirty-one [English] monarchs went seriously awry either before or upon their death. . . . There was only a 22 percent chance that the English throne would pass peacefully down to the legitimate grandson (or other heir of the second generation) of any monarch. (pp. 699–700)

maltreated citizens would depose the incumbent ruling elite requires either the existence or the potential existence of an alternative ruling elite, and this rival must be a genuine outsider. The threat or potential threat posed by a rival ruling elite is akin to the threat of entry of a rival firm that induces an incumbent monopolist to restrain its exercise of market power in a contestable market.

In this regard, the identification of the ruling elite in stable democracies with a political establishment suggests that the electoral rivalry of established political parties, like Democrats and Republicans, who alternate in power according to a stationary stochastic process, is not the key to the accountability of the state to its citizens. As suggested earlier, such parties are likely to be only ostensible rivals, who actually share in appropriating the net revenues of the state. Rather, the key to accountability in democracies would seem to be freedom of entry into the electoral process, which allows new political groups to form and to become effective rivals of the existing political establishment.[10]

13.2 SURVIVAL AND CREDIBILITY

What are the appropriate conditions under which the possibility that maltreated citizens would depose the incumbent ruling elite can cause the proprietary state to act as if it were an agent of its citizens? In deriving these conditions, Grossman and Noh emphasize that the proprietary state's policies must be credible. Their analysis focuses on how the credibility requirement interacts with the possibility that maltreated citizens would depose the incumbent ruling elite to constrain the proprietary state's policy choices.

This interaction is complex in that it involves two underlying components. The first component is that the credibility of the state's policies depends on the survival probability of the incumbent ruling elite. Given this dependence, Grossman and Noh show how, if the ruling elite has a low survival probability, the credibility requirement can negate the

Yet, DeLong and Shleifer also acknowledge a problem in interpreting this evidence.

> Usually the threat came from within the extended family of the king: of the rulers only Oliver Cromwell and William "the Bastard" came from outside the previous royal family. (pp. 699–700)

It seems that more careful study is required to determine which of the successions that went awry involved the deposition of the incumbent ruling elite. But only from such a determination can we infer the degree of insecurity of the English ruling elite, as distinct from the insecurity of its leader.

[10] Even with free entry, however, the frequency with which a new entrant replaces the incumbent ruling elite can be low. This observation suggests that the importance of outsiders like George Wallace and Ross Perot in recent America politics exceeds their modest electoral success.

accountability of the proprietary state to its citizens.[11] The second component is that the survival probability of the incumbent ruling elite, and hence the credibility of the state's policies, depend on the possibility that maltreated citizens would depose the incumbent ruling elite. With this dependence, the possibility that maltreated citizens would depose the incumbent ruling elite becomes a two-edged sword.

To analyze the resulting equilibrium, Grossman and Noh make two assumptions. First, the incumbent ruling elite has a potential survival probability, which can be high or low but which is determined by given sociological and geopolitical factors. Second, the incumbent ruling elite's actual survival probability comes closer to its potential survival probability the more closely the state's policies accord with the interests of its citizens.[12]

Using these assumptions, Grossman and Noh show that dependence of the incumbent ruling elite's actual survival probability on the state's policies causes the proprietary state to act more like an agent of its citizens only if the incumbent ruling elite's potential survival probability is sufficiently high. Furthermore, dependence of the incumbent ruling elite's actual survival probability on the state's policies does not have a monotonic effect on the state's policies, because at some point further increases in this dependence, rather than increasing the accountability of the proprietary state to its citizens, would undermine the state's credibility.

[11] In a typically astute observation, Mancur Olson (1996) argued that in monarchies dynastic succession is popular because in effect it increases a ruler's potential survival probability.

> Perhaps the most interesting evidence about the importance of a monarch's time horizon comes from the historical concern about the longevity of monarchs and from the once-widespread belief in the social desirability of dynasties. There are many ways to wish a King well, but the King's subjects . . . have reason to be sincere when they say "long live the King." If the King anticipates and values dynastic succession, that further lengthens the planning horizon and is good for his subjects. The historical prevalence of dynastic succession, in spite of the near-zero probability that the oldest son of the king is the most talented person for the job, probably owes something to an intuitive sense that everyone in a domain, including the present ruler, gains when rulers have a reason to take a long view. (Olson, 1996, chapter 2, p. 25)

I thank Charles Goodhart for this reference.

[12] Grossman and Noh implicitly focus on the *willingness* of the citizenry to depose the incumbent ruling elite. In contrast, other recent papers focus on the *ability* of the citizenry to depose the incumbent ruling elite. For example, Yoram Barzel (1997), François Bourguignon and Thierry Verdier (1996), and James Robinson (1997) argue that policies that foster economic development can decrease the survival probability of the incumbent ruling elite by enhancing the ability of the citizenry to take effective action against the ruling elite.

Grossman and Noh also show that the higher the incumbent ruling elite's potential survival probability, the more its actual survival probability can depend on the state's policies without causing the credibility requirement to be a binding constraint. Thus, with both a high potential survival probability and a strong dependence of the incumbent ruling elite's actual survival probability on the state's policies, the proprietary state maximizes the wealth of the ruling elite by acting as if the state were an agent of its citizens. Returning to the central question of research strategy, this analysis yields the following conclusion: *If for the state to act as if it were an agent of its citizens is necessary and sufficient for the incumbent ruling elite to have a high survival probability, then characterizing the state as an agent of its citizens provides a useful "as if" framework for positive analysis of economic policy.*

13.3 PATHOLOGIES

These necessary and sufficient conditions fail to obtain most apparently in the many historical examples of ruling elites whose potential survival probabilities have been low. An incumbent ruling elite can have a low potential survival probability for many reasons, of which the most common probably are internal discord associated with ethnic rivalry;[13] threat of conquest by an external foe; and dependence on the support of a capricious external patron. The results discussed earlier imply that, if the incumbent ruling elite's potential survival probability is low, then the proprietary state cannot credibly act as if it were an agent of its citizens. Even worse, if the credibility requirement is a binding constraint, then the possibility that maltreated citizens would depose the incumbent ruling elite further undermines the state's credibility. In extreme cases, with a sufficiently low potential survival probability for the ruling elite, the state is unable to establish a credible regime of nonconfiscatory taxation and secure claims to property and even can be trapped on the wrong side of the Laffer curve.

The proprietary state also fails to act as if it were an agent of its citizens in cases in which the ruling elite's actual survival probability, although high, depends little on the state's policies. Historical examples include the great empires and dynasties of yore, which for generations

[13] Recent empirical analysis by William Easterly and Ross Levine (1997) and Alesina, Baqir, and Easterly (1997) suggests that ethnic diversity is associated with inadequate provision of public goods. To explain this observation, these authors hypothesize that ethnic diversity causes political polarization and a resulting inability to effectuate efficient collective choices. An alternative hypothesis, suggested by the work of Grossman and Noh, is that ethnic diversity causes the ruling elite to have a low potential survival probability, which gives the proprietary state little incentive for adequate provision of public goods, especially public investments.

either deterred or suppressed all threats to the survival of the incumbent ruling elite. In many cases, such states also were able to use coercion to minimize the ability of their subjects to avoid or to evade taxation.

Grossman and Noh show that, if the ruling elite's survival probability is high and largely independent of the state's policies, then the Laffer curve, reflecting the ability of subjects to avoid or to evade taxation, is the only important constraint on the maximization of the stream of rents extracted by the ruling elite. In such cases, the proprietary state is likely to impose tax rates at the peak of the Laffer curve. Even worse, Juan Mendoza (1999) shows that the proprietary state also might shirk the task of enforcing collective choices about the provision of nonexcludable public goods and become a free rider itself. Contemporary examples include many countries in Latin America and Africa and some places in Asia, as well as some neighborhoods in American cities in which the state does little to protect private property and in which citizens must undertake substantial private security measures, such as private guards, gated communities, and walled houses.

In situations in which the ruling elite's survival probability either is unavoidably low or is high and largely independent of the state's policies, we cannot understand economic policy by simply viewing the state as an agent of its citizens. Instead, we have to take explicitly into account that the objective of the proprietary state is to maximize the wealth of the ruling elite. In this context, the identification of the citizenry and the ability of the political system to aggregate and to reconcile the interests of different groups within the citizenry in order to effectuate collective choices are not the main factors determining economic policy. Explicit consideration both of how threats to the survival of the ruling elite affect the credibility of the proprietary state and of how the Laffer curve evolves becomes an essential part of understanding the historical role of the state in promoting economic development.

13.4 THE BRITISH LEGACY

When we look for examples in which viewing the state as an agent of its citizens might be a good historical approximation, we think first of those countries that have adopted and adhered to Anglo-Saxon political traditions. Several of the contributions to this volume rightly emphasize the distinctive British legacy of a state that protects property rights and that is more accountable to its citizens than in most countries. In their often cited analysis of the Glorious Revolution of 1689, Douglass North and Barry Weingast (1989) attempt to explain the emergence in Britain of a regime in which the state's debts were safe from repudiation and in which, as a result, the state was able to borrow large amounts at low interest rates. North and Weingast argue that the key to securing debt and other property rights was the strengthening of Parliament with a heavy representation of property owners together with the preservation of the monarchy as a check on Parliament.[14]

There is no doubt that these new political arrangements of 1689 were important. But the analysis of Grossman and Noh suggests that these new political arrangements were not the entire story. More precisely, these new political arrangements alone would not have been sufficient to create the belief that property was secure from confiscation by the state.

A critical element of the Glorious Revolution of 1689, as North and Weingast themselves point out, was that the new political arrangements had the support of all of the politically powerful parties – Whig and Royalist, commercial and landed – that comprised the citizenry. Further, the military victories of the new king, William III, over the deposed James II and his French supporters, culminating in July 1690 at the Boyne, removed the external threat to the new regime. Because it enjoyed both wide internal support and external security, the new ruling elite, a coalition of Parliament and the monarchy, had a high potential survival probability.

Accordingly, both investors and lenders could confidently expect that the British state now would take a long view. Investors could confidently expect that the state would value its productive subjects for their ability to generate tax revenues over the long run and hence would refrain from opportunistic confiscation of property. Also, lenders could confidently expect that the state would honor its debts and maintain its credit rather than myopically repudiate its debts. Moreover, because the ruling elite had a high potential survival probability, an electoral process with free entry, which would have made it relatively easy for a maltreated citizenry to depose the incumbent ruling elite, served to make the proprietary state accountable to its citizens without undermining the state's credibility.

The British experience leads to the following question: Why have the British institutions of Commons, Lords, and constitutional monarchy, or the American variant of Congress, Supreme Court, and president, not been readily transferable to other nations? The answer, I think, is that the British legacy of a state that protects property rights and that is accountable to its citizens is not attributable to institutional design. Rather, the key to the British legacy, starting with the success of

[14] Barzel (1997) explains why the strengthening of Parliament served the interests of both the monarch and property owners. Avner Greif, Paul Milgrom, and Barry Weingast (1994) offer a similar interpretation of the development of merchant guilds during the late medieval period.

the Glorious Revolution of 1689, is its foundation on a consensus of the citizenry.

This consensus, akin to the Mayflower compact of 1620 on a national scale, supported a stable political coalition, which, together with the achievement of external security, gave the incumbent ruling elite a high potential survival probability and made a regime of secure property credible. Furthermore, because the incumbent ruling elite had a high potential survival probability, dependence of the incumbent ruling elite's actual survival probability on the state's policies made the state accountable to its citizens. Without a high potential survival probability, dependence of the incumbent ruling elite's actual survival probability on the state's policies would have undermined the state's credibility and would have been worse than worthless.

This analysis leaves us with a further series of questions that historians have long pondered. What explains the distinctive properties of the British nation? Why were British people in both Great Britain and America able to establish states in which the ruling elite had a high potential survival probability? How important has been geography in minimizing the threat of conquest by an external foe? How important have been British ethnic homogeneity and the assimilating cultures of the United States and Canada in minimizing the internal discord associated with ethnic rivalry? Most important, what is the source of the remarkable degree of national consensus that characterizes Anglo-Saxon countries? Being only an economist, I leave these questions for others to answer.

REFERENCES

Alesina, Alberto (1988). "Credibility and Policy Convergence in a Two-Party System with Rational Voters," *American Economic Review*, *78*, 796–805.

Alesina, Alberto, Reza Baqir, and William Easterly (1997). "Public Goods and Ethnic Divisions," unpublished.

Austen-Smith, David and Jeffrey Banks (1999). *Positive Political Theory I: Collective Preference*. Ann Arbor: University of Michigan Press.

Barzel, Yoram (1997). "Property Rights and the Evolution of the State," unpublished.

Bourguignon, François and Thierry Verdier (1996). "Oligarchy, Democracy, Inequality, and Growth," unpublished.

Brennan, Geoffrey and James Buchanan (1980). *The Power to Tax: Analytical Foundations of a Fiscal Constitution*. New York: Cambridge University Press.

DeLong, J. Bradford and Andrei Shleifer (1993). "Princes and Merchants: European City Growth before the Industrial Revolution," *The Journal of Law and Economics*, *36*, 671–702; reprinted in Andrei Shleifer and Robert

Vishny, eds., *The Grabbing Hand: Government Pathologies and Their Cures*. Cambridge, MA: Harvard University Press, 1998.

Easterly, William and Ross Levine (1997). "Africa's Growth Tragedy: Policies and Ethnic Divisions," *Quarterly Journal of Economics*, *112*, 1203–50.

Greif, Avner, Paul Milgrom and Barry R. Wiengast (1994). "Coordination, Commitment, and Enforcement: The Case of the Merchant Guild," *Journal of Political Economy*, *102*, 745–76.

Grossman, Herschel I. (1998). " 'Make Us a King': Anarchy, Predation, and the State," unpublished.

Grossman, Herschel I. and Noh, Suk Jae (1990). "A Theory of Kleptocracy with Probabilistic Survival and Reputation," *Economics & Politics*, *2*, 157–71.

(1994)."Proprietary Public Finance and Economic Welfare," *Journal of Public Economics*, *53*, 187–204.

McGuire, Martin C. and Mancur Olson (1996). "The Economics of Autocracy and Majority Rule: The Invisible Hand and the Use of Force," *Journal of Economic Literature*, *34*, 72–96.

Mendoza, Juan (1999). "Private and Public Protection of Private Property: The Government as a Free-Rider," unpublished.

North, Douglass C. and Barry R. Weingast (1989). "Constitutions and Commitment: The Evolution of Institutions Governing Public Choice in Seventeenth Century England," *The Journal of Economic History*, *49*, 803–32.

Olson, Mancur (1996). "Capitalism, Socialism, and Democracy," unpublished.

Robinson, James (1997). "When is a State Predatory?" unpublished.

Rogoff, Kenneth (1985). "The Optimal Degree of Commitment to an Intermediate Monetary Target," *Quarterly Journal of Economics*, *100*, 1169–90.

Taylor, Michael (1982). *Community, Anarchy and Liberty*. New York: Cambridge University Press.

14

Reflections on the Collection

Albert Fishlow

14.1 INTRODUCTION

This is a rich and timely collection of chapters to contemplate. Beyond the skill with which each of the authors crafts his or her contribution, this book is relevant for at least three major innovations.

First, it invokes fiscal and monetary policy as its basic subject, a novelty for the period. We are inclined to take the seventeenth through the nineteenth centuries as the era preceding and including the Industrial Revolution, and to look at economic history through the lens of technological change and establishment of the new manufacturing industries. Here, instead, we focus on government and the public sector as it operated in the Old World as well as the New.

Second, it emphasizes the internal tasks of augmenting tax collection and subsequently appropriating the resources rather than the more typical emphasis upon rapidly increasing international trade and capital flows during this period. As such, it is more focused on the insights originally emanating from Lance Davis, Douglass North, Mancur Olson, Oliver Williamson, and others concerning the relationship between institutional change and the process of development. Transactions costs figure prominently in the broad range of causal forces that lead to changing patterns of taxation and expenditure.

Third, it contrasts the New World, and its institutions, with the Old. One of the obvious and important differences is the historical reliance upon the rate of inflation, and the inflationary tax, that characterized the countries of North and South America. The reliance upon the gold standard that gradually characterized the nineteenth century in Europe was late in coming to the countries on the other side of the Atlantic. Some never conformed, and even those that did – like Argentina – did so imperfectly. Nonetheless, the New World capital markets, including that of the United States, relied importantly on international flows that linked the world in the nineteenth century.

But fourth, the book continues to emphasize the Old World and the New, independent of the fact that the North, on both sides of the Atlantic, did much better economically than the South. Spain and Portugal had much less insertion into the new industrialization than did the United States; Argentina, at the other extreme, managed to evolve into one of the leading economies, at least in terms of per capita income, at the very end of the nineteenth century, without a successful industrialization. These are issues that continue to emerge in the twenty-first century.

Each of these observations merits more elaborate discussion. Successive sections take them up prior to a conclusion.

14.2 THE CENTRAL ROLE OF FISCAL AND MONETARY CAPABILITY

Over the course of the three centuries highlighted in these studies, there was a regular movement toward greater efficiency in tax collection as well as a concerted reduction in public intervention in the economic system. It was the end of mercantilism and the rise of a free and competitive marketplace. These studies illustrate well the national difficulties as well as the particular successes and failures in this secular transformation of public finance.

Clearly, creation of capital markets was an essential precursor to the technological advances in productivity and accelerated economic growth that followed. But these chapters, good as they are, do not much dwell on this issue. To some extent, that is because the question is hardly new. Marx, and before him Smith, devoted attention to the subject. Yet, there is more to say, particularly when contrasting the Old World and the New.

Conditions determining the flow of funds into infrastructure, and subsequently manufacturing activity, were an essential component of the great successes and relative failures of the Industrial Revolution. The rise in national savings that financed this transformation is a central part of the story. And despite the advances in aggregate statistics that have occurred over the last generation, a greater focus on relating those accomplishments more directly to the preceding and accompanying financial reforms would have been most welcome.

This is particularly true in regard to the theme of New World and Old. The countries of the Western Hemisphere became independent just at the time that economic growth was beginning to accelerate. In the North, there was an instantaneous tie; in the South, and in Spain and Portugal, there were long lags before such domestic activity began. Differential interests of large and small landholders, and the role of urban versus rural interests, in the laggards were a central part of the story. So too were the differential resource endowments of the participating countries. But there were also a variety of other factors relating to the public fisc that might have been explored.

To some degree, economic backwardness à la Gerschenkron did not seem to generate the institutional responses in Latin America found within much of Europe that furthered catch-up. Virtually everywhere, there was a distinct lack of political leadership that prevailed until the end of the nineteenth century, and sometimes beyond. And by that time, the gap had become too large to compensate.

Finally, public debt management was another important distinction differentiating countries. This is admirably treated in most of the individual chapters. In the earlier period, war and the emergence of national political authorities were prominent parts of the story. But this then settled down to regular administration. An essential part of the story, for the laggard countries, is the constant process of renegotiation of the external debt. The latter dominated: internal debt was subject to the progressive erosion of inflation. Internal monetary and financial institutions were imperfect and remained so into the twentieth century. And to some extent, their operation was directly related to the external circumstances of the countries in question.

To some degree, the selection of country cases in this volume eliminates the distinction between developmental and revenue default that I emphasized earlier. The latter is found in such countries as Russia, Turkey, and others. The countries here selected more clearly had temporary difficulty in meeting their commitments and would grow into them.

And that logically brings me to the next section, which deals precisely with such external capital flows and their effect upon the development process.

14.3 EXTERNAL VERSUS INTERNAL FORCES

The story told here takes its strength from its emphasis upon the process of internal governmental transformation. Countries are portrayed as gradually accumulating the political capability to enhance their tax collection. This is a relevant and quite interesting tale. In many ways, this is one of the strengths of the volume. Additionally, the application of the new institutional economics, explicitly or implicitly, provides new insights into the transition toward less governmental intervention.

But the focus here upon the national forces seems to give inadequate attention to the international. First of all, the major initial force in virtually all countries' finance was the tariff. This continued to have substantial weight until free trade gradually occurred from the mid-nineteenth century in Great Britain and parts of continental Europe. It remained as the principal basis of revenues in the New World even longer. As a consequence, the extent to which the revenue function of protective barriers assisted the forces calling for import substitution is downgraded.

Additionally, the burden of import duties was applied nationally rather than locally as state authority was progressively enhanced. Where such functions as primary education were controlled locally, as was typically the case in the New World, this placed real burdens on nations' finance, and consequentially on their very existence. In the United States, a major commitment was made to property levies; in Latin America, it was not.

Third, inflows of international capital were important in the New World, including the United States, as substantial additions to public revenues. Well before the commitment to direct foreign investment, largely in railroads in the nineteenth century, such reliance upon foreign finance occurred. It was not always a happy story. The cycle of debt, default, renegotiation, and new flows is a constant part of the process in the nineteenth century. Brinley Thomas emphasized the long swing as a fundamental reality joining the Old World and the New back in the 1950s; his insights remain valid. While he focused on the latter part of the period, from 1870 to 1913, when it also involved Argentina and Brazil, the process clearly had started earlier.

Fourth, the policy impact of the balance of payments – for the long swing spoke equally to the relationship between the flow of agricultural exports from the New World and the earlier inflow of capital – was a matter of some importance. It launched the process of geographic expansion and development of new land as a central part of the process; equally, it provided a market for the rapidly enhanced output of industrial products that emerged from rising productivity; it dealt with the variations in the terms of trade that were important over the nineteenth century; and it was related to the cyclical variation in migration that characterized the same period.

Transactions costs and their influence on governmental decisions are an important part of the story. And these contributions do much to enhance our knowledge of the role they played. But older hypotheses also can help to provide the linkage between the Old World and the New. The long swing is one, and its constituents include an important variation not only in relative but also in absolute prices.

14.4 INFLATION AS A KEY FACTOR

Money creation is a central part of historical development over these centuries. The differential evolution of banking institutions is very much a part of this volume, although the emphasis varies in the individual contributions. But a clear and important reality – and this does not seem to have featured centrally – was the late commitment, if at all, to the gold standard within the New World compared to the Old.

The United States, although a rapid innovator in adapting banking institutions from Great Britain, did not really convert until after the Civil War, and then with a considerable populist reaction eager to monetize silver. The bimetallism found in the United States did differentiate it importantly from most of its Western Hemisphere neighbors in the South. Canada seems to have followed a conservative policy throughout. Argentina did move to the gold standard definitively at the end of the 1890s, after leaving it during the Baring crisis. The consequences, while immediately positive, may not have been so beneficial thereafter in the 1920s. Brazil and Mexico were late, and only partial, acceptors. The former country depended upon cyclical exports of coffee; the latter preferred silver. Colombia, after some experimentation with a silver standard in the 1840s, did not sustain the commitment.

For countries dependent upon capital inflows and characterized by geographic and population expansion over time, the lack of a rigorous standard seemed to make sense. It allowed for an inflationary process in the New World that was of limited magnitude and cyclically related to the expansion of imports, migration, and direct foreign investment. Inevitably expansion came to an end, but the cycles at the end of the nineteenth century do seem positively related to the rapid extension of railroads and subsequent export capability.

An important question is who benefited from the rise in prices. This clearly depended upon the size and distribution of the money stock before and after inflation began. Those entrepreneurs with access to the increased supply of resources gained. Of special interest is the relationship between rural and urban sectors. Another issue is the real source of the inflationary episodes – political, as argued for Brazil, with wars and drought as major factors, or clearly economic, as seems to have been the case of the United States. Finally, there is the matter of the differential evolution of the banking sector and the responsibility of government authority. Foreign banks played a much greater role in nineteenth-century Latin America, related to major exports, than they did in the United States.

Because revenue collection tended to decline as a percentage of gross national product as countries moved toward the Smithean image of capitalism, even the consequences of a low rate of inflation upon real command over resources could have importance over the period studied. I would thus add it to the list that Bordo and Cortés-Conde have already assembled as worthy of future attention.

14.5 OLD VERSUS NEW OR NORTH VERSUS SOUTH

A central objective of this volume is to relate the new countries – originally all colonies – to their European predecessors. What sort of transformation occurred in the process of independence? This is obviously a highly relevant and informative issue. But it is not the only one that can be posed.

In terms of income per capita as well as technological advance, these countries also differed. That separates the United States and Canada – and Argentina at the end of the period – from Brazil, Colombia, and Mexico in the New World; it equally separates Portugal and Spain, and perhaps France early on, from Great Britain and Holland in the Old.

Old and New have an obvious historical basis. But so do North and South in terms of a range of relevant considerations. To what degree was the continued dependence upon agricultural and mineral exports a disadvantage? But why then did the United States and Canada, whose exports fell into similar categories, manage to evolve? W. Arthur Lewis's emphasis upon the different production in the North and South – temperate versus tropical products – seeks to provide answers to these questions. It is wheat that makes the difference. But these matters are neatly put to the side in this volume.

Or consider the issue of education. There is probably a much better relationship between level of development than Old World or New World status in explaining the commitment of funds to human capital. And such investment has significance in explaining the propensity to adapt new techniques in agriculture as well as industry.

Or take even the question of revenue sources that is a highlight of this book. Because of the substantial dependence upon tariff receipts for most of the countries, those with a higher ratio of trade probably found less need to innovate within the public sector than did some of the others. Here dependence upon a national market, as in the United States, coincides as a factor contributing to the rise of industrial production.

These are but a few areas in which a different assembly of the interesting case studies might have contributed to a different set of conclusions than are reached. There is another central matter as well. These country chapters are largely independent rather than comparative in their approach. There are a range of questions relating to government taxes, expenditures, public debt, and so on, like those previously noted, that are well treated in all the individual chapters. But even in their excellent introduction, the editors do not undertake a truly comparative treatment. That will require another volume and a careful selection of relevant hypotheses.

14.6 CONCLUSION

I have exaggerated differences rather than agreements in this brief comment. That is only because of the inherent quality of the contributions. Each will serve as a basic guide to the broad area of fiscal and financial evolution over a considerable interval. Each also, but to a lesser extent, seeks to relate changing institutions to the evolution of property rights. That is a central feature of the chapter on Britain, but it barely appears in some of the others. Each manages to engage the reader through the quality of the narrative and the selectivity of the focus.

So, even after being informed by this collection, originally brought together for the Twelfth World Congress of the International Economic Association, some readers may wish to go deeper. For at least a few of them, I commend a commitment to comparative analysis. That is one of the ways to exploit the careful accumulation of factual material contained in this volume. It is more of a task for a single author and can come only after the basic work has been done, as here.

Index

A Monetary History of Italy
Michele Fratianni and Franco Spinelli
0-521-44315-6

The Economics of World War II
Mark Harrison, editor
0-521-62046-5

Managing the Franc Poincaré
Kenneth Mouré
0-521-39458-9

The Rise of Financial Capitalism
Larry Neal
0-521-45738-6

Between the Dollar-Sterling Gold Points
Lawrence H. Officer
0-521-45462-X

The Credit-Anstalt Crisis of 1931
Aurel Schubert
0-521-36537-6

The Gold Standard and Related Regimes
Michael D. Bordo
0-521-55006-8

Bimetallism
Angela Redish
0-521-57091-3

A History of Banking in Antebellum America
Howard Bodenhorn

(*continued from front of book*)